The Systematic Design of Instruction

seventh edition

The Systematic Design of Instruction

Walter Dick
Florida State University, Emeritus

Lou Carey
University of South Florida

James O. Carey
University of South Florida

Merrill
is an imprint of

Upper Saddle River, New Jersey
Columbus, Ohio

Library of Congress Cataloging-in-Publication Data

Dick, Walter.
  The systematic design of instruction / Walter Dick, Lou Carey, James
O. Carey.—7th ed.
        p.   cm.
  Includes bibliographical references and index.
  ISBN-13: 978-0-205-58556-4 (pbk.)
  ISBN-10: 0-205-58556-6 (pbk.)
  1. Instructional systems—Design.   2. Lesson planning.   I. Carey,
Lou.   II. Carey, James O.   III. Title.
  LB1028.38.D53 2009
  371.3'028—dc22

                                          2008020327

Vice President and Executive Publisher: Jeffery W. Johnston
Publisher: Kevin M. Davis
Editorial Assistant: Lauren Reinkober
Senior Managing Editor: Pamela D. Bennett
Project Manager: Mary Harlan
Production Coordinator: Karla Walsh, Omegatype Typography, Inc.
Design Coordinator: Diane C. Lorenzo
Text Design and Illustrations: Omegatype Typography, Inc.
Cover Design: Jason Moore
Cover Image: SuperStock
Operations Specialist: Laura Messerly
Director of Marketing: Quinn Perkson
Marketing Manager: Erica M. DeLuca
Marketing Coordinator: Brian Mounts

This book was set in Esprit Book by Omegatype Typography, Inc. It was printed and bound by Edwards Brothers Malloy. The cover was printed by Edwards Brothers Malloy.

Photo Credits: Jim Carey, p. 361 (top left, top right, bottom left, bottom right), p. 362 (bottom right), p. 363 (center); EMG Education Management Group, p. 361 (center); NASA Headquarters, p. 362 (top); Prentice Hall School Division, p. 362 (bottom left), p. 363 (top); George Dodson/PH College, p. 363 (bottom).

Pearson® is a registered trademark of Pearson plc
Merrill® is a registered trademark of Pearson Education, Inc.

Pearson Education Ltd., London
Pearson Education Singapore Pte. Ltd.
Pearson Education Canada, Inc.
Pearson Education–Japan
Pearson Education Australia Pty. Limited

Pearson Education North Asia Ltd., Hong Kong
Pearson Educación de Mexico, S.A. de C.V.
Pearson Education Malaysia Pte. Ltd.
Pearson Education Upper Saddle River, New Jersey

Merrill
is an imprint of

www.pearsonhighered.com

10 9
ISBN 13:   978-0-205-58556-4
ISBN 10:   0-205-58556-6

BRIEF CONTENTS

CONTENTS

chapter 1
Introduction to Instructional Design   1

chapter 2
Identifying Instructional Goals Using Front-End Analysis 14

chapter 3
Conducting a Goal Analysis 38

chapter 4
Identifying Subordinate and Entry Skills   58

chapter 5
Analyzing Learners and Contexts   90

chapter 6
Writing Performance Objectives   110

chapter 7
Developing Assessment Instruments   130

chapter 8
Developing an Instructional Strategy   164

chapter 9
Developing Instructional Materials   222

chapter 10
Designing and Conducting Formative Evaluations   256

chapter 11
Revising Instructional Materials   294

chapter 12
Designing and Conducting Summative Evaluations   318

Appendixes   343

PREFACE

Not so many years ago, instruction was typically created by professors or trainers who simply developed and delivered lectures based on their research, experience, and expertise. Over the past thirty-five years, instructional emphasis has shifted dramatically from expert lectures to interactive instruction. This instruction focuses on the main purposes for and anticipated outcomes of the learning, the nature of the environment where acquired knowledge and skills would be used, and the particular characteristics of the learners in relation to the discipline and environment. Effective instruction today requires careful and systematic analysis and description of the intertwined elements that affect successful learning; it requires integral evaluation and refinement throughout the creative process.

The elegance of a generic systematic instructional design process is its inherent ability to remain current by accommodating emerging technologies, theories, discoveries, or procedures. For example, performance analysis and needs assessment will reveal new institutional needs and new performance requirements that must now be accommodated in the instruction; analysis and description of the performance context will uncover novel constraints and new technologies. Likewise, thoughtful analysis of present learners will disclose characteristics not previously observed, and analysis of new instructional delivery options will enable more efficient and cost-effective combinations of media and teaching/learning methods. The inquiry and analysis phases inherent in each step of a systematic instructional model help to ensure the resulting decisions and designs are current, practical, and effective.

The Systematic Design of Instruction simply and clearly introduces you to the fundamentals of instructional design, namely the concepts and procedures for analyzing, designing, developing, and formatively evaluating instruction. The text is designed to aid your learning in several ways. The intuitive chapter organization explains each step in the design process through easily understandable sections including (1) Objectives, (2) Background, (3) Concepts, (4) Examples, (5) Case Study, (6) Summary, (7) Practice, and (8) Feedback. Every chapter leads you through a step of the design model, presenting background research that is carefully illustrated with a wide range of academic and business applications. The contemporary design examples also help you link current theoretical concepts to practical applications. Sample rubrics and exercises provide tools you can use when designing instruction to connect theory to your own real-life applications. Finally, annotated references direct you to resources that help amplify and reinforce each concept in the instructional design process.

Acquiring the instructional design ideas and skills presented here will undoubtedly change the way you approach creating instruction. This is not a textbook to be read and memorized. It is a textbook to be used in order for you to be able to create effective instruction. You will learn a systematic, thoughtful, inquiry-based approach to creation that helps ensure the success of those who use your instruction. For your learning to be most effective, however, we suggest that you choose a relatively small instructional goal in your own discipline and context, and then as you study each chapter, apply the steps in the model to designing instruction for your personal goal. In other words, this is a learn-by-doing textbook. This will help ensure that you can make the instructional design model from this learning experience an integral part of your own instructional design practices.

In this new edition we have retained the features that seem most important to readers of the previous editions and we have added new perspectives and features that keep the text current within the discipline, including:

- Updated references and recommended readings with annotations
- Additional attention to learning and portable digital devices
- Additional attention to the relationship between transfer of learning and the context in which new skills will be used
- Application of instructional design concepts through a serial case study example carried through the steps of the design model in each chapter of the book
- A complete case study in the Appendixes (in addition to the one contained in the chapters) that details the products of design and development activities for each step in the model for a school curriculum goal on writing composition.
- A plan with case study examples for using constructivist learning environments in cognitive instructional design
- An online Instructors' Manual that contains:
  - Course management plans for ten-week and fifteen-week terms
  - Goals and objectives for each step in the model
  - Illustrations of preinstructional materials
  - Goal analyses for each step in the model
  - Rubrics for evaluating instructional design and development products for each step in the model
  - An additional case study
  - Concept quizzes and application quizzes for each chapter of the text
  - An annotated listing of important web resources in the field of instructional design that support each chapter of the text
  - A listing of important organizations and journals in the field of instructional design

For reviewing the seventh edition of *The Systematic Design of Instruction,* we would like to thank Brian Beatty, San Francisco State University; Celina Byers, Bloomsburg University; Kendall Hartley, University of Nevada, Las Vegas; Jane B. Hutchison, William Paterson University; Catherine McCartney, Bemidji State University; and Virginia McGinnis, Edinboro University of Pennsylvania. In the spirit of constructive feedback, always an important component of the systematic design process, the authors welcome reactions from readers about ways in which the text may be strengthened to better meet their needs. Please send comments to the authors at the following e-mail addresses.

Walter Dick   wdick@penn.com
Lou Carey   carey@tempest.coedu.usf.edu
James O. Carey   jcarey@cas.usf.edu

TO THE INSTRUCTOR

We would like to share some of our experiences in teaching with this text. The fundamental decision that must be made by the instructor is to identify the instructional goal for the course. As in any instructional design effort, the nature of the goal will drive the instructional strategy and the evaluation.

The instructional goal can be expressed either as verbal information (i.e., list, describe, or recall various aspects of the instructional design process) or as an intellectual skill (i.e., apply the instructional design process in the creation of instruction). We refer to the first approach as the *knowledge approach* and the latter as the *product approach*.

When knowledge is the course goal, the text serves as a source of information. The role of the instructor is to amplify the principles presented in the materials, to provide examples, and to evaluate students' acquisition of the knowledge. *The Systematic Design of Instruction* is well suited to this type of instruction. It provides students with an instructional design model they can use to understand major concepts in the field of education. Ideas such as performance objectives and formative evaluation can be presented and understood in terms of the overall design, delivery, and evaluation of instruction.

The product approach to teaching instructional design requires that students not only know about designing instruction but also develop instructional materials. It is this approach that we personally have found to be most successful in teaching instructional design. From our experience, students learn more through actually developing instruction. Concepts that appear to be academic in the text become very real to students as they grapple with such decisions as how many test items they need or what kind of practice exercises to use. The personal motivation and involvement of students also tend to increase with each succeeding assignment as they begin to produce instruction in their own content areas. When students reach the one-to-one formative evaluation stage, they often become quite enthusiastic about observing learners as they interact with, and learn from, the materials the students have created. We believe that the product approach to teaching instructional design provides the greatest long-term return for students.

Instructional Strategy

The second major decision you, the instructor, must make in teaching instructional design is the instructional strategy you will use. First is the issue of the sequence of topics. The text presents the model components in the sequence typically followed when designing instruction. If the knowledge approach to the course is used, then it is likely that the components in the model will be presented as they appear in the text. If the product approach is used, then the component sequence and resulting instructional strategy may be different.

One possibility is to have students learn about a component in the model and then complete the developmental assignment related to that component. For example, after students read the chapter on instructional goals, they develop a goal for the instruction they plan to write. Then, after reading about instructional analysis procedures, they do an instructional analysis for their selected goal. This read–develop, read–develop process continues until they complete the model. Even though this approach seems quite rational, students have commented that they would have done things very differently in the beginning of the development of their instructional materials if they had been knowledgeable about the components at the end of the model. Many students also have indicated that they needed more knowledge about the design process before making a significant commitment to developing instruction for a particular topic.

An alternative strategy for the product approach to teaching the class is best described as a cluster approach. In a semester course the students read several chapters in sequence each week. After several weeks, they identify their instructional goal and complete the first stage of analysis, the goal analysis. This demonstrates that they understand what they are going to teach, and the instructor can quickly work with students who are having trouble.

The first report submitted by the students includes their goal statement, goal analysis, subordinate skills analysis, and learner and context analysis. (Our evaluation sheets are shown in Table 1.) While the reports are being graded, students continue with their study of objectives, assessments, and instructional strategies. These then become the major contents of the second report. The students in our courses typically use illustrated text or simple media for the delivery mechanism for their instruction. They learn about developing materials and begin to write their instruction according to their instructional strategy. We have also taught instructional design in conjunction with a second course in computer-based and/or web-based instruction. The students who take both courses convert and present their instruction via computer and/or web.

While the students are writing their instruction, class time is spent learning about formative evaluation, and they begin as soon as possible to conduct their one-to-one evaluations. We require students to do three one-to-ones and use a small group with

t a b l e	**Report Rating Scales**		
1			

Report 1	Points	Score
1. Goal statement	5	_____
2. Goal analysis	10	_____
3. Subskills analysis	10	_____
4. Identification of entry behaviors	3	_____
5. Description of learner interview	3	_____
6. General description of learners	2	_____
7. Description of performance context, implications for instruction	3	_____
Total	36	_____

Report 2	Points	Score
1. Comments on revisions made since Report 1	0	_____
2. Attach copy of revised instructional analysis and goal statement	0	_____
3. Performance objectives	10	_____
4. Sample assessments for each objective	8	_____
5. Describe instructional sequence	2	_____
6. Describe preinstructional activities	2	_____
7. Information/example for each objective	10	_____
8. Practice/feedback for each objective	10	_____
9. Describe strategy for teaching terminal objective	2	_____
10. Describe student groupings and media selections	2	_____
11. Attach copies of pre- and posttests that will be used with the instruction	4	_____
Total	50	_____

t a b l e Continued

1

Report 3	Points	Score
1. Comments on revisions made since Report 2	0	_____
2. Attach copy of instructional analysis and Report 2	0	_____
3. Describe learners, materials, and procedures used in one to ones	5	_____
4. Describe results of one to ones, revisions	10	_____
5. Enclose copy of instructional materials and assessments used in small-group evaluation	20	_____
6. Describe characteristics of small-group learners	3	_____
7. Describe all the materials and instruments used in the small-group evaluation	3	_____
8. Describe the procedures in small-group evaluation	5	_____
9. Present the data from small-group evaluation	12	_____
10. Discuss the small-group data	10	_____
11. Describe revisions to instruction and assessment	12	_____
Total	80	_____

t a b l e Sample Semester Schedule

2

Class Session	Class Topic	Assignments Due
1	Course introduction	
2	Needs assessment and goal analysis	Chapters 1–3
3	Subskills analysis and entry skills	Chapter 4
4	Learner and context analyses	Chapter 5
5	Objectives and assessments	Chapters 6–7
		Report 1 due
6	Developing an instructional strategy	Chapter 8
7	Developing instructional materials	Chapter 9
8	Formative evaluation procedures	Chapter 10
9	Consulting session with students	Begin writing instruction
		Report 2 due
10	Revising instruction	Chapter 11
		Finish writing instruction
11	Discussion of projects	One-to-one formative evaluation
12	Consulting session with students	Small-group evaluation
13	Optional consulting session	Write report 3
14	Summative evaluation	Chapter 12
	Students' reflections on ID project	Report 3 due
15	Course summary	
	Report 3 returned	

at least eight learners. We do not require them to conduct the field trial phase—there just is not enough time in the semester. (See Table 2 for our semester schedule for the course.) We are insistent that students complete the first two phases of the formative evaluation process. Their third and final report consists of their instruction and their formative evaluation.

Classroom Activities

The selection of the knowledge or product approach to instruction has significant implications for course management strategies and, particularly, for the use of class time. If the knowledge approach is chosen, then the course will focus primarily on the knowledge objectives that are stated at the beginning of each chapter in the text. The pace of classroom activities can be slow enough to allow for discussion time and the opportunity to talk about various examples and practice and feedback exercises. Students may learn the concepts best when they are required to provide their own examples.

If the product approach is used, the instructor must carefully monitor the weekly progress of the course to ensure that students have sufficient time to conduct the formative evaluation. In our experience talking with students who have used the text at other institutions, their greatest problem is moving through the course at a pace that allows time for the formative evaluation.

In our product approach to instruction, we provide some lectures to highlight important ideas, but we also use numerous class participation activities. Several sessions during the semester are considered workshops—students work in teams of three or four to review and critique the work of the other students in their group. This is excellent preparation for the group contexts in which many designers will work after graduation.

Evaluation of Student Products

We require that students prepare several reports that document their use of the systematic design process. We base our evaluation of students on these reports and on the instruction that the students create. Table 1 outlines the major components of these reports and shows the points allotted to each component. (The assignment of points is arbitrary; however, the points for the third report are approximately equivalent to the combined points for the first two.) This distribution is proportional to the amount of work represented by the reports and it keeps students motivated throughout the course (i.e., they can make up for early poor performance, or possibly detract from good performance, based on their performance on the final report).

For the instructor, the rating scales for Reports 1, 2, and 3 provide a convenient outline of the content that should be included in the documentation reports and the relative weighting of sections of the reports for evaluation purposes. If a component of a student's report fully meets a stated criterion, then the total points for the component should be assigned to the student. If some of the criteria are not met, then points should be deducted from the component accordingly. If the component is not included in the student's report, then no points should be given for it.

Using the Instructors' Manual

With this edition of the book we have introduced a powerful new feature to support the teaching/learning process for students and teachers. A complete online Instructors' Manual is available. The course models ID practice by providing chapter-by-chapter learning component support for each step in the Dick and Carey Model.

Preinstructional Activities
- Graphic depiction of where the design/development step fits into the model
- Statements of objectives for the design/development step
- Comments on why the design/development step is relevant for ID practitioners
- Descriptions of what is required in order to begin the design/development step

Content Presentation with Examples
- A goal analysis with selected subskills that serves as a "spatial outline" of the skills to be learned in each of the design/development steps
- A complete case study on banking
- A rubric that can be used by students and instructors for evaluating the products of each design/development step

Learner Participation

- A brief quiz with feedback for practicing new information and concepts learned in each design/development step
- A brief quiz with feedback for practicing new applications of knowledge and skills learned in each design/development step

To introduce ID students into the culture of the profession, the Instructors' Manual also includes links to important organizations and journals in the field, as well as annotated links to important web resources in the field. These annotated links are organized in a chapter-by-chapter structure so that they can be used conveniently to supplement assigned readings during a course or workshop.

It is the authors' intent that the Instructors' Manual will provide instructors with new tools that can be woven into the teaching/learning process. It should be particularly valuable in facilitating those teaching instructional design by distance learning because it can be used to provide some of the learning guidance that students normally expect in face-to-face instruction. The authors welcome your comments and suggestions on the Instructors' Manual and, more generally, on your use of *The Systematic Design of Instruction* for teaching ID concepts and practices.

The Systematic Design of Instruction

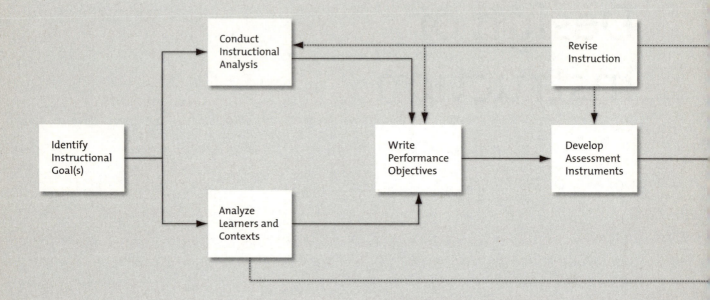

chapter ONE

The Dick and Carey Systems Approach Model for Designing Instruction

In a contemporary e-learning or distance education course, students are brought together with an instructor (perhaps) and are guided through textbook or online content by class activities such as online exercises, question/answer/discussion boards, projects, and interaction with classmates. If student attitudes, achievement, and completion rates are not up to desired levels, such variations as substituting a more interesting textbook, requiring student work groups, or enhancing real-time interaction with the instructor may be tried. If those or other solutions fail to improve outcomes, the instructor or course manager may reorganize the content of the web e-learning portal or, feeling that "E-learning isn't for everyone," may simply make no changes at all.

Attempts to improve student achievement by tinkering with this or that component of a course can be frustrating, often leading an instructor or course manager to explain low performance as a student problem—the students lack the necessary background, aren't smart enough, aren't motivated, or don't have the study habits and perseverance to succeed. However, rather than piecemeal fixes or frustrated rationalizations, a more productive approach is to view e-learning and indeed all purposeful teaching and learning as systematic processes in which every component is crucial to successful learning. The instructor, learners, materials, instructional activities, delivery system, and learning and performance environments interact and work with

Introduction to Instructional Design

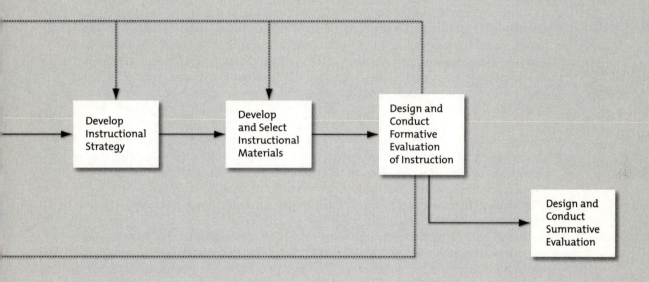

each other to bring about desired student learning outcomes. Changes in one component can affect other components and the eventual learning outcomes; failure to account adequately for conditions within a single component can doom the entire instructional process. Israelite (2004) characterizes e-learning shortfalls in corporate training as a failure to employ systems thinking; for example, the investment in high-tech web portals and delivery technologies frequently has not been accompanied by thorough consideration of other instructional components such as the design of effective learning experiences. Israelite's perspective is usually referred to as the *systems point of view,* and advocates typically use systems thinking to analyze performance problems and design instruction.

Let's first consider what is meant by a system, and then we will provide an overview of the systems approach to instructional design. The term *system* has become very popular as what we do becomes increasingly interrelated with what other people do. A system is technically a set of interrelated parts, all of which work together toward a defined goal. The parts of the system depend on each other for input and output, and the entire system uses feedback to determine if its desired goal has been reached. If it has not, then the system is modified until it does reach the goal. The most easily understood systems are those we create and can control rather than those that occur naturally. For example, you probably have a heating and cooling system in your home in which various components work together to produce a desired temperature. The thermostat is the feedback mechanism through which the system constantly checks the temperature and signals when more heat or cold is needed. At the desired temperature, the system shuts itself off. As long as the thermostat is set and all of the parts are in working order, the system will keep the temperature in a comfortable range. An automobile's braking system, on the other hand, by using a more fallible feedback system—the driver—is a less reliable system. Mechanical failure is seldom the cause of braking-related accidents; rather, it is human failure to recognize and compensate for system components such as slippery road conditions, impaired vision, or distracted attention to a cell phone or a radio while driving in heavy traffic. When human physiological and psychological characteristics are key components of a system, the system becomes less predictable and more difficult to manage for the desired results.

Consider as an example the management of Type 1 (juvenile onset) diabetes. There is a complex, finely balanced set of system components that work together for maintenance of healthy blood sugar levels, particularly (1) diet (what, how much, and when food is eaten), (2) physical exertion, (3) emotional exertion, (4) insulin (when and how much is taken), and (5) each individual's unique metabolic processing of these components. The goal of this system is a stable blood sugar level and the feedback mechanism is periodic blood sugar readings. When the system is out of balance, readings go outside the acceptable range and one or more system components must be adjusted to bring readings up or down as needed. Controlling this system would seem to be a daunting task in the presence of human individual differences. The systems approach, however, enables professionals to identify interacting components of diabetes care, establish normal human ranges for each component as starting points for care, and then adjust and fine-tune a care regimen as needed to accommodate individual differences. An accepted perspective for professionals in diabetes care is that the system is dynamic rather than static, requiring continuous monitoring as individuals grow, age, and change their lifestyles.

In the same way, the instructional process itself can be viewed as a system whose purpose is to bring about learning. The components of the system are the learners, the instructor, the instructional materials, and the learning environment, all interacting to achieve the goal. For example, in a traditional classroom the instructor might guide students through sample problems in the textbook or student manual. To determine whether learning is taking place, a quiz is administered at the end of the class. In the instructional system, the quiz is equivalent to the blood sugar readings in diabetes care. If student achievement is not satisfactory, then components must be modified to make the system more effective and bring about the desired learning outcomes.

The systems view of instruction sees the important roles of all the components in the process. They must all interact effectively, just as the parts in a system of diabetes care must interact effectively to bring about desired outcomes. Success depends not on any one component in the system but rather a determination of the exact contribution of each one to the desired outcome. There must be a clear assessment of the effectiveness of the system in bringing about learning and a mechanism to make changes if learning fails to occur. As in the example of diabetes care, instructional systems include the human component and are therefore complex and dynamic, requiring constant monitoring and adjustment.

Thus far, our discussion of the instructional process has focused only on the "learning moment" when teachers, instructional materials, and learners come together in a classroom with the goal that learning will occur. What about the preparation for the instructional process? How does the instructor decide what to do and when? It is not surprising that someone with a systems view sees the preparation, implementation, evaluation, and revision of instruction as one integrated process. In the broadest systems sense, a variety of sources provide input to the preparation of the instruction. The output is some product or combination of products and procedures that are implemented. The results are used to determine whether the system should be changed, and, if so, how.

The purpose of this book is to describe a systems approach for the design, development, implementation, and evaluation of instruction. This is not a physical system such as home heating and air conditioning but a procedural system. We describe a series of steps, all of which receive input from preceding steps and provide output for the next steps. All of the components work together to either produce effective instruction or, if the system evaluation component signals a failure, determine how instruction can be improved.

Although our model of instructional design will be referred to as a systems approach model, we must emphasize that there is no single systems approach model for designing instruction. A number of models bear the label *systems approach,* and all of them share most of the same basic components. The systems approach model presented in this book is less complex than some but incorporates the major components common to all models including analysis, design, development, implementation, and evaluation. Collectively, these design models and the processes they represent are referred to as *instructional systems development* (ISD). *Instructional design* (ID) is used as an umbrella term that includes all phases of the ISD process. These terms will all become clear as you begin to use the instructional design process.

Instructional design models are based, in part, on many years of research on the learning process. Each component of the model is based on theory and, in most instances, on research demonstrating the effectiveness of that component. The model brings together in one coherent whole many concepts that you may have already encountered in a variety of educational situations. For example, you undoubtedly have heard of *performance objectives* and may have already written some yourself. Such terms as *criterion-referenced testing* and *instructional strategy* may also be familiar. The model will show how these terms, and the processes associated with them, are interrelated and how these procedures can be used to produce effective instruction.

The instructional strategy component of our model describes how the designer uses information from analyzing what is to be taught to formulate a plan for connecting learners with the "instruction" being developed with the ID model. Throughout this text we define the term *instruction* quite broadly as purposeful activity intended to cause, guide, or support learning. As such, instruction encompasses such activities as traditional group lecture/discussion, computer-based drill and practice, moderated small-group online case study analysis, individualized discovery learning, or group problem solving mediated through a network of PDAs. The range of activities that can serve as instruction is limited only by the imagination of teachers, designers, and students.

Our original approach to this component of the model was heavily influenced by the work of Robert Gagné in *The Conditions of Learning,* first published in 1965. *The Conditions of Learning* incorporated cognitive information-processing views of learning, which assume most human behavior to be very complex and controlled primarily by a person's internal mental processes rather than external stimuli and reinforcements. Instruction is seen as organizing and providing sets of information, examples, experiences, and activities that guide, support, and augment students' internal mental processes. Learning has occurred when students have incorporated new information and schemes into their memories that enable new capabilities. Gagné further developed cognitive views of learning and instruction in later editions of *The Conditions of Learning* (1970, 1977, 1985). His influence as one of the founders of the instructional systems development discipline is described in Richey's (2000) book, *The Legacy of Robert M. Gagné.*

Constructivism is a relatively recent branch of cognitive psychology that has had a major impact on the thinking of many instructional designers. Although constructivist thinking varies broadly on many issues, the central point is the view of learning as a unique product "constructed" by each individual learner combining new information with existing knowledge and experiences. Individuals learn by constructing new mental representations of the social, cultural, physical, and intellectual environments in which they live. Because learning in the constructivist view is so entwined with personal experiences, a primary role of the teacher is creating appropriate learning environments—that is, social or technological contexts in which student learning is based on interactions with authentic representations of real practices.

Throughout this text, readers will find elements of behaviorist, cognitivist, and constructivist views adapted as appropriate for the varieties of learners, learning outcomes, learning contexts, and performance contexts that are discussed. The Dick and Carey Model incorporates an eclectic set of tools drawn from each of these three major theoretical positions of the past fifty years and is an effective design framework for guiding pedagogical practices within all three foundational orientations. Although some constructivists may reject the model as forcing practices that are counter to their philosophical foundations, the authors counsel an open-minded view and believe the model, when used by expert professionals, is essentially neutral. Master teachers and instructional designers can translate their own views of learning theory into pedagogical practices based on their own decisions about goals, students, and learning environments. Because the model depicts a set of generic ID practices, it has been adapted successfully by teachers, instructional designers, educational technologists, military trainers, and performance technologists in all kinds of settings. For those interested in historical context, Reiser's (2001) article on the history of instructional design and technology provides a good review of the origins and development of the field.

The model as presented here is based not only on theory and research but also on a considerable amount of practical experience in its application. In the section that follows, we present the general systems approach model in much the same way as a practical cookbook recipe—you do this and then you do that. When you begin to use a recipe in your own kitchen, however, it takes on greater meaning. In essence, your use of your own kitchen, your own ingredients, and your own personal touch will result in a unique product. You may change the recipe, take shortcuts, substitute ingredients, and perform steps out of sequence. So it is with instructional designers. In the beginning they use a model such as the one presented in this book as a scaffold to support their analysis, design, development, implementation, and evaluation work. As students and practitioners of instructional design become more experienced and proficient, they will replace the scaffold with their own unique solution strategies for the multidimensional problems they encounter in designing instruction. As in any complex endeavor those who fail to make the jump from dependence to independence will never master the discipline and will, at best, be good technicians.

As you begin designing instruction, *trust the model*—it has worked for countless students and professionals for more than thirty years. As you grow in knowledge and experience, *trust yourself!* The flexibility, insight, and creativity required for original solutions reside in experienced users and professionals—not in models. The Dick and Carey Model is only a representation of practices in the discipline of instructional design. The purpose for the model is to help you learn, understand, analyze, and improve your practice of the discipline, but all models are oversimplified representations. As you grow in understanding, don't confuse the representation with the reality. The graphical arrangement of boxes and arrows, for example, implies a strict linear process flow, but any experienced instructional designer will attest that in practice the process can sometimes look more like the circular, continuous improvement model in Figure 1.1 or the concurrent processes model in Figure 1.2 that is useful when planning, development, implementation, and revision all occur at the same time or in multiple cycles of simultaneous activities. If you are new to the field of instructional design, these figures may not make a lot of sense now but will come into focus later in the book.

In reading this book you are beginning to study the discipline of instructional design. The Dick and Carey Model gives us a way to distinguish the practices within the broader discipline, similar to distinguishing the individual trees within a forest; mastering a discipline requires that we "see the forest for the trees." In his book *The*

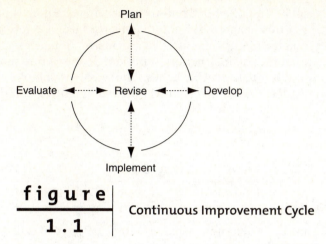

figure
1.1 | Continuous Improvement Cycle

Fifth Discipline: The Art and Practice of the Learning Organization, Peter Senge (1990) accurately defines and depicts what it means to practice a discipline:

> By "discipline" I mean . . . a body of theory and technique that must be studied and mastered to be put into practice. A discipline is a developmental path for acquiring certain skills or competencies. As with any discipline, from playing the piano to electrical engineering, some people have an innate "gift," but anyone can develop proficiency through practice. To practice a discipline is to be a lifelong learner. You "never arrive"; you spend your life mastering disciplines. . . . Practicing a discipline is different from emulating a model. (pp. 10–11)

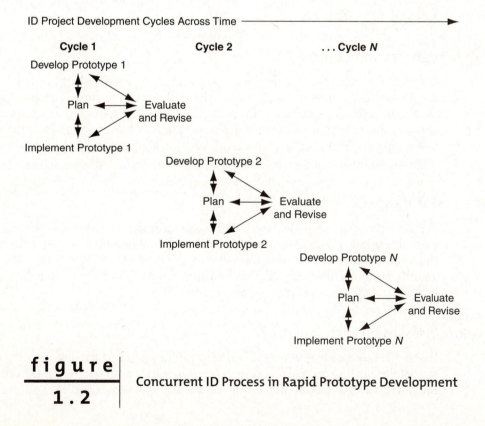

figure
1.2 | Concurrent ID Process in Rapid Prototype Development

The model that will be described in detail in succeeding chapters is presented on the first two pages of this chapter. Ten interconnected boxes represent sets of theories, procedures, and techniques employed by the instructional designer to design, develop, evaluate, and revise instruction. A broken or dotted line shows feedback from the next-to-last box to the earlier boxes. The sequence of boxes represent steps that will be briefly described in the next section and in much greater detail in subsequent chapters.

Components of the Systems Approach Model

Identify Instructional Goal(s)

The first step in the model is to determine what new information and skills you want learners to have mastered when they have completed your instruction, expressed as goals. The instructional goals may be derived from a list of goals, from a performance analysis, from a needs assessment, from practical experience with learning difficulties of students, from the analysis of people who are doing a job, or from some other requirement for new instruction.

Conduct Instructional Analysis

After you have identified the instructional goal, you determine step by step what people are doing when they perform that goal and also look at subskills that are needed for complete mastery of the goal. The final step in the instructional analysis process is to determine what skills, knowledge, and attitudes, known as *entry skills,* are needed by learners to be successful in the new instruction. For example, students need to know the concepts of radius and diameter in order to compute the area and the circumference of a circle, so those concepts would be entry skills for instruction on computing area and circumference.

Analyze Learners and Contexts

In addition to analyzing the instructional goal, there is a parallel analysis of the learners, the context in which they will learn the skills, and the context in which they will use them. Learners' current skills, preferences, and attitudes are determined along with the characteristics of the instructional setting and the setting in which the skills will eventually be used. This crucial information shapes a number of the succeeding steps in the model, especially the instructional strategy.

Write Performance Objectives

Based on the instructional analysis and the description of entry skills, you write specific statements of what learners will be able to do when they complete the instruction. These statements, derived from the skills identified in the instructional analysis, identify the skills to be learned, the conditions under which the skills will be demonstrated, and the criteria for successful performance.

Develop Assessment Instruments

Based on the objectives you have written, you develop assessments that are parallel to and measure the learners' ability to perform what you described in the objectives. Major emphasis is placed on relating the kind of skills described in the objectives to the assessment requirements. The range of possible assessments for judging learners' achievement of critical skills across time includes objective tests, live performances, measures of attitude formation, and portfolios that are collections of objective and alternative assessments.

Develop Instructional Strategy

Based on information from the five preceding steps, you then identify the strategy to use in your instruction to achieve the goal. The strategy will emphasize components to foster student learning including such preinstructional activities as stimulating motivation and focusing attention, presentation of new content with examples and demonstrations, active learner participation and assessment, and follow-through activities that relate the newly learned skills to real-world applications. The strategy will be based on current theories of learning and results of learning research, the characteristics of the media that will be used to engage learners, content to be taught, and the characteristics of the learners who will participate in the instruction. These features are used to develop or select materials and plan instructional activities.

Develop and Select Instructional Materials

In this step you use your instructional strategy to produce the instruction. This typically includes guidance for learners, instructional materials, and assessments. (In using the term *instructional materials* we include all forms of instruction such as instructor's guides, student reading lists, PowerPoint presentations, case studies, videos, podcasts, computer-based multimedia formats, and web pages for distance learning.) The decision to develop original materials will depend on the types of learning outcomes, the availability of existing relevant materials, and developmental resources available to you. Criteria for selecting from among existing materials are also provided.

Design and Conduct Formative Evaluation of Instruction

Following completion of a draft of the instruction, a series of evaluations is conducted to collect data used to identify problems with the instruction or opportunities to make the instruction better. This type of evaluation is called *formative* because its purpose is to help create and improve instructional processes and products. The three types of formative evaluation are referred to as *one-to-one evaluation, small-group evaluation,* and *field trial evaluation.* Each type of evaluation provides the designer with a different set of information that can be used to improve instruction. Similar techniques can be applied to the formative evaluation of existing materials or classroom instruction.

Revise Instruction

The final step in the design and development process (and the first step in a repeat cycle) is revising the instruction. Data from the formative evaluation are summarized and interpreted to identify difficulties experienced by learners in achieving the objectives and to relate these difficulties to specific deficiencies in the instruction. The dotted line in the figure at the beginning of this chapter labeled "Revise Instruction" indicates that the data from a formative evaluation are not simply used to revise the instruction itself, but are used to reexamine the validity of the instructional analysis and the assumptions about the entry skills and characteristics of learners. It may be necessary to reexamine statements of performance objectives and test items in light of collected data. The instructional strategy is reviewed and finally all of these considerations are incorporated into revisions of the instruction to make it a more effective learning experience. In actual practice a designer does not wait to begin revising until all analysis, design, development, and evaluation work is completed; rather, the designer is constantly making revisions in previous steps based on what has been learned in subsequent steps. Revision is not a discrete event that occurs at the end of the ID process, but an ongoing process of using information to reassess assumptions and decisions.

Design and Conduct Summative Evaluation

Although summative evaluation is the culminating evaluation of the effectiveness of instruction, it generally is not a part of the design process. It is an evaluation of the absolute or relative value of the instruction and occurs only after the instruction has been formatively evaluated and sufficiently revised to meet the standards of the designer. Since the summative evaluation is usually not conducted by the designer of the instruction but instead by an independent evaluator, this component is not considered an integral part of the instructional design process per se.

Procedures used for summative evaluation are receiving more attention today than in previous years. This increased attention is due to interest in the effectiveness of web-based instruction across organizations, states, and countries. For example, will web-based instruction developed for learners in Utah, which is very transportable electronically, be effective for students in the Caribbean or China? What would experts in learning conclude about the instructional strategies within very attractive materials that were developed "a world away"? Terms such as *learner verification of materials effectiveness* and *assurances of materials effectiveness* are resurfacing now that materials transportability is much more economical and effortless.

The nine basic steps represent the procedures employed when using the systems approach to design instruction. This set of procedures is referred to as a *systems approach* because it is made up of interacting components that together produce instruction to satisfy needs expressed in a goal. Data are collected about the system's effectiveness so that the final product can be improved until it reaches the desired quality level.

Using the Systems Approach Model

Now that you have read about this model, you should consider several very important questions about its use, discussed in the sections that follow.

Why Use the Systems Approach?

Among the reasons that systematic approaches to instructional design are effective is the required focus, at the outset, on what learners are to know or be able to do when the instruction is concluded. Without this precise statement, subsequent planning and implementation steps can become unclear and ineffective. This focus on outcomes is pertinent for all who are involved in public schools because of the contemporary political climate in education. The most recent standards/accountability movement began with a number of states passing laws establishing tests and performance standards for judging student, school, and school district performance and was cemented when Congress passed the No Child Left Behind Act of 2001. The act mandated state-level development and implementation of assessments of basic skills at selected grade levels. A systems approach to instruction is a powerful tool for planning successful standards-based education because of the tight alignment among learning outcomes, student characteristics, instructional activities, and assessments.

A second reason for the success of the systems approach is this interlocking connection between each component, especially the relationship between instructional strategy and desired learning outcomes. Instruction specifically targeted on the skills and knowledge to be learned helps supply the appropriate conditions for these learning outcomes. Stated another way, the instructional range of activities cannot be loosely related or unrelated to what is to be learned.

The third and perhaps most important reason for the success of the systems approach is that it is an empirical and replicable process. Instruction can be designed for one delivery or for use on multiple occasions with multiple learners. Because it can be reused with similar and scalable student audiences, it is worth the time and effort to evaluate and revise it. In the process of systematically designing instruction, data are collected to determine what part of the instruction is not working, and it is revised until it does work.

The systems approach is an outcomes-based approach to instruction because it begins with a clear understanding of the new knowledge and skills that students will learn. Although widely adopted among educators at all levels, the systems approach finds even more numerous applications in business and industry, government, social services, and the military. In these environments there is a premium on both efficiency of instruction and quality of student performance, with high payoffs for both.

For Which Instructional Types and Student Groupings Is the Systems Approach Appropriate?

The systems approach to designing instruction includes the planning, development, implementation, and evaluation of instruction. Part of this process is choosing the type of instruction. In some instances, it is most appropriate to have an instructor deliver the instruction; in other situations, a variety of media may be employed. In every instance, the systems approach is an invaluable tool for identifying what is to be taught, determining how it will be taught, and evaluating the instruction to find out whether it is effective.

The procedure described in this text for developing an instructional strategy is a generic one. Although systematically designed instruction will not necessarily be individualized, a primary application of the systems approach to instructional design is for the individual learner. Useful for developing simple, tutorial print instruction for individual students, the systems approach is equally applicable to problem solving assignments for small groups of students or complex digital multimedia for distance delivery to a mass audience over the web. The procedure easily fits the requirements of any preferred medium of instruction, noting that most research suggests that it is the analysis process and the instructional strategies, rather than the delivery mode, that determine instructional success. The systems approach is a generic planning process that ensures that materials developed for any type of instruction or student grouping are responsive to the needs of learners and effective in achieving the desired learning outcomes. The reader should be careful to distinguish between the process of designing instruction and the delivery of that instruction. The systems approach is basically a design process, whereas types of instruction, instructional media, and individualized versus group activity are all decisions made within the design process. Ideally, there are no predetermined assumptions about these decisions because a major part of the design process is to determine how the instruction can be delivered most effectively.

Careful attention is paid to determining what must be learned and what learners must already know in order to begin the instruction. The instruction is focused on the skills to be learned and is presented under the best conditions for learning. The learner is evaluated fairly with instruments that measure the skills and knowledge described in the objectives, and the results are used to revise the instruction so that it will be even more effective with succeeding learners. Following this process causes the designer to focus on the needs and skills of the learners and results in the creation of effective instruction.

Who Should Use the Systems Approach?

Teachers As you study the instructional design model and perhaps use it to design specific instruction, you will find that it takes both time and effort. If you are a teacher, you may find yourself saying, "I could never use this process to prepare all my instruction," and you would probably be correct. The individual instructor with day-to-day instructional responsibilities can use the complete process to develop only small amounts of instruction at any given time because of the level of detail included in each step. However, even such limited use can expand any teacher's instructional repertoire. Also, teachers can select and apply some of the steps or even pieces of a single step as appropriate for different instructional planning needs. As you work through the book, however, your goal should be to master the level of detail contained in each step, because mastery of the full model establishes the experience and insight to properly select the right pieces of the instructional design process according to specific instructional needs. What you will learn in this book is a theory-based, systematic way of viewing the teaching–learning process. The ID model provides tools that you can tuck away in a mental toolbox along with all of the other tools that you have picked up through your academic training and your experience. Using these tools will help you sharpen your focus on instructional practices that tend to predict successful learning in students.

We have found that almost every teacher who has studied the process has come away with two reactions. The first is that they will certainly begin immediately to use some of the components in the model, if not all of them. The second reaction is that their approach to instruction will never be the same because of the insights they have gained from using the process. (The reader may be somewhat skeptical at this point; be sure to consider your own reactions *after* you have used this approach.)

ID Professionals The ISD approach can also benefit a diverse range of professionals whose full- or part-time activity is to create instruction that is effective for a given learning outcome with a particular learner population. The instruction is often designed and packaged for use with many learners over a period of time, whether in business, industry, government, social services, the military, or personnel divisions, as well as in instructional support service centers in junior colleges, universities, and some public school districts. Professional titles used by ID professionals include instructional designer, instructional technologist, human performance technologist, educational technologist, trainer or training specialist, human resource development specialist, and others. (In 2002 a task force was convened within the International Society for Performance Improvement—ISPI—for the purpose of developing a process and performance standards for certifying ID professionals. The certification program is in place and awards the designation "Certified Performance Technologist"—CPT—to successful applicants.)

In contrast to the teacher who may be working alone, the ID professional sometimes works with a team of specialists to develop the instruction, often including a content specialist, an instructional technologist, an evaluation specialist, and a manager (who is often the instructional designer). The team approach draws on the expertise of specialists to produce a product that none could produce alone. In these settings there is a premium placed on interpersonal skills because seemingly everyone has ideas on how best to do what needs to be done.

Professors and Instructors This book is suitable for university professors, military instructors, and instructors in any other setting who are interested in improving the effectiveness of their instruction. We are convinced that the model and procedures are equally applicable in both school and nonschool settings. Instructional design skills are critical for those designing instruction for web delivery.

Our examples of various aspects of the application of the systematic design process include instructional contexts for all age groups, from young children to mature adults. We will use the terms *teacher, instructor,* and *designer* interchangeably throughout the book because we truly believe they are interchangeable.

As you read through the chapters that follow, you will find an instructional design case study on group leadership skills for Neighborhood Crime Watch leaders. The example is carried through each step of the design model. You should also note that the appendixes at the end of this text contain a second complete instructional design case study also carried through each step of the model for a school subject (using a variety of sentence types in writing paragraphs). These two case studies were chosen because leading group discussion and writing paragraphs are skills with which all of us are familiar, and group leadership skills are taught in many professional/technical training settings whereas paragraph writing skills are taught at all levels of public and private education.

REFERENCES AND RECOMMENDED READINGS

At the end of each chapter, several carefully selected references are listed. The books and articles supplement the description in the chapter or focus in more detail on an important concept that has been presented.

The references listed for this first chapter are somewhat different. These are a mixture of current books in the field of instructional design or works that have direct implications for the practice of instructional design along with a selection of classic texts and articles. Many of the topics in this book also appear in these referenced texts, which vary in depth and breadth of coverage of topics but should all help to expand your knowledge and understanding of the instructional design field.

Banathy, B. H. (1968). *Instructional systems.* Palo Alto, CA: Fearon Publishers. A classic text placing instruction in a systems context.

Blanchard, P. N., & Thacker, J. W. (Eds.). (2007). *Effective training: Systems, strategies, and practices* (3rd ed.). Englewood Cliffs, NJ: Prentice Hall. Useful combination of theory and practical examples.

Briggs, L. J., Gustafson, K. L., & Tillman, M. H. (Eds.). (1991). *Instructional design: Principles and applications.* Englewood Cliffs, NJ: Educational Technology Publications. An update of an older classic. Many of our chapters parallel chapters in this book.

Dills, C. R., & Romiszowski, A. J. (Eds.). (1997). *Instructional development paradigms.* Englewood Cliffs, NJ: Educational Technology Publications. Presents various models and approaches to instructional design.

Driscoll, M. P. (2005). *Psychology of learning for instruction* (3rd ed.). Boston: Allyn & Bacon. Contemporary approaches to learning that focus on instruction.

Duffy, T. M., & Jonassen, D. H. (Eds.). (1992). *Constructivism and the technology of instruction.* Hillsdale, NJ: Lawrence Erlbaum Associates. Comprehensive review of varying perspectives on constructivism.

Ely, D. P. (1996). *Classic writings on instructional technology.* Englewood, CO: Libraries Unlimited. A tour of the people and writings that shaped instructional technology.

Ertmer, P. A., & Newby, T. J. (1993). Behaviorism, cognitivism, constructivism: Comparing critical features from an instructional design perspective. *Performance Improvement Quarterly, 6*(4), 50–72. Useful comparisons of three theoretical bases with guidelines for instructional designers.

Ertmer, P. A., & Quinn, J. (2003). *The ID casebook: Case studies in instructional design* (2nd ed.). Upper Saddle River, NJ: Merrill/Prentice Hall. Wide array of examples of the application of instructional design processes to real world problems.

Fleming, M. L., & Levie, W. H. (1993). *Instructional message design: Principles from the cognitive and behavioral sciences* (2nd ed.). Englewood Cliffs, NJ: Educational Technology Publications. A classic text that is still used in designing displays and interfaces for contemporary media technologies.

Gagné, R. M. (1985). *The conditions of learning* (4th ed.). New York: Holt, Rinehart and Winston. The final edition of a classic book detailing the linkage between cognitive learning theory and instructional practices.

Gagné, R. M., & Medsker, K. L. (1996). *The conditions of learning: Training applications*. Fort Worth, TX: Harcourt Brace College Publishers. Same model as Gagné's original text by this name, but with the addition of examples from business and industry.

Gagné, R. M., Wager, W. W., Golas, K. C., & Keller, J. M. (2004). *Principles of instructional design* (5th ed.). Belmont, CA: Wadsworth/Thomson Learning. The first new edition of this classic book since 1992 is revised with two new chapters on technology and online learning.

Gredler, M. E. (2005). *Learning and instruction: Theory into practice* (5th ed.). Upper Saddle River, NJ: Merrill/Prentice Hall. A survey of learning theories that includes behaviorist, cognitivist, and constructivist views with applications for instruction.

Hannafin, M. J., Hannafin, K. M., Land, S. M., & Oliver, K. (1997). Grounded practice and the design of constructivist learning environments. *Educational Technology Research and Development, 45*(3), 101–117. This article presents a carefully reasoned argument for grounding instructional practice in theoretical foundations—regardless of the particular practice which one espouses.

Hannum, W. (2005). Instructional systems development: A 30 year retrospective. *Educational Technology Magazine, 45*(4).

Israelite, L. (2004). We thought we could, we think we can, and lessons along the way. In E. Masie (Ed.), *Learning: Rants, raves, and reflections*. San Francisco: Jossey-Bass Pfeiffer. An HRD executive's systems-based view of the importance of maintaining instructional design integrity within the technology decisions and subsequent materials development done by professional and technical trainers.

Jonassen, D. H. (Ed.) (2004). *Handbook of research on educational communications and technology* (2nd ed.). Mahwah, NJ: Lawrence Erlbaum Associates.

Medsker, K. L., & Holdsworth, K. M. (Eds.) (2007). *Models and strategies for training design*. Hoboken, NJ: John Wiley & Sons. A print-on-demand book focusing on ID models in training settings.

Merrill, M. D. (2002). First principles of instruction. *Educational Technology Research and Development, 50*(3), 43–59. The author argues that wide-ranging instructional design theories all include five fundamentally similar principles.

Morrison, G. R., Ross, S. M., & Kemp, J. E. (2007). *Designing effective instruction* (5th ed.). Hoboken, NJ: Wiley. This edition covers many current instructional design concepts as well as planning for project management and instructional implementation.

Newby, T. J., Stepich, D. A., Lehman, J. D., & Russell, J. D. (2005). *Instructional technology for teaching and learning* (3rd ed.). Englewood Cliffs, NJ: Merrill/Prentice Hall. Focus on integrating instruction and technology for the classroom, including planning and developing instruction, grouping learners, selecting delivery formats including distance learning, managing, and evaluating instruction.

Partnership for 21st Century Skills. (2003). *Learning for the 21st century*. Washington, DC: Partnership for 21st Century Skills. This partnership—comprising AOL, Apple, Cable in the Classroom, Cisco Systems, Dell Computer Corporation, Microsoft Corporation, National Educational Association, and SAP—is focused on Pre-K–12 schools, and describes skills and dispositions necessary for improving learning and education. The group has a web site and can be located at their current address through a search engine.

Piskurich, G. M. (Ed.). (2000). *The ASTD handbook of training design and delivery*. New York: McGraw Hill Professional. The book is not as deep or theory-based as some might want, but does provide a well-rounded view of designing and delivering instruction in a training context.

Piskurich, G. M. (2006). *Rapid instructional design: Learning ID fast and right*. San Francisco: Pfeiffer. This is not a book about rapid-prototyping methods in instructional design; rather, it is an instructional design process "how to" with lots of tips and examples.

Reiser, R. A. (2001a). A history of instructional design and technology: Part I: A history of instructional media. *Educational Technology Research and Development 49*(1), 53–64.

Reiser, R. A. (2001b). A history of instructional design and technology: Part II: A history of instructional design. *Educational Technology Research and Development 49*(2), 57–67.

Reiser, R. A., & Dempsey, J. V. (Eds.). (2006). *Trends and issues in instructional design and technology* (2nd ed.). Upper Saddle River, NJ: Merrill/Prentice Hall.

Richey, R. C. (Ed.). (2000). *The legacy of Robert M. Gagné*. Syracuse, NY: ERIC Clearinghouse on Information and Technology. A biographical and historical retrospective that includes five of Gagné's key research papers.

Richey, R. C. (2002). *Instructional design competencies: The standards* (3rd ed.). Syracuse, NY: ERIC Clearing House on Information and Technology: International Board of Standards for Training, Performance, and Instruction.

Rothwell, W. J., & Kazanas, H. C. (2004). *Mastering the instructional design process: A systematic approach* (3rd ed.). San Francisco: Jossey-Bass. A general text on the instructional design process that is focused on professional and technical training.

Seels, B., & Glasgow, Z. (1998). *Making instructional design decisions*. Upper Saddle River, NJ: Merrill/Prentice Hall. Presents an instructional design model for novices and for practitioners.

Senge, P. (1990). *The fifth discipline: The art and practice of the learning organization*. New York: Currency Doubleday. In this modern management classic, Senge identifies systems thinking as the fifth in a set of five disciplines required for growth and development of learning organizations.

Smith, P. L., & Ragan, T. J. (2005). *Instructional design* (3rd ed.). New York: Wiley. Excellent chapters on instructional strategies for various learning outcomes.

Visscher-Voerman, I., & Gustafson, K. L. (2004). Paradigms in the theory and practice of education and training design. *Educational Technology, Research, and Development, 52*(2), 69–89.

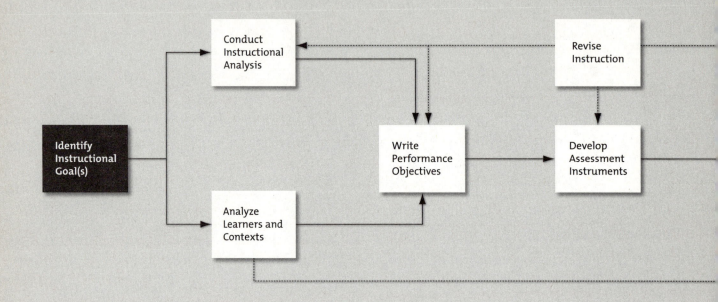

o b j e c t i v e s

➤ Define performance analysis, needs assessment, needs statements, and instructional goals.
➤ Identify an instructional goal that meets the criteria for initiating the design of effective instruction.
➤ Write an instructional goal that meets the criteria for initiating the development of instructional materials.
➤ Evaluate instructional goals for congruence with learner characteristics, learning and performance contexts, and tools available for learners.

Identifying Instructional Goals Using Front-End Analysis

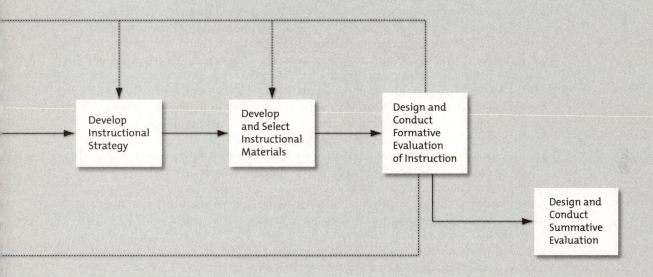

| Develop Instructional Strategy | Develop and Select Instructional Materials | Design and Conduct Formative Evaluation of Instruction | Design and Conduct Summative Evaluation |

Background

Perhaps the most critical event in the instructional design process is identifying the instructional goal. If done improperly, even elegant instruction may not serve the organization's or the intended learners' real needs. Without accurate goals designers run the risk of planning instructional solutions for which needs do not really exist. There are many ways to identify instructional goals, but four common methods that come to mind are the subject-matter expert approach, the content outline approach, the administrative mandate approach, and the performance technology approach.

Every reader of this book could be considered a subject-matter expert (SME, pronounced S-M-E or smee) in some area. You have completed, or will complete, an undergraduate degree in some field. Your knowledge of that field now greatly exceeds that of the general public, so you would be considered a SME. When SMEs are asked to develop instruction in their areas of expertise, they will most likely consider their own learning on the subject. Depending on their evaluation of their own knowledge, they try either to replicate it for students or to improve it. The instructional goals established by SMEs often contain words such as *know* and *understand* with regard to content information. This approach to the teaching–learning process assumes that students need to learn what the SME knows and emphasizes the communication of information from instructor to student in the instructional process.

A second way to identify instructional goals is the content outline approach, in which convincing evidence that a performance problem exists is assumed to be caused by students not having learned the right type or amount of content. This approach often occurs when the "right type and amount of content" are outlined in predefined curriculum standards and frameworks, corporate policies, equipment manuals, training manuals, and so forth. One danger with this method is being locked into content standards that may no longer be relevant or that never were adequate solutions for organizational or social needs. Another danger is assuming that new instruction or more instruction will solve the problem when, in fact, the problem may be due to lack of accountability, lack of incentives, outdated tools, organizational culture, or some other factor.

It often happens that goals are identified for initiating the ID process simply because a person, a panel, a board, an agency, a work team, a supervisor, a program manager, or some other administrative authority issues a mandate that training for the selected goals *will occur*. Goals selected by mandate can be valid if appropriate planning and insight were exercised by the administrator on whose authority the training is based, or if an instructional designer can exercise political savvy and negotiating skills to confirm or redirect goals after the fact. Unfortunately there often is little latitude for negotiation, and this "ready-fire-aim" approach frequently misses the mark. Note that some goals selected through mandate can be valid by definition when required by federal or state law, by union contract, by safety requirements for new employee hires, and so forth. Such goals are true mandates and usually go straight to the training department. The student performance standards enacted by state legislatures are also examples of true mandates in public education and are passed down to school districts and schools for implementation.

Instructional designers favor a fourth approach, performance technology, in which instructional goals are set in response to problems or opportunities within an organization. There are no preconceived notions of what must be learned, of what will be included in an instructional package, or that, in fact, there is any need for instruction at all. Designers attempt to work with those responsible for ensuring that an organization is meeting its quality and productivity goals. These concerns apply to any organization, private or public. Private organizations are motivated to meet productivity goals and their clients' and customers' needs. Public agencies, including public schools, share this motivation and also strive to meet the needs for which taxpayers have mandated the expenditure of public funds. To the extent they are not doing so, changes must be made, and the crucial issue becomes determining the correct modifications.

Designers engage in performance analysis and needs assessment processes to identify the problem precisely, which is not always an easy task. The real problem is not always as it initially appears. After the problem is identified, the designer attempts to discover the causes of the problem, and then enumerates an array of solutions that could be implemented to solve the problem. One step toward a solution could be identifying a set of instructional goals for initiating the ID process, but seldom is instruction the single answer to a problem. Usually a combination of changes is required to solve the problem effectively.

Concepts

The model we use throughout this text is to guide the design, development, and revision of instruction. It has long been accepted that careful analysis is absolutely critical prior to initiating the design of instruction. This analytical work is sometimes referred to as front-end analysis and typically includes performance analysis, needs assessment, and in some cases job analysis. We will provide an overview of these three planning processes in this concepts section, but front-end analysis is not an activity

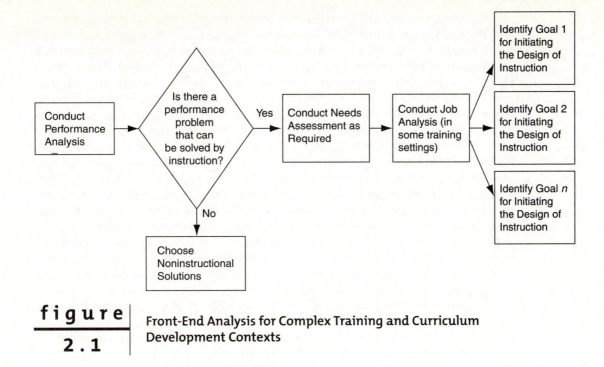

figure

2.1

Front-End Analysis for Complex Training and Curriculum Development Contexts

for which we provide detailed procedures and examples. Figure 2.1 will help to clarify how the skills that you are learning in this text fit into more complex, larger-scale training and curriculum development projects. For most instructional design efforts in school and university settings and for many professional and technical training projects, the brief overview and examples of front-end analysis in this chapter will serve the novice designer well.

Those readers who are using this book as part of a graduate degree program in instructional systems design or instructional technology may find that coursework in evaluation, performance analysis, and needs assessment is part of their programs of study. Others wanting in-depth preparation in front-end analysis are referred to books by Brown and Seidner (1998) for evaluation; Rossett (1999), Mager and Pipe (1997), and Robinson and Robinson (1995) for performance analysis; Kaufman (1998), Kaufman et al. (2002), and Rossett (1987) for needs assessment; and Jonassen, Tessmer, and Hannum (1999) for job analysis. If you are a student using this book you may be designing and developing a unit or lesson of instruction as one of the requirements for your class. If that is the case, you might start your project at the "Conduct Needs Assessment as Required" step in Figure 2.1 and go straight to "Identify Goal 1 for Initiating the Design of Instruction." To provide a broader context for instructional design, the discussion that follows includes an overview of performance analysis with examples from business and public schools.

Performance Analysis

Performance Analysis in a Business Setting   Public and private organizations are continually faced with problems that senior officers and managers must identify and solve. Problems reflect a failure to achieve certain organizational goals or to take advantage of opportunities. Those failures are often seen as resulting from a lack of or improper use of skills; thus, it is not unusual for an officer to identify a problem and assume that training is the solution. Such problems are often presented to the training department with the request that they develop training to solve the problem.

Even when a direct request for training has not been made, the response to some-one saying, "I've got a problem!" has often been, "OK, let's do a needs assessment and find out what training we can provide." Needs assessment is an indispensable tool for solving problems, but a performance technologist would take a different mind-set into the problem situation and do some analysis before deciding that training should be provided. In common terminology this mind-set is called critical thinking. Being a critical thinker is both attitude and intellectual skill; that is, one must *choose* to act like a critical thinker and *master* the analytical techniques employed by a crit-ical thinker. Some of these attitudes and techniques include being open-minded, be-ing objective, seeking root causes, viewing a problem from multiple perspectives, giving a fair hearing to evidence on multiple perspectives, suspending judgment until all per-tinent information has been heard, listening to contrary views, and changing a con-clusion in the face of compelling information. Applying critical thinking attitudes and skills is more difficult from within an organization than from outside. That is why outside consultants are often hired to conduct strategic planning and performance analysis activities. Instructional designers, however, are most often part of the orga-nization in which they practice their profession, so must cultivate this critical think-ing mind-set to be effective performance analysts.

To explain performance analysis further we will consider an example from pro-fessional and technical training. In our example the head of a large information sys-tems (IS) division came to the training manager and said, "The customer service call center has grown so fast that we can't keep up with all of the service orders on their computer workstations. Instead of hiring more service technicians, corporate personnel wants me to accept six transfers from other divisions who are scheduled for termination due to downsizing. I'm going to start screening candidates for trans-fer, but I know they won't have the skills we need. I want you to decide whether we should train them ourselves in desktop troubleshooting and repair or send them outside for training." The training manager replied, "Thanks for the heads-up. I'll check with the customer service manager and get back to you tomorrow morning." The training manager did some homework that night, and the next morning she diplomatically proposed a performance analysis rather than a quick jump into a training program. The director of information systems agreed to hold up the screen-ing process, but only for a week and a half, saying, "Go ahead and see what you can do." Some of the steps she took and information she learned over the next ten days are as follows:

- The computer breakdown problem was in the customer service call center, which had expanded rapidly with many new customer representatives and computer purchases. Current staffing in IS was not sufficient to keep up with the work-station troubleshooting and repair needs.
- One of the business goals for the customer service unit was to improve customer relations.
- One operational target for improved customer relations was customer satisfac-tion with 96 percent of telephone contact opportunities.
- To reach the satisfaction target, the customer service division had set performance standards of "maximum of three automated call menu selections before reaching a live representative" and "maximum average wait time of 90 seconds before reaching a live representative." (There were other performance standards but these are the only ones we will consider here.)
- When the training manager checked the most recent customer follow-up data she found that satisfaction with telephone contact was running at 76 percent, and when she checked telephone log tracking reports she found that average wait time was just over two and a half minutes and wait time for 17 percent of calls was over five minutes. Clearly, a business goal of the customer service unit and a tar-get performance standard were not being met.

- The training manager checked computer workstation problem reports, downtime, and repair logs in IS and found that hiring and training new computer techs to get workstations repaired and back online sooner would, indeed, decrease service interruptions in the call center and thereby lower average caller wait time.

But were there other solutions? Here is what the training manager found when she suspended judgment pending additional information, began to analyze the system of components and relationships among components that could be contributing to the performance problem, and entertained the possibility of alternatives to a training solution.

- She took another look at the telephone logs and checked a sample of transaction records. She discovered that fully a quarter of all calls going to the experienced customer service representatives with specialized training were simple information requests that could be handled by a receptionist-level person without a computer workstation.
- She looked again at the workstation problem reports and repair logs and found that 16 percent of downtime was due to simple configuration fixes and crash reboots with which inexperienced customer service representatives were not familiar.
- She found that computer purchases had barely kept up with the growth of the customer service call center and that IS did not have much shelf inventory to swap a working computer for a broken computer.

At the end of her ten days of performance analysis, the training manager, the head of information systems, and the customer service manager had a meeting and decided to try the following strategies for solving the performance problem and helping the customer service unit achieve its business goal.

- The training manager agreed to work with the telephone systems person in IS to improve call screening by clarifying the contents of the menu choices in the automated answering scripts and by adding another choice in two of the three menu levels. These changes would route a greater percentage of simple information requests to a pool of the newer, less-experienced customer service representatives.
- The training manager agreed to work with IS on a job aid for each workstation, a small laminated card with a decision tree of simple "if this happened, then do that" suggestions for computer "first aid." She also agreed to do a brief interactive training piece that would be available on the company's intranet to step the customer service representatives through the terminology and the process in the decision tree.
- IS decided to accelerate its computer purchase schedule to create some shelf inventory of machines that could be configured and available for service while broken units were being repaired.
- All agreed that it would be a good idea to allow some time for implementing and evaluating the proposed solutions and, in the mean time, to hire temporary computer technicians as needed from an outside employment services agency.

In solving the performance problem described in our example, the training director followed a "performance relationship map" formulated by Robinson and Robinson (1995) for organizing performance analysis efforts. The strategy of the relationship map is to relate a problem that has been voiced to a core organizational or business outcome and then check operational goals and performance standards related to that outcome. Table 2.1 is a summary in question and answer form of the relationship map process for performance analysis.

The purpose of a performance analysis study as depicted in Table 2.1 is to acquire information in order to verify problems and identify solutions. The outcome of a performance analysis study is a clear description of a problem in terms of failure to achieve desired organizational results and the corresponding desired and actual

table 2.1	Application of the Robinson and Robinson (1995) Performance Relationship Map	
Performance Analysis Question		**Performance Analysis Answer**
1. What is the problem that was originally voiced?		1. A training program for six new computer techs for desktop troubleshooting and repair in the customer service call center.
2. Is the voiced problem related to a core organizational outcome?		2. Yes: Improve customer relations.
3. Are there established operational goals for this outcome?		3. Yes: 96 percent customer satisfaction with service contacts by telephone (desired status).
4. Is the operational goal being met?		4. No: 76 percent customer satisfaction with service contacts by telephone (actual status).
5. Is there an operational need?		5. Yes: Eliminate the twenty percentage point gap between the desired status and the actual status.
6. Have job performance standards been set for achieving the operational goal?		6. Yes: Maximum of three automated call menu selections and maximum average wait time of ninety seconds before reaching a live service representative (desired status).
7. Are job performance standards being met?		7. No: Average wait time over two and a half minutes and wait time for 17 percent of calls over five minutes (actual status).
8. Is there a job performance need?		8. Yes: Eliminate the sixty-second gap between the desired status and the actual status.
9. Are there external factors outside the control of local management that are contributing to operational and job performance needs (e.g., government regulations, corporate hiring freeze, labor contract, corporation's national contract with telephone service provider, and so forth)?		9. No: Operational and job performance needs appear to be within the control of local management.
10. Are there internal factors within the control of local management that are contributing to job performance needs?		10. Yes: Work flow, logistics, employee skills, man hours.
11. Are there solutions for the performance needs?		11. Yes: Work flow—redesign call routing. Logistics—accelerate computer acquisitions. Employee skills—create job aid with training. Man hours—hire technicians from temp agency.

employee performance, evidence of the causes of the problem, and suggested cost-effective solutions. Note that while an instructional designer may guide or participate in a performance analysis study, there is no assumption that instruction will be a component of the solution. These studies are often team efforts, and the results reflect what is possible given a wide range of organizational resources. An important consideration in selecting a solution is cost, and instruction is often one of the more expensive alternative solutions. Experience has shown that under careful analysis, many organizational problems that previously were addressed by training are now solved via multicomponent solutions that may or may not include training. If part of the solution is training on new skills or rejuvenating existing skills, then plans for a needs assessment and an instructional design project are made.

Performance Analysis in a Public School Setting   The term *performance analysis* is seldom used in public schools, but the same kind of critical thinking is applied routinely to solve problems involving administrator, teacher, and student performance. For an example focusing on student performance, assume the principal of an elementary school was reviewing results from the state standards test and saw that fifth-grade students were well below the state average for finding and using information resources, and low performance on this section of the test was pulling down the overall fifth-grade performance profile. The principal explained the student performance problem to the assistant principal (AP) for curriculum and said, "We need in-service training for the fifth-grade teachers and the media specialist in information literacy skills. Will you please arrange it?" The AP said she would take care of it, but before she looked into scheduling in-service training she did some investigating. Here are some of the steps she took and information that she found:

- She checked the state standards and found that an information literate person "can recognize when information will help solve a problem, choose the best sources for valid and timely information, organize and synthesize the new information, and write and display the information appropriately for the problem." (*Information literacy* is the current term for library skills or research skills.)
- She compared the state benchmarks and skills in information literacy with sample test items and old exams that had been released to the public. The benchmarks and test items required both recall of information and application of information and concepts to solve problem scenarios. The test items seemed to be valid measures of the skills.
- She looked at scheduling and found that each class rotated through the media center once a week for forty minutes of contact time. She observed several fifth-grade classes during their media center visits and noted that the students had only fifteen to twenty minutes for learning information skills after getting organized and settled down, checking books in, browsing for new books, checking new books out, and taking Accelerated Reader quizzes. The fifteen to twenty minutes of instructional time did seem to be relevant, focused, and on task, but she didn't observe much follow-up when the students went back to their classrooms.

After her investigation, the AP briefed the principal on some tentative conclusions and decided to meet with the fifth-grade teachers and the media specialist. In the meeting she became convinced they all had a good grasp of information literacy skills, but none were very pleased with how they were teaching the content. They all felt they did not have time to go beyond a simple descriptive level and work with the students on applying the skills. The teachers admitted they didn't spend much time in the classroom following up on the instruction in the media center because of pressure to keep test scores up in reading, writing, and arithmetic, confirming the AP's observations of what was happening in the media center and the classrooms. The group concurred on the need for raising students' state test performance on using information resources and, agreeing they had to change their instructional practices, decided on the following action plan:

- Free the media specialist to attend the fifth-grade teachers' group meetings for collaboratively planning a strategy for embedding information skills within classroom language arts instruction.
- Free the media specialist for team teaching time in the fifth-grade classrooms.
- Upgrade from the desktop to the networked version of Accelerated Reader software so students could take AR tests and monitor progress in their own classrooms, thus freeing up instructional time during class visits to the media center.
- Implement an intensive learning improvement program with instruction containing embedded assessments, remediation, and enrichment.

The AP reported to the principal that she and the teachers believed they had a plan for solving the state test performance problem, but it would require some resources. The principal concurred and said the money was available for the software upgrade. Freeing the media specialist would be more difficult but money for a part-time media center clerk might be available from the PTA, the School Improvement Team's discretionary funds, a district budget for performance improvement projects, or from a combination of those sources.

Although the AP would not have described her investigation as performance analysis, she was using good, solid problem-solving methods to look for root causes of the students' poor test performance. In-service training would not have improved student test scores, because the media specialist and teachers knew the content and how to teach it; the constraints in their school schedule prevented them from doing so. The need was for changes freeing sufficient time for students to learn application of the information literacy skills.

The examples from business and education both illustrate instances where instruction was not the primary solution for a problem. *Analyzing Performance Problems* by Mager and Pipe (1997) describes a useful decision process for identifying performance problems caused by circumstances other than instruction. Their process is distilled into a straightforward flowchart that is easy to understand and apply. When instruction is indeed the solution or part of the solution, then needs assessment is an important tool for getting the instructional design process on track for effective results.

Needs Assessment

The processes involved in conducting a large-scale needs assessment can be very sophisticated, but the logic of needs assessment is simple. Needs assessment logic was used as a tool in the performance analysis in Table 2.1. For example, look at steps 3 through 5 and then at steps 6 through 8. There are three components of needs assessment logic. The first is establishing a standard or goal that is referred to as the *desired status*—for example, ten fiction books in the school library for each student enrolled, 90 percent on-time arrivals for city busses, a 40 percent gross profit margin on hardware sales, or 95 percent success rate for students in the school district passing the functional literacy examination. The second component is determining the *actual status* or existing level of performance on the standard or goal—for example, eight fiction books per student, 77 percent on-time arrivals, 43 percent gross profit margin, and 81 percent of students passing. The third component is identifying the *gap* between *desired status* and *actual status,* thereby describing a *need*. Following our examples, the school library needs two more fiction books per student; the city bus system needs 13 percent more on-time arrivals; gross profit margin is fine because actual status exceeds desired status; and the school district needs to increase the percentage of students passing the functional literacy examination by 14 percent. The logic of needs assessment can be summarized as a simple equation: *desired status − actual status = need*.

It has been noted that managers or executives often describe problems in terms of actual status, or the way things are now. Examples would be "Our deliveries are late," "Not enough of our students got to the district spelling bee," "Our sales are down," and "Too many of our students are failing the basic skills test." For actual status and performance to have meaning in needs assessment, the investigator would have to establish standards for a desired status and then further identify exactly *how late* the deliveries are, *how many* students made the district spelling bee, *how far* sales are down, and *what percentage* of the students are failing the basic skills test.

Careful descriptions of both desired and actual status are required, because a *gap or need* is defined as a comparison between the two. The gap of greatest consequence is that in organizational results. If it turns out that there is no gap, then there is no need and no change is required, and obviously there is no requirement for new instruction or training. This is the situation whenever any organizational officer (including a school board member) surveys a situation and indicates that it is satisfactory—the desired and actual are the same and there is no need for change.

We have seen that needs assessment logic is one of the tools used in performance analysis. If performance analysis indicates that training is one of the best solutions for a performance problem, then needs assessment will be used again. This would be called *training needs assessment* or *learning needs assessment* and would result in instructional goals for beginning an instructional design project. Recall that in the example of the customer service performance analysis the training director noted that 16 percent of computer downtime was due to simple configuration fixes and crash reboots with which inexperienced customer service representatives were not familiar. She decided that this was a training problem and volunteered to develop a job aid and training for workstation "first aid." At this point she would probably turn the task over to an ID project manager whose first thought would be "What is the real scope and nature of the performance problem that I want to solve through training?" Training needs assessment would help him answer his question. He would apply the three components of needs assessment logic by (1) working with subject-matter experts in IS to develop realistic standards for workstation first aid performance by customer service representatives (desired status); (2) studying work orders and maintenance logs and observing, interviewing, and perhaps testing customer service representatives (actual status); and (3) describing the gaps between standards for performance and actual performance levels (needs). Through this needs assessment work, the project manager could state a job performance standard for use by management in tracking the success of training and an instructional goal for beginning an ID project. The job performance standard could be "Customer service representatives will solve 95 percent of simple desktop configuration and crash reboot problems," and the instructional goal could be "Using a decision tree job aid, customer service representatives will diagnose simple desktop configuration and crash reboot problems and fix the problems without help from coworkers, supervisors, or IS technicians."

Kaufman (1998), Kaufman, Herman, and Watters (2002), and Kaufman, Oakley-Brown, Watkins, and Leigh (2003) have provided many insights into the needs assessment process, including the distinction between means and ends in terms of what organizations do and areas in which organizations have problems. Consider the following example from the public schools.

It is not unusual to hear principals say their teachers "need" to know more about computers. As a result, a workshop is provided so teachers can all become more competent. In this situation, teacher skills should be viewed as a means to an end, to turn out more competent students. If the real needs assessment issue is "What are the desired computer skill levels and the actual computer skill levels of the students?" and "If there is a gap and a need here, then what are the various solutions to upgrade those skills?" a workshop for all teachers may or may not be the best solution. Kaufman urges us to examine gaps in organizational results rather than internal processes when we begin to identify needs and make plans for spending organizational resources to meet these needs.

Needs assessment is a critical component of the total design process. Trainers and educators must be aware that the creation of unnecessary instruction has a tremendous cost in dollars and encourages detrimental attitudes in students involved in pointless learning activities. Therefore, more emphasis is being placed on front-end analysis, performance analysis, and other approaches for identifying needs more accurately. In the past it was common for survey instruments to be the major means of identifying and documenting training needs. Today surveys are being supplemented or supplanted with more insightful interviews and direct observations of performers.

Job Analysis

For the sake of completing our overview of front-end analysis, we include a brief look at *job analysis,* the process of gathering, analyzing, and synthesizing descriptions of what people do in their jobs. Job analysis is a managerial activity that gained popularity in the late 1800s and early 1900s with time-and-motion studies. It has evolved to serve many roles within the human resource development function, including (1) human resource forecasting and planning, (2) selecting and recruiting personnel, (3) ensuring equality of employment opportunity, (4) designing performance reviews, (5) developing compensation plans, (6) designing and redesigning jobs, and (7) planning training, job aids, performance support systems, and employee development. Current descriptions of what people do in their jobs are particularly useful in an era of constant, rapid, technological change and job dislocation, because descriptions of what people do provide a baseline for making decisions about redesigning jobs for organizational effectiveness, personal productivity, and job satisfaction.

In a typical job analysis, a particular job is characterized in general terms according to the people who work in the job and the environment surrounding the job. Then an inventory is developed of the tasks thought to comprise the job, and these tasks are grouped according to common characteristics into categories called *duties.* After the task inventory is assembled, it is screened by asking subject-matter experts and job incumbents whether the tasks really are a part of the job. After revision, the tasks are formatted as a survey, response scales and directions are added, and the survey is pilot tested. Following a final revision, the survey is duplicated and distributed to a sample of job incumbents. Respondents are typically asked to respond to questions such as: "Is this a task that you perform as part of your job?" "How frequently do you perform this task?" "What percentage of your workday do you spend on this task?" "How critical is this task to the success of your job?" and, "How difficult is this task to perform?" After return of the surveys, responses are summarized on a task-by-task basis, and high-priority tasks are chosen for further review. All of the processes described thus far in this general sequence are called *job analysis.* The process of *task analysis* begins when the tasks chosen for further review are broken down into component elements, the relationships among elements are detailed, the tools and conditions involved in performing each element are described, and standards for successful performance are written. Task analysis work is complex, very labor intensive, and time consuming; therefore, it is usually done only when specifically required for job design and redesign and for the design and development of critical training. When job analysis is conducted in professional and technical training contexts, it is usually to answer questions about what job performance *really* is and to focus training resources on tasks that offer a high probability of gains in job efficiency, effectiveness, and satisfaction.

In summary, instructional goals are ideally derived through a process of performance analysis that establishes rather broad indications of a problem that can be solved by providing instruction. Then a needs assessment is conducted to determine more specifically what performance deficiencies will be addressed, and an instructional goal is stated. Sometimes further examination of that goal is undertaken, either in the context of a curriculum or a job analysis. As a result, more refined specific statements of instructional goals emerge that focus on what learners will be able to do and the context in which they will be able to do it. Regardless of the procedure that is used to generate a goal, it is almost always necessary for the designer to clarify and sometimes amplify the goal in order for it to serve as a firm starting point for the instructional design process. Many goals are abstract or fuzzy, and designers must learn how to cope effectively with them.

Clarity in Instructional Goals

Mager (1997) has described a procedure that the designer can use when a vague, nonspecific goal is encountered. A fuzzy goal is generally some abstract statement about an internal state of the learner, such as "appreciating," "having an awareness of," "sensing," and so on. These kinds of terms often appear in goal statements, but the designer doesn't know what they mean because there is no indication of what learners would be doing if they achieved this goal. Designers assume that at the successful completion of their instruction, students should be able to demonstrate that they have achieved the goal; but if the goal is so unclear that it is not apparent what successful performance would be, then further analysis must be undertaken.

To analyze a vague goal, first write it down. Then indicate the things people would do to demonstrate that they had achieved that goal or what they would be doing if they were performing the goal. Don't be too critical at first; just write everything down that occurs to you. Next, sort through the statements for those that best represent what is meant by your unclear goal. Now incorporate each of these indicators (there may be one or quite a few) into a statement that tells what the learner will do. As a last step, examine the goal statement and ask yourself this: If learners achieved or demonstrated each of the performances, would you agree that they had achieved your goal? If the answer is yes, then you have clarified the goal; you have developed one or more goal statements that collectively represent the achievement of an important goal. In the Examples section of this chapter we demonstrate how this process can be used with vague goals.

The designer should be aware of this type of goal analysis procedure because many critical educational and training goals are not initially stated as clear, concise descriptions of performances of learners. They often are stated in terms that are quite meaningful (in general) to the originator, but have no specifics that the designer can use for developing instruction. Such goals should not be discarded as being useless. An analysis should be undertaken to identify specific performance outcomes that are implied by the goal. Often it will be helpful to use a number of knowledgeable people in the process so that you see the range of ideas that can emerge from the goal and the need for consensus on specific behaviors if truly successful instruction is to be developed.

Learners, Context, and Tools

Whereas the most important aspect of an instructional goal is the description of what learners will be able to do, that description is not complete without an indication of (1) who the learners are, (2) the context in which they will use the skills, and (3) the tools that will be available. A preliminary description of these aspects is important for two reasons. First, they require the designer to be clear about exactly who the learners will be rather than making vague statements or allusions to groups of learners. It is not unheard of for a design project to come to a halt when it is discovered that there are no learners available to receive the instruction. In essence, the instruction has no market.

Likewise, from the very beginning a project designer must be clear about the context in which the skills will be used and whether any aids or tools will be available. We will refer to this as the *performance context*. For example, if learners are going to be using computational skills, will they have access to calculators or computers? In the performance context, will they be working at a desk, or will they be on their feet talking to a customer? Must information be available from memory, or can a computer-based performance support system be used? Information about the performance context and the characteristics of the people who will be receiving the instruction is extremely important as the designer begins to analyze exactly what skills must be included in the instruction. Eventually, the information will be used to select instructional strategies to promote the use of the skills, not only in the learning context but also in the context in which they are eventually intended for application.

A complete goal statement should describe the following:

- The learners
- What learners will be able to do in the performance context
- The performance context in which the skills will be applied
- The tools that will be available to the learners in the performance context

An example of a complete goal statement would be the following: "The Acme call center operators will be able to use the Client Helper Support System to provide information to customers who contact the call center." All four components of a goal statement are included in this statement.

Criteria for Establishing Instructional Goals

Sometimes the goal-setting process is not totally rational; that is, it does not follow a systematic needs assessment process. The instructional designer must be aware that instructional design takes place in a specific context that includes a number of political and economic considerations as well as technical or academic ones. Stated in another way, powerful people often determine priorities, and finances almost always determine the limitations of what can be done on an instructional design project. Any selection of instructional goals must be done in terms of the following three concerns:

1. Will the development of this instruction solve the problem that led to the need for it?
2. Are these goals acceptable to those who must approve this instructional development effort?
3. Are there sufficient resources to complete the development of instruction for this goal?

These questions are of great importance to the institution or organization that will undertake the development.

We cannot overemphasize the importance of being able to relate logically and persuasively the goals of instruction to documented performance gaps within an organization. When instruction is developed for a client, the client must be convinced that if learners achieve the instructional goals, then a significant organizational problem will be solved or an opportunity will be realized through the use of the new skills. This kind of reasoning is as applicable to the development of instruction in public schools as it is to business, military, and public agencies.

The rationale for an instructional goal may help garner support from decision makers, but the designer and managers must be assured that there is sufficient time and resources for both the development of the instruction and its delivery. Most designers would agree that there seldom is sufficient time for either. One reason is that predicting the amount of time required to carry out a project is difficult. Another is that organizations often want something "yesterday!"

Not only is it difficult to predict how long it will take to develop instruction, but it is also difficult to predict how long learners will take to master the instructional goals (i.e., how long will the instruction last?). No readily accepted rules of thumb relate instructional (or learning) time to skills mastered. So many factors are involved that time estimates are difficult to make.

The most likely scenario is that the designer is told, "You have three weeks to develop a four-hour workshop." Until an organization has experience in making these decisions, they are based on immediate conditions in the work setting. Certainly the designer can shorten or lengthen instruction to fit the time available, but the primary instructional concern is to select the best possible instructional strategies for teaching the skills that must be mastered and then determine how much time is required. Obviously, we can make more accurate learning-time estimates after several tryouts of the instruction.

The designer should examine additional questions when contemplating an individual project. Assuming that a need has been established and that time and resources are available, then the designer should determine whether the content is stable enough to warrant the cost of developing it. If it will be out of date in six months, then extensive instructional development is probably not warranted.

In addition, the instructional design process depends heavily on the availability of learners to try out the instruction. Without access to appropriate learners, the designer will be unable to implement the total design process. A few learners are needed to try out rough draft versions of the instruction. If they are not available, then the designer will have to alter the ID process and may want to reconsider the validity of the need.

The final concern is the designer's own expertise in the subject matter of the instruction that will be developed. Experienced professional designers often work in teams involved in a content area that is, at least initially, totally foreign to them. The ability and willingness to work in teams is one of the most important characteristics of a successful designer. A great deal of content learning must take place before the designer can work effectively. For those just learning the design process, it is preferable to begin with a content area in which they already have subject-matter expertise. It is a lot easier to learn one new set of skills, namely instructional design skills, than it is to learn two new sets of skills—both content and process—at the same time.

If you have chosen (or are required) to design an instructional package as you work through the chapters of this book, the process will consume many hours of your time. Before you select or identify an instructional goal, review the criteria listed in this chapter. It is particularly important (1) that you have the expertise to deal with the subject matter, (2) that learners are available to you to help evaluate and revise the instructional materials, and (3) that you have selected a goal that can be taught in a reasonable amount of time.

Examples

Three examples of the procedures used to develop instructional goals may help you formulate or evaluate your own goals. All three examples are based on an identified problem, needs assessment activities, and a prescribed solution to a problem. Each example has its own scenario to help clarify the context of the problem and the process used to identify the goals. The first example concerns providing friendly customer service in a banking context. The second example on group leadership training is the Case Study for this chapter. For a third example from a school learning context, see the School Learning Case Study: Sentence Variety in Appendix A.

Providing Customer Service

For this example a local bank noticed a problem with low customer satisfaction ratings in its branch offices, primarily from customers completing lobby transactions with tellers and with customer service representatives. Informal performance analysis indicated that a satisfaction problem did indeed exist, stemming from customers' perceptions that bank personnel were often impersonal and sometimes short in their dealings. Unable to immediately determine whether bank personnel *didn't know how* or *didn't take the time* to interact in a polite, friendly, businesslike manner, further investigation revealed a common feeling of needing to hurry through a transaction so that other customers would not be kept waiting. However, an even more significant factor was that many employees did not know simple routines for courteous business interactions and did not have strategies for maintaining personalized contact with customers during high-volume times in the lobby. Training would certainly be part of an effective solution and the following instructional goal was identified:

Personnel will know the value of courteous, friendly service.

Although we can all agree that the intentions of this goal are sound, it can be classified as fuzzy and should be clarified. Simply because a goal is fuzzy does not mean it is not worthwhile. Just the opposite—it may be very worthwhile, as in this particular case of a goal that is common to many banks, even though it may still need some work.

First, the phrase *will know the value of* can be changed to *will demonstrate* in order to communicate better what is expected of personnel. Second, we must determine exactly what personnel are expected to demonstrate. We can begin this task by dividing the comprehensive term *service* into more interpretable main parts. We chose to define service as (1) a greeting to the customer, (2) a business transaction, and (3) a conclusion. Even with these two relatively minor changes, the goal is much clearer.

Original Goal	Restated Goal
Personnel will know the value of friendly service.	Personnel will demonstrate courteous, friendly behavior while greeting customers, transacting business, and concluding transactions.

Although the goal is much better in the new form, there are still two terms, *courteous* and *friendly,* that remain to be clarified. By relating these two concepts to each of the three stages of service that have been identified, we can further clarify the goal. Before continuing, remember the five steps included in making a fuzzy goal clearer:

1. Write the goal on paper.
2. Brainstorm to identify the behaviors learners would demonstrate to reflect their achievement of the goal.
3. Sort through the stated behaviors and select those that best represent the goal.
4. Incorporate the behaviors into a statement that describes what the learner will be able to do.
5. Evaluate the resulting statement for its clarity and relationship to the original fuzzy notion.

To help with the brainstorming process of identifying behaviors implied by *courteous* and *friendly,* we described behaviors specific to each of the three stages of service. We also decided to consider behaviors that could be classified as discourteous and unfriendly in a bank setting. The behaviors bank personnel *could* demonstrate and *should not* demonstrate to be considered courteous and friendly are listed in Table 2.2. The descriptions of courteous and discourteous behaviors can be given to bank administrators for additions, deletions, and further clarification.

When the list of representative behaviors is as complete as you can make it, review it at each stage of service to identify key behaviors that best represent the instructional goal. Based on the sample list, we restate the instructional goal as follows. All three forms of the goal are included to enable comparisons for completeness and clarity.

Original Goal   Personnel will know the value of courteous, friendly service.

Revised Version   Personnel will demonstrate courteous, friendly behavior while greeting customers, transacting business, and concluding transactions.

table 2.2

Friendly and Courteous Behaviors During Business Transactions with Customers

---

Greeting the Customer

DO	DON'T
1. Initiate greeting to customer (e.g., "Hello" or "Good morning.").	1. Wait for customer to speak first.
2. Say something to customer to make service appear personal: (a) use customer's name whenever possible, (b) say, "It's good to see you again," or "We haven't seen you for a while."	2. Treat customer like a stranger or someone you have never seen before.
3. If you must complete a prior transaction before beginning work, smile, verbally excuse yourself, and say you will only need a moment to finish your current task.	3. Simply continue working on a task and fail to look up or acknowledge a customer until you are ready.
4. Inquire, "How may I help you today?"	4. Wait for customer to initiate conversation about service needed.

Transacting Business

DO	DON'T
1. Attend to the customers currently waiting in your line. If you must leave your station, simply inform *newly arriving* customers that your line is closing and invite them to *begin* waiting in an alternate line.	1. Shuffle customers to another line after they have waited in yours for a while.
2. Listen attentively to customer as he or she explains problem or service desired.	2. Interrupt customers, even though you believe you know what they are going to say and can see by the paperwork the type of transaction they wish.
3. Keep customer's business as the primary focus of attention during transaction.	3. Chat with employees or other customers, thereby delaying current customer.
4. Complete any missing information on the form yourself, explaining to the customer what you have added and why.	4. Simply inform customers they have incorrectly or incompletely filled out a form, thereby making it their problem.
5. Give complete, clear instructions for additional forms that the customer should complete.	5. Simply say, "Complete these other forms and then come back."

Concluding Transaction

DO	DON'T
1. Inquire whether they need any additional services today.	1. Dismiss a customer by focusing your eyes on the next customer in line.
2. Thank the customer for his or her business.	2. Act like you have done him or her a favor by completing the transaction.
3. Verbally respond to any comments that the customer may have initiated (e.g., the weather, a holiday or upcoming vacation, your outfit or haircut, new decorations, etc.).	3. Let customer-initiated comments drop as though unnoticed.
4. Conclude with a wish for their well-being (e.g., "Take care," "Have a nice trip," "Have a nice day," or "Hurry back.").	4. Allow customers to walk away without a final comment or wish for their well-being.

Final Goal

- Personnel will demonstrate courteous, friendly behavior while greeting customers, transacting business, and concluding transactions by initiating conversation, personalizing comments, focusing attention, assisting with forms, and concluding with a "thanks" and a wish for the customer's well-being.
- *Learners, contexts, and tools:* The learners (personnel) are all bank employees who work directly with customers either in person, by telephone, or through written correspondence. The context is most typically the bank facility and spontaneous, interactive work with customers. Personnel will have no communication aids available to assist them in interacting with customers.

Although the final goal reflects only a subset of the behaviors generated during the brainstorming process, those selected convey the basic intention of the instructional goal. The complete list of courteous and discourteous behaviors that was generated should be saved as input for subsequent instructional analysis activities.

This example related to clarifying a fuzzy goal demonstrates that although taking a first step toward goal clarification can result in a clearer instructional goal, it may still be open to interpretation by instructional designers or instructors. Sometimes the goal must be clarified further by defining the actual behaviors to be demonstrated within each of the general categories included in the instructional goal.

A final concern when identifying instructional goals is the context in which the behavior will be performed. The instructional goal for bank personnel implies that the ultimate performance will be with customers in a bank. The performance context in which the goal is accomplished will have important implications for the instructional strategy.

Case Study: Group Leadership Training

This case study on group leadership training will serve as a running example to help the reader put the ID process together and will be included toward the end of every chapter between the Examples section and the Summary. Training effective group leaders is a common need in organizations ranging from community volunteer groups to business, industry, military, government, and education. Regardless of the context, any course of action dependent on productive group process requires effective group leadership. The setting for our case study is a community volunteer context wherein a need is found for preparing Neighborhood Crime Watch group leaders. The following paragraphs describe planning decisions based on needs assessment, the instructional goal, information for clarifying the instructional goal, and criteria for establishing instructional goals.

Leading Group Discussions

Performance Analysis   In response to rising neighborhood crime rates, a task force was constituted by the state department of law enforcement to conduct an extensive statewide performance analysis of neighborhood policing. In the course of its analysis, the task force documented significant disparities between ideal community policing levels and the actual level of policing that local city and county departments were able to provide. Following a thorough analysis of resources available to local police departments and the constraints under which they operate, one possible solution suggested for improving neighborhood policing services was increasing support for Neighborhood Crime Watch (NCW) organizations. It was noted that across the United States and England, active NCW communities bolstered the effectiveness of local police, improved community–police communications, and reduced the number of crimes committed within their neighborhoods. The panel studying this data called for finding ways to help neighborhoods better help themselves and targeted the Neighborhood Crime Watch Association as an organization worthy of further support.

Needs Assessment   A second task force was appointed to conduct a needs assessment study for Neighborhood Crime Watch organizations to determine how to increase the number of active NCW organizations within an area and improve the effectiveness of existing organizations. This panel concluded that (1) the NCW leader was the key person in determining the effectiveness of NCW groups, (2) leaders of the most effective groups had well-developed group discussion leadership skills, and (3) there was a chronic deficit of effective NCW leaders.

The state, on the recommendation of the two task forces, decided to sponsor a grant to develop training for NCW leader volunteers throughout the state. The instruction was to focus on group discussion leadership skills, and training materials were to be provided to all counties within the state. Support would also be provided to the staffs of local county government in-service training centers who would recruit, manage, and deliver the instruction. Training stipends were provided for one group of twenty NCW leaders per county for each of three years.

Clarifying the Instructional Goal   The instructional goal is (1) a clear, general statement of learner outcomes that is (2) related to an identified problem and needs assessment and (3) achievable through instruction rather than some more efficient means such as enhancing motivation of employees.

What is the instructional goal? In this instance, the instructional goal is for NCW leaders to demonstrate effective discussion group leadership skills in a neighborhood meeting. These discussions should be focused on encouraging neighbors to attend meetings, helping them identify crime problems in their community, and planning programs to help reduce identified problems.

What is the relationship between the goal and the needs assessment study? The instructional goal is directly linked to the law enforcement needs assessment study and to the task force recommendations about effective NCW leadership at the community level. It is also directly related to evidence that effective discussion group leadership was highly correlated with active NCW groups.

Does instruction appear to be the most effective way to achieve the goal? Developing effective discussion group leadership skills is directly related to instruction and practice, and these competencies are not likely to be developed through incentive programs for community volunteers.

Who are the learners? The learners are community volunteers who have agreed to provide leadership for their community NCW organization. They have attained varying levels of education, from high school diplomas to advanced college degrees, and they have developed varying group leadership skills, through community and church organizations, membership in quality teams at work, or formal employment as company owners, department chairs, managers, or supervisors. Most will have had no formal instruction in small-group leadership. They are representative of the citizens living throughout the state who choose to become involved in improving the quality of life for their families and communities.

In what context will the skills be used? NCW leaders will use their group discussion skills in planning for neighborhood NCW meetings and in providing leadership for the discussions that occur during the meetings. These meetings may occur in members' homes or in community centers within the neighborhood.

What tools are available to aid learners' performance in the actual context? There are no formal tools available to the leaders. They do have access to neighborhood police officers, crime prevention experts with the police department, and national, state, and local neighborhood-level crime statistics. Books are available that describe NCW groups, programs, and activities. There is, however, no formal support for further developing and refining discussion group leadership skills other than practice, practice, practice.

Criteria for Establishing Instructional Goals   Instructional designers can use certain criteria to help ensure that instructional goals warrant the cost and effort of designing, developing, and field-testing instruction. The group leadership instructional goal is examined in the following paragraphs using these criteria.

Is the instructional goal acceptable to administrators? In this instance, the design team interviewed local police agencies, county and state NCW association coordinators, and personnel in the county learning centers to determine their perceptions of the importance for and the feasibility of the training. They also interviewed several local NCW leaders concerning their desire to participate in the NCW leadership training sessions. Positive responses about the possibility of the instruction were received from all interviewees.

Are there sufficient resources (time, money, and personnel) to develop instruction? The state grant appears to provide sufficient resources for the instructional development team to develop and field-test the materials. Resources are also available to support the county training centers in managing and delivering the instruction and for trainees to receive the instruction.

Is the content stable? The content and skills underlying effective group discussion leadership are very stable. In fact, traces of John Dewey's 1910 book, *How We Think,* can be seen interwoven in modern texts on problem-solving discussions and productive teamwork in business, education, government, service, and recreation organizations.

Are learners available? Learners are available for participating in both the development and implementation of the instruction. Most current NCW leaders have received no formal leadership training and would therefore provide good feedback to the designers on instructional effectiveness. NCW coordinators have agreed to identify and contact NCW leaders for formative evaluation activities. They will also contact and select the new volunteer members within a county area who will receive the instruction each year.

This case study example demonstrates that instructional goal definition and refinement can be a lengthy, complex process that incorporates many people in the identification of problems, performance analysis, needs assessment, and statements of clear instructional goals. However, if instruction is to address real problems faced by an organization and reflect actual goals, then this process is necessary.

Readers are reminded that a case study focused on school learning is available in the Appendixes. These materials are beneficial in part because they are collected together rather than spread through the chapters of the text. Readers can easily progress from one design document to the next and see the progress of the design. Appendix A provides examples of front-end analysis and determination of instructional goals relevant to this chapter. For additional case studies in instructional design, readers are referred to Ertmer and Quinn's *ID Casebook* (2003).

SUMMARY

Instructional goals are clear statements of behaviors that learners are to demonstrate as a result of instruction. Typically derived through a front-end analysis process and intended to address problems that can be resolved most efficiently through instruction, instructional goals provide the foundation for all subsequent instructional design activities.

Instructional goals are selected and refined through a rational process that requires answering questions about a particular problem and need, about the clarity of the goal statement, and about the availability of resources to design and develop the instruction.

You should answer several questions about the problem and need:

1. Is the need clearly described and verified?
2. Is the need foreseeable in the future as well as currently?
3. Is the most effective solution to the problem instruction?
4. Is there logical agreement between the solution to the problem and the proposed instructional goals?
5. Are the instructional goals acceptable to administrators and managers?

Questions you should answer related to the clarity of the instructional goal include the following:

1. Do the behaviors reflect clearly demonstrable, measurable behaviors?
2. Is the topic area clearly delineated?
3. Is the content relatively stable over time?

Questions to be answered related to resources include the following:

1. Do you have expertise in the instructional goal area or reliable access to those who do?
2. Are the time and resources required to complete the project available to you?
3. Is a group of learners available during the development process in order for you to evaluate and refine your instruction?

Frequently, the instructional goal will be a very general statement of behaviors and content that must be clarified before some of the preceding questions can be answered. The procedure recommended for clarifying instructional goals includes the following steps:

1. Write down the instructional goal.
2. Generate a list of all the behaviors the learners should perform to demonstrate that they have achieved the goal.
3. Analyze the expanded list of behaviors and select those that best reflect achievement of the goal.
4. Incorporate the selected behaviors into a statement or statements that describe what the learners will demonstrate.
5. Examine the revised goal statement and judge whether learners who demonstrate the behaviors will have accomplished the initial broad goal.

RUBRIC FOR EVALUATING INSTRUCTIONAL GOALS

The rubric that follows contains a summary of the criteria you can use to evaluate and refine your instructional goals. It includes the main areas of congruence with the organization's needs, the feasibility of the goal, and its clarity.

Designer note: If an element is not relevant for your project, mark NA for not applicable in the No column.

No	Some	Yes	**A. Congruence with Organization Needs** Is/are the instructional goal statement(s):
___	___	___	1. Linked clearly to an identified problem in the organization?
___	___	___	2. Linked clearly to documented performance gaps?
___	___	___	3. Clearly a solution to the problem?
___	___	___	4. Acceptable to those who approve the instructional effort?

No	Some	Yes	
			B. Feasibility Does the plan include:
___	___	___	1. Stable content/skills over time to warrant investment/resources?
___	___	___	2. Sufficient designer expertise in instructional goal area?
___	___	___	3. Sufficient *people* to design/develop/deliver instruction?
___	___	___	4. Sufficient *time* to design/develop/deliver instruction?
___	___	___	5. An adequate number of learners for development/delivery?
			C. Clarity Do the instructional goal statement(s) describe the:
___	___	___	1. Actions of the learners (what they will *do*)?
___	___	___	2. Content clearly?
___	___	___	3. Intended learners?
___	___	___	4. Performance context?
___	___	___	5. Tools available to learners in performance context?
			D. Other
___	___	___	1.
___	___	___	2.

An appropriate, feasible, and clearly stated instructional goal should be the product of these activities. Using this clarified statement of learner outcomes, you are ready to conduct a goal analysis, which is described in Chapter 3.

PRACTICE

The following list contains several instructional goals that may or may not be appropriate based on the criteria for writing acceptable instructional goals stated in this chapter. Read each goal and determine whether it is correct as written or should be revised. If you believe it can be revised given the information available, revise it and compare your work with the revisions provided in the Feedback section that follows.

1. The district will provide in-service training for teachers prior to the administration and interpretation of standardized tests.
2. Students will understand how to punctuate a variety of simple sentences.
3. Salespersons will learn to use time management forms.
4. Teachers will assign one theme each week.
5. Customers will understand how to balance a checkbook.

The first step in developing a unit of instruction is to state the instructional goal. Several criteria can be used to help you select a suitable goal statement. From the following list of possible considerations for selection, identify all those that are relevant to a designer's selection of an instructional goal.

_____ 6. Personal knowledge and skills in content area

_____ 7. Stable content area

_____ 8. Time required for writing instruction versus the importance of students possessing that knowledge or skill

_____ 9. Students available to try out materials for clarity and revision purposes

_____ 10. Areas in which students have difficulty learning

_____ 11. Few materials available on the topic though instruction is considered important

_____ 12. Content area is fairly logical

An instructional goal must be stated as clearly as possible. From the following lists of considerations select all those within each section that are important for writing instructional goals.

13. Clear statement of behavior
   a. Behavior required of the student is obvious in the goal.
   b. Behavior in the goal can be observed.
   c. Behavior in the goal can be measured to determine whether students have reached the goal.

14. Clear versus fuzzy goals
   a. Instructional goal includes a clearly stated behavior.
   b. Any limitations that will be imposed on the behavior are stated clearly.

15. Time
    a. Approximate instructional time required for students to reach goal.
    b. Approximate time you can devote to developing and revising instruction.

16. Following a districtwide needs assessment on middle school students' writing skills, teachers decided to design special instruction that focused students on:
    - Writing a variety of sentence types based on sentence purpose.
    - Using a variety of sentence structures that vary in complexity.
    - Using a variety of punctuation to match sentence type and complexity.

Through instruction focused directly on the problems identified in the needs assessment, they hoped to change the current pattern of simplistic similarity found in students' compositions. Write an instructional goal for the instruction that can be used in the special unit on writing composition.

17. Write an instructional goal for which you would like to develop a unit of instruction.

FEEDBACK

1. The instructional goal should be revised because it describes what the district is expected to accomplish rather than the teachers. The goal could be rewritten in the following way to reflect two units of instruction commonly provided by school districts. Notice the behavior to be exhibited by teachers has been clarified.
   - Teachers will administer selected standardized tests according to the procedures described in the test manual.
   - Teachers will interpret student performance on both individual and class profile sheets that are provided by the test maker.

2. The goal should be revised because the words "will understand" are too general. The goal could be rewritten to clarify exactly the behavior students will use to demonstrate that they understand how to punctuate sentences. Additionally, the specific punctuation marks to be included in the lesson and used by students are included in the goal.
   - Students will punctuate a variety of simple sentences using periods, question marks, and exclamation points.

3. "Learn to use" states the intended outcome of instruction, but behavior used to describe what sales personnel will actually do might be clarified as follows:
   - Sales personnel will complete time management forms using daily, weekly, and monthly schedules.

4. This is not an instructional goal but a description of the process teachers will use to enable students to practice composition skills; it totally ignores the nature of the skills students are expected to acquire during practice. Not enough information is included in the statement to enable the instructional goal to be rewritten.

5. The phrase "will understand" in the goal is imprecise. The instructional goal could be clarified as follows:
   - Customers will balance a checkbook using canceled checks, a check register, and a monthly bank statement.

6–12. If you selected all of the criteria, you are correct. Each criterion is an important consideration in developing an instructional goal. With regard to personal knowledge of the topic, experienced instructional designers often work with SMEs from a variety of context areas in which the designer has no expertise.

13–15. All of the considerations listed are important.

16. Compare your instructional goal for writing composition with this one: In written composition, students will: (1) use a variety of sentence types and accompanying punctuation based on the *purpose* and *mood* of the sentence and (2) use a variety of sentence types and accompanying punctuation based on the *complexity* or *structure* of the sentence. You will want to examine all the information related to the front-end analysis for the school curriculum case study located in Appendix A, which reflects the beginning point for a complete instructional design case study in a school context. Readers currently working in schools or planning to work in schools should benefit from this school-based example.

17. Refer back to the criteria for evaluating instructional goals listed in the rubric for evaluating

instructional goals shown earlier. Evaluate your topic using each criterion statement.

- Does your goal meet each criterion?
- If it does not meet a particular criterion, can it be revised to do so?
- If it does not meet a particular criterion and cannot be revised to do so, you may want to write another instructional goal and try again.

You may need help in determining whether your goal meets some of the criteria for topic selection such as need or interest, possibly by discussing these issues with colleagues and students. Libraries and the Internet are good sources for determining whether materials on your topic are available and the nature of the available materials. Revise and rewrite your instructional goal as needed to meet the above criteria.

You may check the clarity of your goal by asking colleagues and intended learners to interpret verbally the instructional goal you have written. Do they interpret the goal and the required behavior exactly as you intended? You may need to revise.

If your goal is too big for the instructional time available (thirty minutes, one hour, two hours, etc.), you may want to divide the goal into its logical major parts, reword each part as an instructional goal, and then select the part most suited to your needs and time constraints.

If your goal is too small for the amount of time you desire, consider the skills the student will need to enter your instruction and the skills the student will be ready to learn as a result of completing it. By considering skills related to your goal in this fashion, you can identify the appropriate instruction to include for a specific period of time. Of course you will want to revise your instructional goal to include more skills or information as required.

Rewrite your instructional goal if necessary and begin Chapter 3 after you have developed a clear, behaviorally stated instructional goal that you estimate will fit the desired amount of instructional time.

REFERENCES AND RECOMMENDED READINGS

Barbazette, J. (2006). *Training needs assessment: Methods, tools, and techniques.* San Francisco: Pfeiffer.

Brannick, M. (2002). *Job analysis: Methods, research, and applications for human resource management in the new millennium.* Thousand Oaks, CA: Sage Publications. Thorough treatment of functions and methods of job analysis in the workplace.

Brown, S. M., & Seidner, C. J. (Eds.). (1998). *Evaluating corporate training: Models and issues.* Boston: Kluwer Academic Publishers. This book contains a section on evaluation contexts and models that have relevance for front-end analysis.

Chevalier, R. (Ed.). (2004). *Human performance technology revisited.* Silver Spring, MD: International Society for Performance Improvement. A selection of articles on performance technology compiled from the ISPI journal *Performance Improvement.*

Educational Technology Magazine, 43(1). (2003). Special issue on perspectives on training and performance improvement in business.

Ertmer, P. A., & Quinn, J. (2003). *The ID casebook: Case studies in instructional design* (2nd ed.). Upper Saddle River, NJ: Merrill/Prentice Hall.

Gagné, R. M., Wager, W. W., Golas, K. C., & Keller, J. M. (2004). *Principles of instructional design* (5th ed.). Belmont, CA: Wadsworth/Thomson Learning. Educational goals are related to instructional outcomes, especially as they relate to different categories of learning.

Guidry, J. W., & Simmons, J. L. (2001). Needs assessment: Analyzing performance issues and determining solutions. In L. A. Burke (Ed.), *High-impact training solutions: Top issues troubling trainers.* Westport, CT: Quorum Books.

Gupta, K., Sleezer, C. M., & Russ-Eft, D. F. (2007). *A practical guide to needs assessment* (2nd ed.). San Francisco: Pfeiffer. Models and practical tips for ID practitioners in training and development.

Jonassen, D. H., Tessmer, M., & Hannum, W. H. (1999). *Task analysis methods for instructional design.* Mahwah, NJ: Lawrence Erlbaum Associates. The book has a chapter on job task analysis.

Kaufman, R. (1998). *Strategic thinking: A guide to identifying and solving problems* (revised). Arlington, VA, & Washington, DC: American Society for Training & Development and the International Society for Performance Improvement.

Kaufman, R., Herman, J., & Watters, K. (2002). *Educational planning.* New York: Roman and Littlefield.

Kaufman, R., Oakley-Brown, H., Watkins, R., & Leigh, D. (2003). *Strategic planning for success.* San Francisco: Jossey-Bass/Pfeiffer.

Mager, R. F. (1997). *Goal analysis* (3rd ed.). Atlanta, GA: CEP Press. This brief book describes a process used by the author to help groups clearly identify goals for their instruction.

Mager, R. F., & Pipe, P. (1997). *Analyzing performance problems* (3rd ed.). Atlanta: GA: CEP Press. Latest edition of a classic that describes an approach to determining if training is the solution to a performance problem, or if other solutions should be implemented.

McConnell, J. (2003). *How to identify your organization's training needs: A practical guide to needs analysis.* New York: AMACOM. This resource is available by Internet as a NetLibrary e-book in affiliated libraries.

Pershing, J. A. (Ed.). (2006). *Handbook of human performance technology: Principles, practices, and potential* (3rd ed.). San Francisco: Pfeiffer.

Robinson, D. G., & Robinson, J. C. (1995). *Performance consulting: Moving beyond training.* San Francisco: Berrett-Koehler.

Rosenberg, M. (1990, January). Performance technology: Working the system. *Training,* 43–48. One of the early defining articles on performance technology.

Rossett, A. (1987). *Training needs assessment.* Englewood Cliffs, NJ: Educational Technology Publications. An excellent description of various needs assessment techniques and supporting tools.

Rossett, A. (1999). *First things fast.* San Francisco: Jossey-Bass/Pfeiffer. Approaches to determining if a performance problem exists in an organization.

Rothwell, W. J., & Kazanas, H. C. (1998). *Mastering the instructional design process: A systematic approach.* San Francisco: Jossey-Bass.

Sink, D. L. (2002). ISD—Faster, better, easier. *Performance Improvement, 41*(7), 16–22.

Stolovitch, H. D., & Keeps, E. J. (2004). *Front end analysis and return on investment toolkit.* San Francisco: Jossey-Bass/Pfeiffer. This toolkit facilitates analyzing training efforts on the front end as well as evaluating worth and return on investment (ROI) on the back end of ISD.

Van Tiem, D. M., Moseley, J. L., & Dessinger, J. C. (2005). *Fundamentals of performance technology: A guide to improving people, process, and performance* (2nd ed.). Silver Spring, MD: International Society for Performance Improvement.

Wilmoth, F. S., Prigmore, C., & Bray, M. (2002). HPT models: An overview of the major models in the field. *Performance Improvement, 41*(8), 16–24.

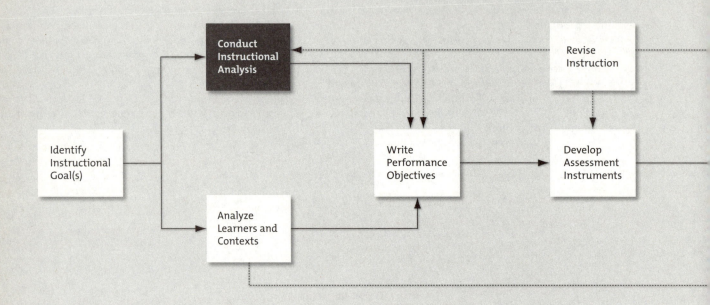

objectives

➤ Classify instructional goals in the following domains: intellectual skill, verbal information, psychomotor skill, and attitude.

➤ Perform a goal analysis to identify the major steps required to accomplish an instructional goal.

Conducting a Goal Analysis

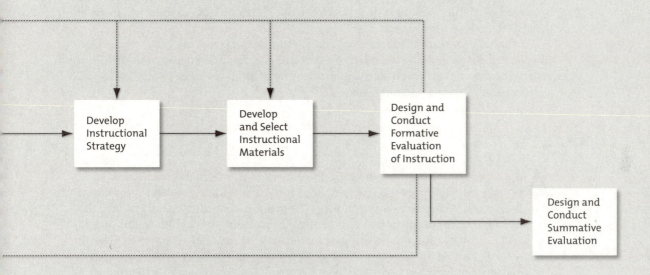

Develop Instructional Strategy → Develop and Select Instructional Materials → Design and Conduct Formative Evaluation of Instruction → Design and Conduct Summative Evaluation

Background

As we move from chapter to chapter in describing the instructional design process, note that the step being discussed is highlighted in the diagram of the model. Also, recall that we begin this step of the design process with a goal that has already been identified and stated. The goal could have been identified through performance analysis and needs assessment or by consulting a state's school performance standards or federal workplace safety standards. However it was derived, the goal should be a clear statement of what learners will be able to do.

The major purpose of instructional analysis is to identify the skills and knowledge that should be included in our instruction. Since this can be a complex process, we have separated it into two major substeps, each addressed in a separate chapter in this book. In this chapter we will discuss how the designer determines the major components of the instructional goal via the use of goal analysis. In the next chapter, we will describe how each step in the goal can be further analyzed to identify subordinate skills. In our experience, ID students are much more successful doing the subskills analysis if they have already worked their way through a successful goal analysis. The total process is referred to as instructional analysis.

The first question for the designer, following the identification of an instructional goal, is "What exactly would learners be doing if they were accomplishing the goal successfully?" Examining instruction by asking such questions is in sharp contrast to creating instruction by first identifying topics or content areas and then determining what information should be included for each topic based on the current views of SMEs. The SME approach tends to stress *knowing,* whereas the instructional design approach stresses *doing.* For example, can you imagine the frustrations of a group of employees at a two-week training session on developing and maintaining a web site after spending the first week studying the history and theory of the Internet? Not until the second week do they get to sit at a computer and begin to experience the excitement of learning to publish their own web page. This is an example of not only destroying learners' motivation but also of not having a procedure for identifying the skills that are *really* required to achieve the instructional goal.

Likewise, rather than describing the content of a course on Shakespeare in terms of a list of the ten plays that a student will read, instructional designers would identify precisely what students will be able to do after completing the course, such as "compare and contrast the element of character development in three of Shakespeare's comedies." Through goal analysis, designers can move beyond simply stating what students will have read when they complete their course on Shakespeare. This chapter will focus on these goal analysis procedures.

It should be stressed that the goal analysis approach is not the only way to identify content that should be included in a set of instructional materials. Using this approach, however, does result in the identification of skills that effectively lead to the achievement of an instructional goal.

Concepts

An instructional analysis is a set of procedures that, when applied to an instructional goal, identifies the relevant steps for performing a goal and the subordinate skills required for a student to achieve the goal. A subordinate skill is a skill that must be achieved in order to learn some higher-level skill, by facilitating or providing positive transfer for the learning of higher-level skills. This chapter focuses on goal analysis, saving the analysis of subskills for the next chapter.

Goal analysis includes two fundamental steps. The first is to classify the goal statement according to the kind of learning that will occur. (The different categories of learning are referred to as *domains of learning.*) The second step is to identify and sequence the major steps required to perform the goal or, for verbal information, identify the major clusters of information that learners must recall.

Review each of the following abbreviated goal statements:

1. Given a list of cities, name the state of which each is the capital.
2. Given a bank statement and a checkbook, balance the checkbook.
3. Set up and operate a digital video camera.
4. Choose to make lifestyle decisions that reflect positive lifelong health concerns.

Each of these goals might serve as the starting point for instructional design, and the question then becomes, "How do we determine what skills must be learned in order to achieve these goals?" The first step is to categorize the goal into one of Gagné's (1985) domains of learning, which is done because of the implications for the goal analysis and the selection of the appropriate subordinate skills analysis techniques discussed in Chapter 4.

Verbal Information

The first of our sample goals requires the learner to name the state for which each of the cities is the capital. There are many ways to teach such a skill and several ways the learner might try to learn it. But basically there is only one answer for each question and only one basic way to ask each question. There is no symbolic manipulation—no problem solving or rule applying. In essence, verbal information goals require the learners to provide specific responses to relatively specific questions.

You can usually spot a verbal information goal by the verb that is used. Often the learner must "state," "list," or "describe." It is assumed that the information to be stated or listed will be taught in the instruction; therefore, the task for the learner is to store the information in memory during the instruction and remember it for the test or when needed for some related task.

Intellectual Skills

Now let's consider goal 2, which deals with balancing a checkbook. By nearly anyone's definition, this is a problem-solving task and is therefore classified as an intellectual skill, defined as skills that require the learner to do some unique cognitive activity—unique in the sense that the learner must be able to solve a problem or perform an activity with previously unencountered information or examples. The four most common types of intellectual skills are making discriminations, forming concepts, applying rules, and solving problems. With these skills the learner can classify things according to labels and characteristics, can apply a rule, and can select and apply a variety of rules in order to solve problems. Any goal that requires a learner to manipulate symbolic information in some way will be an intellectual skill. So, in addition to our problem-solving goal, the following would also be classified as intellectual skills: being able to apply the rule for computing sales tax and being able to classify a variety of creatures as either mammals or reptiles.

It is important to be able to identify the various levels of intellectual skills. Discriminations are mostly simple, low-level learning by which we know whether things are the same or different. We actively teach young children to discriminate between the same and different colors, shapes, textures, sounds, temperatures, tastes, and so forth. Discriminations are seldom taught as individual learning outcomes to older children and adults except in specialized instances such as sounds in foreign language and music, colors and odors in chemistry, and kinesthetic "feel" in athletics. Discriminations are, however, important building blocks that we put together as we learn concepts. Just think of the important discriminations that are involved as a child learns the concept of "hot burner" and the rule "Don't touch the burner if it is hot!"

Learning concepts essentially means being able to identify examples as being members of a certain classification. If the concept is baseball equipment, then the learner would have to be able to determine whether various examples of equipment were baseball equipment. Note that the learner might be asked to identify an actual object or even a picture or description of the object. The learner would have to have mastered the concept by learning the characteristics of baseball equipment that distinguish it from all other sporting equipment and from other objects as well.

Concepts are combined to produce rules. An example of a rule is "a-squared plus b-squared equals c-squared." In this rule, the learner has to have the concepts of a, b, and c, squaring, adding, and square root. The rule shows the relationships among these concepts. The knowledge of the rule is tested by giving the learner a variety of values for a and b and asking for the value of c. The learner must follow a series of steps to produce the correct answer.

The highest level of intellectual skill is problem solving, and there are two types of problems: well structured and ill structured. The more typical is the well-structured problem usually considered to be an application problem. The learner is asked to apply a number of concepts and rules in order to solve a well-defined problem. Typically the learner (or problem solver) is given a lot of details about a situation, a suggestion of what rules and concepts might apply, and an indication of what the characteristics of the solution will be. There is a preferred way of going about determining what the solution should be. Algebra problems are a typical example of well-structured problems that have a preferred process, involve a variety of concepts and rules, and have a "correct" answer.

Researchers also classify some problems as ill structured, in which not all the data required for a solution are readily available to the learner or even the nature of the goal is not clear. Multiple processes can be used to reach a solution, and no one solution is considered the "correct" one, even though the general properties of an adequate solution may be known. There is no better example of an ill-structured problem than the instructional design process itself. Rarely do we know all the critical elements that pertain to the formulation of the need for the instruction or the learners who will receive the instruction. There are various methods of analysis and strategies for presenting the instruction, and there are a variety of ways to assess the effectiveness of the instruction.

Most of the instruction created by instructional designers is in the domain of intellectual skills. It is important to be able to classify learning outcomes according to the various levels of skills and to determine whether the instructional goal could be improved or made more appropriate for learners by elevating it to a higher level of intellectual skill outcome. This is especially true when the designer is presented with an instructional goal in the domain of verbal information.

Psychomotor Skills

The third goal listed above—setting up and operating a digital video camera—would be classified as a psychomotor goal because it involves the coordination of mental and physical activity. In this case, equipment must be manipulated in a very specific way to successfully produce a quality video image.

Psychomotor skills are characterized by learners executing physical actions, with or without equipment, to achieve specified results. In certain situations there may be a lot of "psycho" in the psychomotor goal. That is, there may be a great deal of mental or cognitive activity that must accompany the motor activity. However, for purposes of instructional analysis, if the learner must learn to execute new, nontrivial motor skills or performance depends on the skillful execution of a physical skill, we will refer to it as a psychomotor goal. Consider the following examples. Being able to throw a baseball is a psychomotor skill that requires repeated practice for mastery. Panning smoothly with a video camera to follow a moving object while maintaining correct lead space in the video frame requires practice for mastery; however, programming a VCR to automatically record a late-night program, in which the pushing of buttons is a trivial motor skill for adults, is essentially an intellectual skill. Extended practice in the pushing of buttons is not required for mastery and will not improve the ability to record the late-night program.

Attitudes

If we express a goal statement in terms of having learners choose to do something, as in the fourth example on choosing a healthy lifestyle, then that goal should be classified as an attitudinal goal. Attitudes are usually described as the tendency to make particular choices or decisions. For example, we would like individuals to choose to be good employees, choose to protect the environment, and choose to eat nourishing food. Goal number 4 stated that learners would choose to make lifestyle decisions that reflect a positive lifelong concern for their health. To identify an attitudinal goal, determine whether the learners will have a choice to make and whether the goal indicates the direction in which the decision is to be influenced.

Another characteristic of attitudinal goals is that they probably will not be achieved at the end of the instruction. They are quite often long-term goals that are extremely important but very difficult to evaluate in the short term. As you examine an attitudinal goal, you will find that the only way we can determine whether learners have "achieved" an attitude is by having them do something. That *something* will be a psychomotor skill, intellectual skill, or verbal information; therefore, instructional goals that focus on attitudes can be viewed as influencing the learner to choose, under certain circumstances, to perform an intellectual skill or psychomotor skill or to state certain verbal information. This view of attitudes aligns well with current thinking about teaching dispositions. In her description of dispositions as educational goals, Katz (1993) makes a clear distinction between knowing how to do something and choosing to do it. For example, knowing how to report bullying on the playground or illegal practices in mortgage loan processing is necessary but not sufficient for action; a disposition toward (i.e., a choice for) social conscience, fair play, and ethical behavior is also required.

Cognitive Strategies

Readers familiar with Gagné's work know that he described a fifth domain of learning—cognitive strategies. We mention cognitive strategies here for completeness and to avoid confusion but have deliberately omitted the terminology from the chapters that follow because for our purposes cognitive strategies can be treated similarly to ill-structured problem solving and taught as intellectual skills. Cognitive strategies are the metaprocesses that we use to manage our thinking about things and manage our own learning. Some strategies are as straightforward as mentally repeating the name of new acquaintances several times while visualizing their faces so that you can call them by name the next time you meet them. A more complex cognitive strategy would be figuring out how to organize, cluster, remember, and apply new information from a chapter that will be included on a test. Now consider the very complex combination of ill-structured problems and cognitive strategies that a civil engineer might use in laying out a section of farmland for housing development:

1. The engineer would need to have command of a vast array of physical and intellectual tools, such as computer-assisted design, geographic information system databases, land surveying, soil analysis, hydrology, and water, sewer, and electrical utilities systems.
2. The engineer would need to have command of a variety of "textbook" engineering strategies for the range of problems that would be encountered in a land development project.
3. For a large project, the engineer would have to manage cooperative team efforts for in-house and consulting specialists in environmental, legal, and architectural matters.
4. The engineer would have to organize, manage, and apply all of those tools, solution strategies, and collaboration skills in a formerly unencountered environment. Some tools would be useful; some would not. Some solutions would work; others would be rejected or modified. Some project team members would contribute quickly and reliably; others would require more direction and maintenance. In the end, the final site development would be a one-of-a-kind product of the engineer's ability to orchestrate a variety of resources toward the solution of a unique problem.

The civil engineer in this example would be managing the internal thinking processes required to organize, attack, and solve the multidimensional problems in laying out the housing development, all the while learning new strategies for accomplishing the work assigned. This civil engineer's work can be compared directly with the description previously in this chapter of an instructional designer's work. Both are engaged in solving ill-structured problems. For the instructional design processes described in this text, we will place cognitive strategies with problem solving at the top of the intellectual skills grouping.

Bloom's Domains of Learning Outcomes

In the mid-1950s Benjamin Bloom (1956) and his colleagues published *The Taxonomy of Educational Objectives* as a framework for classifying student learning

| table 3.1 | Types of Learning Required in Bloom's Domains of Learning Outcomes |

Bloom THESE DOMAINS OF LEARNING OUTCOMES	REQUIRE	Gagné THESE TYPES OF LEARNING
Psychomotor Domain		Psychomotor Skills
Affective Domain		Attitude Skills
Cognitive Domain: Knowledge		Verbal Information Skills
Cognitive Domain: Comprehension		Intellectual Skills: Primarily concepts with some rules
Cognitive Domain: Application		Intellectual Skills: Primarily rules with some problem solving
Cognitive Domain: Analysis		Intellectual Skills: Primarily well-defined problem solving
Cognitive Domain: Synthesis		Intellectual Skills: Primarily ill-defined problem solving with some elements of cognitive strategies
Cognitive Domain: Evaluation		Intellectual Skills: Primarily ill-defined problem solving with some elements of cognitive strategies

Note: Most of Bloom's categories within the cognitive domain require combinations of skills. This table is intended to be illustrative rather than a definitive statement of the skills therein.

outcomes according to his views on the complexity of different kinds of skills. Bloom's taxonomy is a popular scheme for categorizing learning in both school and business settings, so we will include it here and compare it in Table 3.1 with Gagné's types of learning. Those familiar with Bloom's categories may want to use the table for translating from Bloom to Gagné. We will use Gagné's scheme throughout the book because his categories provide guidance for how to analyze goals and subskills and how to develop instructional strategies that will be most effective in bringing about learning.

Goal Analysis Procedures

It is important to recognize that the amount of instruction required to teach an instructional goal will vary tremendously from one goal to another. Some goals will represent skills that can be taught in less than an hour, while others will take many hours for students to achieve. The smaller the goal, the easier it is to do a precise analysis of what is to be learned. After we identify the domain of the goal, it is necessary to be more specific in indicating what the learner will be doing when performing the goal.

The best technique for analyzing a goal is to describe, in step-by-step fashion, exactly what a person would be doing when performing the goal. This is not as easy as it first may sound. The person may perform physical activities that are easy to observe, as in a psychomotor skill. On the other hand, the person may process "mental steps" that must be executed before there is any overt behavior, as in an intellectual skill. For example, it would be quite easy to observe the psychomotor steps used to clean a paintbrush and spray equipment but almost impossible to observe directly all the intellectual steps that a person might follow to determine how much paint would be required to cover a building.

As you go through the process of describing the exact steps that a person would take in performing your goal, you may find that one of the steps requires a decision followed by several alternate paths that can be pursued (and, therefore, must be learned). For example, in cleaning a paintbrush, you might find at one point in the cleaning process that the paint will not come out, so an alternative technique must be applied. Similarly, in attempting to solve the mathematics problems related to area and required paint, it may be necessary first to classify the problems as "type A" (smooth surface requiring less paint) or "type B" (rough surface requiring more paint). Based on that outcome, one of two very different techniques might be used to solve the problem. The point is that the learner has to be taught both how to make the decision and how to perform all of the alternative steps required to reach the goal.

Goal analysis is the visual display of the specific steps the learner would do when performing the instructional goal. Each step is stated in a box as shown in the flow diagram below:

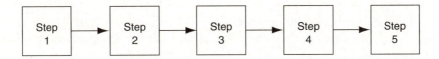

What this diagram indicates is that a learner who had the tools available as described in the goal statement could perform the goal by first doing step 1, which might be adding two numbers or it might be striking a particular key on a keyboard. After doing step 1, the learner would then perform step 2, then 3, 4, and 5. After doing step 5, the process would be complete, and, if done properly, would be considered a demonstration of the performance of the goal.

This sounds straightforward, and it is until you start doing an analysis of your own goal. Then questions arise about how large a step should be. How much can be included in one step? The answer depends primarily on the learner. If the instruction is for very young students or older students who have not "learned how to learn," then the steps should be quite small. If the same topic were taught to older, more proficient learners, the same skills would be included, but they would likely be combined into larger steps. If you take a close look at the systems design model at the beginning of this chapter you will note that the "Conduct Instructional Analysis" step which we are now describing is depicted as a parallel activity with the "Analyze Learners and Contexts" step, rather than as a preceding or following activity. The process of analyzing learners is described in Chapter 5; however, it is important to recognize that elements of that step can be completed simultaneously with goal analysis and that using detailed knowledge of learners while doing a goal analysis will result in more useful, realistic work. Remember that the chapter-by-chapter sequence found in this text is designed to lead you through the process of learning to use a systems design model. As you become proficient at instructional design you will gain a better feel for the sequential, parallel, and cyclical relationships among the steps in the model.

Regardless of how large the steps should be, the statement of each step must include a verb that describes an observable behavior. In our example, we used the verbs *adding* and *striking.* These are behaviors we can observe, or, in the case of *adding,* we can observe the answer written down. What we cannot see, for example, are people reading or listening; there is no direct result or product. If these are part of the goal, then the step should indicate what learners will identify from what they read or hear. Each step should have an observable outcome.

Another behavior that we cannot observe directly is decision making. Obviously it is a mental process based on a set of criteria. The decision-making steps are often critical to the performance of a goal, and depending on what decision is made, a different set of skills is used. If reaching the goal includes decision making, the decision step should be placed in a diamond with the alternate decision paths shown leading from the diamond.

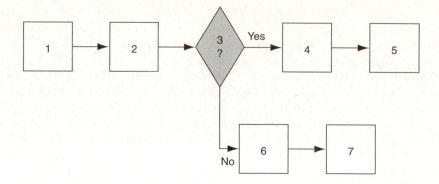

Let's walk through this diagram of the performance of a goal. The performer does step 1 and step 2 sequentially. Then a decision has to be made such as "Does the estimate exceed $300?" or "Is the word spelled correctly on the screen?" If the answer is yes, then the learner continues with steps 4 and 5. Alternatively, if the answer is no, then the learner would do steps 6 and 7.

Several important characteristics about decisions should be noted. First, a decision can be a step in the goal analysis process. The decision is written out with an appropriate verb and displayed in a diamond in the diagram. Second, there have to be at least two different skills to be learned and performed based on the outcome of the decision. An example not requiring a decision diamond would be one in which a step required the learner to "select an apple" and the next step to "peel the apple." The learner might be taught criteria to use for selecting an apple, but regardless of the apple selected, the next step is always to peel it. There are no alternative next steps, and no diamond would be used in the diagram.

If we alter the apple example, the step in the diamond might be to distinguish between ripe and unripe apples. After the distinction is made, the ripe apples might be treated in one manner and the unripe in another. Clearly the learner would have to be able to distinguish between the two types of apples and then be able to perform the appropriate procedure depending on the ripeness of the apple. Note that the question in the diamond would be "Is the apple ripe?" This implies learner ability to make this distinction. If it is likely that students can already do this, then no teaching will be required; they will simply be told to do this at the appropriate point in the instruction. However, in some cases, it will be necessary to treat this as a skill—"The learner will be able to distinguish between ripe and unripe apples"—and eventually to provide instruction for this skill, just as you would for any other steps in the goal analysis process.

Notice also that the numbers in the boxes do not necessarily indicate the sequence in which all of the steps will be performed. In the example, if a person does steps 4 and 5 as a result of the decision made at 3, then the person would not do steps 6 and 7. The opposite would also be true. Also note that step 3, because it is in a diamond, *must* be a question. The answer to the question leads one to *different* steps or skills.

Several other conventions about diagramming a goal are useful to know, such as what to do if you run out of space. Suppose you are working across the page and need room for more boxes. Obviously, you can turn the page on its side. Another solution, shown in the following diagram, is to use a circle after the last box on the line to indicate the point where the process breaks and then reconnects to the boxes after an identical lettered circle. The letter in the circle is arbitrary but should not be the same as any other letter used elsewhere in your analysis diagram. In our example, we have used the letter *M*. You do not have to draw any connecting lines from one circle with an *M* to the identical circle because the reader can locate easily the next circle with the same letter in it.

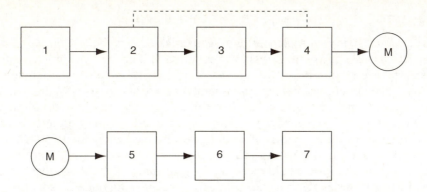

Another solution to the space problem is to drop down to the next line with your boxes and proceed backward from right to left with the description and numbering. As long as the line and arrows indicate the direction of flow, this is acceptable. The arrows are critical to the interpretation of the diagram. Also note the use of the dotted line. This means that when the goal is being performed, it is possible to go back to any number of earlier steps and come forward through the sequence again. Examine the diagram carefully to see the logic of the process being described.

As you analyze your goal, you may find that you have difficulty knowing exactly how much should be included in each step. As a general rule at this stage, you would typically have at least five steps but not more than fifteen for one to two hours of instruction. If you have fewer than five, perhaps you have not been specific enough in describing the steps. If you have more than fifteen steps, then you have either taken too large a chunk to be analyzed or you have listed the steps in too much detail. A very general rule of thumb is to review and revise the steps until you have five to fifteen steps for every one to two hours of instruction.

We have stated that the first step in the goal analysis process is to identify the learning domain of the goal. For either intellectual skills or psychomotor skills, the "steps in a process" method just described is appropriate. However, for verbal information, you would begin the analysis process by thinking, "Now let's see, what will the students be doing? I guess I will ask them to list the major bones in the body, to describe the major causes of bone injuries, and so forth. I'll just ask them on a test to do this, and they'll write down their answers." In a sense, there is no intellectual or psychomotor procedure other than the presentation of a test question and the retrieval of the answer. There is no problem solving with the information nor any decision making required of the learner. Doing the goal analysis would be similar to preparing an outline of the topics contained in the goal, but there is no sequence of steps per se. Boxes could be used to indicate the major topics within the goal, but no arrows would be used to indicate a sequence of steps to be performed. The best sequence for verbal information skills is chronological when a natural chronology can be identified. When there is no natural ordering among the topics, then they should be sequenced based on the inherent relationships among them; for example, spatial, easy to complex, familiar to unfamiliar, common content areas, and so forth.

One special note should be made about the goal analysis of an attitudinal goal. If the goal is an attitude, then it is necessary to identify the behavior that will be exhibited when the attitude is demonstrated. Is it an intellectual skill or a psychomotor skill? If so, use the procedural flowchart process described previously. On the other hand, if the attitude demonstration constitutes verbal information, then your goal analysis will be a list of the major topics contained in the information.

In summary, goal analysis for intellectual and psychomotor skills is an analysis of the steps to be performed, whereas for a verbal information goal, it is a list of the major topics to be learned; either approach can be used depending on the nature of an attitudinal goal.

More Suggestions for Identifying Steps within a Goal

If you cannot state your goal in terms of sequential steps, perhaps it has not been clearly stated in terms of the outcome behavior required. If it has and you still have difficulty, there are several procedures you can use to help identify the steps. First, describe for yourself the kind of test item or assessment you would use to determine whether the learners could perform your goal. Next, think about the steps that the learner would have to go through to respond to your assessment or test. Another suggestion is to "test" yourself; that is, observe yourself, both in the physical and mental sense, performing the goal. Note each of the steps you go through and the decisions you have to make. These are the steps you would record as the goal analysis. Although these procedures may produce a series of steps that seem very simple to you, remember that you are the SME; they probably will not be so simple or obvious to the uninformed learner.

There are several other ways to conduct a goal analysis. In addition to recording your own steps in performing the goal, find others who you know can do it and ask them the steps they would follow. How do their steps compare with yours? Often there will be differences that you should consider in the final representation of the goal. It is sometimes possible to observe others performing your goal. What steps do they follow? It is also a good idea to consult written materials such as textbooks, technical reports, equipment manuals, software instructions, users' guides, policies and procedures booklets, and so forth to determine how the skills in your goal are described. In professional and technical training, the job site (what we call the "performance context" in Chapter 5) is a good place for observing experts performing the goal, for finding existing manuals that document job performance standards, and for talking with employees or supervisors who currently perform or manage performance of the goal. Remember that analyzing contexts is a parallel activity to conducting a goal analysis in the Dick and Carey Model and is very pertinent to the goal analysis.

As an aside, refer for a moment to Figure 2.1 on page 17 and you will see a step right before the goals are identified, labeled "Conduct Job Analysis." A detailed description of the process is outside the scope of this text, but in professional and technical training settings, the results of a job analysis might be available to the instructional designer for use in doing a goal analysis. Stated simply, the results of a job analysis would be a report of the findings from a very careful, detailed examination of the types of job performance information described in the previous paragraph. There are circumstances, however, in which detailed information for goal analysis simply will not be available when you are asked to begin developing instruction. Take for example the case when new training materials are being developed at the same time that a new piece of equipment or software is being developed, so that the manuals, training, and new product can be brought to market simultaneously. When time to market is critical for gaining a competitive advantage, a company will not want to delay product introduction while the training department completes the product package. This circumstance necessitates the "rapid prototyping" approach to instructional design described in Chapter 9.

Doing a goal analysis obviously requires that the designer must either have extensive knowledge about the goal or be working with someone who does. This need for knowledge may have a downside if the designer has already taught the topic or goal in a regular classroom setting. We have routinely observed that novice designers tend to list the steps they would follow in *teaching* a goal rather than the steps that a learner would use in *performing* the goal. Teaching and performing are somewhat different. Verbs to watch for in your description of the steps in your goal analysis are *describe, list, say,* and so forth. These are almost never part of performing psychomotor, intellectual, or attitude goals but rather are words useful in describing how we would teach something. We will reach that point later in the instructional design process. For now we only want to portray, in graphic form, the steps that someone would follow if they were performing your goal.

Another problem in conducting a goal analysis is the inclusion of skills and information that are "near and dear" to the designer but are not really required for the performance of the goal. Designers with a lot of experience in a topic area may be subject to this problem or, more likely, it will arise when the designer is working with a SME who insists on including a certain topic, skill, or information. This becomes a political issue, which can be resolved only through negotiation.

The main purpose of the goal analysis is to provide an unambiguous description of exactly what the learner will be doing when performing the goal. Once the goal analysis has been completed, the designer can identify the exact nature of each skill and any prerequisite skills that must be mastered.

Examples

The first phase of performing an instructional analysis involves two major steps: (1) classifying the goal into a domain of learning and (2) performing a goal analysis by identifying and sequencing the major steps required to perform the goal. Table 3.2 includes four sample instructional goals and a list of the four learning domains previously described. First, we will classify each goal into one of the domains and then identify and sequence the major steps required to perform the goal. The letter of the corresponding learning domain is written in the space provided to the left of each goal statement.

Intellectual Skills Goals

Examine the first goal listed in Table 3.2, determining distances between specified places on a state map. This goal is classified as an intellectual skill because learners will be required to learn concepts, follow rules, and solve problems in performing the goal. With the goal classified, we should identify the major steps required to perform the goal and the best sequence for the steps. A good way for the designer to proceed is to identify the type of test item that would be used to determine if a student could perform this skill. You could obtain a copy of a state map and review how this task can be accomplished using the map as a reference. Checking the map, one sees that there are obviously three separate and distinct ways to determine distance between specified places. One is to use a mileage table, another is to use a mileage scale, and yet another is to add miles printed along highways between the cities. If the student is to be able to use all three methods, then there will be three main methods included in the goal analysis.

Another task would be to decide which of the three identified methods is most appropriate to use in a particular situation. This task implies that there is a decision to

table 3.2	Sample Instructional Goals and Learning Domains	
Domain Letter	**Sample Goals**	**Learning Domain**
B	1. Determine the distance between two specified places on a state map.	A. Verbal information—stating facts, providing specific information (e.g., naming objects)
C	2. Putt a golf ball.	B. Intellectual skills—making discriminations, learning concepts, using rules, and solving problems
D	3. Choose to maximize personal safety while staying in a hotel.	C. Psychomotor skills—physical activity, which usually includes mental activity as well
A	4. Describe the five parts of a materials safety data sheet (MSDS) that are most important for job-site safety.	D. Attitudes—making particular choices or behaving in a manner that implies an underlying belief or preference

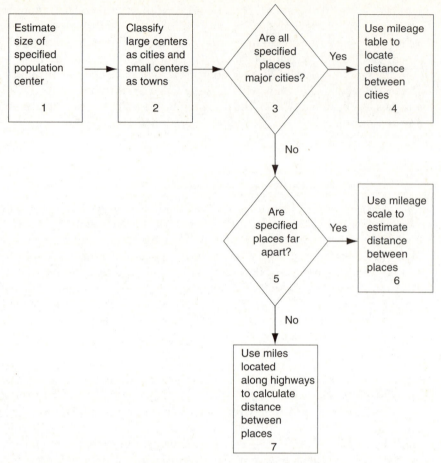

figure 3.1 | **Goal Analysis for an Intellectual Skill**
Goal: Determine distance between specified cities and towns on a state map.
Type of Learning: Intellectual skill

be made; therefore, the criteria necessary to make the decision must be learned. Figure 3.1 contains the major steps required to perform the goal. If learners need to determine the distance between major cities within a state, they will perform tasks 1, 2, 3, and 4. If they need to determine the distance between distant towns or a city and a town, they will use tasks 1, 2, 3, 5, and 6. Similarly, if they need to determine the distance between relatively close cities and towns, which would be the situation if the answer to the first two questions were no, they will do steps 1, 2, 3, 5, and 7. When a choice or decision must be made in order to perform a goal, then when and how to make the decision must be learned together with the other steps. Simply teaching learners to use each of the three procedures would not be adequate for this goal. At this point we have analyzed the instructional goal to provide a framework that will enable us to identify the subordinate skills required to accomplish each major task.

Psychomotor Skills Goals

The second instructional goal presented in Table 3.2, putting a golf ball, should be classified as a psychomotor skill since both mental planning and physical execution of the plan are required to putt the ball into the cup. Neither banging the ball around the green nor simply "willing" the ball into the cup will accomplish the task. Rather, mental planning and calculating, combined with accurately executing the stroke based on mental calculations, are required.

Now that we have the putting goal classified by domain, we should proceed to identify and sequence the major steps learners would take to execute the goal, shown

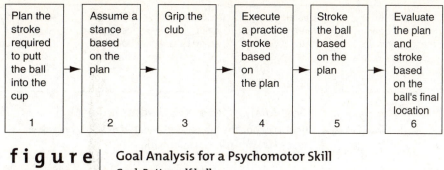

figure 3.2 Goal Analysis for a Psychomotor Skill
Goal: Putt a golf ball.
Type of Learning: Psychomotor

in Figure 3.2. As we watch a golfer preparing to putt the ball, we notice some mental planning activities appear to occur. The steps that follow planning simply provide a broad overview of the complete task from beginning to end. The sequence we have at this point provides us with the framework we will need to identify the subordinate skills required to perform each of the steps already identified.

Attitudinal Goals

The third goal listed in Table 3.2, choosing to maximize personal safety while staying in a hotel, is classified as an attitudinal goal because it implies choosing a course of action based on an underlying attitude or belief. What would learners be doing if they were exhibiting behavior demonstrating safety consciousness while staying in a hotel? The first step to building a framework for this goal would be to visit several hotels and inquire about safety features provided, which would probably result in identifying the three main areas of concern:

1. Hotel fires
2. Personal safety while in hotel room
3. Protection of valuable possessions

Figure 3.3 shows the major steps for maximizing personal safety in relation to hotel fires. This series of steps reflects the actual behaviors performed by a person who *chooses* to maximize fire safety precautions while at a hotel. Each of these major steps

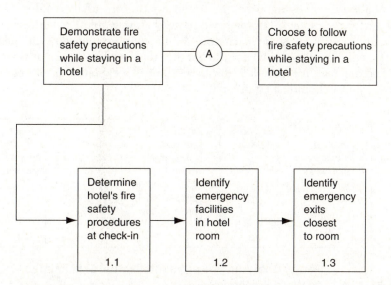

figure 3.3 Goal Analysis for an Attitude Skill
Goal: Choose to maximize personal safety while staying in a hotel.
Type of Learning: Attitude

Describe fire and explosion hazard data	Describe reactivity data	Describe health hazard data	Describe precautions for safe handling and use	Describe control measures
1	2	3	4	5

f i g u r e

3 . 4

Goal Analysis for a Verbal Information Skill

Goal: Describe the five parts of a materials safety data sheet.

Type of Learning: Verbal information

could be broken down further, but, for now, they indicate what a person would be doing to perform the first part of this goal. A similar analysis would be done for the second and third components of the goal related to personal safety and protecting valuable possessions.

Verbal Information Goals

The fourth instructional goal in Table 3.2, describing the five parts of a materials safety data sheet (MSDS) that are most important for job-site safety, is classified as a verbal information goal, because learners are required to recall specific information about the contents of a document. An MSDS is a federally mandated information sheet provided to customers by chemical manufacturers. Performing this goal requires knowledge of five topics, as illustrated in Figure 3.4. Note that for a verbal information goal these are not "steps" in the sense that one goes from one activity to the next. There is no mandated order inherent in the information. Thus, the goal analysis simply indicates the major topics of information that must be covered in the instruction.

Typical First Approach to Goal Analysis

When reading a text such as this, the instructional goal diagrams may appear to have simply flowed from the word processors of the authors. When the reader initially applies the process, however, it does not always seem to work as smoothly and easily. It might be useful to show a typical "first pass" at goal analysis and to point out some of the problems that can be avoided.

Examine Figure 3.5, which shows the analysis of a wordy goal related to the initial use of a word processing program. It appears that the analyst did not say "How would I perform this goal?" but seemed to ask "How would I teach this goal?" We might want to explain some background information to begin the instruction. However, at this point we only want to list the steps in actually performing the goal. Performing the goal in Figure 3.5 does not require an explanation of operating systems; thus, step 1 should be eliminated.

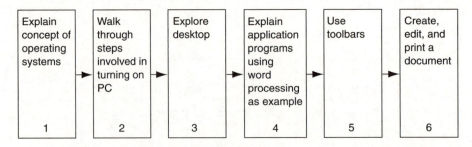

Explain concept of operating systems	Walk through steps involved in turning on PC	Explore desktop	Explain application programs using word processing as example	Use toolbars	Create, edit, and print a document
1	2	3	4	5	6

f i g u r e

3 . 5

Faulty Goal Analysis of an Intellectual Skill Related to Word Processing

Goal: Students will be able to boot up PCs, describe operating systems, and create, edit, and print a document using a word-processing application.

Type of Learning: Intellectual skill

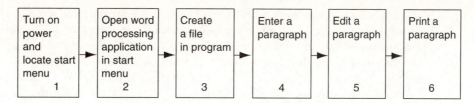

Turn on power and locate start menu	Open word processing application in start menu	Create a file in program	Enter a paragraph	Edit a paragraph	Print a paragraph
1	2	3	4	5	6

figure 3.6

Revised Goal Analysis for a Word-Processing Goal

Goal: Students will be able to operate a word-processing application by entering, editing, and printing a brief document.

Type of Learning: Intellectual skill

Step 2 appears to be a general step related to getting the system up and running. It should be revised to express what the learner would be doing—namely, turn on power and locate start menu. Step 3 should be eliminated because it is a general process for first-time users that would only appear as a substep.

Concerning step 4, the expert who was performing the goal would never stop to explain what an application program is. This may be a subordinate skill somewhere in the instruction, but it doesn't belong here; thus, it too should be eliminated. All we want to do is note the steps in getting the word processing application working. Moving on to step 5 puts us back on track, but what is meant by "use toolbars"? It should be dropped because the substance of the goal is included in step 6.

The final step, step 6, includes writing, editing, and printing a document. This is much too large a step for a goal analysis. It should be broken down into the following separate steps: create a file, enter a paragraph of prose, edit a paragraph, and print a paragraph.

Given this analysis, we would rewrite the goal as follows: Operate a word-processing application by entering, editing, and printing a brief document. The revised steps are shown in Figure 3.6. It looks considerably different from the initial analysis of Figure 3.5. Also note, as you review the steps necessary to carry out the goal, that no one step is equivalent to performing the goal; *all* the steps must be performed in sequence to demonstrate the ability to perform the goal.

Case Study: Group Leadership Training

Turn your attention to the instructional goal in Figure 3.7: "Demonstrate effective discussion group leadership skills." This goal identified in the Case Study section of Chapter 2 is now brought forward for goal analysis in this chapter. The goal

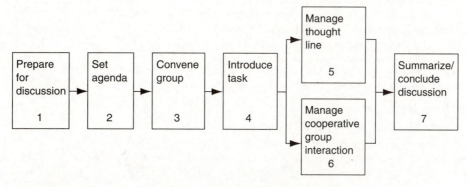

figure 3.7

Goal Analysis for an Intellectual Skill

Goal: Demonstrate effective discussion group leadership skills.

Type of Learning: Intellectual skill

is classified as an intellectual skill since it requires learning concepts and rules as well as solving problems. The seven steps identified to perform this goal and the planned sequence are included in Figure 3.7. There is a natural flow of tasks from left to right because the product developed at each step becomes input for the subsequent one. This step-by-step explanation of the general instructional goal will make subsequent instructional analysis activities much easier. Readers interested in the school curriculum example should study the goal analysis from the case study on writing composition that is included in Appendix B.

SUMMARY

The goal analysis process is begun only after you have a clear statement of the instructional goal. The first step in the goal analysis process is to classify the goal into one of the four domains of learning. It will either be an attitude, an intellectual skill, verbal information, or a psychomotor skill.

The second step in goal analysis is to identify the major steps that learners must perform to demonstrate they have achieved the goal. These major steps should include both the skill performed and relevant content, and they should be sequenced in the most efficient order. For intellectual skill and psychomotor goals, as well as most attitudes, a sequential diagram of the steps to be taken is appropriate. An analysis of verbal information will usually result in a set of topics that can be organized by chronology or by other inherent relationships such as parts of a whole, simple to complex, or familiar to unfamiliar. Remember that perfect frameworks of skills required for a goal are rarely created on the first attempt. Your initial product should be viewed as a draft and should be subjected to evaluation and refinement. Specific problems to look for during the evaluation include steps that are not a natural part of the process, too small or too large, or misplaced in the sequence.

RUBRIC FOR EVALUATING A GOAL ANALYSIS

The following summary rubric can be used to evaluate the quality of your instructional goal analysis. It contains sections for rating the main steps, the diagramming strategy, and other criteria you may identify for your project.

Designer note: If an element is not relevant for your project, mark NA in the No column.

No   Some   Yes   **A. Steps Statements**   Is/are the:

___   ___   ___   1. Verb (behavior/action) included?
___   ___   ___   2. Outcomes visible/observable?
___   ___   ___   3. Content focused/clear?
___   ___   ___   4. Steps focused on learner actions rather than trainer/teacher actions?
___   ___   ___   5. Size chunks comparable in scope, appropriate for learners?
___   ___   ___   6. Steps important/main step in goal?
___   ___   ___   7. Relationships between/among steps clear?
___   ___   ___   8. Relationships among steps reflected in the sequence?
___   ___   ___   9. Redundancy among/between steps avoided?
___   ___   ___   10. (Other)

B. Diagramming   Is/are the:

___   ___   ___   1. Main steps placed in boxes, left to right on page?
___   ___   ___   2. Decision points illustrated by a diamond, question, and branch answers (e.g., yes, no) with arrows illustrating next step?
                  3. Sequencing clearly illustrated with:
___   ___   ___   a. Arrows between steps?
___   ___   ___   b. Numbering system for main steps indicating flow?
___   ___   ___   c. Pairs of matching circles with matching letters for breaks in lines?

No	Some	Yes	C. Other
—	—	—	1.
—	—	—	2.

The final product of your goal analysis should be a diagram of skills that provides an overview of what learners will be doing when they perform the instructional goal. This framework is the foundation for the subordinate skills analysis described in Chapter 4.

PRACTICE

1. Table 3.3 contains a list of learning domains and instructional goals. Read each goal in column two and classify it using the learning domains listed in column one. Space is provided in column three for you to write the rationale you used to classify each goal.

2. On separate sheets of paper, identify and sequence the major areas of activity implied by instructional goals 1, 2, and 3 in Table 3.3.

3. On a separate sheet of paper, identify and sequence the major steps implied by the following instructional goal: In written composition, students will (1) use a variety of sentence types and accompanying punctuation based on the *purpose* and *mood* of the sentence and (2) use a variety of sentence types and accompanying punctuation based on the *complexity* or *structure* of the sentence. Use the rubric to guide and evaluate your work.

table 3.3   **Classify Instructional Goals by Learning Domain**

Learning Domain	Sample Instructional Goal	Rationale
A. Psychomotor Skill B. Intellectual Skill C. Verbal Information D. Attitude	____ 1. Name parts of the human body using common terminology. ____ 2. Separate an egg yolk from the egg white, using the shell as a tool. ____ 3. Choose to behave safely while flying on airplanes.	

FEEDBACK

1. Compare your work with the examples provided in Table 3.4.

2. Compare your decisions about what constitutes the major steps and sequences for each of the

table 3.4   **Feedback for Classifying Instructional Goals**

Learning Domain	Sample Instructional Goal	Rationale
A. Psychomotor Skill B. Intellectual Skill C. Verbal Information D. Attitude	_C_ 1. Name parts of the human body using common terminology.	Requires associating a name with a part of the body. Each part of the body has one name. It does not require anything but recalling labels or names.
	_A_ 2. Separate an egg yolk from egg white, using the shell as a tool.	Requires mental planning and accurate translation of mental plans into physical actions.
	_D_ 3. Choose to behave safely while flying on airplanes.	Behavior implies an underlying attitude about safety.

Name parts of the:

1. Head   2. Arm   3. Hand   4. Trunk   5. Leg   6. Foot

figure 3.8   Goal Analysis for a Verbal Information Skill
Goal: Locate and label various parts of the human body.

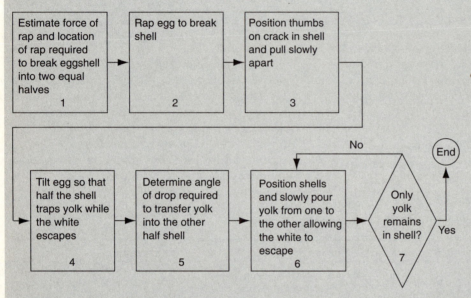

figure 3.9   Goal Analysis for a Psychomotor Skill
Goal: Using the shell as a tool, separate an egg yolk from the egg white.

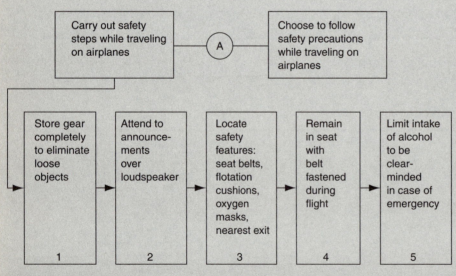

figure 3.10   Goal Analysis for an Attitudinal Skill
Goal: Choose to follow safety precautions while traveling on airplanes.

three instructional goals listed in Figures 3.8 through 3.10. Your analyses will be slightly different from ours because there usually is no one way to analyze the steps in a goal and the wording will always vary.

The second goal, naming parts of the human body, did not have a chronology of events that could be used to develop a logical framework. An organizing method needed to be identified that would enable us to cluster or group information in a logical manner. We chose to organize the content using a "parts of a whole" plan (i.e., main areas of the body). We then selected a sequence for the areas by moving from the top to the bottom—for example, head, arms, hands, trunk, legs, and feet. Note that the words are not connected with arrows because these are not sequential steps that must be performed.

The psychomotor skill required to crack an egg and separate the yolk from the white has a natural sequence of events. The shell could not be pulled apart until it was broken, and the egg white could not be separated until the shell was pulled apart. Like most psychomotor tasks, this one requires practice. The only way your mind can tell your hands how hard to tap the shell or how fast to pour the yolk is to practice the skill. Incorrect estimations and translations result in squashed shells and broken yolks.

The instructional goal on airplane safety has a sequence of sorts that does help with this goal. Carry-on items are stored and then attention is given to safety announcements. The announcements will help in locating safety features on the plane. Then it is necessary to keep the seat belt on and to limit one's alcoholic intake.

3. Compare your goal analysis for writing sentences with the one located in Appendix B.

REFERENCES AND RECOMMENDED READINGS

Bloom, B., Englehart, M., Furst, E., Hill, W., & Krathwohl, D. (1956). *Taxonomy of educational objectives: The classification of educational goals: Handbook 1; The cognitive domain.* New York: W. H. Freeman.

Gagné, R. (1985). *Conditions of learning* (4th ed.). New York: Holt, Rinehart and Winston. This book is a classic in regard to many aspects of instructional design, including the domains of learning and hierarchical analysis.

Gagné, R. M., Wager, W. W., Golas, K. C., & Keller, J. M. (2004). *Principles of instructional design* (5th ed.). Belmont, CA: Wadsworth/Thomson Learning. Provides a number of examples of the application of instructional analysis to intellectual skills.

Jonassen, D. H. (1997). Instructional design models for well-structured and ill-structured problem-solving learning outcomes. *Educational Technology Research and Development, 45*(1), 65–94. Provides definitions and examples of well-structured and ill-structured problem solving.

Jonassen, D. H., Tessmer, M., & Hannum, W. (1999). *Task analysis procedures for instructional design.* Mahwah, NJ: Lawrence Erlbaum Associates. Excellent overview and "how to" guide to instructional design applications of a wide range of techniques for instructional analysis. This book is currently available as an e-book through netLibrary.

Katz, L. G. (1993). *Dispositions: Definitions and implications for early childhood practices.* Urbana, IL: ERIC Clearinghouse on Elementary and Early Childhood Education. An early article that lays the foundations for Katz's writings on teaching dispositions in formal educational settings.

Loughner, P., & Moller, L. (1998). The use of task analysis procedures by instructional designers. *Performance Improvement Quarterly, 11*(3), 79–101.

Mager, R. (1997). Goal analysis: How to clarify your goals so you can actually achieve them. Atlanta, GA: The Center for Effective Performance.

Mellon, C. (1997). Goal analysis: Back to the basics. *Tech Trends, 42*(5), 38–42.

Reigeluth, C. M. (1983). Current trends in task analysis: The integration of task analysis and instructional design. *Journal of Instructional Development, 6*(4), 24–30, 35. Describes substantive and temporal integration of task analysis into the instructional design process.

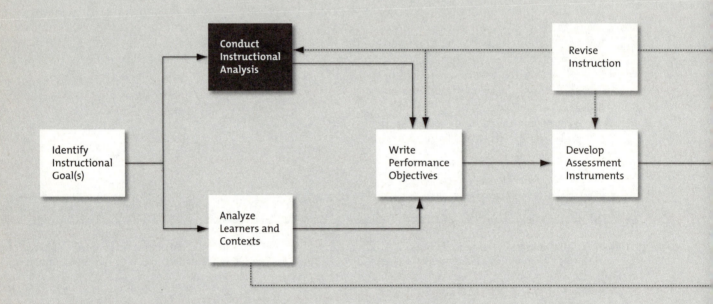

objectives

➤ Describe approaches to subordinate skills analysis including hierarchical, procedural, cluster, and combination techniques.

➤ Describe the relationships among the subordinate skills identified through subordinate skills analysis, including entry skills.

➤ Apply subordinate skills analysis techniques to steps in the goal analysis and identify entry skills as appropriate.

Identifying Subordinate and Entry Skills

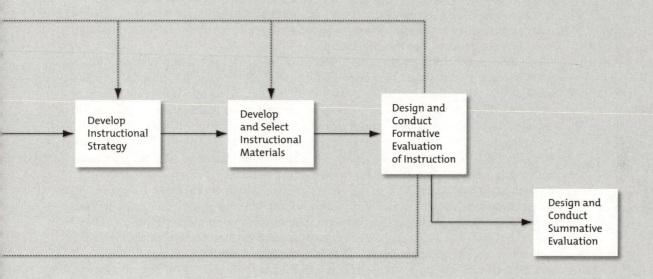

Background

This is the second chapter on the instructional analysis process. In the prior chapter, the procedures for carrying out a goal analysis were described. After the steps in the goal have been identified, it is necessary to examine each step to determine what learners must know or be able to do before they can learn to perform that step in the goal. This second step in the instructional analysis process is referred to as subordinate skills analysis.

The purpose is to identify the appropriate set of subordinate skills for each step. If required skills are omitted from the instruction, and many students do not already have them, then the instruction will be ineffective. On the other hand, if superfluous skills are included, the instruction will take more time than it should, and the unnecessary skills may actually interfere with learning the required skills. The identification of either too many or too few skills can be a problem.

Several processes are used to identify subordinate skills. We will describe each of the techniques and indicate how they can be applied to various types of goals. We will begin with "pure" goals—that is, goals in which the steps are only intellectual or psychomotor skills. Complex goals, however, often involve several domains. A combination approach that can be used with complex goals will also be described.

Concepts

Hierarchical Approach

The hierarchical analysis approach is used to analyze individual steps in the goal analysis that are classified as intellectual or psychomotor skills. To understand the hierarchical approach, consider an instructional goal that requires the student to justify the recommendation that a particular piece of real estate should be purchased at a particular time. This is an intellectual skill goal, and it requires students to learn a number of rules and concepts related to the assessment of property values, the effect of inflation on property values, the financial status of the buyer, and the buyer's short- and long-term investment goals. The skills in each of these areas would depend on knowledge of the basic concepts used in the financial and real estate fields. In this example, it would be extremely important to identify and teach each of the critical rules and concepts prior to teaching the steps for analyzing a particular real estate purchase situation and making a recommendation.

How does the designer go about identifying the subordinate skills a student must learn in order to achieve a higher-level intellectual skill? The hierarchical analysis technique suggested by Gagné (1985) consists of asking the question "What must the student already know so that, with a minimal amount of instruction, this task can be learned?" By asking this question, the designer can identify one or more critical subordinate skills that will be required of the learner prior to attempting instruction on the step itself. After these subordinate skills have been identified, the designer then asks the same question with regard to each of them, namely, "What is it that the student must already know how to do, the absence of which would make it impossible to learn this subordinate skill?" This will result in identifying one or more additional subordinate skills. If this process is continued with lower and lower levels of subordinate skills, one quickly reaches a very basic level of performance, such as being able to recognize whole numbers or being able to recognize letters.

To get a visual understanding of how the designer "builds" the hierarchical analysis, consider the generic hierarchy shown in Figure 4.1. Here a "rule" serves as the immediate subordinate skill required to learn a particular problem-solving skill. It is important to understand that box 2 represents one step in performing the goal. After the rule has been identified (box 2.4), the designer then asks, "What must the student know how to do in order to learn the rule?" The answer is that the student must learn two *concepts,* which are represented in boxes 2.2 and 2.3. When asked, "What must the student know how to do to learn the concept in box 2.2?" the answer is nothing, so no additional skills are listed. For box 2.3, the question results in the identification of a relevant discrimination, which is shown in box 2.1. Figure 4.1 represents how the analysis would appear when laid out in a diagram.

Figure 4.1 is consistent with Gagné's hierarchy of intellectual skills. Gagné has noted that in order to learn how to perform problem-solving skills, learners must first know how to apply the rules that are required to solve the problem. The immediate subskills to the instructional goal are the rules that must be applied in the problem situation.

Further, Gagné has noted that rules are based on recognizing the components or concepts that are combined in the rules. In other words, in order to learn the relationship among "things," you must be able to classify them. The subordinate skills required for any given rule are typically classifying the concepts that are used in the rules. Finally, the learner must be able to discriminate whether a particular example is relevant to the concept.

This hierarchy of skills is helpful to the designer because it can be used to suggest the type of specific subordinate skills that will be required to support any particular step in the goal. If the step is a problem-solving skill (or selecting and using a number of rules), then the subskills should include the relevant rules, concepts, and

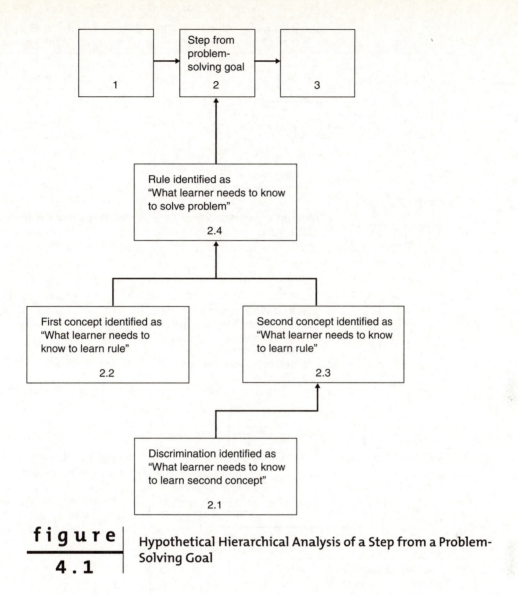

figure 4.1   Hypothetical Hierarchical Analysis of a Step from a Problem-Solving Goal

discriminations. On the other hand, if the application of a single rule is being taught, then only the subordinate concepts and discriminations would be taught.

To apply the hierarchical approach to the steps in the goal analysis, the designer applies it to *each step* in the goal, including any decision steps. The question is asked, "What would the learner have to know in order to learn to do the *first step* in performing the goal?" The question is repeated for each of the subskills for the first step and then for each of the remaining steps in the goal. If this approach were used with the hypothetical problem-solving goal that was shown in Figure 4.1, the result might resemble that shown in Figure 4.2.

Observe in Figure 4.2 that the same subskills have been identified as in the original methodology suggested by Gagné. The fact that no subskills are listed for steps 1, 3, and 4 indicates the designer's determination that there are no relevant skills the learner must master before being taught these steps. This is often a perfectly reasonable assumption.

An example resulting from using the hierarchical instructional analysis technique appears in Figure 4.3. In the diagram it can be seen that step 8 from the goal analysis requires students to estimate to the nearest one-hundredth of a unit (plus or minus

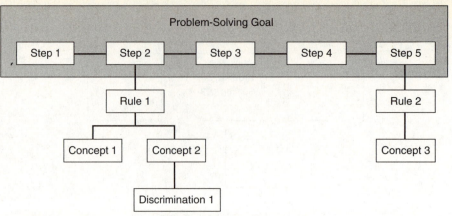

figure 4.2 | Hypothetical Hierarchical Analysis of Steps in a Problem-Solving Goal

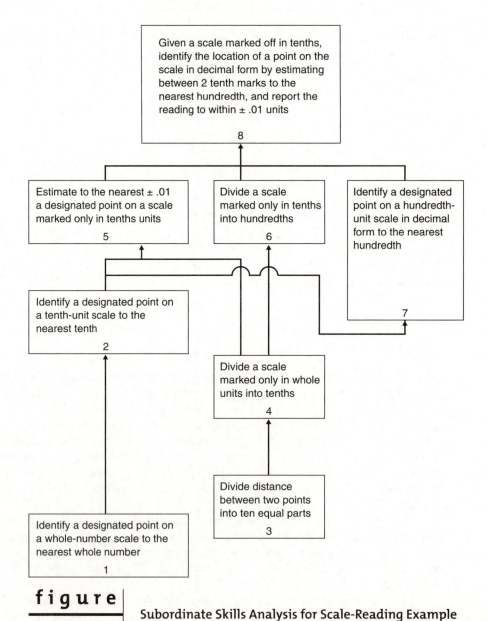

figure 4.3 | Subordinate Skills Analysis for Scale-Reading Example

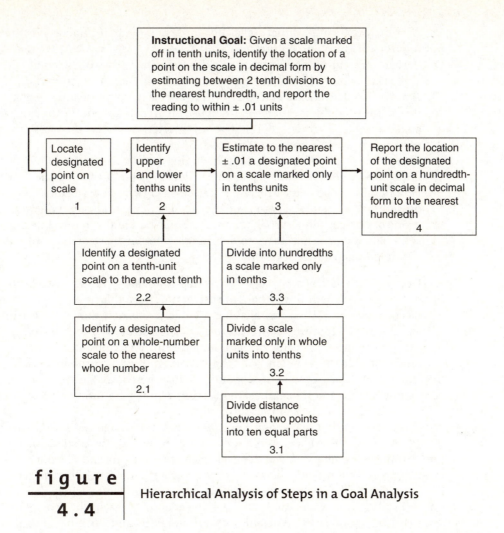

Instructional Goal: Given a scale marked off in tenth units, identify the location of a point on the scale in decimal form by estimating between 2 tenth divisions to the nearest hundredth, and report the reading to within ± .01 units

| Locate designated point on scale 1 | Identify upper and lower tenths units 2 | Estimate to the nearest ± .01 a designated point on a scale marked only in tenths units 3 | Report the location of the designated point on a hundredth-unit scale in decimal form to the nearest hundredth 4 |

Identify a designated point on a tenth-unit scale to the nearest tenth 2.2

Identify a designated point on a whole-number scale to the nearest whole number 2.1

Divide into hundredths a scale marked only in tenths 3.3

Divide a scale marked only in whole units into tenths 3.2

Divide distance between two points into ten equal parts 3.1

figure
4.4

Hierarchical Analysis of Steps in a Goal Analysis

one one-hundredth) a designated point on a linear scale marked only in tenths. Three subordinate skills have been identified for step 8, related to estimating a point to the nearest hundredth on a scale marked only in tenths units, dividing that scale into subunits, and identifying a designated point on a particular scale. Each of these skills has subordinate skills that are identified.

The use of hierarchical analysis is also illustrated in Figure 4.4. Notice that the cognitive task performed by the learner is shown in the four successive substeps labeled 1, 2, 3, and 4 from the goal analysis. In this particular example, the subordinate skills are the same as those identified for the same skill in Figure 4.3; however, it should be noted that they are organized somewhat differently.

These particular analyses were not devised on the basis of one attempt at the process—or even two or three. It takes a number of attempts at identifying the vertical subordinate skills and their interrelationships before you can be satisfied that all the relevant skills are identified and stated appropriately. It is almost impossible to know when an appropriate and valid hierarchical analysis of an instructional goal has been achieved.

After you are satisfied that you have identified all the subskills required for students to master your instructional goal, you will want to diagram your analysis. The following conventions are used when diagramming a hierarchical analysis:

1. The instructional goal is stated at the top. All the steps in the goal appear in numbered boxes at the top of the hierarchy.

2. All subordinate intellectual skills appear in boxes that are attached via lines coming from the tops and bottoms of boxes.
3. Verbal information and attitudinal skills are attached to intellectual and motor skills via horizontal lines, as will be shown in subsequent sections.
4. Arrows should indicate that the flow of skills is upward toward the goal.
5. If two lines should not intersect, then use an arch as shown for the line between box 2 and box 7 in Figure 4.3. The interpretation is that the skill in step 2 is required for steps 5 and 7, but not step 6.
6. Statements of all subordinate skills, including decisions, should include verbs that indicate what the student must be able to do. Avoid boxes that include only nouns.
7. Hierarchies, in the real world, are not necessarily symmetrical, and they can take on all kinds of shapes. There is no one correct appearance for a hierarchy.
8. If one of the steps in the goal analysis is a question and is represented by a decision diamond, it is necessary to determine whether there are subordinate skills required to make that decision.

Doing a hierarchical analysis for each step is not easy because we are not accustomed to thinking about the content of instruction from this point of view. One way to proceed is to ask, "What mistake might students make if they were learning this particular skill?" Often the answer to this question is the key to identifying the appropriate subordinate skills for the skill in question. The kinds of *misunderstandings* that students might have will indicate the *understandings,* also known as *skills,* which they must have. For example, if students might err because they become confused between stalactites and stalagmites, then an important subordinate skill would be the ability to classify examples of these two entities.

It is important to review your analysis several times, making sure that you have identified all the subskills required for students to master the instructional goal. At this point you should again use the backward-stepping procedure, from the highest, most complex skill in your hierarchy to the lowest, simplest skills required by your learners. This will allow you to determine whether you have included all the necessary subskills. It may be possible to check the adequacy of your back-stepping analysis by starting with the simplest skills in your hierarchy and working upward through the subskills to the most complex skills. You should also ask the following questions:

1. Have I included subskills that relate to the identification of basic concepts, such as objects or object qualities? (Example: Can a tetrahedron be identified?)
2. Have I included subskills that enable students to identify abstractions by means of a definition? (Example: Can the student explain what a city is or show what an emulsion is?)
3. Have I included subskills that will enable students to apply rules? (Example: Can the student make sentence verbs agree with subjects or simplify mixed fractions?)
4. Have I included subskills in the analysis that will enable students to learn how to solve problems demonstrating mastery of the instructional goal?

You may be able to identify subskills you have omitted by using these questions to evaluate your instructional analysis. You may also make another type of interesting discovery, namely, that your instructional goal is limited to having students learn how to make discriminations or identify concepts. Although these skills are obviously important, you may want to modify the goal statement by requiring students to use a rule or to solve problems that require the use of the concepts and discriminations that you originally stated in your goal.

You may also find that you have included skills that are "nice to know" but are not really required in order to achieve your goal. Many designers begin with the attitude that these skills are important and should be included. In the end, superfluous tasks often confuse learners or unnecessarily increase the length of the instruction, which can cause the instruction for more important tasks to be rushed or omitted due to time constraints. You do not need to include everything you know about a topic in a hierarchy. The whole point of using the hierarchical approach is to identify just what the learner must know to be successful—nothing more and nothing less. Although it is sometimes tempting not to do so, our best advice is to let the analysis identify the skills for you. It is absolutely the best starting point.

As you proceed with the instructional analysis, it is important to have a clear idea of the distinction between the steps and substeps of performing a goal and subordinate skills. The steps and substeps are the activities that an expert or competent person would describe as the steps in the performance. The subordinate skills would not necessarily be identified by a competent person when describing the process. These are the skills and knowledge that learners will have to learn before they can perform the steps in the goal. For example, if you were teaching someone to boil water, one of the steps would be "Turn on the burner." One of the subordinate skills for that step would be "Identify examples of *burners*." If you were actually boiling water, you would never say, "This is the burner;" you would simply put the pan with the water on the burner. Obviously you must recognize a burner, but verbally identifying it is not a step in the process of boiling water.

Procedural Analysis

Sometimes when looking at the steps in a goal analysis for intellectual or psychomotor skills, one or more of the steps in the goal analysis will be found to contain an additional set of mental or physical steps. When this is the case one simply lists out the skills from left to right in the same step-by-step manner as was done for the original goal analysis, as shown in the following diagram.

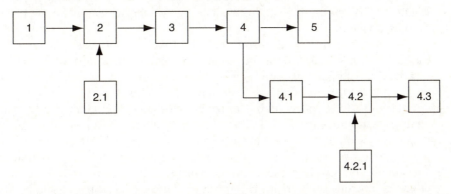

Steps 1 through 5 are the original steps in the goal analysis. Step 2.1 is subordinate to step 2 as in any typical hierarchical relationship. Steps 4.1, 4.2, and 4.3 are subskills of step 4 in that they detail the three additional procedural steps of which step 4 is composed. Step 4.2.1 is subordinate to step 4.2 in a normal hierarchical relationship.

Consider the following examples of steps in an instructional goal. The first is "Place jack under bumper of car." While this could be described as a series of steps for an adult population, it is probably best represented as one step in the process of changing a tire on a car. But what about a problem-solving step like "Conduct needs assessment"? This is a step in a goal of designing instruction that surely is too large to be a single step for any audience. It should be broken down into steps such as "Describe ideal status," "Design instruments for data collection," "Collect data to document current status," and "Determine gap between ideal status and current status." Now consider this final example. Suppose one of the steps in a goal analysis is "boil water." Most adults should know what to do, or they could be taught quickly. For learners who are young children you might want to list the substeps as "Get pan from cupboard," "Fill with water," "Place pan on burner," "Turn on burner," "Is water bubbling?" and "Remove pan." This is an extremely simple example, but it illustrates how substeps are identified. Figure 4.6 later in this chapter (p. 75) is another example of how one step in a goal analysis (step 4) is broken down into additional procedural steps (steps 4.1 through 4.5). For additional description of procedural analysis, readers are referred to Chapter 3 where techniques were covered thoroughly in the description of goal analysis.

Cluster Analysis

Cluster analysis is used when the instructional goal or a main subskill in the goal requires learning verbal information. We demonstrated previously that it makes little sense to try to do a goal analysis of a verbal information goal because no logical procedure is inherent in the goal. Instead, you move directly to the identification of information needed to achieve the goal.

How do you identify the subordinate skills that should be taught? The answer is almost always apparent from the statement of the goal itself. If the student must be able to identify the states associated with each capital city, then there are fifty subskills, one associated with each state and its capital. It would be useless to write those out as part of the analysis. They could easily be reproduced from a text. In contrast, the subskills are sometimes not as apparent, as in the goal "List five major causes of inflation." The answer may depend on a particular economic theory. In this case, it might be worth listing the five major reasons as part of what we will refer to as a cluster analysis.

The most meaningful analysis of a verbal information goal is to identify the major categories of information that are implied by the goal. Are there ways that the information can be clustered best? The state capitals might be clustered according to geographic regions; the bones of the body might be clustered by major parts of the body such as head, arms, legs, and trunk. If the goal were to be able to list all the major league baseball cities, they might be clustered by American and National Leagues and then by divisions.

How do you diagram a cluster analysis? One way is to use the hierarchical technique with the goal at the top and each major cluster as a subskill, clearly labeled as a verbal information cluster analysis and not a hierarchy. It would be just as easy to use an outline format and simply list each of the clusters.

It is sometimes embarrassing for teacher-designers to find that when instructional analysis techniques are used, an instructional goal that they have often taught and for which they would like to develop systematically designed instruction is, in fact, simply verbal information. They can feel guilty that they are not teaching rules and problem solving, but this guilt is sometimes misplaced. There are times when the acquisition of verbal information is critically important. For example, learning vocabulary in a foreign language is verbal information that is the foundation of learning a very complex set of communication skills. The verbal information we must learn as children or as adults is the vehicle we use to develop much more complex concepts and rules. Verbal information goals should not be automatically discarded on discovery but considered for their relevance to other important educational goals. Verbal information is the knowledge base called on when we execute our how-to intellectual skills.

Analysis Techniques for Attitude Goals

In order to determine the subordinate skills for an attitudinal goal, the designer should ask, "What must learners do when exhibiting this attitude?" and "Why should they exhibit this attitude?" The answer to the first question is almost always a psychomotor skill or an intellectual skill. The purpose of the goal is to get the learner to choose to do either a psychomotor or an intellectual skill; therefore, the first half of the analysis for an attitudinal goal requires hierarchical analysis techniques, which aids in identifying the subskills that will be required *if* the learner chooses to do them. If the learner is to choose to jog, then it is necessary to teach the learner to jog. If the learner is to choose to appreciate a certain body of literature, then the student must learn to comprehend and analyze it.

The second part of the analysis is "Why should the learner make a particular choice?" The answer to this question is usually verbal information. The verbal information may either be analyzed using a separate cluster analysis, or it may be integrated, as verbal information, into the basic hierarchical analysis that was done for the first half of the analysis. The verbal information constitutes the persuasive part of attitude shaping, along with modeling and reinforcement, and it should be included as an integral part of the instructional analysis.

In order to represent an attitude on an instructional analysis chart, simply write the attitude goal in a box *beside* the psychomotor or intellectual skill goal that will be analyzed. Connect the two main boxes with a line like this:

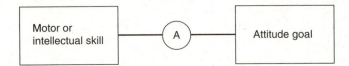

This connecting line shows that the motor or intellectual skill is supporting the attitudinal goal. At this point it is obvious that we are beginning to combine the various analysis techniques. These combinations, sometimes called information maps, are described in the following section.

Analysis Techniques for Combination Domains

We have just described how an attitudinal goal can be analyzed using a hierarchical analysis. It is quite common to find that the instructional analysis process results in identifying a combination of subordinate skills from several domains for a goal that was classified as belonging to only one domain.

Consider, for example, the combination of intellectual skills and verbal information. It is not unusual when doing a hierarchical analysis to identify knowledge that the learner should "know." Just "knowing something" is not an intellectual skill as we have defined it here and therefore would not, by the rules, appear on an intellectual skills hierarchy. But often it is important that this knowledge, which is verbal information, appear as a part of the analysis of what must be learned to achieve the instructional goal. Briggs and Wager (1981) therefore suggest that the verbal information be shown in the diagram with a connecting line like this:

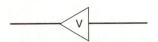

This indicates that the verbal information in the right-hand box is used in support of the intellectual skill in the left-hand box. In a hierarchy, it might look like this:

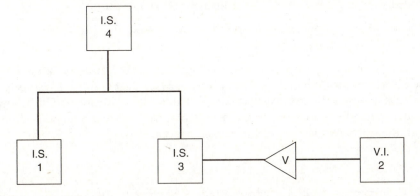

Boxes 1, 3, and 4 represent intellectual skills, whereas box 2 is verbal information.

What happens if you put all the diagramming techniques together? It is conceivable that an attitude goal with a psychomotor component might require subordinate intellectual skills and verbal information and look something like this:

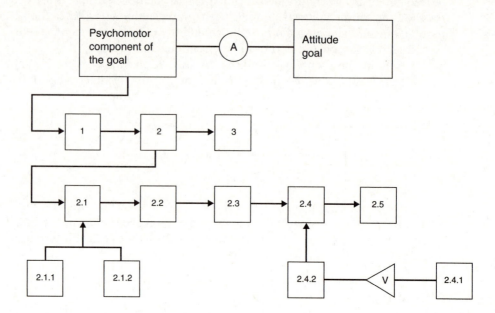

The diagram indicates that the primary goal is for learners to develop an attitude that will be demonstrated by the execution of some psychomotor skill. The psychomotor skill is composed of three steps—1, 2, and 3. A subskill analysis of skill 2 indicates that it includes five steps, 2.1 through 2.5. Two intellectual skills, 2.1.1 and 2.1.2, are subordinate to step 2.1. The intellectual skill 2.4.2 requires verbal information, 2.4.1, in order to support step 2.4.

Instructional Analysis Diagrams

At this point we will review the diagramming procedures for doing an instructional analysis. The first step, of course, is to classify your instructional goal and perform a goal analysis. Then select the appropriate technique(s) for identifying the subordinate skills.

Type of Goal or Step	Type of Subordinate Skills Analysis
Intellectual skill	Hierarchical*
Psychomotor skill	Hierarchical*
Verbal information	Cluster
Attitude	Hierarchical* and/or cluster

*Note that hierarchical analyses can contain sequences of procedural steps.

As the designer proceeds with the analysis, the subordinate skills are visually displayed in diagrams. When diagrammed, any particular set of subskills required to reach a terminal objective can have a variety of structural appearances. The following diagram is generally used to represent a goal analysis. There are no subordinate skills, so all the skills are diagrammed in one continuous line.

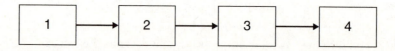

It is also traditional to place superordinate skills above the skills on which they are dependent. In this way, the reader will automatically recognize the implied learning relationship of the subskills. This is illustrated in the following diagram. Notice that subskills 1.1, 1.2, and 1.3 do not depend on each other, but that learning skill 1 requires the previous learning of 1.1, 1.2, and 1.3. Objectives 2, 3, and 4 are not interdependent; 4.1 and 4.2 must be learned prior to 4.

Instructional goal

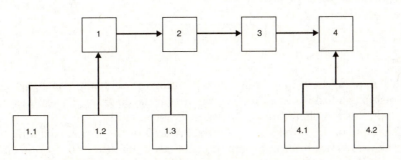

The following diagram illustrates the dependence of subsequent skills on those preceding them.

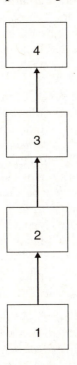

The student must learn subskill 1 in order to learn to perform subskill 2. Likewise, before subskill 4 can be learned, subskills 1, 2, and 3 must be mastered; thus, these skills form a hierarchy. Note, this does not mean that 1, 2, 3, and 4 are performed in sequence. If they were, then they would be the substeps of a superordinate skill, and would be diagrammed as follows:

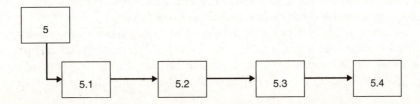

In addition, we noted that attitudinal goals can be indicated by the following:

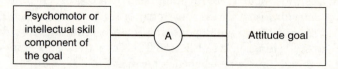

Verbal information is indicated by connecting it to an intellectual skill via a line and a triangle containing the letter *V*.

Skill in using these diagramming conventions should help you grasp the implied relationship of subskills in an instructional analysis diagram. The order for learning each skill is also implied through the sequencing of skills.

Take note of the numbers that have appeared in the various diagrams of subordinate skills. Do not interpret them to mean more than they do. At this point in the instructional design process, the numbers in the boxes are used simply as a shorthand method for referring to the box; they *do not* represent the sequence in which the skills will be taught. Using these numbers, we can discuss the relationship between box 7 and box 5 without describing the skills that are involved. We should not be thinking about how we will teach these skills but rather ensuring that we have the correct skills included in our analysis. At a later point in the design process, it will be necessary to decide on the instructional sequence for the skills, and you may wish to renumber the skills at that time.

Why is the instructional analysis process so critical to the design of instruction? It is a process the instructional designer can use to identify those skills really needed by the student to achieve the terminal objective—and to help exclude unnecessary skills. This may not appear to be a terribly strong argument when considered in light of a particular instructional goal that you might select. You might feel that you are so thoroughly familiar with the content and skills required of the student that this type of analysis is superfluous. You may be assured, however, that as you become involved in a variety of instructional design projects you cannot be a subject-matter expert in all areas. It will be necessary to engage in analytic processes of this type with a variety of subject-matter specialists to identify the critical skills that will result in efficient and effective instruction.

Entry Skills

The instructional analysis process serves another important function that we have not yet discussed. It helps the designer identify exactly what learners will already have to know or be able to do *before* they begin the instruction, called *entry skills* because learners must already have mastered them in order to learn the new skills included in the instruction. We will describe how the designer identifies entry skills and indicate why this is so important.

The procedure used to identify entry skills is directly related to the subordinate skills analysis process. You know that with the hierarchical analysis you ask, "What does the learner need to know in order to learn this skill?" The answer to this question is one or more subordinate skills. With each successive set of subordinate skills, the bottom of the hierarchy will contain very basic skills.

Assume you have such a highly developed hierarchy representing the array of skills required to take a learner from the most basic level of understanding up to your instructional goal. It is likely, however, that your learners already have some of these skills, making it unnecessary to teach all the skills in the extended hierarchy. To identify the entry skills for your instruction, examine the hierarchy or cluster analysis and identify those skills that a majority of the learners will have already mastered before beginning your instruction. Draw a dotted line above these skills in the analysis chart. The skills that appear above the dotted line will be those you must teach in your instruction, whereas those below the line are called entry skills.

Why are entry skills so important? Defined as the skills that fall directly below the skills you plan to teach, they are the initial building blocks for your instruction, the basis from which learners can begin to acquire the skills presented in your instruction. Without these skills, a learner will have a very difficult time trying to learn from your instruction. Entry skills are a key component in the design process. An example of how entry skills can be identified through the use of a hierarchy appears in Figure 4.5. This is basically the same hierarchy that appeared in Figure 4.3; however, three more skills have been added to the analysis chart. A dotted line has been drawn across the page indicating that all skills above the line will be taught in the instructional materials. All the skills listed below the line are assumed as skills already attained by students before beginning the instruction.

Each skill below the line was derived directly from a superordinate skill that already appeared on the instructional analysis chart, derived by asking the question, "What does the learner have to be able to do in order to learn this skill?" Note that even the entry skills identified in Figure 4.5 have a hierarchical relationship to each other. The derived skills include the ability to interpret whole and decimal numbers. These are skills that *must* be mastered in order to learn skills 1 and 7, but they will not be taught in this instruction. Students will have to have mastered these skills *before* they begin the instruction on reading a scale.

Instructional designers should identify expected entry skills of learners by continuing the instructional analysis to the point that skills identified become basic for their learners. The designer must assume that most, if not all, of the learners will have these skills. It is then a matter of simply drawing a dotted line through the instructional analysis chart to separate those skills to be included in the instruction from those skills that learners in the target population are assumed to have already mastered.

The description thus far has related entry skills to a hierarchical instructional analysis. Similarly, if a cluster or combination approach is used in which subordinate skills and knowledge are identified, then the identification process can be continued until basic skills are identified and so indicated by the dotted line.

You should be aware that the examples we have used have rather clearly described specific skills related to specific instructional goals. There are some descriptors of learners that may be considered as either entry skills for a particular instructional unit or as descriptive of the general target population. Consider the question of students' reading levels.

It is apparent that instructional materials typically depend heavily on the reading ability of students; students must have some minimum level of reading ability to become involved with the materials. Is the specification of reading level a description of a general characteristic of the learners or is it a specific entry skill that students must possess before beginning instruction? Clear arguments could be made on either side of this issue. You may be able to identify other skills that would produce similar problems.

A possible technique to appropriately classify such an ability is to determine whether it would be worthwhile or feasible to test a learner for that particular skill prior to permitting the learner to begin the instruction. If the answer to that question is "Yes, it would be worth the time to test the learner," then you have probably defined a specific entry behavior. If, on the other hand, it would seem to be inappropriate to test the skill of the learner (such as giving a reading test) before instruction, then the factor you have identified is probably better classified as a general characteristic of the learners for whom the unit is intended.

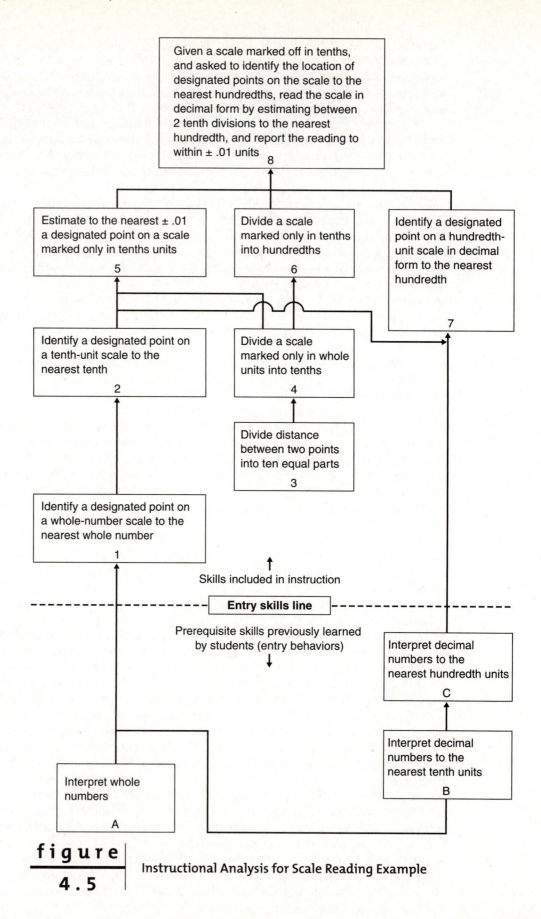

Instructional Analysis for Scale Reading Example

How you identify the specific entry skills for your materials will depend on where you stopped when you conducted your instructional analysis. If you identified only those tasks and skills that you plan to include in the instructional materials, then you will need to take each of the lowest skills in the hierarchy and determine the subordinate skills associated with them. These would be listed on your instructional analysis chart beneath a line that clearly differentiates them from subordinate skills that will be included in the instructional materials. If your subordinate skills analysis were already carried out to the point of identifying basic low-level skills, then it should be possible for you simply to draw a dotted line through the chart above those skills that you assume most learners have already acquired.

Also note that when developing instructional materials about topics of general interest that emphasize information objectives, there sometimes are apparently no required entry skills other than the ability to read the materials and to use appropriate reasoning skills to reach the instructional goal. If you have identified such an area, then it is perfectly legitimate to indicate that, although the materials are intended for a certain group of learners, there are no specific entry skills required to begin the instruction.

The Tentativeness of Entry Skills

The identification of entry skills is one of the real danger spots in the instructional design process, because the designer is making assumptions about both what the learners must know and should already know. Obviously, the designer can err in one of two directions, and each has consequences. For example, with curriculum materials designed for only the brightest students, the subordinate skills analysis dotted line separating skills to be taught from skills assumed to be known would be placed relatively high on the chart, suggesting that learners already have mastered most of the skills described on the chart. When the assumed entry skills are not already mastered by the majority of the target population, the instructional materials lose their effectiveness for a large number of learners. Without adequate preparation in the entry skills, learners' efforts are inefficient and the materials are ineffective.

The second error occurs when the dotted line is drawn too low on the instructional analysis, presuming that learners have few or none of the skills required to achieve the instructional goal. An error of this type is costly both in terms of developing instructional materials that are not really needed by learners and in terms of the time required for learners to study skills they have already mastered.

It should be noted that the designer is making a set of assumptions at this early point about the learners who will use the instruction. If time is available, a tryout sample of group members should be tested and interviewed to determine if most of them have the entry skills derived from the subskills analysis. Procedures for doing this will be discussed in later chapters. If time does not permit this, then the assumptions will have to be tested at a later time in the development process. Delaying this verification of entry skills, however, can lead to a situation in which a lot of development has taken place improperly because of a mismatch between the learner and the instruction.

If there is not a good alignment between the entry skills of the learners and the skills planned for inclusion in the instruction, then a fundamental question must be answered. Is specific content being taught, or is the target population being taught? If it is the former, then little or no change is required in entry skills. One simply keeps looking until a group of learners with the right entry skills is found. Your instruction is for them! If your purpose is to teach a specific group of learners, however, then the instruction must be modified by the addition or subtraction of instruction to match the entry skills that do exist within the group. There is no one correct answer to this dilemma. Each situation must be considered in light of the needs assessment that resulted in the creation of the instructional goal.

In the same manner, it is often found that only some of the intended learners have the entry skills. What accommodation can be made for this situation? It may be possible to have several "starting points" within the instruction, and learners' scores on entry skills tests can be used to place them at the appropriate starting point. Or the solution may again be that the instruction was designed for learners with certain entry skills. Those who do not have these skills must master them somewhere else before beginning the instruction. There are usually no easy answers to this all-too-common situation.

Examples

In this section we illustrate combination analysis procedures for a psychomotor skill and an attitude. In the Case Study that follows, there are two examples of combination analysis procedures for intellectual skills and verbal information.

Subordinate Skills Analysis of a Psychomotor Skill

Instructional Goal   Putt a golf ball into the cup.

Psychomotor skills usually require a combination of intellectual and motor skills, and the intellectual skills often require supporting verbal information. The chronological procedure to follow in putting a golf ball was illustrated in Figure 3.2 (p. 51). At this point we need to continue the instructional analysis to identify the subordinate skills and information required to perform each step previously identified. As an illustration, we will first analyze the subordinate skills required to perform step 1: Plan the stroke required to putt the ball into the cup. The analysis appears in Figure 4.6.

Note in the diagram that the subordinate skills required to plan the stroke are all intellectual skills—the *psycho* component of the psychomotor skill. The *motor* component occurs when the golfer translates the plan into action. Observing someone putting, the designer can readily see the motor part of the skill, whereas the mental part remains hidden. All of the mental activity required to plan the stroke should be completed prior to moving to step 2: Assume a stance based on the plan.

The first step in this psychomotor skill is an intellectual skill, so we apply the hierarchical analysis procedure. In response to the question, "What would the student need to be able to do in order to learn how to plan the stroke?" we determine that the plan consists of predictions on the direction the ball should be hit and the force with which it should be hit. In turn, direction of the putt depends on knowing the required trajectory of the ball, which in turn depends on knowledge of the "lay of the land." A similar analysis has been used to identify the subordinate skills associated with determining how hard to hit the ball.

Two items are of importance in this example. The first is that step 1 in the goal, namely, making a plan about how to hit the ball, is a step that cannot be taught until students have learned about direction and force and their accompanying subordinate skills. These skills can then be combined into the step of making a plan.

Second, examining the four subskills beneath step 4, you should again go through the process of determining whether each is an intellectual skill, and, if so, whether further hierarchical analysis is required. Steps 4.1, 4.3, 4.4, and 4.5 are motor skills that should require no further analysis. Step 4.2 is an intellectual skill, however, and it requires the use of the plan as well as all the accompanying subordinate skills listed for step 1. It is not necessary to repeat all these skills in the chart. This dependency can be noted by simply putting 1 in a circle under step 4.2 to indicate that all of step 1 must be learned *before* this step.

Each of the other steps in the putting procedure would need to be analyzed to identify the subordinate skills required to perform it. Skill is acquired through both

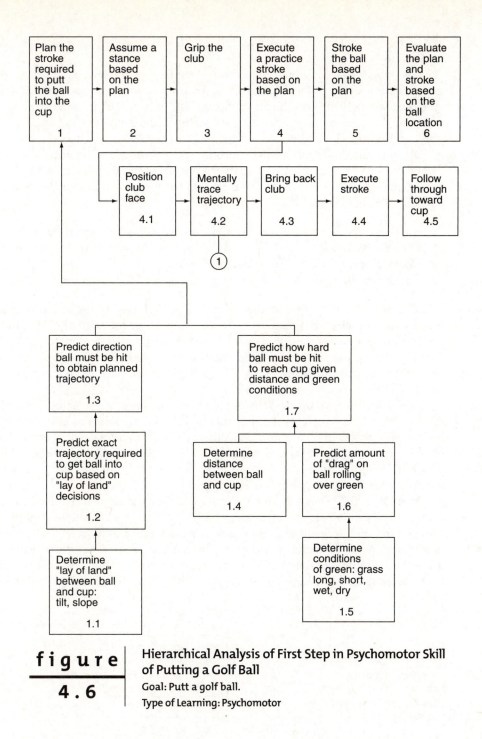

figure 4.6

Hierarchical Analysis of First Step in Psychomotor Skill of Putting a Golf Ball

Goal: Putt a golf ball.

Type of Learning: Psychomotor

accurate mental predictions and practice at translating the predictions into physical actions. Much practice is required for accurate translations.

Subordinate Skills Analysis of an Attitudinal Goal

The attitudinal goal analysis example that follows will illustrate one technique you could use to develop an instructional analysis for such a goal. Starting with the goal statement, the necessary skills and information are identified in a step-by-step sequence.

Instructional Goal   The learner will choose to maximize personal safety while staying in a hotel.

The choice to follow safety precautions while registered in a hotel requires that learners know about potential dangers to themselves, know the procedures to follow, and then actually follow the procedures. The attitudinal instructional goal was introduced in Chapter 3 and preliminary analysis and sequence decisions were illustrated in Figure 3.3 (p. 51).

To continue the analysis, we focus only on fire hazards. What procedures should a hotel occupant follow to minimize the risk of being harmed during a hotel fire? We identified a procedure that contains three basic steps, placed in a sequence that fits a natural order of events.

1. Inquire about hotel's fire safety rules, procedures, and precautions when checking into the hotel.
2. Check emergency facilities in assigned room.
3. Check emergency exits closest to room.

The next step is to analyze the information and skills an individual would need to accomplish each step. Remember that one important component of shaping an attitude, and thereby increasing the chances that people will demonstrate the desired behavior, is to provide them with information about why they should act in a certain way. In your analysis of these tasks, be sure to include reasons that each should be accomplished.

Begin with the first task. Why should someone request fire safety information? Reasons would include facts about death and injury due to fires in hotels. Facts about the frequency of hotel fires, additional hazards in high-rise hotels, or perhaps the number of persons killed or injured annually in hotel fires could be included. The purpose of this information is to get their attention and help them realize that they, too, are at risk while registered in hotels.

Moreover, they must be able to judge whether the hotel's reported safety precautions and procedures are adequate, which means they will need information about routine fire safety precautions that they can expect to find in hotels. Thus, the first task in our procedure includes supporting information describing why patrons should gather fire safety information about hotels and what they should expect to find. The first subordinate skill and the supporting information could be diagrammed as follows:

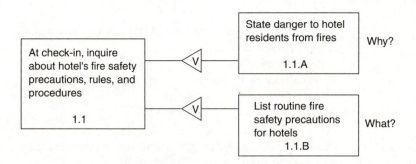

If we were to observe hotel patrons inquiring about fire safety procedures while checking into the hotel, we could correctly infer that they were choosing to maximize their personal safety while staying in the hotel (our original attitudinal goal).

From here, move to the second subordinate skill: check emergency facilities in assigned room. Again, they will need to know why they should do this and what they could expect to find, which could be diagrammed in the following manner:

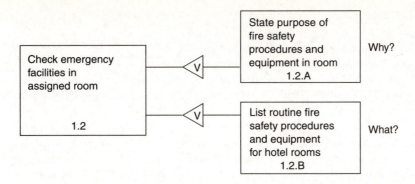

The third subordinate skill is related to why hotel guests should check emergency exits close to their assigned rooms and what they should expect to see, as shown in the next illustration.

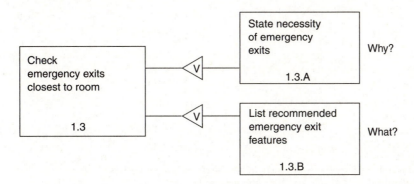

A completed analysis for the fire precaution skill appears in Figure 4.7. Notice in the diagram that the main subordinate skills are placed horizontally. Blocks of information required to perform each step in the procedure are connected to the appropriate box using this symbol:

After completing the analysis of skills 2 and 3, it would be wise to check each set of subordinate skills to determine whether they are related to the original attitudinal goal. If patrons were performing the tasks as specified, could we infer that they were demonstrating an attitude toward maximizing their personal safety while staying in a hotel? If the answer is yes, then we have not strayed from our original goal.

Identification of Entry Skills

Consider the psychomotor instructional analysis of putting a golf ball illustrated previously in Figure 4.6. Identifying appropriate entry skills depends on the current skill level of the learner. We would probably not identify any entry skills for "weekend duffers" who enjoy playing golf without knowledge and skill beyond how to score the game and successive approximations of putting the ball into the cup. For experienced golfers with skill, however, we may want to place the entry skills line between the subordinate skills for step one (subskills 1.1 through 1.7) and main step one. The only way to know for sure is to observe sample learners from the target group actually putting the ball.

Now, review the attitude instructional analysis on personal safety in a hotel included in Figure 4.7. Where would you place the entry skills line? We would assume that all steps in the procedures, and the information required for each step, were needed; therefore, no entry skills line needs to be included in the diagram.

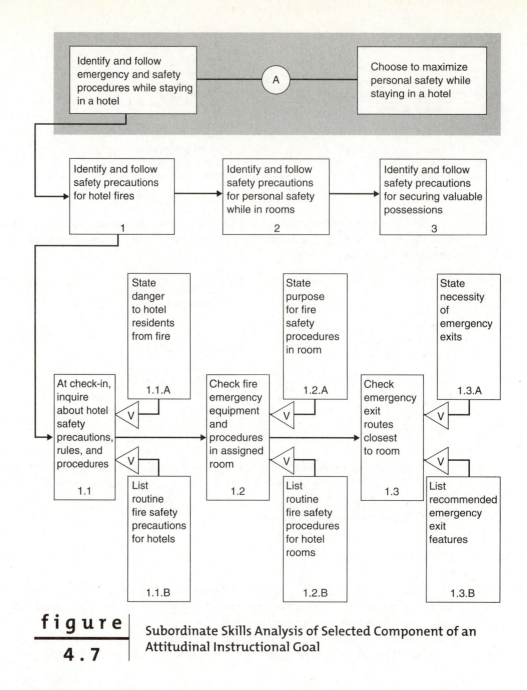

figure 4.7 Subordinate Skills Analysis of Selected Component of an Attitudinal Instructional Goal

Case Study: Group Leadership Training

We continue now with the case study on leadership training for Neighborhood Crime Watch group leaders. We will select only pieces of the goal analysis work begun in Chapter 3 for more detailed subskills analysis work here, because complete analyses of all steps in the goal would become too lengthy and unwieldy for inclusion in this text. We will illustrate subskills analysis for both intellectual skills and verbal information.

Hierarchical Analysis of an Intellectual Skill

Instructional Goal Demonstrate effective discussion group leadership skills.

The hierarchical approach was selected to continue the instructional analysis of step 6 from the goal analysis shown in Figure 3.7 (p. 53). Three main discussion leader actions were identified as behaviors that would aid in managing cooperative group interaction—engendering cooperative member behaviors, defusing blocking behaviors, and alleviating group stress during a meeting. These three actions are illustrated and sequenced in the following diagram. Since they are not hierarchically related, there is some latitude in how they are sequenced. Engendering cooperative action is listed first because it is the most straightforward and positive of the three actions. Defusing blocking behaviors is listed second because it is a complement to positive actions, and alleviating group stress is listed last. In the superordinate skill, skill 6, the learner will integrate the use of the three subordinate skills in order to manage cooperative group interaction.

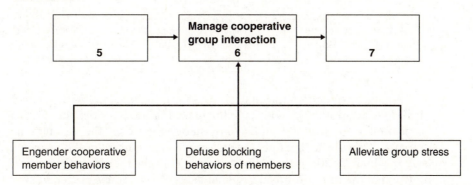

We can continue the hierarchical analysis by identifying the skills subordinate to each of the management skills, focusing on one task at a time. Beginning with the first, in order for leaders to engender cooperative behaviors, they will need to be able to recognize strategies for engendering cooperative behavior and to recognize group members' cooperative actions. More specifically, they will need to be able to name strategies for encouraging cooperative interaction and name member actions that facilitate cooperative interaction. Because these latter tasks are verbal information, they are connected to their respective classification tasks using verbal information symbols, which could be diagrammed as follows:

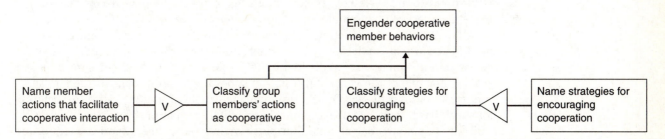

Now let's turn our attention to the second task in the diagram: defusing blocking behaviors of group discussion members. To demonstrate this skill, leaders would need to classify strategies for defusing blocking behaviors as well as group member actions that block cooperative interaction. Each of these behaviors has a verbal information component consisting of naming defusing strategies and naming member actions that block cooperative interaction, as the following diagram illustrates:

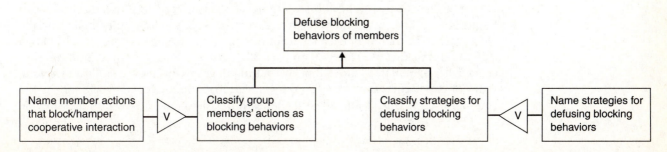

We are now ready for the third skill: alleviating group stress. Similar to the first two tasks, leaders need to classify leader actions for alleviating group stress and symptoms of group stress. These two tasks are supported by verbal information tasks related to naming the strategies and naming the symptoms, which can be diagrammed as follows:

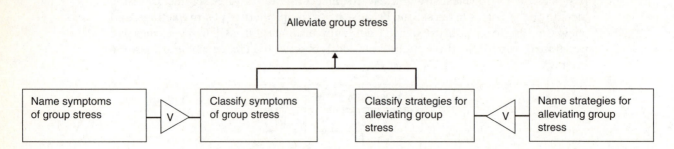

A completed draft of the analysis thus far is included in Figure 4.8 to demonstrate the relationship among subtasks in the hierarchy. First, notice that the original seven steps provide an overview and step-by-step sequence for the instructional goal written at the top of the diagram. Second, notice the hierarchical substructure beneath step 6, which identifies the subordinate skills in the hierarchy for only step 6. Third, notice that the three group management steps have been arranged horizontally (subordinate skills 6.5, 6.10, and 6.15), which implies that they are not hierarchically related. To complete the instructional analysis for the instructional goal, you would identify the information to be included in the remaining verbal information tasks and the subordinate skills for the other major steps identified in the instructional goal. As you can see from this example, a thorough analysis of an intellectual skill can become quite elaborate.

Cluster Analysis for Verbal Information Subordinate Skills

Subordinate Skills   Name member actions that facilitate cooperative interaction and name member actions that block or hamper cooperative interaction.

Although some instructional goals are verbal information tasks, more often we need to perform an analysis of verbal information subordinate skills that are embedded within an intellectual skills hierarchy. Table 4.1 on page 82 contains a cluster analysis for two of the verbal information subordinate skills tasks in the managing cooperative group discussion analysis depicted in Figure 4.8. Verbal information for subskill 6.1, name member actions that facilitate cooperative interaction, and subskill 6.6, name member actions that block or hamper cooperative interaction, are included. Task 6.1 contains one cluster of information: spontaneous actions when introducing and reacting to new ideas. Task 6.6 contains two clusters of information: spontaneous, unplanned actions and planned, purposeful actions. Each of the three clusters has its own column in Table 4.1.

Identification of Entry Skills

Next consider the hierarchical instructional analysis in leading group discussions in Figure 4.8. Which tasks do you believe should be labeled as entry skills for the Neighborhood Crime Watch leaders? For this very heterogeneous group, we label two skills as entry skills in Figure 4.9 on page 83. Suppose the target population were instead college graduates who had prior training in group discussion skills and several years of experience serving as chairs for various committees at work and in the community. For this group, all skills beneath 6.5, 6.10, and 6.15 would possibly be

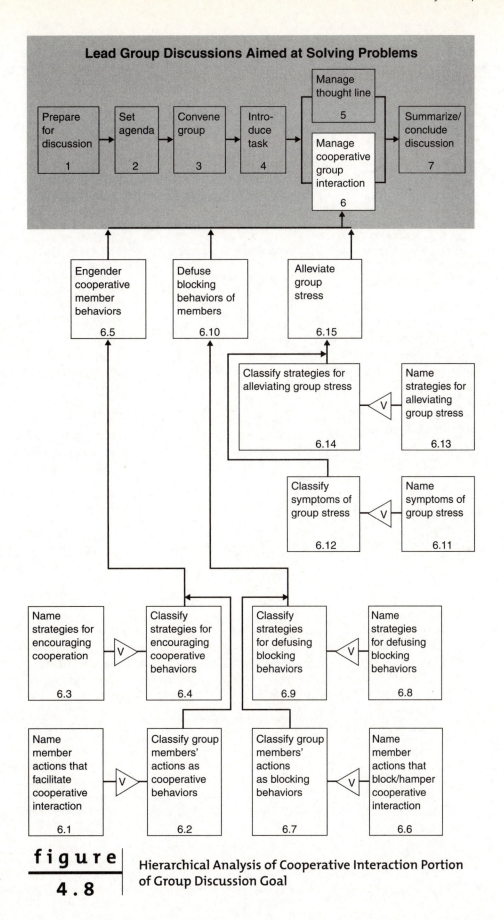

figure 4.8

Hierarchical Analysis of Cooperative Interaction Portion of Group Discussion Goal

t a b l e	**Cluster Analysis of Verbal Information Tasks for Goal on Leading Group Discussion**
4 . 1	

NAME MEMBER ACTIONS THAT FACILITATE COOPERATIVE INTERACTION 6.1	NAME MEMBER ACTIONS THAT BLOCK OR HAMPER COOPERATIVE INTERACTION 6.6	
Spontaneous, Unplanned Actions:	**Spontaneous, Unplanned Actions:**	**Planned, Purposeful Actions:**

Spontaneous, Unplanned Actions:

6.1.1 When introducing and reacting to new ideas:

1. treats all members' ideas fairly (impartiality) and with due consideration
2. comes with open mind
3. listens and considers others' comments
4. volunteers information and ideas
5. expects others to have sincere motives
6. invites others to participate
7. demonstrates good will constantly
8. resists pressures to conform
9. appreciates loyalties members feel toward others and other groups

6.1.2 When *ideas* are questioned by group members:

1. admits personal errors in ideas, judgment
2. resists tendency to abandon ideas too quickly
3. explains ideas further to enable fair examination
4. helps modify ideas for group acceptance

Spontaneous, Unplanned Actions:

6.6.1 When introducing and reacting to new ideas:

1. neglects comments made by colleagues who:
   a. rarely speak
   b. lack influence
2. neglects comments because they:
   a. are poorly phrased
   b. are unpopular
   c. lack immediate appeal
3. accepts ideas too quickly due to:
   a. desire to make quick progress
   b. advocacy by popular, articulate, experienced member (favoritism)
   c. desire to be considered cooperative
   d. novelty
4. comes with fully formed conclusions
5. proposes and exhorts
6. only remarks when invited
7. misconstrues others' motives
8. neglects other's comments, ideas
9. rewards/punishes others for ideas
10. pressures others to conform
11. demeans members' loyalties to others

6.6.2 When *ideas* are questioned by group members:

1. refuses to admit personal error
2. shows dogmatic commitment to own ideas
3. views questions as personal attack (oversensitive)
4. reacts to questions defensively

Planned, Purposeful Actions:

6.6.3 Attempts to control others by building a personal image through:

1. adopting a sage role ("I've been here longer and I know."); remains quiet early, then saves the group with reasonable recommendations
2. dropping names, places, experiences
3. collusion (feeding cues to colleagues, opening opportunities for each other)
4. moving faster than others, suggests solutions before others get started
5. taking extreme position, then moving to center to appear cooperative
6. overresponding (listening and responding to feint cooperativeness)
7. showing specious earnestness ("That's such a gooood idea yoooou have.")
8. using trendy language for popular appeal

6.6.4 Attempts to control others by inducing feelings of inadequacy in them through:

1. using technical language unnecessarily
2. demanding definitions repetitively
3. displaying studied disregard of another's comments (going back to previous speaker as though nothing was said)
4. usurping leader's functions repeatedly

6.6.5 Attempts to control others by delaying work of group through:

1. summarizing unnecessarily at short intervals
2. cautioning against moving too fast
3. deceptively showing deliberation and adjustment (posture/gestures)

6.6.6 Attempts to control others by putting them off balance through:

1. inappropriately changing pace, tone, volume
2. distorting another's ideas to make them appear contradictory, extreme, unreasonable
3. abruptly switching from logic to sentimentality
4. disparaging important matters with over casual reaction or verbal minimization
5. studied misrepresentation

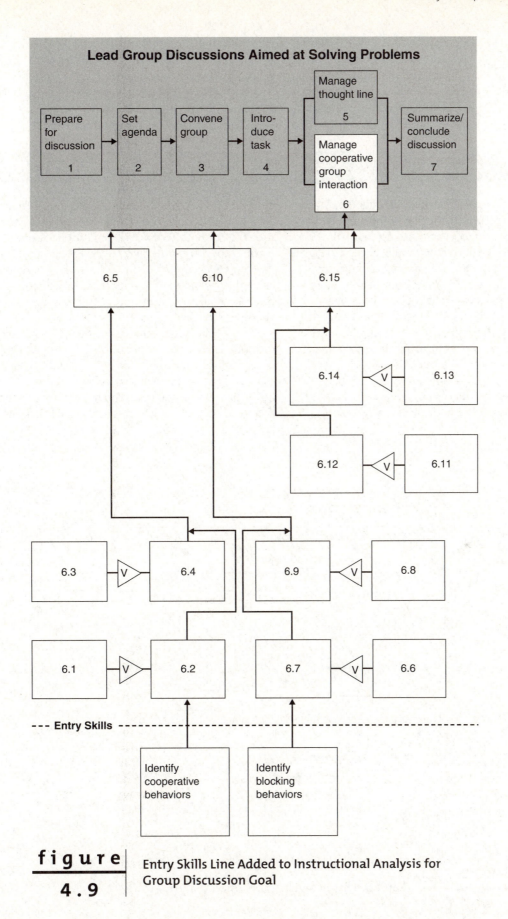

figure 4.9 | Entry Skills Line Added to Instructional Analysis for Group Discussion Goal

classified as entry skills. The instruction for this group could focus on practicing these three leadership skills in interactive groups with detailed feedback on their verbal and nonverbal management actions during the meetings.

Readers interested in a school curriculum example should study the subordinate skills analysis and identification of entry skills contained in Appendix C.

SUMMARY

In order to begin a subordinate skills analysis, it is necessary to have a clear description of the main tasks learners need to perform in order to accomplish the instructional goal. The derivation of these major steps was described in Chapter 3. To conduct a subordinate skills analysis, you must analyze each of the major steps in a goal. If a step is verbal information, a cluster analysis would be done. Hierarchical analysis should be used with intellectual and psychomotor skills. Sometimes sequences of procedural steps will be included in a hierarchical analysis.

Goal analysis of an attitude identifies the behaviors that would be exhibited if someone held that attitude. During the subordinate skills analysis phase,

each of the behaviors would need to be analyzed. These behaviors can be intellectual skills, psychomotor skills, or both. Verbal information required to perform either the intellectual or psychomotor skill would be placed within the framework to support the related steps in the hierarchy. This information might include what to expect and why a particular action should be performed.

For each of the skills identified during this subordinate skills analysis, the process is repeated. That is, each of the identified subordinate skills is analyzed to identify its respective subordinate skills. This step-down process is used until you believe that no further subordinate skills remain to be identified. At this

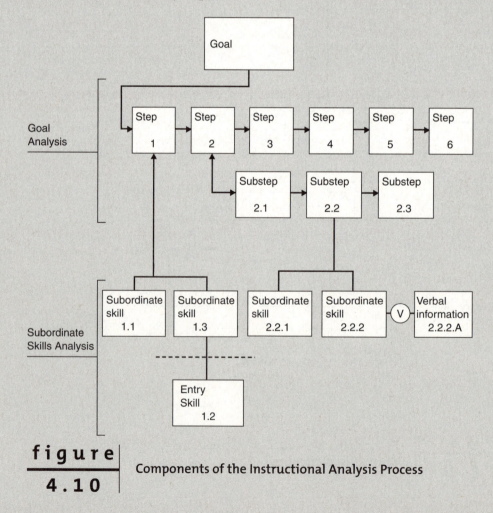

figure
4.10

Components of the Instructional Analysis Process

point, the designer identifies the entry skills that will be required of learners by drawing a dotted line below those skills that will be taught and above those that will not. The skills identified in the analysis that will not be taught are referred to as *entry skills*.

The final product of the subordinate skills analysis is a framework of the subordinate skills required to perform each main step of the instructional goal. The total instructional analysis includes the instructional goal, the main steps required to accomplish the goal, the subordinate skills required to accomplish each main step, and the entry skills. This framework of skills is the foundation for all subsequent instructional design activities.

It is important to evaluate the analysis of learning tasks before proceeding to the next phase of design activities, because many hours of work remain to be completed. The quality of the analysis will directly affect the ease with which succeeding design activities can be performed and the quality of the eventual instruction. Specific criteria to use in evaluating the analysis include whether all relevant tasks are identified, superfluous tasks are eliminated, and the relationships among the tasks are clearly designated through the configuration of tasks on the chart and the placement of lines used to connect the tasks. Producing an accurate, clear analysis of tasks typically requires several iterations and refinements.

Figure 4.10 summarizes the major concepts from the last two chapters. The goal is translated into a diagram of steps and substeps via the goal analysis process. Those steps, in turn, are used to derive the subordinate skills and the entry skills for the goal. The overall process is referred to as an instructional analysis. Careful instructional analysis can be complex and time consuming. In large ID projects where there is pressure to complete new curriculum materials or get a product to market, designers will sometimes use rapid prototyping techniques to speed up the overall ID process. There is an overview of these techniques in Chapter 9.

RUBRIC FOR EVALUATING SUBORDINATE AND ENTRY SKILLS

Following is a rubric for evaluating subordinate and entry skills. The three sections of criteria include skills statements, diagramming, and other criteria you may identify for your goal analysis project.

Designer note: If an element is not relevant for your project, mark NA in the No column.

No	Some	Yes	
			A. Intellectual and Psychomotor Skills Does the analysis:
—	—	—	1. Identify critical rules and concepts for main steps in goal?
			2. Illustrate the hierarchical relationship among skills by:
—	—	—	a. Progressing downward from problem solving to rules, to concepts, to discriminations?
—	—	—	b. Using upward pointing arrows to link hierarchical skills?
—	—	—	c. Using codes—e.g., 4.2 (step 4 skill 2)—to link related skills?
—	—	—	3. Have procedural subskills linked to main steps using procedural boxes left to right, arrows, and skills code numbers?
—	—	—	4. Have required verbal information linked to appropriate skill?
			B. Verbal Information Does the analysis:
—	—	—	1. Use main areas of content as headings?
—	—	—	2. Use appropriate size chunks/depth for learners?
—	—	—	3. Present information in logical order (e.g., spatial, chronological, familiar to unfamiliar)?
—	—	—	4. Avoid noncritical information?
—	—	—	5. Use appropriate format for scope (e.g., matrix, cluster, box, outline)?
—	—	—	6. Link information directly to related attitude or skill using "V" triangle?
			C. Attitudes Are attitudes clearly linked to appropriate:
—	—	—	1. Behaviors that reflect the attitude (positive and negative)?
—	—	—	2. Verbal information needed to support the attitude?
—	—	—	3. Psychomotor skills needed to act in certain ways?
—	—	—	4. Intellectual skills needed to reason appropriately (e.g., what to do, rewards, consequences)?
—	—	—	5. Skills and attitudes using "A" circle and horizontal lines?
			D. Other.
—	—	—	1.
—	—	—	2.

In the exercises that follow, you will be asked to complete a subordinate skills analysis for psychomotor, intellectual, and verbal information goals. The topics and goals used in the examples are purposely different from those used in previous examples. Working with new goals at this point will provide you with a broader base of experience that should be beneficial when you select a topic and goal of your own.

Work through each example, and then compare your analysis with the sample one in the Feedback section. If your analysis is different, locate the differences and determine whether you would like to make any revisions in yours. You may like your analysis better than the sample provided, but you should be able to explain and justify the differences.

1. Do an instructional analysis for the following psychomotor skill.

   Topic Changing a tire.

   Demonstrate your ability to do a procedural analysis by identifying the subskills required to perform step 2 for the following instructional goal on tire changing.

   Instructional Goal Change the tire on an automobile.

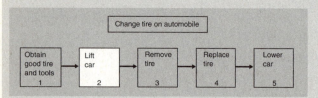

2. Complete a hierarchical analysis for the following intellectual skill.

   Topic Map skills.

   Demonstrate your ability to do a hierarchical analysis by identifying the subordinate skills required to perform each of the four main steps for the instructional goal on map reading.

   Instructional Goal Use a map of your town to locate specific places and determine the distances between them.

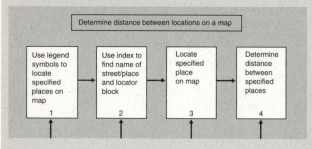

To aid your analysis, you may want to obtain a copy of a local city map and use it to perform each of these main steps. As you work, note what tasks you must perform and what information and skills you need to perform each one.

3. Complete a hierarchical analysis for the following intellectual skill.

   Topic Writing Composition

   Demonstrate your ability to do a combination intellectual skills and verbal information instructional goal analysis for the following goal on writing composition.

   Instructional Goal In written composition, (1) use a variety of sentence types and accompanying punctuation based on the *purpose* and *mood* of the sentence, and (2) use a variety of sentence types and accompanying punctuation based on the *complexity* or *structure* of the sentence.

4. Complete a cluster analysis for verbal information.

   Topic Parts of the body.

   Instructional Goal Name the parts of the body using common terminology.

   One strategy for this analysis might be to proceed from the head to the feet.

5. Review the psychomotor instructional analysis on changing a tire in Figure 4.11, assuming a target population of high school juniors with temporary driver's licenses. For any steps in the procedure identify the entry skills that you believe are relevant for this analysis. Modify the procedural analysis in the diagram to reflect your work.

6. Review the hierarchical analysis on reading a map located in Figure 4.12. Assume a target population of sixth-grade students who are below average, average, and above average in reading and arithmetic skills. Which tasks in the analysis would you predict are entry skills and which do you believe should be included in instruction for the sixth-grade group? Modify the diagram in Figure 4.12 to reflect your work.

7. Consider the verbal information on naming parts of the human body in Figure 4.13. Assume a target population of third-grade students. Which tasks do you believe should be considered entry skills? Remember that the task requires students to name parts, which requires spelling. Modify Figure 4.13 to show your work.

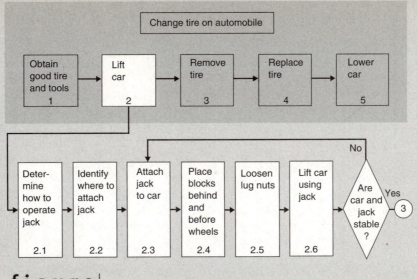

figure
4.11

Instructional Analysis for Changing an Automobile Tire

---

1. Compare your subskills analysis for changing a tire with the one shown in Figure 4.11. You may also have identified some subskills below the skills labeled 2.1 through 2.6. For example, one would need to know the rule that "lug nuts loosen by turning counterclockwise" to complete step 2.5 successfully.

2. Compare your hierarchical analysis for reading a map with the one shown in Figure 4.12. Analyze and see if you can explain differences between your work and Figure 4.12.

3. Compare your hierarchical analysis for writing composition with the one provided in the case study in Appendix C.

4. Compare your verbal information cluster analysis on parts of the body with the one shown in Figure 4.13.

5. No subordinate skills are included in the instructional analysis on changing a tire that should be designated as entry skills for this high school learner group.

6. Probably only two subordinate skills in the instructional analysis for the map reading goal would be considered entry skills; these are subordinate skill 4.8, multiply by whole numbers, and skill 4.10, multiply by fractions. Students who cannot multiply by whole numbers or fractions would need either to have step 4 excluded from their instruction or receive modified instruction where they calculate distance using only addition.

7. Entry skills identified for the verbal information cluster analysis include the ability to discriminate among the head, arms, hands, trunk, leg, and foot. Correct spelling of terms will be covered in the instruction; thus, it is not included as an entry skill.

REFERENCES AND RECOMMENDED READINGS

Briggs, L., & Wager, W. (1981). *Handbook of procedures for the design of instruction* (2nd ed.). Englewood Cliffs, NJ: Educational Technology Publications. This classic text in instructional design provides one of the most detailed step-by-step procedures for carrying out the ID process.

Gagné, R. M. (1985). *Conditions of learning* (4th ed.). New York: Holt, Rinehart and Winston. This book is a classic in regard to many aspects of instructional design, including the domains of learning and hierarchical analysis.

Gagné, R. M., Wager, W. W., Golas, K. C., & Keller, J. M. (2004). *Principles of instructional design* (5th ed.).

Belmont, CA: Wadsworth/Thomson Learning. Provides a number of examples of the application of hierarchical analysis to intellectual skills.

Gottfredson, C. (2002, June/July). Rapid task analysis: The key to developing competency-based e-learning. *The E-Learning Developer's Journal*. Retrieved December 19, 2007, from www.elearningguild.com/pdf/2/062502DST.pdf. Details of a procedure with examples for instructional analysis.

Jonassen, D. H. (1997). Instructional design models for well-structured and ill-structured problem-solving

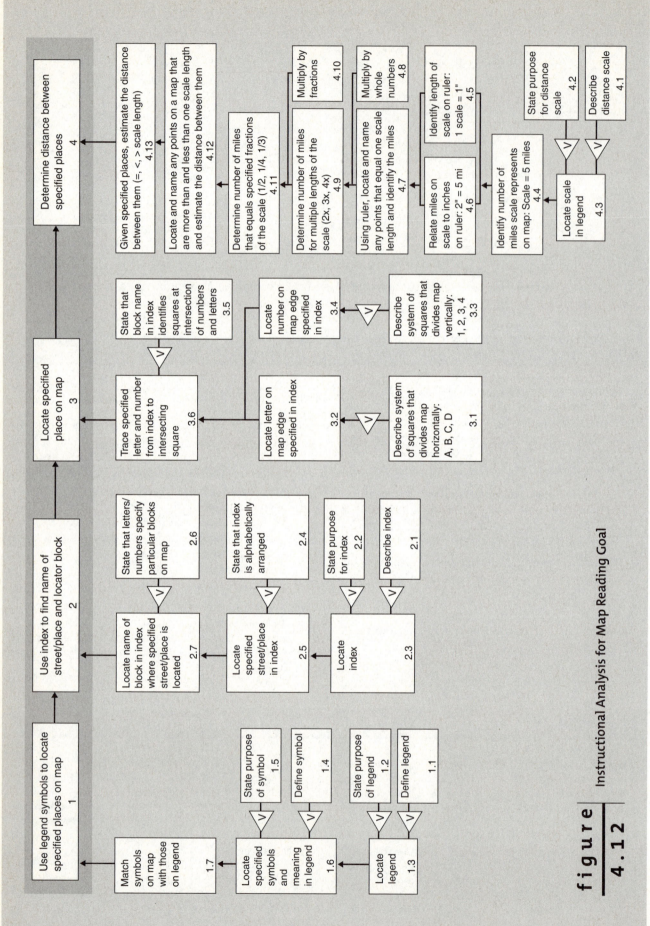

figure
4.12 Instructional Analysis for Map Reading Goal

Name parts of the head 1.0	Name parts of the arm 2.0	Name parts of the hand 3.0	Name parts of the trunk 4.0	Name parts of the leg 5.0	Name parts of the foot 6.0
Name:	Name:	Name:	Name:	Name:	Name:
			Front		
1.1 scalp	2.1 armpit	3.1 back	4.1 shoulder	5.1 thigh	6.1 heel
1.2 hair	2.2 upper arm	3.2 palm	4.2 collarbone	5.2 knee	6.2 arch
1.3 ear	2.3 elbow	3.3 finger	4.3 chest	5.3 calf	6.3 sole
1.4 forehead	2.4 forearm	3.4 thumb	4.4 breast	5.4 shin	6.4 toe
1.5 eyebrows	2.5 wrist	3.5 knuckle	4.5 rib cage	5.5 ankle	6.5 toe joint
1.6 eyes		3.6 fingertip	4.6 ribs		6.6 toe nail
1.7 eyelids		3.7 fingernail	4.7 waist		
1.8 cheeks		3.8 identifying pattern (print)	4.8 navel		
1.9 nose			4.9 hip bones		
1.10 nostrils			4.10 hip joint		
1.11 mouth			Back		
1.12 lips			4.11 shoulder blades		
1.13 teeth			4.12 rib cage		
1.14 tongue			4.13 waist		
1.15 jaw			4.14 hips		
1.16 neck					
1.17 Adam's apple					

figure 4.13 Cluster Analysis of a Verbal Information Task
Goal: Name the various parts of the human body.
Type of Learning: Verbal information

learning outcomes. *Educational Technology Research and Development, 45*(1), 65–94. This paper includes a step-wise look at approaches to solving well-structured and ill-structured problems that can be used during instructional analysis.

Jonassen, D. H., Tessmer, M., & Hannum, W. (1999). *Task analysis procedures for instructional design.* Mahwah, NJ: Lawrence Erlbaum Associates. Excellent overview and "how to" guide to instructional design applications of a wide range of techniques for job and task analysis. This book is currently available as an e-book through netLibrary.

Lee, J., & Reigeluth, C. M. (2003). Formative research on the heuristic task analysis process. *Educational Technology Research and Development, 51*(4), 5–24.

Loughner, P., & Moller, L. (1998). The use of task analysis procedures by instructional designers. *Performance Improvement Quarterly, 11*(3), 79–101.

Mager, R. (1997). *Goal analysis: How to clarify your goals so you can actually achieve them.* Atlanta, GA: The Center for Effective Performance.

Merrill, P. F. (1987). Job and task analysis. In R. M. Gagné (Ed.), *Instructional technology: Foundations.* Hillsdale, NJ: Lawrence Erlbaum Associates.

Reigeluth, C. M. (1983). Current trends in task analysis: The integration of task analysis and instructional design. *Journal of Instructional Development, 6*(4), 24–35. Describes integration of task analysis into the instructional design process.

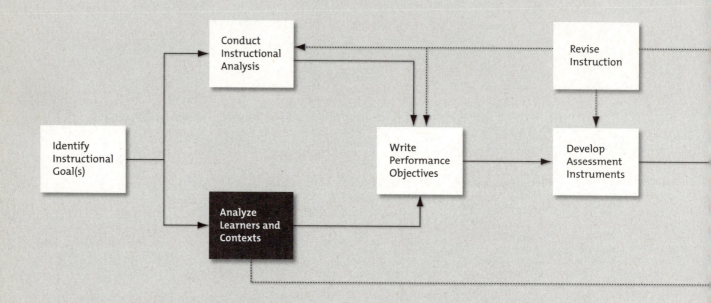

objectives

- ➤ Name the general characteristics of a target population that are important to consider when developing instruction.
- ➤ Name contextual characteristics of the eventual setting in which acquired skills will be performed.
- ➤ Name contextual characteristics of the instructional setting.
- ➤ For a given instructional goal and context, describe methods and sources for obtaining information about the target population, performance setting, and instructional setting.
- ➤ Analyze and describe the general characteristics of a target population.
- ➤ Analyze and describe the contextual characteristics of the eventual performance and instructional settings.
- ➤ Review instructional analysis work in light of learner and context information and revise as indicated.

Analyzing Learners and Contexts

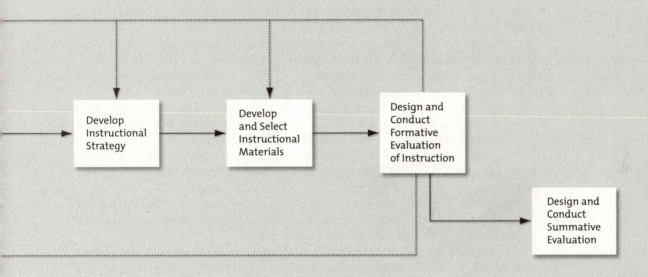

Develop Instructional Strategy	Develop and Select Instructional Materials	Design and Conduct Formative Evaluation of Instruction

Design and Conduct Summative Evaluation

Background

The previous chapters have focused on identifying the skills and knowledge to be taught. From a needs assessment a goal was identified that, in turn, was analyzed to determine the specific steps included in the goal. Additional analysis was used to identify (1) the subordinate skills that must be included in the instruction and (2) the entry skills that learners must have to begin the instruction.

Not only must the designer determine what is to be taught but also the characteristics of the learners, the contexts in which the instruction will be delivered, and the contexts in which the skills will eventually be used. We refer to these types of analyses as learner analysis and context analysis. They provide the details that help shape both what is taught and, especially, how it is taught.

What do we need to know about the people we are instructing? Answers vary greatly on this question. One approach is to learn as much as possible in order to design instruction that is most appropriate for the learners. However, data collection can be expensive and time consuming, and it may yield information that is not very useful. Another approach is to assume that as designers we already know enough about the learners to forgo collecting information about them. For some designers, this may be true, but for others who are designing for new learner populations, assumptions about learners may be inaccurate, causing significant problems when the instruction is delivered.

Historically, educational psychologists have examined an array of individual difference variables and their relationship to learning. Studies of intelligence and personality traits fill the literature. From an instructional design perspective, we want to know which variables significantly affect the achievement of the group of learners we will instruct, since designers create instruction for groups of learners having common characteristics. In this chapter we identify a set of variables indicated by research to affect learning. By describing your learners in terms of these variables, you can modify your instructional strategy to enhance learning.

Of equal importance at this point in the design process are analyses of the context in which learning will occur and the context in which learners will use their newly acquired skills. In some instances, a learner is taught a skill in a classroom, demonstrates mastery on a posttest, and that is the end of the matter. Likewise, a student may use the mathematics skill learned this year in a mathematics class next year. In these situations, the context for learning and the context for using the skill are essentially the same.

In contrast, consider a course on interpersonal skills for managers. These skills may be taught and practiced in a training center, yet used in a variety of corporate settings. These different contexts should be reflected in the media selected for instruction, in the instructional strategy, and in evaluations of the learners.

Another reason for the designer to analyze the learners and contexts is that these analyses cannot be done in one's office. Designers should talk with learners, instructors, and managers; they should visit classrooms, training facilities, and the learners' workplace to determine the circumstances in which learners will be acquiring and using their new skills. All of these experiences significantly enhance designers' understanding of what is being taught and how it will be used.

As noted in Chapters 3 and 4, the instructional analysis steps and analyses of learners and contexts are often performed simultaneously instead of sequentially, so that information gathered from each informs the other.

In this chapter, we will first discuss what we need to know about learners (*learner analysis*), then next what we need to know about the setting in which learners will apply their new skills (*performance context analysis*), and finally what we need to know about the setting in which learners will acquire their new skills (*learning context analysis*).

Concepts

Learner Analysis

Let's begin by considering the learners for any given set of instruction, referred to as the *target population*—the ones you want to "hit" with the appropriate instruction.

Sometimes the target population is also referred to as the *target audience* or *target group*. It is described by such identifiers as age, grade level, topic being studied, job experience, or job position. For example, a set of materials might be intended for systems programmers, fifth-grade reading classes, middle managers, or high school principals. These examples are typical of the descriptions usually available for instructional materials. But the instructional designer must go beyond these general descriptions and be much more specific about the skills required of the learners for whom the materials are intended.

It is important to make a distinction between the target population and what we will refer to as *tryout learners*. The target population is an abstract representation of the widest possible range of users, such as college students, fifth graders, or adults. Tryout learners, on the other hand, are learners available to the designer while the instruction is being developed. It is assumed that these tryout learners are members of the target population—that is, they are college students, fifth graders, and adults, respectively. But the tryout learners are *specific* college students, fifth graders, or adults. While the designer is preparing the instruction for the target population, the tryout learners will serve as representatives of that group in order to plan the instruction and to determine how well the instruction works after it is developed.

What information do designers need to know about their target population? Useful information includes (1) entry skills, (2) prior knowledge of the topic area, (3) attitudes toward content and potential delivery system, (4) academic motivation, (5) educational and ability levels, (6) general learning preferences, (7) attitudes toward the organization giving the instruction, and (8) group characteristics. The following paragraphs elaborate each of these categories.

Entry Skills   Prior to beginning instruction, target population members must have already mastered certain skills (i.e., entry skills) associated with the learning goal. The research literature also discusses other characteristics of learners, categorized as either specific or general in nature, that relate to learners' knowledge, experience, and attitudes. These also influence the outcome of instruction. Interested readers may want to consult the work of Richey (1992) for a detailed review of this research.

Prior Knowledge of Topic Area   Much of the current learning research emphasizes the importance of determining what learners already know about the topic that will be taught; rarely are they completely unaware or lacking in at least some knowledge of the subject. Further, they often have partial knowledge or misconceptions about the topic. When we teach, learners may try to interpret what is being said in light of the associations they can make with their prior learning. They construct new knowledge by building on their prior understanding; therefore, it is extremely important for the designer to determine the range and nature of prior knowledge.

Attitudes toward Content and Potential Delivery System   Learners may have impressions or attitudes about the topic that will be taught and perhaps even how it might be delivered. For example, the target population may have no interest in mastering the rules and techniques required for keeping an electronic day planner because they have no interest in entering their old paper and pencil day planner into their desktop computer. They might, however, be interested in learning the new skills if the company provides them with a personal digital assistant (PDA) that will synchronize files with their desktop computer. The designer should determine, from a sample set of learners, the range of prior experience, knowledge, and attitudes toward the content area that will be covered in the instruction. Designers also should determine learners' expectations regarding how the instruction might be delivered.

Academic Motivation (ARCS)   Many instructors consider the motivation level of learners the most important factor in successful instruction. Teachers report that when learners have little motivation or interest in the topic, learning is almost impossible. Keller (1987) developed a model of the different types of motivation necessary for successful learning, and he suggested how to use this information to design effective instruction. Called the ARCS model (attention, relevance, confidence, and satisfaction), the model will be discussed in detail in the chapter on instructional strategies (Chapter 8); it will be used here to show how to obtain information from learners during the learner analysis.

Keller suggests asking learners questions such as these: How relevant is this instructional goal to you? What aspects of the goal interest you most? How confident are you that you could successfully learn to perform the goal? How satisfying would it be to you to be able to perform the goal? The answers to these questions will provide insight into the target population and into potential problem areas in the design of instruction. Do not *assume* that learners are very interested in the topic, find it relevant to their interests or job, feel confident that they can learn it, and will be satisfied when they do. These assumptions are almost never valid. It is important to find out how learners feel *before* you design the instruction rather than while it is being delivered. We will discuss the implications of learners' academic motivation and describe procedures for collecting motivational data after considering more general characteristics of the learners.

Educational and Ability Levels Determine the achievement and general ability levels of the learners. This information will provide insight into the kinds of instructional experiences they may have had and perhaps their ability to cope with new and different approaches to instruction.

General Learning Preferences Find out about the target population's learning skills and preferences and their willingness to explore new modes of learning. In other words, are these learners seemingly fixated on the lecture/discussion approach to learning, or have they experienced success with seminar-style classes, case studies, small-group problem-based learning, or independent web-based courses? Much has been written about "learning styles" and assessing a student's personal learning style so that instruction can be adapted for maximum effectiveness. Research indicates that personal styles can be identified, but such styles are often derived from learners' expressions of personal preferences for listening, viewing, reading, small-group discussion, and so forth, rather than measurement of psychological traits that will predict how a student will learn best. We will treat learning styles as an aspect of learning preferences until a body of research emerges that confirms practical gains in learning efficiency, effectiveness, and attitudes through individualizing instruction based on identification of learning styles.

Attitudes toward Training Organization Determine the target population's attitudes toward the organization providing the instruction. Do they have a positive, constructive view of both management and their peers, or are they somewhat cynical about senior leadership and their ability to provide appropriate training? Researchers have indicated that such attitudes are substantial predictors of the success of instruction in terms of the likelihood of newly learned skills being used on the job. Those with positive attitudes about the organization and their peers are more likely to use the skills.

Group Characteristics A careful analysis of the learners will provide two additional kinds of information that can be influential in the design of instruction. The first is the degree of heterogeneity within the target population on important variables. Obviously, finding ways to accommodate diversity is important. The second kind of information is an overall impression of the target population based on direct interactions with them. This is not simply accepting a stereotypical description or a management description of the learners; this requires interaction with learners in order to develop an impression of what they know and how they feel.

These learner variables will be used to select and develop the objectives for instruction, and they will especially influence various components of the instructional strategy. They will help the designer develop a motivational strategy for the instruction and will suggest various types of examples that can be used to illustrate points, ways in which the instruction may (or may not) be delivered, and ways to make the practice of skills relevant for learners.

Data for Learner Analysis

There are various ways to collect data about learners. One method would involve a site visit for structured interviews with managers, instructors, and learners. These interviews might yield valuable information about learners' entry skills, personal goals, attitudes about the content and training organization, and self-reported skill levels. During the site visit, the designer could also observe learners in the performance and instructional contexts. Either on site or using distance technology, designers could administer surveys and questionnaires to obtain similar information about learners' interests, goals, attitudes, and self-reported skills. In addition to self-report and supervisor judgment, designers could administer pretests in order to identify learners' actual entry skills and prior knowledge and skills.

Output   The results of a learner analysis include a description of the learners' (1) entry skills and prior knowledge of the topic, (2) attitudes toward the content and potential delivery system, (3) academic motivation, (4) prior achievement and ability levels, (5) learning preferences, (6) general attitudes toward the organization providing training, and (7) group characteristics. Good instruction that precisely fits the learners' needs and characteristics will be in vain, however, if the performance context does not enable and support application of the new skills.

Performance Context Analysis

The designer must be concerned about the characteristics of the setting in which the skills and knowledge will be used. Instruction should be part of satisfying a need that has been derived from a needs assessment, which should be based on identifying performance problems that can be solved through instruction or opportunities that instruction can provide for an organization. The instruction must contribute to meeting an identified need by providing learners with skills and attitudes that will be used, if not in the workplace, certainly somewhere other than the classroom. Seldom is something learned simply for the purpose of demonstrating mastery on a test at the end of the instruction; therefore, as designers it is important for us to know the environment in which our learners will be using their new skills. From a constructivist perspective, a careful context analysis is critical for aiding the designer in creating appropriate elements of the learning environment and enabling the learner to build optimal conceptual frameworks for learning and remembering. Accurate analysis of the performance context should enable the designer to develop a more authentic learning experience, thereby enhancing the learners' motivation, sense of instructional relevance, and transfer of new knowledge and skills to the work setting. In fact, the reason for analyzing the performance context before the learning context is to ensure, to the greatest extent possible, that requirements for applying the new skills are present while new skills are being learned.

Managerial or Supervisor Support   We must learn about the organizational support that learners can expect to receive when using the new skills. Research indicates that one of the strongest predictors of use of new skills in a new setting (called *transfer of training*) is the support received by the learner. If managers, supervisors, or peers ignore or punish those using new skills, then use of the new skills will cease. If personnel recognize and praise those using new skills and emphasize how the skills are contributing to progress within the organization, then skills will be used, and hopefully their use will address the problem identified in the original needs assessment.

If management support is not present, then the designer (or the training organization) has an added problem associated with this project, namely recruiting their support. It is often helpful to include managers in project planning, ask them to serve as subject-matter experts, and perhaps ask them to serve as mentors or coaches for the learners when they return to the workplace.

Physical Aspects of the Site   The second aspect of the context analysis is to assess the physical context in which the skills will be used. Will their use depend on equipment, facilities, tools, timing, or other resources? This information can be used to design the training so that skills can be practiced in conditions as similar as possible to those in the workplace.

Social Aspects of the Site   Understanding the social context in which skills are to be applied is critical for designing effective instruction. In analyzing social aspects, some relevant questions to ask include the following: Will learners work alone or as team members? Will they work independently in the field, or will they be presenting ideas in staff meetings or supervising employees? Are the skills to be learned already used proficiently by others in the organization, or will these learners be the first?

Relevance of Skills to Workplace   To ensure that new skills meet identified needs, we should assess the relevance of the skills to be learned by employees currently working in the performance site. This is a reality check to ensure that instruction really will be the solution, or part of a solution, to the needs that were originally identified. Designers should assess whether physical, social, or motivational constraints to the use of the new skills exist. Physical constraints might include lack of work space, outdated equipment, inadequate time or scheduling, or too few personnel. For example, it would do little good to provide customer service training for a receptionist who has a constant stream of customers, all four telephone lines lit, and a thirty-minute delay for customers with appointments. Likewise, training in new instructional software is irrelevant for teachers who have severely outdated computers in their classrooms that won't run current software applications.

Data for Performance Context Analysis

Although some instructional analyses can be done in the office, context analyses require designers to observe in the appropriate setting. These observations influence the entire future course of the project because they provide critical information not only for direct input to the project but also for enhancing the skills and knowledge of designers.

On-site visits for purposes of context analysis should be planned well in advance, and one or more visits should be made. Ideally these visits should occur at the same time that instructional analysis is being conducted. The sites will be situation specific, and some may have been identified in the needs assessment.

The purpose for the visits is to gather data from potential learners and managers and to observe the work environment where the new skills will be used. The basic data-gathering procedures include interviews and observations. The interviews should be conducted using written questions that focus on the issues presented in this chapter. Answers to the questions are situation or project specific and depend on the unique nature of each setting.

Output   The major outputs of this phase of the study are (1) a description of the physical and organizational environment where the skills will be used, and (2) a list of any special factors that may facilitate or interfere with the learners' use of the new skills.

Learning Context Analysis

There are two aspects to the analysis of the learning context that determine what is and what should be. The *what is* is a review of the setting in which instruction will take place. This might be only one site, such as a corporate training center, or it could be one of many sites that a client has available. The *what should be* is facilities, equipment, and resources that adequately support the intended instruction.

In the learning context analysis, the focus is on the following elements: (1) the compatibility of the site with instructional requirements, (2) the adaptability of the site for simulating aspects of the workplace or performance site, (3) the adaptability of the site for using a variety of instructional strategies and training delivery approaches, and (4) the constraints present that may affect the design and delivery of instruction. The following paragraphs briefly elaborate each of these areas.

Compatibility of Site with Instructional Requirements   In the instructional goal statement prepared in the first step of the model, the tools and other support items required to perform the goal were listed. Does the learning environment that you are visiting include these tools? Can it accommodate them if they are provided? The most common "tool" today is probably a computer. Are computers available? Are they compatible with the computers in the training organization? And, of great importance, are they compatible with those in other training sites that may be used for the instruction?

Adaptability of Site to Simulate Workplace   Another issue is the compatibility of the training environment with the work environment. In training, an attempt must be made to simulate those factors from the work environment that are critical to performance. Will it be possible to do so in the designated training context? What would have to be changed or added?

Adaptability for Delivery Approaches   The list of tool requirements from the goal statement indicates the *what should be* with regard to the learning context and, obviously, for the performance context as well. There may be other limitations or requirements that should be noted at this point in the analysis. These relate to organizational mandates that have been placed on your instruction. The organization may have decided that the instruction must be deliverable in typical corporate training centers in the United States, that the instruction must be deliverable by web to employees' desktops worldwide, or that the instruction is intended for the "typical" fourth-grade classroom. Determine what delivery approach can be used in the proposed instructional sites.

Learning Site Constraints Affecting Design and Delivery   For whatever reason, an upfront decision may have been made that this instruction will be computer-based and self-instructional. The decision may not have been made on the basis of an analysis of the capability of a computer system to deliver the desired instruction. In such cases, the context analysis of the learning environment becomes critically important. The designer may find that the computers in various training sites or on employees' desks are incompatible, and it will triple the cost of the project to provide compatible computers. Or the organization may recognize the benefit of compatible delivery systems and use this opportunity to conform. The major point is that the development of the instruction should *never* be initiated before addressing such matters. Most experienced designers have, at one time or another, regretted the omission of constraints analysis in the design process.

In an ideal situation, the location of the training and the means of delivering it would be decided on the basis of an analysis of the requirements for teaching the instructional goal. In the extreme, some argue that training should not be delivered until the individual has need of it. It should be delivered just in time where needed in the workplace, not in a group setting in a classroom. Traditional practice is a long way from that vision. An instructor teaching twenty to twenty-four learners in a classroom is still the predominant method of corporate training. Public education is teacher-led with typically twenty to forty students. However, more e-learning is being accessed from the web at home or at a workstation. The instruction can be individualized or can be set in a virtual learning community using real-time interaction with other students, a group leader, or an instructor. The new skills being learned may even be supported by performance support software on the student's desktop in the job site. Such systems are a very real part of current training technology and make systematic design principles even more applicable for the development of efficient, effective instruction.

Data for Learning Context Analysis

The analysis of the learning context is similar, in many ways, to that of the workplace. The major purpose of the analysis is to identify available facilities and limitations of the setting. The procedure for analyzing the learning context is to schedule visits to one or more training sites and schedule interviews with instructors, managers of the sites, and learners, if appropriate. As with performance context analysis, have interview questions prepared in advance. If the learners are similar to those who will be taking your instruction, they may be able to provide valuable information about their use of the site. It is also important to observe the site in use and to imagine its use for your instruction. Additionally, determine any limitations on your use of the site and the potential impact on your project.

Output   The major outputs of the learning context analysis are (1) a description of the extent to which the site can be used to deliver training on skills that will be required for transfer to the workplace and (2) a list of any limitations that may have serious implications for the project.

Public School Contexts

Before summarizing this section, it is worth reviewing learner and context analysis from the perspective of the designer who will be developing instruction for public schools. Designers who support learner and learning environment analyses may believe they are already familiar with them in the public school sector, and no further analysis is necessary. We encourage you to renew your experience base by doing the proposed analyses with learners, teachers, and typical classrooms. We also encourage you to think beyond the accepted textbook and curriculum guide approach to public schooling, which has led to the criticism that most public education emphasizes factual recall over conceptual understanding and textbook problems over authentic application. Constructivist theorists have been justifiably sharp in their criticism of teaching/learning activities that are abstracted from, and thus not relevant to, authentic physical, social, and problem contexts. This leads not only to diminution of student motivation but also to inability to transfer learning for application in meaningful, real-life problem situations outside the school walls.

The importance cannot be overemphasized of analyzing the context in which skills learned in school classrooms will ultimately be used. Those who work in vocational education see the immediate relevance of this step to their design efforts. They want to provide vocational graduates with skills that can be used and supported in the workplace. However, consider something like fifth-grade science instruction. What is the "performance site" for skills learned in such a course? One way to answer the question is to identify where the skills will be used next in the curriculum and talk with those teachers about the contexts in which the skills are used and about how well prepared students have been in these skills in the past.

Another analysis of the performance context relates to the use of the skills and knowledge outside the school. Why are the students learning these skills? Do they have any application in the home or the community, in hobby or recreational interests, or in vocational or higher educational pursuits? If so, carefully note performance context applications and bring them to the instructional strategy stage of design. These applications are exactly what is needed to boost motivation, provide context for new content and examples, and design practice activities that are seen as relevant by students. In essence, we believe the learner and context analysis step in the instructional design model is just as important to the public school designer as it is to one who will be working with adult populations in diverse training and work environments.

Evaluation and Revision of the Instructional Analysis

Most designers review and revise design analyses *before* the first draft of instruction is created. One component of the design process for which a preliminary tryout can be made is the instructional analysis. The reason we are discussing the tryout in this chapter, rather than in Chapter 10, is that the tryout can occur at the same time the designer is conducting the learner and context analyses. Those analyses bring the designer into contact with potential learners, or recent learners, who can review the instructional analysis with the designer.

The instructional analysis diagram indicates the goal, the steps required to perform the goal, the subordinate skills, and the required entry skills. In order to review the reasonableness of your analysis, select several people who have the characteristics of the target population. Sit with each person and explain what the analysis means. State the goal and explain what someone would do if he or she were able to do it. You might provide an example in which you go through the steps. Then explain how each of the sets of subskills supports one or more of the steps in the goal. Explain what is meant by entry skills, and ask whether the person knows or can do each of the entry skills you have listed for your instruction.

What is the purpose of this explanation? You hear yourself explaining your ideas as you have represented them in the analysis. Sometimes just the act of explaining the analysis will lead to insights about duplications, omissions, unclear relationships, illogical sequences, or unneeded information. Almost without regard to what the learner says during the explanation, you may find changes you want to make.

In addition to your personal reactions, you need to see how a learner from the target population reacts to the skills you will be teaching. You will be "explaining" and not "teaching," but you will want to stop occasionally to ask questions of the learner. Does the learner understand what you are talking about? How would the learner describe it in his or her own words? Can the learner perform the entry skills? These questions focus on the task, but you can include learner analysis questions as well, asking if he or she understands the relevance of the skills, has knowledge of the topic area, or sees how learning and using the skills will alleviate a problem or need.

If you do this review with several learners, perhaps somewhat divergent in their backgrounds and experiences but still members of the target population, you will gain information to refine the instructional analysis.

You might also explain your materials to supervisors in the work setting to obtain their input. Supervisors can provide insights from both content-expert and context-feasibility perspectives. Input from target learners and supervisors will aid revising the instructional analysis before you begin the next phase of the design process, writing performance objectives and assessments, which depend entirely on information from the instructional analysis.

This description of an early review and revision of instructional analysis work highlights the iterative nature of the ID process. Recall that in a system the components interact; a change in inputs from one component affects the outputs of another component. As instructional designers do their work, they frequently "circle back" to fine-tune earlier decisions based on new information discovered as they progress through the ID process.

Examples

Identifying learner characteristics and the contextual characteristics of the performance and learning settings are important early steps in designing instruction. In this section we illustrate how learner characteristics, the performance context, and the learning context can be described using a two-dimensional matrix format, which allows designers to record a lot of information in a limited amount of space and to find it readily as they work on various aspects of the instruction. Table 5.1 is an example form for analyzing learner characteristics; Table 5.2 is an example form for analyzing the performance context; and Table 5.3 is an example form for analyzing the learning context. The first and second columns of each table list suggestions for categories of information and data sources that could be useful in your analyses, which could be more or less important in your analyses depending on the learners and contexts under consideration. For specific examples of how these forms would be filled out, see the case study that follows and the one in Appendix D.

table 5.1 Example Form for Analyzing Learner Characteristics

Information Categories	Data Sources	Learner Characteristics
1. Entry skills	Interview target learners, supervisors; Pretest	
2. Prior knowledge of topic area	Interview target learners, supervisors; Observe in performance setting; Pretest	
3. Attitudes toward content	Interviews Questionnaires Observations	
4. Attitudes toward potential delivery system	Interviews Questionnaires Observations	
5. Motivation for instruction (ARCS)	Interviews Questionnaires Observations	
6. Educational and ability levels	Interviews Questionnaires Observations	
7. General learning preferences	Interviews Questionnaires Observations	
8. Attitudes toward training organization	Interviews Questionnaires Observations	
9. General group characteristics a. Heterogeneity b. Size c. Overall impressions	Interviews Questionnaires Records	

table

5.2

Example Form for Analyzing Performance Context

Information Categories	Data Sources	Performance Site Characteristics
1. Managerial/ supervisory support	**Interviews:** Current persons holding position, supervisors, administrators **Organization Records:**	Reward system (intrinsic—personal growth opportunities; extrinsic— financial, promotion, recognition) Amount (time) and nature of direct supervision Evidence of supervisor commitment (time, resources)
2. Physical aspects of site	**Interviews:** Current persons holding position, supervisors, administrators **Observations:** Observe one to three sites considered typical	Facilities: Resources: Equipment: Timing:
3. Social aspects of site	**Interviews:** Current persons holding position, supervisors, administrators **Observations:** Observe typical person performing skills at sites selected	Supervision: Interaction: Others effectively using skills:
4. Relevance of skills to workplace	**Interviews:** Current persons holding position, supervisors, administrators **Observations:** Observe typical person performing skills at sites selected	Meet identified needs: Current applications: Future applications:

table

5.3

Example Form for Analyzing Learning Context

Information Categories	Data Sources	Learning Site Characteristics
1. Number/ nature of sites	**Interviews:** Managers **Site visits: Observations:**	Number: Facilities: Equipment: Resources: Constraints: Other:
2. Site compatibility with instructional needs	**Interviews:** Managers, instructors **Site visits: Observations:**	Instructional strategies: Delivery approaches: Time: Personnel: Other:
3. Site compatibility with learner needs	**Interviews:** Managers, instructors, learners **Site visits: Observations:**	Location (distance): Conveniences: Space: Equipment: Other:
4. Feasibility for simulating workplace	**Interviews:** Managers, instructors, learners **Site visits: Observations:**	Supervisory characteristics: Physical characteristics: Social characteristics: Other:

Case Study: Group Leadership Training

Learner and context analyses are critical in instances where heterogeneous groups of learners who are not known to the instructional designer will be learning in unfamiliar contexts and performing their new skills in self-regulated contexts. This is the case in the group leadership training example in this case study. You may want to refer back to the Case Study section of Chapter 2 in order to refresh your memory of the Neighborhood Crime Watch scenario.

Learner Analysis

Table 5.4 contains an example of a learner analysis for new Neighborhood Crime Watch leaders. The first column of the table names the categories of information considered, the second column names data sources for obtaining the information, and the third column contains information specific to the NCW leaders as they enter the group leadership instruction. Notice, as you read through the categories, how you begin to form a picture of the group of NCW leaders.

table 5.4 | **Description of Learner Characteristics for Newly Appointed Neighborhood Crime Watch (NCW) Leaders**

Information Categories	Data Sources	Learner Characteristics
1. Entry skills	**Interviews and Observations:** Three current and three newly elected NCW chairs; the county NCW supervisor; three police liaison officers	**Performance Setting:** Learners have no prior experience as Neighborhood Crime Watch chairpersons, and most have no prior experience in serving as the leader in problem-solving discussions.
	Test Data: Posttest performance from group membership training	Learners have served as members in work- or community-related committee meetings; however, most have had no formal training in problem solving through interactive discussions.
		Learning Setting: Learners have successfully completed our training for group members in problem-solving, interactive discussions.
2. Prior knowledge of topic area	**Interviews and Observations:** Same as above	Learners have general knowledge of the group leadership area from participating as members in group discussions and from observing different leaders they have had through the years. As adults who have interacted more-or-less successfully with colleagues, they possess, at least at an awareness level, many of the skills required to be effective discussion leaders.
3. Attitudes toward content	**Interviews and Observations:** Same as above	Learners believe the group problem-solving skills they will learn are beneficial and will help them become good, contributing members of team efforts. They also believe that acquiring the upcoming group leadership skills will help them ensure that their committee meetings will be effective and productive.
4. Attitudes toward potential delivery system	**Interviews and Observations:** Same as above	Learners have experience learning through live lectures, web-based instruction, and live group problem-solving simulations as a result of the prior instruction. They liked the convenience of the web-based instruction, and they believe that the simulations were helpful.

table

5.4

Continued

Information Categories	Data Sources	Learner Characteristic
5. Motivation for instruction (ARCS)	**Interviews and Observations:** Same as above **Questionnaires:** Sent to all current NCW chairpersons in the county	Learners are positive about their selection of leaders, and are anxious to develop/refine their leadership skills. They believe the leadership skills are *relevant* to their jobs as Neighborhood Crime Watch chairpersons, and they are *confident* they can become effective group discussion leaders. These factors, along with the interactive nature of the instruction, should help ensure that learners are *attentive* during instruction.
6. Educational and ability levels	**Interviews and Observations:** Same as above **Records:** Biographical data from NCW Chairperson Application Form **Test Data:** Posttest performance from group membership training	**Education Levels:** Learners vary in their formal education with some completing high school, some college, and some graduate degrees. **Ability Levels:** Besides academic progress, learners' interpersonal skills are a concern. Based on experiences in the prior "group member" training, it seems that learners are heterogeneous with some high in interpersonal skills, some moderate, and some low.
7. General learning preferences	**Attitude Data:** Questionnaire from group membership training **Interviews and Observations:** All 16 learners in group membership training session	Learners are experienced with a variety of learning formats; however, they prefer not to be publicly "put on the spot" until they are completely clear about trainer and group expectations and the skills they are to demonstrate in a group setting. In workshop settings, they prefer a short cycle of (1) presentation (What do you expect of me?), (2) private rehearsal (How can I best accomplish this?), and then (3) interactive "on the spot" simulations (Can I manage group interaction/progress with real people and problems?). They like simulations and like to be involved.
8. Attitudes toward training organization	**Interviews:** NCW supervisor, police liaison officers, current NCW leaders	Respondents have positive feelings about the organization developing the materials, about web-based instruction, and about the county learning center they used during prior training. All think the training is a good idea for helping new NCW leaders plan and manage their organizations. They also believe the training is helping them become acquainted with other NCW leaders from across the county and that these relationships will help them build an interpersonal network of support.
9. General group characteristics a. Heterogeneity b. Size c. Overall impressions	**Interviews:** NCW supervisor, police liaison officer **NCW Records:** Needs assessment, history with NCW leaders, biographical forms for leaders **Observations:** Three current NCW leaders conducting neighborhood meetings	**Heterogeneity:** Learners are extremely heterogeneous in that they come from various neighborhoods throughout a county; come from a wide variety of work settings and areas of expertise; have varying years of work experience; and represent a mix of age, gender, and cultural backgrounds. **Size:** There will be a total of twenty learners per training site to maximize learning efficiency for live group interactive work. **Overall impressions:** Instruction will need to be efficient, effective, and convenient or "volunteer" participants may choose not to read materials, complete computer-based activities independently, or attend all group sessions.

Performance Context Analysis

A performance context analysis is shown in Table 5.5. Again, information categories are listed in column 1, data sources are included in column 2, and performance site characteristics are described in column 3. Gathering such information about the arena in which NCW leaders work will aid designers in choosing the best instructional strategies to use

table 5.5 | **Description of Performance Context for Neighborhood Crime Watch (NCW) Leaders**

Information Categories	Data Sources	Performance Site Characteristics
1. Managerial/ supervisory support	**Interviews:** Three current Neighborhood Crime Watch (NCW) chairpersons; 3 police support/liaison persons; and the county NCW program administrator **Records:** Studied NCW charter and literature; studied records for NCW leaders (function, duties, etc.)	Supervision of NCW chairpersons is minimal. Supervision mainly takes the form of providing current information. For example, they receive organizational bulletins, materials, and information from NCW web site. They receive immediate notification of current crimes committed in their neighborhoods, details of those crimes, and statistical summaries of local and area crimes on NCW web site from assigned police liaison person. Police liaison person also serves as on-call resource person for chairpersons seeking information, and attends NCW meetings as resource person for total group questions.
2. Physical aspects of site	**Interviews:** Same as above **Observations:** Attended 3 NCW meetings in different regions of the county	**Facilities:** There are no facilities provided by NCW Association or police for scheduled NCW meetings. Meetings typically occur within the neighborhood in a committee member's home or in a neighborhood association facility. **Resources:** No money is provided for NCW member meetings. Any resources required (meeting announcements, materials distributed to attendees, refreshments, etc.) for operating the meetings are sponsored by participating NCW members. **Equipment:** No particular equipment is required for the NCW meetings. **Timing:** Meetings are typically scheduled by the chairperson two to three times per year and at additional times if a particular situation warrants it.
3. Social aspects of site	**Interviews:** Same as above **Observations:** Same as above	**Supervision:** The chairperson has no supervision during the conduct of the meeting. **Interaction:** The chairperson is actively interacting with community members who attend the NCW meetings. This interaction is as a leader to manage the work of the group. The chairperson has a police officer at meetings to serve as a content expert on crime and the law, and can invite other experts to meetings as the topic to be discussed warrants. **Others effectively using skills:** There are no others effectively using discussion leadership skills in the meetings because the chairperson is the single designated NCW leader for the community. Others in the group may have discussion leadership skills developed in the workplace or in other community settings.
4. Relevance of skills to workplace	**Interviews:** Same as above **Observations:** Same as above **Records:** Reviewed needs assessment study describing characteristics of effective/ineffective NCW leaders	**Meet identified needs:** The leadership training should meet NCW's identified needs of improving the effectiveness of NCW chairpersons in the problem solving/solutions meetings. New chair persons will be able to use the skills for their first neighborhood meeting session, and the skills will serve them well in the future meetings.

for maximizing the transfer of skills to the performance site. In this case, the leaders will be working in a public arena gathering information, organizing meetings and programs, and performing group management tasks during formal and informal meetings. They are unsupervised and receive little support except for the county NCW coordinator and the assigned local police support person. Providing these support individuals with information and strategies for supporting the NCW leaders in their communities could prove very beneficial for enhancing each leader's effectiveness in the community.

Learning Context Analysis

Table 5.6 contains a learning context analysis for the group leadership instructional goal. A list of the information categories appears in the first column, the data sources in the second column, and learning context characteristics in the third column. From this information, we can infer that the design team has a very good instructional situation. The importance of the neighborhood crime problem and the political/social priority currently attached to it has created the financial and professional resources, facilities, equipment, and personnel to provide quality instructional products and training sessions. The only apparent limitations placed on the designers are those related to balancing learning efficiency and cost effectiveness. For the school curriculum example see the analysis of learners and contexts in Appendix D.

table **5.6**	Description of Learning Context for Neighborhood Crime Watch (NCW) Leaders	
Information Categories	**Data Sources**	**Learning Site Characteristics**
1. Number/ nature of sites	**Interviews:** Managers **Site Visits:** **Observations:**	**Number:** One site per county in each of fifty counties across state. **Facilities:** The web-based instruction will be delivered directly into the new NCW leaders' homes. The group instruction is to occur in each county's government training facility. Typical facilities across the state contain one lecture hall for eighty to one hundred persons; three to five classrooms for twenty to twenty-five persons; one conference room for sixteen to twenty persons; one learning center open 8:00 a.m. until 8:00 p.m. with one to two managers available for materials distribution, equipment assistance, and learner guidance; one administrative office. Depending on scheduling conflicts; all facilities are available for the NCW chairperson training. **Equipment:** Typical centers contain whiteboards, overhead projection screens and projectors, LCD projector for computer display projection onto screens, newsprint pads and stands, five to six multimedia computer workstations. **Resources:** A state grant is provided to create centrally the web-based instruction that will be distributed statewide. In addition, the grant will fund for each county a group instructor, instructional materials, mailings, and secretarial assistance (scheduling/communication). **Constraints:** 1. The learning center is busy. Scheduling instruction may be difficult; however, there is less use evenings and weekends when planned training will occur for community volunteers. 2. The regular instructors available in each site are not content experts in group discussion leadership. Instructor training will need to be developed and implemented. One expert trainer may need to be available for troubleshooting across the sites.

(continued)

table

5.6

Continued

Information Categories	Data Sources	Learning Site Characteristics
2. Site compatibility with instructional needs	**Interviews:** Managers, Instructors **Site Visits:** **Observations:**	**Instructional strategies:** A variety of instructional strategies can be employed including self-study print materials, computer-based instruction, classroom presentations and discussion, and simulated, small-group discussion sessions in conference rooms. **Delivery approaches:** Support is available for production and use of all typical print and nonprint materials. Support is also available for Internet-based instruction and other computer based, multimedia formats. The training center is also equipped for local area and wide area telecommunications, teleconferencing, and synchronous interaction via the web. **Time:** Instructional time in the center is limited to fifteen hours for project due to constraints placed by volunteer NCW leaders. This time is typically divided into ten weekly, ninety-minute periods. Independent study time is possible off site between these scheduled sessions. **Personnel:** Each site has an administrator, several trainers, technicians, and secretaries. There are no trainers present who have provided small-group leadership instruction for NCW volunteers, although they have provided leadership training for city and county government employees.
3. Site compatibility with learner needs	**Interviews:** Managers, Instructors, Learners **Site Visits:** **Observations:**	**Location (distance):** The learning centers are located centrally within each county area, making transportation for group sessions convenient. **Conveniences:** Restaurants are located in the areas, and there is a coffee shop within most of the centers. **Space:** The classrooms can be used for group simulations and the conference rooms for smaller group "meeting" rehearsals. **Equipment:** If needed, the five to eight computer workstations can be scheduled to avoid time conflicts with NCW leaders.
4. Feasibility for simulating workplace	**Interviews:** Managers, Instructors, Learners **Site Visits:** **Observations:**	**Supervisory characteristics:** This cannot be simulated since leaders will have no supervision and little support in their neighborhoods (county NCW coordinator and local police officer). **Physical characteristics:** The physical characteristics can be simulated since volunteers typically meet in neighborhood homes and community centers. **Social characteristics:** Within the neighborhood, learners will work as the leaders of Neighborhood Crime Watch interactive group discussions. These discussions with learners as leaders can readily be simulated in the centers.

SUMMARY

To begin this stage of instructional design, you should have completed or be working on the goal analysis and the subordinate skills analysis including the identification of entry skills. You should also have general ideas about the target population for which instruction will be developed, using general descriptions such as kindergarten children, seventh graders, college freshmen, ambulance drivers, or automobile operators convicted of reckless driving following a serious accident.

The first task is to identify the general characteristics that members of the target population bring to the instruction, such as reading levels, attention span, previous experience, motivation levels, attitudes toward school or work, and performance levels in previous instructional situations. Another important characteristic is the extent and context of related knowledge and skills that members of the target population already possess. One outcome from these target group analysis activities is a description of learner characteristics that will facilitate later design considerations such as appropriate contexts, motivational information and activities, materials formatting, and the amount of material to be presented at one time.

The second task is to describe the performance context, or environment, where learners will assume their natural roles as students, employees, citizens, or clients and actually use the information and skills prescribed in the instructional goal. Performance site features that are important to describe include whether the learner will receive managerial or supervisory support in the performance context, the physical and social aspects of the performance site, and the relevance of the information and skills to be learned to the performance site.

The final task in this section is to describe the learning context. Critical issues in the learning context are discovered through a review of resources that could support instruction and constraints that could inhibit instruction or limit instructional options. Both resources and constraints are usually analyzed in categories such as finances, personnel, time, facilities, equipment, and local culture. In addition, you should describe the compatibility of the learning site with your instructional needs and the learners' needs. Finally, you should describe the feasibility of simulating the performance site within the learning site. The closer you can simulate the performance site, the more likely learners will be able to transfer and implement newly acquired skills.

RUBRIC FOR EVALUATING ANALYSIS OF LEARNERS AND CONTEXTS

The following rubric is a summary of the criteria you can use to evaluate statements of learners' characteristics (achievement, experience, and attitudes), performance, and instructional contexts.

Designer note: If an element is not relevant for your project, mark NA in the No column.

No	Some	Yes	
			A. Achievement and Ability Does the description include *relevant* information for instruction related to goal, subordinate skills, and entry behaviors, for:
___	___	___	1. Age?
___	___	___	2. Grade/education level?
___	___	___	3. Achievement level?
___	___	___	4. Ability level?
			B. Experience Does the description include a summary of learners':
___	___	___	1. Current job?
___	___	___	2. Prior experience?
___	___	___	3. Entry behaviors?
___	___	___	4. Prior knowledge of topic area?
			C. Attitudes Does the description include a summary of learners':
___	___	___	1. Attitudes toward content?
___	___	___	2. Attitudes toward delivery system?
___	___	___	3. Academic motivation (attention, relevance, confidence, satisfaction)?
___	___	___	4. Expectations for instruction?
___	___	___	5. Learning preferences?
___	___	___	6. Attitude about training organization?
___	___	___	7. Group characteristics (heterogeneity, overall impression)?

No	Some	Yes	**D. Performance Context** Does the analysis include whether:
___	___	___	1. Goal is based on needs assessment and identified problem or opportunity?
___	___	___	2. Project has managerial support?
___	___	___	3. Physical aspects are positive (or a constraint)?
___	___	___	4. Social aspects of site are positive (or a constraint)?
___	___	___	5. Goal and skills are relevant to target group and managers in the workplace?
___	___	___	6. Other

E. Learning Context   Does the analysis include whether site:

No	Some	Yes	
___	___	___	1. Is compatible with instructional requirements?
___	___	___	2. Can be adapted to simulate workplace?
___	___	___	3. Can be adapted to accommodate planned delivery approaches?
___	___	___	4. Has constraints that will affect instructional design and delivery?
___	___	___	5. Other

With the analyses of learners, performance context, and learning context complete, you are ready to begin the next design phase: writing performance objectives appropriate for the prescribed skills, learners, and contexts.

PRACTICE

The main instructional design concepts in this chapter are learner analysis, performance context analysis, learning context analysis, and the evaluation/revision of the instructional analysis. In the exercises that follow, the purposes for each of these design activities are named, data to be gathered for each are described, and data-collection procedures are identified. For each of the analysis statements, identify the related type(s) of analysis. If the element named is associated with more than one analysis type, place the letters of all types involved in the space preceding the element. If it is not associated with any, place the letter *d* in the space.

a. Learner analysis
b. Performance context analysis
c. Learning context analysis
d. None of these

Purposes for Analysis

_____ 1. Identify facilities, resources, and limitations of site

_____ 2. Examine relevance of skills to workplace

_____ 3. Describe learners' entry skills

_____ 4. Review instructional equipment and systems

_____ 5. Describe social aspects of site

_____ 6. Describe learners' motivation for learning

Information Gathered for Analysis

_____ 7. Skills and experience of trainers and teachers

_____ 8. Attitudes of managers toward instructional content

_____ 9. Relevance of skills to workplace

_____ 10. Prior knowledge and experiences

_____ 11. Number and nature of training sites

_____ 12. Attitudes of supervisors and managers toward learners

Persons Involved in Analysis

_____ 13. Instructional designers

_____ 14. Supervisors or managers

_____ 15. Directors, trainers, or teachers

_____ 16. Learners

17. Assume that you have been hired by a large school district as an instructional designer. Your first project is to create the Internet-based writing instruction for sixth-grade students described in Appendixes A through C. Imagine a typical set of sixth-grade students in a very large school district and develop a table of learner characteristics for the project.

18. Create an analysis table to describe the performance and learning contexts. These are typically the same in a middle school setting.

FEEDBACK

1. b, c   4. c   7. c   10. a
2. b   5. b, c 8. b   11. c
3. a   6. a   9. b   12. b

13–16. All the individuals named could be involved in each of the three types of analysis.

17. Compare your learner characteristics with those in Appendix D, section 1.

18. Compare your performance/learning context with the one in Appendix D, section 2. Remember, your analyses are expected to differ in some ways because this is an ill-structured problem.

REFERENCES AND RECOMMENDED READINGS

Duffy, T. M., Lowyck, J., & Jonassen, D. H. (Eds.). (1993). *Designing environments for constructive learning*. Berlin: Springer-Verlag. Describes various learning environments, with special attention to constructivism and its implications for instruction and learning.

Holton, E. F., & Baldwin, T. T. (Eds.). (2003) *Improving learning transfer in organizations*. San Francisco: Jossey-Bass.

Keller, J. M. (1987). Strategies for stimulating the motivation to learn. *Performance and Instruction, 26*(8), 1–7. Useful framework for considering characteristics of learners.

Mager, R. F., & Pipe, P. (1997). *Analyzing performance problems* (3rd ed.). Atlanta: GA: CEP Press. The decision flowchart in the text is useful for deciding what aspects of the performance context to include in an analysis.

McCombs, B. L. (1982). Transitioning learning strategies research and practice: Focus on the student in technical training. *Journal of Instructional Development, 5*(2), 10–17. This research stresses the importance of considering the entry knowledge and learning skills that learners bring to the instructional setting.

Pershing, J. A., & Lee, H. K. (2004). Concern matrix: Analyzing learner's needs. In A. M. Armstrong (Ed.), *Instructional design in the real world* (pp. 1–10). Hershey, PA: Information Science Publishing (IGI Global). This chapter focuses on analyzing learners' values and needs.

Richey, R. (1992). *Designing instruction for the adult learner*. London: Kogan Page. Excellent analysis of the impact of motivation on instructional effectiveness.

Rothwell, W., & Kazanas, H. C. (1992). *Mastering the instructional design process*. San Francisco: Jossey-Bass, 83–95. Excellent set of questions to ask about delivery and application environments.

Schuble, L., & Glaser, R. (1996). *Innovations in learning: New environments for education*. Mahwah, NJ: Lawrence Erlbaum Associates. This text describes the impact of learning environments on instructional design.

Tessmer, M., & Harris, D. (1993). *Analyzing the instructional setting*. London: Kogan Page. A complete process for examining the environment in which learning will take place.

Tobias, S. (1987). Learner characteristics. In R. M. Gagné (Ed.), *Instructional technology: Foundations*. Hillsdale, NJ: Lawrence Erlbaum Associates. Summarizes areas of research on learner characteristics.

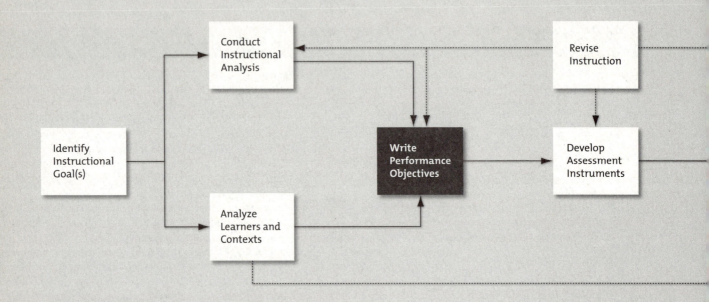

objectives

- ➤ Differentiate among the terms *instructional goal, terminal objective, subordinate skill, subordinate objective, behavioral objective, performance objective,* and *instructional objective.*
- ➤ Name and describe the parts of a properly written performance objective.
- ➤ Write a terminal objective that includes relevant information about the instructional context and/or the performance context.
- ➤ Write performance objectives for skills that have been identified in an instructional analysis. These objectives should include the conditions under which the skill will be performed, the skill to be performed, and the criteria to be used to assess learner performance.

Writing Performance Objectives

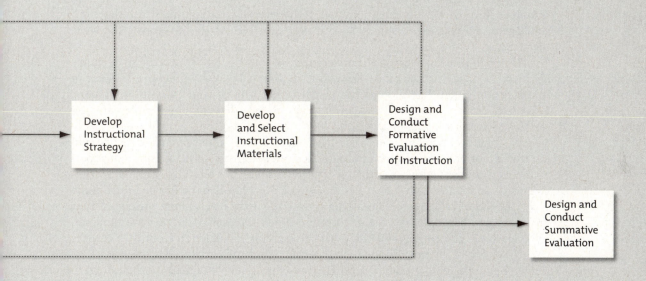

Develop Instructional Strategy

Develop and Select Instructional Materials

Design and Conduct Formative Evaluation of Instruction

Design and Conduct Summative Evaluation

Background

Perhaps the best-known part of the instructional design model is the writing of performance objectives, or, as they are often called, *behavioral objectives*. Since publication of his book on objectives in 1962, Robert Mager has influenced the educational community through his emphasis on the need for clear, precise statements of what students should be able to do when they complete their instruction. The term *behavioral objective* became familiar to many educators in the 1960s.

During that time, workshops were set up for public school teachers throughout the country. Thousands of teachers were trained to write behavioral objectives in order to become accountable for their instruction. Two major difficulties emerged, however, when the process of defining objectives was not included as an integral part of a total instructional design model.

First, without such a model it was difficult for instructors to determine how to derive objectives. Although instructors could master the mechanics of writing an objective, there was no conceptual base for guiding the derivation of objectives. As a result, many teachers reverted to the tables of content in textbooks to identify topics for which they would write behavioral objectives.

The second and perhaps more critical concern was what to do with the objectives after they were written. Many instructors were simply told to incorporate objectives into their instruction in order to become better teachers. In reality, most objectives were written and then placed in desk drawers, never to affect the instructional process.

Researchers have investigated whether using objectives makes any difference in learning outcomes. In almost all the research studies, this question has been asked in the context of an operational instructional setting. In a typical experiment, one group of students receives a sequence of instruction preceded by statements of what they should be able to do when they complete the instruction. A control group receives the same instructional materials, but without the statements of the instructional objectives. The results have been ambiguous. Some studies have shown significant differences in learning for those students who receive objectives; other studies have shown no differences. Summary analyses of the research findings indicate a slight but significant advantage for students who are informed of the objectives for their instruction.

Although these investigations are of interest, they do not address the importance of objectives in the process of designing instruction. Objectives guide the designer in selecting content and developing the instructional strategy and assessment process. Objectives are critical to the design of instruction, regardless of whether they are presented to learners during instruction.

Statements of what learners should be able to do when they complete instruction are useful not only to designers but also to students, instructors, curriculum supervisors, and training administrators. If objectives for a unit or course are made available to students, they have clear-cut guidelines for what is to be learned during the course and tested afterward. Few students are likely to be lost for long periods of time, and more are likely to master the instruction when they know what they are supposed to be learning. Informing students of the purpose for instruction from the outset is congruent with current notions of learner-centered instruction. Knowledge of intended outcomes aids students in linking new knowledge and skills to their current knowledge and experiences.

Objections to the use of behavioral objectives have been raised. For example, detractors can point to the seemingly trivial objectives in some instructional materials. However, these objectives typically are not based on a carefully conducted instructional analysis illustrating the relationship of each new skill to ones previously acquired. Similarly, many educators acknowledge that writing objectives in areas such as humanities or interpersonal relations is more difficult than in other disciplines. However, because instructors in these disciplines usually are required to assess learner performance and communicate acceptability (e.g., grades and personnel evaluations), the development of objectives supports these instructors by taking them through the following tasks: (1) specifying the skills, knowledge, and attitudes they will teach, (2) determining the strategy for instruction, and (3) establishing criteria for evaluating student performance when instruction ends.

Although some instructors might see objectives as detrimental to free-flowing classroom discussion, they actually serve as a check on the relevance of discussion. Objectives also can increase the accuracy of communication among instructors who must coordinate their instruction. Statements describing what learners should be able to do when they complete their instruction provide a clear framework for what should be covered, thus helping to prevent instructional gaps or duplication. Objectives can also indicate to parents or supervisors what students or employees are being taught. General course goals, which are often used for this purpose, may sound interesting and challenging, but seldom indicate what it is that learners will know or be able to do when instruction is completed.

Concepts

Performance Objective

This chapter's most important concept is the performance objective—a detailed description of what students will be able to do when they complete a unit of instruction. First, it should be pointed out that three terms are often used synonymously when describing learner performance. Mager (1997) first used the term *behavioral objective* in 1975 to emphasize that it is a statement describing what the student will be able to do. Some educators have strongly objected to this orientation. Other, perhaps more acceptable, terms have been substituted for *behavioral*. You will therefore see in the literature the terms *performance objective, learning objective,* and *instructional objective*. When you see these you can assume that they are synonymous with behavioral objective. You should not be misled to think that an instructional objective describes what an instructor will be doing. It describes instead the kinds of knowledge, skills, or attitudes that the students will be learning.

We have said previously that the instructional goal describes what learners will be able to do when they complete a set of instructional materials. It describes what learners will be able to do in a real-world context, outside the learning situation, using the skills and knowledge. When the instructional goal is converted to a performance objective, it is referred to as the *terminal objective*. The terminal objective describes exactly what the student will be able to do when he or she completes a unit of instruction. The context for performing the terminal objective is created within the learning situation, not the real world. Similarly, the skills derived through an analysis of the steps in a goal are called *subordinate skills*. The objectives describing the skills that pave the way to the achievement of the terminal objective are referred to as *subordinate objectives*. Though this paragraph may seem to be filled with jargon, these terms will become meaningful as you use the instructional design model. In summary, the goal is a statement of what students will be able to do in the performance context that you described in Chapter 5. The goal is rephrased as a terminal objective describing what students will be able to do in the learning context, and subordinate objectives describe the building-block skills that students must master on their way to achieving the terminal objective.

Performance objectives are derived from the skills in the instructional analysis. One or more objectives should be written for each of the skills identified in the instructional analysis. Sometimes, this includes writing objectives for the skills identified as entry skills. Why should objectives be written for entry skills if they are not included in instruction? Most importantly, objectives for entry skills form the basis for developing test items to determine whether students actually have the entry skills you assumed they would have, which helps ensure the appropriateness of given instruction for particular students. In addition, these objectives will be useful for the designer should it be determined necessary to develop instruction for previously assumed entry skills not actually possessed by the target population.

Table 6.1 contains a summary of how performance objectives are derived. It links the steps in the ID process to their results and their related type of objective.

The Function of Objectives

Objectives serve a variety of purposes, not just as statements from which test items and tasks are derived. Objectives have quite different functions for designers, instructors, and learners, and it is important to keep these distinctions in mind. For the designer, objectives are an integral part of the design process, the means by which the skills in the instructional analysis are translated into complete descriptions of what students will be able to do after completing instruction. Objectives serve as the input

t a b l e	Derivation of Performance Objectives	
6 . 1		

Step in the ID Process	Results of the Step	Name When Stated as an Objective
Goal Identification (Chapter 2)	Instructional Goal or Goals	Terminal Objective or Objectives
Goal Analysis (Chapter 3)	Major Steps and/or Clusters of Information Required to Master the Goal	Subordinate Objectives
Subordinate Skills Analysis (Chapter 4)	Subskills	Subordinate Objectives
Subordinate Skills Analysis (Chapter 4)	Entry Skills	Subordinate Objectives

documentation for the designer or test construction specialist as they prepare the test and the instructional strategy. It is important that designers have as much detail as possible for these activities.

After the instruction has been prepared for general use, the objectives are used to communicate to both the instructor and learners what may be learned from the materials. To accomplish this, it is sometimes desirable to either shorten or reword the objectives to express ideas that are clear to learners based on their knowledge of the content. Designers should be aware of this shift in the use of objectives and reflect this distinction in the materials they create.

Consider how a comprehensive list of objectives created during the design process can be modified for inclusion in instructional materials. How do these modified objectives differ from those used by designers? First, few objectives for subordinate skills used during the development of materials are included. Generally only major objectives are provided in the course syllabus, textbook introduction, or main web page. Second, the wording of objectives appearing in such materials is modified. The conditions and criteria are often omitted to focus learners' attention on the specific skills to be learned, resulting in better communication of this information. Finally, students are more likely to attend to three to five major objectives than to a lengthy list of subordinate objectives.

Parts of an Objective

How are objectives written for the goal statement, steps in the goal, subordinate skills, and entry skills? The work of Mager continues to be the standard for the development of objectives. His model for an objective is a statement that includes three major parts. The first part describes the skill identified in the instructional analysis, describing what the learner will be able to do. This component contains both the *action* and the *content* or *concept*. In the distance estimation problem described in Figure 4.3 (p. 62), the skill or behavior is to "identify the location of a point on the scale in decimal form by estimating between 2 tenth divisions to the nearest hundredth."

The second part of an objective describes the conditions that will prevail while a learner carries out the task. Will learners be allowed to use a computer? Will they be given a paragraph to analyze? These are questions about what will be available to learners when they perform the desired skill. In the distance estimation problem, the conditions are "given a scale marked off in tenths."

The third part of an objective describes the criteria that will be used to evaluate learner performance. The criterion is often stated in terms of the limits, or range, of acceptable answers or responses, indicating the tolerance limits for the response. The criterion may also be expressed in terms of a qualitative judgment, such as the inclusion of certain facts in a definition or a physical performance judged to be acceptable

table

6.2

Parts of a Performance Objective

Parts of an Objective	Description of Parts	Example of Parts
Conditions (CN)	A description of the tools and resources that will be available to the learner when performing the skill	1. In a work-team meeting (CN) 2. Using a web search engine (CN) 3. From memory (CN)
Behavior (B)	A description of the skill that would include actions, content, and concepts	1. Manage the line of discussion (B) 2. Use Boolean operators (B) 3. Describe the emergency response procedure when a gas detection indictor goes off (B)
Criteria (CR)	A description of acceptable performance of the skill	1. So the meeting stays on track (CR) 2. To narrow the number of relevant hits by half (CR) 3. Exactly as detailed in the company policy manual (CR)

by an expert. In the distance estimation problem, the criterion for an acceptable answer is "report the reading to within ± .01 units."

The following statement contains all three parts of the objective: "Given a scale marked off in tenths, identify the location of a point on the scale in decimal form by estimating between 2 tenth divisions to the nearest hundredth, and report the reading to within ± .01 units."

Sometimes an objective may not convey any real information, even though it may meet the formatting criteria for being an objective. For example, consider the following objective: "Given a multiple-choice test, complete the test and achieve a score of at least nine out of ten correct." Although this may be a slightly exaggerated example, it can be referred to as a universal objective in the sense that it appears to meet all the criteria for being an objective and is applicable to almost any cognitive learning situation. It says nothing, however, in terms of the actual conditions or the behavior that is to be learned and evaluated. You should always make sure that your objectives are not universal objectives. Table 6.2 summarizes the parts of a performance objective with some more examples.

Derivation of Behaviors

It has been stated that objectives are derived directly from the instructional analysis; thus, they must express precisely the types of behavior already identified in the analysis. If the subskill in the instructional analysis includes, as it should, a clearly identifiable behavior, then the task of writing an objective becomes simply the addition of criteria for assessment and description of the conditions under which the behavior must be performed. For example, if the subskill is "divides a scale into tenths," then a suitable objective might be stated: "Given a scale divided into whole units, divide one unit into tenths. The number of subunits must be ten, and the size of all units must be approximately the same."

Sometimes, however, the designer may find that subskill statements are too vague to write a matching objective. In this circumstance, the designer should carefully consider the verbs that may be used to describe behavior. Most intellectual skills can be described by such verbs as *identify, classify, demonstrate,* or *generate.* These verbs, as described by Gagné, Wager, Golas, and Keller (2004), refer to such specific activities as grouping similar objects, distinguishing one thing from another, or solving problems. Note that Gagné et al. have not used the verbs *know, understand,* or *appreciate* because they are too vague. When these words are used (inappropriately) in objectives, *know* usually refers to verbal information, *understand* to intellectual skills, and *appreciate* to attitudes. These vague terms should be replaced by more specific performance verbs.

The instructor must review each objective and ask, "Could I observe a learner doing this?" It is impossible to observe a learner "knowing" or "understanding." Often these verbs are associated with information that the instructor wants the students to learn. To make it clear to students that they are supposed to learn certain skills, it is preferable to state in the objective exactly how students are to demonstrate that they *know* or *understand* the skills. For example, the learner might be required to state that New York and California are approximately 3,000 miles apart. If students are able to state (or write) this fact, it may be inferred that they know it.

Objectives that relate to psychomotor skills usually are easily expressed in terms of a behavior (e.g., running, jumping, or driving). When objectives involve attitudes, the learner is usually expected to choose a particular alternative or sets of alternatives. On the other hand, it may involve the learner making a choice from among a variety of activities.

Derivation of Conditions

With the knowledge, skill, or attitudinal part of the objective clearly identified, you are ready to specify the conditions part of the objective. Conditions refer to the exact set of circumstances and resources that will be available to the learner when the objective is performed. In selecting appropriate conditions you need to consider both the behavior to be demonstrated and the characteristics of the target population. You should also consider the purposes that the conditions serve in an objective. These purposes include specifying (1) whether a cue will be provided that learners will use to search the information stored in their memory, (2) the characteristics of any resource material required to perform the task, (3) the scope and complexity of the task, and (4) relevant or authentic contexts for the real-world performance setting.

Cue or Stimulus   Consider first the cue or stimulus provided for learners. This is an especially important consideration for testing verbal information tasks. Suppose you wanted to ensure that learners could associate a particular concept with its definition, or vice versa. It is common to find the conditions for this type of task simply written as, "From memory, define . . . ," or as, "Given a paper and pencil test, define . . ." Neither of these examples identifies the cue or stimulus the learners will use to search their memory or schema for the related information.

There are several conditions that could be used to describe the stimuli learners will be given to aid their recall of verbal information. Consider the following list of stimuli (conditions) and behaviors, each of which could enable learners to demonstrate that they know or can associate the concept with the definition.

Condition	Behavior
Given the term, ⟶	write the definition.
Given the definition, ⟶	name the term.
Given the term and a set of alternative definitions, ⟶	select the most precise definition.
Given an illustration of the concept, ⟶	name and define the concept illustrated.
Given the term, ⟶	list its unique physical characteristics.
Given the term, ⟶	list its functions or roles.

Although each of these conditions is "from memory," it more clearly specifies the nature of the stimulus material or information that learners will be given in order to search their memory for the desired response. Each condition could also imply a paper and pencil test, a computer touch screen, or an online interactive form, but merely specifying the method by which the test will be administered as the condition leaves the issue of an appropriate stimulus undefined.

Resource Materials The second purpose for including conditions in an objective is to specify any resource materials that are needed to perform a given task. Such resource materials might include the following: (1) illustrations such as tables, charts, or graphs; (2) written materials such as reports, stories, or newspaper articles; (3) physical objects such as rocks, leaves, slides, machines, or tools; and (4) reference materials such as dictionaries, manuals, databases, textbooks, or the web. Besides naming the resources required, the conditions should specify any unique characteristics the resources should possess.

Control Task Complexity The third purpose for conditions is to control the complexity of a task in order to tailor it to the abilities and experiences of the target population. Consider how the following conditions control the complexity of a map-reading objective.

1. Given a neighborhood map containing no more than six designated places, . . .
2. Given a neighborhood map containing no more than twelve designated places that are spaced more than one inch apart, a locator grid and index, and a scale with one inch equal to one mile, . . .
3. Given a commercial map of a city, . . .

Such conditions limit or expand the complexity of the same task to make it appropriate for a given target group.

Aiding Transfer The fourth purpose is aiding the transfer of knowledge and skill from the instructional setting to the performance setting. The conditions element is used to specify the most real-world, authentic, or relevant materials and contexts possible given the resources in the instructional setting.

In deciding the conditions that should be specified, the primary considerations should be the performance and instructional contexts, the nature of the stimulus material, and the characteristics of the target population. Special resources required in either of the two contexts and limitations on task complexity are both conditions that are directly related to the nature of appropriate stimuli and the capabilities of the group.

Although the preceding examples have focused on intellectual skills and verbal information, conditions appropriate for demonstrating psychomotor skills and attitudinal choices should also be considered carefully. For psychomotor tasks, you will need to consider the nature of the context in which the skill will be performed and the availability of any required equipment for performing the task. For example, if learners are to demonstrate that they can drive an automobile, you need to consider whether they will be required to maneuver a subcompact, an SUV, or both. You also need to consider whether the driving demonstration will involve inner-city freeways, interstate highways, downtown streets, two-lane country roads, or all of these. Such decisions will influence the equipment required, the nature of instruction, the time required for practicing the skills, and the nature of the driving test.

Specifying the conditions under which learners will demonstrate that they possess a certain attitude also requires careful consideration. Three important issues are the context in which the choice will be made, the nature of the alternatives from which the learner will choose, and the maturity of the target population. These considerations are important because choices may be situation-specific. For example, choosing to demonstrate good sportsmanship during a tennis match may depend on the importance of the match in terms of the consequences for winning or losing. It may also depend on the player's sense of freedom to "act out" feelings of frustration and anger without negative repercussions. It will also depend on the age and corresponding emotional control of the players. Demonstrating the true acquisition of a sportsmanlike attitude would require a competitive match where attitudes could be expressed without fear of reprisal. Simply stating the appropriate behavior on a pencil and paper test or demonstrating it under the watchful eye of the coach will not suffice.

Specifying conditions for both psychomotor skills and attitudinal choices can be tricky. An appropriate set of conditions may be difficult to implement in the instructional and testing setting. For this reason, simulations are sometimes required. When they are, the designer must remember that the actual demonstration of the attitude has been compromised.

The conditions associated with an objective will shape the instruction every bit as much as the behavior in the objective. For example, does the learner have to memorize the information in the objective? Why does it have to be memorized? Can the information be looked up in a reference manual, or will there not be time for that? In this particular example, if learners only need to be able to find the information, then the instruction will consist of opportunities, with feedback, to look for various bits of information related to the objective. If information must be immediately available in a crisis situation, however, then the focus of the practice will be on ways to store and quickly retrieve the information from memory without taking time to look it up in notes or reference materials.

How does the designer decide exactly what the conditions should be? Sometimes it is simply a matter of SME judgment. Often the designer can use the context analysis as the basis for describing conditions of performance. After all, the context analysis describes the situations under which the desired behavior will occur, and that is what we want to describe in the conditions of an objective.

Derivation of Criteria

The final part of the objective is the criterion for judging acceptable performance of the skill. In specifying logical criteria, you must consider the nature of the task to be performed. Some intellectual skill and verbal information tasks have only one response that would be considered correct. Examples include balancing a ledger sheet, matching the tense or number of subjects and verbs, and stating a company safety policy. In such instances, the criteria are that learners can produce the precise response. Some designers add the word *correctly* to this type of objective, whereas others state no criterion and assume that it is implicit in the conditions and behavior. However you choose to treat such objectives, you should keep in mind that specifying the number of times that learners are to perform the task (e.g., two out of three times or correctly 80 percent of the time) does not indicate the objective criterion. The question of "how many times" or "how many items correct" and similar statements are questions of mastery. The designer must determine how many times a behavior must be demonstrated in order to be sure that learners have mastered it. This decision is usually made when test items are developed. The important point is that the criterion in the objective describes what behavior will be acceptable or the limits within which a behavior must fall.

Some intellectual skills and verbal information tasks do not result in a single answer, and learners' responses can be expected to vary. Examples include dividing a line into equal parts and estimating distance using a scale. In these instances the criteria should specify the tolerance allowed for an acceptable response. Other tasks that result in a variety of responses include designing a solution to a business problem, writing paragraphs, answering essay questions on any topic, or producing a research report. The criteria for such objectives should specify any information or features that must be present in a response for it to be considered accurate enough. For complex responses, a checklist of response features may be necessary to indicate the criteria for judging the acceptability of a response.

The criteria for judging the acceptability of a psychomotor skill performance may also need to be specified using a checklist to indicate the expected behaviors. Frequency counts or time limits might also be necessary. A description of the body's appearance as the skill is performed may need to be included (e.g., the position of the hands on a piano keyboard).

Specifying criteria for attitudinal goals can be complex. Appropriate criteria will depend on such factors as the nature of the behavior observed, the context within which it is observed, and the age of members of the target population. It might include a tally of the number of times a desirable behavior is observed in a given situation. It could also include the number of times an undesirable behavior is observed. You may find that a checklist of anticipated behaviors is the most efficient way to specify criteria for judging the acquisition of an attitude. A frequent problem with criteria for attitude measurement is the evaluator's ability to observe the response within a given time period and circumstance; thus, compromise may be necessary.

One problem that can arise in certain instructional settings is a statement that expert judgment or instructor judgment is the criterion for judging learner performance. It is wise to begin with a determination to avoid listing expert judgment as the criterion for an objective since it is not helpful to you or the learners. It only says that someone else will judge the learner's performance. In situations in which a judge must be used, try to consider the factors you would consider if you were the expert judging the performance. Develop a checklist of the types of behaviors and include these in the statement of the objective to ensure a clear understanding of the criteria.

A second problem is that criteria for an answer, product, or performance can be complex and specified in a variety of categories, such as (1) adequate form of a response (i.e., the physical structure of a response); (2) adequate function of the response (i.e., meeting the specified purpose or intention for the response); and (3) adequate qualities or aesthetics. Let's consider two examples using these three categories to clarify the idea of complex criteria. Suppose that learners were to produce chairs. The chair can be judged by its features and strength (physical structure), by whether it is comfortable (function or purpose), and by its aesthetic appearance (color, balance, coordination, etc.).

Now consider the criteria in these categories that might be applied to a written paragraph. Related to form, criteria might include whether it is indented and formatted according to structural rules. For function or purpose, criteria such as conveying information on one topic, persuading a reader, or providing adequate directions might be appropriate. Related to qualities or aesthetics, criteria might include clarity, interest value, logical chronology and transition, and creativity.

Many other different categories of criteria can be applied to learners' answers, products, and performances. Other examples include categories such as social acceptability, environmental soundness, economic viability, parsimony, and so forth. Designers will need to analyze the complexity of the task to be performed and, during this analysis, derive appropriate categories of criteria that should be considered in judging a learner's response. Mastery should be judged based on whether learners' responses adequately meet the criteria categories and qualities within each category. Many instructional designers use rubrics or checklists to define complex criteria for acceptable responses.

Process for Writing Objectives

In order to make objectives, and subsequent instruction, consistent with the context analysis, designers should review the goal statement before writing objectives. Does it include a description of the ultimate context in which the goal will be used? If not, the first step should be to edit the goal to reflect that context.

The second step is to write a terminal objective. For every unit of instruction that has a goal, there is a terminal objective. The terminal objective has all three parts of a performance objective, and its conditions reflect the context that will be available in the *learning environment*. In other words, the goal statement describes the context in which the learner will ultimately use the new skills while the terminal objective describes the conditions for performing the goal at the end of the instruction. Ideally these two sets of conditions would be the same, but, by necessity, they may be quite different.

After the terminal objective has been established, the designer writes objectives for the skills and subskills included in the instructional analysis. The next step is to write objectives for the subordinate skills on the instructional analysis chart. This will include intellectual skills, verbal information, and, in some cases, psychomotor skills and attitudes. You will find in later chapters that for each objective you write you will have a specific assessment of that skill and you will have a component of instruction that will teach that skill.

But what do you do when you get to the entry skill line? You have to make another decision. If the entry skills consist of such basic skills and information that you think almost all members of the target population know them and would be insulted to be tested on them, then no objectives are required. On the other hand, if the entry skills reflect skills and information that may not be known to all learners, then write objectives for these skills.

The steps in writing objectives are as follows:

1. Edit goal to reflect eventual performance context.
2. Write terminal objective to reflect context of learning environment.
3. Write objectives for each step in goal analysis for which there are no substeps shown.
4. Write an objective for each grouping of substeps under a major step of the goal analysis, or write objectives for each substep.
5. Write objectives for all subordinate skills.
6. Write objectives for entry skills if some students are likely not to possess them.

Evaluation of Objectives

The rubric at the end of this chapter contains a list of criteria for evaluating objectives. The rubric serves as a summary of the qualities of well-written objectives, and it is intended for use by readers who are writing objectives for an ID project. In addition to using a rubric to judge an objective, you can take the evaluation a step further to evaluate the clarity and feasibility of an objective. Construct a test item that will be used to measure the learners' accomplishment of the task, and if you cannot produce a logical item yourself, then the objective should be reconsidered. Another way to evaluate the clarity of an objective is to ask a colleague to construct a test item that is congruent with the behavior and conditions specified. If the item produced does not closely resemble the one you have in mind, then the objective is not clear enough to communicate your intentions.

You should also evaluate the criteria you have specified in the objective, which may be done by using the criteria to evaluate existing samples of the desired performance or response. These may be samples produced by you, by colleagues, or by anyone who has performed the task. You should specifically attend to whether each criterion named is observable within the specified conditions and time frame. Determining the observability of criteria usually is easier for verbal information and intellectual skill tasks than it is for psychomotor skill and attitudinal objectives, as you might suspect.

While writing objectives, the designer must be aware that these statements of criteria will be used to develop assessments for the instruction. The designer might again check the clarity and feasibility of objectives by asking, "Could I design an item or task that indicates whether a learner can successfully do what is described in the objective?" If it is difficult to imagine how this could be done in the existing facilities and environment, then the objective should be reconsidered.

Another helpful suggestion is that you should not be reluctant to use two or even three sentences to describe your objective adequately. There is no requirement to limit objectives to one sentence. You should also avoid using the phrase "after completing this instruction" as part of the conditions under which a student will perform a skill as described in an objective. It is assumed that the student will study the materials prior to performing the skill. Objectives do not specify *how* a behavior will be learned.

One final word: Do not allow yourself to become deeply involved in the semantics of objective writing. Many debates have been held over the exact word that must be used in order to make an objective "correct." The point is that objectives have been found to be useful as statements of instructional intent. They should convey to the designer or subject matter specialist in the field what it is that the student will be able to do; however, objectives have no meaning in and of themselves. They are only one piece of the total instructional design process, and only as they contribute to that process do they take on meaning. The best advice at this point is to write objectives in a meaningful way and then move on to the next step in the instructional design process.

Examples

This section contains examples of performance objectives for psychomotor skills and attitudes. To aid your analysis of each example, the conditions are highlighted using the letters *CN*, the behaviors are identified with a *B*, and the criteria are indicated using the letters *CR*. You would not include these letters in your own objectives. Following each set of examples is a discussion that should also aid your analysis. For examples of performance objectives for verbal information and intellectual skills, see the Case Study section of this chapter and the school curriculum case study in Appendix E.

Psychomotor Skills

Figure 4.11 (p. 87) contains an abbreviated goal analysis for changing an automobile tire. The subordinate objectives in Table 6.3 are based on the substeps included in the analysis.

As noted previously, writing performance objectives for psychomotor skills is more complex than writing objectives for verbal information and for many intellectual skills. In this abbreviated list of examples, notice the increased specificity in the conditions. Any special circumstances must be prescribed. Notice in objective 2.4 that the designer does not want the learner to be given blocks or to be reminded to obtain them. Obviously part of the demonstration will be for the learner to recall as well as to perform this step.

The verbs are also important and may require some translation to ensure that the behaviors are observable. Notice the shifts in 2.1 from "determine how to" to "operate the." To measure whether the learner has "determined how to," observable behaviors needed to be identified, thus the shift in the verb.

Notice, also, how the criteria are written. Specifying the criteria for steps in a psychomotor skill typically requires listing the substeps that must be accomplished. The criteria for each of these objectives contain such a list.

Another interesting feature about objectives for psychomotor skills should be noted. Although each objective has its own conditions, the conditions, behaviors, and criteria in preceding examples are often conditions for performing any given step.

t a b l e	Sample Psychomotor Skills and Matching Performance Objectives
6.3	

Steps	Matching Performance Objectives
2.1 Determine how to operate jack.	2.1 Given a standard scissors jack and detached jack handle (that is not placed beneath a car) (CN), operate the jack (B). Attach the handle securely, pump the handle so the jack lifts, release the safety catch, and lower the jack to its closed position (CR).
2.2 Identify where to attach jack to car.	2.2 Given an unattached scissors jack and a car to be lifted that is perched precariously on the brim of the road (CN), prepare for attaching the jack (B). Relocate the car to a flat, stable location; locate the best place on the frame of the car in proximity to the wheel to be removed; then position the jack squarely beneath the frame at that location (CR).
2.3 Attach jack to car.	2.3 Given a scissors jack placed squarely beneath the frame at the appropriate spot (CN), attach the handle and raise the jack (B). Jack is squarely beneath frame at appropriate spot and raised just to meet car frame. Contact between jack and car is evaluated for balance and adjusted if necessary. Car is *not* lifted and lug nuts are *not* loosened (CR).
2.4 Place blocks behind and before wheels that remain on ground.	2.4 Without being given blocks and without being told to locate appropriate blocks (CN), locate blocks and place behind wheels to remain on ground (B). Locate enough brick-size blocks of a sturdy composition and place one before and behind each wheel that is away from jack (CR).
Goal: Change the tire on an automobile.	**Terminal Objective:** Given an automobile with a flat tire, all tools required to change the tire secured in their normal positions in the trunk, and an inflated spare tire secured normally in the wheel well (CN), replace the flat tire with the spare tire (B). Each step in the procedure will be performed in sequence and according to criteria specified for each step (CR).

For example, an implied condition for objective 2.2 is the successful completion of objective 2.1. Similarly, an implied condition for objective 2.3 is the successful completion of objective 2.2.

Finally, notice the criteria listed for the terminal objective. Actually listing all the criteria for performing this objective would require listing again all of the specific criteria for each step in the process, because completing all the steps constitutes performing the terminal objective. For this reason, the criteria listed for each objective should be placed on a checklist that could be used to guide the evaluation of the learner's performance.

Attitudes

Developing objectives for the acquisition of attitudes can also be complex in terms of conditions, behaviors, and criteria. The examples listed in Table 6.4 are taken from the attitudinal goal on hotel safety included in Figure 4.7 (p. 78), and they serve as good illustrations of problems the designer could encounter.

The first thing you should notice about the conditions in these objectives is that they would be very difficult to implement, for several reasons. Individual rights and privacy are two problems, and gaining access to rooms to observe whether doors were bolted and jewelry and money were put away is another. In such instances the designer would undoubtedly need to compromise. The best compromise would probably be to ensure that individuals know what to do should they choose to maximize their

table 6.4	Sample Attitudes and Matching Performance Objectives

Attitudes	Matching Performance Objectives
1. Choose to maximize safety from fires while registered in a hotel.	1.1 Unaware that they are being observed during hotel check-in (CN), travelers always (CR): (1) request a room on a lower floor and (2) inquire about safety features in and near their assigned room such as smoke alarms, sprinkler systems, and stairwells (B).
2. Choose to maximize safety from intrusion while registered in a hotel.	2.1 Unaware they are being observed as they prepare to leave the hotel room for a time (CN), travelers always (CR): (1) leave radio or television playing audibly and lights burning, and (2) they check to ensure the door locks securely as it closes behind them (B).
	2.2 Unaware that they are being observed upon reentering their hotel rooms (CN), travelers always (CR) check to see that the room is as they left it and that no one is in the room. They also keep the door bolted and chained (B) at all times (CR).
3. Choose to maximize the safety of valuables while staying in a hotel room.	3.1 Unaware that they are being observed during check-in (CN), travelers always (CR) inquire about lockboxes and insurance for valuables. They always (CR) place valuable documents, extra cash, and unworn jewelry in a secured lockbox (B).
	3.2 Unaware that they are being observed upon leaving the room for a time (CN), travelers never (CR) leave jewelry or money lying about on hotel furniture (B).

personal safety while in a hotel. An objective test on related verbal information or a problem-based scenario test may be the best the designer can do.

Consider another attitude example that is more manageable. Recall the courteous, friendly bank tellers in Chapter 2. The attitude goal and objectives included in Table 6.5 for teller attitudes appear to be observable and measurable. This particular example will enable us to illustrate some important points. First, the conditions are exactly the same for all four of the selected behaviors; thus, they are written once before the behaviors to avoid redundancy. Recall that the measurement of attitudes requires that the tellers know how to act while greeting a customer and why they

table 6.5	Manageable Attitude and Matching Performance Objectives

Attitude	Matching Performance Objectives
Tellers will choose to treat customers in a friendly, courteous manner.	Unaware they are being observed during transactions with customers on a busy day (CN), tellers will always (CR):
	1. Initiate a transaction with a customer by: (a) smiling, (b) initiating a verbal greeting, (c) saying something to make the service appear personalized, (d) verbally excusing themselves if they must complete a prior transaction, and (e) inquiring how they can be of service (B).
	2. Conduct a customer's transaction by: (a) listening attentively to the customer's explanation, (b) requesting any necessary clarifying information, (c) providing any additional forms-required, (d) completing or amending forms as needed, (e) explaining any changes made to the customer, and (f) explaining all materials returned to the customer (B).
	3. Conclude each transaction by: (a) inquiring about any other services needed, (b) verbally saying, "Thank you," (c) responding to any comments made by the customer, and (d) ending with a verbal wish (e.g., "Have a nice day," "Hurry back," or "See you soon") (B).

should act in this manner. They also must believe they are free to act in the manner they choose, which means that they cannot know that they are being observed. Another condition is that they choose to be courteous even when they are very busy. The designer could infer that a teller who chooses to greet customers in a friendly manner under these conditions possesses the desired attitude.

Second, the criterion for acceptable performance, which is *always,* is also the same for all four objectives. This criterion therefore precedes the list of behaviors in order to avoid redundancy.

Finally, the expected behaviors are listed separately beneath the conditions and criteria. This brief list of behaviors could be expanded to include those behaviors that tellers are never (*CR*) to exhibit while greeting a customer (e.g., wait for the customer to speak first and fail to look up or acknowledge a customer until ready).

With these objectives a supervisor could develop a checklist for tallying the frequency with which each behavior occurs. From such tallies, the supervisor could infer whether the teller possessed the prescribed attitude.

Case Study: Group Leadership Training

We pick up the case study again with examples of objectives for verbal information and intellectual skills. Only selected objectives are included here, but a complete ID process would include one or more objectives for each of the subskills identified in the instructional analysis. The conditions are again highlighted using the letters *CN*, the behaviors identified with a *B*, and the criteria indicated using the letters *CR*. As before, you would not ordinarily include these letters in your own objectives. A brief discussion follows each set of examples to point out important features of the objectives.

Verbal Information and Intellectual Skills

Table 6.6 includes the instructional goal and the terminal objective for the performance and instructional contexts. The intellectual skills in Tables 6.6 and 6.7 and the verbal information tasks in Table 6.7 are taken from Figure 4.8 (p. 81), which illustrated the instructional analysis for the instructional goal "Lead group discussions aimed at

table 6.6 Sample Instructional Goal with Performance Context and Terminal Objective with Learning Context for the Goal: Lead Group Discussions Aimed at Solving Problems

Instructional Goal	Instructional Goal with Performance Context Added
Lead group discussions aimed at solving problems.	During actual Neighborhood Crime Watch (NCW) meetings held at a designated neighborhood site (e.g., member home, neighborhood social/meeting facility) (CN), successfully lead group discussions aimed at solving crime problems currently existing in the neighborhood (B). Member cooperation will be used to judge achievement of this goal (CR).

	Terminal Objective with Learning Context Added
	During simulated Neighborhood Crime Watch (NCW) meetings attended by new NCW leadership trainees and held at a county government training facility (CN), successfully lead group discussions aimed at solving given problems (B). Member cooperation will be used to judge the achievement of this goal (CR).

table 6.7

Sample Performance Objectives for Verbal Information and Intellectual Skills Tasks for the Instructional Goal "Lead Group Discussions Aimed at Solving Problems"

Main Step in Instructional Goal	Performance Objective for Main Step
6. Manage cooperative group interaction.	6.1 During simulated Neighborhood Crime Watch (NCW) meetings comprised of new NCW leadership trainees and held at a county government training facility (CN), manage cooperative group interaction (B). Discussion members should participate freely, volunteer ideas, cooperate fully with leader and other members (CR).

Subordinate Skills	Sample Subordinate Objectives for Main Step
6.1 Name member actions that facilitate cooperative interaction.	6.1.1 When requested either orally or in writing (CN) to name group member actions that facilitate cooperative interaction, name those actions (B). At least six facilitating actions should be named (CR).
	6.1.2 When asked either orally or in writing (CN) to indicate what members should do when their ideas are questioned by the group, name positive reactions that help ensure cooperative group interaction (B). Learner should name at least three possible reactions (CR).
6.2 Classify member actions as cooperative behaviors.	6.2.1 Given written descriptions of a group member's actions during a meeting (CN), indicate whether the actions are cooperative behaviors (B). Learner should classify correctly at least 80 percent of the actions demonstrated (CR).
	6.2.2 Given videos of staged NCW meetings depicting members' actions (CN), indicate whether the actions are cooperative (B). Learner should classify correctly at least 80 percent of the actions demonstrated (CR).
6.3 Name strategies for encouraging member cooperation.	6.3.1 When asked in writing to name leader actions that encourage and stifle member discussion and cooperation (CN), name these actions (B). Learner should name at least ten encouraging and corresponding stifling actions (CR).
6.4 Classify strategies for encouraging cooperation.	6.4.1 Given written descriptions of group leader's actions during a meeting (CN), indicate whether the actions are likely to encourage or stifle cooperative group interaction (B). Learner should correctly classify at least 80 percent of the actions depicted (CR).
	6.4.2 Given videos of staged NCW meetings depicting staged leader's actions (CN), indicate whether the leader's actions are likely to encourage or stifle member cooperation (B). Learner should classify correctly at least 80 percent of both the encouraging and corresponding stifling actions demonstrated (CR).
6.5 Engender cooperative member behaviors.	6.5.1 In simulated NCW problem-solving meetings with learner acting as group leader (CN), initiate actions to engender cooperative behavior among members (B). Group members cooperate with each other and with leader during discussion (CR).

problem solving." Table 6.7 contains the objectives for a sample of subordinate intellectual skills and verbal information tasks depicted in Figure 4.8.

Verbal Information   In the example of verbal information objectives in Table 6.7, notice that the conditions specify key terms that must be used in test items presented to learners. For example, in subordinate objectives 6.1.1 and 6.1.2 for skill 6.1, key terms prescribed are *"member actions that facilitate cooperative interaction"* and *"what members should do when their ideas are questioned."* These key terms will function as cues the learner will use to locate related information stored in memory. Although there are many different ways that corresponding test items could be formatted (e.g., as complete questions or as brief statements), the key terms must be presented to the learner. Notice that the manner in which the key terms will be presented to learners is made clear, *in writing*. Notice also that the behaviors used in the subskill and the objective are the same. Even in cases when they are not exactly the same, the behaviors used should enable learners to demonstrate the same covert skill (e.g., "name" versus "list"). Finally, consider the criterion in each objective. Because the number of actions named by learners will undoubtedly vary, the number of actions that should be named by learners is prescribed.

Intellectual Skills   In the intellectual skills examples (e.g., 6.2.1 and 6.2.2 for skill 6.2) notice that the conditions part of the objective is similar to that used in the verbal information objectives. Not only is key terminology included (e.g., "group member's actions during a meeting"), but the manner in which these actions will be presented is prescribed as well (e.g., "written descriptions of group actions" and "videos of staged NCW meetings depicting members' actions"). In objective 6.5.1, there are no key terms stated in the conditions; however, the examination will take place in "simulated NCW problem-solving meetings with learner acting as group leader." Notice that the conditions in these three intellectual skills help prescribe the complexity of the task. Detecting positive leader and member actions is probably easier in a written script than in a video of interactive dialogue, which is probably easier than detecting the same actions when you are "ego involved"—leading the meeting yourself and processing the verbal and nonverbal behaviors of colleagues you are actively facilitating. Notice that the behaviors in the subordinate skills and corresponding objectives are congruent. Even when alternative terms are used, the skill demonstrated will be the one prescribed in the subordinate skill. Notice the criteria included in these objectives. In subordinate objectives 6.2.1 and 6.2.2, the learner is required to locate 80 percent of the cooperative behaviors demonstrated in the scenarios and videos. On the other hand, the criterion for objective 6.5.1 is that members within the leader's interactive groups need to cooperate with each other and the leader. In other words, the behavior of members within the group will provide evidence of the leader's success. Readers can also examine the subordinate skills and performance objectives for the school curriculum case study in Appendix E.

SUMMARY

Before beginning to write performance objectives, you should have a completed instructional analysis. You should also have completed your learner and context analysis. With these products as a foundation, you are ready to write performance objectives for your goal, all steps and substeps in that goal, and subordinate skills.

To create each objective, you should begin with the behaviors that are described in the skill statements. You will need to add both conditions and criteria to each skill to transform it into a performance objective. In selecting appropriate conditions, you should consider (1) appropriate stimuli and cues to aid the learners' search of their memories for associated information, (2) appropriate characteristics for any required resource materials, (3) appropriate levels of task complexity for the target population, and (4) the relevance or authenticity of the context in which the skill will be performed. For attitudinal objectives, you will also need to consider circumstances in which the learners are free to make choices without reprisal.

The final task is to specify a criterion or criteria appropriate for the conditions and behavior described and appropriate for the developmental level of the target group. When there is only one correct response possible, many designers omit criteria as they are clearly implied, whereas other designers choose to insert the term *correctly*. When the learners' responses can vary, as they can for tasks in all four domains, criteria that describe the characteristics of an acceptable response must be added. Deriving criteria for psychomotor skills and attitudes typically is more complex in that several observable behaviors generally need to be listed. These behaviors, however, are very useful for developing required checklists or rating scales. In specifying criteria, designers must be careful *not* to rely on imprecise criteria such as "expert judgment." There are several categories of criteria that designers can consider in selecting those most appropriate for a given learner response, such as structure, function, aesthetics, social acceptability, environmental soundness, economic viability, and so forth.

RUBRIC FOR EVALUATING PERFORMANCE OBJECTIVES

Criteria you can use for constructing and evaluating elaborated goals, terminal objectives, and performance objectives are summarized in the following rubric to facilitate your work. Space is provided on the left side for marking your judgments and criteria are listed in the right column. You may want to copy the checklist to provide to various reviewers of your materials.

Designer note: If an element is not relevant for your project, mark NA in the No column.

No   Some   Yes   **A. Goal Statement**   Does the goal statement:

___   ___   ___   1. Describe the ultimate performance context?
___   ___   ___   2. Describe a context that is authentic and realistic?

B. Terminal Objective   Is there congruence between the terminal objective:

___   ___   ___   1. Conditions and the context of the learning environment?
___   ___   ___   2. Behavior and the behavior in the goal statement?
___   ___   ___   3. Criteria and the criteria in the goal statement?

C. Performance Objective Conditions   Do/will the conditions:

___   ___   ___   1. Specify the cue or stimulus provided to learners?
___   ___   ___   2. Specify resource materials/tools needed?
___   ___   ___   3. Control complexity of task for learners' needs?
___   ___   ___   4. Aid transfer to performance context (authentic)?

D. Performance Objective Behavior   Is the behavior:

___   ___   ___   1. Congruent with the behavior in the anchor step of the instructional goal analysis?
___   ___   ___   2. The *actual* behavior rather than a description of how learners will respond (e.g., "classify" rather than "circle")?
___   ___   ___   3. Clear and observable rather than vague?

___   ___   ___   **E. Performance Objective Content**   Is the content congruent with the anchor step in the instructional goal analysis?

F. Performance Objective Criteria   Are/do criteria:

___   ___   ___   1. Included only when needed to judge a complex task?
___   ___   ___   2. Include physical or form attributes?
___   ___   ___   3. Include purpose/function attributes?
___   ___   ___   4. Include aesthetic attributes?
___   ___   ___   5. Include other relevant attributes (e.g., social acceptability, health, environment, economy, parsimony)?

No	Some	Yes	
—	—	—	**G. Overall Performance Objective** Is the performance objective:
—	—	—	1. Clear (you/others can construct an assessment to test learners)?
—	—	—	2. Feasible in the learning and performance contexts (time, resources, etc)?
—	—	—	3. Meaningful in relation to goal and purpose for instruction (not insignificant)?
			H. (Other)
—	—	—	1.

Your complete list of performance objectives becomes the foundation for the next phase of the design process, developing criterion-referenced test items for each objective. The required information and procedures are described in Chapter 7.

PRACTICE

Judge the completeness of given performance objectives. Read each of the following objectives and judge whether it includes conditions, behaviors, and a criterion. If any element is missing, choose the part(s) omitted.

1. Given a list of activities carried on by the early settlers of North America, understand what goods they produced, what product resources they used, and what trading they did.
   a. important conditions and criterion
   b. observable behavior and important conditions
   c. observable behavior and criterion
   d. nothing

2. Given a mimeographed list of states and capitals, match at least 35 of the 50 states with their capitals without the use of maps, charts, or lists.
   a. observable response
   b. important conditions
   c. criterion performance
   d. nothing

3. During daily business transactions with customers, know company policies for delivering friendly, courteous service.
   a. observable behavior
   b. important conditions
   c. criterion performance
   d. a and b
   e. a and c

4. Students will be able to play the piano.
   a. important conditions
   b. important conditions and criterion performance
   c. observable behavior and criterion performance
   d. nothing

5. Given daily access to music in the office, choose to listen to classical music at least half the time.
   a. important conditions
   b. observable behavior

   c. criterion performance
   d. nothing

Convert instructional goals and subordinate skills into terminal and subordinate objectives. It is important to remember that objectives are derived from the instructional goal and subordinate skills analyses. The following instructional goal and subordinate skills were taken from the writing composition goal in Appendix E. Demonstrate conversion of the goal and subordinate skills in the goal analysis by doing the following:

6. Create a terminal objective from the instructional goal:

   In written composition, (1) use a variety of sentence types and accompanying punctuation based on the *purpose* and *mood* of the sentence, and (2) use a variety of sentence types and accompanying punctuation based on the *complexity* or *structure* of the sentence.

7. Write performance objectives for the following subordinate skills:

   5.6 State the purpose of a declarative sentence: to convey information

   5.7 Classify a complete sentence as a declarative sentence

   5.11 Write declarative sentences with correct closing punctuation.

Evaluate performance objectives. Use the rubric as an aid to developing and evaluating your own objectives.

8. Indicate your perceptions of the quality of your objectives by inserting the number of the objective in either the Yes or No column of the checklist to reflect your judgment. Examine those objectives receiving No ratings and plan ways the objectives should be revised. Based on your analysis, revise your objectives to correct ambiguities and omissions.

FEEDBACK

1. c
2. d
3. e
4. b
5. d
6–7. Examine the sample terminal objective and performance objectives for the subordinate skills in the writing composition case study in Appendix E.

8. Evaluate your goal elaborations, terminal objectives, and your performance objectives using the rubric. If you want further feedback on the clarity and completeness of performance objectives you have written, ask a colleague for a critique using the rubric.

REFERENCES AND RECOMMENDED READINGS

Caviler, J. C., & Klein, J. D. (1998). Effects of cooperative versus individual learning and orienting activities during computer-based instruction. *Educational Technology Research and Development, 46*(1), 5–17. Demonstrates the effectiveness of providing objectives to learners.

Gagné, R. M., Wager, W. W., Golas, K. C., & Keller, J. M. (2004). *Principles of instructional design* (5th ed.). Belmont, CA: Wadsworth/Thomson Learning. The authors describe a five-part performance objective and relate objectives to the various domains of learning.

Gronlund, N. E. (2004). *Writing instructional objectives for teaching and assessment* (7th ed.). Upper Saddle River, NJ: Pearson/Merrill/Prentice Hall. Gronlund describes the derivation of objectives for various types and levels of learning and their use in both teaching and classroom assessment.

Mager, R. F. (1997). *Preparing instructional objectives* (3rd ed.). Atlanta, GA: Center for Effective Performance. This is the latest edition of Mager's 1962 book on objectives. Mager's humor is well served by the branching programmed-instruction format.

Plattner, F. B. (1997). *Instructional objectives*. Alexandria, VA: American Society for Training and Development.

Roberts, W. K. (1982). Preparing instructional objectives: Usefulness revisited. *Educational Technology, 22*(7), 15–19. The varied approaches to writing objectives are presented and evaluated in this article.

Strayer, J. (Ed.). (2003). *Instructional systems design revisited*. Silver Springs, MD: International Society for Performance Improvement. This e-book compilation of articles from the ISPI journal *Performance Improvement* is available for download from several outlets.

Yelon, S. L. (1991). Writing and using instructional objectives. In L. J. Briggs, K. L. Gustafson, & M. H. Tillman (Eds.), *Instructional design: Principles and applications*. Englewood Cliffs, NJ: Educational Technology Publications.

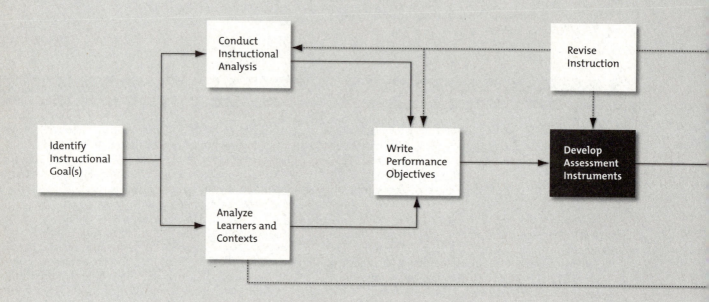

objectives

➤ Describe the purpose for criterion-referenced tests.

➤ Describe how entry skills tests, pretests, practice tests, and posttests are used by instructional designers.

➤ Name four categories of criteria for developing criterion-referenced tests and list several considerations within each criterion category.

➤ Given a variety of objectives, write criterion-referenced, objective-style test items that meet quality criteria in all four categories.

➤ Develop instructions for product development, live performance, and attitude assessments; develop rubrics for evaluating learners' work.

➤ Evaluate instructional goals, subordinate skills, learner and context analyses, performance objectives, and criterion-referenced test items for congruence.

Developing Assessment Instruments

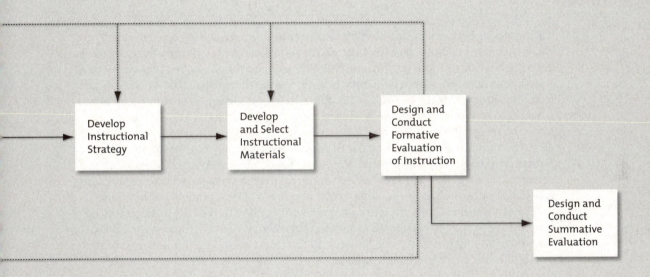

Background

Achievement testing is currently at the forefront of the school-reform movement in the United States, and learner-centered assessment permeates the school-reform literature. Learning-centered assessment tasks are expected to function as learning events, and in this model, learners are encouraged to engage in self-assessment on their path to assuming responsibility for the quality of their own work.

The definitions of learner-centered assessment are congruent with traditional definitions of criterion-referenced testing, a central element of systematically designed instruction. Learner-centered assessments are to be criterion-referenced (i.e., linked to instructional goals and an explicit set of performance objectives derived from the goals). This type of testing is important for evaluating both learners' progress and instructional quality. The results of criterion-referenced tests indicate to the instructor exactly how well learners were able to achieve each instructional objective, and they indicate to the designer exactly which components of the instruction worked well and which ones need to be revised. Moreover, criterion-referenced tests enable learners to reflect on their own performances by applying established criteria to judge their own work. Such reflection aids learners in becoming ultimately responsible for the quality of their work.

You may wonder why test development appears at this point in the instructional design process rather than after instruction has been developed. The major reason is that the test items must correspond one to one with the performance objectives. The performance required in the objective must match the performance required in the test item or performance task. Likewise, the nature of the test items that will be given to learners serves as a key to the development of the instructional strategy.

In this chapter we discuss how designers construct various types of assessment instruments. We use the term *assessment* because "testing" often implies paper and pencil multiple-choice tests. *Assessment* is used as a broader term that includes all types of activities effective for demonstrating learners' mastery of new skills. At this point in the design process, it is necessary to construct sample assessments for each objective.

Concepts

The major concept in this chapter is criterion-referenced assessment, usually an instrument composed of items or performance tasks that directly measure skills described in one or more performance objectives. The term *criterion* is used because assessment items serve as a benchmark to determine the adequacy of a learner's performance in meeting the objectives; that is, success on these assessments determines whether a learner has achieved the objectives in the instructional unit. More and more often the term *objective-referenced* is being used rather than *criterion-referenced* in order to be more explicit in indicating the relationship between assessments and performance objectives. Assessment items or tasks are referenced directly to the performance described in the objective for the instructional materials. You may therefore consider these two terms—*objective* and *criterion*—essentially synonymous.

Another use of the word *criterion* relates to specification of the adequacy of performance required for mastery. Examples of this second type of criterion include such benchmarks as the student will "answer all the items correctly," "follow all six steps in the safe storage of flammable liquids," and "cut an angle with an accuracy level of five degrees." This type of criterion specification may be established for one test item written for one performance objective, several test items written for one objective, or several test items written for many objectives. Clarity in specifying objectives and criteria for adequate performance is necessary as a guide to adequate test construction. Based on a particular performance objective using established criteria, a posttest may require only one test item or it may require many.

Four Types of Criterion-Referenced Tests and Their Uses

There are basically four types of tests the designer may create, including the entry skills test, the pretest, practice or rehearsal tests, and posttests. Each of these test types has a unique function in designing and delivering instruction. Let's look at each type of test from the viewpoint of the person who is designing instruction. What purposes do they serve within the instructional design process?

Entry Skills Tests   The first type of test, an entry skills test, is given to learners before they begin instruction. These criterion-referenced tests assess learners' mastery of prerequisite skills, or skills that learners must have already mastered before beginning instruction. Prerequisite skills appear below the dotted line on the instructional analysis chart. If there are entry skills for an instructional unit, test items should be developed and used with learners during the formative evaluation.

It may be found that, as the theory suggests, learners lacking these skills will have great difficulty with the instruction. In contrast, it may be found that for some reason the entry skills are not critical to success in the instruction. It should be noted that if there are no significant entry skills identified during the instructional analysis, then there would be no need to develop corresponding objectives and test items.

Also, if some skills are more questionable than others in terms of being already mastered by the target population, then it is these questionable skills that should be assessed on the entry skills test.

Pretests   The purpose of a pretest is not necessarily to show a gain in learning after instruction by comparison with a posttest but rather to profile the learners with regard to the instructional analysis. The pretest is administered to learners before they begin instruction for the sake of efficiency—to determine whether they have previously mastered some or all of the skills that are to be included in the instruction. If all the skills have been mastered, then the instruction is not needed. On the other hand, if the skills have only been partially mastered, then pretest data enable the designer to be most efficient in the creation of instruction. Perhaps only a review or a reminder is needed for some skills, saving time-consuming direct instruction with examples and rehearsal for the remainder.

Designers have some latitude in determining which enabling skills to include on a pretest, and they must use their judgment in selecting the objectives that are most important to test. Deciding which skills to include is probably unique to each instructional goal and particular context. The pretest typically includes one or more items for key skills identified in the instructional analysis, including the instructional goal.

Since both entry skills tests and pretests are administered prior to instruction, they are often combined into one instrument, which does not, however, make them one and the same test. Different items assess different skills from the instructional goal diagram, and the designer will make different decisions based on learners' scores from the two sets of items. From entry skills test scores designers decide whether learners are ready to begin the instruction. From pretest scores they decide whether the instruction would be too elementary for the learners and, if not too elementary, how to develop instruction most efficiently for a particular group.

Should you always administer a pretest covering the skills to be taught? Sometimes it is not necessary. If you are teaching a topic that you know is new to your target population, and if their performance on a pretest would only result in random guessing, it is probably not advisable to have a pretest. A pretest is valuable only when it is likely that some of the learners will have partial knowledge of the content. If time for testing is a problem, it is possible to design an abbreviated pretest that assesses the terminal objective and several key subordinate objectives.

Practice Tests   The purpose for practice tests is to provide active learner participation during instruction. Practice tests enable learners to rehearse new knowledge and skills and to judge for themselves their level of understanding and skill. Instructors use students' responses to practice tests to provide corrective feedback and to monitor the pace of instruction. Practice tests contain fewer skills than either the pretest or posttest, and they are typically focused at the lesson rather than the unit level.

Posttests   Posttests are administered following instruction, and they are parallel to pretests, except they do not include items on entry skills. Similar to the pretest, the posttest measures objectives included in the instruction. As for all the tests that are described here, the designer should be able to link the skill (or skills) being tested with its corresponding item on the posttest.

Related to selecting skills from the instructional goal analysis, the posttest should assess all of the objectives, especially focusing on the terminal objective. Again, as with the pretest, the posttest may be quite long if it measures all the subordinate skills, and it may be more comprehensive in terms of having more items on more of the skills in the instructional goal analysis. If time is a factor and a briefer test must be developed, then the terminal objective and important subskills should be tested. Items should be included to test those subskills that are most likely to give learners problems on the terminal objective.

Eventually the posttest may be used to assess learner performance and to assign credit for successful completion of a program or course; however, the initial purpose for the posttest is to help the designer identify the areas of the instruction that are not working. If a student fails to perform the terminal objective, the designer should be able to identify where in the learning process the student began not to understand the instruction. By examining whether each item is answered correctly and linking the correct and incorrect responses to the anchor subordinate skill, the designer should be able to do exactly that.

All four types of tests are intended for use during the instructional design process. After the formative evaluation of the instruction has been completed, however, it may be desirable to drop part or all of the entry skills test and the pretest. It would also be appropriate to modify the posttest to measure only the terminal objective. In essence, much less time would be spent on testing when the design and development of the instruction is complete. A summary of the test types, design decisions, and the objectives typically included on each type of test follows.

Test Type	Designer's Decision	Objectives Typically Tested
Entry skills test	• Are target learners ready to enter instruction? • Do learners possess the required prerequisite skills?	• Prerequisite skills or those skills below the dotted line in the instructional analysis
Pretests	• Have learners previously mastered the enabling skills? • Which particular skills have they previously mastered? • How can I most efficiently develop this instruction?	• Terminal objectives • Main steps from the goal analysis
Practice tests	• Are students acquiring the intended knowledge and skills? • What errors and misconceptions are they forming? • Is instruction clustered appropriately? • Is the pace of instruction appropriate for the learners?	• Knowledge and skills for a subset of objectives within the goal • Scope typically at the lesson rather than the unit level
Posttests	• Have learners achieved the terminal objective? • Is the instruction more or less effective for each main step and for each subordinate skill? • Where should instruction be revised? • Have learners mastered the intended information, skills, and attitudes?	• The terminal objective • Main steps and their subordinate skills

Test Design

How does one go about designing and developing a criterion-referenced test? A primary consideration is matching the learning domain with an item or assessment task type. Objectives in the verbal information domain typically require objective-style test items, typically including formats such as short-answer, alternative response, matching, and multiple-choice items. It is relatively easy to examine learners' verbal information responses, whether written or oral, and judge whether they have mastered a verbal information objective. Learners either recall the appropriate information or they do not.

Objectives in the intellectual skills domain are more complex, and they generally require either objective-style test items, the creation of a product (e.g., musical score, research paper, widget), or a live performance of some type (e.g., conduct an orchestra, act in a play, or conduct a business meeting). At higher levels of intellectual skills, it is more difficult to create an assessment item or task, and it is more difficult to judge the adequacy of a response. What if an objective requires the learner to create a unique solution or product? It would be necessary to write directions for the learner to follow, establish a set of criteria for judging response quality, and convert the criteria into a checklist or rating scale, often called a rubric, that can be used to assess those products.

Assessment in the attitudinal domain can also be complex. Affective objectives are generally concerned with the learner's attitudes or preferences. Usually there is no direct way to measure a person's attitudes (e.g., whether they support diversity within the organization). Items for attitudinal objectives generally require that either the learners state their preferences or that the instructor observes the learners' behavior and infers their attitudes from their actions. For example, if learners voluntarily engage in advocacy for the promotion of minority employees on three different occasions, the instructor may infer that they support diversity. From these stated preferences or observed behaviors, inferences about attitudes can be made.

Test items for objectives in the psychomotor domain are usually sets of directions on how to demonstrate the tasks, and they typically require the learner to perform a sequence of steps that collectively represents the instructional goal. Moreover, criteria for acceptable performances need to be identified and converted into a checklist or rating scale that the instructor uses to indicate whether each step is executed properly. The checklist can be developed directly from the skills and execution qualities identified in the instructional analysis. The designer may also wish to test the subordinate skills for the motor skills. Often these are intellectual skills or verbal information that can be tested using an objective-item format before having the student perform the psychomotor skill. On occasion the performance of a psychomotor skill, such as making a ceramic pot, results in the creation of a product. It is possible to develop a list of criteria for judging the adequacy of this product.

Mastery Levels

For each performance objective you write there must be a criterion level specified, which indicates how well the student must perform the skill described in the objective on the assessments you provide. In essence, the criterion indicates the mastery level required of the student. The concept of mastery level, as opposed to criterion level, is more often applied to a test for an entire unit of instruction or an entire course. An instructor may state that, in order for learners to "master" this unit, they must achieve a certain level of performance. The question remains, "How do you determine what the mastery level should be?"

Researchers who work with mastery learning systems suggest that mastery is equivalent to the level of performance normally expected from the best learners.

This method of defining mastery is clearly norm-referenced (i.e., a group comparison method), but sometimes it may be the only standard that can reasonably be used.

A second approach to mastery is one that is primarily statistical. If designers want to make sure that learners "really know" a skill before they go on to the next instructional unit, then sufficient opportunities should be provided to perform the skill so that it is nearly impossible for correct performance to be the result of chance alone. When multiple-choice test items are used, it is fairly simple to compute the probability that any given number of correct answers to a set of items could be due to chance. With other types of test items it is more difficult to compute the probability of chance performance but easier to convince others that performance is not just a matter of chance. Simply exceeding the chance level of performance, however, may not be a very demanding mastery level. Setting it higher than chance often is a rather arbitrary decision.

An ideal mastery level is one defined by an exact, explicit level of performance that defines mastery. It might be argued that in order for soldiers to learn to send encoded messages, they must be able to spell standard military terms. In this circumstance, a mastery level of 100 percent for a unit on spelling military terms is not entirely arbitrary. It is based on the criticality of the skill in question to the learning of subsequent skills. The greater the relationship between the two, the higher the mastery level should be set. As a general principle, mastery level for any performance should be considered with respect to both evaluating the performance at that point in time and enhancing the learning of subsequent, related skills in the unit or in the rest of the course.

In some situations, the best definition of mastery is the level required to be successful on the job. With many complex skills there is a continuum of performance, with the novice or beginner at one end and the experienced expert at the other. What level is required in the workplace or on the transfer task that the learner will eventually be expected to perform? The performance context analysis can yield useful information regarding the expected level of performance and can be used in the design of the criterion-referenced assessment process. If no one is currently using the skills, then managers or subject-matter experts must use their professional judgment to estimate mastery levels. If the levels prove to be unrealistic, they can be adjusted in the future.

Test Item Criteria

Regardless of the type of learning involved in the objective, appropriate test item writing techniques should be applied to the development of criterion-referenced tests. There are four categories of test item qualities that should be considered during the creation of test items and assessment tasks. These categories are goal-centered criteria, learner-centered criteria, context-centered criteria, and assessment-centered criteria. Each category of quality is described in the following paragraphs.

Goal-Centered Criteria   Test items and tasks should be congruent with the terminal and performance objectives. They should match the behavior, including the action and concepts, prescribed. To match the response required in a test item to the behavior specified in the objective, the designer should consider the learning task or verb prescribed in the objective. Objectives that ask the student to *state* or *define, perform with guidance,* or *perform independently* will all require a different format for questions and responses.

It is critical that test items measure the exact behavior described in the objective. For example, if an objective indicates that a student will be able to match descriptions of certain concepts with certain labels, then the test items must include descriptions of concepts and a set of labels, which the student will be asked to match.

Let's look at an example. Given a scale marked off in tenths and asked to identify designated points on the scale, label the designated points in decimal form in units of tenths. Corresponding test items for this objective follow:

_____ 1. In tenths of units, what point on the scale is indicated at the letter A?
_____ 2. In tenths of units, what point on the scale is indicated at the letter B?

You can see in this example that the objective requires the learner to read exact points on a scale that is divided into units of one-tenth. The test item provides the learner with such a scale and two letters that lie at specified points on the scale, for which the learner must indicate the value of each in tenths.

You will encounter more illustrations similar to this in the Examples, Case Study, and Practice sections. It is important to note carefully the behavior described by the verb of the objective. If the verb is to *match,* to *list,* to *select,* or to *describe,* then you must provide a test item that allows a student to match, list, select, or describe. The objective will determine the nature of the item. You do not arbitrarily decide to use a particular item format such as multiple choice. Test and item format will depend on the wording of your objectives.

Test items and tasks should meet the conditions specified in the objective. If a special item format, equipment, simulations, or resources are prescribed, they should be created for the assessment. An open-book examination differs greatly from an examination in which reference material is forbidden. The expected conditions of performance included in the performance objective serve as a guide to the test-item writer.

Test items and tasks should provide learners with the opportunity to meet the criteria necessary to demonstrate mastery of an objective. One must determine the number of items required for judging mastery of each objective assessed and whether all the required criteria are included on the checklist or rating scale.

The performance objective also includes the criteria used to judge mastery of a skill. No absolute rule states that performance criteria should or should not be provided to learners. Sometimes it is necessary for them to know performance criteria and sometimes it is not. Learners usually assume that, in order to receive credit for a question, they must answer it correctly.

Note that an assessment for the terminal objective should also be created. Consider how you would respond if someone asked how learners would demonstrate that they had achieved your instructional goal. What would you ask learners to do to demonstrate that they had reached mastery? The answer should describe an assessment that requires the learner to use the major steps in the goal successfully. Typically there would also be separate assessments for each step in the process to determine, as the instruction proceeds, whether learners are mastering each step as it is taught.

Learner-Centered Criteria   Test items and assessment tasks must be tailored to the characteristics and needs of the learners, including considerations such as learner needs, vocabulary and language levels, developmental levels for setting appropriate task complexity, motivational and interest levels, experiences and backgrounds, special needs, and freedom from bias (e.g., cultural, racial, gender).

The vocabulary used in the directions for completing a question and in the question itself should be appropriate for the intended learners. Test items should not be written at the vocabulary level of the designer unless that level is the same as that expected for the target learners. Learners should not miss questions because of unfamiliar terms. If the definition of certain terms is a prerequisite for performing the skill, then such definitions should have been included in the instruction. The omission of necessary terms and definitions is a common error.

Another consideration related to familiarity of contexts and experiences is that learners should not miss an item or task because they are asked to perform it in an unfamiliar context or are using an unfamiliar assessment format. Items made unnecessarily difficult by placing the desired performance in an unfamiliar setting not only test the desired behavior but also test additional, unrelated behaviors as well. Though this is a common practice, it is an inappropriate item-writing technique. The more unfamiliar the examples, question types, response formats, and test-administration procedures, the more difficult successful completion of the test becomes. One example of this "staged" difficulty is creating problems using contrived, unfamiliar situations. The setting of the problem, whether at the beach, the store, school, or office, should be familiar to the target group. Learners can better demonstrate skills using a familiar topic rather than an unfamiliar one. If an item is made unnecessarily difficult, it may hamper accurate assessment of the behavior in question.

An exception to this guideline regarding unfamiliar contexts when assessing higher-order intellectual skills, some psychomotor skills, and some attitudes applies when the successful transfer of newly learned skills into unencountered performance contexts is the goal of the instruction. Even in this circumstance, however, the test item should be situated in a *logical* performance context for the new skill, and strategies for analyzing and adapting to unencountered contexts should be included in the instruction.

Designers must also be sensitive to issues of gender and diversity in creating items and tasks. Items that are biased either on the surface or statistically against any particular group are not only inappropriate but unethical as well. Finally, designers should consider how to aid learners in becoming evaluators of their own work and performances. Self-evaluation and self-refinement are two of the main goals of all instruction since they can lead to independent learning.

Context-Centered Criteria   In creating test items and assessment tasks, designers must consider the eventual performance setting as well as the learning or classroom environment. Test items and tasks must be as realistic or authentic to the actual performance setting as possible. This criterion helps to ensure transfer of the knowledge and skills from the learning to the performance environment.

Feasibility and resources in the learning environment are often a consideration as well. Sometimes the learning setting fails to contain the equipment necessary to reproduce exact performance conditions. Designers must sometimes be creative in their attempts to provide conditions as close to reality as possible. The more realistic the testing environment, the more valid the learners' responses will be. For example, if the behavior is to be performed in front of an audience, then an audience should be present for the exam.

Assessment-Centered Criteria   Learners can be nervous during assessment, and well-constructed, professional-looking items and assessment tasks can make the assessment more palatable to them. Test-writing qualities include correct grammar, spelling, and punctuation as well as clearly written and parsimonious directions, resource materials, and questions.

To help ensure item and task clarity and to minimize test anxiety, learners should be given all the necessary information to answer a question before they are asked to respond. Ideally, the learners should read a question or directions, mentally formulate the answer, and then either supply the answer or select it from a given set of alternatives.

Items written to "trick" learners often result in testing skills or behaviors not specified in the objective. Designers should spend their time constructing good simulation items rather than inventing tricky questions. If the object is to determine how well learners can perform a skill, then a series of questions ranging from very easy to extremely difficult would provide a better indication of their performance levels than one or two tricky questions (e.g., double negatives, misleading information, compound questions, incomplete information).

There are also many rules for formatting each type of objective test item, product and performance directions, and rubric. These rules are most often related to producing the clearest item and assessment tasks possible. Ideally, learners should err because they do not possess the skill and not because the test item or assessment is convoluted and confusing. Designers who are unfamiliar with formatting rules for items and directions should consult criterion-referenced measurement texts that elaborate formatting rules for assessments.

Mastery Criteria

In constructing the test, a major question that always arises is, "What is the proper number of items needed to determine mastery of an objective?" How many items must learners answer correctly to be judged successful on a particular objective? If learners answer one item correctly, can you assume they have achieved the objective? Or if they miss a single item, are you sure they have not mastered the concept? Perhaps if you gave the learners ten items per objective and they answered them all correctly or missed them all, you would have more confidence in your assessment. There are some practical suggestions that may help you determine how many test items an objective will require. If the item or test requires a response format that will enable the student to guess the answer correctly, then you may want to include several parallel test items for the same objective. If the likelihood of guessing the correct answer is slim, however, then you may decide that one or two items are sufficient to determine the student's ability to perform the skill.

If you examine the question of the number of items in terms of the learning domain of the objective, it is easier to be more specific. To assess intellectual skills it is usually necessary to provide three or more opportunities to demonstrate the skill. With verbal information, however, only one item is needed to retrieve the specific information from memory. If the information objective covers a wide range of knowledge (e.g., identify state capitals), then the designer must select a random sample of the instances and assume that student performance represents the proportion of the verbal information objective that has been mastered. In the case of psychomotor skills, there also is typically only one way to test the skill, namely, to ask the student to perform the skill for the evaluator. The goal may require the student to perform the skill under several different conditions. These should be represented in repeated performances of the psychomotor skill.

Test Item Format and Performance Objectives

Another important question to consider is, "What type of test item or assessment task will best assess learner performance?" The behavior specified in the objective provides clues to the type of item or task that can be used to test the performance. In Table 7.1 the column on the far left lists the types of behavior prescribed in the performance objective. Across the top are the types of test items that can be used to evaluate student performance for each type of behavior. The table includes only suggestions. The "sense" of the objective should suggest what type of assessment is most appropriate.

As the chart indicates, certain types of performance can be tested in several different ways, and some test item formats can assess specified performance better than others. For example, if it is important for learners to remember a fact, asking them to state that fact is better than requesting reactions to multiple-choice questions. Using the objective as a guide, select the type of test item that gives learners the best

table 7.1 Type of Behavior and Related Test Item Types

Type of Behavior Stated in Objective	COMPLETION	SHORT ANSWER	MATCHING	MULTIPLE-CHOICE	ESSAY	PRODUCT DEVELOP.	LIVE PERFORM.
State/Name	X	X					
Define	X	X	X	X			
Identify	X	X	X	X			
Discriminate		X	X	X			
Select		X	X	X			
Locate		X	X	X			
Evaluate/Judge		X	X	X			
Solve		X	X	X	X	X	X
Discuss					X		X
Develop					X	X	X
Construct					X	X	X
Generate					X	X	X
Operate/Perform							X
Choose (attitude)							X

opportunity to demonstrate the performance specified in the objective. There are other factors to consider when selecting the best test item format. Each type of test item has its strengths and its limitations. To select the best item type from among those considered adequate, weigh such factors as the response time required by learners, the scoring time required to analyze and judge answers, the testing environment, and the probability of guessing the correct answer.

Certain item formats would be inappropriate even when they speed up the testing process. It would be inappropriate to use a true/false question to determine whether a student can state the correct definition of a term. Given such a choice, the student does not state from memory but discriminates between the definition presented in the test item and the one learned during instruction. In addition to being an inappropriate response format for the behavior specified in the objective, the true/false question provides learners with a fifty-fifty chance of guessing the correct response.

Test items can be altered from the "best possible" response format to one that will save testing time or scoring time, but the alternate type of question used should still provide learners with a reasonable opportunity to demonstrate the behavior prescribed in the objective. When the instruction is implemented, it is important that instructors be able to use the evaluation procedures. The designer might use one type of item during development of the instruction and then offer a wider range of item formats when the instruction is ready for widespread use.

The testing environment is also an important factor in item format selection. What equipment and facilities are available for the test situation? Can learners actually perform a skill given the conditions specified in an objective? If equipment or facilities are not available, can realistic simulations, either paper and pencil or other formats, be constructed? If simulations are not possible, will such questions as "List the steps you would take to . . ." be appropriate or adequate for your situation? The farther removed the behavior in the assessment is from the behavior specified in the objective, the less accurate is the prediction that learners either can or cannot perform the behavior prescribed. Sometimes the exact performance as described in the objective is impossible to assess, and thus other, less desirable ways must be used. This will also be an important consideration when the instructional strategy is developed.

Objective Tests

Objective tests include test items that are easy for learners to complete and designers to score. The answers are short, they are typically scored as correct or incorrect, and judging correctness of an answer is straightforward. Objective formats include completion, short answer, true/false, matching, and multiple-choice. Test items that should be scored using a checklist or rubric, including essay items, are not considered to be objective items, and they are described in the next section on alternative assessments.

Writing Objective Test Items Whether centered on goals, learners, contexts, or assessments, designers can use all four main criteria in developing effective objective test items. These criteria were described in detail previously, and they are presented in the rubric at the end of the chapter for your convenience.

Sequencing Items There are no hard and fast rules that guide the order of item placement on a test of intellectual skills or verbal information, but there are suggestions that can guide placement. Final decisions are usually based on the specific testing situation and the performance to be tested.

A typical sequencing strategy for designers who need to hand-score constructed responses and to analyze responses within objectives is to cluster items for one objective together, regardless of item format. The only type of item excepted from this strategy is the lengthy essay question. Such questions typically are located at the end of a test to aid learners in managing their time during the test. A test organized in this fashion is not as attractive as one organized by item format, but it is far more functional for both the learner and the instructor. It enables the learner to concentrate on one area of information and skill at a time, and it enables the instructor to analyze individual and group performance by objective without first reordering the data.

Writing Directions Tests should include clear, concise directions. Beginning a test usually causes anxiety among learners, who will be judged according to their performance on the test. There should be no doubt in their minds about what they are to do to perform correctly on the test. There are usually introductory directions to an entire test and subsection directions when the item format changes.

Test directions change according to the testing situation but usually include the following kinds of information:

1. The test title suggests the content to be covered rather than simply saying "Pretest" or "Test I."
2. A brief statement explains the objectives or performance to be demonstrated and the amount of credit that will be given for a partially correct answer.
3. Learners are told whether they should guess if they are unsure of the answer.
4. Instructions specify whether words must be spelled correctly to receive full credit.
5. Learners are told whether they should use their names or simply identify themselves as members of a group.
6. Time limits, word limits, or space limits are spelled out. In addition, learners should be informed whether they need anything special to respond to the test, such as number 2 pencils, machine-scorable answer sheets, a special text, or equipment such as computers, calculators, or maps.

It is difficult to write clear and concise test directions. What is clear to you may be confusing to others. Write and review directions carefully to ensure that learners have all the information they need to respond correctly to the test.

Objective tests are not the only means of assessment. The next section describes procedures for developing alternative assessments including live performance, product development, and attitudes.

Alternative Assessment Instruments for Performances, Products, and Attitudes

Developing alternative assessment instruments used to measure performance, products, and attitudes does not involve writing test items per se but instead requires writing directions to guide the learners' activities and constructing a rubric to frame the evaluation of the performances, products, or attitudes. Many complex intellectual skills have both process and product goals. For example, consider a course in which this textbook might be used. The instructional goal could be "Use the instructional design process to design, develop, and evaluate one hour of self-instructional materials." Students would be required to document each step in the process and produce a set of instructional materials. The instructor could assess the process by examining the students' descriptions of their use of the process and their intermediate products such as an instructional analysis and performance objectives. A rating scale would be used to evaluate each step in the process. A separate scale would be used to evaluate the instruction that is produced.

Clearly, there are situations in which the process is the major outcome, with little concern for the product in the belief that with repeated use of the process the products will continue to improve. In other situations, the product or result is all important, and the process used by the learner is not critical. As the designer, you must have the skills to develop both traditional tests and novel approaches that employ other forms of observation and rating-scale types of assessments. In this section, the methods to use when developing such instruments are described.

Writing Directions   Directions to learners for performances and products should clearly describe what is to be done and how, including any special conditions such as resources or time limits. In writing your directions, you also need to consider the amount of guidance that should be provided. It may be desirable to remind learners to perform certain steps and to inform them of the criteria that will be used in evaluating their work. In such instances (e.g., developing a research paper or making a speech), examinees can be given a copy of the evaluation checklist or rating scale that will be used to judge their work as a part of the directions. In other circumstances (e.g., answering an essay question or changing a tire), providing such guidance would defeat the purpose of the test. Factors you can use in determining the appropriate amount of guidance are the nature of the skill tested, including its complexity, the sophistication level of the target learners, and the natural situations to which learners are to transfer the skills as determined in your context analysis.

Instructions to examinees related to the measurement of attitudes differ from those given for measuring performances and products. For accurate evaluation of attitudes, it is important for examinees to feel free to "choose" to behave according to their attitudes. Examinees who are aware that they are being observed by a supervisor or instructor may not exhibit behaviors that reflect their true attitudes. Covertly observing employees, however, can be problematic in many work settings. Agreements are often made between employees and employers about who can be evaluated, who can conduct the evaluation, what can be evaluated, whether the employee is informed in advance, and how the data can be used. Even with these understandable limitations, it is sometimes possible through planning and prior agreements to create a situation where reasonable assessment of attitudes can occur.

Developing the Instrument   In addition to writing instructions for learners, you will need to develop a rubric to guide your evaluation of performances, products, or attitudes. There are five steps in developing the instrument:

1. Identify the elements to be evaluated.
2. Paraphrase each element.

3. Sequence the elements on the instrument.
4. Select the type of judgment to be made by the evaluator.
5. Determine how the instrument will be scored.

Identify, Paraphrase, and Sequence Elements Similar to test items, the elements to be judged are taken directly from the behaviors included in the performance objectives. Recall that categories of elements typically include aspects of the physical form of the object or performance, the utility of the product or performance, and the aesthetic qualities of the product or performance. You should ensure that the elements selected can actually be observed during the performance or in the product.

Each element should be paraphrased for inclusion on the instrument. The time available for observing and rating, especially for an active performance, is limited, and lengthy descriptions such as those included in the objectives will hamper the process. Often only one or two words are necessary to communicate the step or facet of a product or performance to the evaluator. In paraphrasing, it is also important to word each item such that a Yes response from the evaluator reflects a positive outcome and a No response reflects a negative outcome. Consider the following examples for an oral speech:

Incorrect	Yes	No	Correct	Yes	No
1. Maintains eye contact	___	___	1. Maintains eye contact	___	___
2. Pauses with "and, uh"	___	___	2. Avoids "and, uh" pauses	___	___
3. Loses thought, idea	___	___	3. Maintains thought, idea	___	___

In the incorrect example the paraphrased list of behaviors mixes positive and negative outcomes that would be very difficult to score. In the correctly paraphrased list, items are phrased such that a yes response is a positive judgment and a no response is a negative one. This consistency will enable you to sum the Yes ratings to obtain an overall score that indicates the quality of the performance or product.

After elements are paraphrased, they should be sequenced on the instrument. The order in which they are included should be congruent with the natural order of events, if there is one. For example, an essay or paragraph evaluation checklist would include features related to the introduction first, to the supporting ideas second, and to the conclusions last. The chronological steps required to change a tire should guide the order of steps on the checklist. The most efficient order for bank tellers' behaviors would undoubtedly be greeting the customer, conducting the business, and concluding the transaction. In general, the goal analysis sequence is useful for suggesting the sequence of elements.

Developing the Response Format The fourth step in developing an instrument to measure performances, products, or attitudes is to determine how the evaluator will make and record the judgments. There are at least three evaluator response formats including a checklist (e.g., yes or no); a rating scale that requires levels of quality differentiation (e.g., poor, adequate, and good); a frequency count of the occurrence of each element considered; or some combination of these formats. The best evaluator response mode depends on several factors including the following: (1) the nature and complexity of the elements observed; (2) the time available for observing, making the judgment, and recording the judgment; (3) the accuracy or consistency with which the evaluator can make the judgments; and (4) the quality of feedback to be provided to the examinee.

Checklist. The most basic of the three judgment formats is the checklist. If you choose the checklist, you can easily complete your instrument by including two columns beside each of the paraphrased, sequenced elements to be observed, a Yes column to indicate that each element was present and a No column to indicate either the absence or inadequacy of an element. Benefits of the checklist include the number of different elements that can be observed in a given amount of time, the speed with which it can be completed by the evaluator, the consistency or reliability with which judgments can be made, and the ease with which an overall performance score can be obtained. One limitation of the checklist is the absence of information provided to examinees about why a No judgment was assigned.

Rating Scale. A checklist can be converted to a rating scale by expanding the number of quality level judgments for each element where quality differentiation is possible. Instead of using two columns for rating an element, at least three are used. These three columns can include either not present (0), present (1), and good (2), or poor (1), adequate (2), and good (3). Including either a (0) or (1) as the lowest rating depends on whether the element judged can be completely missing from a product or a performance. For example, some level of eye contact will be present in an oral report, and the lowest rating should be a 1. A paragraph, however, may have no concluding sentence at all; thus a score of 0 would be most appropriate in this instance. The particular ratings selected depend on the nature of the element to be judged.

Similar to checklists, rating scales have both positive and negative features. On the positive side, they enable analytical evaluation of the subcomponents of a performance or product, and they provide better feedback to the examinee about the quality of a performance than can be provided through a checklist. On the negative side, they require more time to use because finer distinctions must be made about the quality of each element evaluated. They also can yield less reliable scores than checklists, especially when more quality levels are included than can be differentiated in the time available or than can be consistently rated. Imagine a rating scale that contains ten different quality levels on each element scale. What precisely are the differences between a rating of 3 and 4 and a rating of 6 and 7? Too much latitude in making the evaluations will lead to inconsistencies both within and across evaluators.

Two strategies for developing scales can help ensure more reliable ratings. The first is to provide a clear verbal description of each quality level. Instead of simply using number categories and general terms such as (1) inadequate, (2) adequate, and (3) good, you should use more exact verbal descriptors that represent specific criteria for each quality level. Consider the following example related to topic sentences in a paragraph.

	General			
	Missing	**Poor**	**Adequate**	**Good**
1. Topic sentence . . .	0	1	2	3

	Improved			
	Missing	**Too broad/ specific**	**Correct specificity**	**Correct specificity and interest value**
1. Topic sentence . . .	0	1	2	3

Both response scales have four decision levels. The first example contains verbal descriptors for each rating, but the question of what constitutes a poor, adequate, and good topic sentence remains unclear. In the improved response format, the criterion for selecting each rating is more clearly defined. The more specific you can be in naming the criterion that corresponds to each quality level, the more reliable you can be in quantifying the quality of the element judged.

The second strategy you can use for developing scales is to limit the number of quality levels included in each scale. There is no rule stating that all elements judged should have the same number of quality levels, say a four- or five-point scale. The number of levels included should be determined by the complexity of the element judged and the time available for judging it. Consider the following two elements from a paragraph example.

	Yes	No					
1. Indented	___	___	1. Indented	0	1	2	3
2. Topic sentence	___	___	2. Topic sentence	0	1	2	3

In the checklist on the left, the elements could each reliably be judged using this list. Considering the rating scales on the right, you can see an immediate problem. Indenting a paragraph and writing a topic sentence differ drastically in skill complexity. Imagine trying to differentiate consistently four different levels of how well a paragraph is indented! Yet, as indicated in the preceding example, four different levels of the quality of a topic sentence would be reasonable.

A good rule for determining the size of the scale for each element is to ensure that each number or level included corresponds to a specific criterion for making the judgment. When you exhaust the criteria, you have all the levels that you can consistently judge.

Frequency Count. A frequency count is needed when an element to be observed, whether positive or negative, can be repeated several times by the examinee during the performance or in the product. For example, in a product such as a written report, the same type of outstanding feature or error can occur several times. During a performance such as a tennis match, the service is repeated many times, sometimes effectively and sometimes not. In rating behaviors such as those exhibited by bank tellers, the teller can be observed during transactions with many different customers and on different days. The instances of positive and negative behaviors exhibited by the teller should be tallied across customers and days.

A frequency count instrument can be created by simply providing adequate space beside each element in order to tally the number of instances that occur. Similar to the checklist, the most difficult part of constructing a frequency count instrument is in identifying and sequencing the elements to be observed.

Scoring Procedure   The final activity in creating an instrument to measure products, performances, and attitudes is to determine how the instrument will be scored. Just as with a paper and pencil test, you will undoubtedly need objective-level scores as well as overall performance scores. The checklist is the easiest of the three instrument formats to score. Yes responses for all elements related to one objective can be summed to obtain an objective-level score, and Yes responses can be summed across the total instrument to obtain an overall rating for the examinee on the goal.

Objective-level scores can be obtained from a rating scale by adding together the numbers assigned for each element rated within an objective. A score indicating the examinee's overall performance on the goals can be obtained by summing the individual ratings across all elements included in the instrument.

Unlike objective tests, checklists, and rating scales, determining an appropriate scoring procedure for a frequency count instrument can be challenging. The best procedure to use must be determined on a situation-specific basis, and it depends on the nature of the skills or attitudes measured and on the setting. For example, when rating the interactive performance of classroom teachers or sales personnel, some instances of the behaviors you want to observe will occur during the evaluation, whereas others will not. In such cases you must consider whether a lack of occurrence is a negative or neutral outcome. In another situation such as tennis, you will have many opportunities to observe an element such as the service and to readily count the number of strategically placed first serves, foot faults, or let serves. It is quite easy to tally the total number of serves made by a player and to calculate the proportion of overall serves that were strategically placed first serves, foot faults, let services, and so forth. Yet, once these calculations are made, you must still decide how to combine this information to create a score on the instructional goal related to serving a tennis ball.

Regardless of how you decide to score a frequency count instrument, it is important that you consider during the developmental process how it will be done and compare the consequences of scoring it one way versus an alternative way. The manner in which you need to score an instrument may require modifications to the list of elements you wish to observe; therefore, scoring procedures should be planned prior to beginning to rate learner performances. When no feasible scoring procedure can be found for a frequency count instrument, you might reconsider using either a checklist, a rating scale, or a combination format instead.

All the suggestions included in this discussion should be helpful in the development of criterion-referenced tests. If you are an inexperienced test writer, you may wish to consult additional references on test construction. Several references on testing techniques are included at the end of this chapter.

Portfolio Assessments

Portfolios are collections of criterion-referenced assessments that illustrate learners' work. These assessments might include objective-style tests that demonstrate progress from the pretest to the posttest, products that learners developed during instruction, or live performances. Portfolios might also include assessments of learners' attitudes about the domain studied or the instruction.

Portfolio assessment is defined as the process of meta-evaluating the collection of work samples for observable change or development. Objective tests are assessed for learner change or growth from pretests through posttests, and products and performances are tracked and compared for evidence of learner progress. There are at least five criteria for designing quality portfolio assessments:

1. The instructional goals and objectives included in portfolio assessment should be very important and warrant the increased time required for this assessment format.
2. The work samples must be anchored to specific instructional goals and performance objectives.
3. The work samples should be the criterion-referenced assessments that are collected during the process of instruction.
4. The assessments are the regular pretests and posttests, regardless of test format, and typically no special tests are created for portfolio assessment.
5. Each regular assessment is accompanied by its rubric with a student's responses evaluated and scored, indicating the strengths and problems within a performance.

With the set of work samples collected and sequenced, the evaluator is ready to begin the process of assessing growth, which is often accomplished at two levels. The first level, learner self-assessment, is one of the tenets of the learner-centered assessment movement. Learners examine their own materials, including test scores, products, performances, and scored rubrics, and they record their judgments about the strengths and problems in the materials. They also describe what they might do to improve the materials. Instructors then examine the materials set, without first examining the evaluations by the learner, and record their judgments. Following the completion of the instructor's evaluation, the instructor and the learner compare their evaluations, discussing any discrepancies between the two evaluations. As a result of this interview, they plan together next steps the learner should undertake to improve the quality of his or her work.

Portfolio assessment is not appropriate for all instruction since it is very time consuming and expensive. The instruction would need to span time so that the learner has time to develop and refine skills. The instruction should also yield the required products or performances for the assessment.

A course in instructional design would be an appropriate situation for portfolio assessment since many products are developed and refined over a span of several months. The products created by the learner include an instructional goal, an instructional analysis, an analysis of learners and contexts, performance objectives, assessment instruments and procedures, an instructional strategy, a set of instructional materials, often a formative evaluation of the materials, and a description of the strengths in the instruction as well as refinement prescriptions for identified problems. During the design and development process, a rubric would be used to score each element in the process. At the conclusion of the course, a meta-evaluation of all the materials and initial rubrics would be undertaken. This is often the point where learners say, "If only I knew then what I know now."

Congruence in the Design Process

In the systems approach to instructional design, the output from one step is the input to the next. Therefore, it is important to stop periodically to determine whether products being created are consistent from step to step in the process.

At this point in the design process, the goal has been analyzed, subordinate skills identified, learners and contexts analyzed, objectives written, and assessments developed. It is imperative that the skills, objectives, and assessments all refer to the same skills, so careful review is required in order to ensure this congruence.

Materials for Evaluating the Design   You will need all the materials produced thus far to complete the design evaluation, including the instructional analysis diagram, performance objectives, summaries of learner characteristics as well as performance and learning contexts, performance objectives, and assessments. Recall that there are four main categories of criteria to be considered for evaluating your overall design to this point—goal, learner, context, and assessment criteria. These criteria are woven through the evaluation of your design.

Procedures for Evaluating the Design   Using these main criteria, there are five steps in evaluating the design:

1. Organize and present the materials to illuminate their relationships.
2. Judge the congruence between the information and skills in instructional goal analysis and the materials created.
3. Judge the congruence between the materials and the characteristics of the target learners.
4. Judge the congruence between the performance and learning contexts and the materials.
5. Judge the clarity of all the materials.

Organization. How can you best organize and present your materials to evaluate them at this point in the instructional design process? Each component builds on the product from the previous one; therefore, the materials should be presented in a way that enables comparison among the various components of your design. The designer should be able to see at a glance whether the components are parallel, which

table 7.2	Structure of the Design Evaluation Chart		
	Subskill	**Performance Objective**	**Sample Assessment**
	1	Objective 1	Test item
	2	Objective 2	Test item
	3	Objective 3	Test item
	Instructional Goal	Terminal Objective	Test item

can be achieved by organizing the materials such that related components are together. Consider the structure in Table 7.2. The first column is a list of the subskills from the instructional goal analysis, the second column includes performance objectives for each skill, and the third column shows test items for each objective. The last line should contain the instructional goal, the terminal objective, and the test item(s) for the terminal objective. Using such a table, the evaluator can, at a glance, determine whether the materials are congruent. Table 7.3 includes an example of the type of material that would be listed in each section of Table 7.2.

The sequence of subskills presented on your chart is important. If you place them in the order you believe they should be taught, then you will be able to receive additional feedback from a reviewer concerning the logic you have used for sequencing skills and presenting instruction. This additional feedback may save steps in rewriting or reorganizing your materials at a later point. The topic of sequencing skills will be addressed in greater detail in the next chapter.

You should have other documents available for evaluators to use with your design evaluation table. These include the instructional analysis diagram, the table of target learner characteristics, and the table describing the performance and learning contexts. All items in the design table should be keyed to the numbering of the subskills in the analysis diagram. This complete set of materials represents your instructional design to this point.

Congruence. The second step requires using the goal-centered criteria to judge the congruence among your materials. The congruence among the subordinate skill in the goal framework, its intended performance objective (conditions, behavior, and content), and the intended test items is critically important to the quality of your materials.

A recommended procedure to follow for this part of the analysis is to compare the (1) subordinate skills in instructional goal analysis with the subordinate skills listed in the design evaluation table, (2) subordinate skills in the table with the performance objectives in the table, and (3) performance objectives (conditions, performance, and criteria) with the test items prescribed in the table.

table 7.3	Example of a Design Evaluation Chart		
	Skill	**Performance Objective**	**Test Item(s)**
	1. Write the formula for converting yards to meters.	1. From memory, correctly write the formula for converting yards to meters.	1. In the space provided below, write the formula used to convert yards to meters.
	2. Convert measures in yards to comparable meters.	2. Given different lengths in yards, convert the yards to meters, correct to one decimal place.	2. 5 yds = _____ meters 7.5 yds = _____ meters 15 yds = _____ meters

The wording of the subordinate skills in the goal analysis diagram and the design evaluation table should be the same. Once this congruence is established, the goal analysis can be set aside. Your subordinate skills and performance objectives should differ only in that conditions and perhaps criteria have been added. Finally, determine whether the performance objectives and test items match in conditions, performance, and criteria. Are students given the information and materials in the items that were prescribed in the objective? Once the design is parallel in content, evaluators can turn to examining the congruence between the performance objectives and the characteristics of the learners.

Learner Characteristics. The third step is to compare the materials with the characteristics of the learners. For this analysis evaluators should judge the congruence between the materials and learners' ability, vocabulary, interests, experiences, and needs. The best materials in the world are ineffective if intended learners cannot use them effectively. Do reviewers believe the performance objectives and assessments are set at the right scope and complexity for the defined target group? Are the objectives broken down finely enough or too much? Are the test items at the appropriate level of complexity for the learners?

Contexts. The fourth step is to judge the congruence of the performance and learning contexts with the performance objectives and test items in the design evaluation table. Reviewers should judge the *authenticity* of the tasks prescribed for the performance context because this authenticity helps ensure transfer of skills from the learning to the performance context. They should also examine the *feasibility* of the tasks for the learning context. Can the designer expect the resources required (e.g., costs, time, personnel, facilities, equipment) to implement the implied instruction and assessments to be available in the learning context?

Materials Clarity. With congruence among the materials and the goal, contexts, and learners established, the final step is for reviewers to judge the clarity of the materials. Unfortunately, this step is sometimes where the evaluation begins, but without determining the alignment of the design documents, clarity may be a moot point. During this step, evaluators should be asked whether the structure and scope of the goal analysis make sense to them. Are the subordinate and entry skills correctly identified, and are they in the correct order? Are the performance objectives clearly written, and do they know what is meant by each? What is their perception of the quality of the test items including language clarity; vocabulary level; grammar, spelling, and punctuation; assessment format; and professional appearance?

After you have received feedback concerning the adequacy of your design and made appropriate revisions in your framework, you will have the input required to begin work on the next component of the model, namely developing an instructional strategy. Having a good, carefully analyzed, and refined design at this point will facilitate your work on the remaining steps in the process.

Examples

When you examine test items and assessments in this section, you can use the four categories of criteria summarized by the rubric at the end of the chapter to help focus your attention on particular aspects of the item.

A Checklist for Evaluating Motor Skills

In measuring the performance of motor skills, you will need instructions for the performance and a rubric you can use to record your evaluations of the performance.

figure	Directions for a Psychomotor Skill Test (Changing a Tire)
7.1	

Using the equipment provided in the trunk of the car, remove from the car any one of the tires designated by the instructor. Replace that tire with the spare tire secured in the trunk. The test will be complete when you have (1) returned the car to a safe-driving condition, (2) secured all tools in their proper place in the trunk, (3) secured the removed tire in the spare tire compartment in the trunk, and (4) replaced any lids or coverings on the wheel or in the trunk that were disturbed during the test.

Your performance on each step will be judged using three basic criteria. The first is that you remember to perform each step. The second is that you execute each one using the *appropriate* tools in the *proper* manner. The third is that you perform each step with safety in mind. For safety reasons, the examiner may stop you at any point in the exam and request that you (1) perform a step that you have forgotten, (2) change the manner in which you are using a tool or ask that you change to another tool, or (3) repeat a step that was not performed safely. If this occurs, you will not receive credit for that step. However, you will receive credit for correctly executed steps performed after that point.

The examples provided are based on the automobile tire changing performance objectives included in Table 6.3 (p. 122).

The directions for the examinee are contained in Figure 7.1. The directions differ slightly from the terminal objective in Table 6.3. For the examination, the car will not have the specified flat tire. Instead, the learner is to replace any tire designated by the examiner. Imagine the logistical problems of having to evaluate fifteen or twenty learners on these skills and having to begin each test with a flat tire on the car. Other information included in the instructions also is based on the practicality of administering the test. Notice that the student is required to return and secure all tools, equipment, and parts to their proper place. While helping to ensure that the examinee knows how to perform these tasks, it also ensures that the equipment and car are ready for the next examinee.

Information is also provided for the examinee about how the performance will be judged. These instructions tell examinees that in order to receive credit, they must: (1) recall each step, (2) perform it using the appropriate tool, (3) use each tool properly, and (4) always be safety conscious in performing each step. Given this information, they will understand that failure to comply with any one of these four criteria will mean a loss of credit for that step. They are also told that they can be stopped at any point during the test. Knowing that this can happen, why it can happen, and the consequences of it happening will lessen their anxiety if they are stopped during the exam.

A partial checklist that can be used to evaluate performance is included in Figure 7.2. Only main step 2, lifts car, is illustrated. Notice that the main headings within step 2 are numbered consistently with the steps in the goal analysis (Figure 4.11, p. 87) and the performance objectives in Table 6.3. The criteria listed in each objective in Table 6.3 are paraphrased and assigned letters (e.g., a, b, c, etc.) for the checklist. Two columns are provided for the evaluator's response.

The next step in developing the instrument was to determine how learners' scores would be summarized. It was decided to obtain both main step scores (e.g., lifts car) as well as a total score for the test. To facilitate this scoring plan, blanks are placed to the left of each main step. The total number of points possible in step 2 is recorded in parentheses beneath the space. The number of points earned by each student can be determined by counting the number of Xs in the Yes column. This value can be recorded in the blank beside main step 2. In the example, you

figure	Partial Checklist for Evaluating a Psychomotor Skill (Changing a Tire)

7.2

Name _____Karen Haeuser_____ Date ___6-12___ Score _____
( )

_____ 1. Obtains spare and tools
(11)

_____ 2. Lifts car   *Yes*   *No*
(13)

    2.1 Checks jack operation
      a. Attaches jack handle securely   X   ___
      b. Pumps handle to lift jack   X   ___
      c. Releases and lowers jack   X   ___

    2.2 Positions jack
      a. Checks car location, stability   X   ___
      b. Relocates car, if needed   X   ___
      c. Locates spot on frame to attach jack   X   ___
      d. Positions jack in appropriate spot   X   ___

    2.3 Attaches jack to car
      a. Raises jack to meet frame   X   ___
      b. Evaluates contact between jack/car   ___   X
      c. Adjusts jack location, if needed   ___   X

    2.4 Places blocks beside wheels
      a. Locates appropriate blocks   X   ___
      b. Places block before wheels   X   ___
      c. Places block behind wheels   X   ___

_____ 3. Removes tire
( )
_____ 4. Replaces tire
( )
    Etc.

can see that the examinee earned eleven of the possible thirteen points. Summing the points recorded for each main step in the left-hand column will yield a total score for the test, which can be recorded at the top of the form beside the name. The total possible points for the test can be recorded in the parentheses beneath the total earned score.

One final observation should be made. The evaluator needs to determine how to score items 2.2b and 2.3c when no adjustment to the car or jack is needed. One strategy would be to place an X in the column for each of these steps even when they are not needed. Simply leaving them blank or checking the No column would indicate that the student committed an error, which is not the case.

Instrument for Evaluating Behaviors Related to Attitudes

For rating behaviors from which attitudes can be inferred, you will need either a checklist, rating scale, or frequency count. Our example is based on the courteous bank teller illustrations in Chapter 2 and Table 6.5. Because a teller should be evaluated in the performance site using several example transactions with a customer, a frequency count response format will undoubtedly work best. A sample instrument is contained in Figure 7.3.

Notice that at the top of the instrument there is space for identifying the teller and the date or dates of the observations. There is also space for tallying the number of transactions observed. This information will be needed later to interpret the data.

figure 7.3

A Frequency Count Instrument for Evaluating Behaviors from Which Attitudes Will Be Inferred (Courteous Service)

Name _Robert Jones_ _____   Date(s) _4/10, 17, 24_

Total Transactions Observed ~~HH HH HH~~ Total _+186_   Total _−19_

A. Customer Approaches and Teller:	Yes	No
1. Smiles	~~HH~~ ~~HH~~	~~HH~~
2. Initiates verbal greeting	~~HH~~ ~~HH~~ ~~HH~~	
3. Personalizes comments	~~HH~~ ~~HH~~ ~~HH~~	
4. Excuses self when delayed	////	//
5. Inquires about services	~~HH~~ ~~HH~~ ////	/
6. Attends to all in line	~~HH~~ ~~HH~~	///
7. Other:		

B. During Transaction, Teller:		
1. Listens attentively	~~HH~~ ~~HH~~ ~~HH~~	
2. Requests clarifying information	~~HH~~ ////	
3. Provides forms required	~~HH~~ ////	
4. Completes/amends forms	~~HH~~ ////	
5. Explains changes made	~~HH~~ ////	
6. Explains materials returned	~~HH~~ ~~HH~~ //	///
7. Other:		

C. Concluding Transaction, Teller:		
1. Inquires about other services	~~HH~~ ~~HH~~ ~~HH~~	
2. Says, "Thank you"	~~HH~~ ~~HH~~ ~~HH~~	
3. Responds to customer comments	~~HH~~ ~~HH~~	~~HH~~
4. Makes concluding wish	~~HH~~ ~~HH~~ ~~HH~~	
5. Other:		

There is also space to record the total number of positive and negative behaviors exhibited by the teller during the observations.

The particular behaviors sought are paraphrased in the far left column. Similar to the checklist, there are two response columns for the evaluator. The only difference is that space is provided in this example for tallying many behaviors during several different transactions.

In determining how to score the instrument, both the behaviors perceived as positive (186) and those perceived as negative (19) were tallied. Reviewing the summary of this simulated data, it appears that the teller behaved in a courteous manner toward customers in the vast majority of the instances. This information can be interpreted in two ways, depending on the teller's knowledge of the observations. If the teller was unaware of the observations and chose to behave in this manner, then the evaluator could infer that the teller indeed displayed a positive attitude in providing courteous, friendly service. Conversely, if the teller was aware of the examination, then the evaluator could infer that the teller knew how to behave courteously during transactions with customers and chose to do so while under observation.

Case Study: Group Leadership Training

To this point in the case study we have identified a goal and completed a goal analysis, a subskills analysis, an analysis of learners and contexts, and written performance objectives. Having demonstrated in the examples section procedures for developing instruments for a psychomotor skill and an attitude, in the case study that follows we demonstrate how test items would be written for several verbal information and intellectual skills objectives. We then pause in the ID process to evaluate the design work to this point.

Test Items for Verbal Information and Intellectual Skills

Sample performance objectives from Table 6.7 (p. 125; Instructional goal, "Lead group discussions aimed at solving problems": Step 6, "Manage cooperative group interaction") are repeated in column 1 of Table 7.4. A test item or set of items is illustrated for each of the objectives.

Performance Objectives   As you examine the test items, first notice the congruence between the performance objective and the item relative to objective conditions, behavior, and criteria. For example, examine the congruence between performance objective 6.5.1 and its corresponding test directions for learners on the right side of the table. The objective conditions prescribe a simulated meeting with the learner serving as leader. The task directions to the learners describe them as leading the meeting. The behavior in the objective is to initiate actions to engender group members' cooperation. The task directions on the right side prescribe that the leader initiates actions to engender group members' cooperation during the meeting. The criteria in the objective would appear on the designer's rubric for observing leader behaviors during the meeting and not in the task directions to learners.

Congruence with Learner Characteristics   Second, examine items for their appropriateness for the NCW leaders. You will need the test items (Table 7.4) and the description of learner characteristics (Table 5.4, pp. 102–103) for this analysis. Judge the complexity of the language used in the items and the complexity of the tasks required. The language appears to be at an appropriate level for adults who have at least completed high school. The task complexity also appears to be appropriate for adults who have volunteered for the training to become community leaders in the NCW program.

Performance and Learning Sites   Third, examine the test items (Table 7.4) for appropriateness in the learning and performance sites (Tables 5.5, p. 104, and 5.6, p. 106). The last section of Table 7.4 contains the learning site and performance site assessment for main step 6 to aid your assessment for this criterion. At the posttest point, learners will be observed as they lead group discussions and the evaluator will use an observation form in the learning site to note the behaviors exhibited by leaders and tally the frequency with which each occurs.

Clarity   Finally, examine the test items in Table 7.4 for their general clarity. Readers may want to use the rubric (pp. 158–159) to assist their evaluation. Note that key terms are highlighted in the items to direct learners' attention. The items appear to be clear in that all information required to answer an item is presented before the learner is expected to respond. Grammar, punctuation, and spelling are correct, and the items have a professional appearance.

Once the items and directions are written, evaluated, and refined, you are ready to create the design evaluation table and review the materials developed to this point.

table 7.4

Parallel Test Items for the Verbal Information and Intellectual Skills Performance Objectives in Table 6.7 for the Instructional Goal "Lead Group Discussions Aimed at Solving Problems"

Performance Objectives for Subordinate Skills	Parallel Test Items
6.1.1 When requested in writing to name group member actions that facilitate cooperative interaction (CN), name those actions (B). At least six facilitating actions should be named (CR).	1. List positive actions you and committee members should take to *facilitate* cooperative group interaction during NCW meetings. (Create response lines for nine responses.)
6.1.2 When asked in writing to indicate what members should do when their ideas are questioned by the group (CN), name positive reactions that help ensure cooperative group interaction (B). Learner should name at least three possible reactions (CR).	1. Suppose you introduce a new idea during a NCW meeting and the value of your idea is questioned by one or more committee members. What positive reactions might you have to *facilitate* cooperative group interaction? (Create response lines for four responses.)
6.2.1 Given written descriptions of a group member's facilitating actions during a meeting (CN), indicate whether the actions are cooperative behaviors (B). Learner should correctly classify at least 80 percent of the actions described (CR).	1. Read the script of the NCW meeting. Each time the leader or a member of the NCW group exhibits a cooperative behavior, place a checkmark beside that line in the script.
6.2.2 Given videos of staged NCW meetings depicting member's actions (CN), indicate whether the actions are cooperative (B). Learner should classify correctly at least 80 percent of the actions demonstrated (CR).	(*Reader note:* This video and response sheet are both located in the practice test section on the NCW web-based training site.) **Directions** **Skill:** Classify Cooperative NCW Leader and Member Actions. Click on the Videos button on the left of your screen and select Video 1 from the video table of contents that appears. Then: (a) Highlight and print the Leader Response Form for Video 1. (b) Study the response form, reading the directions for marking your responses. (c) Locate the Video 1 title button on your screen and click on the Video 1 title when you are ready to complete the assessment. (d) When you are finished (you may view the video twice in the process of completing your ratings), click on the Feedback-Video 1 title in the video menu. (e) Compare your ratings with those provided in the Feedback-Video 1 and note any discrepancies. (f) Keep your response form and notes about discrepancies, and bring them to the next instructional session at the center.
6.3.1 When asked in writing to name leader actions that encourage and stifle member discussion and cooperation (CN), name these actions (B). Learner should name at least ten encouraging and corresponding stifling actions (CR).	List twelve positive actions and their corresponding stifling actions that you as an NCW leader can take to affect member interaction during NCW meetings. (Create double response lines for twelve responses with headings of Positive Actions and Stifling Actions.)
6.4.1 Given written descriptions of group leader's actions during a meeting (CN), indicate whether the actions are likely to encourage or stifle cooperative group interaction (B). Learner should correctly classify at least 80 percent of the actions depicted (CR).	1. Read the script of an NCW meeting. Each time the leader of the NCW group exhibits a behavior that is likely to encourage member cooperation, place a check mark (✓) on the left side of the script in the corresponding script line. In contrast, each time the leader exhibits a behavior likely to stifle member cooperation, place a check mark on the right side of the script beside that line.
6.4.2 Given videos of staged NCW meetings depicting staged leader's actions (CN), indicate whether the leader's actions are likely to encourage or stifle member cooperation (B). Learner should classify correctly at least 80 percent of the encouraging and stifling actions demonstrated (CR).	(*Reader note:* This video and response sheet are both located in the practice test section on the NCW web-based training site.) **Directions:** **Skill:** Classify NCW Leader Actions Likely to Encourage and Stifle Member Cooperation. (a) Highlight and print the Leader Response Form 2.

table
7.4

Continued

Performance Objectives for Subordinate Skills	Parallel Test Items
	(b) Study the sheet, reading the directions for marking your responses.
	(c) Locate Video 2 in the videos menu on your screen and click on the Video 2 title when you are ready to complete the assessment.
	(d) When you are finished (you may view the video twice in the process of completing your ratings), click on the Feedback-Video 2 title in the video menu.
	(e) Compare your ratings of the leader's actions with those provided in the web site and note any discrepancies.
	(f) Keep Response Form 2 and notes about discrepancies, and bring them to the next instructional session at the center.
6.5.1 In simulated NCW problem-solving meetings with learner acting as group leader (CN), initiate actions to engender cooperative behavior among members (B). Group members cooperate with each other and with leader during discussion (CR).	**Directions:** **Skill:** Engender cooperative behavior among members. During the NCW meeting today, you will serve as NCW leader for thirty minutes. During your meeting, a member (staff) will introduce a problem not previously discussed in the group. You will lead the group discussion as the problem is discussed and demonstrate personal actions before the group that you believe will engender members' cooperative participation. If you have questions about your actions or the actions of others, do not raise them with staff or members of your group until the thirty minutes has passed.

Performance Objective for Main Step	Prescription for Frequency Count Observation Instrument (used by evaluator during simulations and actual meetings)
6. During simulated NCW meetings comprised of new NCW leadership trainees and held at a county government training facility, manage cooperative group interaction. Discussion members should participate freely, volunteer ideas, cooperate fully with leader and other members. During actual NCW meetings held at a designated neighborhood site (e.g., member home, neighborhood social/meeting facility), lead group discussions aimed at solving crime problems currently existing in the neighborhood.	The following categories will be used relative to main step 6: Manage cooperative group interaction in both the learning and performance contexts. A. Engendering actions demonstrated Frequency 1. _____ _____ 2. _____ _____ (etc.) B. Defusing actions demonstrated Frequency 1. _____ _____ 2. _____ _____ (etc.) C. Stress-alleviating actions demonstrated Frequency 1. _____ _____ 2. _____ _____ (etc.) D. Rating of overall quality of cooperative group interaction (circle one) Mild 1 2 3 4 5 Excellent

Your role will be to organize the materials, locate appropriate reviewers, facilitate the review process, explain materials, answer questions, and take notes. The reviewers' role will be to study the documents provided and make the requested judgments.

Design Evaluation

Again, the four main criteria reviewers will use to judge the quality of the design to this point involve goal, learner, context, and assessment considerations. In evaluating the congruence among the various design elements, the following steps were taken:

1. Organize and present the materials.
2. Judge the congruence among the materials and the instructional goal.
3. Judge the appropriateness of the materials for the target learners.
4. Judge the congruence of the performance objectives and test items with the performance and learning contexts.
5. Judge the clarity of the materials.

Organization   Table 7.5 contains a partial design evaluation chart for the instructional goal on leading group discussions. The first column contains selected subordinate skills for step 6, "Manage cooperative group interaction," the second column contains the performance objectives for the selected skills, and the third column includes matching test

table 7.5   A Section of a Design Evaluation Chart for the Instructional Goal "Lead Group Discussions Aimed at Solving Problems," Step 6, "Manage Cooperative Group Interaction"

Skill	Performance Objectives	Test Items
6.3 Name actions for encouraging cooperation.	6.3.1 When asked in writing to name actions for encouraging and stifling discussion member cooperation, name these actions. Learner should name at least ten ways.	1. There are several strategies you can use as a NCW leader to *encourage and stifle cooperative discussion* during your meetings. What direct actions might you take as the leader to encourage member participation and cooperation? (Create response lines for ten responses.)
6.4 Classify strategies for encouraging and stifling cooperation.	6.4.1 Given written descriptions of group leader's actions during a meeting, indicate whether the actions are likely to encourage or stifle cooperative group interaction. Learner should correctly classify at least 80 percent of the actions depicted.	Place a plus (+) before those group leader actions most likely *to encourage* and a minus (−) before those actions likely *to stifle* cooperative group interaction. ___ 1. Introduces all members who attend the meeting. ___ 2. Emphasizes status differences among group members. ___ 3. Glances around the group welcomingly. ___ 4. Names a particular group member to start discussions. ___ 5. Comments positively after each person as commented. (etc.)
6.5 Engender cooperative member behaviors.	6.5.1 In simulated NCW problem-solving meetings with learner acting as group leader, initiate actions to engender cooperative behavior among members. Group members cooperate with each other and with leader during discussion.	As you observe (name) manage the meeting, what actions did he/she take *to engender* or encourage cooperative group behavior? Actions to Engender Cooperation Frequency 1. _____ _____ 2. _____ _____ 3. _____ _____ (etc.)

items for each of the objectives. Only a few of the skills, objectives, and test items are needed to illustrate the analysis process. A thorough analysis would include all the skills, objectives, and items developed to this point. In addition to the chart, a copy of the goal analysis (Figure 4.8), learner characteristics (Table 5.4), performance site characteristics (Table 5.5), and learning site characteristics (Table 5.6), should be available for the reviewers. They could also benefit from the summary of assessment criteria included in the rubric. With the materials organized, the second step of judging the congruence between the materials and the goal can be undertaken.

Congruence   For this analysis reviewers will need the goal analysis (Figure 4.8) and the subordinate skills in Table 7.5. Notice that the subordinate skills illustrated are worded the same as those in the goal analysis except for the addition of the term *stifling* that has been added to subordinate skill 6.4. Reviewers and designers would need to discuss this addition to determine whether it was appropriate and intended or an inadvertent addition that should be corrected.

Using Table 7.5 only, reviewers should compare the subordinate skills in column one with the performance objectives in column two. The skills do appear to be exactly the same except for skill 6.4 where the action term is *classify* whereas the objective specifies *indicate*. There is no meaningful difference between these two terms in this instance.

Finally reviewers should compare the congruence between the performance objectives in column two and the test items in column three. Examine the items for their congruence with the conditions, behavior, and criteria separately rather than holistically. Reviewers followed the same process the designer used in the previous section, and they judged the items and objectives to be congruent across conditions, behavior, and criteria.

Contexts   The third step is to judge the congruence of the performance and learning contexts with the goal, objectives, and test items in the design evaluation table. Because reviewers have previously judged the goal, subordinate skills, and performance objectives for congruence and decided they were consistent, they can simply concentrate on the performance objectives (Table 7.5) and the description of contexts (Tables 5.5 and 5.6). Following their review, they believed that leaders could transfer the skills described in the materials to their community NCW meetings. The meetings will be informal and held in homes in the neighborhood or community centers. Little additional resources (e.g., costs, resources, time, personnel, and facilities) would be needed. They also thought it feasible to conduct the training in the counties' learning centers based on government support, grant funding, personnel, and the availability of the Internet instructional system and training facilities.

Learners   The congruence among the goal, skills, objectives, and test items has already been established; thus, reviewers will need to review the feasibility of the materials (Figure 4.8 and Table 7.5) for the learner (Table 5.4). Reviewers who had greater familiarity with target learners concluded that attaining the instructional goal, "Lead group discussions aimed at solving problems," appeared to be feasible for adult community NCW volunteers. They also believed that community volunteers would most likely succeed in managing cooperative meetings given instruction, and this might lead to better community participation. They thought the performance objectives and test items were reasonable and should assist the leaders in developing skills that would be usable not only in the community but also on their jobs. Additionally, they judged the materials to be free of bias (e.g., gender, cultural, or racial).

Materials Clarity   Finally reviewers considered the clarity of the materials; they needed the goal analysis (Figure 4.8) and the design evaluation chart (Table 7.5) to complete their work. They perceived the structure of the goal analysis to be logical with the six main steps describing the chronology of events in managing a meeting.

The verbal information tables (e.g., Table 4.1) were judged to be necessary to illuminate the designer's intended meaning of the linked subordinate skills. They thought that neither the learners nor the instructors would know what to do if these tables were eliminated from the materials. They also considered the content to be appropriate in scope for NCW leaders and thought leaders could succeed given review and instruction in performing the tasks. Reviewers could interpret the performance objectives and test items and thought these materials were clear. In addition, they judged the test items to be consistent with the assessment criteria stated in the rubric.

Readers interested in school curriculum examples should review the subordinate skills, performance objectives, and corresponding assessments for the writing composition case study in Appendix E.

SUMMARY

In order to develop criterion-referenced tests, you will need the list of performance objectives based on the instructional analysis. The conditions, behavior, and criteria contained in each objective will help you determine the best format for your assessment instrument.

An objective test format will be best for many verbal information and intellectual skill objectives; however, you still must decide what objective-style item format would be most congruent with the prescribed conditions and behaviors. Objective items should be written to minimize the possibility of correctly guessing the answer, and they should be clearly written so that all stimuli or cues prescribed in the objective are present in the item or instructions. You must also decide how many items you will need to measure adequately student performance on each objective. In determining the number of items to produce, you need to consider how many times the information or skill will be tested. Enough items to support the construction of pretests and posttests should be produced. Whenever possible, learners should be presented with a different item each time an objective is measured.

Some intellectual skills cannot be measured using objective test items. Examples include writing a paragraph, making a persuasive speech, and analyzing and contrasting certain features of two different methods for predicting economic trends. Intellectual skills that result in a product or a performance, psychomotor skills, and behaviors related to attitudes should be measured using tests that consist of instructions for the learner and an observation instrument for the evaluator. In creating these instruments you must identify, paraphrase, and sequence the observable elements of the product, performance, or behavior. You will also need to select a reasonable judgment format for the evaluator and determine how the instrument will be scored.

RUBRIC FOR EVALUATING CRITERION-REFERENCED ASSESSMENTS

The following rubric contains a summary of criteria to use in developing and evaluating criterion-referenced assessments. The first section contains criteria appropriate regardless of the assessment format, and the second section describes criteria appropriate for alternative assessments including product development, live performances, and attitudes.

Designer note: If an element is not relevant for your plan, mark NA in the No column.

No	Some	Yes	
			A. All Assessment Formats (Objective and Alternative)
			1. Goal-Centered Criteria Are the items, directions, and rubrics congruent with the components of the terminal and performance objectives including:
—	—	—	a. Conditions?
—	—	—	b. Behavior?
—	—	—	c. Content?
—	—	—	d. Criteria?
			2. Learner-Centered Criteria Are the items and directions congruent with target learners':
—	—	—	a. Vocabulary, language level?
—	—	—	b. Developmental level (e.g., complexity, abstractness, guidance)?
—	—	—	c. Background, experience, environment?

No	Some	Yes	
——	——	——	d. Experience with testing format and equipment?
——	——	——	e. Motivation and interest?
——	——	——	f. Cultural, racial, gender needs (lack bias)?

3. Context-Centered Criteria for Assessments   Is/are:

No	Some	Yes	
——	——	——	a. Items and directions authentic for the contexts?
——	——	——	b. Items and directions feasible for the contexts?
——	——	——	c. Required equipment/tools available?
——	——	——	d. Adequate time available for administration, scoring, analysis?
——	——	——	e. Adequate personnel available for administration?

4. Assessment-Centered Criteria   Is/are:

No	Some	Yes	
——	——	——	a. All information required to answer provided?
——	——	——	b. Language clear and parsimonious?
——	——	——	c. Grammar, spelling, and punctuation correct?
——	——	——	d. Item formatting rules followed (consult measurement text)?
——	——	——	e. Format feasible given resources (time, personnel, costs)?
——	——	——	f. Professional looking?

B. Product, Live Performance, and Attitude Assessments

1. Directions   Do directions clearly indicate:

No	Some	Yes	
——	——	——	a. What is to be done?
——	——	——	b. How it is to be done?
——	——	——	c. Any needed resources, facilities, equipment?
——	——	——	d. Any constraints on time, format, etc.?
——	——	——	e. Appropriate guidance for task and learner needs?

2. Elements or Features to be Rated   Are elements:

No	Some	Yes	
——	——	——	a. Important?
——	——	——	b. Observable?
——	——	——	c. Paraphrased?
——	——	——	d. Sequenced in natural order of occurrence?
——	——	——	e. Stated either neutrally or positively for consistent rating direction?

3. Rating or Quality Judgment   Are the rating categories:

No	Some	Yes	
——	——	——	a. Consistent in directionality (Yes is positive rating, No is low)?
——	——	——	b. Labeled using both numbers and verbal descriptions?
——	——	——	c. Low in number of rating levels (rarely over three/four)?
——	——	——	d. Fair in that "zero" used only when element is totally missing?
——	——	——	e. Likely to yield reliable ratings (consistent across raters and time)?

The quality of your items and instruments depends on the quality of your objectives, which in turn depends on the quality of your instructional analysis and goal statement. After reviewing the items you have developed for your objectives, you should stop forward progress in the design process and evaluate your overall design to this point, revising your work if needed for overall quality and congruence.

Following this overall design evaluation, you can proceed to the next chapter on instructional strategies. During this phase of the design process, you will determine what tests to include in your instructional package and how they will be used. In the subsequent chapter on developing instructional materials, you will use your sample objective items and test plan to construct the objective tests you will need. If you have developed rating instruments instead of objective items, you will plan how and when to use these instruments related to the instructional strategy and materials.

PRACTICE

Judge whether each of the following statements about criterion-referenced tests is correct. If it is, place a C in the space before the item. If it is incorrect, state briefly why it is incorrect. Check your answers in the Feedback section.

_____ 1. A criterion-referenced test is composed of items that measure behavior.

_____ 2. A criterion-referenced test is the same as an objective-referenced test.

_____ 3. Test items in criterion-referenced tests need not measure the exact type of behavior described in a performance objective.

_____ 4. Test items for criterion-referenced tests are developed directly from skills identified in the instructional analysis.

_____ 5. It is always a good idea to construct entry skill test items for the pretest.

_____ 6. Entry skill test items are developed to measure skills learners should possess before beginning instruction.

_____ 7. Pretests are used before instruction to indicate students' prior knowledge about what is to be taught as well as their knowledge of prerequisite entry skills.

_____ 8. Criterion-referenced test items are written directly from performance objectives, which in turn are written directly from the skills in an instructional analysis.

Using the instructional analysis diagram that follows, indicate by box number(s) the skills that should be used to develop test items for the:

_____ 9. Entry skills test

_____ 10. Pretest

_____ 11. Posttest

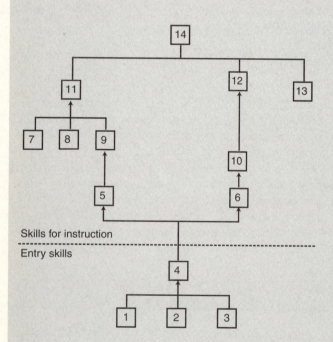

Skills for instruction

Entry skills

Write parallel assessments for performance objectives. On a separate sheet of paper, write a test item or other assessment that is congruent with the conditions, behavior, and content prescribed in each of the following performance objectives on writing composition. Assume the following:

- Your target group consists of average and above-average middle school students.

- The performance and learning contexts are their school classroom and other areas of the school and community where they might be expected to write. In Appendix D students will have access to their teachers and to Blackboard for the instruction and appropriate assessments.

You can use the rubric as an aid to constructing your items and for evaluating those you create.

12. Write a _terminal objective_ for the following: In written composition, use a variety of sentence types and accompanying punctuation based on the _purpose, mood, and complexity_ of the sentence. Sentences will be judged on format for sentence type, punctuation, sentence type by sentence purpose, and sentence variety within paragraphs.

13. Write _performance objectives_ for the following items taken from Appendix D:

5.6 Given the terms _declarative sentence_ and _purpose,_ state the purpose of a declarative sentence. The purpose should include to convey/tell information.

5.7 Given several complete simple sentences that include declarative, interrogative, and exclamatory sentences that are correctly or incorrectly closed using a period, locate all those that are declarative.

5.11 Write declarative sentences on: (1) selected topics and (2) topics of student choice. Sentences must be complete and closed with a period.

14. Develop a test that includes instructions for the learner and evaluation forms for the psychomotor skill of putting a golf ball. The following performance objectives are based on the instructional analysis in Figure 4.6. The test should have two parts, including putting form and putting accuracy. Compare the instructions you write with the ones included in the corresponding item of the Feedback.

Objectives: On a putting green and using a regulation ball and putter:

5.1 Demonstrate good form while putting the golf ball. The body must be relaxed and aligned with the target, and the club must be comfortably gripped at the correct height. The stroke must be the appropriate height, speed, and direction for the target and smoothly executed. The face of the putter should be square throughout the stroke.

6.1 Putt uphill, downhill, and across hill on a sloped putting green; from distances of ten, fifteen, and twenty-five feet; putt accurately enough for the balls to reach a distance of no less than three feet from the cup.

15. Plan a design evaluation, creating a chart with three columns: skills, objectives, and assessments. In addition to the design evaluation chart you construct, what design document will help you determine the congruence of the information in column 1 of your chart? What information will you need to judge the congruence and quality of the information in column 2 of your chart? What information will you need to judge the congruence and quality of the information in column 3 of your chart? How are these various design elements related during the evaluation?

FEEDBACK

1. C
2. C
3. They must measure the behavior in the objective.
4. They are derived from objectives.
5. There may be no entry skills that require testing.
6. C
7. C
8. C
9–11. Generally speaking, performance objectives for which test items should be included are:

   Entry skills: skills 1 through 4

   Pretest: skills 5 through 14

   Posttest: skills 5 through 14

12–13. Compare your test items with those in Appendix E. In addition to these examples, you will want to review the more complete design evaluation chart for writing composition located there.

14. We have provided instructions to learners for the putting exam below and you can also compare the evaluation form you designed with the one contained in Figure 7.4.

Putting Assessment Instructions

The putting exam will consist of two parts: putting form and putting accuracy. You will be required to execute twenty-seven putts for the exam.

Your putting form will be judged throughout the test using the top part of the attached rating sheet. The aspects of your form that will be rated are listed in columns A and B. Your score depends on the number of OKs circled in the column labeled (1). You can receive a total score of ten on putting form if you do not consistently commit any of the mistakes named in the errors column. In the example, the student received a total score of seven. The errors consistently committed were all related to the swing: low backswing and follow-through and slow swing speed.

Your putting accuracy will also be judged on the twenty-seven putts. Nine of the putts will be uphill, nine will be downhill, and nine will be across the hill to the cup. From each area, three putts will be from ten feet, three from fifteen feet, and three from twenty-five feet. Your accuracy score will depend on the proximity of each putt to the cup. Three rings are painted on the green at one-foot intervals from the cup to make a target area. The following points will be awarded for each area:

In cup = 4 points
Within 1 foot = 3 points
Within 2 feet = 2 points
Within 3 feet = 1 point
Outside 3 feet = 0

Balls that land on a ring will be assigned the higher point value. For example, if a ball lands on the one-foot ring, you will receive three points.

Each of your twenty-seven putts will be tallied on the form at the bottom of the sheet. The example is completed to show you how it will be done. Putting uphill from ten feet, the student putted two balls in the cup and another within the one-foot ring. Eleven points $(4 + 4 + 3)$ were earned for putting uphill from ten feet. Look at the fifteen feet across hill section. One putt was within a foot, one was within three feet, and one was outside three feet for a total of four points $(3 + 1 + 0)$. In summing the student's scores, all putts from each distance and from each area are added. For example, the student has a ten-feet score of 27 and an uphill score of 25. The student's overall score is 56.

The following score levels will be used to evaluate your overall putting performance on the test:

Acceptable = 27 or (27×1)
Good = 41 or (27×1.5)
Excellent = 54 or (27×2)
Perfect! = 108 or (27×4)

Before reporting for your test, be sure to warm up by putting for at least fifteen minutes or thirty putts. Remain on the practice greens until you are called for the exam.

15. See Figure 7.5 and the discussion in the text.

figure

7.4

Checklist and Tally for Evaluating Putting Form and Accuracy

Name _____ *Mary Jones* _____ Date ___ *3/26*

	A	B	(1)	Type of Errors			
1.	Body	Comfort	(OK)	TNS			
		Aligned	(OK)	RT	LFT		
2.	Grip	Pressure	(OK)	TNS			
		Height	(OK)	HI	LOW		
3.	Backswing	Height	OK	HI	(LOW)		
		Direction	(OK)	RT	LFT		
4.	Follow-through	Height	OK	HI	(LOW)		
		Direction	(OK)	RT	LFT		
5.	Speed		OK	FST	(SLW)	JKY	
6.	Club face		(OK)	OPN	CLS		

Total **7**

(10)

Putting Accuracy Score

Area:	Uphill					Downhill					Across Hill					Totals
Points:	4	3	2	1	0	4	3	2	1	0	4	3	2	1	0	Totals
10'	//	/					/	/	/		/		/	/		*27*
15'		//	/				/	/	/			/		/	/	*18*
25'	/		/		/		/	/	//				/		//	*11*
Totals		*25*					*18*					*13*				*56*

figure

7.5

Design Elements Gathered and Used in Conducting a Design Evaluation

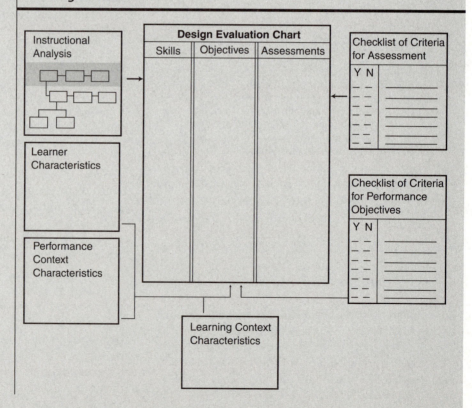

REFERENCES AND RECOMMENDED READINGS

Airasian, P. W. (2007). *Classroom assessment* (6th ed.). New York: McGraw-Hill.

Arter, J. A., & McTighe, J. (2001). *Scoring rubrics in the classroom: Using performance criteria for assessing and improving student performance.* Thousand Oaks, CA: Corwin Press. Integrating assessment with instruction to improve student performance.

Carey, L. M. (2001). *Measuring and evaluating school learning* (3rd ed.). Boston: Pearson. Deriving and writing test items, product, performance, attitude directions and rubrics, and portfolio assessment. Terminology is consistent with this text.

Educational Testing Service, Stiggins, R., Arter, J. A., Chappius, J., & Chappius, S. (2008). *Classroom assessment for student learning: Doing it right—Using it well.* Upper Saddle River, NJ: Prentice Hall.

Educational Testing Service, Arter, J. A., & Chappius, J. (2008). *Creating and recognizing quality rubrics.* Upper Saddle River, NJ: Prentice Hall.

Fishman, J. A. (2003). *Introduction to test construction in the social and behavioral sciences: A practical guide.* Lanham, MD: Rowman & Littlefield. Good perspective on test construction that begins with the end goal as a first consideration in instrument design.

Gagné, R. M., Wager, W. W., Golas, K. C., & Keller, J. M. (2004). *Principles of instructional design* (5th ed.). Belmont, CA: Wadsworth/Thomson Learning. The chapter on assessing student performance includes not only the development of objective-referenced assess-ments, but also the concept of "mastery" and norm-referenced measures.

Kubiszyn, T. (2007). *Educational testing and measurement: Classroom application and practice* (8th ed.). New York: Wiley. Good general textbook on criterion-referenced assessment. Contains information on item writing criteria, developing alternative assessments, and portfolio assessment.

McMillan, J. H. (2007). *Classroom assessment: Principles and practice for effective standards-based instruction* (4th ed.). Boston: Allyn & Bacon.

Miller, M. D., Linn, R. L., & Gronlund, N. E. (2009). *Measurement and assessment in teaching* (10th ed.). Upper Saddle River, NJ: Merrill.

Nitko, A. J., & Brookhart, S. M. (2007). *Educational assessment of students* (4th ed.). Upper Saddle River, NJ: Merrill/Prentice Hall. Good section on assessment of higher-order thinking, problem solving, and critical thinking.

Popham, W. J. (2008). *Classroom assessment: What teachers need to know* (5th ed.). Upper Saddle River, NJ: Prentice Hall.

Shrock, S. A., & Coscarelli, W. C. (2007). *Criterion-referenced test development: Technical and legal guidelines for corporate training* (3rd ed.). San Francisco: Pfeiffer.

Stiggins, R. (2008). *Introduction to student involved assessment for learning* (5th ed.). Upper Saddle River, NJ: Merrill/Prentice Hall.

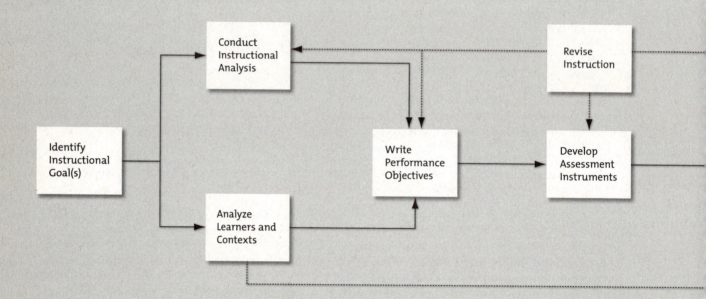

objectives

➤ Describe considerations in selecting an instructional delivery system.

➤ Sequence and arrange content in lesson-level clusters.

➤ Name the five learning components of an instructional strategy and list the primary considerations within each.

➤ Plan the learning components of an instructional strategy, including preinstructional activities, content presentation and learning guidance, learner participation, assessment, and follow-through activities, for a set of objectives for a particular group of learners.

➤ Specify learning components that are congruent with learners' maturity and ability levels and the type of learning outcome.

➤ Select appropriate student groupings and media for the learning components of an instructional strategy.

➤ Consolidate media selections and confirm or select a delivery system.

Developing an Instructional Strategy

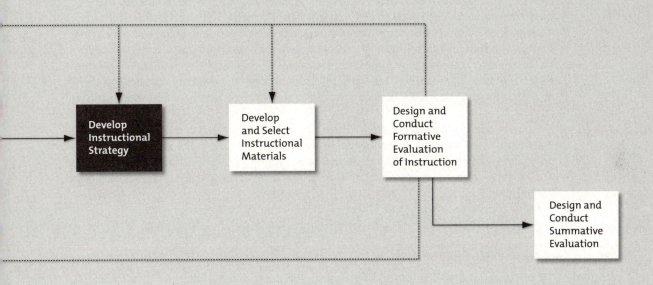

Develop Instructional Strategy	Develop and Select Instructional Materials	Design and Conduct Formative Evaluation of Instruction

Design and Conduct Summative Evaluation

Background

As the title indicates, this chapter addresses the ways that a designer identifies how instruction will be presented to and engage learners. The term *instructional strategy* suggests a huge variety of teaching/learning activities, such as group discussions, independent reading, case studies, lectures, computer simulations, worksheets, cooperative group projects, and so on. These are essentially microstrategies. They are only pieces of an overall macrostrategy that must take learners from a motivational introduction to a topic through learners' mastery of the objectives. To examine the difference between micro- and macrostrategies, consider the format of a typical textbook.

If you have another textbook nearby, pick it up and look it over. In what ways is the book structured to facilitate learning by the reader? The typical text, particularly for adults, has an introduction, a body of information, references, and an index. Sometimes review questions have been prepared and appear at the end of the chapters, or test items may be included in an instructor's manual. In essence, a textbook is a microstrategy that serves primarily as a source of information and, as such, is incomplete instruction. The macroinstructional strategy (the complete instruction) is usually created by an instructor who must do nearly everything to bring about learning: define the objectives, write the lesson plan and tests, motivate the learners, present the content, engage the students as active participants in the learning process, and administer and score the assessments.

A well-designed set of instructional materials contains many of the strategies or procedures that a good teacher might normally use with a group of learners. When designing instruction, it is necessary to develop an instructional strategy that employs, to the degree possible, the knowledge we have about facilitating the learning process.

Educational psychologists have conducted much research over the past seventy-five years to determine how people learn. If you have read any of this research, you may feel that it often seems esoteric and generally removed from real-life learning situations. Psychologists have been successful, however, in identifying several major components in the learning process that, when present, almost always facilitate learning. Three of these components are motivation, prerequisite and subordinate skills, and practice and feedback.

Many of the psychologists whose work influenced the original approaches to instructional design thirty to forty years ago were behaviorists. Some behaviorist views were later modified by cognitive explanations of learning, with corresponding modifications and amplifications to the instructional design process. More recently, constructivists have made telling criticisms of instructional practices for higher-order learning and suggested new approaches. Several of their ideas are reflected in later sections of this chapter. The model used in this text can be viewed as a generic process in which experienced designers can accommodate a variety of psychological points of view.

In this chapter, procedures will be described that can be used to design an instructional strategy for different types of instructional objectives. In the next chapter you will be shown how this instructional strategy applies directly to the selection or development of instructional materials and the development of classroom procedures.

Concepts

The instructional design steps we have covered in previous chapters have basically dealt with the question of what to teach. With that now determined, we turn to the question of how to teach it. The term *instructional strategy* is used generally to cover the various aspects of choosing a delivery system, sequencing and grouping clusters of content, describing learning components that will be included in the instruction, specifying how students will be grouped during instruction, establishing lesson structures, and selecting media for delivering instruction. Each of these pieces of an instructional strategy will be defined and described in turn through the rest of this chapter.

Selection of a Delivery System

In any kind of formal educational experience, there is usually a general methodology that is used for managing and delivering the teaching and learning activities that we call *instruction*. This general methodology is referred to as the *delivery system*. Delivery systems and instructional strategies are not synonymous. A delivery system is only part of an overall instructional strategy, and novice instructional designers must guard against being seduced by flashy technologies and ending up ascribing far too much weight to how instruction is packaged and delivered at the expense of the careful planning of the teaching–learning activities that should be included in the instruction. The delivery system is either an assumption that the designer takes into the development of an instructional strategy, or it is an active decision that is made as part of developing an instructional strategy. In either case, choosing a delivery system can be either a lesson-level, course-level, or curriculum-level management decision.

The best way to define *delivery system* more precisely is through a list of examples. The following are a few examples of common delivery systems (mixed in with some instructional methods) for conducting instruction:

- Traditional model—instructor with group of learners in classroom, training center, or lab
- Large-group lecture with small-group question and answer follow-up
- Telecourse by broadcast, webcast, or two-way interactive videoconference
- Computer-based instruction
  - Can range from independent study to instructor-facilitated
  - Can range from textual drill and practice to fully interactive multimedia
  - Can include simulation, gaming, intelligent tutoring, and virtual reality
- Internet or intranet web-based instruction
  - Can range from independent study to instructor-facilitated
  - Can range from textual drill and practice to fully interactive multimedia
  - Can range from a simple online syllabus to a comprehensive solution organized within a learning portal that includes content, instruction, interaction, and assessment
- Self-paced (sometimes open-entry, open-exit) programs that include a variety of combinations of instructor or tutor and print or mediated learning
- Site-based internship and mentoring
- Electronic performance support ranging from simple, searchable job aids to contextually sensitive smart systems
- Combinations and unique, custom systems

In an ideal instructional design process, one would first consider the goal, learner characteristics, learning and performance contexts, objectives, and assessment requirements, and then work through the following considerations and decisions to arrive at the selection of the best delivery system:

1. Review the instructional analysis and identify logical clusters of objectives that will be taught in appropriate sequences.
2. Plan the learning components that will be used in the instruction.
3. Choose the most effective student groupings for learning.
4. Specify effective media and materials that are within the range of cost, convenience, and practicality for the learning context.
5. Assign objectives to lessons and consolidate media selections.
6. Select or develop a delivery system that best accommodates the decisions made in steps 1 through 5.

This represents an ideal path for choosing a delivery system because the choice is based on careful consideration of needs and requirements before a solution is named. In this view, selecting a delivery system (step 6) is an output of the process of careful deliberation about teaching/learning requirements (steps 2–5). Reversing the sequence and choosing a delivery system first would impose a solution (and its inherent constraints) before the requirements for delivering effective instruction are fully known.

There are three considerations to note about this ideal path to choosing a delivery system. First is that it almost never happens this way! One reason is that instructors and instructional designers often have preferred modes of course delivery, so in their minds the delivery system has been chosen before the instructional design process has even begun. A second reason is that the delivery system can be dictated by the learning context in which the organization delivers its instruction. The designer is typically required to work within this context, changing it only slightly for any given course or workshop. If the designer is working within a public school context, then the assumption may be that the teacher in a traditional classroom setting will be the delivery system. The same assumption can be made regarding training in business and industry that still is, for the most part, instructor-led platform instruction, in spite of the increase in business training that now assumes web delivery at the outset. A third reason is the increasingly common situation in which new delivery systems such as proprietary software for e-learning portals have been purchased and installed and the designer is told that this system will be used for the delivery of instruction, often in an attempt to justify the purchase of the system. Now that Internet (and in some settings intranet) access is ubiquitous and web technology has advanced so rapidly, it is often chosen a priori as the delivery system when distribution of instruction to the home or desktop is desired across time and distance. When such preestablished situations prevail, as they usually do, the designer must be flexible and get everything out of the system that it is capable of delivering. If there is a mismatch between the skills to be taught and the system specified for delivering the instruction, then the designer must make appropriate adaptations or make the case and propose an alternative system. Figure 8.1 graphically depicts the development of an instructional strategy that distinguishes between assuming a delivery system at the outset of the process as opposed to selecting a delivery system as a logical conclusion of the process.

A second consideration to note about the previously described ideal approach to selecting a delivery system is that the numbering 1 through 6 gives the appearance of a linear, stepwise sequence, when in fact steps 2, 3, and 4 are frequently considered at the same time. For example you may decide that a practice and feedback sequence is required for student mastery (step 2). While specifying that activity you would also be deciding that it would be most effective to do the practice and feedback in small groups of three to five learners (step 3) with three different scenarios prerecorded on a video (step 4). The parallel nature of these three steps is illustrated in Figure 8.1. Discussion will continue later in this chapter about putting together these pieces of an instructional strategy.

A final note is that the systems design model you are using is equally applicable whether the delivery system is chosen earlier or later in the process, and the generic instructional design steps that you are taking in this model are as relevant for a print-based correspondence delivery system as for a digital, interactive multimedia delivery system. We have included this discussion of selecting delivery systems at this point in the instructional strategy because it is where it usually happens in practice. The discussion will be reintroduced later in this chapter at the point where specifying media and selecting delivery systems would ideally occur.

Content Sequencing and Clustering

Content Sequence   The first step in developing an instructional strategy is identifying a teaching sequence and manageable groupings of content. What sequence should you follow in presenting content to the learner? The most useful tool in determining the answer to this question is your instructional analysis. You would begin with the lower-level skills, that is, those just above the line that separates the entry skills from the skills to be taught and then progress up through the hierarchy. At no point would you present information on a particular hierarchical skill prior to having done so for all related subordinate skills.

The instructional sequence for a goal would, of course, logically be sequenced from the left, or the beginning point, and proceed to the right. If there are subordinate capabilities for any of the major steps, then they would be taught prior to going on to the next major component.

Because the goal analysis indicates each step that must be performed, and the subordinate skills analysis indicates the skills that must be acquired prior to learning the major steps in the goal, the instructional sequence tends to be a combination of bottom to top and left to right. That is, the subordinate skills for step 1 are taught first,

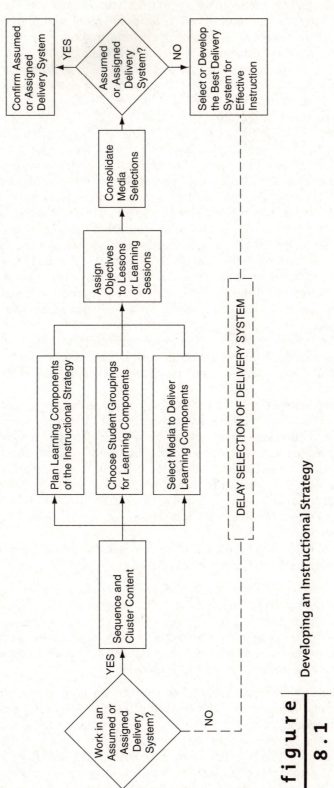

figure

8.1 Developing an Instructional Strategy

then step 1. Next the subordinate skills for step 2 are taught, then step 2 itself. This sequence is continued until all the steps are taught. Finally, there is instruction on integrating and practicing all the steps in the instructional goal. See Figure 4.10 (p. 84) for an example of this approach. The boxes are numbered in the sequence in which they would be taught, beginning at the bottom, and working up to each major step.

There are three exceptions to this general approach to sequencing. The first occurs when two or more steps in a goal are the same and/or have the same subordinate skills. In this situation, it is not necessary to teach these skills again. The learner can simply be informed that a skill that has been previously learned will be used again at this point in the procedure.

A second exception to the general sequencing approach is when the instruction includes the use of several pieces of equipment or the parts of a single piece of equipment. The instructional analysis may indicate that the learner will be required, for example, to be able to identify and locate various pieces of equipment at various points in the instruction. To avoid having to go back and forth to make identifications, it is usually both possible and desirable to present all of this instruction at the beginning of your unit. Similarly, it is sometimes desirable to present all the lower-level verbal information objectives, such as definitions, at one time at the beginning of the instruction. Use caution when doing this because you may be removing the context required to make the definitions meaningful. It may also make it more difficult for learners to store the information in memory and to retrieve it using contextual cues. Learners may also think that learning verbal information out of context is irrelevant and boring.

A third exception is when boredom would result from a predictable, tedious, step-by-step sequence. If this would be the result, it is better to sacrifice some of the efficiency of the ideal sequence and break it up to sustain interest and motivation.

Clustering Instruction   The next question in your instructional strategy deals with the size of the cluster of material you will provide in your instruction. At one extreme of the continuum is the linear programmed-instruction approach, which tends to break all the information down into very small units and requires constant responding by the learner. At the other extreme of the continuum is the conventional textbook in which a chapter is usually the unit of information. You may decide that you will present your information on an objective-by-objective basis with intervening activities, or you may wish to present the information on several objectives prior to any kind of learner activity.

You should consider the following five factors when determining the amount of information to be presented (or the size of the "cluster"):

1. The age level of your learners
2. The complexity of the material
3. The type of learning taking place
4. Whether the activity can be varied, thereby focusing attention on the task
5. The amount of time required to include all the events in the instructional strategy for each cluster of content presented

For example, how much time will be required for informing learners of the prerequisites, presenting content, and providing practice? For younger children it is almost always advisable to keep the instruction, and the clusters within it, relatively small. More mature learners will be able to handle larger clusters of content. Regardless of the age of the learners, when content is varied with performance and feedback activities, the learners do not seem to tire of the activity as quickly.

The designer is often faced with clustering instruction into two- or three-day workshops or semester-long courses. How much goes into a half-day or a day? The nature of the delivery system will make a big difference. With self-instructional formats, such as stand-alone computer-based instruction and typical e-learning, the designer need not worry about exact time constraints. The nature of these systems allows time to vary among learners; however, instructor-led, group process, and television or webcast approaches, for example, require accurate time estimates, and there are no magic formulas for predicting time requirements. Develop a typical segment of instruction and try it out to estimate how long a total course or workshop might take. If timing is an important issue, then do not wait until all of the instruction is developed to estimate how much time is required to deliver it.

Learning Components of Instructional Strategies

An instructional strategy describes the general components of a set of instructional materials and the procedures that will be used with those materials to enable student mastery of learning outcomes. You should note that an instructional strategy is more than a simple outline of the content that will be presented to the learner. For example, it would be insufficient to say that, in order to have students learn how to add two-digit numbers, you would first teach them single-digit numbers without carrying and then present the main concept of adding two-digit numbers. This is certainly a part of an instructional strategy and refers to content sequencing and clustering, but this says nothing about what you will do before you present that content, what learners will do with that content, or how it will be tested or transferred to a performance context.

The concept of an instructional strategy originated with the events of instruction described in Gagné's *Conditions of Learning* (1985). In this cognitive psychologist's view, nine events represent external instructional activities that support internal mental processes of learning:

1. Gaining attention
2. Informing learner of the objective
3. Stimulating recall of prerequisite learning
4. Presenting the stimulus material
5. Providing learning guidance
6. Eliciting the performance
7. Providing feedback about performance correctness
8. Assessing the performance
9. Enhancing retention and transfer

Gagné's fifth event, providing learning guidance, has specific meaning within his system of instructional prescriptions for different domains of learning outcomes, but in a general sense, it is useful to think of all of the instructional events as forms of learning guidance. Learning is internal, occurring in the mind of the learner, and the purpose for developing an instructional strategy is planning how to guide learners' intellectual processing through the mental states and activities that psychologists have shown will foster learning. Gagné's cognitive view of instruction is often characterized as quite purposeful and prescriptive, more teacher-centered than student-centered. The Dick and Carey model is based on this cognitive perspective, and we teach it in this text for several reasons:

- It is grounded in learning theory.
- It conforms to currently prevailing views of instruction in public education (standards-based accountability), higher education accreditation (outcomes assessment), and business/industry/military training (performance-based).
- It is a necessary foundational system of instructional design for new students of the field and the most intuitive system to learn.

Later in this chapter, after working through the cognitive approach to ID, we will offer our view of blending constructivist learning environments with more prescriptive strategies.

To facilitate the instructional design process, we have organized Gagné's events of instruction into five major learning components that are part of an overall instructional strategy:

1. Preinstructional activities
2. Content presentation
3. Learner participation
4. Assessment
5. Follow-through activities

We will briefly describe each of these components and then provide detailed examples of how strategies could be developed for goals in each domain of learning.

Preinstructional Activities   Prior to beginning formal instruction, you should consider three factors. These factors include motivating the learners, informing them of what they will learn, and stimulating recall of relevant knowledge and skills that they already should know.

Motivating Learners.   One of the typical criticisms of instruction is its lack of interest and appeal to the learner. One instructional designer who attempts to deal with this problem in a systematic way is John Keller (1987), who developed the ARCS model based on his review of the psychological literature on motivation. The four parts of his model are <u>A</u>ttention, <u>R</u>elevance, <u>C</u>onfidence, and <u>S</u>atisfaction. In order to produce instruction that motivates the learner, these four attributes of the instruction must be considered throughout the design of the instructional strategy.

The first aspect of motivation is to gain the attention of learners and subsequently sustain it throughout the instruction. Learners must attend to a task in order to learn to perform it. Their initial attention can be gained by using emotional or personal information, asking questions, creating mental challenges, and perhaps the best method of all, using human-interest examples.

According to Keller, the second aspect of motivation is relevance. Although you may be able to gain learners' attention for a short period of time, it will be difficult to sustain when they do not perceive the subsequent instruction as relevant to them. When instruction is thought irrelevant, learners ask, "Why do we have to study this?" and employees question the relationship between training and their jobs. When you use information from the learner and context analyses (Chapter 5) to help learners understand the relevance of the skills included in instruction, you will sustain their motivation; if not, you undoubtedly will lose them. In other words, instruction must be related to important goals in the learners' lives.

The third major component of the ARCS model is confidence. For learners to be highly motivated, they must be confident that they can master the objectives for the instruction. If they lack confidence, then they will be less motivated. Learners who are overconfident are also problematic; they see no need to attend to the instruction because they already know it all. The challenge with under- and overconfident learners is to create the appropriate level of expectation for success. Learners who lack confidence must be convinced that they have the skills and knowledge to be successful, whereas overconfident learners must be convinced that there are important details in the instruction that remain to be learned. On the other hand, if learners have, in fact, already mastered the instruction, they should be given more advanced instruction that more nearly meets the four aspects of the ARCS model.

The final component of Keller's model is satisfaction. High motivation depends on whether the learner derives satisfaction from the learning experience. Some would refer to this as reinforcement. Sometimes satisfaction is sustained through the use of *extrinsic* rewards for successful performance such as free time, a high grade, a promotion in the workplace, or some other form of recognition. Of greater importance is the *intrinsic* satisfaction a learner can gain by mastering a new skill and being able to use it successfully. Self-esteem can be greatly enhanced through meaningful learning experiences.

When taken alone, any of the four aspects of Keller's model may not be sufficient to keep a learner on task in a learning situation. When you can incorporate all four—attention, relevance, confidence, and satisfaction—into your strategy, the likelihood of maintaining the learners' interest is greatly increased.

There is a direct relationship between the five main learning components of the instructional strategy and the four aspects of motivation included in Keller's ARCS model. This relationship is illustrated in Figure 8.2. Following exposure to each component of the instruction, learners can ask themselves three questions. The first question relates to the relevance of the content presented or activity performed. If the materials are perceived as relevant to personal needs and interests, then attention is gained and maintained. The second relates to how confident they are that they can be successful. If they understand the material and are confident that they will be successful, then motivation is sustained. The third question relates to how satisfied they are that the content presented and activities provided meet their needs. If they are satisfied with each component, then motivation is maintained.

In designing the instructional strategy, we must devise ways to present each component to help ensure that learners continue to answer the three questions affirmatively. In order to do this, we can use the content from the learner analysis. We must understand their needs, interests, and performance levels well enough to infer how *they* will perceive the content and activities. In designing each learning component of the instructional strategy for the goal, designers should ask, "How does this relate to the learners' needs and interests and to their feelings of confidence and satisfaction?"

The most important aspect of maintaining learners' perceptions of relevance appears to be the congruence between the learners' expectations and the instruction they encounter. For example, the initial motivating material must be congruent with the learners' perceptions of their needs and interests. What material would best meet learners' initial expectations and hook them into the instruction? If you judge that the congruence of the material in any component would not be immediately obvious to the learner, then devise ways to illustrate the congruence so that they will perceive

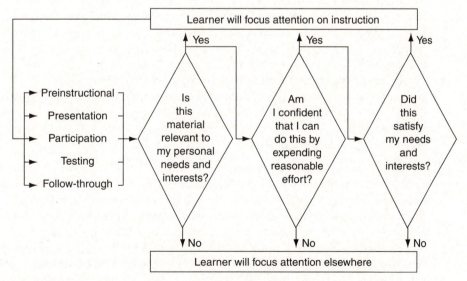

figure

8.2

The Relationship between Each Major Component of Instruction and ARCS

it as relevant. Problems will result when learners fail to see the relationships among their initial expectations, the content presented, the examples described, the practice activities provided, and the test questions administered.

As you develop the subsequent sections of your strategy, continued in the following pages, you will want to continue to be aware of motivational concerns. For example, you will want to present the objectives so that the learners perceive them as achievable instead of overwhelming. A list of thirty or forty technically worded objectives would be likely to shatter the learners' confidence. A list of three or four global objectives written in the learners' language would tend to build confidence. Learners who are sure that they have previously mastered all prerequisites will be more confident than those who doubt their skill and knowledge.

Learners will have an immediate reaction to the volume of material presented initially; are learners more likely to feel comfortable and confident or overwhelmed with the amount of material you have chosen? Considering practice exercises, are learners likely to succeed on those you have provided and thus gain confidence in themselves? Has enough instruction preceded the practice for learners to be successful? You should also consider how learners will perceive pretests in deciding whether it is advisable to administer one. Will pretests demonstrate competence in the skills to be learned or create doubt and insecurity instead?

Learner satisfaction is the third general area of consideration. Will learners be rewarded for learning the skills? Will they consider the proposed rewards as adequate for the amount of effort required? Should you provide additional content to point out potential rewards? On your practice exercises, are they likely to succeed and thus gain intrinsic feelings of satisfaction and accomplishment? Are they likely to perceive the feedback you have designed as verification of their success or as criticism? After they complete your posttest, are they likely to be satisfied with their progress? Will they perceive the effort they had to expend as justified by what they learned? Will they believe that the promises you made in the preinstructional materials were realized? Will they feel that they can do something better? If they believed that the rewards would be forthcoming, yet the rewards failed to materialize, then your task in motivating them for a subsequent unit undoubtedly will be more difficult. Remember that the most powerful, long-lasting rewards are intrinsic feelings of accomplishment that are relevant to a learner's own internal system of values.

Informing the Learner of the Objectives. The second component of the preinstructional activities is to inform the learners of the objectives for the instruction. Have you ever studied a text and wondered which key concepts you should be learning? If you had been informed of the objectives, then you would have known what to memorize, to solve, or to interpret.

By providing learners with the objectives, you help them focus their study strategies on these outcomes. They should not feel they are responsible for "knowing everything" but rather for being able to do certain specific things. Not only does this information help learners to use more efficient study strategies, but it also helps them determine the relevance of the instruction.

Stimulating Recall of Prerequisite Skills. The third preinstructional component is informing learners of the prerequisite skills required to begin your instruction, first as a quick reality check to make sure that learners get an initial view of the relationship between the new content and what they already know. This can be done either by briefly testing learners on entry skills and requiring demonstrated mastery before continuing or by briefly describing required entry skills and telling learners that instruction will proceed on the assumption that they can perform these skills. Informing learners of prerequisites prepares them for the instruction that is to follow. If a test is used, it provides designers with information on the variability of students' entry skills, which helps an instructor plan remediation and interpret student achievement in the new instruction.

The second, and more important, purpose for this component is to promote learners' active recall of relevant mental contexts in which the new content can be integrated. In fact, all three preinstructional activities, taken together, can be viewed as the important first step in activating the mental processing that will enable learners to tie what they are learning with what they already know. This linking of new with old makes initial learning easier and eventual recall more successful.

Content Presentation and Learning Guidance   The next step is to determine exactly what information, concepts, rules, and principles need to be presented to the learner. This is the basic explanation of what the unit is all about. Content presentation usually follows one of two general patterns—deductive or inductive. In the deductive pattern, a textbook, an instructor, or mediated materials show the learner how to distinguish the pieces of new learning and the structural relationships among the pieces in order to put them all together into a coherent whole. The inductive pattern is most associated with discovery learning in which students are guided, or guide themselves, through experiences from which they glean the pieces of new learning and the structural relationships needed to build the coherent whole. If we consider those in our lives whom we consider to be good teachers, we can usually see how they were able to blend deductive and inductive patterns in their instruction.

Content presentation is always interwoven with *learning guidance,* which concerns formatting new content in ways that help us "get it" and remember it when needed in the future. A textbook contains the simplest example of learning guidance in the way text is laid out with section headings, subheadings, paragraph headings, bulleted lists, and so forth. This embedded outline is our cue to the structure of the content and makes it easier to learn and remember. It is important not only to introduce new content but also to explain its structure and interrelationships with other content. Making learning more memorable by depicting structure and relationships can be accomplished in many ways—outlining (as in the textbook example), diagramming, modeling (two-dimensional representations and three-dimensional real objects), illustrating with still and motion graphics, highlighting, flowcharting, talking through progressive levels of abstraction, ranking by size, importance, or complexity, and so forth.

Another common form of learning guidance is the use of examples. You will need to determine the types and number of examples you will provide with the new content. Many research studies have investigated how we use examples and nonexamples to learn new skills. A nonexample is a deliberate attempt by the designer to point out why a particular example is wrong. We know that learning is facilitated by the use of examples and nonexamples, so, generally, they should be included in your instructional strategy. In a later section we will consider, in more detail, what learning guidance should be included in content presentation and learner participation for objectives in different domains of learning. Throughout this and following chapters, we will use the term *content presentation* to mean the totality of what is to be learned along with relevant learning guidance in the form of examples and nonexamples, illustrations, diagrams, demonstrations, model solutions, scenarios, case studies, sample performances, and so on. It is important to remember that the primary error in this step is to present too much content, especially when much of it is unrelated to the objective.

Learner Participation   One of the most powerful components in the learning process is that of practice with feedback. You can enhance the learning process greatly by providing learners with activities that are directly relevant to the objectives, giving learners an opportunity to practice what you want them to be able to do. One approach is to embed practice tests (as described in Chapter 7) into the instruction. The more common approach is to provide informal opportunities within the instruction for students to "try out" what they are learning at the time that they are learning it.

Not only should learners be able to practice, but they should also be provided feedback or information about their performance. Feedback is sometimes referred to as *knowledge of results*. For simple learning tasks students can be told whether their answer is right or wrong or can be shown a copy of the right answer or an example from which they must infer whether their answer is correct. For more complex learning tasks students can also be told why their practice work is right or wrong, and guidance can be provided to help them understand, learn, and correct their work. Feedback may also be provided in the form of reinforcement. For adult learners, knowledge of correct completion of a task is often the best reinforcement and can be accompanied by positive statements such as "Great, you are correct." Young children often respond favorably to forms of reinforcement such as an approving look from the teacher in classroom instruction, pop-up animations and audio flourishes in multimedia instruction, recognition in front of peers, special privileges, or the opportunity to do some other activity.

When the learning components are chosen, it is typical to provide content, examples, practice, and feedback for each objective in the instructional analysis. Sometimes, it is more efficient and appropriate to combine several objectives into a cluster in order to provide more integrated content, examples, and practice with feedback. The decision to cluster the objectives is a subjective one, made by the designer based on knowledge of both the content and the learners. When it is an inappropriate decision, it will become apparent during the formative evaluations.

The learning components chosen for teaching each objective should include components for the terminal objective. It cannot be assumed that just because you have taught each objective in your analysis that learners will be able to integrate all of the skills and information to perform the terminal objective. The final element of your content and learner participation should be a summary of all of the instruction. It is structured like any other objective; namely there is a summary of the content that has been presented and examples of how to perform the terminal objective. Then the learner is given the opportunity to do a sample activity that includes the terminal objective and to receive feedback on the activity. When that is done, the learner will then complete the assessment described in the next section.

Assessment   Four basic criterion-referenced tests were described in Chapter 7: entry skills tests, pretests, practice tests, and posttests. The general function of each was described as well as how to develop them. At this point you must decide exactly what your strategy as a designer will be for assessing what learners have accomplished. This strategy may differ significantly from that which is eventually chosen by an instructor who uses your completed instruction.

First, you know that you will be using practice tests of some sort as part of the learner participation component of your instruction; then you must decide the following:

- Will I test entry skills? When will the assessment be administered?
- Will I have a pretest over the skills to be taught? When will it be administered? Exactly what skills will be assessed?
- When and how will I administer the posttest?

A careful distinction needs to be made here between *developing draft materials* in preparation for formative evaluation and *producing materials in their final form* after formative evaluation and revision. The draft form of your instruction developed at this stage may be "test heavy," because you want to be able to locate missing entry skills and track student performance carefully to pinpoint ineffective sequences in the instruction.

In addition to the formal testing that has been described, the designer may want to consider using embedded attitude questions, which indicate learners' opinions of the instruction at the time that they encountered it. For example, rather than wait until the end of the unit of instruction to ask general questions about the quality of the illustrations, ask questions during the instruction about the illustrations just presented. These attitude or opinion questions can be physically located directly in self-paced instruction or included in unit guides. Later, after formative evaluation and revision, the embedded attitude questions would probably be removed from the instruction and the overall testing strategy would become "leaner."

What types of attitude items are most helpful? Items that are as specific as possible will provide the most information to the designer when the time comes to do the formative evaluation. The questions could refer to such aspects of the instruction as the clarity of a specific example or illustration, the sufficiency of a set of practice problems, or the general interest level of the content.

Sometimes there will be parts of the instruction in which the designer uses a special procedure or approach—either from a content or a pedagogical point of view. At these points in the instruction, the designer can insert very specific questions about learners' reactions to what has been done. This approach does not seem to be disruptive to the learners but instead provides on-the-spot specific reactions to the instruction rather than the general reactions that are often received on a questionnaire administered at the end of an instructional unit. The end-of-unit questions can help the designer obtain an overall reaction to the instruction, but the embedded attitude questions will provide more precise, targeted information.

Follow-Through Activities   The final learning component in the instructional strategy, follow-through, is a review of the entire strategy to determine whether learner memory and transfer needs have been addressed. These questions can be answered first by reviewing the performance context analysis, which should describe the conditions under which the learners will have to perform the instructional goal.

Memory Skills.   Consider what learners will be doing when performing the instructional goal and consider what they will have to recall from memory. Is there anything that must absolutely be retrieved from memory? Must it be done rapidly and without prompts or reference materials? If so, then many of the techniques suggested later in this chapter for teaching verbal information are critical for inclusion in the instructional strategy.

Often the answer to the question of what learners need to remember is that memorization is not critical, just as long as they carry out the skill successfully. If this is the case with your goal, then you might want to consider the use of a job aid. A job aid is any device that is used by the performers to reduce their reliance on their memory to perform a task. For example, could the learner follow a checklist while performing the task? If so, this would greatly reduce the need to memorize a lot of information and could possibly reduce the length of the instruction.

Transfer of Learning.   The second question to ask about your instructional goal is "What is the nature of the transfer of learning that will have to take place?" That is, "How different will the performance context be from the learning context?" Let's look at two somewhat extreme examples to make our case.

Suppose the instructional goal is to use a new computer application program, and it is taught in the training center on computers that are identical to those used in the workplace. During the training, learners work with actual forms used in their department while learning to use the application. It is expected that the learners will use the new application after they have completed their training.

From our description, it can be assumed that if the training is well designed, then there should be 100 percent transfer to the workplace. Transfer will occur because the systems and the application will be the same, and the forms will be similar to those used in training. The remaining components in the transfer context are the installation of the application on the learners' computers and the support environment established by their managers for learners' successful use of the new application.

Now consider a situation in which the instructional goal is to become effective participants in employee quality-improvement teams. The employees to be trained are from different divisions within the company; have various types of expertise, levels of education, commitment to the company, and attitudes about their supervisors; and face diverse problems in their respective divisions.

A situation like this requires careful consideration of the transfer of skills learned during training. First of all, it is assumed that the designer has been able to determine the steps that lead to effective participation on a team. The content and examples should draw on a variety of situations from various parts of the company. The learners should receive ample opportunities to practice working on a team that seeks new solutions to troublesome problems. Unfortunately, the trainer will not be able to create practice situations that exactly match the job conditions, because people mixes on quality-improvement teams will vary, as will the nature of the problems. Will the learners be praised for using their new skills? Will anyone even notice them? Will they have the desired effect in terms of increasing the effectiveness of the teams?

Research indicates that, in general, learners transfer only some of what they learn to new contexts (Schunk, 2004). Learning tends to be situation-specific. The designer must therefore be aware of the tendency of learning not to transfer and to use every means possible to counter this tendency. Broad and Newstrom (2001) have reviewed the literature on transfer and organized it in terms of what the trainer, the manager, and the learner can do to increase the probability that transfer will occur.

In addition to making the training and performance as similar as possible, it is also very helpful to require learners to develop a plan that indicates how they will use their new skills in the transfer context. The plan should include a list of possible problems the learner may have and suggestions for how these can be overcome. Commitment to the plan and periodic review of the plan will help to remind the learner of the skills that were learned and how they can be used.

Transfer of training from the classroom to the performance site is emerging as one of the most critical concerns of educators and trainers. No longer is end-of-instruction posttest performance considered the major criterion by which instructional effectiveness will be judged. Instruction is effective if learners can use it to further their study of more advanced topics or to perform skills on the job that make a difference in their organization's effectiveness. If these criteria are not met, then there are serious questions about the need for the instruction. Was it the wrong instruction, was it not taught effectively, were learners not motivated, or did it simply not transfer to the performance site? When we examine instruction that does not work, we can find potential problems at a variety of points in the instructional design process—from the needs assessment to the strategy for promoting transfer of learning.

Summary of Learning Components   The learning components of a complete instructional strategy are summarized below in their typical chronological sequence.

A. Preinstructional activities
   1. Gain attention and motivate learners
   2. Describe objectives
   3. Describe and promote recall of prerequisite skills
B. Content presentation
   1. Content
   2. Learning guidance
C. Learner participation
   1. Practice
   2. Feedback
D. Assessment
   1. Entry skills test
   2. Pretest
   3. Posttest

E. Follow-through activities
   1. Memory aids for retention
   2. Transfer considerations

Note that components B and C are repeated for each instructional objective or cluster of objectives. Components B and C are also repeated in summary form for the terminal objective. Components A and D are repeated selectively as needed for objectives or clusters of objectives based on the content, lesson length, flow of the instruction, needs of learners, and so forth.

Learning Components for Learners of Different Maturity and Ability Levels

Before beginning a discussion of instructional strategies for various learning outcomes we will take a moment to consider different learners' needs for instructional strategies. First, recall that the learning components of an instructional strategy are intended to guide learners' intellectual processing through the mental states and activities that foster learning. Ideally, all learners could manage their own intellectual processing; that is, they would be independent learners or we could say that they had "learned how to learn." Indeed, this is an outcome of schooling that is now found in many mission statements for public, private, elementary, secondary, and postsecondary educational institutions.

This ideal exists, to a lesser or greater extent, in all of us. Generally speaking, younger students and less able students cannot manage their learning processes as well as older students and more able students. There is thus a greater need to provide the former the learning components in an instructional strategy, whereas older students and more able students can provide many of their own learning components. The learning components of an instructional strategy should be planned selectively rather than being provided slavishly for all learners in all instructional settings. Instruction for a first-grade student learning the concept of fractions should include all learning components. In contrast, a one-day in-service seminar for electrical engineers on the latest materials for circuit boards might include only content presentation with examples, practice, and feedback in the form of live question and answer discussion sessions. In this situation, a transfer activity might be conducted after the seminar in work group problem discussions using groupware on the company intranet. The intent in planning instructional strategies should be to match learning components with the amount of guidance needed by the intended learners.

This same consideration is critical when designing instruction for distance students. Moore and Kearsley's (1996) theory of transactional distance is a "pedagogical" theory to be used as guidance for developing a distance course that will meet the needs of the intended student population. The implications of the theory are illustrated in Table 8.1; that is, more autonomous distance learners can manage greater transactional distance, thus requiring less course structure and course dialogue (meaning student interaction) for an effective course experience. The opposite is true for less autonomous learners. It can be seen that one would not provide a low-structure, low-dialogue course for students who are not self-directed. On the other hand, any combination of structure and dialogue can work quite well for independent learners. Structure makes intellectual content acquisition manageable and predictable whereas dialogue personalizes the student's experience and facilitates learner participation. Although not synonymous with our description of learning components, it is clear that course structure and dialogue are important vehicles for carrying the learning components of an instructional strategy. The value of course structure and learner interaction is supported in studies of distance learning students' perceptions of what works for them in distance courses (Moore & Kearsley, 1996).

table 8.1	The Structure and Dialogue Dimensions of Moore and Kearsley's Theory of Transactional Distance			
	Level of Course Structure	**Level of Course Dialogue**	**Transactional Distance**	**Suitability for Learner Autonomy Level**
	Low: a flexible course in which student has control of course management	*Low:* little interactive communication with the instructor	*Greater*	Highly autonomous learner
	↕	↕	↕	↕
	High: a rigid course in which student conforms to a detailed course structure	*High:* lots of interactive communication and guidance from instructor (or through tutor, classmate, course materials, computer, etc.)	*Lesser*	Less autonomous learner who has not "learned how to learn" *or* Any range of learner autonomy up to and including the most independent learner

Learning Components for Various Learning Outcomes

The basic learning components of an instructional strategy are the same regardless of whether you are designing instruction for an intellectual skill, verbal information, a motor skill, or an attitude. They can thus be used as an organizing structure for your design. Within each component, however, there are distinctions you should consider for each type of learning outcome. These are noted in the sections that follow. Developing strategies to help ensure that material is motivational is omitted from this discussion because it was presented earlier in this chapter.

Intellectual Skills   Each of the five learning components should be considered when designing instruction for intellectual skills.

Preinstructional Activities. In addition to considering motivation, informing the learner of objectives, and promoting recall of prerequisites, the designer should be aware of both the way learners may have organized their entry knowledge in memory and the limits of their ability to remember new content. The strategy should provide ways for the learner to link new content to existing prerequisite knowledge in memory. When the links may not be obvious to the learner, direct instruction about the links and relationships between existing knowledge and new skills should be provided.

Content Presentation and Learning Guidance. In presenting content for intellectual skills, it is important to recall the hierarchical nature of intellectual skills in determining the sequence for presentation. Subordinate skills should always come first. It is also important to point out the distinguishing characteristics of concepts that make up rules, which may include physical characteristics or role and relationship characteristics. It is also important to focus learners' attention on irrelevant characteristics that may be present, as well as on common errors that learners make in distinguishing among concepts or in applying rules. These "prompts," however, must eventually disappear from instruction in ill-defined problem solving, because the nature of this type of learning requires that students be able to make their own decisions about the relevance and interrelatedness of various components of the problem being solved.

In selecting examples and nonexamples of a concept, the designer should select both clear and questionable examples and nonexamples to illustrate gross and fine distinctions. Direct information about why the examples fit or do not fit the definition may need to be provided. You should also ensure that the examples and illustrations selected are familiar to the learner. Teaching an unknown using an unfamiliar example unnecessarily increases the complexity of the skill for the learner; thus, you should select instances and examples likely to be contained in the learner's experience and memory. To enhance transfer, you could progress from familiar examples to less familiar ones and to new instances. When students are learning to solve ill-defined problems, the new examples will usually take the form of case studies, problem scenarios, and student-selected examples that can be carried over into practice and feedback activities.

The strategy should also provide the learner with ways of organizing new skills so they can be stored along with relevant existing knowledge and thus be recalled more easily. This is particularly critical when students are learning to solve ill-structured problems for which they must "pull together" and synthesize a range of new and old learning to develop solution strategies.

Often at the end of presentation activities, designers say, "I taught all the subordinate skills, and I taught each of the steps in the goal. What is left to teach?" Yes, learners have been taught each of the steps, but they have not typically put them all together at one time. The content presentation for the terminal objective should therefore be at least a review of all of the steps that are required to perform the goal and an example of complete, correct performance of the goal.

Learner Participation. There are several important considerations when designing practice exercises for intellectual skills. One is the congruence of the practice to the conditions and behaviors prescribed in the objectives and covered in the instruction. This criterion helps separate relevant practice from busywork. Others are ensuring the link between prerequisite knowledge and new skills and progressing from less difficult to more complex problems. Yet another is providing a familiar context within which the skill can be rehearsed. Imagine having to practice analyzing an instructional goal in an unfamiliar skill area or having to write a paragraph on a topic you know nothing about. When you are skilled in performing the instructional goal, you are able to focus on the goal analysis process; when you are familiar with the paragraph topic, you are able to concentrate on the structure of the paragraph and the design of the message. As with designing the presentation of new content and examples, structuring practice exercises using unfamiliar contexts may unnecessarily increase the complexity of the skill for the learner.

There are three caveats regarding the complexity of practice exercises. First, practice toward the end of instruction should replicate conditions found in the performance context for optimum transfer. If this authentic practice seems too unfamiliar to learners, then additional practice (and perhaps content) is required to engage learners in increasingly less familiar contexts until the performance context can be approximated. A second, and related, caveat is that practice for learning to solve ill-defined problems must eventually be in unfamiliar contexts, because that is the only way that learners will be able to try out the problem-solving strategies they are learning in a way that enables transfer out of the classroom and into real-world applications. The third is that the learner should be given the opportunity to practice the terminal objective and to receive corrective feedback before the posttest.

The nature of feedback to learners is also important. It should be balanced in focusing on both the successes and failures in students' practice. Focusing only on errors may cause learners to perceive that nothing they did was meritorious, which is seldom the case. When errors are committed, learners should be provided with information about why their responses were inadequate. Learners tend to perceive corrective feedback as information rather than criticism, especially when they can use the feedback to improve their performance. As learners move from lower-level to higher-level intellectual skills the nature of feedback will change from pointing out features that make practice responses "right" or "wrong" to a combination of guidance for students on their responses *and* on the process that they used to arrive at their responses.

Assessment. The strategy for assessing learners' performance of intellectual skills involves determining when and how to test the skills. In order to make these decisions, the designer should consider how the test results will be used by both the designer and the learner. Premature testing, or tests administered prior to learners' readiness for them, can be more damaging than beneficial, because they tend to discourage learners and to provide incorrect information about the adequacy of the instruction. In designing tests for complex intellectual skills, it is often desirable to test whether learners have mastered concepts and relationships and can describe the correct steps for performing a procedure prior to asking them to perform the terminal objective. For example, you might want to test whether students can describe the characteristics of a good paragraph and the criteria for judging paragraph quality prior to asking them to write paragraphs. Practicing incorrect constructions will not improve students' ability to write. Testing their writing skills prior to their mastery of subordinate skills will yield paragraphs that require a great amount of feedback from the instructor and frustration for the students.

Just as damaging as premature testing is applying inappropriate standards for judging the quality of intellectual skill products and performances. You should carefully consider levels of performance that reflect outstanding work, acceptable work, and unacceptable work for a given target group. Setting these standards is somewhat arbitrary, but they must be based on a realistic conception of what is possible for a particular age or ability group in a given situation. Remember that the standard for judging the quality of students' solutions to ill-structured problems cannot be a single correct answer, because by their nature ill-structured problems can have more than one correct solution. Solutions are usually judged using a rubric that accounts for how well the students' solution process identifies and handles the components of the problem as well as how closely the answer embodies the *characteristics* of an adequate solution to the problem.

Follow-Through. It is critical to consider the requirements for retention and transfer of learning for hierarchically related skills, especially when the skills from one instructional unit are subordinate to those in a subsequent one. You must consider whether corrective feedback following the posttest will suffice or whether additional instruction with practice and feedback will be required. You should also use data from the posttest to target additional instruction on specific subordinate skills where it is needed.

The review of the strategy for memory and transfer requirements is extremely important with intellectual skills. Where will the skill eventually be used, and has there been sufficient preparation for transfer to occur? Have learners been given authentic tasks to perform and a variety of tasks similar to those that will be encountered in the workplace? If the skill must be used from memory in the performance context, have sufficient cues been provided in the instructional practice? Is it appropriate to create a job aid that enables, for example, animated pop-up explanations for each of the icons in the toolbar of a new computer interface, or could the steps for calibrating a quality-control instrument be listed on a card for use as needed? What about the environment in which the skills will be used? Has this been reproduced, both physically and interpersonally, in the instruction? And, finally, is the performance site prepared to support the learner? Are managers and supervisors aware of what is being taught and how the learners will expect to use the skills? Are teachers familiar with the performance context, and have they included instruction on how to integrate new skills into the work environment? Prompting the organization to encourage and reward the new skills of learners is a critical aspect of the overall instructional strategy. You can begin this part of the process, if it hasn't already been done, when you begin to try out the instruction.

A critical transfer requirement for higher-order intellectual skills is learning not only strategies for solving problems but also the ability to reflect on, evaluate, and improve the manner in which one derives and manages those strategies. This ability to monitor and direct one's own cognitive processes is the heart of "learning how to learn" and requires attention throughout all five learning components of an instructional strategy. Briefly, the tactic in all five learning components is to gradually transfer the responsibility for structuring the learning experience from the teacher and materials to the learner. This is the ultimate goal of transfer. Our wish for all students-become-citizens is that they have learned to regulate their own learning and profit from their experiences. For further study, readers are referred to constructivist psychology where the term *reflexivity* is used to describe self-regulated learning and strategies are described for fostering habits of reflexive thought during instruction. Kolb's (1984) theory of experiential learning also emphasizes the role of observation and reflection in self-regulation of the learning process.

Verbal Information   This section considers each learning component in relation to verbal information goals and subordinate skills.

Preinstructional Activities. Designing preinstructional activities is important for verbal information outcomes. When informing learners of the objectives, you should consider how the objectives can be summarized using organizational structures. You could also consider advising learners on ways to use the information.

Presentation Activities. In presenting verbal information, the context for storing and recalling it when needed is extremely important. Strategies linking new information to knowledge currently stored in memory will improve the effectiveness of the instruction. This linking process is referred to as *elaboration* and the more detailed the elaboration or linking procedure, the greater likelihood that learners will store new information in a logical place and recall it later. Elaboration strategies include providing analogies or asking learners to use an imaginary image or example from their own experience for facilitating storage and recall of new information. These contextual links form the cues learners will use to recall the information.

Another recommended strategy for presenting verbal information is to group like information in subsets and to provide direct instruction relating items in the subset and among different subsets, referred to as *organization*. Procedures recommended for aiding students in organizing new information include providing them with an outline or table that summarizes information by related subsets.

When information is entirely new and unrelated to prior learning, then the strategy should include a memory device, or *mnemonic,* to aid the learner in recalling the information. In developing mnemonics, however, those logically related to the material to be recalled are recommended. Cueing letters that form a familiar word or an easily recalled acronym and that are logically related to the information to be remembered can work well. Illogical mnemonics, however, can be as difficult to recall as the information they are designed to help retrieve.

Learner Participation. What does it mean to "practice" verbal information? Rote repetition of unrelated facts has limited effectiveness in helping learners recall information over time. Designing practice activities that strengthen elaborations and cues and that better establish an organizational structure are believed to be better. Practice in generating new examples, in forming mental images that cue recall, and in refining the organizational structure should also help. Focusing the exercise on meaningful contexts and relevant cues is another consideration for the strategy.

Just as with intellectual skills, feedback about the accuracy of verbal information recalled should be provided. Whenever possible the feedback should include the correct response and information about why a given response is incorrect.

Assessment. In testing verbal information you will want to be sure to provide learners with cues that will be available in the performance context for recalling the information. You may also want to sequence verbal information items near related intellectual skills, motor skills, or attitudes to provide a relevant context for recalling the information. As noted previously, such a sequencing strategy for tests would suggest that all test items related to definitions and facts not be placed in a separate section at the beginning or end of the test.

Follow-Through. Facilitating memorization of verbal information can be problematic, involving additional elaboration and organization strategies. However, it may also require a better motivational strategy. You may need to create something for learners to "do" with the information to hook them into learning it. Your strategy might include such activities as crossword puzzle contests for teams of learners that are not only fun but allow them to aid each other in recalling information. Such a team approach may provide them with practice in recalling for themselves as they coach their teammates. Fun for learners, it can enrich elaborations and help ensure that the additional cues provided by teammates are based on prior knowledge and are meaningful to them.

Because this is a verbal information goal, the assumption is that consideration has been given to why the learner must achieve it. With such goals, the learner does not use a job aid or other provided reference material. The motivation of the learner and the adequacy of practice are therefore critical. Also review the context in which the information will be used. Is the application context adequately represented in the learning context?

Motor Skills The learning of a motor skill usually involves several phases. Initial learning concerns the development of an "executive routine," which consists of the "directions" that the learner is to follow. The mental statement of each step in the routine is followed by the performance of that step. With repeated practice and appropriate feedback, the steps in the routine begin to smooth out, there is less hesitation between each step, the mental rehearsal of the executive routine decreases, and the skill begins to assume its final form. Expert performance is often represented by the absence of dependency on the executive routine and an automatic execution of the skill. What are the implications of this description of the learning of a typical motor skill for the presentation of content, examples, practice, and feedback? One very apparent implication is the requirement of some form of visual presentation of the skill. Obviously video can be used to capture movement, but often sequences of photos or drawings can be used, at least at the initial stages of learning a motor skill. The categories of content and examples in a strategy usually take the form of a verbal description of the skill followed by an illustration.

Preinstructional Activities. It is typically easier to gain learners' attention and motivate them prior to receiving instruction on a motor skill than other types of learning. Motor skills are concrete and can be demonstrated; thus, learners do not need to be "told" what they are going to learn. They can see for themselves. This ability to observe what is to come can be very motivational. Additionally, they can be shown persons they admire performing the skill and receiving praise or coveted rewards. Most of us work very hard for praise, medals, and ribbons. One caution in this situation is how to motivate less able learners who have learned that they do not want to perform psychomotor skills publicly.

Presentation Activities. It is important to determine an effective way to group information on a motor skill. It is not unusual to cluster meaningful parts of the skill, which can later be integrated into the complete skill. In our earlier example of learning how to putt a golf ball, we showed that this skill can be broken down into lining up the ball with the cup, the backswing, hitting the ball, and follow-through. Whether to present the skill as a whole or in parts may depend on the skill level of the learners, the complexity of the skill, and the time available for learners to master the skill.

Participation. Practice and feedback are the hallmarks of psychomotor skills. Research has shown that learners can benefit from mentally visualizing the performance of a skill before they physically engage in it. Actual practice of a skill should be repetitious. Immediate feedback on correct execution of the skill is very important, since incorrect rehearsal will not promote skill improvement.

A special problem with a motor skill involving the use of equipment is deciding when the learner should interact with the equipment. At one extreme all instruction is received before the learner practices on the actual equipment. Logistically this is the easiest approach, but it puts a great burden on the student to remember all the details of the instruction. The other extreme is to have the learner interact with the equipment at each step in the instruction. Although there is less of a memory problem, this approach can require one piece of equipment per learner.

One solution to this instructional problem, which may later become a performance problem, is to provide the learner with a job aid. For example, perhaps the learner must enter a coded number into a piece of equipment to make it operate in a particular way. If there is no reason to require the learner to memorize all the possible codes, they could instead be listed on a plate on the equipment or on a card that the learner could easily review. Job aids can also include lists of steps to be executed or criteria to be used to evaluate a product or performance. If the designer chooses to incorporate a job aid into the training, obviously the learner must be taught how to use it.

Assessment. The ultimate question in testing any motor skill is "Can the learner execute the skill that has been taught?" To answer this, they must demonstrate the skill with the intended equipment and environment. Performances are public, assessment is quick, and learners can be quite ego involved in the situation. If other learners are present during the performance, they must be quiet and supportive of the individual performing or they will negatively impact the performance and motivation to participate.

Follow-Through. Transfer of learning must also be addressed with motor skills. What are the conditions under which this skill must be performed? If possible, requirements found in the performance context should be present as the skill is practiced during instruction and should also be present for the posttest. Learners should also be encouraged to continue rehearsal following instruction. For example, few if any musicians or athletes become expert following instruction if they do not have the motivation to continue rehearsal on their own.

Attitudes   Researchers believe our attitudes consist of three components: feelings, behaviors, and cognitive understandings. Feelings, in this case, can be described as pleasures or displeasures that are expressed through our tendency to approach or avoid a situation. This tendency is thought to depend on our success or failure in prior similar situations or our observation of others in these situations. This is the key to a successful instructional strategy for an attitude.

Preinstructional Activities. Designing preinstructional activities is also important for attitudes. Similar to psychomotor skills, motivation for acquiring an attitude may best be accomplished through firsthand observation by the learners. For attitudes, however, the observation should evoke empathic identity with the character observed so that learners experientially feel the emotion of the character. In terms of informing the learners of the objectives, it is possible that the objective is communicated through the film or video. In other situations it may be best to state the objectives directly prior to the video or following it. Likewise, linking the upcoming learning to the learner's current feelings, skills, and knowledge may be accomplished through the characters in a carefully crafted or selected video. It may also be helpful to have a recap discussion of the video where learners reflect on and discuss similar situations and people in their lives.

Presentation Activities. The content and example portion of the strategy should be delivered by someone or by an imaginary character who is respected and admired by the learners. This "human model" should display the behaviors involved in the attitude and indicate why this is an appropriate attitude. If possible, it should be obvious to the learner that the model is being rewarded or takes personal satisfaction in displaying this attitude.

The substance of the instruction for an attitude consists of teaching the behavior that is to be demonstrated by the learner, such as personal cleanliness, as well as the supporting information about why this is important. The behaviors should be demonstrated under the conditions described in the performance objectives.

You may also need to consider in your strategy whether you are developing an attitude or reshaping one. For existing negative behaviors (and attitudes) such as unrestrained public emotion or anger as a response to frustration, you may need to focus instruction on self-awareness and teaching alternative ways of behaving in the circumstance. Creating simulations that evoke emotions that can lead to damaging behaviors may be required. Guiding learners to more positive behaviors as responses to the same emotions can be difficult. You may wish to consider strategies such as video recording them as they respond in context and then working with them as they analyze how they felt and reacted. You may want them to hear how others in the situation judged their reactions. You may want them to observe someone they admire react positively in a similar circumstance and, through remaining calm, direct the conclusion of the interaction to the anticipated outcome.

Undoubtedly the strategy you choose for instruction related to an attitude hinges on multiple factors. In addition to attempting to develop or reshape an attitude, several questions should be considered. Are the learners volunteers for the program because they perceive a need and wish to change? Are they satisfied with themselves but have been directed or "sentenced" to the program by a supervisor, school administrator, or judge? Are the attitude and behaviors ones the learners care little about, or do they represent strong convictions or sensitive feelings? How free can you be in delivering instruction, creating simulations, and providing feedback? Will group instruction suffice, or will individualized instruction be required? The answers to all such questions should have been obtained in the learner and context analyses and should be considered in designing an instructional strategy for attitudes.

Learner Participation. How can the learner practice an attitude? First, practice and feedback should be provided for any information, intellectual skills, and motor skills that are part of the attitude. Making inappropriate or ineffective choices that are followed by ineffective or even positive feedback will not help the learner make better choices. Practice, therefore, must incorporate opportunities to choose followed by consistent feedback (rewards/consequences/rationales) to help ensure that a given behavior becomes associated with a given response. Role playing is frequently used because of the difficulty in recreating the performance context for attitudes within an instructional setting. Opportunities for verbal testimonials regarding the desired choices can enhance the effectiveness of role playing. The feedback should include information about what the learner did right and what the learner did wrong. Related to inappropriate responses, information about more appropriate responses should be provided.

Because attitudes can be learned vicariously, mental rehearsals may prove beneficial for practicing them. Such rehearsals might include dramatic scenes that present respected models who are faced with alternatives. Following the presentation of alternatives, the learners can observe the model reacting in positive ways and can observe the model receiving extrinsic rewards or expressing intrinsic satisfaction considered positive and relevant by the learners. Additionally, other models could be observed reacting in negative ways and receiving negative consequences. These story simulations are especially useful because characters affected by the negative model's attitudes and behaviors can be observed by learners. When respected characters are injured, insulted, or angered by the "bad" model, the learner can associate or empathize with these reactions, helping the learner rehearse associating the attitude and behavior with the unpleasant consequences. These reactions of the respected characters constitute feedback to the learner. Reactors can be seen discussing the behavior of the negative model, and they can provide informative feedback by describing alternative ways the model should have behaved.

Assessments. As discussed previously, an important consideration when designing tests for attitudes is whether learners will know they are being observed. Other considerations include tests of verbal information related to knowledge of the expected behaviors and the potential rewards and consequences for behaving in certain ways. The assessment strategy should also encompass any intellectual or motor skills required for exhibiting the required behaviors. For example, it would be difficult to demonstrate positive attitudes toward safe driving if one could not drive a car, could not state the rules of the road, and could not solve safety problems encountered while driving. Although this is an extreme example, it illustrates the point.

You may want to design questionnaires with situations and questions for the learners about how they would react to hypothetical circumstances. However, you should be aware that research demonstrates little relationship between our professed attitudes in a hypothetical situation and our actual behavior when confronted with a similar situation in real life. To the extent possible, the designer should try to create hypothetical situations that simulate those in which the attitude would influence learner choices and behaviors.

Follow-Through. Perhaps the most important consideration in the instructional strategy for teaching an attitude is the adequacy of the components that will promote transfer. Rarely are we interested in a demonstration of an attitude in the presence of an instructor other than to show that the learner has mastered the skill associated with the attitude. We want the skill to be chosen by the learner as the desired behavior in situations when the instructor is not present. It is therefore critical to provide the learner with practice contexts that are similar to those in which we hope to see the attitude occur. The learner should also be provided with valid feedback to this attitude as part of the practice activity.

Learning Components for Constructivist Strategies

Overview Less-prescriptive learner-centered approaches to education and constructivist theories can have valuable roles in the design and management of instruction. After looking at a radical constructivist view that there is no objective reality, that knowledge is constructed internally and individually by learners and is therefore unpredictable, an instructional designer might ask, "How can instructional designers determine what students need, prescribe instructional activities, and assess learning outcomes?" The answer is that it can be done, but it must be done differently.

As described in Chapter 1, the Dick and Carey model is rooted in cognitive psychology, and we have called it a *cognitive* model. Constructivism also has roots in cognitive psychology and has two branches: cognitive constructivism and social constructivism. In common usage it is referred to just as *constructivism,* and we will follow that convention. Several information-processing assumptions of cognitive psychology conflict with the assumptions of pure constructivist thinking. Designers on the extreme ends of the continuum between cognitive and constructive theories would choose to reject, out of hand, the design of instruction using the other theory; however, we believe that a blending of these theories can be a productive path for effective instruction and learning. Our experience as professors working with hundreds of university students and their instructional design projects, as instructional designers and developers of our own courses, and as designers, evaluators, and observers of ID projects in school, university, business, military, and government contexts has convinced us that selected constructivist practices can effectively overlay the learning components of a cognitive ID model. Constructivist psychologists have been particularly effective in describing instructional strategies for learning to solve ill-defined problems, and it is for this domain of learning that a blending of constructivist practices deserves serious consideration.

Carey (2005) and Ertmer and Newby (1993) provide balanced analyses of how aspects of a constructivist approach can be compatible with aspects of a cognitive approach for specified types of learners and learning outcomes. Moreover, Dede (2008) suggests that in many situations, a combination top-down (cognitive) and bottom-up (constructive) approach might be the instructional strategy of choice. Anyone familiar with the work of master teachers has observed the beneficial and seamless meshing of these two approaches in the classroom. Readers should be clear about our intent in this discussion of constructivism. It is not to set aside the cognitive model and provide a comprehensive explanation of constructivist instructional design; that has been done well by Jonassen (1999) and others. Our purpose is, rather, to describe aspects of constructivist practice that we believe can be blended effectively into the cognitive ID model. Our approach will be to compare the elements of a generic cognitive ID process with planning practices in the design of constructivist learning environments (CLEs). Then we will comment on blending CLEs into the Dick and Carey design model and summarize some of the critical aspects of constructivist theory that must be maintained to be faithful to that pedagogy. We will finish this section with a brief review of considerations for designing and managing CLEs. A succinct working definition of *constructivist learning environments* for beginning this discussion is "learners in collaborative groups with peers and teachers consulting resources to solve problems." Discovery learning, inquiry-based learning, and problem-based learning are instructional strategies that are roughly synonymous with constructivist learning environments.

Cognitive ID Models and Constructivist Planning Practices   Table 8.2 provides a comparison of the steps in a cognitive ID model with constructivist planning practices. A careful look at the table makes two points very clear. First, constructivism is not an easy way out of the planning process required in cognitive ID. If CLEs are the instructional strategy of choice because designers seek the constructivist learning outcomes predicted by relevant theory, then there will still be planning tasks regarding goals, content, learners, contexts, and so forth. Learner-centered instruction does not remove the instructor from planning or participation. The roles still exist; they are just different.

A second observation illustrated in Table 8.2 is that a designer following the Dick and Carey model through Chapter 7 on the design of assessment will have completed the planning useful for designing CLEs. There are some theoretical issues in constructivist design that dictate how to use the planning work that has been done for goals, content and objectives, and assessments, and we will discuss those momentarily. The point here is that the analysis and design work has been accomplished and can be used, so this is an effective place in the Dick and Carey Model to introduce a blend with constructivism. Next we will describe how to manage some theoretical issues in blending CLEs into a cognitive model.

Theoretical Considerations   A theoretical difference pervading comparisons of cognitive and constructivist views is rooted in the roles of content and the learner. The cognitive assumption is that the content drives the system whereas the learner is the driving factor in constructivism. The former focuses more on products and outcomes,

table 8.2 Cognitive ID Models and Constructivist Practices

Cognitive ID Phases	Dick and Carey ID Processes	Constructivist Planning Practices
Analyze	Needs	Places learning within the mission and requirements of the organization.
	Goals	Maintains focus during preparation prior to student engagement and process during student engagement. Includes process outcomes that may not be present in cognitive strategies.
	Content	Assembles and references domain knowledge resources that will be needed by students in the learning environment; seldom done in the detail of a hierarchical subordinates skills analysis.
	Learners	Places learners in zone of proximal social, cultural, and intellectual development (matching learning environment to learners).
	Learning Context Performance Context	Emphasizes situated learning (authentic social, cultural, physical attributes) in constructivist learning environments (CLEs).
Design	Objectives	Usually written but fewer than cognitive frameworks and not stated as formal three-part objectives. Sometimes broken into learning objectives and process objectives because of requirements for learners' collaboration and task management in CLEs.
	Assessments	Mandatory joint responsibility of teacher, learner, and other learners assessing progress, products, and process. More holistic with less focus on testing subskills. No single correct solution, so criteria describe properties of an adequate solution.
	Instructional Strategies • Content clustering and sequencing • Learning components • Student groupings • Delivery system/media	The CLE is the instructional strategy. Learners in collaborative groups with peers and teachers consult resources to solve problems. Group meetings can be face to face or computer mediated in synchronous or asynchronous time or in virtual spaces. Resources must be accessible, pertinent, and sufficient. Problems must be complex, relevant, and situated in the real world. Learners must be actively engaged, reflective, and aware. Teachers must motivate and encourage learners, manage group process/progress, and provide adaptive learning guidance including scaffolding, coaching (tutoring, feedback, and direct instruction), modeling, and mentoring.
Develop	Instructional materials	Focuses less on prescriptive print or mediated instructional materials; focuses more on inquiry, access, and resource-based learning. Carefully describes for students goal, problem scenario, group process, milestones, and resources.
	Assessments	Assessments are usually rubrics and portfolios with guidance on process for collaborative evaluation.
	Course management	Prescriptive instructor's guide is replaced by document describing learning context, intended learners, goal and objectives, content domain and problem scenario, process/activities overview, required tools/resources/scaffolding, and assessment instruments/processes.

whereas the latter focuses more on process. These assumptions cause differences in how cognitivists and constructivists view goals, content and objectives, and assessment, and these differences must be taken into account if one plans to blend CLEs into cognitive ID with theoretical integrity.

Planning and documentation for CLEs always includes goals regarding the content domain that will be explored, and just as in cognitive models, these goals should reflect the needs and learning priorities of the organization. The CLE is an instructional strategy, however, that by definition includes goals for learners that spring from the inquiry process instead of from the content domain. These goals are inseparable from constructivist theory and part of the CLE strategy even if not written out in documentation under the heading of "Goals." Driscoll (2005) describes five aspects of constructivism that should be considered in ID. These desired outcomes (goals) of learner-centered inquiry when supported by adaptive learning guidance are (1) reasoning, critical thinking, and problem solving; (2) retention, understanding, and use; (3) cognitive flexibility; (4) self-regulation; and (5) mindful reflection and epistemic flexibility. Numbers 3, 4, and 5 collectively can be called *metacognition* and are the capabilities that Gagné described as *cognitive strategies*. The designer who chooses to blend CLEs into the cognitive model should recognize these constructivist goals, make them explicit in project documentation, and account for them in design of the CLE and the assessments. The most compelling reason for choosing CLEs is when the original goal is learning to solve ill-defined problems and develop cognitive strategies; however, the authors have seen many instances in which creative designers have chosen to blend a CLE into the design as a motivational vehicle for other learning outcomes.

Content analysis is completed down through the subordinate skills level in cognitive design to discover the structure of the content, enabling the designer to decide what must be learned in order to master the goal and whether there is a required sequence for learning it. After the analysis, objectives are written that mirror the structure of the content. This objective view of reality becomes a theoretical problem when blending CLEs into a cognitive model. Hannafin et al. (1997, p. 109) make this difference between cognitive and constructivist views clear.

> For constructivists objects and events have no absolute meaning; rather, the individual interprets each and constructs meaning based on individual experience and evolved beliefs. The design task, therefore, is one of providing a rich context within which meaning can be negotiated and ways of understanding can emerge and evolve. Constructivists tend to eschew the breaking down of context into component parts in favor of [learning] environments wherein knowledge, skill, and complexity exist naturally.

If choosing CLEs as the instructional strategy, cognitive designers need not alter the content analysis that has been completed; rather, they must alter the way the content analysis is used. The CLE should not be shaped by imposing a content structure on it; instead, the CLE should be structured so that learners find the content structure within it as part of the process of guided inquiry. The designer can, however, use the content analysis as a resource for selecting a robust problem scenario and providing access to content resources sufficient for solving the problem therein. Another use for the subordinate skills analysis in CLEs is for tutoring and scaffolding in ill-defined problem solving when students need guidance for putting together relationships among concepts, rules, and principles. The content analysis can also be used for designing tutorials as resource material for students in CLEs, following Jonassen's (1997) description of cognitive strategies for teaching well-defined problems. Because objectives mirror the goal analysis and subskills analysis in cognitive design, they are subject to the same theoretical problem denoted in Hannafin's comment above. As such, subordinate objectives could be reserved for use in developing tutorials or job aids as resources for learners in the CLE but would not be distributed to learners to guide their progress or process.

As mentioned previously, the cognitive model is content driven and the result is a parallel relationship among skills, objectives, and assessments. This relationship imposes a structure on the instruction that does not exist in CLEs and influences the nature of assessment. The assessments developed in cognitive design can be used to inform the assessment of constructivist learning but cannot be *the* assessment of outcomes in CLEs. Ill-structured problems have many correct solutions, so designers choosing to blend CLEs into a cognitive design must create a description of the functional characteristics of correct solutions instead of a description of the correct solution. Designers must also create assessment strategies that address the explicit inquiry goals found in constructivist theory. That requires *authentic assessment,* characterized by learners performing realistic tasks that typically result in a product of some type (e.g., a problem solution, a journal article, a dramatic video, or a computer program) or performances of skills and procedures (e.g., demonstrating steps used to develop a software solution, managing progress of a work team, diagnosing illnesses, or producing a newsletter).

A second characteristic of authentic assessment is an interactive, joint evaluation of the resulting product or process by the learner and instructor. This evaluation could also include others such as experts in the field or peer work team members. Interactive evaluative discussions typically include illuminating first the features of the product or performance that are well done, and from that positive perspective, discussions of other parts of the work that need to have additional refining.

Finally, these assessments should involve the joint determination of the criteria that will be used to evaluate the quality of students' work. One of the goals of education is for learners to (1) acquire information about the qualities of objects or performances (e.g., form, function, aesthetics, parsimony), (2) use these criteria in judging the work of others, (3) apply the criteria during their own work, and (4) use them in judging the results of their work. The self-assessment aspect moves assessment from being a test of the learner to being a learning outcome. Self-assessment is key to cognitive flexibility, self-regulation, and reflection. Now we turn our attention to some details of designing and managing CLEs.

Designing Constructivist Learning Environments   Five theory-based goals of all CLEs were described in the section on theoretical considerations. The five goals can be viewed as a set of minimum specifications or requirements for designing CLEs. They are repeated below with relevant constructivist learning conditions suggested by Driscoll (2005). The discussion follows the pattern of organization used by Chieu (2005).

The goal of reasoning, critical thinking, and problem solving is best supported by planning CLEs that are complex, realistic, and relevant. Complexity is required in the problem scenarios used in CLEs if students are to transfer learning experiences to life experiences; however, the range of complexity available within the problem must challenge students of different achievement and ability without inducing undue frustration. The CLE must situate students in a realistic, relevant problem scenario. Situated learning requires a context with which students can identify for motivation and transfer. The context should include realistic elements of the physical, social, and cultural world in which the students operate but need not be "the real world." Learning can be situated effectively in such contexts as play-acted fairy tales, mock court trials, computer simulations, or computer-based micro worlds. A problem scenario should be relevant on two levels. First, problem scenarios must be planned such that students are able to discern pattern and structure in the problem through their inquiry process; otherwise, the problem has little relevance to the desired learning of reasoning and critical thinking skills. The second level of relevance is in the generalizability of the problem-solving process and strategies that are being learned. Odd, one-of-a-kind problems may be interesting and instructive in some ways but essentially irrelevant for the desired transfer to applying and practicing problem-solving strategies in a variety of unencountered circumstances.

Retention, understanding, and use are best accomplished by providing for interaction among learners, peers, and teachers. The interaction should be integral to the inquiry process such that students are placed in positions where they need to probe, consider, defend, refine, and perhaps reconceptualize their construction of new knowledge. This social interaction provides opportunities for the practice and feedback that promote retention and understanding. Social interaction needs to be managed to maintain a productive balance between what is purely social and what is task oriented, whether organized in face-to-face settings or mediated in chat rooms, blogs, wikis, discussion forums, or electronic mailing lists.

Cognitive flexibility is the ability to adapt and change one's mental organization of knowledge and mental management of solution strategies for solving new, unexpected problems. Cognitive flexibility is engendered when students are exposed to multiple representations of the content domain and multiple solution strategies for the same problem and when students are challenged to examine and evaluate their own strategies for solving a problem. CLEs should provide opportunities for confronting dissimilar problems that require reorganization of content domain knowledge and exploration of alternative solutions. Self-assessment and collaborative assessment are critical for developing cognitive flexibility, as they provide opportunities for low-threat encounters with disparate perspectives and opportunities for formative attempts at shaping problem solutions.

Self-regulation involves identifying learning outcomes of personal interest or value and choosing to pursue them. This goal is best supported by creating environments in which students can practice choosing and pursuing their own learning goals. Less mature learners will typically require guidance as they learn through experience which goals are realistic, achievable, and personally rewarding. CLEs that use project-based learning can offer opportunities for students to choose among multiple problem scenarios within the same general content domain.

Mindful reflection and epistemic flexibility are reflected by learners who maintain awareness of their own process of constructing knowledge and choosing ways of learning and knowing. Support for this goal is similar to support for cognitive flexibility but goes beyond providing multiple perspectives to encouraging students to weigh, compare, and decide on the merits of differing perspectives. If social negotiation of meaning requires discussion with others to construct meaning, then mindful reflection and epistemic flexibility can be thought of as a mental discussion with oneself about meaning, how one judges something to be true, and whether there are other, perhaps better, ways to know the truth. As with cognitive flexibility, self-assessment and collaborative assessment are critical in acquiring this goal. Now we will turn our attention to some considerations in planning and managing CLEs, providing a template for organizing design and development efforts.

Planning Constructivist Learning Environments   Whether to embark on a cognitive or constructivist instructional strategy or a blend thereof requires consideration of several factors, including how well any of the approaches meet the defined needs of the organization. The designer must also decide the best path for learners to achieve the instructional goal approved by the organization. Considerations of learners' characteristics, including their ability, maturity, and experience, are certainly important factors. In choosing a constructivist strategy or blending constructivism with a cognitive strategy, the skills of the teacher, trainer, or instructional manager become an important consideration, because managing a CLE and the students engaged in the CLE is quite different from the pedagogical style with which most teachers are accustomed. Moreover, the features of the performance and learning contexts, especially in light of resources, will influence the selection of the best strategy for learning.

The planning that goes into CLEs was summarized in the right-hand column of Table 8.2 opposite the "Analyze" and "Design" phases, and the point was made that effective CLEs require thoughtful preparation. Table 8.2 could be used as a template for planning CLEs, but Table 8.3 is focused more on planning needs for a constructivist strategy. For Table 8.3 we assume the analysis and design steps through Chapter 7 of this book have already been completed and the designer is choosing to use a CLE

t a b l e	Planning for a Constructivist Learning Environment (CLE)
8 . 3	

Planning Needs	**Planning Activities**
Planning the Learning Environment	*Describe here the designs and materials needed to launch the CLE.* • Goal • Learning objectives • Rationale • Constructivist focus • Pedagogical model (problem-based, project-based, case-based, etc.) • Scenario (overview of problem, project, case, etc.) • Learning resource materials • Learner groupings • Delivery system, media, and personnel
Planning for Learner Engagement	*Describe here the procedures and activities anticipated during engagement given the nature of the learners, instructional goal, and pedagogical model.* • Engage (first encounter with problem and material, gain attention, arouse curiosity, establish personal relevance in minds of learners) • Explore (involvement, questioning, hypothesizing, information seeking, interaction, sharing) • Explain (describe phenomena, use terminology, share ideas, propose explanations, test solutions, defend interpretations) • Elaborate (transfer and expand knowledge, apply in new settings, see relationships, recognize patterns, make connections, test in new contexts, relate to life experiences) • Evaluate (collaborate, negotiate outcomes, define criteria, diagnose and prescribe, note incremental improvement, provide product and performance rubrics, reflect, refine)

Planning Learning Guidance	*Describe here materials and activities anticipated for adaptive learning guidance during learner engagement in the CLE.*
	
	• Scaffolding
	  • Models
	  • Graphic organizers
	  • Worked examples
	  • Job aids
	  • Concept maps
	  • Questioning
	  • Guided feedback
	  • And so forth
	• Coaching
	• Modeling
	• Tutoring and peer tutoring
	• Mediated tutorials
	• Direct instruction
	• And so forth

Planning Authentic Assessment	*Describe here the materials and procedures anticipated for authentic assessment for the goal, the learners, and the CLE.*
	
	• Rubrics and other instruments
	• Categories of criteria
	  • Form
	  • Function
	  • Aesthetic
	  • Legal
	  • And so forth
	• Prompts for reflection and self-assessment
	• Model solutions
	• And so forth

instead of the cognitive instructional strategy emphasized in this chapter. Under these assumptions, planning the CLE becomes a combination of modifying existing planning so it addresses constructivist assumptions and addresses additional requirements that are unique to the CLE. Although the table divides planning activities into considerations for the learning environment, learner engagement, learning guidance, and assessment, most of the planning activities would be completed prior to launching the environment and engaging learners.

Authentic assessment and learning guidance are, of course, part of learner engagement, but they are presented in separate rows of Table 8.3 because of their critical contributions to the success of students' progress through CLEs. The popular 5 Es scheme developed by the Biological Science Curriculum Study (BSCS) team is included in the table for planning for learner engagement, but designers can substitute any scheme that matches their preferences and the pedagogical model being used. In the category of planning for learning guidance in Table 8.3, everything could be considered scaffolding as long as it supports students as needed and is withdrawn as the student develops proficiency. Designers can structure this category in whatever manner suits their concept of learning guidance. See the Examples and Case Study sections at the end of this chapter as well as the appendixes for examples of how Table 8.3 would be filled out.

Now we shift from our discussion of constructivist ID back to the design of an instructional strategy per Figure 8.1, but first, one final note for those following the Dick and Carey Model. If the decision is made to use a constructivist instructional strategy (to blend CLEs into the model) and to do it with theoretical integrity, then recognize that some content-based assumptions of the Dick and Carey Model may be changed. This could have implications for the assessment of student learning outcomes, formative evaluation, revision, accountability, and replicability of instruction. The instructional strategy specified in the school learning case study in Appendix H is an example of blending a CLE into the Dick and Carey Model with *no impact* on the cognitive design assumptions, because the problem-based student newsletter activities are used as authentic motivation for the middle-school students' participation in the direct instruction on using a variety of sentences when writing paragraphs. Beyond the instruction on sentence variety, the CLE would also have great utility for other direct instruction and for higher-order skills across the middle-school curriculum. This is a desirable blend of cognitive and constructive strategies, because the benefits of both models will be realized. The instructional strategy specified in the group leadership case study at the end of this chapter is also an example of blending a CLE into the Dick and Carey Model, but in this instance there would be an impact on some of the cognitive design assumptions. Although the web-based instruction for participants would be provided within typical cognitive-design guidelines, the group-based problem-solving sessions, in which participants set their own agendas and choose their own priorities, would result in different learning outcomes for different groups and varying levels of mastery by individual learners within groups. This makes replication with predictable outcomes difficult, and the variability in performance presents problems for formative evaluation, revision, and certification of achievement. The authors, however, have chosen to specify the CLE for the case study for two reasons. First, the prerequisite skills were covered in the web-based instruction. Second, the group-based problem-solving sessions would elicit active participation in more authentic performance than could have been offered in direct instruction. As in most decisions for planning instruction, choosing instructional strategies will be guided by careful analysis of instructional goals and thorough understanding of the needs of learners and the parent organization.

Student Groupings

When you are planning the learning components of an instructional strategy, you also need to plan the details of student groupings and media selections. Although all three are considered simultaneously, the learning components of the strategy remain the primary planning units, because they determine learning effectiveness. The emphasis should always be on planning student groupings and media selections *within* learning components. If a delivery system requiring distance learning or individualized instruction has been prescribed, then some limits on student groupings may exist; in most cases, however, this decision is in the hands of the instructional designer.

The primary question to ask when making decisions about student groupings is whether requirements for social interaction exist in the performance and learning contexts, in the statements of learning objectives, in the specific learning component being planned, or in one's foundational views of the teaching process. The type of student grouping (individual, pairs, small group, large group) depends on specific social interaction requirements and is often mixed within and among the learning components in a lesson or unit. Remember that motivation is a key learning component and that social interaction and changes in student groupings provide variety and interest value even when not specifically required in the performance context or objectives. In other instances, pedagogical methods such as active learning and problem-based learning employ a variety of student groupings for managing different learning components of the instructional strategy. The considerations for deciding about student groupings are the same whether meetings are face to face or mediated at a distance through technology.

Selection of Media and Delivery Systems

Selections of media and delivery systems share many considerations, so the two topics will be addressed together. As we begin this discussion of media selection, it is a good time for all of us to think back to our own school experiences. Do you remember those few teachers who always seemed to have a video reserved for that last class on Friday afternoon? You remember the routine: class starts—lights off—video starts—video ends—lights on—bell rings—goodbye! Was that good instruction? Usually not, but why not? Think about the learning components of an instructional strategy described in this chapter. Would the Friday afternoon video be a complete strategy or just a part of an overall set of unit activities? The video probably could fit into a unit as part of preinstructional activities and content presentation, but what about the other learning components that are part of a complete strategy? They just did not happen on those Friday afternoons. This example illustrates the point of view in this chapter that media are useful to the extent that they effectively carry required learning components of an instructional strategy.

This chapter's initial discussion on the selection of a delivery system noted that it most often occurs early in the instructional design process. When working under the constraint of an assigned or assumed delivery system, media selection becomes a choice among those formats available in that system. There are two reasons why this limit on available media is not as problematic as one might think. First, research on effects of media on students' learning—beginning with military training films in the 1940s and continuing through radio, television, slide shows, computer-based multimedia and simulation, and web-based distance learning—generally concludes that the medium itself does not make a significant difference in how much students learn. Clark's (1983) review of research established the basic argument that the design of instruction rather than the medium used to deliver it determines student learning. In a summary of research eighteen years later, Russell (2001), focusing more on distance learners' achievement, reached conclusions very similar to Clark's. Although Russell's updated web site (http://nosignificantdifference.wcet.info/about.asp) lists a number of studies reporting improved student performance in mediated distance learning, it is difficult to attribute the positive results to the medium itself because of changes in instructional strategies for the distance learning treatments that were not controlled in the studies. The implication for the instructional designer (with some qualifications discussed in the following paragraphs) is that almost any media will work for most teaching–learning requirements.

Second, designing instruction under an imposed delivery system does not particularly limit the media formats available. Common media formats ranging from text, graphics, audio, hypertext, and motion video through simulations, real objects, and authentic environments can be displayed or represented in a low-tech delivery system with an instructor or AV equipment in a classroom or a high-tech delivery system via computer or the web. Regardless of whether instruction is low tech or high tech, the learning components of an instructional strategy are still the key predictors of learner success, and must be provided by the instructor, by mediated materials, or by classmates, workmates, colleagues, family, friends, or the learners themselves.

At this ideal point in the instructional design process, once decisions have been made about content sequencing and clustering and the learning components have been planned, appropriate decisions can be made regarding media selection and a delivery system. How are these choices made? Certainly there are practical considerations one immediately thinks of in terms of availability of resources and personnel. But there are prior decisions that should be made that relate to the selection of appropriate media for the various domains of learning and for certain task requirements found in objectives.

Media Selection for Domains of Learning   Gagné et al. (2004) have developed a matrix for choosing effective instructional media and delivery methods. The matrix brings together considerations of domains of learning, Gagné's events of instruction, delivery methods and strategies, and types of media. The matrix is accompanied by a table with summary decisions about media characteristics that should be excluded or selected for different domains of learning. Interested readers may want to consult the source for details of the media selection logic and the decision table. In our view the critical decision points in the matrix and table can be distilled down to two questions: (1) Is practice with intelligent, adaptive feedback required for learning? and (2) Is physical practice required for learning? The answers to both of these questions are found in the domain of learning represented by the objectives being taught.

Intellectual Skills. Consider the analysis of media used to teach intellectual skills. Research suggests that learners should be provided precise corrective feedback to responses made during the learning process. Often there is more than one "correct answer." In order to provide responsive feedback to learners' practice, one would choose interactive media such as a human instructor, a peer tutor, a mentor, a trainer, or a computer-based smart system. If one-way media such as large-group lecture or informational web pages were chosen, then supplemental student materials that require responses and provide feedback could be developed, or study groups could be organized. The key is that the medium of choice must be intelligent and adaptive, because feedback and guidance to learners will change based on their practice responses.

Verbal Information. If the instructional goal is in the domain of verbal information, there is still the requirement of eliciting responses from learners, but there is less need for intelligent, adaptive feedback. Students can easily compare their own responses to the correct answers, so there is less need for interactive media with verbal information goals.

Psychomotor Skills. When learning a motor skill begins by learning an executive routine (describing what the learner will do and how under various circumstances), this first phase can be treated as an intellectual skill. As the learner masters the executive routine, however, practice and feedback are required either using simulators or in the real physical environment with any real equipment and objects described in the instructional goal. Simulators can be designed to provide feedback but an instructor often provides a debriefing that includes feedback after a simulation session. When psychomotor learning includes practice with real objects, a peer, coach, or instructor is often required for feedback; however, advanced learners can analyze their own performance using practice aids and/or audio-video recordings.

Attitudes. Research about how we learn attitudes suggests that one of the most powerful methods is to observe a person we regard highly doing something for which they are rewarded or have received approval. It is then more likely that we will tend to make the same choice when we are in a similar situation. For teaching attitudes then, the visual media, such as television or digital video, are often suggested. Role playing, which is also effective for learning attitudes, requires interaction that can be face to face, online, or simulated in games or virtual meeting spaces.

The purpose of this review has been to suggest that although media is less important than other factors, some differences in learning outcomes are reflected in the media used to deliver instruction. However, it cannot be assumed that the objectives are all in the same domain. This choice will be simpler for a short lesson, in which all of the objectives might be intellectual skills or verbal information. As the size of instruction increases—for example, to a forty-hour course—there most likely will be a mixture of domains represented in the objectives, making it necessary to select media for clusters of similar objectives or attempt to mix compatible media for a variety of objectives.

Media Selection for Certain Learner Characteristics

There are two instances in selecting media in which learner characteristics are critical considerations. First, media for learners with sensory, cognitive, or learning disabilities must comply with requirements of the Americans with Disabilities Act for accommodating disabilities, or assistive means must be chosen that supplement the media to accommodate the disabilities. Sometimes it is the design of the medium that enables accommodations for disabilities. For example, blind Internet users have access to design features such as screen reader software, speech-enabled browsing, or Braille display. The key for enabling such access requires following established design standards for what are termed "accessible" web pages. The second instance in which learner characteristics can dictate media selection is for a target audience of nonreaders or which includes nonreaders, for whom audio and pictorial media will have obvious benefits.

Media Selection for Certain Task Requirements Found in Objectives

In addition to matching media to learning domains and learner characteristics, task requirements found in objectives can limit media choices. First the designer should ask whether specific sensory discriminations (visual, auditory, tactile, etc.) are required to master the objective. If the answer is yes, then the medium or combination of media must be capable of managing the sensory requirements in content presentation, learner participation, and assessment. A second question the designer should ask is whether social interaction is required for mastery of the objective. If the answer is yes, this requirement will need to be accommodated in learner participation and most certainly in assessment. As mentioned previously, social interaction may not require face-to-face encounters and could be managed for some purposes online or simulated in virtual reality.

Media Selection for Replacing the Need for Instruction

It is worth reminding designers at this point in the ID process that education and training are expensive; alternate paths to mastering skills and improving performance are worth considering. It is easy to focus one's attention narrowly on the instruction to be developed when it is possible that job aids, performance support tools (PSTs), or electronic performance support systems (EPSSs) could replace some or all of the instruction. We mentioned job aids and performance support earlier in this chapter but will provide more detail here because they are forms of media. Job aids are any tools that support performance of a task or skill. Some examples of job aids that replace instruction are informative signage in a library to guide students to information resources, a table of the periodic elements on the front wall for student reference in a chemistry classroom, a government employee's "cheat sheet" of acronyms for different agencies, a decision map that an auto repair technician uses to troubleshoot your car, or a calculator programmed to run quality control algorithms for a production manager. PSTs and EPSSs are higher-tech, computer-based forms of job aids. If there is a distinction between the PSTs and EPSSs, it would be that PSTs are more stand-alone and not as integrated into the performance context, but the distinctions between the two are disappearing in common usage. Performance support tools basically do three things: streamline and automate procedures, provide information needed for a task, and provide logic required for making decisions. These three tasks are supported through such functional tools as databases, hypermedia, tutorials, expert systems, wizards, task tracking, process modeling and visualization, and so forth. Examples of performance support systems include the interview sequence in TurboTax, the wizards in Microsoft Office software, the tutorials in Adobe Photoshop, the customized software a day trader uses to track the market and time stock trades, and the incident-tracking software integrated with GPS that a police dispatcher uses to route officers to emergency calls.

Using job aids or performance support as a substitute for instruction can be as simple as laminating a "how-to" card for use at a computer workstation or as involved as authoring a complex software system. In most instances job aids and performance support won't eliminate instruction completely, but can shorten learning time and improve precision in job performance. For those interested in investigating job aids and performance support further, we recommend Gery's (1991) original book on EPSSs, Brown's (1996) book on developing EPSSs, Dickelman's (2003) collection of articles, and Rossett and Schafer's (2006) book on job aids and performance support.

Practical Considerations in Choosing Media and Delivery Systems

An important factor in delivery system selection is the projected availability of various media for the environment in which the instructional package will be used. If the materials will be used in the learning resource center of a public school, community college, or university, then a whole array of media devices would probably be available to the learner and instructor. In contrast, if the package is designed for home study or use on the job or a community center where equipment may be limited, you must either develop a means of making that equipment available or limit media selection to reasonable expectations of availability. The ubiquity of computers and online access in recent years has changed how we think about "reasonable expectations of availability." If an Internet-capable computer is not available at home, then access can be obtained at work, school, or public library, thus opening media selection to the web and in some cases to CD, DVD, and proprietary software.

Computers, the web, and broadband access have enabled delivery of text, graphics, audio, video, and interactivity by means of a single medium or as discrete items using a single access point. This consolidation of stimulus features into a single delivery system simplifies media selection and distribution of instruction. Concerns regarding the ability of instructors and students to manage the computer or web interface and associated software are decreasing as delivery of audio, video, and interactivity becomes more and more intuitive, seamless, and platform independent. This trend is seen most clearly in e-learning portals and the porting of web content for handheld computers, PDAs, and cell phones, and the ease of accessing/downloading blogs, RSS feeds, newsfeeds, webcasts, and podcasts, as well as photo, video, and audio sharing.

A related factor in media selection is the ability of the designer or an available expert to produce materials in a particular medium. For example, you may find that computer-assisted instruction would be an ideal medium for a particular instructional objective, but because you do not already have the skills to develop instruction using computers or the time to learn them, or because there is no staff available to do it, another choice must be made.

The flexibility, durability, and convenience of the materials within a specified medium are other factors. If the materials are designed so that they require equipment found only in a learning center, is there a learning center available? Is it open during hours when students can participate in independent study? Are the materials in a form that students can handle alone without destroying either the materials or equipment required for the materials? Should the materials be portable and, if so, how portable can they be with the media you have chosen?

The final factor is the cost effectiveness, over the long run, of one medium compared to others. Some materials may be initially cheaper to produce in one medium than another, but these costs may be equalized when one considers costs in other areas such as lecturers, evaluators, and feedback personnel. It might be cheaper to videotape a lecture for a large group of students to view again and again as needed, which frees the lecturer or specialist to work with small groups of students or to help individuals solve problems.

All the factors discussed here represent either theoretical or practical criteria that must be met. These criteria illustrate the importance of media selection in the instructional development process. In theory it would be ideal to delay the choice of a delivery system until media have been chosen for the components of the instructional strategy; however, in practice, nearly all projects begin with the delivery system already established. Regardless of the circumstance, most delivery systems offer a range of media alternatives. Matched with a thorough front-end analysis and learning context analysis, the designer can maximize the effectiveness of the instruction with a variety of media formats in a course or workshop.

Examples

This Examples section synthesizes the steps a designer would take in the process of developing an instructional strategy. Procedures and criteria for evaluating the strategy are also described.

The Process of Developing an Instructional Strategy

Assigning objectives to lessons and consolidating media selections are two steps in developing an instructional strategy (Figure 8.1; p. 169) that have not yet been discussed. Both of these are process steps that integrate some of the work of developing an instructional strategy, so they will be described in this section.

Now that you have an idea of what is included in an instructional strategy, you can see that it would be inappropriate to go directly from a list of performance objectives to writing instructional materials without first planning and documenting your instructional strategy. The instructional strategy is a product that can be used as any of the following:

- Prescription to develop instructional materials
- Set of criteria to evaluate existing materials
- Set of criteria and a prescription to revise existing materials
- Framework from which instruction can be organized and managed and student participation can be planned

Regardless of the availability of existing instructional materials, the instructor should develop an instructional strategy for a set of performance objectives before selecting, adapting, or developing instruction.

What is needed to develop an instructional strategy? The instructor should begin with an instructional design that includes: (1) an instructional goal and goal analysis,

(2) subskills identified through an instructional analysis, (3) a list of performance objectives, (4) associated test items, (5) learner analysis, (6) learning context analysis, and (7) performance context analysis.

Having completed all these steps, you are ready to develop your instructional strategy, realizing that you have already completed some of the work needed. You have already (1) identified objectives, (2) identified prerequisite knowledge (through your analysis of the relationship among subskills in the instructional analysis), (3) identified the sequence for presenting instruction (when you completed your design evaluation table and your analysis diagram), (4) identified the content required (when you analyzed the knowledge and skills during the instructional analysis), and (5) identified appropriate test items for each objective. All this information, already included in your design evaluation table, will serve as input for the development of the instructional strategy.

Even though we recommend that learning components in an instructional strategy occur in the order presented in the previous section (preinstructional activities, presentation of content, student participation, assessment, and follow-through), we do not recommend that you try to develop your instructional strategy in this order. The developmental sequence differs from the suggested order in which students encounter learning components during a lesson.

The best sequence for developing your instructional strategy is as follows:

1. Indicate the sequence of objectives and how you will cluster them for instruction. To do this, consider both the sequence and the size of clusters that are appropriate for the attention span of students and the time available for each session. In designing the sequence, remember to include review or synthesizing activities when needed. The decisions you make about sequence and clusters can be summarized using a form such as that shown in Table 8.4. Later, this prescription will help you assign objectives to lessons.

2. Indicate your approach to preinstructional activities, assessment, and follow-through. The relevant issues, listed in Figure 8.3, can be answered in narrative form with reference to each of the headings in the figure. Note that decisions about student groupings and media selection are made while these components of the strategy are

table 8.4

Performance Objectives for Main Step 6 from Table 6.7 Sequenced and Clustered

Clusters*	Instructional Goal Steps			
1	Main step 1: Prepare for discussion			
2	Main step 2: Set agenda			
3	Main step 3: Convene group			
4	Main step 4: Introduce task			
5–8	Main step 5: Manage thought line			
	Cluster 5	Cluster 6	Cluster 7	Cluster 8
9–12	Main step 6: Manage cooperative group interaction			
	Cluster 9 Objectives:	Cluster 10 Objectives:	Cluster 11 Objectives:	Cluster 12 Objectives:
	6.1.1 6.3.1	6.6.1 6.7.1	6.11.1	6.1: Main step 6
	6.1.2 6.4.1	6.6.2 6.7.2	6.12.1	
	6.2.1 6.4.2	6.6.3 6.8.1	6.12.2	
	6.2.2 6.5.1	6.6.4 6.9.1	6.13.1	
		6.6.5 6.9.2	6.14.1	
		6.6.6 6.10.1	6.14.2	
		6.6.7	6.15.1	
13	Main step 7: Summarize/conclude discussion			
14	Terminal objective			

*All clusters are designed to require approximately two hours (allocated time in learning center).

| **f i g u r e**

8 . 3 | Format for Writing Preinstructional, Assessment, and Follow-Through Learning Components Including Their Student Groupings and Media Selections Plans |

PREINSTRUCTIONAL ACTIVITIES

MOTIVATION: Explain how you will gain learners' attention and maintain it throughout instruction.

OBJECTIVES: Explain how you will inform the learners about what they will be able to do when they finish your lesson. Explain why doing this is important to the learners.

ENTRY SKILLS: Explain how you will inform learners about skills they should already possess and how you will promote learners' active recall of relevant mental contexts in which the new skills can be integrated.

STUDENT GROUPINGS AND MEDIA SELECTIONS: Explain how you will group students (e.g., individualized, small subgroups, total group). Describe the media selection (e.g., live lecture, videotape, print, web-based).

ASSESSMENT

PRETEST: Explain whether you will test for entry skills and what you will do if a learner does not have them. Explain also whether you will test for skills you will teach.

PRACTICE TESTS: Explain how you will use practice tests and rehearsal activities and where they will be located in the instruction.

POSTTEST: Explain when and how the posttest will be administered.

STUDENT GROUPINGS AND MEDIA SELECTIONS: Explain how you will group students for assessments (e.g., individualized, small subgroups, total group). Describe the media selection (e.g., paper and pencil, product development, live performance or video, computer-administered and scored).

FOLLOW-THROUGH ACTIVITIES

MEMORY AID: Describe any memory aids that will be developed to facilitate retention of information and skills.

TRANSFER: Describe any special factors to be employed to facilitate performance transfer.

STUDENT GROUPINGS AND MEDIA SELECTIONS: Explain how you will group students (e.g., individualized, small subgroups, total group). Describe the media selection (e.g., live lecture, videotape, print, web-based).

---

planned. Note also that these components of the instructional strategy apply to all of your objectives; that is, they are normally planned once for your total unit or lesson. The next section will apply to individual objectives or clusters of objectives.

3. Indicate the content to be presented and student participation activities for each objective or cluster of objectives, for which you may wish to use a form similar to the one included in Figure 8.4. The objective number from your list of performance objectives is identified at the top of the form. Your form should include two main sections: content to be presented and student participation. The presentation section should briefly describe the required content and learning guidance. In selecting examples for guidance, remember to choose congruent examples that are most likely to be familiar and interesting to learners. The participation section should illustrate a sample practice exercise and the type of feedback that will be provided in the instruction. Figure 8.4 will be used as part of the information required for assigning objectives to lessons and for developing or selecting instructional materials. Don't forget to include a component that indicates your strategy for teaching the terminal objective at the end of your instruction, and remember to include notes about student groupings and media selection.

<table>
<tr><td rowspan="10">figure

8.4</td><td>Format for Writing Content Presentation and Student
Participation Learning Components</td></tr>
<tr><td>Objective Number</td></tr>
<tr><td>CONTENT PRESENTATION</td></tr>
<tr><td>CONTENT:
EXAMPLES:
STUDENT GROUPINGS AND MEDIA SELECTIONS:</td></tr>
<tr><td>STUDENT PARTICIPATION</td></tr>
<tr><td>PRACTICE ITEMS AND ACTIVITIES:
FEEDBACK:
STUDENT GROUPINGS AND MEDIA SELECTIONS:</td></tr>
</table>

4. Review your sequence and clusters of objectives, preinstructional activities, assessment, content presentation, student participation strategies, and student groupings and media selections. Using this information—coupled with the amount of time available for each lesson and the predicted attention span of target learners—assign objectives to lessons or learning sessions. The first session will undoubtedly contain preinstructional activities, and the last will include the posttest or feedback from the posttest. Intervening lessons should include time for any needed review, presentation, and participation.

5. Review the entire strategy again to consolidate your media selections and either (1) confirm that they fit an imposed delivery system or (2) select a delivery system that is compatible with the learning and performance context.

Several things should be noted about developing an instructional strategy as outlined here. First of all, certain instructional components must be considered in terms of the entire sequence of instruction; that is, preinstructional, assessment, and follow-through activities apply to the whole lesson. On the other hand, the content presentation, practice, and feedback sections must be completed for each objective or cluster of objectives, including your terminal objective. It is not intended that you write the whole lesson in the strategy. If you do, then you have written too much. The purpose of the written strategy is to require you to think through the entire lesson before you start developing or selecting any instruction.

Instructional Strategy Evaluation

With the completion of the instructional strategy, you are at another important checkpoint in the instructional design process. Now is a good time to do some more checking with both SMEs and learners. Their reactions will save needless writing and revision later on. The time required is small compared to the value of the feedback.

Subject-matter experts and individuals familiar with the needs, interests, and attention spans of learners can be asked to review all three of your strategy tables and to pinpoint potential problems. Spending a short time with selected reviewers now may save hours during later stages of the instructional development process. You may need to provide reviewers with additional information such as a description of your instructional goal, a list of your objectives, and a description of the characteristics of your intended learners. This information will help reviewers judge the quality of the information included in your strategy.

Now is also the time to try out your instructional strategy and assessments with one or two learners. The procedure is to explain to the learners that you are developing some instruction and would like to see whether you have an adequate outline of what you are going to teach. Go through the strategy just as you have written it, but in this case simply explain it to the learners. You might show them some of the examples and ask them to do the practice activities. Do they understand, and can they participate? Give them some or all of your test items and see how they do. This is a very informal process, but it can yield valuable information that you can use to revise the strategy before you begin to write the instructional materials or instructor guide, create a storyboard, or prepare a web-based instructional lesson.

Case Study: Group Leadership Training

There are two versions of an instructional strategy in this case study. The first version illustrates the five phases of a cognitive instructional strategy that follows the Dick and Carey model. The second version uses a constructivist learning environment for the same goal. For additional cognitive and constructivist examples of instructional strategies, refer to the school-based example in Appendixes F, G, and H at the end of the book.

Cognitive Instructional Strategy

The five phases to planning the cognitive instructional strategy for a unit of instruction are as follows:

1. Sequence and cluster objectives.
2. Plan preinstructional, assessment, and follow-through activities for the unit with notes about student groupings and media selections.
3. Plan the content presentations and student participation sections for each objective or cluster of objectives with notes about student groupings and media selections.
4. Assign objectives to lessons and estimate the time required for each.
5. Review the strategy to consolidate media selections and confirm or select a delivery system.

We will consider each of these in turn, with examples from the group leadership case study that we have carried throughout the book.

Sequence and Cluster Objectives   The first step in planning the instructional strategy is to sequence and cluster performance objectives. The subskills and instructional goal from Figure 4.8 (p. 81), Lead Group Discussions Aimed at Solving Problems, are included in Table 8.4. Fourteen clusters of objectives are identified, and two hours of instruction are planned for each cluster. Although not broken out for this illustration, the objectives for main steps 1 through 4 are each assigned to their own cluster. The objectives for main step 5, "thought line," are divided into four separate clusters. The objectives for main skill 6, "Manage cooperative group interaction," are broken out into clusters 9 through 12. The content and nature of the objectives in each cluster were analyzed to ensure that they represented a logical set of skills. Cluster 9 contains the objectives related to recognizing and engendering cooperative behavior, and cluster 10 includes objectives for recognizing and defusing blocking behaviors of group members. Cluster 11 deals with recognizing and alleviating group stress. Cluster 12 focuses on objectives for all subordinate skills of main step 6 addressed together. Cluster 13 includes all objectives subordinate to main step 7, "Summarize/conclude discussion." Cluster 14 contains the terminal objective of all seven main steps and their subordinate skills. This cluster reflects the entire leadership process.

The clusters of subskills planned and the amount of time assigned may need to be revised as you continue to develop the strategy. This initial structure, however, will help you focus on lessons rather than on individual objectives.

Plan Preinstructional, Assessment, and Follow-Through Activities These learning components of the instructional strategy relate to the overall lesson or lessons and do not refer to individual instructional objectives within a lesson. First, how will you design preinstructional activities? Remember, this area contains three separate sections: motivation, objectives, and entry skills. Figure 8.5 shows the instructional strategy plans for these components. Notice that the information used in the lessons is not included in the figure, the objectives are not written out, and the entry skills are not listed. Instead, what you will need to do when developing the instruction is briefly described, along with notes about student groupings and media selection.

Focusing now on the assessment and follow-through phases of the instructional strategy for the instructional goal, how would you plan these activities for NCW leaders? Figure 8.6 includes plans for pretests, posttests, and follow-through activities. A pretest focused directly on the objectives included in each session will be administered at the beginning of the session except for clusters 8, 12, and 14. No pretest will be administered in these sessions because pretest data for these objectives, main steps 5, 6, and the terminal objective, will have been collected in preceding sessions. Likewise, a cluster-focused posttest will be administered at the conclusion of each session. A terminal objective posttest will be administered during the final session. Given the characteristics of the leaders and their situation as volunteers in their neighborhoods, the posttests will be administered informally and represented as practice activities rather than as tests. It will be made clear to learners that the assessments are included to help them focus and practice skills and to help the staff learn about the strengths and weaknesses in the instruction.

The bottom portion of Figure 8.6 contains the designers' prescriptions for follow-through activities. Included are plans for memory aids and transfer support as leaders plan and conduct meetings in their neighborhoods. Student groupings and media selections are also noted in the figure.

---

f i g u r e

8 . 5

Preinstructional Learning Components for Unit on Leading Group Discussion with Student Groupings and Media Selections

---

PREINSTRUCTIONAL ACTIVITIES

MOTIVATION: Prior to main step 1, "Prepare for discussion," the County NCW Coordinator will welcome the new leaders, provide praise for the volunteers, and discuss the critical role of NCW leaders in improving and maintaining the quality of life in the community. A uniformed police officer will welcome participants, discuss the relationship between NCW associations and the police department, present statistics on current crime and trends in neighborhoods (nature and frequency) around the state, discuss the financial and emotional costs of such crimes to families, and present actual statistics on the effectiveness of local NCW programs in reducing neighborhood crime. Actual local instances of NCW *leader* effectiveness will be highlighted.

OBJECTIVES: The critical role of the discussion leader in NCW groups will be described. An overview of the tasks leaders perform before and during meetings will be presented. A video of an actual group discussion, highlighting the role of the leader at each step, will be shown.

ENTRY SKILLS: Learners will all have completed the instruction on problem-solving group discussion methods. They will be heterogeneous in their group discussion skill levels due to their varying ages, education levels, work experience, and group problem-solving experience. They will enter the leadership instruction regardless of their posttest performance levels in the group membership instruction.

STUDENT GROUPINGS AND MEDIA SELECTIONS: Instructor-led, large-group discussion; video playback.

figure	Testing and Follow-Through Learning Components
8.6	for Unit on Leading Group Discussion

ASSESSMENT

PRETESTS: Due to the heterogeneous nature of the NCW leaders and the varied group participation experiences they have had, a pretest will be administered at the beginning of each of the sessions. The pretest will be informal and administered as an instructional activity to be collected. For sessions 1 through 3, the pretest will be a print document. For sessions 4 through 14, it will consist of a staged NCW meeting (video) that leaders watch. During viewing, they will use an observation form to tally the number of times named leader behaviors occur in the meeting. After instructional materials are developed and formative evaluation activities are complete, trainers may choose to dispense with the pretest for evaluation purposes. They may choose, however, to maintain the pretest as a preinstructional learning tool to focus learner attention on the objectives.

STUDENT GROUPING AND MEDIA SELECTION: Individualized, web-based; streaming video; downloadable observation form.

POSTTESTS: A small learning site posttest will be administered at the conclusion of each session. Clusters 8 and 12 will each consist of a performance posttest that requires leaders to manage the discussion thought line and manage the cooperative group interaction.

A final posttest will be administered during the last evening of training. To maximize the authenticity of the assessment, the examination will be designed to accommodate learners who are volunteers in a community setting, and it will be completed in three sections: a product section, a process section, and an analysis/feedback section.

The product part of the final posttest will require learners to complete the first three main steps (1. Prepare for discussion; 2. Set agenda; and 3. Convene group) in preparation for the first actual NCW meeting they will lead in their own neighborhoods. Leaders will independently make these preparations between the thirteenth and fourteenth instructional sessions and bring copies of their plans and materials to the last session. They will submit one copy of their plans (product) for review.

For the process portion of the posttest, leaders will break into small groups of four persons. Within their small groups, each member will lead a fifteen-minute group discussion on the "problem" topic he or she has prepared for the first community meeting. Their leadership performances will be videorecorded within each group.

For the last part of the posttest, learners will discuss the leadership performances of members within their groups. During these discussions, members will focus on each leader's strengths relative to introducing the task, managing the thought line, engendering cooperative member behaviors, defusing blocking behaviors, and alleviating group stress. Through these discussions, members will receive feedback on the positive aspects of their performances. Leaders may also review the videos of their own meetings to "watch themselves in action."

The effectiveness of the overall instruction will be assessed through the plans learners submitted, the videos of their leadership, and the interactive discussion in which learners critiqued each other's performances.

STUDENT GROUPING AND MEDIA SELECTIONS: Small and individual grouping; print, videorecording with playback.

FOLLOW-THROUGH ACTIVITIES

MEMORY AID: Memory aids planned include checklists of member and leader behaviors that leaders can use to focus their attention as they read meeting transcripts or view videos of simulated meetings. Leaders will take copies of the

(*continued*)

figure

8.6

Continued

checklists with them for reference as they plan for meetings in their neighborhoods.

TRANSFER: The NCW area coordinator schedules biannual meetings with NCW leaders. During these meetings successes, issues, and problems encountered in leading group discussions within the neighborhoods will be shared. In addition, the NCW coordinator will remain on call for leaders as they plan their meetings. Leaders will also be given names and telephone numbers of all NCW leaders attending the training sessions. Hopefully, these leaders will form a network of support for each other, sharing ideas and plans. Finally, a sample of leaders will be selected for a performance site posttest. Information gathered during these sessions on any assistance needed by leaders will be shared with the local NCW coordinator and local police representatives.

STUDENT GROUPING AND MEDIA SELECTIONS: Individualized, large- or small-group discussion; print job aid.

Plan Content Presentation and Learner Participation   Content presentation and learner participation sections make up the interactive part of the lesson. They are considered the exchange or interface point. The presentation section has two parts—namely, the content and learning guidance. The learner participation component has two areas: sample practice items and activities and the planned feedback strategy.

Figure 8.7 includes performance objectives for main step 6, "Manage cooperative interaction," as an illustration of how this format is used to sketch out the instructional strategy. Each objective is stated, followed by a description of the content and examples to be presented. In cases where videos will be used to present content, a description of the action is provided. All instruction and practice will be web-based up to objective 6.5.1. Notice that no new content about the objective is included for objective 6.5.1 because the skill-related content was presented online in the preceding objectives. Instead, media, materials, and general instructions for interactive meetings are described. In this instance the content presentation and student participation components are intertwined. This example illustrates how hierarchical skills build on each other and how the table format can be adapted for each objective.

At this point, we have completed examples of how to design the instructional strategy for the following: (1) sequencing and clustering objectives; (2) planning preinstructional, assessment, and follow-through activities; and (3) identifying content presentation and learner participation activities. Student groupings and media selections have also been noted as the learning components were planned.

Assign Objectives to Lessons   With this information complete, we should review it and allocate prescribed activities to lessons. Lesson prescriptions are included in Figure 8.8 on page 211. Compare the strategy for individual sessions in Figure 8.8 with the initial sequence and cluster of objectives in Table 8.4. Notice that we predicted a total of fourteen two-hour clusters in Table 8.4, but added an additional two hours of instruction for fifteen sessions in Figure 8.8. This was necessary to allow for preinstructional, motivational, and pretest activities in the first session. Within the remaining sessions, pretest and posttest activities are added. Again, you must consider the timelines tentative until you have developed the instruction and tested it with actual learners.

figure

8.7

Content Presentation and Student Participation Learning Components for Cluster 9 Performance Objectives (Main Step 6, Manage Cooperative Group Interaction) with Student Groupings and Media Selections

PERFORMANCE OBJECTIVES SUBORDINATE TO MAIN STEP 6

STUDENT GROUPING AND MEDIA SELECTIONS: All objectives 6.1.1 through 6.4.2, Individualized; web-based; streaming video where required; practice and feedback online.

6.1.1 When requested in writing to name group member actions that facilitate cooperative interaction, name those actions. At least six facilitating actions should be named.

CONTENT PRESENTATION

CONTENT: Cooperative interaction within group discussions depends on spontaneous positive actions that group members demonstrate when introducing their own ideas and when reacting to ideas introduced by others. An annotated NCW meeting dialogue will be provided with characters in the meeting demonstrating positive actions that foster cooperative group interaction. The annotation will point out the particular actions used by group members. The dialogue format will be used for its interest value and context validity.

EXAMPLES:

Personal actions
1. Prepares for discussion before meeting
2. Readily volunteers ideas and information
3. Invites others to participate
4. Demonstrates goodwill
5. Demonstrates open-mindedness

Reactions to others in discussion
1. Considers all members' ideas impartially
2. Listens attentively to others' comments
3. Gives others credit for their ideas
4. Demonstrates trust in others' motives
5. Resists pressures to conform
6. Respects others' loyalties and needs

STUDENT PARTICIPATION

PRACTICE ITEMS AND ACTIVITIES:
1. List positive personal **actions** that group members can take to facilitate cooperative interaction during problem-solving discussions.
2. List positive personal **reactions** to others that group members can take to facilitate cooperative interaction during problem-solving discussions.
3. Think back over interactive discussions you have had in the past. Name the actions and reactions of others that made you feel that those conversing with you were interested in you, in your comments, and in the problem being discussed.

FEEDBACK: Repeat list of positive personal actions and reactions group discussion members can demonstrate.

6.1.2 When asked in writing to indicate what members should do when their ideas are questioned by the group, name positive reactions that help ensure cooperative group interaction. Learner should name at least three possible reactions.

CONTENT PRESENTATION

CONTENT: Problem-solving group discussions naturally require give and take and a good deal of interactive brainstorming that often includes proposals of half-baked ideas. During brainstorming sessions, a member's ideas may be questioned for a myriad of reasons. The manner in which a member responds to these questions can demonstrate her or his goodwill and open-mindedness and can help ensure cooperative group interaction.

(continued)

figure	Continued
8.7	

EXAMPLES:
1. Listens attentively to members' questions (without interrupting)
2. Explains ideas more fully to help others understand the ideas and direction
3. Resists abandoning ideas too quickly just because they are questioned
4. Participates in modifying initial ideas to make them more acceptable to the group
5. Readily admits errors in ideas or judgment

STUDENT PARTICIPATION

PRACTICE ITEMS AND ACTIVITIES:
1. List positive **reactions** a group member can make when her or his proposals or ideas are questioned by other group members.
2. Think back over interactive discussions you have had in the past. Name the **positive reactions** that you have seen others make when their ideas were questioned or not readily accepted by other members of the group.

FEEDBACK: Restate positive reactions to others' questions.

6.2.1 Given written descriptions of group members' facilitating actions during a meeting, indicate whether the actions are likely to facilitate cooperative group interaction. Learner should correctly classify at least 80 percent of the actions depicted.

CONTENT PRESENTATION

CONTENT: A written NCW meeting scenario will be presented with actual characters and dialogue. The dialogue will include both positive personal actions and positive personal reactions of meeting participants.

EXAMPLES: (See 6.1.1)

STUDENT PARTICIPATION

PRACTICE ITEMS AND ACTIVITIES:
Using a checklist of positive personal actions and reactions, identify characters in the written scenario who demonstrate each positive action or reaction.

FEEDBACK: Complete checklist with characters' names inserted for each action and reaction.

6.2.2 Given videos of staged NCW meetings depicting facilitating member actions, indicate whether the members' actions are likely to facilitate cooperative group interaction. Learner should classify correctly at least 80 percent of the actions demonstrated.

CONTENT PRESENTATION

CONTENT: A simulated NCW discussion group will be staged and videorecorded with discussion members exhibiting positive personal actions and reactions during the meeting. Learners will watch the group members in action as they propose and discuss ideas.

EXAMPLES: (See 6.1.1)

STUDENT PARTICIPATION

PRACTICE ITEMS AND ACTIVITIES:
Using a checklist of positive personal actions and reactions, identify characters in the simulated meeting who demonstrate each positive action or reaction.

FEEDBACK: Complete checklist with characters' names inserted for those actions and reactions demonstrated.

6.3.1 When asked in writing to name leader actions that either encourage or stifle discussion and member cooperation, name these actions. Learner should name at least ten encouraging and corresponding stifling actions.

CONTENT PRESENTATION

CONTENT: As the discussion group leader, there are several actions you can take that encourage cooperative group interaction. For each of these cooperating actions, there are corresponding actions that tend to stifle group cooperation.

figure

8.7

Continued

EXAMPLES:

Cooperation encouraging actions	Cooperation stifling actions
1. Suggests points of discussion as questions	1. Prescribes topics for the group to consider
2. Uses an investigative, inquiring tone	2. Uses an authoritative tone
3. Uses open terms such as *perhaps* and *might*	3. Uses prescriptive terms such as *must* or *should*
4. Hesitates and pauses between speakers	4. Fills quiet gaps with personal points of view or solutions
5. Willingly turns over the floor to group members who interrupt	5. Continues to talk over interrupting member or interrupts member
6. Encompasses total group with eyes and invites all to participate freely	6. Focuses gaze on a few members
7. Nonverbally (eyes, gestures) encourages speaker to address group	7. Holds speaker's attention
8. Uses comments that keep discussion centered in the group	8. Encourages discussion to flow through leader by evaluating member comments
9. Encourages volunteerism (e.g., "Who has experience with . . .")	9. Designates speakers and speaking order (e.g., "Beth, what do you think about . . .")
10. Refers to *us, we, our*	10. Refers to *I, me, mine,* or *your*
11. Acknowledges group accomplishments	11. Acknowledges own accomplishments or those of particular members
12. Praises group effort and accomplishment	12. Singles out particular people for praise

STUDENT PARTICIPATION

PRACTICE ITEMS AND ACTIVITIES:

1. List strategies you can use as group discussion leader to encourage cooperative group interaction.
2. Think back over interactive discussions you have had in the past. Name the actions and reactions of the discussion leader that you believe engendered cooperative interaction among group members.

FEEDBACK: Repeat list of positive leader actions and reactions that engender cooperative interaction among group members.

6.4.1 Given written descriptions of a group leader's action during a meeting, indicate whether the leader exhibits actions that are likely to encourage or stifle cooperative group interaction. Learner should correctly classify at least 80 percent of the actions depicted.

CONTENT PRESENTATION

CONTENT: A written NCW meeting scenario will be presented with actual characters and dialogue. The dialogue will focus particularly on leader actions and reactions designed to encourage positive member interaction and participation.
EXAMPLES: (See 6.3.1)

STUDENT PARTICIPATION

PRACTICE ITEMS AND ACTIVITIES:
Using a checklist of actions the leader can take to encourage or stifle positive member interaction, identify the particular behaviors exhibited by the leader in the written scenario.
FEEDBACK: Complete checklist with described leader actions checked.

(continued)

figure
8.7

Continued

6.4.2 Given videos of staged NCW meetings depicting staged leader's actions, classify the leader's actions that are likely to encourage or stifle member cooperation. Learner should classify correctly at least 80 percent of the encouraging and stifling actions demonstrated.

CONTENT PRESENTATION

CONTENT: A simulated NCW discussion group will be staged and recorded with video. The group leader will exhibit actions designed to encourage or stifle member interaction during the meeting. Learners will watch the leader "in action" managing the group.
EXAMPLES: (See 6.3.1)

STUDENT PARTICIPATION

PRACTICE ITEMS AND ACTIVITIES:
Using a checklist of actions the leader can take to encourage and stifle positive member interaction, identify the particular behaviors exhibited by the leader in the video.
FEEDBACK: Complete checklist with exhibited leader actions checked.

6.5.1 In simulated NCW problem-solving meetings with learner acting as group leader, initiate actions to engender cooperative behavior among members. Group members cooperate with each other and with leader during discussion.

CONTENT PRESENTATION

CONTENT: Learners will break into small groups of four and each group will receive a written description and background information for a particular neighborhood safety problem as well as a meeting agenda for discussing the given problem. After reading the material, one member will serve as the discussion leader and the remaining three members will serve as group members. (Different problem scenarios will be provided for each of the four group members to enable each to rehearse group interaction leadership.)
STUDENT GROUPING AND MEDIA SELECTIONS: Small-group role play; print scenario.

STUDENT PARTICIPATION

PRACTICE ITEMS AND ACTIVITIES: The leader will introduce the problem to the group, set the climate for cooperative interaction, and lead a simulated group discussion for ten minutes.
FEEDBACK: Following the discussion, group members will discuss positive aspects of the leader's performance. These discussions will be held within the small group only.
STUDENT GROUPING AND MEDIA SELECTIONS: Small-group discussion among group members

Consolidate Media Selection and Confirm or Select Delivery System The last phase of planning is to review the instructional strategy to consolidate media selections and ensure compatibility with the delivery system. While planning the instructional strategy, consider how to mediate instruction by noting the domain of learning in each objective and examining the conditions, behavior, and content in the objective. Also consider which medium would best replicate conditions in the learning and performance contexts. Begin by selecting the ideal media formats for the domains of learning and objective components, but compromise and choose the best medium given constraints such as budget, personnel, equipment, and delivery system and learning site constraints. After choosing the best medium for each objective or cluster of objectives, it makes sense to examine the entire set of selections for patterns or common media prescriptions across the objectives.

figure 8.8

Lesson Allocation Based on Instructional Strategy

SESSION	ACTIVITIES
1	Introductory and motivational materials: 1. NCW coordinator gives welcome, praise for leader volunteers, and overview of workshop (objectives). 2. Police officer gives welcome, presentation of statewide/nationwide neighborhood crime problems, and presentation of crime-reducing influence of active NCW groups. 3. Pretest with group discussion feedback pointing to main steps in leadership process.
2	Pretest; introduction; instruction and practice activities on objectives for main step 1, "Prepare for discussion"; and posttest.
3	Pretest; introduction; instruction and practice activities on objectives for main step 2, "Set agenda"; and posttest.
4	Pretest; introduction; instruction and practice activities on objectives for main step 3, "Convene group"; and posttest.
5	Pretest; introduction; instruction and practice activities on objectives for main step 4, "Introduce task"; and posttest.
6–9	Each of these sessions will contain a pretest; introduction; instruction and practice activities on objectives for main step 5, "Manage thought line"; and posttest. Session 6 — 2 hours Session 7 — 2 hours Session 8 — 2 hours Session 9 — 2 hours
10–13	Sessions 10, 11, and 12 will contain a pretest; introduction; instruction and practice activities on objectives for main step 6, "Manage cooperative group interaction"; and posttest. Session 13 will contain an introduction and interactive groups in which leaders manage group interaction. No pretest or posttest will be administered. A debriefing and discussion session will follow group rehearsals. Session 10 Objectives: 6.1.1 6.3.1 / 6.1.2 6.4.1 / 6.2.1 6.4.2 / 6.2.2 6.5.1 Session 11 Objectives: 6.6.1 6.7.1 / 6.6.2 6.7.2 / 6.6.3 6.8.1 / 6.6.4 6.9.1 / 6.6.5 6.9.2 / 6.6.6 6.10.1 / 6.6.7 Session 12 Objectives: 6.11.1 / 6.12.1 / 6.12.2 / 6.13.1 / 6.14.1 / 6.14.2 / 6.15.1 Session 13 Objectives: 6.1: Main step 6
14	Pretest; introduction; instruction and practice activities on objectives for main step 7, "Summarize/conclude discussion"; and posttest.
15	Give welcome, instructions for session, and three-part posttest for terminal objective, debriefing.

Table 8.5 contains a summary of media prescriptions taken from the instructional strategy for the instructional goal "Lead group discussions aimed at solving problems, Step 6: Manage cooperative group interaction." The first column contains the class sessions and the second column contains the objectives in each session. The third column identifies the initial media selections based on the domain of learning, the objective, resources available for materials development, and facilities and equipment present in the county learning centers. In the fourth column the media selections are consolidated and final decisions about a delivery system are recorded.

table 8.5	Consolidation of Media Selections and Choice of Delivery System for Main Step 6, Sessions 10 through 13 (from Figure 8.8)

Session	Objectives	Initial Student Groupings and Media Selections	Consolidated Media Selections and Delivery System(s)
10	6.1.1 & 6.1.2	Individualized, web-based, distance	Individualized; web-based distance; streaming video
	6.2.1 & 6.2.2	Individualized, web-based, distance	
		Individualized; web-based distance; streaming video	
	6.3.1	Individualized, web-based, distance	
	6.4.1 & 6.4.2	Individualized, web-based distance	
		Individualized; web-based distance; streaming video	
11	6.6 through 6.9		Individualized; web-based distance; streaming video
12	6.11 through 6.14		Individualized; web-based distance; streaming video
13	6	Large-group presentation for motivation and directions	Large-group presentation for motivation and directions
	6.5		
	6.10		
	6.15	Small group, simulation and interactions	Small group, simulation and interactions
		Videos of small-group sessions	Videos of small-group sessions and small-group discussion of videos

Considering the entire set of prescriptions in column 3 of Table 8.5, you can see that a pattern exists: live group simulations, videos, and individualized web-based instruction are each repeated several times. In the performance site, newly trained leaders will work interactively within a group, so using live group simulations during instruction will closely resemble the context within which NCW leaders must work. They will also need to make inferences from group interactions, so observing televised groups as they interact will help support concept acquisition. Providing printed dialogue scripts of meetings rather than didactic descriptions of meetings is also prescribed for authenticity, because interpreting meeting dialogue and members' actions will be the focus during learners' actual work.

The first delivery system considered was individualized web-based distance instruction because of costs and convenience. For authenticity and transfer, however, the live-group simulations would have to be retained for advanced practice, feedback, and posttesting. These media consolidation and delivery system decisions are reflected in column 4 of Table 8.5.

The decision for independent, web-based instruction was made for several reasons. The learners are mature, motivated adults who have volunteered for the NCW responsibility, and the novelty value and convenience of distance learning should engender some initial motivation. Most learners have computers with Internet access in their homes, and others have access at work or in a local branch library. Although the initial audience for the instruction is not large, the training program will be repeated and could be exported to other counties promoting development of NCW groups. There is some turnover in the job and new NCW volunteers could be trained with a combination of the web instruction and peer tutoring from successful NCW leaders. From a practical perspective, the distance learning format will standardize instruction, ensure uniform results, save instructor time, and reduce learner travel time and miles. Finally, there is sufficient money in the grant budget to pay for web development, formative evaluation, and revision, and the county information systems division has agreed to provide server space and software maintenance.

After consolidating media selections and confirming or selecting a delivery system, it may be necessary to revisit the previous step, "Allocate activities to lessons," and touch up some of that planning. This is particularly true if selection of a delivery system was delayed until this point in the design process. In most instructional design contexts the delivery system would have been assumed or imposed at the outset of the process, and the designer merely confirms delivery system capability for the media selections. One can see in Table 8.5 that skills 6.5, 6.10, and 6.15 have all been moved to session 13 with main step 6. This was done because these require learners to come to the center and cannot be delivered via the web. The reader is referred back to Figure 8.1 for a visual representation of the overall process of developing an instructional strategy and choosing a delivery system. The instructional strategy for main step 6, "Manage cooperative group interaction," is now complete, and we have the prescriptions necessary to begin developing materials.

Constructivist Instructional Strategy

A constructivist instructional strategy is quite different than the one just described, and it could be created in many different ways due to the flexibility afforded by a constructivist model. Table 8.6 includes a constructivist strategy for main step 6 from the goal analysis in Figure 4.9 (p. 83). The left column focuses the designer on planning needs and the right column identifies planning activities that should be completed. Notice in the sample strategy the increased responsibility placed both on the instructor/coaches and on the learners for creating and managing the learning environment.

table 8.6	Planning for a Constructivist Learning Environment for Main Step 6, Manage Cooperative Group Interaction

Planning Needs	**Planning Activities**
Planning the Learning Environment	**Designs and materials needed to launch the CLE** • Goal: Lead group discussions aimed at solving problems • Learning objectives: Addressed at main step level during sessions; subordinate skills excluded except as job aids or direct requests; 14 two-hour instructional sessions possible (covered by grant); apportioned to the 7 main skills steps; number of sessions per main step negotiated on ongoing basis by the learners and coaches • Learning objective for main step 6, Manage cooperative group interaction: Learners serve as team leaders in NCW meeting and exhibit actions for *diffusing* committee members' blocking behaviors, *engendering* members' cooperative behaviors, and *alleviating* members' stress • Rationale: Leaders, through skill in managing problem-solving discussions, encourage community members to become involved and to stay involved in cooperative community meetings aimed at reducing crime in neighborhoods • Constructivist focus: Critical thinking, problem solving, and cognitive flexibility • Pedagogical model: Problem-based learning (PBL) • Scenario: A group of new NCW community leaders addressing crime problems in their neighborhood and identifying ideas for reducing local crime activity; key question driving problem scenario for session is "How do I manage my NCW community meetings to bring about effective and continued participation by community members?" • Learning Resource Materials • Instructional goal analysis illustrating subordinate skills for main step 6, Manage cooperative group interaction

(continued)

table

8.6

Continued

Planning Needs	Planning Activities

	• Web-based instruction and quizzes for all subskills for main step 6 to be used as follow-up assignment with groups/ individuals if needed and for statewide distribution to county government learning centers.
	• The materials learners produce individually and in groups following their learning interaction in session 2 (NCW meeting agendas) and session 4 (NCW meeting task statements)
	• Job aids
	   • Leader actions that can engender cooperative group behavior (subskill analysis for 6.5)
	   • Recognizing and diffusing members' blocking behaviors (subskill analysis for 6.10)
	   • Actions leader can take to alleviate group stress (subskill analysis for 6.15)
	   • Draft rubric for evaluating leader actions during simulated meeting
	• Learner groupings: Total of 20 learners per site with learners forming own work groups of four to five individuals (four teams) to ensure that each member has at least 15 to 20 minutes to serve as leader of a group problem-solving meeting
	• Delivery system, media, and personnel
	   • Internet access during sessions and between sessions for learner research
	   • Blogging space for group interaction between sessions
	   • County web-based learning portal
	   • Video equipment for recording interactive meetings
	   • Trained facilitator/coach for each meeting group (four, each site)
	   • Technology specialist to manage video recording and playback for teams
	   • Instructional designer to create direct instruction for web-based portal

Planning for Learner Engagement	**Procedures anticipated during engagement**
	• Engage
	   • View video of community members who express disappointment with their interactions at problem-solving community meetings. All cited the cause as ineffective leaders who did not control group stress levels or members' blocking behaviors and who did not make members feel that their ideas were welcome or accepted. Following video, members discuss similar situations in their own experiences and the important role of leaders in gaining and sustaining community member participation in NCW meetings.
	• Explore
	   • Group and coach plan session organization to enable both interactive meetings and debriefing, reflection, and review (e.g., group size, meeting length, breaks)
	   • Group and coach discuss the learning outcome related to video interviews as well as the three meeting management job aids they can use (as both leaders and members) during the simulated meetings
	   • Group and coach critique job aids and remove/add leader actions based on their own experiences.
	   • Learners take turns serving as group leaders exploring actions they can take to diffuse committee members' blocking behaviors, *engender* their cooperative behaviors, and *alleviate* committee members' stress as learners discuss crime issues in their community and identify potential solutions and strategies

table | Continued
8.6

Planning Needs	Planning Activities
	• Explain: Following each person's leadership turn, he or she talks with team members and coach about his or her actions and consequences (actions/feelings) within the group • Elaborate: Members share ideas about alternative strategies they or group leader might use for better problem-solving interactions; discuss alternative, effective strategies they have observed leaders use at work and in other meetings within the community • Evaluate: (see authentic assessment in a later section of table)

Planning Learning Guidance	**Materials and activities anticipated for adaptive learning guidance**
	• Scaffolding
	  • Demonstrate member blocking behaviors and stress if actions are not forthcoming from group members in meetings
	  • Assist members in focusing on important aspects of leader/member actions
	  • Refer to job aids when needed
	  • Model
	    • Diffusing behaviors when not forthcoming from leader
	    • Stress alleviating behaviors when not forthcoming from leader

Planning Authentic Assessment	**Materials and procedures anticipated for authentic assessment**
	• Reflection prior to viewing videos; prompts for group members
	• Reflect on consequences of particular actions or reactions within the group
	  • Reflect on the effectiveness of leader and committee member actions demonstrated during meeting
	  • Discuss their rational for actions they believe were effective and ineffective in their own leadership
	  • Explain their reasoning about particular actions they judge as effective and ineffective
	  • Evaluate the rubric provided to add/remove actions they believe should be critiqued in their leadership
	• While viewing videos produced of the meetings (which can be paused), when needed, prompts for group members
	  • Reflect on consequences of particular actions or reactions observed within the group meeting
	  • Reflect on actions demonstrated that appear to be very effective or not effective
	  • Consider the types of information needed to refine skills in meeting management
	• Following the reflections, prompts for learner discussion
	  • Whether they want to schedule another meeting simulation where they can serve as leaders, and if so, how they would like it to proceed
	  • The emphasis they would like in a subsequent meeting (e.g., step 5, managing thought line; step 6, managing group interaction; a combination of the two)
	  • Information they believe necessary for the meeting (e.g., actual crime statistics from the town, resource officers)
	• Remind learners of group blog and invite them to reflect on any part of this session's simulated meetings (their role or that of teammates); some members may want to post information or job aids they gather or develop for the group

SUMMARY

Materials you will need in order to develop your instructional strategy include the instructional goal, the learner and context analyses, the instructional analysis, the performance objectives, and the assessment items. You will need to reference these materials several times as you design your strategy.

The instructional strategy is a prescription that will be used for developing or selecting instructional materials. The first consideration is sequencing the content for teaching and making clusters of logical groupings of skills in the instructional analysis.

Some educational psychologists view instructional strategy as having four main learning components that guide learners' intellectual processing through the mental states and activities that foster learning. These four components of an essential instructional strategy are preinstructional activities, content presentation, student participation with feedback, and follow-through activities. The fifth learning component—assessment—is included in the strategy to facilitate instructional management. Assessment enables us to tailor instruction to the needs of learners, to evaluate the quality of instructional materials, and to evaluate the progress of learners. Although the major function of assessment in the strategy is management, it also can support learning when corrective feedback about performance is provided to learners. As these components are being planned, the designer specifies student groupings and selects one or more media that can be used to deliver each component. The selection decision is based on theory and administrative (or logistical) considerations.

Instruction is presented to students in the sequence of the named components in the strategy; however, the strategy is not designed in this order. The first step in designing the strategy is to sequence and cluster objectives for presentation. The second is to prescribe the preinstructional, assessment, and follow-through learning components. The third is to prescribe the content presentation and student participation components. The fourth is to assign objectives to lessons. The final step is to review the instructional strategy to consolidate media selections and confirm or select a delivery system.

The type of instructional goal is an important consideration when designing your strategy. Whether intellectual skills, verbal information, motor skills, or attitudes, careful consideration of all five of the learning components is important. Each type of goal, however, may require unique activities for each of the learning components.

In creating each component of your strategy, you should also consider the characteristics of your target students—their needs, interests, and experiences—as well as information about how to gain and maintain their attention throughout the five learning components of instruction. Keller's ARCS model provides a handy structure for considering how to design materials that motivate students to learn.

RUBRIC FOR EVALUATING AN INSTRUCTIONAL STRATEGY

Before developing materials based on your strategy, you should seek evaluation from content experts as well as from one or more of your target learners. The following is a rubric that you can use as a job aid in developing your strategy and that reviewers can use to assess it.

Designer note: If an element is not relevant for your plan, mark NA in the No column.

No	Some	Yes	**A. Content Sequence** Is/does the plan:
___	___	___	1. Appropriate for type of learning?
___	___	___	2. Have logical order (e.g., chronological, simple to complex, concept to rule to principle)?
___	___	___	3. Follow main steps?
___	___	___	4. Cover all skills/information within a main step before moving to next step?

B. Content Clusters (chunks)   Is the plan appropriate for:

No	Some	Yes	
___	___	___	1. Skill complexity?
___	___	___	2. Learners' age and ability?
___	___	___	3. Type of learning?
___	___	___	4. Content compatibility?
___	___	___	5. Time available (hour, day, week, semester)?
___	___	___	6. Delivery format (self-paced, instructor-led, televised, web-based, combination, etc.)?
___	___	___	7. Time required for all instructional events per cluster?

No	Some	Yes	
—	—	—	**C. Preinstructional Activities** Is/does the plan:
—	—	—	1. Appropriate for learners' characteristics?
—	—	—	2. Motivational for learners (gain attention, demonstrate relevance)?
—	—	—	3. Inform learners of objectives and purpose for instruction?
—	—	—	4. Cause learners to recall prerequisite knowledge and skills?
—	—	—	5. Inform learners of input needed to complete tasks required?

D. Presentation Materials   Does the plan include:

No	Some	Yes	
—	—	—	1. Materials appropriate for the type of learning?
—	—	—	2. Clear examples and nonexamples for learners' experience?
—	—	—	3. Appropriate materials such as explanations, illustrations, diagrams, demonstrations, model solutions, and sample performances?
—	—	—	4. Learner guidance through the presentation materials?
—	—	—	5. Aids for linking new content and skills to prerequisites?
—	—	—	6. Progression from the familiar to the unfamiliar?
—	—	—	7. Organization?

E. Learner Participation   Is the plan likely to be:

No	Some	Yes	
—	—	—	1. Appropriate for learning type?
—	—	—	2. Congruent with objectives?
—	—	—	3. Congruent with learner characteristics?
—	—	—	4. Congruent with instruction?
—	—	—	5. Likely to be motivational (aid learner in building confidence)?
—	—	—	6. Appropriately placed in instruction (not too soon, often, infrequent)?

F. Feedback   Does the plan appear to be:

No	Some	Yes	
—	—	—	1. Appropriate for learning type?
—	—	—	2. Congruent with objectives?
—	—	—	3. Congruent with learner characteristics?
—	—	—	4. Informative, supportive, and corrective?
—	—	—	5. Likely to aid learner in building confidence and personal satisfaction?

G. Assessments   Is the plan appropriate for:

No	Some	Yes	
—	—	—	1. Readiness/Pretests?
—	—	—	2. Posttests?
—	—	—	3. Type of learning (objective, alternative)?
—	—	—	4. Learner characteristics (age, attention span, ability)?
—	—	—	5. Yielding valid and reliable information about learner status and attitudes?

H. Follow-Through Activities   Is the plan likely to:

No	Some	Yes	
—	—	—	1. Aid retention of the new information and skills?
—	—	—	2. Support transfer of skills from learning to performance environment (e.g., working with supervisors, forming support teams)?

I. Student Groupings   Are groupings appropriate for:

No	Some	Yes	
—	—	—	1. Learning requirements (e.g., learning type, interaction, objective clusters)?
—	—	—	2. Learning context (e.g., staff, facilities, equipment, media, delivery system)?

J. Media and Delivery System   Are plans appropriate for:

No	Some	Yes	
—	—	—	1. Instructional strategy?
—	—	—	2. Assessments?
—	—	—	3. Practical constraints (e.g., context, personnel, learners, resources, materials)?
—	—	—	4. Media and delivery systems available?
—	—	—	5. Materials considerations (durability, transportability, convenience)?

With your strategy complete, you can begin to develop instruction based on the prescriptions in the strategy. For readers who are doing an instructional design project as they work through this text, we suggest that you read Chapter 9 before developing your instructional strategy, paying particular attention to our recommendation that first-time designers plan individualized instruction.

PRACTICE

1. **Sequence subordinate skills.** Examine the instructional analysis in Appendix C for the writing composition goal. Notice that the subordinate skills for each main step have a code that begins with the number of the main step. For example the code 5.4 reflects a subordinate skill for skill 5.5, and 5.32 reflects a subordinate skill for main step 5. Assume these skill codes signal the order each of the subordinate skills will be presented to the learner. Given this information, evaluate the sequence of instruction implied by the skill codes. Is this order correct or should the skill codes be reordered to reflect a better sequence for learning the skills?
   a. The order of the subordinate skills for instruction is appropriate.
   b. All the verbal information skills should be presented first (e.g., 5.1, 5.2, 5.4, 5.6, etc).
   c. Instruction should begin with the discrimination skills (e.g., 5.3, 5.5, 5.7, etc.)
   d. The order actually does not matter since these skills can be sequenced in any order as long as they are taught before main step 5.

2. **Cluster subordinate skills for instruction.** Assume the preinstructional session is complete, you have already planned instruction for main skills 1 through 4, and you are planning a forty-minute instructional session for main step 5. The students are in the sixth grade, and they are average or above average in prior writing achievement. You should follow an educated hunch at this point if you are unfamiliar with sixth-grade students. Which of the following clusters of objectives would be best for the first forty-minute instructional session related to main step 5?
   a. Main step 5 plus all subordinate skills 5.1 through 5.32.
   b. Skill 5.32 plus subordinate skills 5.11, 5.17, 5.24, and 5.31.
   c. Subordinate skills 5.7, 5.9, 5.10, 5.11, and 5.32 (related only to declarative sentences).
   d. All subordinate skills from 5.1 through 5.32.

3. **Preinstructional materials: Motivation.** Assume that you are planning the overall motivational presentation for the goal to "hook the students" into the instruction. Which of the following motivational plans would be effective? Choose all the plans that might work.
   a. This step is unnecessary given the limited amount of time available for the unit.
   b. Compare a story or newsletter article written with only declarative sentences and written again with a variety of sentence types based on purpose and mood.
   c. Present a story or article with content of interest to sixth-grade students.
   d. Present the information from the perspective of persons whose opinions the students would value.
   e. Illustrate a student receiving positive attention from teachers and peers for writing a good newsletter article.

4. **Design preinstructional materials: Inform learner of objectives.** Select the statement that would be most effective for *introducing* students to the unit. In written composition, use a variety of sentence types and accompanying punctuation based on the *purpose, mood,* and *complexity* of the sentence. Choose all that are appropriate.
   a. The instruction will be a brief thirty minutes so there is no need to provide objectives for just this one lesson.
   b. Write sentences based on purpose and mood.
   c. Write declarative, interrogative, imperative, and exclamatory sentences.
   d. Given an assignment to write an interesting newsletter article, write declarative, interrogative, imperative, and exclamatory sentences appropriate for the purpose and mood of the sentence with 90 percent accuracy.

5. **Design preinstructional materials: Informing learner of prerequisites.** Which of the following plans appears best for the students in the lesson on choosing and writing declarative sentences?
   a. There are no entry skills identified for this unit so none should be included.
   b. Any entry skills should be identified for the whole unit in the preinstructional materials.
   c. Students should be reminded of skills 5.1 through 5.5.
   d. Prerequisite skills for subordinate skills 5.11, 5.17, 5.24, and 5.31 should be described.

6. **Plan content presentation and examples.** Consider the following subordinate skill from Appendix C: Classify a complete sentence as a declarative sentence. How many examples should you include in the instruction?
   a. One: This is an intellectual skill rather than verbal information.
   b. Two: This is a complex skill and should be demonstrated more than once.

c. Four or more: At least two example sentences and two nonexample sentences should be presented.

d. Twelve: Allow opportunities to illustrate many examples and nonexamples for each type pf sentence.

7. **Planning learner participation.** Which of the following strategies would be best (considering feasibility or time/resource requirements) for practice and feedback for the skills in the following subordinate skill: Write a declarative sentence using correct closing punctuation? Choose all that apply.

a. Objective tasks: Multiple-choice format.

b. Objective tasks: Short-answer format.

c. Alternative assessment: Live performance with teacher observing.

d. Alternative assessment: Product development and rubric scoring.

e. A combination of objective tasks and alternative assessments.

8. **Planning assessment.** Which of the following assessment plans appears to be most useful for main step 5 in Appendix C? Choose all that apply.

a. Administer an objective-style readiness test to ensure that learners can classify complete sentences for all four sentence types.

b. Administer a readiness/pretest in an objective format covering the entry skills, all subordinate skills, and main step 5.

c. Administer a posttest in an objective format covering skills 5.11 through main step 5.

d. Administer an alternative assessment *product* test over main step 5. The assessment should include directions for the learner and a rubric for scoring students' declarative sentences.

9. **Planning for transfer.** Which of the following rehearsal and posttest strategies might best support transfer of the writing skills to the home environment? Choose all that apply.

a. Completing an objective-style posttest and making a good grade.

b. Completing an alternative assessment in a product development format and making a good grade.

c. Participating in writing articles for the planned newsletter and posting them on the web for other students.

d. Participating as an editor or editorial board member for the newsletter.

10. **Media selection for task requirements.** Examine the following enabling skill from Appendix C: Recognize a declarative sentence with correct closing punctuation. Based on the nature of the skill (rather than feasibility and economics), which of the following media do you believe would provide a good vehicle for delivering the instruction? Choose all that apply.

a. Teacher-led instruction.

b. Inexpensive and practical paper module that can be reused by students next year.

c. Web-based management program such as Blackboard with teacher facilitation and elaboration.

d. Straight web-based management program such as Blackboard.

11. Develop an instructional strategy for the preinstructional activities for the instructional goal:

In written composition, students will:

• use a variety of sentence types and accompanying punctuation based on the *purpose* and *mood* of the sentence.

• use a variety of sentence types and accompanying punctuation based on the *complexity* or *structure* of the sentence.

12. Plan a constructivist learning for the instructional goal:

In written composition, students will: (1) use a variety of sentence types and accompanying punctuation based on the *purpose* and *mood* of the sentence and (2) use a variety of sentence types and accompanying punctuation based on the *complexity* or *structure* of the sentence.

What pedagogical model and procedural plans would you use to promote an interactive student/teacher learning environment for this goal? You may want to use a planning template such as the one in Table 8.3 to guide your work.

FEEDBACK

1. a

2. c

3. b, c, d, e

4. b, c

5. c

6. c

7. b

8. b, c

9. c, d

10. a, b, c, d

11. Plan for a cognitive instructional strategy: Compare your preinstructional activities with those provided in Appendix F. Review the remainder of Appendix F and G to see the entire instructional strategy.

12. Plan for a constructivist learning environment: Compare your plan with the sample provided in Appendix H. Review both sections 1 and 2 of this appendix.

REFERENCES AND RECOMMENDED READINGS

Atkinson, R. K., Derry, S. J., Renkl, A., & Wortham, D. (2000). Learning from examples: Instructional principles from the worked examples research. *Review of Educational Research, 70*(2), 181–214. Synthesis of research with principles for providing instructional guidance.

Broad, M. L., & Newstrom, J. W. (2001). *Transfer of training*. New York: Da Capo Press. Describes many factors regarding transfer that should be considered before, during, and after instruction.

Brown, L. A. (1996). *Designing and developing electronic performance support systems*. Newton, MA: Digital Press.

Carey, J. O. (2005). Applying principles of instructional design for quality assurance in e-learning: Issues and dilemmas in higher education. In *Quality assurance of e-learning in higher education*. Report of the National Institute of Multimedia Education International Symposium, November 9–10, 2005 (pp. 69–80). Chiba, Japan: NIME.

Chieu, V. M. (2005). Constructivist learning: An operational approach for designing adaptive learning environments supporting cognitive flexibility (Doctoral thesis, Catholic University of Louvain, 2005). Retrieved August 25, 2007, from www.ifi.refer.org/rapports/theses/these-vu_minh_chieu.pdf.

Clark, R. (1983). Reconsidering research on learning from media. *Review of Educational Research, 53*(4), 445.

Dede, C. (2008). *How Web 2.0 tools are transforming learning and knowledge*. Paper presented at the annual Florida Educational Technology Conference, Orlando, FL.

Derry, S. J. (1996). Cognitive schema theory in the constructivist debate. *Educational Psychologist, 31*(3/4), 163–174.

Dickelman, G. J. (Ed.). (2003). EPSS revisited: A lifecycle for developing performance-centered systems. Silver Springs, MD: ISPI.

Dillon, A., & Gabbard, R. (1998). Hypermedia as an educational technology: A review of the quantitative research literature on learner comprehension, control, and style. *Review of Educational Research, 68*(3), 322–349. This summary of research concludes that learning gains from the use of hypermedia are limited.

Dills, C. R., & Romiszowski, A. J. (Eds.). (1997). *Instructional development paradigms*. Englewood Cliffs, NJ: Educational Technology Publications. A handbook that addresses many instructional strategy issues along with many other issues related to the field of instructional design.

Driscoll, M. P. (2005). *Psychology of learning for instruction* (3rd ed.). Boston: Allyn & Bacon.

Educational Technology Magazine 47(3), (2007). Special issue on highly mobile computing; i.e. hold in one hand devices for social interaction and information access including PDAs, cell phones, tablet computers, UMPCs, gaming systems, iPods, motes.

Educational Technology Research and Development, 56(1), (2008). Special issue on scaffolded learning with hypermedia.

Ertmer, P., & Newby, T. (1993). Behaviorism, cognitivism, constructivism: Comparing critical features from an instructional design perspective. *Performance Improvement Quarterly, 6*(40), 50–72. Excellent review of theories that affect instructional design practice. Indicates implications for the instructional designer.

Gagné, R. M. (1985). *Conditions of learning* (4th ed.). New York: Holt, Rinehart and Winston. Gagné describes in detail the factors that should be present to stimulate learning in each of the learning domains.

Gagné, R. M., & Medsker, K. L. (1996). *The conditions of learning: Training applications*. Fort Worth, TX: Harcourt Brace College Publishers. This book integrates much of Gagné's early work on conditions of learning with the current world of training in business and industry.

Gagné, R. M., Wager, W. W., Golas, K. C., & Keller, J. M. (2004). *Principles of instructional design* (5th ed.). Belmont, CA: Wadsworth/Thomson Learning. Chapters 9–12 in this book will provide additional background on developing instructional strategies.

Gery, G. (1991). *Electronic performance support systems*. Tolland, MA: Gery Performance Press. This is the original text by Gloria Gery, who coined the term *EPSS*.

Hannafin, M. J., Hannafin, K. M., Land, S. M., & Oliver, K. (1997). Grounded practice and the design of constructivist learning environments. *Educational Technology Research and Development, 45*(3), pp. 101–117.

Hannafin, M. J., & Hooper, S. R. (1993). Learning principles. In M. Fleming & W. H. Levie (Eds.), *Instructional message design*. Englewood Cliffs, NJ: Educational Technology Publications. Description of fundamental principles for instructional presentations, practice, and feedback.

Hannum, W. H. (2007). When computers teach: A review of the instructional effectiveness of computers. *Educational Technology, 47*(2), 5–13.

Hmelo-Silver, C. E. (2006). Design principles for scaffolding technology-based inquiry. In A. M. O'Donnell, C. E. Hmelo-Silver, & G. Erkens (Eds.), *Collaborative reasoning, learning and technology.* Mahwah, NJ: Lawrence Erlbaum Associates.

Hmelo-Silver, C. E., Ravit, G. D., & Clark, A. C. (2007). Scaffolding and achievement in problem-based and inquiry learning: A response to Kirschner, Sweller, and Clark. *Educational Psychologist, 42*(2), 99–107.

Jonassen, D. H. (1997). Instructional design models for well-structured and ill-structured problem-solving learning outcomes. *Educational Technology Research and Development, 45*(1), 65–94. Provides examples and procedures for designing and developing both well-structured and ill-structured problem-solving instruction.

Jonassen, D. H. (1999). Designing constructivist learning environments. In C. M. Reigeluth (Ed.), *Instructional design theories and models* (Vol. II). Mahwah, NJ: Lawrence Erlbaum Associates.

Jonassen, D. H. (2004). *Learning to solve problems: An instructional design guide.* San Francisco: Pfeiffer.

Jonassen, D. H. (2006). On the role of concepts in learning and instructional design. *Educational Technology Research and Development, 54*(2), 177–196.

Keirns, J. L. (1999). *Designs for self-instruction: Principles, processes and issues in developing self-directed learning.* Boston: Allyn & Bacon. Looks at instructional strategies for individualized learning.

Keller, J. M. (1987a). Strategies for stimulating the motivation to learn. *Performance and Instruction, 26*(8), 1–7.

Keller, J. M. (1987b). The systematic process of motivational design. *Performance and Instruction, 26*(9), 1–8.

Keller, J., & Burkman, E. (1993). Motivation principles. In M. Fleming & W. H. Levie (Eds.), *Instructional message design.* Englewood Cliffs, NJ: Educational Technology Publications. Review of both learner and text characteristics that are important to the designer.

Kolb, D. (1984). *Experiential learning.* Englewood Cliffs, NJ: Prentice Hall.

Kruse, K., & Keil, K. (2000). *Technology-based training: The art and science of design, development, and delivery.* San Francisco, CA: Jossey-Bass Pfeiffer.

Lee, W. W., & Owens, D. L. (2004). *Multimedia-based instructional design: Computer-based training; web-based training; distance broadcast training; performance-based solutions* (2nd ed.). San Francisco: Jossey-Bass Pfeiffer. This text demonstrates that the same instructional design model can be used for all media.

London, M. (2003). *Job feedback: Giving, seeking, and using feedback for performance improvement* (2nd ed.). Mahwah, NJ: Lawrence Erlbaum Associates. Utilization of feedback in job settings and assessment centers, and for fostering a continuous-learning environment.

McManus, P., & Rossett, A. (2006). Performance support tools. *Performance Improvement, 45*(2), 8–17.

Moore, M. G., & Kearsley, G. (1996). *Distance education: A systems view.* New York: Wadsworth. 197–212. A good overview of distance education with summaries of research findings.

O'Donnell, A. M., Hmelo-Silver, C. E., & Erkens, G. (Eds.). (2006). *Collaborative reasoning, learning and technology.* Mahwah, NJ: Lawrence Erlbaum Associates. 147–170.

Reiser, B. J. (2004). Scaffolding complex learning: The mechanisms of structuring and problematizing student work. *Journal of the Learning Sciences, 13,* 273–304.

Romiszowski, A. J. (1993). Psychomotor principles. In M. Fleming & W. H. Levie (Eds.), *Instructional message design.* Englewood Cliffs, NJ: Educational Technology Publications. One of the few sources that describes the principles of motor skills instruction for the designer. Excellent summary of the fundamentals.

Rossett, A., & Schafer, L. (2006). *Job aids and performance support: Moving from knowledge in the classroom to knowledge everywhere.* San Francisco: Pfeiffer.

Russell, T. L. (2001). *The no significant difference phenomenon: A comparative research annotated bibliography on technology for distance education* (5th ed.). Montgomery, AL: IDECC.

Russell, T. L. (2008). The no significant difference web site. Retrieved October 12, 2007, from http://nosignificantdifference.wcet.info/about.asp. The NSD website has been updated and now reports studies through 2007.

Schunk, D. (2004). *Learning theories: An educational perspective* (4th ed.). Upper Saddle River, NJ: Merrill/Prentice Hall.

Sims, R. S. (1998). *Reinventing training and development.* Westport, CT: Quorum Books. Provides overview of Kolb's model of experiential learning and how debriefing is used to enhance transfer.

Smith, P. L., & Ragan, T. J. (2005). *Instructional design* (3rd ed.). New York: Wiley. In-depth descriptions of a variety of instructional strategies.

Schwartz, P., Mennin, S., and Webb, G. (2001). *Problem-based learning: Case studies, experience, and practice.* London: Kogan Page.

Windschitl, M. (2002). Framing constructivism in practice as negotiation of dilemmas: An analysis of the conceptual, pedagogical, cultural, and political challenges facing teachers. *Review of Educational Research, 72*(2), 131–175. An analysis of the difficulties encountered by teachers implementing constructivist methods in school settings.

Woo, Y., Herrington, J., Agostinho, S., & Reeves, T. (2007). Implementing authentic tasks in web-based learning environments. *Educause Quarterly 30*(3), 36–43. Retrieved February 8, 2008, from http://connect.educause.edu/Library/EDUCAUSE + Quarterly/ImplementingAuthenticTask/44835.

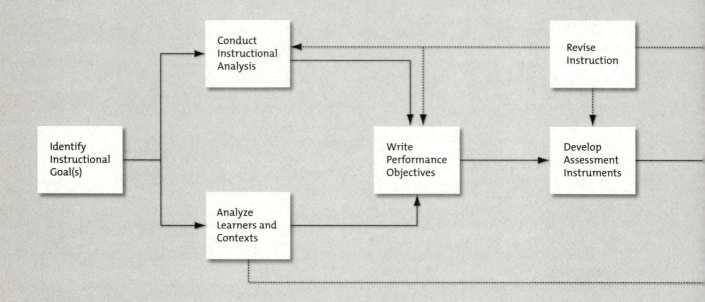

objectives

➤ Describe the designer's role in materials development and instructional delivery.
➤ Describe factors that may cause revisions in media selections and delivery systems for a given instruction.
➤ Name and describe the components of an instructional package.
➤ List four categories of criteria for judging the appropriateness of existing instructional materials.
➤ Name appropriate rough draft materials for various final media.
➤ Given an instructional strategy, describe the procedures for developing instructional materials.
➤ Develop instructional materials based on a given instructional strategy.

Developing Instructional Materials

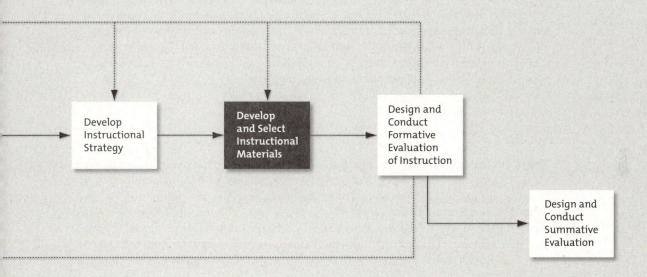

Develop Instructional Strategy

Develop and Select Instructional Materials

Design and Conduct Formative Evaluation of Instruction

Design and Conduct Summative Evaluation

Background

In a typical classroom setting, the instructor plans and performs functional activities that we describe as being components of an instructional strategy. The instructor is often the motivator, the content presenter, the leader of practice activities, and the evaluator. The instructor makes decisions that affect the whole group as well as individual students. Instructors are usually required to use strategies whereby they must move the whole class forward through a sequence of instruction or retain the whole class at a particular point in the instruction until they feel that sufficient skill and knowledge have developed within a majority of the group.

The hallmark of individualized instruction is that many of the instructional events typically carried out by the instructor with a group of students are now presented to the individual student through instructional materials. As we have said elsewhere, this does not necessarily mean that the instructor is removed from the instructional setting. The instructor's role is different and even more important than in lockstep instruction. The instructor is still the motivator, as well as a counselor, evaluator, and decision maker; and the instructor usually feels added responsibility for each student's mastery of the objectives.

We recommend that you produce self-instructional materials in your first attempt at instructional design; that is, the materials should permit the student to learn the new information and skills without any intervention from an instructor or fellow students. Once having performed this feat as a designer of print or mediated materials, you can move to instructor-led or various combinations of mediated materials with an instructor. As a first effort, however, learning components such as motivation, content, practice, and feedback should be built into the instructional materials. If you were to start your development with the instructor included in the instructional process, it would be very easy to use the instructor as a crutch to deliver the instruction. In your first effort as a designer, we recommend that you see how much can be done without having an instructor actively involved in the instructional process. Not only will this test your design skills and give you added insight into the learning components of an instructional strategy, but it will also give you a defined, replicable product to take into the formative evaluation process in Chapter 10.

In this chapter we provide concepts, guidelines, and criteria for developing instructional materials. We do not focus on media production techniques, because those techniques encompass vast skill sets for which excellent resources are available in books and online text, tutorials, and interactive user groups. We begin with an overview of instructional materials development and then discuss considerations therein, finishing with the detailed steps in the process.

Concepts

With the instructional strategy in hand, the designer is ready to bring the instruction to life. The analysis and design work serve its purpose by ensuring an instructional product that is responsive to the needs that gave rise to the original goal. Once developed in rough draft form the materials are evaluated and revised as needed following the processes in Chapters 10 and 11. The four broad tasks in Table 9.1 guide instructional materials development, but before discussing each of them we will consider various roles that the instructional designer can play in materials development and delivery.

The Designer's Role in Materials Development and Instructional Delivery

When the Designer Is Also the Materials Developer and the Instructor   In many instructional settings, the person who designs the instruction also develops materials and teaches students. For example, a human resources generalist in a small company may design, develop, and deliver all new employee orientation, benefits training, and "soft skills" training. Teachers and professors do their own lesson plans and

table 9.1   Overview of Instructional Materials Development

Task	Outcome
Reconsider delivery system and media selection	Compromises in delivery system and media selection based on availability of existing materials, cost constraints, and the instructor's role
Determine components of the instructional package	A clear conception of what the materials will include and how they will look
Consider existing instructional materials	Decisions about whether to adopt or adapt any existing materials for use in the instruction
Develop instructional materials	Rough draft materials and the management information that will be needed for formative evaluation

syllabi, materials, and instruction, and professionals in all fields routinely design, develop, and present their own workshops and in-service training.

When designers are also developers and instructors they will take on different teaching responsibilities based on the types of materials that were prescribed in the instructional strategy. When instructors design and develop individualized materials, or materials that can be delivered independently of an instructor, their role in instructional delivery is passive, but their role as a facilitator is very active. In this case, their task during instruction is to monitor and guide the progress of students through the materials. Students can progress at their own speed through the instruction, with the instructor providing additional help for those who seem to need it. Except for the pretests and posttests, all learning components are included within the materials. In some materials, even these tests are included and submitted to the instructor when learners complete them.

On the other hand, when instructors select and adapt materials to suit their instructional strategy, it is probable that the instructor will have an increased role in delivering instruction. Some available materials may be instructor independent, but when they are not, the instructor must provide learning components specified in the strategy but not found in the materials. This mixed bag of resource-based learning and direct instruction is probably the most common instructor-managed teaching and learning. When an instructor uses a variety of instructional resources, he or she plays a greater role in materials management. By providing a learner guide for available materials, instructors may be able to increase the independence of the materials and free themselves to provide additional guidance and consultation for students who need it.

A third case is the very traditional model in which the instructor personally delivers all instruction according to the instructional strategy that has been developed. This commonly occurs in public schools or in other settings where there is a small budget for materials or where the content to be taught changes rapidly. The instructor uses the instructional strategy as a guide in producing outlines for lecture notes and directions for group exercises and activities. In professional and technical training, the designer often develops a formal instructor's guide that provides detailed lesson plan–like guidance for lectures, discussions, and participant activities, while in educational settings, daily lesson plans or the course syllabus serve this purpose.

This type of instruction has both advantages and disadvantages. A major advantage is that the instructor can constantly update and improve instruction as changes occur in the content. Instructors spend the majority of their time, however, lecturing and delivering information to a group, leaving little time to help individual learners with problems. Progress through a lesson is difficult because when the instructor stops to answer a question for one learner, the progress of the entire group is halted.

The intended delivery mode for instruction is a very important consideration in the development of materials based on the planned instructional strategy. If instruction is intended to be independent of an instructor, then the materials will have to include all the learning components in the strategy. The instructor is not expected to play a role in delivering instruction.

If the instructor plans to combine available materials, then instructional delivery will combine materials and instructor presentation. The instructor may not be required to develop any new materials in this mode but may be required to deliver some of the needed instruction. The amount of original materials developed for this type of instruction will depend on available time, budget, and staff support.

If instructors plan to deliver all the instruction with materials such as lecture notes, a multimedia projector, and a whiteboard, then they may need to develop little besides lecture outlines, electronic presentations, practice worksheets or active learning exercises, and formal tests.

As the instructional designer you made decisions about the intended delivery system and media formats in planning your instructional strategy. Now in the case when you are also the materials developer and the instructor, you may need to modify and adapt your original decisions to reflect existing materials, the realities of development and production costs, and changes in your thinking about your role as instructor. These decisions will affect materials development activities as well as the required budget and staff.

When the designer is also the developer and the instructor, the whole process of materials development is rather informal; that is, much of what would be formal specification and communication between designer and materials developer remains as mental notes or informal planning notes. The thought also tends to reside in the back of the designer's mind that, as the instructor, "I will be able to manage the instruction, adapting and accommodating as needed on the fly." This thought results in less concern for the nitty-gritty details of developing and implementing instruction.

Another commonly practiced arrangement assigns responsibility for design with the instructor but not sole responsibility for materials production. Unusual in public schools, it occurs more often in higher education, business, government, and military settings where there is often technical assistance available for production of complex media such as video, web-based, and multimedia. The designer usually works collaboratively with an in-house media production specialist rather than turning over specifications.

When the Designer Is Not the Instructor   In large companies with a significant training and development function, an instructional designer may work with a team responsible for design, development, and implementation of training. Similar teams also exist in instructional design (ID) consulting firms, personnel training and development companies, and many universities. The functions represented on such a team are usually manager, instructional designer, subject-matter expert, materials developer (or coordinator), and evaluator.

In a smaller ID setting, one individual may be responsible for more than one function, while in a larger setting, multiple individuals may be assigned to each function. The team would also interact regularly with a representative of the internal or external client and sometimes with an instructor or instructional program manager. In ID teams it is common for the manager to be a senior-level instructional designer and for the instructional designer also to be a materials developer or at least have working-level knowledge of a variety of media formats. The combination of instructional design and materials development skills is desirable, particularly in computer-based and web-based materials development, because of pressure to bring "just in time" training products to users as quickly as possible. Michael Greer (1992) is a good source for exploring team-based instructional design and ID project management, and Brill, Bishop, and Walker (2006) describe project management competencies validated through a Delphi study.

Earlier in this section we mentioned that the process of specifying and developing materials is fairly informal when the designer is also the materials developer and the instructor. When the designer is neither the developer nor the instructor, however, a premium is placed on precision specifications and working in a team environment requiring communication and collaboration skills. There is no such thing as a standard operating procedure for the communication that occurs between a designer and a materials developer. It is always a unique collaboration that is determined by the mix of design and development skills possessed by each participant and the division of responsibilities in the team setting.

For example, a creative instructional designer with good television production skills and the time necessary might turn over a full production script with storyboarding to the materials developer. At the other extreme, a busy designer without production experience would probably meet with the developer, go over the learner and context analyses, review the instructional strategy, solicit production ideas from the developer, and then meet later to review a storyboard and script notes prepared by the developer. The best way for a designer to establish methods for communicating media specifications is to meet with and learn from the developer, because materials developers will already have planning and production tools that they use routinely in their media trade. The instructional designer should adopt the planning tools with which materials developers in a particular shop are comfortable.

Another reason for introducing the idea of an ID team is to point out a common problem in the instructional design process that stems from the relationship, or lack thereof, between the designer and the learners. When the designer is also the instructor of a given set of learners, the designer-instructor has a good understanding of the interests and motivations of the learners, of their preferences and expectations, and their general and specific knowledge of the content area. It is often the case, however, in team ID settings that the designer is not the instructor and is unfamiliar with the learners for whom the instruction is intended and may have little or no direct contact with them. In such cases the designer can depend on careful learner and context analyses, but in lieu of good information, may depend on his or her own stereotypes of what the learners are like. Such assumptions may result in more problems than if the designer had no knowledge of the learners at all.

If possible, designers should have conducted the on-site learner and context analyses themselves to observe a sample of the learners for whom the instruction is being designed. This step is equally important whether observing schoolchildren, military recruits, adult volunteer learners, middle-management trainees, or any others for whom instruction is to be designed. If the designer did not do the original learner and context analyses, then an opportunity for at least casual observation should be pursued. Based on these observations, the designer makes decisions as diverse as the size of content clusters, the features of a graphical user interface, or the types of role models that should be used to foster attitudes. Although it is impossible to indicate all the characteristics of a learner population that might be important to the design of new instruction, the instructional designer must become as knowledgeable as possible about the target population.

The Delivery System and Media Selections

At this point in the instructional design process, a delivery system is specified and the instructional strategy has been developed, including clustering and sequencing, learning components, student groupings, and tentative media selections. If the designer will be working within an assumed or imposed delivery system, then the range of options will be limited and the media selections that have been made will probably be fairly stable. If one made open selections of media formats and an ideal delivery system, however, the likelihood is high that specifications will be revised during materials development. The point here is that our choices of theoretically best practice will run into a reality check as a natural part of the materials development process; some conflict is expected, and the resulting compromises usually help ensure a workable educational product that fits the learning environment. Three factors often cause compromise in selections of media and delivery system: (1) availability of existing instructional materials, (2) production and implementation constraints, and (3) the amount of facilitation that the instructor will provide during instruction.

Availability of Existing Instructional Materials   Sometimes existing materials are an attractive alternative to going through the development and production process.

Existing materials could be substituted for planned materials on a scale ranging from a single motivational sequence in one lesson to an entire course or curriculum. Consider the example of our Neighborhood Crime Watch leadership training design. In Chapter 8 we specified a web-based delivery system, but suppose a review of existing materials turned up an appropriate, current instructional television series on group leadership skills developed by a junior college consortium. If the duplication and distribution rights were not prohibitive, then distribution by mail of student workbooks and VHS tapes or DVDs might be a viable substitute for the time and cost of developing web-based instruction; alternatively, with proper permission appropriate video excerpts could be digitized for web distribution.

Production and Implementation Constraints   Media formats and delivery systems that look expensive *are* expensive. Cutting production corners to save money will usually not impact student learning, but it will impact attention and perceptions of relevance and authority. Novice designers who have not worked with complex media often severely underestimate the costs of hiring commercial production and equally underestimate the expertise, infrastructure, and time requirements for in-house production. Sometimes after development is completed, the costs of duplication, distribution, and maintenance can be just as prohibitive as unanticipated production costs. It is essential to anticipate such constraints by due diligence during the learning context analysis and to maintain an open, flexible viewpoint when entering the materials production phase. When faced with these dilemmas, the best strategy is to back down to simpler media formats and produce them well rather than sticking with complex media formats and producing them poorly. Using our Neighborhood Crime Watch example again, if it became apparent that quality, web-based streaming video was simply out of reach, it would be better to drop back to a good PowerPoint presentation developed for web delivery than to do an amateurish video.

Amount of Instructor Facilitation   The first steps in adoption of a new technology are usually attempts to replicate the features of the old technology; thus, as we began using instructional television, computer software, or web-based instruction, we tried to replicate features of the classroom experience for our students. Instructor facilitation is a particular feature of classroom instruction that has implications for how we develop instructional materials. Later in this chapter we will discuss how the facilitation factor affects development of face-to-face instruction but here we will look at how it affects implementation of distance learning delivery systems. Instructor facilitation is a point at which distance learning philosophies sometimes diverge between academic programs and professional and technical training programs, as shown in Table 9.2, which includes the familiar open university model of distance learning as a reference point. Note that these models are not mutually exclusive and that the features of each are not as discrete as the tabular format might imply.

There are several implications in Table 9.2 for the development of materials in distance learning delivery systems. Recalling our discussion from Chapter 8 of Moore and Kearsley's concept of transactional distance, high levels of course dialogue in the academic model encourage learners' perceptions of a more personal experience and feelings of group affiliation. Much of this dialogue is instructor participation in online discussion and practice with feedback, and it is generally reflected in more positive student evaluations of the course and the instructor. This is a feature of classroom instruction that the academic model attempts to replicate in distance learning. When discussion and feedback are provided by the instructor, initial materials development costs are lower; however, per-student costs are high and the course cannot be scaled up in size without hiring additional instructors. The open university model uses

table

9.2

Levels of Instructor Facilitation in Three Models of Distance Learning

	Academic Model of Distance Learning	Open University Model of Distance Learning	Professional and Technical Training Model of Distance Learning
Delivery Systems	Web, two-way interactive television, videoconferencing	Web, broadcast television	Web, computer-based training
Purpose	Replicate classroom experience	Replicate large lecture hall experience	Replace classroom experience
Instructor Facilitation	• Instructor centered • Learning facilitated by instructor's active participation	• Instructor centered or materials centered • Learning facilitated by differentiated staff (e.g., proctor, learning center staff, graduate assistant, adjunct, tutor)	• Materials and software centered • Independent learning facilitated by software
Learners	Suitable for all learner independence levels	Suitable for fairly independent learners	Suitable for highly independent learners
Accountability	• Student learning outcomes • Student attitude about course • Student rating of faculty	• Student learning outcomes • Student attitude about course • Student rating of instructor and differentiated staff	• Student learning outcomes • Student attitude about course • Supervisor rating of student's job performance
Class Size Scalability and Per-Student Cost	• Limited scalability and high per-student cost • Add students by adding additional faculty	• More scalable, moderate to high per-student costs • Add students by adding additional staff	• Scalable, per-student costs dependent on sufficient audience size to amortize cost of development
Development and Implementation	• Low startup costs if technological infrastructure is in place • Can be developed and managed independently by a faculty member	• Low to high startup costs, depending on medium and sophistication of materials • Can require production team and will require network of facilitators	• High startup costs for intensive materials development and evaluation • Production team, but primary management task after implementation is accountability

differentiated staffing to limit instructor costs and still maintain a personalized course that accommodates large student audiences. The per-student costs, however, can still be high due to personnel and administrative expenses. The most notable practitioner of the online open university model is the University of Phoenix, now claiming the title of "nation's largest university."

The professional and technical training model of distance learning opts for higher initial development expenses by assigning learning components to the instructional materials rather than to an instructor, and then it relies on distribution to large numbers of students to bring down the per-student cost. Initial choices of ideal delivery system and media formats are often compromised when the instructional designer is faced with distance learning materials development and delivery cost options that are based on varying levels of instructor facilitation. The decision regarding the role of the instructor in instructional delivery needs to be considered and affirmed before selecting or developing materials.

The academic and open university models of online learning have succeeded beyond expectations, experiencing exponential growth in recent years, but reviews in the training and development world have been mixed regarding the success of online learning. Some training managers and performance consultants speculate that problems in online learning have arisen when content from instructor-led training was converted for web delivery without in-depth consideration of the learning components for which the instructor had been responsible in the face-to-face learning environment. Such components as motivating learners, promoting active recall of prerequisites, providing practice with corrective feedback, and promoting transfer could be missing from the online learning experience. One response has been to provide an instructor presence in the online environment, and another response is seen in the trend toward "blended learning" wherein self-paced online experiences are joined with face-to-face classroom or work group experiences. Regardless of the media or the delivery system, the designer's foundation for creating instructional materials must be the learning components specified in the development of the instructional strategy.

Components of an Instructional Package

Having reconsidered the delivery system and media selections, you are ready to start selecting existing instructional materials, developing materials yourself, or writing specifications for someone else who will be developing the materials. Before you begin you should be aware of the several components that usually make up an instructional package, noting that the term *package* includes all forms of print and mediated materials.

Instructional Materials   The instructional materials contain the content—either written, mediated, or facilitated by an instructor—that a student will use to achieve the objectives. This includes materials for the major objectives and the terminal objective and any materials for enhancing memory and transfer. Instructional materials refer to any preexisting materials that are being incorporated, as well as to those materials that will be specifically developed for the objectives. The materials may also include information that the learners will use to guide their progress through the instruction. Templates for such student guidance are now available as part of commercial web-based online course management portals such as Blackboard. Student workbooks, activity guides, problem scenarios, computer simulations, case studies, resource lists, and other such materials would also be part of the instructional materials.

Assessments   All instructional materials should be accompanied by objective tests or by product or performance assessments. These may include both a pretest and a posttest. You may decide that you do not wish to have the tests as a separate component in the materials, preferring to have them appear as part of the instructor's materials so they are not available to students. The package will be incomplete, however, unless you have included at least a posttest and the other assessments that are necessary for using the instructional package.

Course Management Information   There often is a general description of the total package, typically called an instructor's manual, that provides an overview of the materials and shows how they might be incorporated into an overall learning sequence for students. The manual might also include the tests and other information that you judge to be important for implementing the course. In addition to the student guidance templates provided in commercial web-based instructional management systems, there is also course management support for the instructor, often including automated class listing, student tracking, online testing, project monitoring, grade book, and a variety of communication and messaging mechanisms. Some types of self-paced independent learning do not have course instructors per se, so the instructor's guide is really a course management guide that can be customized for site-specific applications. Special attention should be paid to the ease with which course management information can be used by the instructor or course manager, and it should undergo the same type of formative evaluation as would tests and instruction.

Considerations for adding suggestions for a constructivist learning environment to the course management information include the needs of the organization, the appropriateness of the environment for the goal and for the learners' ability and motivation, the performance and learning contexts, and the resources available for supporting the environment (e.g., time, personnel, facilities, equipment, money). Caution must be used in including such information, because learning environments are often situation-specific and, by definition, need to evolve within the context rather than be prescribed.

Existing Instructional Materials

The next step following the development of the instructional strategy is to determine whether there are existing materials that fit your objectives. In some content areas you will find an abundance of materials available, either superficial or greatly detailed, which are not really directed to the target population in which you are interested. On the other hand, occasionally it is possible to identify materials that will at least partly serve your needs. When you consider the cost of developing a video or a multimedia presentation, it is clearly worth the effort to spend several hours examining existing materials to determine whether they meet your needs.

A recent development in selecting existing instructional materials is the Sharable Content Object Reference Model (SCORM), which is a set of e-learning standards for interchangeability of learning objects. A learning object is what might have been traditionally called a lesson or module that would include a cluster of content with the required learning components of an instructional strategy. *Educational Technology Magazine* (2006) devoted a special issue to learning objects, and Churchill (2007) describes classes of learning objects. If a learning object is SCORM compliant then it could be "dropped" into a SCORM-compliant course shell and the shell would be capable of launching and displaying the object, tracking and managing students through the object. The theory of SCORM is that cost savings could be realized by distributing learning objects across agencies that teach the same learning outcomes; for example, many companies teach new employees about 401(k) retirement plans, most universities teach students how to evaluate and cite web pages for use as references in research papers, and all branches of the military teach their military police common tactical procedures. A fascinating feature of the SCORM standard is that interchangeability is virtual; that is, a course shell could be on a computer in the physics department at Georgia Tech and the learning object could be on a computer in one of the colleges at Cambridge, England. The SCORM concept is promising, but practice in sharable objects currently lags well behind theory; however, treating learning objects as existing materials for selection and use is becoming more popular. You can access examples of interactive learning objects and additional information about their use at Churchill's Learning Objects web site (www.learnactivity.com/lo).

To aid planning your materials evaluations, recall from Chapter 7 three of the categories of criteria for creating assessments—goal-centered, learner-centered, and context-centered criteria. We will use these and add two more categories— learning-centered and technical criteria.

Goal-Centered Criteria for Evaluating Existing Materials   Goal-centered criteria focus on the content of instruction, and your instructional analysis documents will provide a basis for determining the acceptability of the content in various instructional materials. Specific criteria in this area include (1) congruence between the content in the materials and your terminal and performance objectives, (2) adequacy of content coverage and completeness, (3) authority, (4) accuracy, (5) currency, and (6) objectivity.

Learner-Centered Criteria for Evaluating Existing Materials   Your learner analysis documentation should provide the foundation for consideration of the appropriateness of instructional materials for your target group. Specific criteria include the appropriateness of the materials for your learners' (1) vocabulary and language levels; (2) developmental, motivation, and interest levels; (3) backgrounds and experiences; and (4) special language or other needs. Other important learner-centered criteria include the materials' treatment of diversity and whether gender, cultural, age, racial, or other forms of bias appear to be present. Using these criteria to judge available materials can help you determine the appropriateness of the materials for your specific target group.

Learning-Centered Criteria for Evaluating Existing Materials   Your instructional strategy can be used to determine whether existing materials are adequate as is, or whether they need to be adapted or enhanced prior to use. Materials can be evaluated to determine whether they include (1) preinstructional materials (e.g., performance objectives, motivational information/activities, prerequisite skills); (2) correct content sequencing and presentation that is complete, current, and tailored for learners; (3) student participation and congruent practice exercises; (4) adequate feedback; (5) appropriate assessments; (6) adequate follow-through directions that enhance memory and transfer; and (7) adequate learner guidance for moving students from one component or activity to the next. The instructional strategy should be used to evaluate each potential resource. It may be possible to combine several resources to create a complete set of materials. When materials lack one or more of the necessary learning components—such as motivation, prerequisite skills, and so on—it may be economically advantageous to make adaptations so that the missing components are made available for use by students. It may also make sense to "complete" existing materials by writing assessments and an instructor's guide.

Context-Centered Criteria for Evaluating Existing Materials   Your instructional and performance context analyses can provide the foundation for judging whether existing materials can be adopted as is or adapted for your settings. Criteria within the context category include the authenticity of the materials for your contexts and learners and the feasibility of the materials for your settings and budget.

Technical Criteria for Evaluating Existing Materials   Materials should also be judged for their technical adequacy, according to criteria related to (1) the delivery system and media formats (appropriate for the objectives and the learning context), (2) packaging, (3) graphic design and typography, (4) durability, (5) legibility, (6) audio and video quality, and, when appropriate, (7) interface design, navigation, and functionality.

If suitable materials are found, it may change some of your decisions about delivery system, media, and components of the instructional package. If no appropriate materials are found that can be adopted or adapted for your instructional strategy, you are in the instructional materials development business. You must specify how you or a media production specialist will move from an instructional strategy to an instructional product that you can take into formative evaluation.

Instructional Materials and Formative Evaluation

Rough Draft Materials   We all know what the term *rough draft* means, because we have all written rough drafts of papers that have subsequently been revised into a final form. *Rough draft* means about the same thing when applied to instructional materials, but it carries the additional meaning that the product is developed in alternate, simpler, less-expensive media formats.

The purpose for doing a rough draft of materials is to create a quick low-cost version of your design to have something to guide final production and to take into formative evaluation and try out with a subject-matter expert, several learners, or a group of learners. The thought is that the time to catch any problems with the instructional materials is when they can still be revised without great expenditures of time and money. The design model we have been following throughout this book has a feedback line, "Revise instruction," that marks the point where rough draft materials will encounter that revision process.

A troublesome thought at this point might be "How can I determine whether my instructional planning and materials are effective from a rough draft version?" Research in learning from different media formats suggests that where actual mastery of knowledge and skills is concerned, there is very little difference between rough draft and finished product. For example, a student most often will learn just as much from watching a video as from looking at hand-drawn storyboard cards and listening to a person read the script. As one would expect, the attention and motivational effects of the experience will be different, but rough draft tryouts are used routinely in formative evaluation of complex, expensive media. Developers even use illustrator art or computer-generated art to determine whether children will like and identify with cartoon characters that will later be created for film or video. Table 9.3 lists examples of rough draft versions for a few final media formats. As you look at the suggested rough draft formats, recall that the purpose for the draft is a quick, cheap product to take into formative tryouts.

Rapid Prototyping   Anyone experienced in multimedia authoring knows the time and energy requirements for developing and testing complex computer-based instruction. The thought of "doing it several times" for the sake of formative evaluation is daunting, but that is exactly what happens in an instructional materials development process called *rapid prototyping,* a term borrowed from manufacturing where computer-aided design (CAD) technology has enabled direct reproduction of 3-D computer models into physical prototypes made of wood, plastic, or some other material for evaluating design specifications. In many learning contexts, technologies and training requirements change so quickly that instructional designers have rethought some of the traditional approaches to instructional design. The first strategy used in rapid prototyping is to go light on the early analysis steps of an instructional design model, then develop prototype instructional materials rapidly, and use quick iterative cycles of formative evaluation and revision to shape the final form of the materials. Rapid prototyping can be thought of as a series of informed, successive approximations, emphasizing the word *informed* because this developmental approach relies absolutely on information gathered during tryouts to ensure the success of the final product.

table **9.3**	Examples of Suggested Rough Draft Formats

If Final Medium Will Be:	Then Rough Draft Version Could Be:
• Illustrated text	Word processed, loose-leaf notebook with hand-drawn or clip-art illustration
• Laminated booklet	8½-by-11-inch card stock
• Activity centers and learning centers	"Flimsy" versions of materials that, in final form, will need to be "heavy duty" to resist wear and tear
• Presentation graphics program such as PowerPoint	These programs are so user-friendly that it is easiest to create rough draft materials directly in the presentation program using drawing tools and a good clip art collection, and then type lecture notes or narration into the "notes view"
• Video	Hand-drawn storyboards with script notes or full script are still used; although technological advances such as mini DVD camcorders and user-friendly desktop video editing programs have made it possible to record inexpensive draft footage and rough cut it into AVI or Quicktime format for formative tryouts
• Multimedia computer-based instruction (e.g., Authorware, Director, IconAuthor, Toolbook II)	Hand-drawn screen designs with flowchart of decision points, media events, and hyperlinks; mock-ups with limited functionality are often developed for proof-of-concept and formative review; mockups are sometimes developed for testing in user-friendly, lower-tech programs (e.g., rough draft in PowerPoint but final version in Authorware)
• Web-based and multimedia web-based instruction	Same as above (all programs mentioned can be ported for web access)

The second strategy used in rapid prototyping is concurrent design and development; that is, much of the front-end analysis work is conducted while the first rough draft materials are being developed. This might seem like getting the cart before the horse, but recall that rapid prototyping occurs primarily in high-tech, quickly changing learning contexts. The thinking here is that trainers designing cutting-edge technological products will not know answers to critical design questions unless they are also involved in product development with those technologies. Figure 1.2 in Chapter 1 (p. 5) is a diagram of concurrent design and development. In team instructional design settings there is a premium on accurate, continuous communication between those working in design and those working in materials development if the benefits of simultaneous activity are to be realized. Jones and Richey (2000) report an interesting case study detailing rapid prototyping methodology.

The concept of using rough draft materials for tryouts still holds in this type of prototyping, with the focus of early approximations being on the functionality of the user interface, the flow of program events, learner navigation through the instruction, and learners' performance. In later iterations as the instruction nears its final form, the fancy artwork and graphics are added to the product.

The rapid prototyping process is quite complex in large instructional development projects involving interactive computer-based and web-based multimedia. In such efforts, many stages of instructional design, materials development, and formative evaluation occur simultaneously. For example, in production of computer-based instruction, one feature could be in the design phase while another was undergoing development and yet another was in prototype testing. It is easy to fall into a pattern of thinking that instructional design is a strictly linear process, but this is misleading because tracking design and development activities would reveal a sequence of overlapping, circular patterns that duplicates the iterative product design and development process.

Materials Development Tools and Resources   Production of mediated materials requires a whole set of skills, both artistic and technical, that can range from simple word processing to converting materials for web-based delivery. To develop familiarity and skills with typical materials planning and production tools, readers are referred to the References and Recommended Readings section at the end of this chapter. Smaldino, Lowther, and Russell (2007) provide overviews of current instructional media formats, along with guidelines and tips for materials planning, design, and development. Several references at the end of this chapter include instruction on digital audio and video and on computer-based and web-based multimedia. Technologies change so quickly that listings in this book could soon be outdated; however, there are two good sources for this type of specialized information. Paperback literature available in computer stores, bookstores, and through web-based vendors comprise the "how-to" manuals that quickly follow new releases of computer applications, programming, and authoring tools. The other source is the web itself. To find the most current information on a computer application or authoring tool that you are using, just type the brand name into a web index or search engine, and you will likely find web sites maintained by the publisher and other users as well as references for newsgroups, user forums and e-mailing lists, blogs, conferences, and webinars.

Examples

In order to facilitate your work, this Examples section synthesizes the steps in the process of developing instructional materials based on the instructional strategy.

The Materials Development Process

Earlier in this chapter we discussed the advantages for a first-time instructional designer of developing self-paced materials rather than instruction presented by an instructor. By doing so, you will be able to work through development of materials for all of the learning components of the instructional strategy. This is good advice if your target audience is upper-elementary students through adults, but you will probably want to include a teacher as part of your instructional delivery if you have chosen young learners up to second or third grade as your target audience. If you do use a teacher, be sure to provide prescriptive plans for carrying out the learning components that you have specified. By doing so you will be able to collect usable data during tryouts of the instruction and make meaningful revisions after completing formative evaluation.

Another piece of advice for the novice designer is that the first materials development be done in illustrated text format or simple media formats. This natural starting point avoids the need for complex media development skills. Even those with well-developed skills in multimedia production should remember that the desired outcome is rough draft materials for formative evaluation. Anyone with decent word processing skills can quickly create rough drafts of text and either draw by hand or electronically insert pictorial and graphic illustrations; most of us have learned PowerPoint or other simple presentation software, for which there are abundant good examples of text design and media formatting that you can emulate for a wide range of content and learner ages. Even low-end, user-friendly desktop publishing applications such as Broderbund's Print Shop Pro Publisher and Microsoft's Publisher include style guides and templates that make good-looking illustrated text easy to produce. Sticking with illustrated text or simple media formats also keeps one's focus on the whole point of this book—that is, the design, development, and validation of effective instruction—rather than production of mediated materials. The purpose for the materials development step in this chapter is to produce only a draft product that will communicate well enough to allow a formative tryout with intended learners. Illustrated text or simple media can be used to take a manageable product into formative evaluation where the focus can be on learning outcomes rather than media production variables.

We will show in our case study how the instructional strategy is used as a guide for developing the first draft of your instruction. The strategy should keep you on track as you write your materials to motivate and inform the learners, present each objective, provide practice and feedback, and implement your assessment and memory and transfer strategies. The next section summarizes the general steps you will follow from the development of the instructional strategy to the completion of the first draft of the instruction and support materials.

Steps in the Development of Instruction

1. Review the instructional strategy for each objective in each lesson.
2. Review your analysis of the learning context and your assumptions about resources available for developing materials. Reconsider the delivery system and the media chosen to present the materials, to monitor practice and feedback, to evaluate, and to enhance learner memory and transfer.
3. Decide on the components of the package of instructional materials.
4. Survey the literature and ask subject-matter experts to determine what instructional materials are already available.
5. Consider how you might adopt or adapt available materials.
6. Determine whether new materials need to be designed. If so, go to step 7. If not, begin organizing and adapting available materials, using the instructional strategy as a guide.
7. Review your analysis of learners and for each lesson consider the instructor's role in facilitating instruction and determine the degree to which you want the instruction to be self-paced, group-paced, or mixed.
8. Plan and write the instructional materials based on the instructional strategy in rough draft form. You will be amazed at how stick figures and rough illustrations can bring your ideas to life for a first trial. Printed, visual, or auditory materials in this rough form will allow you to check your sequence, flow of ideas, accuracy of illustration of ideas, completeness, pace, and so on. Make a rough set of materials as complete as is reasonably needed for each instructional activity.
9. Review each completed lesson or learning session for clarity and flow of ideas.
10. Using one complete instructional unit, write the accompanying instructions to guide the students through any required activities.
11. Using the materials developed in this first inexpensive rough draft, begin evaluation activities. Chapter 10 introduces and discusses procedures and activities for evaluating and revising instructional materials.
12. You may either develop materials for the instructor's manual as you go along or you can take notes as you develop and revise the instructional presentations and activities. Using the notes, you can write the instructor's guide later.

The best way to provide examples of developing rough draft materials is to go right into the case study to see how instructional strategy specifications from Chapter 8 are turned into instructional materials.

Case Study: Group Leadership Training

Selected parts of the instructional strategy for the group leadership unit will be used to illustrate materials development. From the many performance objectives that could be illustrated we have chosen two: objective 6.3.1, "Naming strategies that encourage and stifle member cooperation," and objective 6.4.1, "Classifying strategies that encourage and stifle member cooperation." See Figure 8.8 (p. 211) for a complete list of the objectives included in Session 10.

All materials illustrated are scripts for web-based distance instruction. Learners study independently at home. They come to the learning center only for interactive meeting participation and interactive group leadership associated with objective 6.5.1, "In simulated NCW problem-solving meetings with learner acting as group leader, initiate actions to engender cooperative behavior among group members."

These examples of rough draft materials development assume that the instructional designer is sharing development responsibilities with a production specialist. The designer specified web-based instruction in the instructional strategy and has now scripted what will appear on the web pages. For the specific objectives illustrated in the example, the production specialist will use the scripting to create a web page design with cartoon characters and dialogue balloons simulating a comic book style. In the example that follows, a comment on mediation is included as each component of the instructional strategy is described. Readers should note that the materials specified for web-based delivery in this example lesson could have been specified with equivalent learning effectiveness for broadcast television with a workbook, illustrated text on DVD, traditional classroom instruction with role playing, or many other delivery systems. However, any delivery system chosen for the entire unit on group leadership skills would need to preserve students' opportunities to observe and participate in small-group interaction with adaptive feedback.

Preinstructional Activities

Mediation of Preinstructional Activities   The web-based instructional materials prescriptions for this session are scripts for web presentations as well as any of the inexpensive graphic and color enhancements that are readily available for web-based instruction. These enhancements are intended to stimulate motivation and interest value.

Motivation Materials and Session Objectives   Table 9.4 shows an example of motivational materials and session objectives written by an instructional designer (see Figure 8.5 on page 204 for the instructional strategy using these materials). The left column identifies particular learning components from the instructional strategy and the right column contains the instruction, which highlights the links between instruction and instructional strategy, making the relationships easier for you to follow. (The session information and left-hand column material would not appear in the actual instruction.)

t a b l e 9 . 4	Preinstructional Activities for the Group Leadership Instructional Goal

Learning Component	Instruction
Introduction/ motivation	Throughout America, we as citizens have good intentions of working together to make our neighborhoods safe for our families and us. We bond together in times of crisis, forming search parties for a missing neighbor or chaperoning schoolchildren to and from a bus stop. We always work relentlessly until the crisis is resolved. When there is no immediate crisis, however, we often have difficulty forming cohesive groups that persist in systematic efforts to improve and sustain neighborhood safety. We have seen illustrations of the positive differences that effective NCW associations can make in our neighborhoods, and we have examined the activities and impact of several NCW associations around the state. The key factor in forming and maintaining an effective NCW group is **leadership**. In your neighborhood, *you* are the key ingredient to an effective NCW association and improved safety for all citizens.
Linking to previous skills	During previous sessions we practiced group leadership skills related to planning and preparation skills for NCW meetings. You also rehearsed techniques for managing the thought line for the group, and you experienced the difference you can make using thought line management techniques during a problem-solving meeting. To this point in discussion groups, your actions have been rather directive: preparing materials, inviting participants, and keeping the group on the topic with thought line management techniques. Your direction in these areas is critical for helping your neighbors examine different facets of safety issues and plan safety programs.
Session objectives	There is another important ingredient in effective group leadership: **managing cooperative group interaction during meetings**. Regardless of the topic of the meeting, the level of members' preparation, or the resulting plan of action, participants are most likely to view the NCW association and your meetings as worth their time and effort when their interaction in the group is comfortable and cooperative. Leader actions for managing cooperative interaction are more democratic than those we have covered to this point; their purpose is to draw out participants. These actions are interwoven in a discussion with actions you use to manage the thought line. In this session, however, we will set aside thought line actions and focus specifically on actions for encouraging cooperative group interaction. You can use three main strategies as the NCW leader to manage cooperative group interaction during meetings: 1. Engender cooperative member behaviors. 2. Recognize and defuse members' blocking behaviors if they occur. 3. Recognize and alleviate group stress if it appears. You will spend the next four sessions practicing and refining your leadership skills in these three main areas. During this session, our focus will be on skills related to engendering cooperative member behaviors, and we will work on the following three main skills: 1. Recognizing cooperative member behaviors 2. Recognizing leader actions that encourage and stifle member cooperation during meetings 3. Using leader actions ourselves to encourage member cooperation during meetings Many of you have participated in problem-solving discussion groups in the past, and a few of you have served as leaders for discussion groups. As a beginning, watch a NCW leader lead a group-discussion meeting and see how many of these leader behaviors you already recognize.

figure 9.1 Graphic Example of How Preinstructional Text Material Can Be Converted Using Graphics for Web-Based Delivery

Figure 9.1 includes an illustration of how graphics and comic book characters can be used to convert these preinstructional activities scripts to web-based instructional materials. This sample of how the materials developer creates the web presentation is provided to spark your imagination and illustrate how scripts can be given personality and interest value. Imagine converting the remaining materials to web-based instruction after you study the scripts, focusing on the nature of the content and its relationship to the components of the instructional strategy.

Pretest   The pretest for Session 10 covers only objective 6.4.2, "Given videos of staged NCW meetings, classify leaders' actions that are likely to encourage or stifle member cooperation." Objectives 6.3.1 and 6.4.1 are both subordinate to 6.4.2 and are embedded in the pretest exercise for 6.4.2. Objective 6.5.1, the highest-level skill in this cluster, is not included in the pretest because it requires the learner to lead an actual interactive group meeting. Requiring a public demonstration of skill prior to instruction on the skills does not seem appropriate for this adult group of volunteers.

Mediation of Pretest   As prescribed in the objective and instructional strategy, the pretest consists of directions for learners, a learner response form, and a streaming video of a simulated NCW meeting. Learners print from the web site a "working copy" of the response form to use as they view the video. For the pretest, they can view the video only twice, marking their responses on the response form as they watch. Following the second viewing, they access the interactive pretest form on the web site and respond to questions about the number and type of leader and member actions they observed in the meeting. Figure 9.2 contains the directions and the learners' response sheet.

Content Presentation and Learning Guidance

Mediation of Instruction   We present in this chapter only a segment of the lengthy instruction needed for the objectives in Session 10. Assume that instruction for

figure

9.2

Sample Pretest for Group Leadership Instructional Goal (Session 10, Objective 6.4.2 in Table 8.10 and Instructional Strategy in Table 8.9)

Learning Component	Pretest Directions
Pretest	Detecting leader behaviors that encourage or stifle group cooperation during meetings
	Directions: Print web form 6.1, then watch web video 6.1: *Leader Behaviors that Encourage and Stifle Cooperative Learning*. In the video, an NCW meeting is under way, and members are discussing neighborhood problems with vandalism. They are examining possible actions they can take to eliminate opportunities for vandals and community actions that can lessen vandalism in the future.
	The form that you printed contains twelve specific **leader actions** that either encourage or stifle group members' cooperation during a meeting. Study the list carefully. Can you pick out these actions used by the group leader in the meeting? As you watch the video presentations:
	1. Check all the *purposeful actions* that Eloise McLaughlin, the NCW leader, directly makes during the meeting to *encourage her neighbors' participation and cooperation*. She may exhibit some of the behaviors more than once and others not at all. Each time she exhibits an encouraging behavior, place a checkmark (✓) in the "Do" column next to the behavior.
	2. Check in the "Don't" column each time that Eloise takes one of the actions that stifles cooperation. For example, if Eloise uses questions as a way to suggest points of discussion five times, you should place a checkmark (✓) in the "Do" column of your checklist each time she demonstrates this skill. On the other hand, if she directly tells the group what she wants them to discuss two times, you should place a checkmark in the "Don't" column each time she directly tells the group what to discuss. Notice how her actions are recorded on the response form in the following example:

Example:

DO TALLY	ELOISE'S COOPERATION-ENCOURAGING ACTIONS	ELOISE'S COOPERATION-STIFLING ACTIONS	DON'T TALLY
✓ ✓ ✓ ✓ ✓	Suggests points of discussion as questions	Prescribes topics for the group to consider	✓ ✓

The NCW meeting segment you will watch runs for eight minutes. Watch the video meeting straight through; then watch it a second time. As you watch the meeting progress, use the form to record your judgments about the group management skills Eloise exhibits during the meeting. When you finish marking your checklist, go to web pretest 6.1. Use the form you have been working on to fill in the pretest and click the "send pretest" button when you are done.

figure 9.2

Continued

DO TALLY	ELOISE'S COOPERATION-ENCOURAGING ACTIONS	ELOISE'S COOPERATION STIFLING ACTIONS	DON'T TALLY
	1. Suggests points of discussion as questions.	1. Prescribes topics for the group to consider	
	2. Uses an investigative, inquiring tone	2. Uses an authoritative tone	
	3. Uses open terms such as *perhaps* and *might*	3. Uses prescriptive terms such as *must* or *should*	
	4. Hesitates and pauses between speakers	4. Fills quiet gaps with personal points of view or solutions	
	5. Willingly turns over the floor to group members who interrupt	5. Continues to talk over interrupting members or interrupts member	
	6. Encompasses total group with eyes, inviting all to participate freely	6. Focuses gaze on a few members	
	7. Nonverbally (eyes, gestures) encourages speaker to address group	7. Holds speaker's attention	
	8. Uses comments that keep discussion centered in the group	8. Encourages discussion to flow through leader by evaluating member comments	
	9. Encourages volunteerism (e.g., "Who has experience with . . .")	9. Designates speakers and speaking order (e.g., "Beth, what do you think about . . .")	
	10. Refers to *us, we, our*	10. Refers to *I, me, mine,* or *your*	
	11. Acknowledges group accomplishments	11. Acknowledges own accomplishments or those of particular members	
	12. Praises group effort and accomplishment	12. Singles out particular people for praise	

objectives 6.1.1 through 6.2.2 is already complete and that we are developing instruction only for objectives 6.3.1 and 6.4.1. Instruction is web-based and although intended for participants to access in their homes, those without home equipment can access the materials in the learning center's computer laboratory, their local library, or at another site more convenient to their homes. The web-based instruction for these two objectives will be created using a comic book instructor and a conversational format such as illustrated in Figure 9.3 for objective 6.4.1, which

figure 9.3

Rough Example of Content Presentation Script in Table 9.4 Converted for Web-Based Instruction

roughly illustrates how the NCW committee members will appear in the web-based instruction. Jackson, the NCW leader in this example, is offering introductory comments to the group. Encouraging behaviors are highlighted for learners using call-out boxes and arrows.

Instruction   Figure 9.4 shows the content and learning guidance in session 10 for objectives 6.3.1 and 6.4.1, naming and recognizing leader actions that encourage or stifle cooperative interaction among members. Notice that for objective 6.4.1, an actual script of an NCW meeting is provided. The numbers beside each person's comments during the meeting form a key that link the comments to the leader actions presented in objective 6.3.1. This presentation exercise begins to link verbal information actions to interactive human actions during a meeting.

Learner Participation

Mediation of Learner Participation and Feedback   The learner participation component will also be formatted for web-based instruction enabling learners to study independently and at home throughout the county. Learners can print the pages containing the script, locating and marking all instances of behavior directly on the printed pages. After completing the exercise, they can scroll down to the feedback section which repeats the meeting script with the behaviors *enhancing* and *stifling* marked. Learners can then compare their classification of the behaviors with those made by the designer, marking any discrepancies. These discrepancies can then be discussed in person at the learning center when NCW leaders come for the next interactive session.

Learner Participation Script   The learner participation script for the web-based materials is illustrated in Figure 9.5 on pages 247–248. Only a part of the script is illustrated; the actual script would continue until all twelve cooperation encouraging and corresponding stifling behaviors are illustrated. We stop before the end of the script because the nature of the student participation is established.

figure

9.4

Content Presentation and Learning Guidance for Group Leadership Instructional Goal

---

Session 10, Engendering Cooperative Member Behaviors: Content and Examples for Objective 6.3.1, When asked in writing to name leader actions that encourage or stifle member discussion and cooperation, name these actions

---

As the discussion leader, there are many actions you can take to encourage co-operation among group members. All of these actions are designed to draw out members' ideas and suggestions and to demonstrate the importance of their participation. Your actions during a discussion should place participating members in the foreground while placing yourself in the background. Your personal ideas, solutions, and conclusions are put on hold during the meeting; your job is to get all members actively involved in examining the problem, volunteering ideas and suggestions, weighing the strengths and weaknesses of ideas suggested, and settling on "best solutions" that will alleviate or minimize given problems in the community. Remember that good solutions identified in meetings are most likely to be carried out if group members participate in forming the solutions and have a personal commitment to them.

Although many actions can encourage or stifle cooperative behavior during a discussion, let's focus our attention on twelve key actions that enhance cooperation, each of which has a complementary stifling counterpart (e.g., do this [encouraging] rather than that [stifling]). The twelve action pairs (encouraging and stifling) can be divided into four main categories with three pairs each, as illustrated by the following list.

Leader actions that facilitate or stifle cooperative interaction
(Notice that each encouraging and stifling action pair is bridged with the terms *rather than*.)

I. Appearing open-minded and facilitating to group members *rather than* directive when introducing or changing the topic or suggesting paths the group might take. You can take specific actions during a meeting to achieve this impression:
  1. Suggesting points of discussion as questions *rather than* prescribing topics for the group to consider
  2. Using an investigative inquiring tone *rather than* an authoritative one
  3. Using open terms such as *perhaps* and *might rather than* prescriptive terms such as *must* or *should*

II. Demonstrating a genuine desire for others to contribute *rather than* treating them as providing you with an audience. Certain actions effectively leave this impression with your group members:
  4. Hesitating and pausing between speakers *rather than* filling quiet gaps by offering personal points of view or solutions
  5. Willingly turning over the floor to group members who interrupt you *rather than* continuing to talk over the interrupting member
  6. Encompassing total group with eyes, inviting all to participate freely, *rather than* focusing your gaze on a few members you know are ready contributors

III. Helping group members focus on themselves, their needs, and their ideas *rather than* on you as the leader. You can achieve this objective through these actions:
  7. Nonverbally (eyes, gestures) encouraging speakers to address the group *rather than* addressing only you
  8. Using comments that keep discussion centered in the group *rather than* encouraging discussion to flow through you (e.g., "Are there any more thoughts on that idea?" rather than "I like that, Karen, tell me more about it")
  9. Encouraging volunteerism *rather than* designating speakers and speaking order (e.g., "Who has experience with . . ." rather than "Beth, what do you think about . . .")

(continued)

figure 9.4   **Continued**

IV. Moving ownership of ideas from individual contributors to the whole group. Ownership transfer can be accomplished in the following ways:

10. Referring to *us, we, our, rather than I, me, mine,* or *your*

11. Acknowledging group accomplishments *rather than* your own or those of particular members

12. Praising group efforts and accomplishments *rather than* singling out particular people for praise

When you consistently exhibit these twelve encouraging behaviors in leading group discussions, group members will be more productive and reach better decisions than if you use the alternative stifling behaviors.

Session 10, Engendering Cooperative Member Behaviors: Content and Examples for Objective 6.4.1, Given written descriptions of a group leader's actions during a meeting, indicate whether the actions are likely to encourage or stifle cooperative group interaction

It may be helpful to examine an NCW leader using each of these twelve cooperation-encouraging actions while leading a group discussion. In the following NCW meeting script, Jackson, the leader, demonstrates each of the behaviors. The meeting script appears in the right column and the left column is used to highlight particular actions. The actions are linked to the previous list by number (1–12).

LEADER ACTIONS	NEIGHBORHOOD WATCH MEETING SCRIPT
6. Eyes group inclusively 10. Use of terms *us, our, we* 11. Praises group for accomplishment 12. Does not praise individuals	**Jackson:** (*Smiling, eyes encompassing whole group*) I'm pleased that so many of *us* can be here tonight. During *our* last meeting, *we* discussed the problems we are having with graffiti and planned ways to try to reduce the amount of graffiti we see. *Our* three point program *appears to be having an incredible impact;* the old graffiti is gone, and we have fewer instances of new graffiti.
	Sam: (*Addressing Jackson*) I think the new paint on buildings and fences looks good. It dresses up the community.
4. Hesitates, waiting for others to join	(*Jackson does not verbally respond; he awaits other members' comments.*)
	Dorothy: I think we should send letters of appreciation to the businesses who contributed the paint and to the student–parent groups that volunteered their time through the school to paint out the graffiti that had been building for so . . .
	Frank: (*Interrupting Dorothy*) The letters have been sent.
	Dorothy: Good.
6. Eye contact with all 10. *We* agreed 1. Pose topic as question	**Jackson:** (*Looking around group*) Last meeting *we agreed* to invite Officer Talbot to talk with us about ways we can help protect ourselves from home burglaries. Is this still the area we wish to address this evening?

figure 9.4

Continued

LEADER ACTIONS	NEIGHBORHOOD WATCH MEETING SCRIPT
9. Not designating speaker	*(Jackson again looks around the group and hesitates without calling on a particular member.)*
	Gwen: *(Addressing Jackson)* I want to talk about ways to protect ourselves from burglars. As I told you, our house was robbed last month while we were visiting John's mother in Pittsburgh.
7. Nonverbal gesture for speaker to address group	*(Jackson gestures with eyes and hands for Gwen to address her comments to the group.)*
	Gwen: *(Continuing to group)* I thought we had done everything we needed to do by stopping the mail and newspaper, but obviously that wasn't enough.
4. Hesitates	*(Jackson hesitates, awaiting other members' responses to Gwen.)*
	Sam: *(Looking at Jackson)* I would like some information on the nature of burglaries in our neighborhood.
8. No comment, evaluation	*(Jackson does not comment; instead, he looks inquiringly at Officer Talbot, the resource officer.)*
	Officer Talbot: During the past year, there were 125 burglaries in our community, and over 90 percent of them occurred between 10:00 a.m. and 3:00 p.m. when you were at work and the children were at school. Most burglaries have been crimes of opportunities . . . we have made entering our homes relatively easy. The intruders entered homes through unlocked doors and windows, especially through garage doors, bathroom windows, and back doors and windows where they were less likely to . . .
	Gwen: *(Interrupting Talbot)* Our doors and windows *were* locked. Still they entered. They broke the kitchen window on the back porch and crawled in over the sink!
	Officer Talbot: It does happen, Gwen. I'm sure your intruders felt more safe entering your house from the back side. They are typically looking for cash or items they can readily sell for cash such as jewelry, electronic equipment, silver, guns, or other valuables easy to carry away. Typical burglars in this neighborhood are local male teenagers. Only 15 percent of our burglaries have been committed by individuals who are pros.
	Sam: Thank you.

(continued)

figure

9.4

Continued

LEADER ACTIONS	NEIGHBORHOOD WATCH MEETING SCRIPT
2. Uses inquiring tone 3. Uses terms *perhaps, might*	**Jackson:** (*Using inquiring tone*) It seems that the majority of our crimes are opportunities. Perhaps we might consider ways of removing . . . **Sam:** (*Interrupting Jackson*) Exactly. How can we remove the opportunities?
5. Willingly turns over floor	(*Jackson turns interestedly to Sam.*) **Frank:** I found a home security survey that helps homeowners locate areas where they might be lax. **Officer Talbot:** I have seen those. What areas does your survey cover? **Frank:** Let's see. It covers examining windows, doors, garages, landscaping, exterior lights, and interior lights. It's in a checklist format and would be easy for us to use and to share with all members of the neighborhood.
12. Doesn't praise individual 2. Inquiring tone and response	**Jackson:** (*Does not praise Frank, although he believes that bringing the survey to the meeting was a good idea since it will provide a catalyst for further group discussion*) May we make a copy of the survey to share around the group? Is it copyrighted? **Officer Talbot:** These surveys are typically provided by public service groups, and citizens are encouraged to copy and use them. **Frank:** Yes. We can copy and distribute it. It is produced and distributed from the county sheriff's office. In fact, it gives a number here for obtaining more copies. I thought it was a good idea for our meeting this evening, so I brought enough copies for everyone. (*He passes copies of the survey to members around the table.*) **Officer Talbot:** I'll contact the office and get the extra copies. How many copies will we need?
3. Using term *probably* 12. Not praising individual 10. Moving ownership of survey from Frank to group with "our survey"	**Jackson:** We will probably want enough copies for all homes in our four-block area. (*Turning to the group, without addressing or praising Frank*) Well, what does our survey say?

Notice that during Jackson's meeting, he exhibited each of the twelve positive behaviors at least once. Each of these group-encouraging behaviors is so subtle that it often is unnoticed by group members. The behaviors taken together, however, communicate clearly to group members that Jackson believes their input is valuable, he wants them to contribute, and he is not going to broker who gets to speak or when. Jackson's actions demonstrate clearly that he does not perceive his neighbors to be an audience or backdrop for him and one or two of his friends in the community.

figure	Learner Participation for the Group Leadership Instructional Goal
9.5	

Session 10, Engendering Cooperative Member Behaviors: Learner Participation for Objective 6.4.1

Directions: Can you locate each time one of these twelve key interaction leadership actions occurs in the following NCW meeting? Darcy, the new NCW leader, is a law student who recently moved to a residence located in a high-crime area near the university. She has had several leadership roles in college, but this is her first community-based leadership activity. Young and inexperienced, she may commit errors or stifling actions as she manages her group's interaction. Having completed communications courses and participated in problem-solving discussions in college, however, she will undoubtedly demonstrate several of the encouraging actions as well. Each time Darcy demonstrates an encouraging action, write the number of the action with a plus sign (+) in the left column of the same line. If she uses the action incorrectly (stifling), write the action number with a minus sign (−). For example, if Darcy suggests a point of discussion as a question, you would place a + 1 in the left column of that line. On the other hand, if she tells the group what to discuss, you will place a −1 in the left column preceding the line. Use a list of numbered leader actions identical to the one used in the pretest to aid your responses.

MARK LEADER ACTIONS IN THIS COLUMN	NEIGHBORHOOD WATCH MEETING SCRIPT
	Darcy: Thank you all for coming this morning. I am so pleased to see this many of you returning and also to see several new faces. Why don't we begin by introducing ourselves? Some of you may want to share your reasons for joining us. Shall we start here on my left?
	(*The fourteen neighbors in attendance begin to introduce themselves.*)
	Darcy: At the conclusion of the last meeting, several of you suggested that we discuss ways to be more safe as we move about the neighborhood and campus. On this topic, I have invited Sharon Wright, who will share some of the strategies they use with students who come to the Victims' Advocacy Center on campus.
	Darcy: (*Turning to Sharon*) Thank you for coming this morning, Sharon. Some of you may know Sharon. We are certainly lucky to have her with us. She has her Ph.D. in criminology with a master's in counseling and victim advocacy.
	Sharon: Thank you, Darcy. I am very pleased to have been invited.
	Darcy: (*Looking around total group, smiling*) I have also made a list of topics suggested in Mann and Blakeman's book *Safe Homes, Safe Neighborhoods* on personal safety in the neighborhood.
	Darcy: (*Continuing*) Our basic plan this morning is to generate information for a personal safety tips brochure that we will stuff in all community mailboxes and that Sharon will distribute through the Victims'

(*continued*)

<table>
<tr><td>

f i g u r e

9 . 5
</td><td>

Continued
</td></tr>
</table>

MARK LEADER ACTIONS IN THIS COLUMN	NEIGHBORHOOD WATCH MEETING SCRIPT
	Advocacy Center on campus. I think we should begin with the issue of safety in the home since we are having such problems with robberies. **Ben:** I think that street safety is more problematic here, so . . . **Darcy:** (*Interrupting Ben*) That's a very good idea, Ben, and we should get to street safety as well. (*Darcy remains quiet, looking around room for other suggestions from group.*) **Sharon:** We should perhaps discuss safety in public parking lots on campus and at the mall. There are several strategies we can use there to improve our chances of being safe. **Darcy:** That's a good idea, Sharon. Well, that's three good topics. Home safety, street safety, and parking lot safety. Let's begin with these and see where they take us. Bob, you haven't said anything yet. Where would you like to start? **Bob:** Like Ben, I understand there are a lot of problems in our neighborhood with street crimes such as muggings, purse snatchings, and so forth. Let's consider this area since most of us walk from campus down Third Street and across Garfield. Those are some of the most dangerous sidewalks in this city! . . .
	The student participation script continues until all twelve cooperation and corresponding stifling behaviors are illustrated. We stop here because the nature of the student participation is established.

Feedback   Figure 9.6 illustrates feedback for a segment of the participation exercise. Learners would locate this feedback after completing the exercises in Figure 9.5. In Figure 9.6, the pluses and minuses shown in the left column indicate the designer's classification for whether the action was seen as enhancing (+) or stifling (−). Learners compare their classifications with those of the instructor. The right-hand column repeats the script in Figure 9.5 so that learners are not required to scroll up and down the screen to match the participation and feedback materials. Learners continue with the feedback material until they have compared all their responses and marked their inconsistent ratings for group discussion.

Following the learner feedback for objective 6.4.1, participants will begin instruction for objective 6.4.2, "Classifying leaders' actions during interactive meetings." A streaming video will be used in which learners observe segments of three NCW meetings in progress. The information presentation and example segments demonstrate each of the encouraging and discouraging behaviors as well as show how the leader could have molded each of the stifling actions into complementary, encouraging actions.

As a participation activity, learners again classify all the encouraging actions the leader takes during the meeting session. In addition, for each stifling action encountered, they prescribe the action the leader should have taken instead. The feedback for this objective is also delivered using streaming video, with guided trips through the same meeting to revisit particular leader behaviors. During the feedback trip, as each stifling action is revisited, the leader changes actions before the learner's eyes, using complementary and encouraging behavior instead. Following instruction on objective 6.4.2, the learners finish session 10 with objective 6.5.1

figure	Feedback for the Group Leadership Instructional Goal
9.6	**Session 10, Engendering Cooperative Member Behaviors: Feedback for Objective 6.4.1 (to illustrate feedback, only a segment of the exercise follows)**

Directions: Once you have finished analyzing Darcy's cooperation enhancing and stifling actions, you should compare your marked script with the following. Each time your behaviors column does not match, circle the behavior on your script that differs from this script. Reread the script at the point of difference to see whether you wish to change your mind about the category. If not, we will discuss differences before moving on.

MARK LEADER ACTIONS THIS COLUMN	NEIGHBORHOOD WATCH MEETING
+1 +3, +10 +1	**Darcy:** Thank you all for coming this morning. I am so pleased to see this many of you returning and also to see several new faces. *Why don't we begin by introducing ourselves?* Some of you *may* want to share your reasons for joining *us*. Shall *we* start here on my left? (*The fourteen neighbors in attendance begin to introduce themselves.*)
+11, +10 −10	**Darcy:** At the conclusion of the last meeting, *several members suggested* that *we discuss* ways to be more safe as we move about the neighborhood and campus. On this topic, I have invited Sharon Wright, who will share some of the strategies they use with students who come to the Victims' Advocacy Center on campus.
−11, −12	**Darcy:** (*Turning to Sharon*) Thank you for coming this morning, Sharon. Some of you may know Sharon. *We are certainly lucky to have her with us. She has her Ph.D. in criminology with a master's in counseling and victim advocacy.*
	Sharon: Thank you Darcy. I am very pleased to have been invited.
+6 −10 −1, +10 −10, +10 −3 +10	**Darcy:** (*Looking around total group, smiling*) *I have* also made a list of topics suggested in Mann and Blakeman's book *Safe Homes, Safe Neighborhoods* on personal safety in the neighborhood. *Our basic plan* this morning is to generate information for a personal safety tips brochure that we will stuff in all community mailboxes and that Sharon will distribute through the Victims' Advocacy Center on campus. *I think we should* begin with the issue of safety in the home since *we* are having such problems with robberies.
	Ben: I think that street safety is more problematic here, so . . .
−5, −8 +10, −3 +4	**Darcy:** (*Interrupting Ben*) *That's a very good idea*, Ben, and *we should* get to street safety as well. (*Darcy remains quiet, looking around room for other suggestions from group.*)
	Sharon: We should perhaps discuss safety in parking lots on campus and at the mall. There are several strategies we can use there to improve our chances of being safe.
−8 −1	**Darcy:** *That's a good idea* Sharon. Well that's three good topics. Home safety, street safety, and parking lot safety. *Let's begin with these* . . .

and lead a small-group discussion of their own during a face-to-face session at the community center.

For a school curriculum example of developing instructional materials, see Appendixes I, J, and K in this book.

SUMMARY

You have the following resource materials for developing your instruction:

- Instructional goal
- Instructional analysis
- Performance objectives
- Sample test items
- Characteristics of the target learners
- Characteristics of the learning and performance contexts
- Instructional strategy that includes prescriptions for the following:
  - Cluster and sequence of objectives
  - Preinstructional activities
  - Assessments to be used
  - Content presentation and learning guidance
  - Learner participation (practice and feedback)
  - Strategies for memory and transfer skills
  - Activities assigned to individual lessons
  - Student groupings and media selections
  - Delivery system

Some of your resources should be kept close at hand while writing materials. The performance objectives in the design evaluation chart (see Tables 7.2 and 7.3 and Figure 7.1 on pages 148 and 150) will help ensure congruence between the instruction created and the objective. Other critical resources include the learner analysis, the context analysis, and the instructional strategy documents. Constant reference to these documents while you work will keep your efforts targeted and help avoid introducing interesting—but extraneous—information. Focus carefully on the conditions specified in the objectives as well as the characteristics and special needs of the learners.

When you complete this phase of the instructional design, you should have a draft set of instructional materials, draft assessments, and a draft instructor's manual. Do not feel that any materials you develop on the first attempt will stand for all time. It is extremely important to consider the materials you develop as draft copies and expect review and revision based on feedback from learners, instructors, and subject-matter experts. You should not begin any elaborate and expensive production procedures and should instead rely on crude pictures or clip art rather than finished artwork, storyboards and "desktop" videos rather than studio-produced tapes, and PowerPoint rather than complex multimedia. Delay any expensive mediated materials until you have completed at least one revision of your instruction.

You can be assured that no matter how humble your materials at this point, there will be associated costs that should be minimized until the needed data is available to make correct decisions about the final version. We will have more to say about this in succeeding chapters.

RUBRIC FOR EVALUATING INSTRUCTIONAL MATERIALS

Criteria for evaluating instructional materials are included in the following rubric. This checklist is a useful job aid to evaluate the completed materials developed during this course. Despite the draft stage of your materials, the last section on technical criteria will be useful for selecting existing instructional materials.

Designer note: If an element is not relevant for your project, mark NA in the No column.

No	Some	Yes	**A. Goal-Centered Criteria** Are the instructional materials:
___	___	___	1. Congruent with the terminal and performance objectives?
___	___	___	2. Adequate in content coverage and completeness?
___	___	___	3. Authoritative?
___	___	___	4. Accurate?
___	___	___	5. Current?
___	___	___	6. Objective in presentations (lack of content bias)?

No	Some	Yes	
			B. Learner-Centered Criteria Are the instructional materials appropriate for learners':
___	___	___	1. Vocabulary?
___	___	___	2. Developmental level (complexity)?
___	___	___	3. Background, experience, environment?
___	___	___	4. Experiences with testing formats and equipment?
___	___	___	5. Motivation and interest?
___	___	___	6. Cultural, racial, gender needs (lack bias)?
			C. Learning-Centered Criteria Do the materials include:
___	___	___	1. Preinstructional materials?
___	___	___	2. Appropriate content sequencing?
___	___	___	3. Presentations that are complete, current, and tailored for learners?
___	___	___	4. Practice exercises that are congruent with the goal?
___	___	___	5. Adequate and supportive feedback?
___	___	___	6. Appropriate assessments?
___	___	___	7. Appropriate sequence and chunk size?
			D. Context-Centered Criteria Are/do the instructional materials:
___	___	___	1. Authentic for the learning and performance sites?
___	___	___	2. Feasible for the learning and performance sites?
___	___	___	3. Require additional equipment/tools?
___	___	___	4. Have congruent technical qualities for planned site (facilities/delivery system)?
___	___	___	5. Have adequate resources (time, budget, personnel availability and skills)?
			E. Technical Criteria Do the instructional materials have appropriate:
___	___	___	1. Delivery system and media for the nature of objectives?
___	___	___	2. Packaging?
___	___	___	3. Graphic design and topography?
___	___	___	4. Durability?
___	___	___	5. Legibility?
___	___	___	6. Audio and video quality?
___	___	___	7. Interface design?
___	___	___	8. Navigation?
___	___	___	9. Functionality?
___	___	___	10. Other?

PRACTICE

1. What are the three major components of an instructional package?

2. What types of learning components would you be most likely to include in the instructional materials?

3. What would you be likely to include in the instructor's guide portion of course management information?

4. Number the following materials showing your preferred order of development: ( ) instructional materials, ( ) assessments, and ( ) instructor's guide. (There is no set answer to this question, but with your developmental project in mind, it is time to give the developmental procedure some thought. This will enable you to collect pertinent information at the proper time.)

Designers use five families of criteria to evaluate existing instructional materials. Match each of the following criteria with its family by placing the letter of the family in the space before each criterion.

    a. Goal-centered criteria
    b. Learner-centered criteria
    c. Learning-centered criteria
    d. Context-centered criteria
    e. Technical criteria

_____ 5. Screen design quality

_____ 6. Complexity of vocabulary

_____ 7. Congruence with subordinate skills

_____ 8. Feasibility for learning environment

_____ 9. Authenticity for learning performance

_____ 10. Content expert's authority

_____ 11. Navigation ease

_____ 12. Adequacy feedback for learners

_____ 13. Audio or video quality

_____ 14. Currency of content

15. Although you are undoubtedly creating instructional materials for your own project, it might be helpful for you to develop some instructional materials for the writing composition case study. Develop instructional materials for only the preinstructional activities prescribed in the following instructional strategy from Appendix F. Recall that the learning environment parts of the strategy were completed in Chapter 8. For this exercise, focus only on the writing skills described.

- You are developing instruction for the sixth-grade target group.

- The instruction will be delivered using an Internet-based instructional delivery system.

- Students will access your instruction using their laptop computers.

Motivation: Writing Different Types of Sentences: A newsletter article will be used as an introduction. It will be on a topic of high interest to sixth graders, and it will contain all four sentence types to illustrate variety and increasing interest in the article through varying sentence type.

Objectives: Each of the four types of sentences in the sample story will be highlighted and described in the introduction. The purpose of the unit, learning to write stories that contain a variety of sentence types, will be included.

Entry Skills: Since there are several entry skills noted in the instructional analysis, a test will be developed and administered to determine whether students have the required prerequisite skills.

It may help you to use the script format used earlier to develop your material. Simply divide a sheet of paper into three sections and label each component and objective as you work. This format will help keep you on track. Of course you would not use this format when field-testing your own instruction. The first two columns would be omitted.

FEEDBACK

1. Instructional materials, assessments, and course management information

2. Instructional materials include:

   - Preinstructional activities, including objectives and review materials as well as motivational materials and activities.

   - Content that must be presented to students to enable them to achieve your objectives, including examples and nonexamples of information, concepts, or skills that need to be learned

   - Participation activities that enable students to practice or to try out the concept or skills for themselves and feedback on students' performance to enable reconsideration of their ideas or adjustment of their techniques

   - Assessments of learners' mastery of new information and skills

   - Activities that enhance memory and transfer

3. Instructors' guide would include:

   - Information about the target population for the materials

   - Suggestions on how to adapt materials for older, younger, higher-achieving, or lower-achieving students

   - Overview of the content

   - Intended learning outcomes of the instruction

   - Suggestions for using the materials in a certain context or sequence

   - Suggestions for a constructivist learning environment when appropriate (goals, learners, contexts, resources)

   - Suggestions for materials management for individualized learning, small-group learning, learning-center activities, or classroom activities

   - Retention and transfer activities

   - Tests that can be used to evaluate students' performance on terminal objectives

   - Evidence of the effectiveness of the materials when used as suggested with the intended target populations

   - Suggestions for evaluating student work and reporting progress

   - Estimation of time required to use the materials properly

   - Equipment or additional facilities needed for the materials

4. No rigid pattern of development exists, though the following order shows an example of procedure suitable for an instructional strategy, a unit of instruction, or whole course (subject to constraints on time, materials, and resources):

- Assessments that were probably completed in a previous design step and may just need final formatting
- Instructional materials
- Course management information including the instructor's guide and other information for implementing distance learning and self-paced instructional programs

5. e.

6. b

7. a

8. d

9. d

10. a

11. e

12. c

13. e

14. a

15. See the preinstructional materials in Appendix I. Notice the use of peer teachers to present the information and guide students through the information. They represent a purposeful attempt to balance gender and culture for the students. In addition to these preinstructional materials, readers will want to review the other instructional materials developed for the case study in Appendixes K and L. It would be good to compare the materials illustrated in Appendixes I, J, and K with the instructional strategies in Appendixes F, G, and H. Readers should imagine the additional benefits of placing these materials on the web site. The additional space, color, highlighting, and navigation in that medium increase the attractiveness and clarity of these materials many times over.

REFERENCES AND RECOMMENDED READINGS

Aldrich, C. (2005). *Learning by doing: A comprehensive guide to simulations, computer games, and pedagogy in e-learning and other educational experiences*. San Francisco: Jossey-Bass. Integrates content, simulations, games, and pedagogy.

Barron, A., Ivers, K., Lilavois, N., & Wells, J. (2006). *Technologies for education: A practical guide* (5th ed.). Englewood, CO: Libraries Unlimited. A survey of technologies for use in educational settings with guidance for effective utilization.

Berg, G. A. (2003). *Knowledge medium: Designing effective computer-based learning environments*. Hershey, PA: IGI Publishing. Includes theory and practices, media theory, and film criticism.

Brill, J. M., Bishop, M. J., & Walker, A. E. (2006). The competencies and characteristics required of an effective project manager: A web-based Delphi study. *Educational Technology Research and Development* 48(2), 115–140.

Churchill, D. (2007). Towards a useful classification of learning objects. *Educational Technology Research and Development, 55*(5), 479–497.

Clark, R. C., & Mayer, R. E. (2007). *E-learning and the science of instruction: Proven guidelines for consumers and designers of multimedia learning* (2nd ed.). San Francisco: Pfeiffer. E-learning in training and development settings.

Driscoll, M. (2002). *How to design self-directed and distance learning*. San Francisco: Pfeiffer. Multimedia design based on a systematic ID process.

Driscoll, M. (2005). *Advanced web-based training strategies: Unlocking instructionally sound online learning*. San Francisco: John Wiley & Sons.

Educational Technology Magazine, 46(1). (2006). Special issue on learning objects.

Educational Technology Magazine, 47(1). (2007). Special issue on the role of pedagogical agents in providing learning guidance. Pedagogical agents are the interface animations that come to life on the screen and provide information, suggestions, and guidance, or "peer buddies" that interact with the user in intelligent tutoring systems, or the interactive avatars in role playing games.

Fenrich, P. (2005). *Creating instructional multimedia solutions: Practical guidelines for the real world*. Hershey, PA: Information Science Publishing. Includes information on design teams, authoring tools, and digital media development.

Fleming, M., & Levie, W. H. (Eds.). (1993). *Instructional message design*. Englewood Cliffs, NJ: Educational Technology Publications. Excellent chapters on concept learning, problem solving, psychomotor skills, attitude change, and motivation.

Gibbons, A. S., & Fairweather, P. G. (1999). *Computer-based instruction: Design and development*. Englewood Cliffs, NJ: Educational Technology. Authoring tools, interface design, and message design for delivering instruction by computer or web.

Greer, M. (1992). *ID project management: Tools and techniques for instructional designers and developers*. Englewood Cliffs, NJ: Educational Technology Publications. Good guide to ID team organization and management with chapters on creating and testing rough draft materials.

Gustafson, K. L., & Brance, R. M. (1997). Revisioning models of instructional development. *Educational Technology Research and Development, 45*(3), 73–89. This article includes commentaries on electronic performance support systems and rapid prototyping.

Hannafin, M. J., & Peck, K. L. (1988). *The design, development, and evaluation of instructional software*. New York: Macmillan. This older text is still an excellent source for process of developing computer-based materials from instructional strategy prescriptions.

Hew, K. F., & Brush, T. (2007). Integrating technology into K–12 teaching and learning: Current knowledge gaps and recommendations for future research. *Educational Technology Research and Development, 55*(3), 223–252.

Horton, W. (2000). *Designing web-based training: How to teach anyone anything anywhere anytime*. New York: John Wiley & Sons.

Islam, K. A. (2007). *Podcasting 101 for training and development: Challenges, opportunities, and solutions*. San Francisco: Pfeiffer.

Ivers, K. S., & Barron, A. E. (2002). *Multimedia projects in education: Designing, producing, and assessing*. Westport, CT: Libraries Unlimited. Focus on student and teacher multimedia production in PK–12 settings.

Jonassen, D. H. (Ed.). (1982). *The technology of text* (Vol. I). Englewood Cliffs, NJ: Educational Technology Publications. Principles for designing and displaying text.

Jonassen, D. H. (Ed.). (1985). *The technology of text* (Vol. II). Englewood Cliffs, NJ: Educational Technology Publications. Special issue to examine theory, research, and practice on the design of instructional text.

Jonassen, D. H. (1996). *Computers in the classroom*. Englewood Cliffs, NJ: Merrill/Prentice Hall.

Jonassen, D. H., Peck, K. L., & Wilson, B. G. (1999). *Learning with technology: A constructivist perspective*. Upper Saddle River, NJ: Merrill/Prentice Hall. Focuses on the use of technology for engaging students in meaningful learning rather than the use of technology to deliver instructional content to learners.

Jones, T. S., & Richey, R. C. (2000). Rapid prototyping methodology in action. *Educational Technology Research and Development 48*(2), 63–80.

Lee, W. W., & Owens, D. L. (2004). *Multimedia-based instructional design: Computer-based training; web-based training; distance broadcast training; performance-based solutions* (2nd ed.). San Francisco: Pfeiffer.

Mann, S., & Blakeman, M. C. (1993*). Safe homes, safe neighborhoods: Stopping crime where you live*. Berkeley: Nolo Press.

McConnell, D. (2000). *Implementing computer supported cooperative learning*. London: Kogan Page. Useful coverage of group work and computer conferencing in distance education.

Morrison, G. R., & Lowther, D. L. (2002). *Integrating computer technology into the classroom* (2nd ed.). Upper Saddle River, NJ: Merrill/Prentice Hall.

Newby, T. J., Stepich, D. A., Lehman, J. D., & Russell, J. D. (2005). *Instructional technology for teaching and learning* (3rd ed.). Englewood Cliffs, NJ: Merrill/Prentice Hall. Focus on integrating instruction and technology for the classroom, including planning and developing instruction, grouping learners, selecting delivery formats including distance learning, managing, and evaluating instruction.

Rothwell, W. J., & Kazanas, H. C. (2004). *Mastering the instructional design process: A systematic approach*. San Francisco: Jossey-Bass. Part 5 of the book is a sequence of chapters on managing ID projects.

Santos, S. A. (2006). Relationships between learning styles and online learning: Myth or reality? *Performance Improvement Quarterly, 19*(3), 73–88. The paper concludes that a student's preferred way of learning does not relate to their success in online learning, and using learning-style instruments to develop online accommodations or to advise students on taking online courses is not recommended.

Simpson, O. (2003). *Student retention in online, open, and distance learning*. London: Kogan Page.

Sinclair, J. T., Sinclair, L. W., & Lansing, J. G. (2002). *Creating web-based training: A step-by-step guide to designing effective e-learning*. New York: AMACOM Books. Guide to managing web-based training projects using proprietary authoring programs in high-budget training and development settings.

Slatkin, E. (1991). *How to write a manual*. Berkeley, CA: Ten Speed Press. This booklet is old but still available and provides good suggestions for writing and formatting information.

Smaldino, S. E., Lowther, D. L., & Russell, J. D. (2007*). Instructional technology and media for learning* (9th ed.). Upper Saddle River, NJ: Merrill/Prentice Hall. This standard reference in educational technology now includes consideration of all current instructional strategies and media.

Smith, P. J. (2007). Workplace learning and flexible delivery. *Review of Educational Research, (73)*1, 53–88. This review organizes research around cognitive conceptualizations of workplace learning and addresses the challenges of delivering flexible learning programs therein.

Tomei, L. A. (Ed.). (2007). *Online and distance learning: Concepts, methodologies, tools, and applications*

(Vols. 1–6). Hershey, PA: IGI Publishing. This six-volume set is a compilation of articles, research reports, case studies on web-based learning. The set is expensive and targeted for libraries and information centers.

Zettle, H. (2006). *Television production handbook* (9th ed.). Belmont, CA: Wadsworth. This edition of the standard in TV production includes the latest in analog and digital technologies.

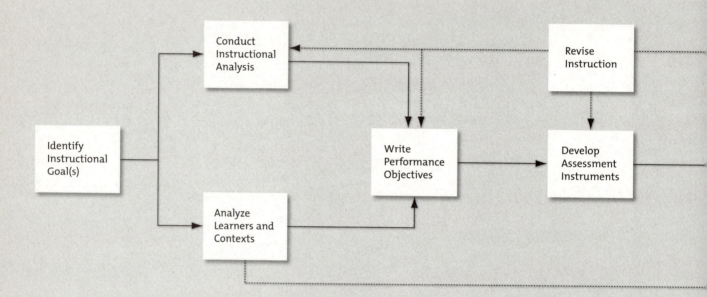

objectives

➤ Describe the purposes for and various stages of formative evaluation of instructor-developed materials, instructor-selected materials, and instructor-presented instruction.

➤ Describe the instruments used in a formative evaluation.

➤ Develop an appropriate formative evaluation plan and construct instruments for a set of instructional materials or an instructor presentation.

➤ Collect data according to a formative evaluation plan for a given set of instructional materials or instructor presentation.

Designing and Conducting Formative Evaluations

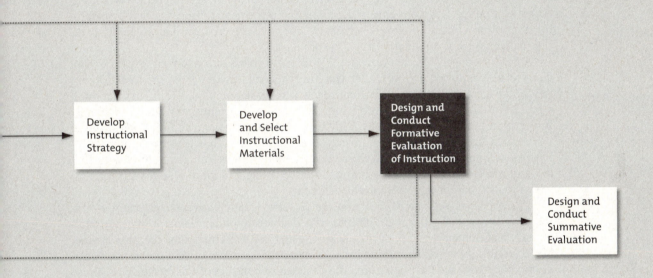

Background

If you had been developing instructional materials forty years ago, it is likely that your initial draft, or perhaps a revised draft, of those materials would have been put into final production and distributed to the target population. The almost certain problems that would occur due to the limited effectiveness of first draft instructional materials would have probably been blamed on poor teaching and poor learning when, in fact, the materials were not sufficient to support the instructional effort.

The problem of untested materials was magnified in the 1960s with the advent of large curriculum development projects. At that time the concept of *evaluation* tended to be defined as a comparison of the effectiveness of an innovation with other existing products. When such studies were carried out, researchers often found a relatively low level of student achievement with the new curriculum materials. In reviewing this situation, Cronbach (1975) and Scriven, Tyler, and Gagné (1967) concluded that we must expand our concept of evaluation to what has come to be called *formative evaluation*—the collection of data and information during the development of instruction that can be used to improve the effectiveness of the instruction.

Studies have shown that thousands of the instructional products sold in the United States each year have not been evaluated with learners and revised prior to distribution. Other studies have demonstrated that simply trying out materials with a single learner and revising the materials on the basis of that data can make a significant difference in the effectiveness of materials. This component of the instructional design model therefore emphasizes the necessity of gathering data from members of the target population about the use and effectiveness of materials and using that information to make the materials even more effective.

You should note that all of the design and development steps in the instructional design process are based on theory, research, and some common sense. At this point, you are about to become an evaluator as you collect data about the effectiveness of your own instructional materials. By following the instructional design model, you hope you have generated instructional materials that will produce significant achievement for learners who initially cannot perform your terminal objective. You are now at the point of testing that assumption.

Formative evaluation was originally used as a process to improve instruction after the first draft of instruction was developed. Experienced designers, however, found that it was better to try out earlier components of the design process, thereby avoiding a lot of problems that would otherwise not be discovered until after the draft of the instruction was complete.

Recall we suggested that during the context analysis you use your instructional analysis to explain what you will be teaching to some learners from the target population. We also suggested a similar approach when you completed your instructional strategy—that you use it to "teach" some learners in an attempt to find the problems in the strategy prior to its use as a guide for developing the instruction. Both of these procedures can be referred to as formative evaluations in that you are gathering information from learners in order to revise the materials before proceeding with the design process. Now you will be doing the same thing, in a more systematic manner, with the instruction that you have developed.

A rather arbitrary division of content has been made between this chapter and the next. We typically think about formative evaluation and revision of instructional materials as one major step. For the sake of clarity and to emphasize the importance of reexamining the whole instructional design process when instructional materials are to be revised, we have separated the design and conduct of the formative evaluation study from the process of revising the instructional materials.

In this chapter we will discuss how to apply formative evaluation techniques to newly developed materials, to selected and adapted materials, to instructor-delivered instruction, and to combinations of these three presentation modes. We will also show how to apply these techniques to instructional procedures as well as to instructional materials to ensure that instruction, regardless of the presentation mode, is properly implemented and managed.

Concepts

The major concept underlying this chapter is *formative evaluation,* which is the process designers use to obtain data for revising their instruction to make it more efficient and effective. The emphasis in formative evaluation is on the collection and analysis of data and the revision of the instruction. When a final version of the instruction is produced, other evaluators may collect data to determine its effectiveness. This latter type of evaluation is often referred to as *summative evaluation*. It is summative in that the instruction is now in its final form, and it is appropriate to compare it with other similar forms of instruction.

There are three basic phases of formative evaluation. First in one-to-one or clinical evaluation, the designer works with individual learners to obtain data to revise the materials. The second stage of formative evaluation is a small-group evaluation. A group of eight to twenty learners representative of the target population study the materials on their own and are tested to collect the required data. The third stage of formative evaluation is usually a field trial. The number of learners is not of particular consequence; often thirty are sufficient. The emphasis in the field trial is on testing procedures required for installing the instruction in a situation as close to the "real world" as possible. The three phases of formative evaluation are typically preceded by the review of instruction by interested specialists who are not directly involved in the instructional development project but have relevant expertise.

Formative Evaluation Designs

What frame of reference can you use to design the formative evaluation? Keeping in mind the purpose of formative evaluation is to pinpoint specific errors in the materials in order to correct them, the evaluation design—including instruments, procedures, and personnel—needs to yield information about the location of and the reasons for any problems. Focusing the design only on the goals and objectives of the instruction would be too limited. Data on learners' achievement of goals and objectives would be insufficient, though important, because these data will only provide information about where errors occur rather than why they occur. Similarly, a shotgun approach to the collection of data would also be inappropriate. Although collecting data on everything you can imagine will produce a variety of information, it may yield some data that are irrelevant and incomplete.

Perhaps the best anchor or framework for the design of the formative evaluation is the instructional strategy. Since the strategy was the foundation for creating the materials, it is likely to hold the key to the nature of errors you made in producing them. Using the instructional strategy as the frame of reference for developing evaluation instruments and procedures should help you avoid designing a formative evaluation that is either too narrowly focused or too broad.

One way the instructional strategy can be used to aid the design of the formative evaluation is to create a matrix that lists the components of the instructional strategy along one side and the major categories of questions about the instruction along the other. In the intersecting boxes of the component-by-question matrix, you can generate questions that should be answered in the evaluation related to each area and component. Using these questions, you can then plan the appropriate instruments and procedures to use and the appropriate audiences to provide the information.

The different components of the strategy should be quite familiar to you by now. What general questions should be asked about each component of the materials? Although there are undoubtedly unique questions for a given set of materials, the five following areas of questions directly related to the decisions you made while developing the materials would be appropriate for all materials.

1. Are the materials appropriate for the type of learning outcome? Specific prescriptions for the development of materials were made based on whether the objectives were intellectual or motor skills, attitudes, or verbal information. You should be concerned whether the materials you produced are indeed congruent with suggestions for learning each type of capability. The best evaluator of this aspect of the materials would undoubtedly be an expert in the type of learning involved.
2. Do the materials include adequate instruction on the subordinate skills, and are these skills sequenced and clustered logically? The best evaluator for this area of questions would be an expert in the content area.
3. Are the materials clear and readily understood by representative members of the target group? Obviously, only members of the target group can answer these questions. Instructors familiar with target learners may provide you with preliminary information, but only learners can ultimately judge the clarity of the materials.
4. What is the motivational value of the materials? Do learners find the materials relevant to their needs and interests? Are they confident as they work through the materials? Are they satisfied with what they have learned? Again, the most appropriate judges of these aspects of the materials are representative members of the target group.
5. Can the materials be managed efficiently in the manner they are mediated? Both target learners and instructors would be appropriate to answer these questions.

Table 10.1 contains an example of the suggested framework for designing the formative evaluation. Using such a framework will help ensure that you include relevant questions about different components of the materials and that appropriate groups and individuals are included.

Notice the two rows at the bottom of the matrix. The first indicates the individuals or groups most appropriate for evaluating each aspect of the materials. The second provides a reminder that you must consider how to gather each type of information needed from the evaluators. You may want to create a checklist or list of questions to accompany the materials for soliciting information from the specialists you choose. You may also want to interview them to determine why they believe particular parts of the material are inadequate and to obtain their suggestions about how the materials might be improved.

In designing instrumentation for gathering information from learners, you must consider the phase (i.e., one-to-one, small-group, and field trial), the setting (learning or performance context), and the nature of the information you are gathering. In the one-to-one evaluations, the materials themselves make up one instrument. You will want learners to circle words or sentences and to write comments directly in the materials. The questions included in the intersecting blocks of the matrix should help you develop other instruments such as checklists to guide your observations and questions to include in your interviews and questionnaires. It is important to note that although different areas of questions about the materials are described separately here, it does not mean to imply that they must be on separate instruments. The instruments you produce should be efficient in gathering information from participants.

table 10.1 | **Example Framework for Designing a Formative Evaluation**

MAIN COMPONENTS OF MATERIALS					
	Main Areas of Questions about Materials				
	TYPE OF LEARNING	CONTENT	CLARITY	MOTIVATION	MANAGEMENT
Preinstructional Initial motivation Objectives Entry skills					
Presentation Sequence Size of unit Content Examples					
Participation Practice Feedback					
Assessment Pretests Posttests Performance context					
Who judges?	Learning Specialists	Content Expert	Target Learners	Target Learners	Target Learners/ Instructors
How are data gathered?	Checklist Interview	Checklist Interview	Observations Interviews Tests Materials	Observations Interviews Surveys	Observations Interviews

At a minimum, the types of data you will probably want to collect include the following:

- Reactions of the subject-matter expert. It is the responsibility of this person to verify that the content of the module is accurate and current.
- Reactions of a manager or supervisor who has observed the learner using the skills in the performance context.
- Test data collected on entry skills tests, pretests, and posttests.
- Comments or notations made by learners to you or marked on the instructional materials about difficulties encountered at particular points in the materials.
- Data collected on attitude questionnaires and/or debriefing comments in which learners reveal their overall reactions to the instruction and their perceptions of where difficulties lie with the materials and the instructional procedures in general.
- The time required for learners to complete various components of the instruction.

In the following sections the roles of subject matter, learning, and learner specialists in formative evaluation are described. The three learner-oriented phases of formative evaluation are then elaborated.

Role of Subject-Matter, Learning, and Learner Specialists in Formative Evaluation

Although the formative evaluation process focuses on the acquisition of data from learners, it is also important to have the instruction reviewed by specialists. It is assumed that the designer is knowledgeable about the content area or is working with a content specialist and is also knowledgeable about the target population. Still, there are several good reasons to have the instruction reviewed by outside specialists.

When the first draft of the instruction has been written, designers appear to experience a "forest and trees" problem. They have seen so much that they cannot see anything; it is invaluable to the designer to get others to review what has been developed. A type of reviewer outside the project who has special expertise in the content area of the instruction, called a subject-matter expert (SME), should comment on the accuracy and currency of the instruction. Although many suggestions for improvement may be received, the designer should give considerable thought before making any changes that are counter to the instructional strategy already developed. Another type of reviewer is a specialist in the type of learning outcome involved. A colleague familiar with the suggestions for instruction related to the type of learning might be able to critique your instructional strategy related to what is known about enhancing that particular type of learning.

It is also helpful to share the first draft of the instruction with a person who is familiar with the target population—a person who can look at the instruction through the target population's eyes and react. This specialist may be able to provide insights into the appropriateness of the material for the eventual performance context.

The designer is not obligated to use the suggestions of these specialists. There may be some recommendations that the designer may want to consider after data from learners have been collected and summarized. At least the designer is sensitized to potential problems before learners become involved in the formative evaluation process.

One-to-One Evaluation with Learners

In this discussion of the three phases of formative evaluation of instruction, we will assume that the designer has developed original instruction. In subsequent sections we will discuss the differences in procedures when existing materials are used or when instructor-led instruction has been created.

The purpose of the first stage of formative evaluation, the one-to-one stage, is to identify and remove the most obvious errors in the instruction and to obtain initial performance indications and reactions to the content by learners. During this stage of direct interaction between the designer and individual learners, the designer works individually with three or more of learners who are representative of the target population.

Criteria   During the development of the instructional strategy and the instruction itself, designers and developers make a myriad of translations and decisions that link the content, learners, instructional format, and instructional setting. The one-to-one trials provide designers with their first glimpse of the viability of these links and translations from the learners' perspective. The three main criteria and the decisions designers will make during the evaluation are as follows:

1. Clarity: Is the message, or what is being presented, clear to individual target learners?
2. Impact: What is the impact of the instruction on individual learner's attitudes and achievement of the objectives and goals?
3. Feasibility: How feasible is the instruction given the available resources (time/context)?

The one-to-one trials help verify whether the designers' and developers' hunches were correct or reflected misconceptions of the target group.

Selecting Learners   One of the most critical decisions by the designer in the formative evaluation is the selection of learners to participate in the study. This is not an experiment; there is no need for random selection of large numbers of learners. Actually, the designer wants to select a few learners who represent the range of ability in the group because prior learning or ability is usually one of the major determiners of ability to learn new skills and information. The designer therefore selects at least one learner from the target population who is above average in ability (but certainly not the top student), one who is average, and at least one learner who is below average. The designer then works on an individual basis with each learner. After the initial evaluations with the three learners, the designer may wish to select more learners from the target population to work in a one-to-one mode, although three is usually sufficient.

The designer should be aware of learner characteristics other than ability that may be highly related to achievement and therefore should be systematically represented in the formative evaluation. As noted in Chapter 5, attitudes and previous experience can be very important, and such variables should be a consideration during formative evaluation. For the one-to-one phase of the formative evaluation, the designer may wish to select one learner with a very positive attitude toward that which is being taught, one who is neutral, and one who is negative. Likewise, if experience on the job is an important factor, select someone who has been on the job ten or more years, one who has been there two to five years, and someone who has been there for less than a year. The point is that ability might not be the only critical factor in selecting learners for a formative evaluation. The designer will have to make this decision for each particular instructional design situation.

Data Collection   The three main criteria and the decisions to be made during one-to-one trials help evaluators focus on the kinds of information that would be useful. Table 10.2 contains the types of information that can be obtained for comparisons with clarity, impact, and feasibility criteria. The lists in each criterion category are intended to be illustrative rather than exhaustive because the degree of relevance of each kind of information may differ by learner maturity, instructional content, and delivery method.

For *clarity of instruction,* there are three main categories of illuminating information—message, links, and procedures. The first category, *message,* relates to how clear the basic message is to the learner determined by such factors as vocabulary,

table **10.2**	Formative Evaluation Criteria for One-to-One Trials and the Types of Information for Each Criterion

Criteria			
	MESSAGE	LINKS	PROCEDURES
Clarity of Instruction	• Vocabulary level • Sentence complexity • Message complexity • Introductions • Elaborations • Conclusions • Transitions	• Contexts • Examples • Analogies • Illustrations • Demonstrations • Reviews • Summaries	• Sequence • Segment size • Transition • Pace • Variation
	ATTITUDES	ACHIEVEMENT	
Impact on Learner	• Utility of the information and skills (relevance) • How easy/difficult the information and skills are to learn (confidence) • Satisfaction with skills learned	• Clarity of directions and items for posttests • Scores on posttests	
	LEARNER	RESOURCES	
Feasibility	• Maturity • Independence • Motivation	• Time • Equipment • Environment	

sentence complexity, and message structures. Regardless of whether the learner reads, hears, or sees the message, he or she must be able to follow it. The second category, *links,* refers to how the basic message is tailored for the learner, including contexts, examples, analogies, illustrations, demonstrations, and so forth. When these links are also unfamiliar to the learner, the basic message will undoubtedly be more complex. The third area, *procedures,* refers to characteristics of the instruction such as the sequence, the size of segment presented, the transition between segments, the pace, and the variation built into the presentation. The clarity of instruction may change for the learner when any one of these elements is inappropriate for her or him. The instruction can be so slow and iterative that the learner loses interest, or it can proceed so quickly that comprehension becomes difficult.

Descriptive information rather than quantitative data will probably yield the best information about clarity for revising the instruction. If the instruction is delivered through print, whether on paper or on a computer screen, the learner can be directed to underline or highlight in some way all unfamiliar words and unclear examples, illustrations, and paragraphs, and to mark directions within any figures or tables that are confusing. The learner can be directed to jot down unclear terms and note confusing material when using a video or slides or directed to stop the equipment at any point in order to interact with the evaluator about confusing passages or terms. Regardless of the delivery format during a one-to-one trial, the learner can be asked about the procedural characteristics of the instruction such as segment size and pace. Information about the procedural characteristics can also be collected by observation as the learner listens to the instructor, reads the material, or watches a screen. Such observations can help the evaluator determine whether anxiousness, boredom, fatigue, or all three conditions become apparent at different points in the instruction.

The second criterion in Table 10.2, *impact on learner,* relates to the learner's attitudes about the instruction and her or his achievement on specific objectives. The evaluator needs to determine whether the learner perceives the instruction as being (1) personally relevant to her or him, (2) accomplishable with reasonable effort, and

(3) interesting and satisfying to experience. Related to achievement, posttests will help determine whether the individual can recall the information and perform the tasks. The format of these achievement measures will differ depending on the instructional delivery medium. Questions or directions for performance can be presented orally by the instructor. Learners can be asked to respond (1) using paper and pencil or keyboard, (2) orally in response to the instructor's questions, or (3) by developing or performing something requested.

The third criterion in Table 10.2, *feasibility,* relates to management-oriented considerations that can be examined during the one-to-one trial, including the capability of the learner, the instructional medium, and the instructional environment. Examples of questions of interest include the following: (1) How will the maturity, independence, and motivation of the learner influence the general amount of time required to complete the instruction? (2) Can learners such as this one operate or easily learn to operate any specialized equipment required? (3) Is the learner comfortable in this environment? and (4) Is the cost of delivering this instruction reasonable given the time requirements?

Procedures　　The typical procedure in a one-to-one evaluation is to explain to the learner that a new set of instructional materials has been designed and that you would like his or her reaction to them. You should say that any mistakes that learners might make are probably due to deficiencies in the material and not theirs. Encourage the learners to be relaxed and to talk about the materials. You should have the learners not only go through the instructional materials but also have them take the test(s) provided with the materials. You might also note the amount of time it takes a learner to complete the material.

Instructional designers have found this process invaluable in preparing materials. When learners use the materials in this manner, they find typographical errors, omissions of content, missing pages, graphs that are improperly labeled, inappropriate links in their web pages, and other kinds of mechanical difficulties that inevitably occur. Learners often are able to describe difficulties that they have with the learning sequence and the concepts being taught. They can critique the tests in terms of whether they think they measure your objectives. You can use all of this information to revise your materials and tests and correct relatively gross problems as well as small errors.

In contrast to the earlier stages of instructional design, which emphasize the analytical skills of the designer, the first critical hallmark of the one-to-one formative evaluation is its almost total dependence on the ability of the designer to establish rapport with the learner and then to interact effectively. The learner has typically never been asked to critique instruction; the assumption has been made that if learning does not occur, it is the student's fault. Learners must be convinced that it is legitimate to be critical of what is presented to them. This is sometimes particularly difficult for the young person who is being asked to criticize an authority figure. The designer should establish an atmosphere of acceptance and support for any negative comments from the learner.

The second critical hallmark of the one-to-one approach is that it is an *interactive process*. The power of the process is greatly diminished when the designer hands the instruction to the learner and says, "Here, read this and let me know whether you have any problems." Sitting diagonally beside the learner, the designer should read (silently) with the learner and, at predetermined points, discuss with the learner what has been presented in the materials. The dialogue may focus on the answers to practice questions or may be a consideration of special points made in the content presentation. Before each one-to-one session, the designer should formulate a strategy about how the interaction will take place and how the learner will know when it is appropriate to talk with the evaluator.

It is clear that a one-to-one session can take place with only one learner at a time. It is simply not feasible to do the process with two or more learners. As the designer proceeds with the evaluation, it is necessary to note the comments and suggestions made by the learner as well as any alternative explanations made by the designer that seem effective. These can be noted on one copy of the instruction, or a tape recorder can be used during the session, to which students seem to adapt quite readily.

Assessments and Questionnaires   After the students in the one-to-one trials have completed the instruction, they should review the posttest and attitude questionnaire in the same fashion. After each item or step in the assessment, ask the learners why they made the particular responses that they did. This will help you spot not only mistakes but also the reasons for the mistakes, which can be quite helpful during the revision process. You will also find that some test items that appear to be perfectly clear to you will be totally misinterpreted by the learner. If these faulty items remain in the assessment for the small-group evaluation, there will be major problems in determining whether only those items or the instruction is defective. Exert as much care in evaluating your assessment instruments as you do the instruction itself.

Test directions and rubrics to evaluate performances and products should also be formatively evaluated before they are actually used to evaluate examinees' work. Just as with paper and pencil tests, you must ensure that the directions are clear to the learner and that learners can follow the instructions to produce the anticipated performance or product.

You must also evaluate the utility of the evaluation instrument, particularly the following elements: (1) the observability of each of the elements to be judged, (2) the clarity of the manner in which they are paraphrased, and (3) the efficiency of the sequencing order. Related to the evaluator's responding format, you should check whether the response categories and criteria are reasonable in terms of the number and type of judgments you need to make and the time available for you to observe, judge, and mark the judgment. If you are unable to keep up with the performer, then the accuracy of your judgments will be affected.

The reliability of your judgments should be evaluated by rating the same performance or product two or more times with an intervening time interval. You can also check reliability by having two or more evaluators use the instrument to judge the same performance or product. When the multiple ratings obtained from a single evaluator on a single product differ or the ratings of multiple evaluators differ for a single product, the instrument should be revised in such areas as the number of elements to be judged, the number of levels of judgments to be made, and the clarity of the criteria for each level. The number of elements to be observed and the number of judgment categories should be reduced to a point where consistency is obtained. This implies that several iterations of instrument evaluation are necessary to verify the utility of the instrument and the consistency of judgments made using it.

Finally, you should evaluate your scoring strategy. Using the data you gather during the formative evaluation of the instrument, combine or summarize element-level scores as planned. Review these combined scores in terms of objective level and overall performance. Are the scores logical and interpretable? Can they be used to evaluate particular parts of the instruction and performance? If not, then modify the rating and/or scoring procedure until usable data are obtained.

Learning Time   One design interest during one-to-one evaluation is determining the amount of time required for learners to complete instruction, which is a very rough estimate, because of the interaction between the learner and the designer. You can attempt to subtract a certain percentage of the time from the total time, but experience has indicated that such estimates can be quite inaccurate.

One final comment about the one-to-one evaluation process is in order. Rarely are learners placed in such a vulnerable position and required to expose their ignorance. Even adults must sometimes admit not knowing the meaning of a fairly common word—they always meant to look it up in the dictionary but forgot. In the one-to-one stage, the designer is in control and thus has the responsibility for providing a comfortable working situation. Because learners may hesitate to reveal deficiencies in their current state of knowledge, every possible effort should be made to be both objective about the instruction and supportive of the learner. Without the learner, there is no formative evaluation.

Data Interpretation   The information on the clarity of instruction, impact on learner, and feasibility of instruction needs to be summarized and focused. Particular aspects of the instruction found to be weak can then be reconsidered in order to plan revisions likely to improve the instruction for similar learners. One caution about data interpretation from one-to-one trials is critical. Take care not to overgeneralize the data gathered from only one individual. Although ensuring that the participating target learner is representative of the intended group will help ensure that reactions are typical of other target group members, there is no guarantee that a second target learner will respond in a similar manner. Differing abilities, expectations, and personal abilities among members of the target group result in different data from each. Information gathered from the one-to-one trial should be viewed as a "first glimpse" that may or may not generalize. Gross errors in the instruction will likely become apparent during the trial and will lead to immediate, accurate revisions. Other areas of the instruction that are questionable may not be revised until after the instruction is retried with other individuals or with a small group.

Outcomes   The outcomes of one-to-one trials are instruction that (1) contains appropriate vocabulary, language complexity, examples, and illustrations for the participating learner; (2) either yields reasonable learner attitudes and achievement or is revised with the objective of improving learner attitudes or performance during subsequent trials; and (3) appears feasible for use with the available learners, resources, and setting. The instruction can be refined further using small group trials.

In the next chapter, we will discuss how to summarize the information from the one-to-one trials and how to decide what revisions should be made. In this chapter, we will continue with our discussion of the next phase of formative evaluation, which takes place after the revisions from the one-to-one evaluation have been completed.

Small-Group Evaluation

There are two primary purposes for the small-group evaluation. The first is to determine the effectiveness of changes made following the one-to-one evaluation and to identify any remaining learning problems that learners may have. The second purpose is to determine whether learners can use the instruction without interacting with the instructor. (At this point in our discussion, we are continuing to assume that the designer is creating some form of self-instructional materials.)

Criteria and Data   Typical measures used to evaluate instructional effectiveness include learner performance scores on pretests and posttests. Pretests typically encompass entry skills as well as instructional objectives, and posttests measure learners' performance on the subordinate and terminal objectives for the instruction. Besides learner performance levels, their attitudes about the instruction are obtained through an attitude questionnaire and sometimes a follow-up interview. Information gathered about the feasibility of the instruction usually includes the following: (1) the time required for learners to complete both the instruction and the required performance measures, (2) the costs and viability of delivering the instruction in the intended format and environment, and (3) the attitudes of those implementing or managing the instruction.

Selecting Learners   For the small-group evaluation, you should select a group of approximately eight to twenty learners. If the number of learners is fewer than eight, the data will probably not be very representative of the target population. On the other hand, if you obtain data on many more than twenty learners, you may find that you have more information than you need and that the data from additional learners does not provide a great deal of additional information.

The selection of learners to participate in your small-group trial is important. The learners who evaluate the materials should be as representative of your target population as possible. In an ideal research setting, you would select the learners randomly, which would enable you to apply your findings generally to the entire target population. In typical school, industrial, and adult education settings, however, true randomization is often impossible and perhaps not even desirable. When you cannot select your learners at random or when the group you have available to draw from is relatively small, you want to ensure that you include in your sample at least one representative of each type of subgroup that exists in your population, possibly including the following:

- Low-, average-, and high-achieving students
- Learners with various native languages
- Learners who are familiar with a particular procedure (e.g., web-based instruction) and learners who are not
- Younger or inexperienced learners as well as more mature learners

When your target group is homogeneous, these subgroups are not a problem. When the target population is made up of persons with varied skills and backgrounds, the designer should consider including representatives of each group in the small-group sample. For example, it is almost impossible to predict how a low-achieving learner will perform on your materials based on the efforts of a high-achieving learner. By selecting a representative sample, you will be able to be more insightful about changes you may need to make in your instruction.

Small-group participants are sometimes a biased sample because they consist of people who participate more willingly than the group at large. The designer must be aware of this problem and obtain the most representative group possible, considering all the constraints usually present in obtaining participants for small-group trials. It is also important to note that while this stage is referred to as *small-group evaluation*, the term refers to the number of learners and not the setting in which the learners actually use the materials. For example, if your materials require the use of highly specialized equipment, and you have access to only one piece of equipment, then you would attempt to obtain eight to twenty learners who would use your materials in an individualized setting. It is not necessary to get all the learners together in one room at one time to conduct a small-group evaluation.

Procedures   The basic procedures used in a small-group evaluation differ sharply from those in a one-to-one evaluation. The evaluator (or the instructor) begins by explaining that the materials are in the formative stage of development and that it is necessary to obtain feedback on how they may be improved. Having said this, the instructor then administers the materials in the manner in which they are intended to be used when they are in final form. If a pretest is to be used, then it should be given first. The instructor should intervene as little as possible in the process. Only in those cases when equipment fails or when a learner becomes bogged down in the learning process and cannot continue should the instructor intervene. Each learner's difficulty and the solution should certainly be noted as part of the revision data.

Assessments and Questionnaires   Additional steps in small-group evaluation are the administration of an attitude questionnaire and, if possible, in-depth debriefings with some of the learners in the group. The primary purpose for obtaining learner reactions to the instruction is to identify, from their perceptions, weaknesses and strengths in the implementation of the instructional strategy. The questions should therefore reflect various components of the strategy. The following questions would usually be appropriate:

- Was the instruction interesting?
- Did you understand what you were supposed to learn?

- Were the materials directly related to the objectives?
- Were sufficient practice exercises included?
- Were the practice exercises relevant?
- Did the tests really measure your knowledge of the objectives?
- Did you receive sufficient feedback on your practice exercises?
- Did you feel confident when answering questions on the tests?

These questions might be included in an attitude questionnaire and then pursued at some depth in a discussion with learners. By using questions directed at components of the instructional strategy, such as those just described, it is possible to relate the learners' responses directly to particular components of the instructional materials or procedures. In the discussion with the learners after the materials have been completed, the instructor can ask questions about such features as the pacing, interest, and difficulty of the materials.

Data Summary and Analysis   Both the quantitative and descriptive information gathered during the trial should be summarized and analyzed. Quantitative data consist of test scores as well as time requirements and cost projections. Descriptive information consists of comments collected from attitude questionnaires, interviews, or evaluator's notes written during the trial.

Outcomes   The goal of the small-group trial and instructional revisions is refined instruction that should be effective with most target learners in the intended setting. Refinements required in instruction may be simple, such as changing examples and vocabulary in test items or increasing the amount of time allocated for study. Modifications might also require major changes in the instructional strategy (e.g., motivational strategies, sequence of objectives, instructional delivery format) or in the nature of information presented to learners. Once instruction is adequately refined, the field trial can be initiated.

In the next chapter, we will illustrate how to summarize this data and determine the implications they have for the revision process. In this chapter, we have focused our concern on the formative evaluation study and the collection of data.

Field Trial

In the final stage of formative evaluation the instructor attempts to use a learning context that closely resembles the intended context for the ultimate use of the instructional materials. One purpose of this final stage of formative evaluation is to determine whether the changes in the instruction made after the small-group stage were effective. Another purpose is to see whether the instruction can be used in the context for which it was intended—that is, is it administratively possible to use the instruction in its intended setting?

In order to answer these questions, all materials, including the tests and the instructor's manual, should be revised and ready to go. If an instructor is involved in implementing the instruction, the designer should not play this role.

Location of Evaluation   In picking the site for a field evaluation, you are likely to encounter one of two situations. First, if the material is tried out in a class that is currently using large-group, lockstep pacing, then using self-instructional materials may be a very new and different experience for the learners. It will be important to lay the groundwork for the new procedure by explaining to the learners how the materials are to be used and how they differ from their usual instruction. In all likelihood you will obtain an increase in interest, if not in performance, simply because of the break in the typical classroom instructional pattern. Second, if the materials are tried out in an individualized class, then it may be quite difficult to find a large enough group of learners who are ready for your instructional materials because learners will be "spread out" in the materials they are studying.

Criteria and Data   The field trial is much like the final dress rehearsal in theater since the instruction is polished and delivered in a manner that is as close as possible to the final format. Also, similar to dress rehearsals, the main purpose of the field trial is to locate and eliminate any remaining problems in the instruction. There are many similarities between the small-group trial and the field trial. The decisions to be made during both types of trials are whether learner performance is adequate and delivery of instruction is feasible. Another similarity to the small-group trial is that information is gathered on learner achievement and attitudes; instructor procedures and attitudes; and resources such as time, cost, space, and equipment. The main differences between the two trials are in the actual sophistication of the materials, learners, procedures, instructors, and setting.

Selecting Learners   You should identify a group of about thirty individuals to participate in your field trial. Again, the group should be selected to ensure that it is representative of the target population for which the materials are intended. Because a "typical" group is sometimes hard to locate, designers often select several different groups to participate in the field trial. This ensures that data will be collected under all intended conditions such as an open classroom, traditional instruction, Internet-based instruction, and/or some combination of methods.

   The use of multiple tryout sites may be necessary if such sites will vary a great deal. The designer may not be able to be present while the instruction is used; therefore, it is important that the designer inform the instructor about the procedures to be followed and the data to be collected.

Procedure for Conducting a Field Trial   The procedure for conducting the field trial is similar to that for the small group, with only a few exceptions. The primary change is in the role of the designer, who should do no more than observe the process. The instruction should be administered or delivered by a typical instructor, for whom the designer may have to design and deliver special training so that he or she will know exactly how to use the instruction.

   The only other change might be a reduction in testing. Based on experience in the small group, the pretest and posttest might be modified or reduced to only assess the most important entry behaviors and skills to be taught. The reasoning is that by this point in the development process the main concern in the formative evaluation is feasibility in the learning context.

   The questionnaire may be modified to focus on the environmental factors that the designer thinks will be critical to the success of the instruction. Essentially, the questions should focus on anything that might interfere with the success of the instruction. Observation of the instruction in use and interviews with learners and the instructor will be very valuable.

Data Summary and Interpretation   Data summary and analysis procedures are the same for the small-group and field trials. Achievement data should be organized by instructional objective, and attitudinal information from both learners and instructors should also be anchored to specific objectives whenever possible. Summarizing the data in these formats will aid locating particular areas where the instruction was and was not effective. This information from the field trial is used to plan and make final revisions in the instruction.

Outcomes   The goal of the field trial and final revisions is effective instruction that yields desired levels of learner achievement and attitudes and that functions as intended in the learning setting. Using data about problem areas gathered during the field trial, appropriate revisions are made in the instruction. With the revisions complete, we can begin the formative evaluation in the performance context.

Formative Evaluation in the Performance Context

We have discussed three phases of formative evaluation that focus on gathering information and data about learner performance and attitudes toward the instruction. The context of the instruction changes in each phase from an informal setting in the one-to-one trials to the actual learning context in the field trial. But the question remains about whether the learner can use the new skills in what we have called the *performance context*—the site where the skills are ultimately required.

Almost no newly learned skills are intended for use only during the learning process; the goal is their use at some other time, in some other location. The designer cannot ignore this, but rather should, when appropriate and feasible, include it in the formative evaluation plan. The designer should determine whether the skills that have been taught are retained and used in the performance context and whether the use of the skills has the desired effect on the organization. If negative results are obtained, the designer must determine what the implications are for revising the training. The process described next for doing formative evaluation in the performance context could be used after any of the three phases of learning context formative evaluation.

The purpose of the performance context formative evaluation is to make three fundamental determinations. First, do the learners find that it is appropriate to use their new skills in the workplace and have they been doing so? Second, if they have been used, what has been the impact on the organization? Third, what suggestions do the learners and others that they work with have for improving the instruction? Instruction that works fine in terms of learner performance on a posttest may not result in learner success on the job.

Criteria and Data   Criteria and data in the performance site will vary greatly from one context to another, and appropriate methods for the evaluation must be tailored to the site. In selecting the most appropriate procedures for collecting evidence of training impact, you should consider performance data from both direct observation and company records. Also include perceptual information such as views and attitudes from learners, from those who work with them, and perhaps from customers. Basic questions, possible data sources, and data-gathering methods are compiled in Table 10.3. In framing your own questions, be more specific about *which* skills are of interest in your evaluation.

t a b l e

1 0 . 3

Questions, Data Sources, and Data-Gathering Methods for Performance Context Formative Evaluation

Questions	Data Sources	Methods
1. Did the skills transfer? 2. How are the skills used (frequency, context)? 3. What physical, social, managerial factors enhanced transfer and use of the skills? 4. What physical, social, managerial factors inhibited transfer and use of the skills? 5. Does using the skills help resolve the original need? How? What is the evidence? 6. How might training be refined or improved?	• Learners • Colleagues/peers of learners • Subordinates of learners • Supervisors • Customers • Company records	• Interviews • Questionnaires • Observations • Records analysis

Sometimes it is important to allow time to pass before asking prior learners to comment on their transfer of knowledge and skills to the performance context. Time can enable the learner to arrange the work environment to accommodate the skills, try the skills initially, and refine them. A template that can be used to create a questionnaire to assess learners' perceptions of training outcomes is included in Figure 10.1. The left side of the form lists statements of the main skills covered during instruction. The right side includes five overall training impact responses that learners in the work environment are asked about each of the skills. Four of these responses are based on Rogers's (1995) theory of change diffusion, which was translated for the health community by Prochaska and DiClemente (1986) and for the education community by Hall and Hord (1987). Generally, change is proposed to have at least five stages:

1. *Precontemplation.* Learners do not see a problem with themselves or the organization; thus, they are not using the new skills on the job.
2. *Contemplation.* Learners are thinking about using the skills, but they do not have a plan for doing so.
3. *Preparation.* Learners have or are developing a plan to use the new skills, including such ideas as getting new equipment, seeking more training, or working with others who use the skills.
4. *Action.* Learners are beginning to use the new skills and are refining the skills, their equipment, or the work environment.
5. *Maintenance.* Learners are routinely using the skills smoothly.

The five responses on the survey in Figure 10.1 include "not using," which is intended to reflect both the precontemplation and contemplation stages; "planning to use," which corresponds to the preparation stage; "starting to use," which corresponds to the action stage; and "using routinely," which corresponds to the maintenance stage. The fifth response, "was using before," is not a part of the stages of change, but is included in the set by us to identify those who may not have needed the training at all.

You may assume that performance context formative evaluation only applies to workshops and skills training. This is not necessarily the case, although it is easier to conceptualize in those situations. The greatest barrier to the use of this procedure may be timing. For some instruction, learners will begin using the skills immediately because the skills are part of a hierarchical flow (such as the use of sentence writing skills to write essays), and the designer can do a follow-up within weeks. But what about the public school student who might not be using the skills for years or a training manager who rarely gets to use newly learned skills? For some instruction, this delay can be tolerated because of the length of the overall project and the importance of the information.

Selecting Respondents   Who should participate in this phase of the formative evaluation? Certainly all of the one-to-one learners should participate if the evaluation is done following that phase. Perhaps only a sample of the learners from the small group and field trial would be included. They could be specifically selected based on their performance on the posttest and attitude questionnaire. It would be appropriate to select several high achievers and several low achievers, along with any other learners who presented special circumstances of interest to the designer. These same evaluation questions should be presented to the manager or supervisor of the learner. Their reactions might be identical to the learners or quite different. Peers and subordinates may also offer insights into the effectiveness of the instruction. Did they notice the learners using the skills? Were the learners effective? How could they have performed better?

Procedure   At the completion of the formative evaluation, regardless of the phase, the learners should be told that they will be contacted sometime in the future to discuss

figure

10.1

Template for Assessing Learners' Perceptions of the Impact of Instruction in the Performance Context

Reflections on Residuals from (*name instruction/workshop here*)

During (*date*) you were selected to participate in (*name of workshop, training, course*) that had the defined expected outcomes of: (*insert your goals and objectives here*)

1. Name first goal/objective
2. Name second goal/objective
3. Name third goal/objective
4. *Etc.*

(*name time*) has passed since the conclusion of the (*instruction*), which has provided time for you to transfer the new knowledge and skill to your job and to reflect on how you and your work have been influenced by the (*workshop*) experience. We would like for you to share your reflections on how you and your work have been influenced by the experience. Your comments are anonymous, and all information gathered will be used to assess and improve the (*workshop*). Thank you in advance for your time.

A. To what degree are you using these skills in your work?

Outcomes	Not using	Planning to use	Starting to use	Using routinely	Was using before
1. *Insert outcome 1 here*	○	○	○	○	○
2. *Insert outcome 2 here*	○	○	○	○	○
5. *Etc.*	○	○	○	○	○

B. If you responded "not using" to any of the intended outcomes, please indicate your reason. For any outcome, choose as many reasons as apply. *Designer note: Add your own reasons below that are relevant to the organization & skill.*

Outcomes	Not relevant for my work	Need more training	Need more supervisor support	Need more resources	Need more assistance
1. *Insert outcome 1 here*	○	○	○	○	○
2. *Insert outcome 2 here*	○	○	○	○	○
5. *Etc.*	○	○	○	○	○

Please comment here on other reasons why you are not currently using the skills learned in the instruction.

C. As a direct result of the workshop, have you noticed positive changes related to these outcomes in your knowledge, skills, and attitudes/perspectives?

1 = No, 2 = Some, 3 = A lot

Outcomes	Knowledge	Skills	Attitudes/perspectives
1. *Insert outcome 1 here*	① ② ③	① ② ③	① ② ③
2. *Insert outcome 2 here*	① ② ③	① ② ③	① ② ③
5. *Etc.*	① ② ③	① ② ③	① ② ③

D. For each outcome, please comment on the (*instruction/workshop*) strengths and your suggestions for improvements.

Outcomes	Strengths	Suggestions for Improvement
1. *Insert outcome 1 here*		
2. *Insert outcome 2 here*		
5. *Etc.*		

the instruction they have just completed and its usefulness. When sufficient time has passed to permit the skills to be used—and this will vary according to the nature of the goal—the learners should be contacted. Ideally, the designer would go to the location where the skills are being used, but the contact could be done via telephone.

Outcomes Data gathered during the performance site formative evaluation are used to document the strengths and weaknesses in the instruction, the transfer of skills to the performance site, the use of skills, and the degree to which the original need was reduced or eliminated through the instruction. These data should be summarized and shared with learners, their supervisors, and those requesting the instruction as a way to reduce or eliminate the original need. In addition, problems detected in the workplace that block transfer and implementation of the new skills should be described and shared with the organization. The performance site formative evaluation documents (1) the strengths and weaknesses in the instruction, (2) areas in which transfer and use of skills can better be supported, and (3) suggestions for revising instruction to remove any instructional barriers to implementing the new skills in the work setting. In the next chapter we will indicate how this documentation will be used to refine instruction by eliminating observed weaknesses.

Formative Evaluation of Selected Materials

The three phases of formative evaluation previously described are not totally applicable when the instructor has selected existing materials to try with a group of learners. The kinds of editorial and content changes that are made as a result of one-to-one and small-group evaluations are typically not used with existing materials. These procedures are avoided not because they would be unproductive in improving the instruction, but because in reality the instructor who selects existing materials seldom has the time or resources to conduct these phases. In this circumstance the instructor should proceed directly to a field trial with a group of learners, both to determine whether they are effective with a particular population and in a specific setting and to identify ways that additions to or deletions from the materials or changes in instructional procedures might be made to improve effectiveness.

Preparations for the field trial of existing materials should be made as they would be for a field trial of original materials. An analysis should be made of existing documentation on the development of the materials, the effectiveness of the materials with defined groups, and particularly any description of procedures used during field evaluations. Descriptions of how materials are to be used should be studied, any test instruments that accompany the materials should be examined for their relationship to the performance objectives, and the need for any additional evaluations or attitude questionnaires should be determined.

In the field trial study, the regular instructor should administer the pretest unless he or she knows the learners already have the entry skills and lack knowledge of what is to be taught. A posttest and an attitude questionnaire should certainly be available to evaluate learners' performance and their opinions of the materials.

The instructor who conducts a field trial is able to observe the progress and attitudes of learners using a set of adopted or adapted materials. It is even possible to examine the performance of different groups of learners using modified or unmodified materials to determine whether the changes increased the effectiveness of the materials. The instructor should certainly take the time following the field evaluation to thoroughly debrief the learners on their reactions to the instruction because additional insights about the materials or procedures can be gained during such debriefing sessions. After completing a field trial of selected materials, the instructor should have collected approximately the same types of data that would have been collected if original materials were being formatively evaluated.

Formative Evaluation of Instructor-Led Instruction

If the instructor plans to deliver the instruction to a group of students using an instructor's guide, then the purposes of formative evaluations are much the same as they are for the formative evaluation of independent instructional materials: to determine whether the instruction is effective and decide how to improve it. Once again, the formative evaluation of an instructional plan most nearly approximates that of the field trial phase for instructional materials. In all likelihood, there will be little time for one-to-one or even small-group evaluation.

In preparing for a field trial of instructor-led instruction, the instructor should be concerned with the entry skills and prior knowledge, the posttest knowledge, and the attitudes of learners. In addition, the instructor is in a unique position to provide interactive practice and feedback, which should be included in the instructional strategy to provide learners with the opportunity to demonstrate specific skills they have acquired. These sessions also serve to identify those skills not yet acquired. This form of in-progress practice and assessment may be administered in one of two formats, either orally to a variety of learners while keeping notes on their performance or by periodically distributing various printed practice and feedback exercises during the lesson. This latter approach provides concrete evidence of learners' progress.

The instructor can also use the field trial as an opportunity to evaluate instructional procedures. Observation of the instructional process should indicate the suitability of grouping patterns, time allocations, and learner interest in various class activities.

Many instructors already use these types of formative evaluation in their instruction. Our point is to stress the thorough and systematic use of these techniques to collect and analyze data in order to revise the lesson plan. To identify weak points in the lesson plan and to provide clues to their correction, in-progress data can be compared to results obtained with the posttest, attitude questionnaire, and students' comments during debriefing sessions.

Very often, the field testing of selected materials and the field testing of instructor-led instruction are interwoven. Frequently the use of selected materials will require an interactive role for the instructor and, likewise, the use of an instructor's guide may well involve the use of some prepared instructional materials. Under either circumstance, approximately the same types of field evaluation procedures should be employed and similar types of revisions carried out.

Data Collection for Selected Materials and Instructor-Led Instruction

Much of the information dealing with the collection of data in a field trial of original instructional materials applies equally well to the data collection procedures used in the evaluation of selected materials and instructional procedures. For example, it is critically important that any equipment to be used during instruction is in good running order and that the environment in which the field trial is conducted be conducive to learning.

When an instructor evaluates self-instructional materials, selected materials, or an instructor's guide, existing rapport with learners can be a great advantage. It is important during the evaluation of materials and guides that students understand the critical nature of their participation in and contributions to the study. The instructor, in working with familiar learners, also has knowledge of the learners' entry skills and, quite possibly, is able to predict accurately the pretest performance of students. The instructor should, however, avoid relying entirely on such predictions. If there is any doubt at all concerning the learners' performances, they should be tested to verify the need for instruction in specified skills.

When the instructor selects materials to implement an instructional strategy, a number of unique concerns arise. Information can be gathered about these concerns by observation and the use of questionnaires. The major question will be "Did the instruction have unity?" To answer this question, the instructor should determine the adequacy of the learner guide in directing students to various resources.

Redundancy and gaps in the instructional materials should be noted. Was sufficient repetition and review built into the strategy? If the instructor is presenting the instruction, then events that reflect the same types of problems should be noted as the presentation progresses. The types of questions raised by learners will provide a key to the strategy's inadequacies.

Concerns Influencing Formative Evaluation

The formative evaluation component distinguishes the instructional design process from a philosophical or theoretical approach. Rather than speculating about the instructional effectiveness of your materials, you will be testing them with learners. You will therefore want to do the best possible job of collecting data that truly reflect the effectiveness of your materials. There are several concerns about the formative evaluation context and the learners who participate in the evaluation that the designer should keep in mind when planning and implementing data-collection procedures.

Context Concerns   For proper evaluation of materials, ensure that any technical equipment is operating effectively. More than one instructor has been discouraged because a new set of instructional materials was tried with a particular piece of equipment and the equipment failed to operate correctly. Data from learners were invalid, and the instructor learned little more than that the equipment must operate effectively to try out materials.

It is also important in the early stages of formative evaluation, especially in the one-to-one trials, that you work with learners in a quiet setting in which you can command their full attention. At this point you are concerned about how the materials will work under the best possible conditions. As you move to the small-group sessions and field trial you are increasingly concerned with how the materials will work in more typical contexts. If the typical setting is an individualized classroom that has a relatively high noise level, then you will want to know whether the materials work in that situation. But you should not begin the formative evaluation under these conditions.

Concerns about Learners   In the selection of learners for participation in any phase of formative evaluation, avoid depending entirely on the instructor to assess entry knowledge of the learners. Whenever possible, administer entry-skills tests to learners to verify that they are actually members of the target population for whom the materials are intended. Experience has shown that instructors, for whatever reason, sometimes make poor estimates of the readiness of learners who are recommended for participation in formative evaluation studies. Do what you can to verify the entry knowledge of the learners.

When you get the information on entry knowledge and skills of learners, you sometimes encounter the problem of what to do with those learners who have already mastered some or all of the skills to be taught or learners who do not have the required entry skills. Do you drop them from the formative evaluation? It is preferable to include some learners who do not exactly match the skill profile of the real target population. Those who already know some of the content can serve as "subject-matter sophisticates" who can be indicators of how other students who do not know the content will respond. You can also determine whether your instruction can bring these learners up to approximately 100 percent performance. If it does not work for these learners, then it is unlikely to be effective with learners who have less entering knowledge.

Learners who do not have the entry skills should also be included in a formative evaluation. The entry skills have been theoretically derived and therefore are in need of validation. If the learners who cannot demonstrate the entry skills do, in fact, struggle through the instruction with little success, whereas those with the entry skills are successful, it suggests that you have identified skills that learners must have to begin the instruction. If, on the other hand, learners without the entry skills are successful with the instruction, then you must seriously reconsider the validity of the entry skills you have identified.

We have suggested that in the one-to-one formative evaluation, the designer should use at least three learners—one high, one average, and one low in ability. This is a vague recommendation that can be made more specific by identifying a high-ability learner as one who already knows some of the content to be taught. The average learner can be identified as one who has the entry skills but no knowledge of the skills to be taught, and the low-ability learner as one who does not have some or all of the entry skills. By using these definitions the designer can be much more sure of getting the desired range of abilities. Research indicates that these three types of learners will provide different but useful information to the designer, and thus all three should be included in the formative evaluation.

Concerns about Formative Evaluation Outcomes

A final word of caution: Be prepared to obtain information that indicates your materials are not as effective as you thought they would be after going through such an extensive instructional design process. It is common to become tremendously involved when putting a great deal of time and effort into any kind of project. It is just as common to be sharply disappointed when you find that your efforts have not been entirely satisfactory.

You should note, however, that in the formative evaluation process, positive feedback from students provides you with little information about how you might proceed to change anything. Positive feedback only indicates that what you have is effective with the students who used the materials. You can then only make the limited inference that the materials would be effective with learners who are of similar ability and motivation.

As you move through the formative evaluation process, it might be helpful to pretend that another instructor has developed the materials and that you are merely carrying out the formative evaluation for that person. We do not suggest that you mislead the learners about it, but rather that you adopt this noninvolved psychological set in order to listen to what learners, instructors, and subject-matter experts might say. These kinds of feedback must be integrated into an objective assessment of the extent to which your materials are meeting the objectives you have set for them and how they can be improved.

Concerns with Implementing Formative Evaluation

Although the ideal instructional design process is to conduct three phases of formative evaluation prior to distributing instruction for general use, it is sometimes simply not possible to follow this procedure. In many cases, there is not enough time to conduct the formative evaluation or no funds have been budgeted to do so. What responsibility does the designer have in this situation?

The first consideration should be to determine whether any kind of formative evaluation can be conducted before the formal usage of the instruction. Are there ways to combine some of the one-to-one techniques with the field trial? Can we get someone to read through the materials and see whether they make sense? Can we walk through a role play to make sure it works? Most designers would acknowledge that using newly designed instruction without some type of tryout is extremely risky, but sometimes it is unavoidable.

If instruction is being used with the target population without the benefit of any formative evaluation, it is still possible to use that opportunity to gather information useful for revising the instruction. In these situations, the procedures typically applied are those of the field trial. Questionnaire data and assessment information can be combined with observations of learners and direct discussions of the instruction to determine what kinds of changes should be made.

The general principle for the designer is that formative evaluations are always conducted; it is just a question of when, where, and how. Sometimes there is enough time and resources to conduct the three phases of formative evaluation that have been described in this chapter. When it is not possible to do so, it is the designer's responsibility to improvise ways to gather as much information as possible about the instruction so that it can be appropriately revised.

Problem Solving during Instructional Design

In the instructional design process the designer is often faced with questions that can best be answered with data from learners. It is interesting to find how often it is possible to settle a design argument by saying, "Let's have the learners tell us the answer to that." The whole formative evaluation process is one of gathering data from learners to answer questions you may (or may not) have had about your instruction.

Assume that following a series of one-to-one evaluations, it becomes clear that there is a question about the use of illustrations in your instruction. Several students liked and used them, whereas several others said they were of no use. Since it may be expensive to use illustrations in instruction, a significant question must be answered: "Should illustrations be used in your instruction?"

In order to answer this question, the designer might develop two versions of the instruction for use in the small-group evaluation. Ten randomly selected learners might receive the instruction with illustrations, whereas ten receive it with no illustrations. Then the performance and attitudes of both groups could be compared. How did they do on the posttest? How did they do on those items directly related to the illustrations? What did they say on the attitude questions about their use of (or the absence of) the illustrations? How did the learning times of the two groups compare?

Is this research? Not really. The purpose is to make a decision about what to do with a particular unit of instruction, not to determine the benefits of using illustrations in instruction. The designer could collect enough data in the formative evaluation about the illustrations to make at least a tentative decision about their continued use in the instruction. This same methodology can be used to answer a wide array of questions that will inevitably arise during the design process.

Examples

The following list includes information that you can use for planning a one-to-one, a small-group, and a field trial evaluation. While looking through these suggested procedures, assume that you know your intended target population but are unsure whether they possess the required entry skills. The examples that follow are not offered as the only activities you should pursue in formative evaluation but as a list of suggestions you can use to begin thinking about your own project. You may be able to identify other activities for your project.

Formative Evaluation Activities

One-to-One Evaluation

I. Participation by subject-matter experts
   A. You should provide the expert with the following:
      1. Instructional analysis
      2. Performance objectives
      3. Instruction
      4. Tests and other assessment instruments

      These materials should be in rough form because major revisions could well be the outcome of this one-to-one testing. You may want to present your materials in the order described above.

   B. You should be looking for verification of the following:
      1. Objective statements
      2. Instructional analysis

   3. Accuracy and currency of the content

   4. Appropriateness of the instructional materials in vocabulary, interest value, sequence, chunk size, and learner participation activities

   5. Clarity and appropriateness of test items and assessment situations

   6. Placement of this piece of instruction relative to prior and subsequent instruction

  C. The number of subject-matter experts you should approach for assistance will vary with the complexity of the information and skills covered in your materials. For some instruction one expert will be sufficient, whereas for others four may still seem inadequate. The nature of the learning task will dictate the number and type of expert consultants you will need.

 II. Participation by learners from the target population

  A. Identify learners who are typical of those you believe will be found in the target population. (Include each major type of learner that can be found in the target population.)

  B. Arrange for the learner(s) to participate.

  C. Discuss the process of a one-to-one evaluation of the materials with each learner separately.

  D. Evaluate the pretest you have constructed to measure entry skills.

   1. Can the learner read the directions?

   2. Does the learner understand the problems?

   3. Does the learner have the required prerequisite skills?

  E. Sit with the learner while he or she studies the materials.

   1. Instruct the learner to write on the materials to indicate where difficulty is encountered or to discuss ideas and problems.

   2. If the learner fails to understand an example, then try another verbal example. Does this clarify the issue? Note in writing the changes and suggestions you make as you go through the materials.

   3. If the learner fails to understand an explanation, then elaborate by adding information or changing the order of presentation. Does this clarify the issue? Note the changes you make in writing.

   4. If the learner appears to be bored or confused while going through the materials, you may want to change the presentation to include larger or smaller bits of information before practice and feedback. Record your ideas concerning the regrouping of materials as you go along.

   5. Keep notes on examples, illustrations, information you add, and changes in sequence during the formative evaluation process. Otherwise, you may forget an important decision or idea. Note taking should be quick and in rough form so the learner is not distracted from the materials.

  F. You may choose to test another learner from the target population before you make any changes or revisions in your materials in order to verify that the changes are necessary. If errors pointed out by your first learner "consultant" are obvious, then you may want to make revisions before testing the next learner. This will save testing time and enable the next learner to concentrate on other problems that may exist in the materials.

 III. Outcomes of one-to-one formative evaluation

  A. Consider again the types of information you are looking for in the one-to-one testing:

   1. Faulty instructional analysis

   2. Errors in judgment about entry skills of learners in the target population

   3. Unclear or inappropriate objectives and expected outcomes

   4. Inadequate information presentation and examples

    a. Examples, graphs, or illustrations that are too abstract

    b. Too much or too little information at one time

    c. Wrong sequence of information presented

    d. Unclear examples

   5. Unclear test questions, test situations, or test directions

   6. Faulty wording or unclear passages

IV. Performance context formative evaluation

  A. Determine whether it is appropriate and feasible to contact learners after they complete the one-to-one evaluation.

  B. By phone, Internet, or in person, determine when and how learners use skills taught in the training.

  C. Determine the organizational level of support from managers for using the skills.

  D. Observe learners as they use skills, interview peers and subordinates, or both.

  E. Determine whether using skills resolved the problems identified through the needs assessment.

  F. Ask for suggestions for revision of the instruction.

Small-Group Evaluation

I. Participation by learners from the target population

  A. Identify a group of learners that typifies your target population.

  B. Arrange for a group to participate.

   1. Adequate time should be arranged for required testing as well as instructional activities.

   2. Learners should be motivated to participate.

   3. Learners should be selected to represent the types of people expected in the target population. You may want to include several learners from each expected major category in your target population.

  C. During the pretest, instruction, and posttest, you may want to make notes about suggestions for instructors who will use the materials. You may also note changes you want to make in the instruction or procedures as a result of your observation of learners interacting with the materials.

  D. Administer the pretest of required entry skills if one is appropriate.

   1. Check the directions, response patterns, and questions to ensure that the wording is clear.

   2. Instruct learners to circle words they do not understand and place a check beside questions or directions that are unclear.

   3. Do not stop to discuss unclear items with learners during the test unless they become bogged down or stop.

   4. Record the time required for learners to complete the entry test.

  E. Administer the pretest of skills to be taught during instruction. This test and the test of required entry skills could be combined into one pretest if desirable.

   1. Have learners circle any vocabulary that is unclear to them.

   2. Have learners place a check beside any directions, questions, or response requirements that are unclear to them.

   3. Have learners write additional comments in the test if they desire.

   4. Do not discuss problems with learners during the test.

  F. Administer the instructional materials. Have the instructional setting close to reality with all required equipment and materials present. Any instructional assistance required should also be available during the trial.

   1. Instruct learners that you will need their help in evaluating the materials.

   2. Have learners sign their work so you can compare their performance on the lesson with their performance based on their entry behaviors.

   3. Instruct learners to circle any unclear words and place a check beside any illustrations, examples, or explanations that are unclear in the instruction. Learners should keep working through the materials to the end without stopping for discussion.

4. Record the time required for learners to complete the instructional materials. Time required may be more than anticipated if learners need instruction on unfamiliar equipment or procedures.

G. Administer the posttest.

1. Have learners sign their posttest to enable comparisons with the pretest and questionnaires.

2. Have learners circle any unclear vocabulary and place a check beside any unclear directions, questions, or response requirements.

3. Have learners respond to as many items as they can, regardless of whether they are sure of the answer or just guessing. Often incorrect guesses can provide clues to inadequate instruction. You may want them to indicate which answers reflect guessing.

4. Record the time required for learners to complete the posttest.

H. Administer an attitude questionnaire to learners.

1. You may want to ask questions such as these:
   - Did the instruction hold your attention?
   - Was the instruction too long or too short?
   - Was the instruction too difficult or too easy?
   - Did you have problems with any parts of the instruction?
   - Were the cartoons or illustrations appropriate or distracting?
   - Was the use of color appealing or distracting?
   - What did you like most?
   - What did you like least?
   - How would you change the instruction if you could?
   - Did the tests measure the material that was presented?
   - Would you prefer another instructional medium?

I. Arrange for learners to discuss the pretest, instruction, and/or posttest with you or their instructor after they have completed all the work.

1. You may want to structure the discussion with planned questions.

2. You may want to ask questions such as "Would you change the exercises in section X?" or "Did you like the example in section X?"

J. See Section IV under one-to-one evaluation for ideas on the performance context formative evaluation. You may want to continue to evaluate only a sample of the learners in the small-group evaluation.

Field Trial

I. Select an appropriate sample from the target population.

A. Arrange for the selected group to try the materials.

1. Ensure that there is an adequate number of learners in the group. Thirty is often suggested as the number of learners to participate in a field trial.

2. Ensure that selected learners reflect the range of abilities and skills of learners in the target population.

3. Ensure that there are adequate personnel, facilities, and equipment available for the trial.

B. Distribute the instructional materials as well as the instructor's guide, if it is available, to the instructor conducting the field test.

C. Discuss any instructions or special considerations that may be needed if the instruction is out of context.

D. Personally play a minimal role in the field trials.

E. Conduct performance context formative evaluation as previously described.

F. Summarize the data you have collected. Summarized data may include a report of the following:

1. Scores on the entry skill part of the pretest

2. Pretest and posttest scores on skills taught

3. The time required for students to complete each test used

4. The time required for students to complete the instruction
5. The attitudes of learners as well as participating instructors

Formative Evaluation of Selected Materials and Instructor-Led Instruction

I. Selected materials

In addition to the formative suggestions for self-instructional materials, you should determine whether the following are true:

A. All parts of the instructional strategy are accounted for in the selected materials or provided by the instructor.
B. The transitions between sources are smooth.
C. The flow of content in the various instructional resources is consistent and logical.
D. The learners' manual or instructor adequately presents objectives.
E. Directions for locating instruction within each source are adequate.
F. Sections of the instructional strategy that must be supplied by the instructor are adequate.
G. The vocabulary used in all the sources is appropriate.
H. The illustrations and examples used are appropriate for the target group.

II. Instructor-Led Instruction

A major factor in evaluating instruction that is delivered by instructors is that they are an interactive part of the instruction. In addition to all the considerations we have mentioned previously, several important evaluation considerations are unique to this type of instruction.

A. Is the instructor convincing, enthusiastic, helpful, and knowledgeable?
B. Is the instructor able to avoid digressions to keep instruction and discussions on relevant topics and on schedule?
C. Does the instructor make presentations in an interesting, clear manner?
D. Does the instructor use the chalkboard and other visual aids to help with examples and illustrations?
E. Does the instructor provide good feedback to learners' questions?
F. Does the instructor provide adequate practice exercises with appropriate feedback?

You should record events that occur during instruction so that you can study them for what they imply about the effectiveness of the instruction.

Case Study: Group Leadership Training

The following illustrations are based on the instructional analysis and strategy of main step 6, "Manage cooperative group interaction" presented in Chapter 8. Again, the target population is Neighborhood Crime Watch leaders of varying levels of knowledge and skills. Conduct of the one-to-one and small-group formative evaluations is described in this section. Examples of the field trial and performance context evaluation are included in the Practice and Feedback sections of this chapter. In reading each of these types of evaluations, you should remember the purposes for the evaluations, the nature of the leadership instruction, and the characteristics of the NCW leaders.

One-to-One Formative Evaluation Procedures

Materials for the One-to-One Trials   The materials consisted of loose typed pages containing directions, instruction, and assessments. The videos were presented as paper storyboards at this point. Illustrations consisted of rough hand drawings and clip art. Materials for each objective and any required leader responses were placed on one page, with feedback on the following page. This facilitated evaluating the sequence and clustering of the objectives and ensured that both could be readily changed if needed. The pages were divided into two columns leaving ample room for tryout students as well as the designer to comment and write suggestions directly in the materials. Six copies of the rough materials were produced: one for each learner, one for the designer, and one for tallying results and making revisions.

Participants and Instructions   Four NCW leaders were selected for the one-to-one evaluation. The sample consisted of new NCW leaders with differing educational levels: one owned his own company but had not completed high school, one was a high school graduate and postal worker, one was a graduate student at a local university, and another had a graduate degree and several years of experience leading group meetings at work. All participants were from the same town.

Participants were thanked for attending, and coffee, soft drinks, and bagels were offered to help ensure a social rather than judgmental environment. The purpose for the session was explained and participants were told there were no incorrect answers, only areas in which the developers may not have been as clear or complete as needed. Before beginning, they were told that the developers wished them to check vocabulary, reading level, and pacing, as well as the clarity of examples, exercises, and feedback. They were also asked to comment on their experiences in leading group discussions, whether they believe some of the sections could have been skipped, and whether they believe more information and examples should be added.

Preinstructional Materials   As participants worked through each section of the materials, in order to help them begin critiquing, the designers asked them to comment on whether: (1) the initial motivation material was clear and interesting, (2) the objectives were clear and relevant to them, and (3) they already possessed any of the skills in the objectives. They were asked to write their comments directly on the pages in the large margin provided. The designer paraphrased their verbal comments in the margin as well.

Content Presentation   Leaders identified and marked unclear or confusing directions or management information, and they circled unfamiliar vocabulary in the written materials, including the video scripts. The designer asked them to orally comment on the clarity of descriptions and examples used and to orally suggest other examples from their experiences. These experiences were paraphrased in the margin by the designer. They were also prompted to comment on the adequacy of sequence of content and chunk size. It was not possible to judge pace due to the interactive nature of the evaluation.

Learner Participation   Leaders were asked to complete all practice items and activities and to comment on whether they were interesting and assisted them in learning and remembering the skills. The designer asked the participants to comment on items they missed (without telling the learner that the items were missed) in order to gather more information on their misconceptions and incomplete learning. Through these conversations, the designer identified areas for which more information and examples were needed. Learners were also asked to evaluate the clarity and helpfulness of the feedback provided and to write in the margin questions that remained after studying the feedback.

Assessments   For both the pretest and the posttest, learners were asked to provide information about the clarity of the test instructions, vocabulary used, and questions or tasks required. They marked unclear or confusing words, questions, or directions.

As participants responded, the designer asked probing questions when an item was missed on the posttest to identify the source of errors or misconceptions. Learners' comments were paraphrased by the designer in the margins beside the missed questions.

Following the one-to-one evaluation, learners were asked to reflect back over the instruction and comment on its clarity and utility overall. This interview provided insights into the relevance of the instruction for their tasks as leaders and for its utility in helping them better perform their jobs. They were also asked to comment on any materials they believe should be improved or eliminated.

Following each one-to-one evaluation, the comments of the learner were reviewed and synthesized, and the materials were revised to eliminate obvious mistakes. The revised set of materials was then produced for the next evaluation session. With the one-to-one evaluations completed and the materials revised as needed, the instruction should undergo a small-group evaluation to identify any problems with the materials or their administration in the intended format.

Small-Group Formative Evaluation Procedures

Materials for the Small-Group Trial   The instructional materials were completely developed to the intended level of sophistication, including the web-based instruction, simulations, instructor-led sessions, videos, and assessments, so that either management or learning problems could be identified during the evaluation. The instructor's guide was also complete and tested to help ensure that various instructors in learning centers throughout the state could use the materials effectively. To facilitate learners' evaluation of the instructor-led, web-based, and video instruction, an evaluation form naming each objective and its related activities was given to learners to complete immediately after they completed each part of the instruction. The form also included a rating scale for judging the interest, clarity, and utility of each activity as well as a column for their suggested improvements. It used the general format shown in Figure 10.2.

Participants and Instructions   Twenty new NCW leaders were selected for the small-group formative evaluation. There were six learners with high school educations, six with bachelor's degrees, and eight with at least some graduate school course

figure 10.2   Form Learners Can Use during the Formative Evaluation of Nonprint Materials

Group Leadership Training Materials Evaluation Form for Nonprint Media

Rating responses
1 = Not at all
2 = Somewhat
3 = Mostly
4 = Very

Use this column to write your ideas and suggestions for how to improve this piece of the instruction.

INSTRUCTIONAL PIECE	PLEASE CIRCLE THE QUALITY LEVEL:	WHAT WOULD MAKE IT BETTER?
6.1.1 Pretest	Interesting: 1 2 3 4	
Video on Web Site	Clear: 1 2 3 4	
Video # 6	Useful: 1 2 3 4	
6.2.2 Web Site	Interesting: 1 2 3 4	
Video of NCW	Clear: 1 2 3 4	
Discussion Group	Useful: 1 2 3 4	

(And so forth for the remaining nonprint objectives and activities.)

work completed. Some of the participants at each education level had prior experience with group leadership either at work, in their places of worship, or in the community. Two of the participants with bachelor's degrees had formal course work in communication and group discussion management.

One small-group evaluation was conducted at this point, although another may need to be scheduled after the results are evaluated and the materials and instructor's guide revised. Some of the revisions may result in learning or management improvements; others may not.

Preinstructional Materials Learners followed directions and participated as instructed. For the web-based pretest, a free response form was inserted following the pretest and learners were invited to enter comments on any unclear information in the directions. Learners were directed to answer all the questions to the best of their ability. Following the questions, learners received another essay-style response form, and they were invited to identify and comment on any questions that were unclear or confusing. Questions were organized within objectives and objectives were organized within instructional goals. Data were summarized by identifying the percentage of students in the group answering each question correctly and the percentage of items answered correctly by each learner. In addition, the designer tallied items and directions marked as unclear and vocabulary words marked as unfamiliar. Learners were not stopped to ask questions about the interest value or clarity of the motivational materials or objectives.

Content Presentation and Practice Learners were not stopped or interviewed during instruction. Prior to beginning, however, they were invited to mark directly on print materials any explanations, examples, illustrations, vocabulary, practices, and feedback that they considered unclear. For video and web-based materials, the evaluation form was again provided for learners to mark as they worked through the instruction. Learners were instructed to complete all participation items and activities within the materials.

Assessments The posttests were marked in the same manner as the pretests. Similarly, questions were organized within objectives and objectives were organized within instructional goals. Data were summarized by identifying the percentage of learners in the group answering each question correctly as well as the percentage of items and objectives answered correctly by each participant. Again, a tally of questions marked as unclear and vocabulary words marked as unfamiliar was made. Finally, the time required for learners to complete the pretest, instruction, and posttest was recorded including the shortest time, longest time, and average time taken by the group. With these data gathered and organized by objective and goal, the process of identifying problems and solutions began.

Instruments for Assessing Learners' Attitudes about Instruction

Instruments for assessing learners' achievement of group leadership skills were illustrated and discussed in the preceding chapter. No attitude questionnaires, however, were presented, and good formative evaluation includes assessing both achievement and attitudes.

Figure 10.3 contains an attitude questionnaire for the instructional goal, "Lead group discussions aimed at solving problems." The questionnaire is designed to be administered following session 10: "Engender cooperative member behaviors" (objectives 6.1.1 through 6.5.1 in Table 6.7, p. 125). It contains six sections. Four of the sections relate to facets of Keller's ARCS model including attention, relevance, confidence, and satisfaction. Another section enables learners to rate the clarity of in-

figure

10.3

Attitude Questionnaire for Main Step 6: Manage Cooperative Group Interaction, Session 10, Objectives 6.1.1 through 6.5.1

Session 10: Engendering Cooperative Member Behaviors   **Date** _____

Instructions: Use the following questionnaire to judge the effectiveness of today's session on engendering cooperative member behaviors. Please rate the quality of the instruction in each of the five main categories included on the form. For each of the instructional areas listed on the left, circle the response on the right that best reflects your perception of the quality level. At the bottom of the form, please comment on aspects of tonight's session that you consider to be particular strengths or problems. Thank you.

I. Attention: To what degree did the following instructional activities hold your interest or attention?

INSTRUCTIONAL AREAS   ATTENTION LEVEL (CIRCLE ONE LEVEL FOR EACH AREA)

A. Reading, analyzing annotated dialogues
    of NCW meetings illustrating:
    1. Member actions that aid cooperative   Little   1   2   3   4   5   Very attentive
        interaction
    2. Strategies leaders use to encourage   Little   1   2   3   4   5   Very attentive
        group cooperation
B. Watching, analyzing videotapes of NCW
    meetings depicting:
    3. Positive member actions that aid   Little   1   2   3   4   5   Very attentive
        cooperative interaction
    4. NCW leaders engendering cooperative   Little   1   2   3   4   5   Very attentive
        member behaviors
C. Performing myself as group leader to:
    5. Engender cooperative member   Little   1   2   3   4   5   Very attentive
        behaviors in my group

II. Relevance: To what degree do you believe the following skills are *relevant* for helping you provide effective leadership in NCW problem-solving meetings?

                                                             RELEVANCE LEVEL

    6. Recognizing cooperative member   Little   1   2   3   4   5   Very relevant
        behaviors during meetings
    7. Engendering cooperative member   Little   1   2   3   4   5   Very relevant
        behaviors during meetings

III. Confidence: What level of *confidence* do you have that you can effectively use these group interaction management skills in NCW problem-solving discussions?

                                                             CONFIDENCE LEVEL

    8. Recognizing cooperative member   Little   1   2   3   4   5   Very confident
        behaviors during meetings
    9. Engendering cooperative member   Little   1   2   3   4   5   Very confident
        behaviors during meetings

IV. Clarity: What level of *clarity* do you believe the following instructional materials and activities have?

                                                             CLARITY LEVEL

    10. Session introduction   Little   1   2   3   4   5   Very clear
    11. Objectives for session   Little   1   2   3   4   5   Very clear
    12. Annotated written dialogues of NCW   Little   1   2   3   4   5   Very clear
         meetings
    13. Videos of NCW meetings   Little   1   2   3   4   5   Very clear
    14. Performing ourselves as group leaders   Little   1   2   3   4   5   Very clear
    15. Instructions for our group leadership   Little   1   2   3   4   5   Very clear
         activity

(*continued*)

figure	Continued	
10.3		

16. Checklists we used to find positive
    leader actions — Little 1 2 3 4 5 Very clear
17. Feedback on exercises for positive
    member and leader actions — Little 1 2 3 4 5 Very clear

V. Satisfaction: Overall, how satisfied were you with:

SATISFACTION LEVEL

18. The facilities — Little 1 2 3 4 5 Very satisfied
19. The instructor(s) — Little 1 2 3 4 5 Very satisfied
20. The pace — Little 1 2 3 4 5 Very satisfied
21. The instruction — Little 1 2 3 4 5 Very satisfied
22. Yourself, relative to the new skills you
    have developed/refined — Little 1 2 3 4 5 Very satisfied

VI. Comments: Please comment on aspects of this session that were strengths or problems for you personally.

	Strengths	**Problems**
Introduction:		
Objectives:		
Annotated dialogues:		
Videos:		
Interactive leadership session:		
Assessments:		
Other:		
Other:		

struction. The last section asks learners to provide their comments on the strengths and weaknesses of instruction from their perspective. To aid their work, different aspects of instruction are named in the far-left column. The last two rows, marked "Other," are included to invite learners to comment on aspects of the instruction that were not specifically named on the form.

It may also be important to assess learners' attitudes after they return to the performance context. One year following the instruction for Neighborhood Crime Watch leaders, a survey will be sent to them requesting information about how well they were able to transfer the information and skills they learned during instruction to their work within the community. Figure 10.4 contains the survey that participants will receive through an e-mail invitation to participate and a link to an online survey program such as Survey Monkey (www.surveymonkey.com). Only the first two of the seven skills included in the training are included in the sample survey to illustrate the procedure.

figure
10.4

Survey for Assessing Learners' Perceptions of the Impact of Instruction in the Performance Context

Reflections on Residuals from the
Neighborhood Crime Watch Group Leadership Training

Last April you participated in the county's group leadership training for community leaders. The training program had the defined expected outcomes that you would use effective group leadership skills in conducting meetings for solving community problems including

1. Preparing for meetings and discussions
2. Setting meeting agendas
3. Convening the group
4. Introducing the task
5. Managing the thought line
6. Managing cooperative group interaction
7. Summarizing and concluding the discussion

One year has passed since you successfully completed the workshop at the county learning center. Hopefully, this has provided the time necessary for you to transfer your leadership skills to your work with groups in the community. We would like for you to share your reflections on how you and your work have been influenced by the leadership workshops. The survey will take only a few minutes, and your comments are anonymous. All information gathered will be used to assess the effectiveness of the workshops for our community leaders. Thank you in advance for your time.

A. To what degree are you using these skills in your work as an NCW leader?

Outcomes	Not using	Planning to use	Starting to use	Using routinely	Was using before
1. Preparing for meetings and discussions	○	○	○	○	○
2. Setting meeting agendas	○	○	○	○	○
7. *Etc.*	○	○	○	○	○

B. If you responded "not using" to any of the skills, please indicate your reason. For any outcome, choose as many reasons as apply

Designer note: Add your own reasons below that are relevant to the organization & skill.

Outcomes	Not relevant for my work	Need more training	Need more supervisor support	Need more resources	Need more assistance
1. Preparing for meetings and discussions	○	○	○	○	○
2. Setting meeting agendas	○	○	○	○	○
7. *Etc.*	○	○	○	○	○

Please comment here on other reasons you are currently using the skills learned in the instruction.

C. As a direct result of the workshop, have you noticed *positive* changes related to these outcomes in your knowledge, skills, and attitudes/perspectives?

1 = No, 2 = Some, 3 = A lot

Outcomes	Knowledge			Skills			Attitudes/ perspectives		
1. Preparing for meetings and discussions	①	②	③	①	②	③	①	②	③
2. Setting meeting agendas	①	②	③	①	②	③	①	②	③
7. *Etc.*	①	②	③	①	②	③	①	②	③

Please comment on how your work in the community has been influenced.

(continued)

figure	Continued
10.4	**D. For each outcome, please comment on the workshop's strengths and your suggestions for improvements.**

Outcomes	Strengths	Suggestions for Improvement
1. Preparing for meetings and discussions		
2. Setting meeting agendas		
7. *Etc.*		

In addition to evaluating the instruction, instruments used to gather information are also assessed for their clarity and utility during the formative evaluation. For example, if several learners ask questions about instructions or particular items on the attitude questionnaire or tend to leave items or sections blank, then the related areas should be examined for clarity and modified. In addition, if any section of the instrument does not yield data useful for pinpointing strengths and weaknesses and for revising instruction, then it should also be revised or eliminated.

For additional learning support and the school curriculum examples of formative evaluation, be sure to go to Appendix L, sections 1 through 7.

SUMMARY

Formative evaluation of instructional materials is conducted to determine the effectiveness of the materials and to revise them in areas where they are ineffective. Formative evaluations should be conducted on newly developed materials as well as existing materials that are selected based on the instructional strategy. Evaluations are necessary for both mediated and instructor presented materials. The evaluations should be designed to produce data to pinpoint specific areas where the instruction is faulty and to suggest how it should be revised.

An iterative process of formative evaluation containing at least three cycles of data collection, analysis, and revision is recommended. Each cycle focuses on different aspects of quality. The first cycle, one-to-one evaluation, is conducted to pinpoint gross errors in the materials. These errors typically relate to both the clarity of vocabulary, concepts, and examples used, and the motivational value of all five components of the instructional materials. Evaluations can also be conducted with content experts and individuals familiar with the characteristics of target learners. One-to-one evaluations must be conducted with representatives of the target population. An interactive interview process is used so the evaluator can learn what was wrong with the materials and why it was wrong.

The second cycle, the small-group evaluation, follows the correction of major errors identified in the instruction. The group typically consists of from eight to twenty representative members of the target population. The purpose of the small-group evaluation is to locate additional errors in the instructional materials and management procedures. The elements of the instructional strategy are again the anchor for the evaluation instruments and procedures. During this cycle the evaluator plays a less interactive role, performance and attitude data are collected, and in-depth debriefings are conducted to obtain both quantitative and qualitative data.

The final cycle, a field trial, is conducted following refinement of the materials based on the small-group evaluation. The purpose of this evaluation is to pinpoint errors in the materials when they are used as prescribed in the intended setting. Similar to the first two cycles, evaluation instrumentation and procedures should be anchored in the five components of the instructional strategy. Instruments to gather data on learner performance and attitudes are important. The gathering of management data such as the time required to use the materials and the feasibility of the management plan is also important. During the trial, the evaluator does not interfere as data are gathered from the learners or instructor, although observation while materials are used can provide insights for interpreting data.

Following any phase of formative evaluation, the designer should determine the feasibility of collecting additional data from the learners as they return to the context in which they will use the skills learned in the instruction. The intent is to find out whether the skills are being used and with what effect. The resulting information is used in the revision of the instruction.

RUBRIC FOR EVALUATING FORMATIVE EVALUATION PROCEDURES

The summary rubric located below is appropriate for evaluating the processes used during formative evaluation. The rubrics for evaluating the actual *materials* during a formative evaluation are included in Chapters 8 and 9.

Designer note: If an element is not relevant for your project, mark NA in the No column.

No	Some	Yes	
			A. Overall Formative Evaluation Design Is/does the design:
—	—	—	1. Based on an instructional strategy (e.g., preinstruction, presentation, participation, assessment, and transfer)?
—	—	—	2. Use multiple data-gathering strategies?
—	—	—	3. Include summaries of reviewers' comments to locate strengths and problems?
—	—	—	4. Provide for adjusting/refining materials and procedures prior to subsequent evaluation phases?
			B. Experts Did the evaluation include expert review for:
—	—	—	1. Type of learning by learning specialists?
—	—	—	2. Content accuracy and currency by content specialists?
—	—	—	3. Appropriate complexity by learner specialists?
—	—	—	4. Feasibility and transfer by content specialists?
—	—	—	5. Clarity and effectiveness by target learners?
			C. Target Learners Did learners:
—	—	—	1. Represent target group?
—	—	—	2. Receive an orientation to provide instruction and put them at ease?
—	—	—	3. Receive all necessary materials (preinstruction through transfer)?
—	—	—	4. Complete and comment on pretest (including entry skills)?
—	—	—	5. Mark unclear passages and underline unfamiliar vocabulary?
—	—	—	6. Question unfamiliar examples and suggest alternatives?
—	—	—	7. Question perspectives and focus?
—	—	—	8. Participate in practice and rehearsal activities and comment on the helpfulness of feedback?
—	—	—	9. Complete the posttest and comment on unclear items?
—	—	—	10. Complete the attitude questionnaire and comment on the clarity of questions as well as their opinions?
—	—	—	11. Appear comfortable with media and delivery system?
			D. Evaluators Did evaluators:
—	—	—	1. Interact with learners during evaluation to question, clarify, elaborate, etc.?
—	—	—	2. Summarize learners' comments and responses?
—	—	—	3. Identify strengths and pinpoint problems?
—	—	—	4. Revise materials for obvious errors between one-to-one trials?
			E. Performance Context Were the following types of information collected and summarized:
—	—	—	1. Learners' ability to transfer the new knowledge and skills?
—	—	—	2. Frequency of skill application (actual/ideal)?
—	—	—	3. Context for skill application?
—	—	—	4. Factors inhibiting use of the skills on the job?
—	—	—	5. Evidence that original problems within organization were resolved?
—	—	—	6. Positive changes in learners' skills, work, or attitudes related to instruction?

   This chapter has focused on the design of the formative evaluation and the data-gathering procedures. Chapter 11 describes data analysis and materials revision based on the data.

PRACTICE

The following exercises are based on the instructional analysis and strategy of main step 5, "Prescribe best sentence type(s) to introduce and develop each main point" presented in Appendices C, F, and G. The target population is sixth-grade students who are average and above average in writing skills. For a field trial formative evaluation, consider the questions and identify decisions you would make based on the purposes of the evaluation, the nature of the instruction, and the target population.

1. Why would the designer be interested in a field trial of the materials on writing composition?

2. What information would the designer collect during the field trial for this instruction that would not have been collected during the small-group evaluation session?

3. Describe an appropriate sample group and instructional setting that could be used to evaluate the instructional materials.

4. What materials would the designer include in the field trial?

5. Would the designer do a performance context formative evaluation for any of the phases?

6. If so, which one(s), and why?

7. How would the designer's procedures differ if he or she were conducting a field trial of adapted or adopted materials rather than a set of original materials?

8. Describe the major procedural differences between the field trial of selected materials and the field trial of instructor-led instruction.

9. Develop an attitude questionnaire to use with learners when conducting the small-group evaluations and field trials. Make your questionnaire appropriate for sixth-grade students who are participating in the formative evaluation of the writing composition materials.

FEEDBACK

1. Materials are field-tested to determine their effectiveness with the target population when used under specified conditions. Field trials answer the question "Do these materials work for given learners when used in the planned learning context, and are there any improvements that can be made?" It helps to determine the instructional effectiveness of the materials in the absence of coaching by an instructor. It also aids in determining whether the materials are actually ready for use. The materials, tests, and instructions for both learners and instructors should be examined during the field trial. Have the materials had enough revision, or is more revision required? Revision at this point can be either in the materials themselves or in suggestions for using the materials.

2. The designer would probably want to collect the same types of information that were obtained during the small-group evaluation. Other information might include learners' attitudes about the following:

- Was instruction interesting?
- Was instruction too easy, too difficult, or just right?
- Was instruction too fast, too slow, or just right?
- Were the materials easy to use or were they complicated?

The designer might also want to include instructors' attitudinal information: whether the materials are easy to use, complicated, or just right, and why the instructors hold these opinions.

3. An appropriate population for a field trial for the writing composition instruction would be one or more sixth-grade classes in the district that are heterogeneous in writing achievement (e.g., contains both average and above-average students). The class or classes should have teachers who are interested in the project and who are experienced in using Internet-based instruction with the class. They should also be experienced in working with students who are receiving their instruction using personal computers, because this introduces

new challenges for group management (e.g., students working on lessons rather than communicating with friends or surfing the Internet).

4. All materials developed should be included and evaluated in the field trial. This should include all print materials, web-based materials, equipment, assessments, and the instructor's guide.

5. No.

6. The learning context and the performance context are the same in this case study. The designer might, however, wish to see how well learners are participating in the students' newsletter (follow-through activity for motivation and transfer) and how well the newsletter is received by other students, teachers, and perhaps parents.

7. The major difference between field evaluation of selected materials and original materials is that the instructor is present during the evaluation of selected existing materials. This provides the instructor with the opportunity to observe the use of the materials and to determine the adequacy of the various components of the instructional strategy.

8. With instructor-led instruction, the instructor interacts with the learners while delivering the instruction. The instructor controls the practice and feedback components of the instruction. The instructor is more passive when evaluating selected materials.

9. The attitude questionnaire (see Appendix L, section 7) can be given to learners to complete during the small-group and field trials. During the one-to-one trials, however, you should use the questionnaire as an interview form. You can write responses learners make on the form. The one-to-one trials will help you formatively evaluate the attitudinal questionnaire to determine whether the questions you have asked are clear. If you get several "I don't know" responses, then rephrase the questions until the learner understands the question and expresses an opinion. Note on the questionnaire changes you need to make to clarify what you are asking. The attitudinal questionnaire can be used as an interview guide during the debriefing session as well. It will help you focus the evaluation on important components in the materials.

REFERENCES AND RECOMMENDED READINGS

Bernhardt, V. (2007). *Translating data into information to improve teaching and learning.* Larchmont, NY: Eye on Education Press. This book does not focus on lesson-level evaluation, but does have good procedures for summarizing data for decision making at the school level.

Bodzin, A. M., Price, B., & Heyden, R. (2004). A formative evaluation approach to guide the development of a webtext biology curriculum. Paper presented at the National Association of Biology Teachers Annual meeting, November 7–12, 2004, Montreal, Quebec, Canada. Retrieved December 12, 2007, from www.usingexploringlife.com/downloads/nabt2001.pdf. This presentation reports methods for a formative evaluation of a large-scale field trial of online biology curriculum.

Broad, M. L. (2005). *Beyond transfer of training: Engaging systems to improve performance.* San Francisco: Pfeiffer. Links results of training to original performance improvement needs.

Brown, S. M., & Seidner, C. J. (Eds.). (1998). *Evaluating corporate training: Models and issues.* Boston: Kluwer Academic Publishers. With contributions from authors, this text describes evaluation models and standards from business and education.

Cambre, M. (1981). Historical overview of formative evaluation of instructional media products. *Educational Communications and Technology Journal 29*(1), 1–25. Good historical perspective on formative evaluation in ID.

Carey, L. M. (2001). *Measuring and evaluating school learning.* Boston: Allyn & Bacon. Chapter 10, Evaluating group performance; Chapter 11, Analyzing items, tasks, and tests; and Chapter 12, Evaluating individual performance and instruction will all be very helpful for the designer interested in more detail in synthesizing and interpreting data to evaluate learning and instruction.

Cronbach, L. J. (1975). Course improvement through evaluation. Reprinted in D. A. Payne & R. F. McMorris (Eds.), *Education and psychological measurement.* Morristown, NJ: General Learning Press, 243–256. This is one of the original articles on the need for formative evaluation of instructional materials.

Dessinger, J. C., & Moseley, J. L. (2003). *Confirmative evaluation: Practical strategies for valuing continuous improvement*. San Francisco: Pfeiffer. Describes techniques for evaluation of the impact of training several months after the implementation of instruction.

Dick, W. (2002). Evaluation in instructional design: The impact of Kirkpatrick's four-level model. In R. A. Reiser & J. V. Dempsey (Eds.), *Trends and issues in instructional design and technology*. Upper Saddle River: Merrill/Prentice Hall.

Dick, W., & Carey, L. M. (1991). Formative evaluation. In L. J. Briggs, K. L. Gustafson, & M. H. Tillman (Eds.), *Instructional design: Principles and applications*. Englewood Cliffs, NJ: Educational Technology Publications.

Dick, W., & King, D. (1994). Formative evaluation in the performance context. *Performance and Instruction, 33*(9), 3–10. Discussion of follow-up evaluation in the workplace.

Druin, A. (1999). *The design of children's technology*. San Francisco: Morgan Kaufmann Publishers. This book includes methodology for formative evaluation and revision of computer-based instruction and support.

Hale, J. (2002). *Performance-based evaluation: Tools and techniques to measure the impact of training*. San Francisco: Pfeiffer. Contains good descriptions of collecting and using data for judging effectiveness in training and development.

Hall, G. E., & Hord, S. M. (1987). *Change in schools*. Albany, NY: SUNY Press. Describes stages of change that are useful for evaluating the impact of training in a performance context.

Kirkpatrick, D. L., & Kirkpatrick, J. D. (2005). *Transferring learning to behavior: Using the four levels to improve performance*. San Francisco: Berrett-Koehler Publishers. The authors focus on learning transfer for results, the fourth level of evaluation in Kirkpatrick's training evaluation model.

Martin, F., & Dunsworth, Q. (2008). A methodical formative evaluation of computer literacy course: What and how to teach. *Journal of Information Technology Education, 6*, 123–134. Retrieved January 21, 2008, from http://jite.org/documents/Vol6/JITEv6p123–134 Martin217 .pdf. A case study of formative evaluation in a university setting.

Morrison, G. R., Ross, S. M., & Kemp, J. E. (2007). *Designing effective instruction* (5th ed.). Hoboken, NJ: Wiley. This text includes designs for formative evaluation, data displays, and interpretations.

Nathenson, M. B., & Henderson, E. S. (1980). *Using student feedback to improve learning materials*. London: Croom Helm. A detailed description of the use of the formative evaluation process with Open University courses in England.

Performance and Instruction Journal, 22(5). 1983. Special issue on formative evaluation. This issue carries a number of articles of interest to the designer. See especially: Wager, One-to-One and Small Group Formative Evaluation; Komoski, Formative Evaluation;

Lowe, Clinical Approach to Formative Evaluation; and Golas, Formative Evaluation Effectiveness and Cost.

Prochaska, J. O., & DiClemente, C. C. (1986). Towards a comprehensive model of change. In W. R. Miller & N. Heather (Eds.), *Treating addictive behaviors: Processes of change*. New York: Plenum Press.

Reeves, T. C., & Hedberg, J. G. (2003). *Interactive learning systems evaluation*. Englewood Cliffs, NJ: Educational Technology Publications. The book presents six levels of evaluation and includes formative techniques for e-learning processes and materials.

Rogers, E. M. (1995). *Diffusion of innovations* (4th ed.). New York: The Free Press.

Royse, D. D. (2001). *Program evaluation: An introduction*. Belmont, CA: Brooks/Cole-Wadsworth Thompson Learning. This text contains a chapter on formative and process evaluation readers will find informative.

Russell, J. D., & Blake, B. L. (1988). Formative and summative evaluation of instructional products and learners. *Educational Technology, 28*(9), 22–28. This article distinguishes between the formative evaluation of instruction and the formative evaluation of learners.

Scott, R. O., & Yelon, S. R. (1969). The student as a co-author—The first step in formative evaluation. *Educational Technology,* October, 76–78. This is one of the few articles that describes procedures to be used in one-to-one formative evaluation with students.

Scriven, M., Tyler, R., & Gagné, R. (1967). *Perspectives of curriculum evaluation*. AERA Monograph Series on Curriculum Evaluation. Chicago: Rand McNally. In this monograph, the authors made the first functional distinction between formative and summative evaluation.

Shambaugh, R. N., & Magliaro, S. G. (1997). *Mastering the possibilities*. Boston: Allyn & Bacon.

Smith, P. L., & Ragan, T. J. (2005). *Instructional design* (3rd ed.). New York: Wiley. Contains chapters on formative and summative evaluation with data displays and interpretations for revision.

Tessmer, M. (1993). *Planning and conducting formative evaluations*. London: Kogan Page. A complete description of the major phases of formative evaluation.

Tessmer, M. (1994). Formative evaluation alternatives. *Performance Improvement Quarterly, 7*(1), 3–18.

Tessmer, M. (1996). Formative evaluation. In P. Kommers, S. Grabinger, & J. C. Dunlap (Eds.), *Hypermedia learning environments: Instructional design and integration*. Mahwah, NJ: Lawrence Erlbaum Associates. This chapter addresses formative evaluation procedures for electronic teaching/learning context.

Thiagarajan, S. (1991). Formative evaluation in Performance Technology. *Performance Improvement Quarterly, 4*(2), 22–34. Discusses follow-up evaluation six months after implementation. Excellent references.

Weston, C. B., LeMaistre, C., McAlpine, L., & Bordonaro, T. (1997). The influence of participants in formative evaluation on the improvement of learning from written instructional materials. *Instructional Science, 25*(5), 369–386. This empirical study using print materials concluded that formative revisions that incorporate learner feedback have the most impact on improving student learning.

Weston, C. B., McAlpine, L., & Bordonaro, T. (1995). A model for understanding formative evaluation in instructional design. *Educational Technology Research and Development 43*(3), 29–49. The article presents a model that depicts the feedback relationships among various ID processes.

Many of the references at the end of Chapter 7 are useful sources for data synthesis, analysis, and interpretation.

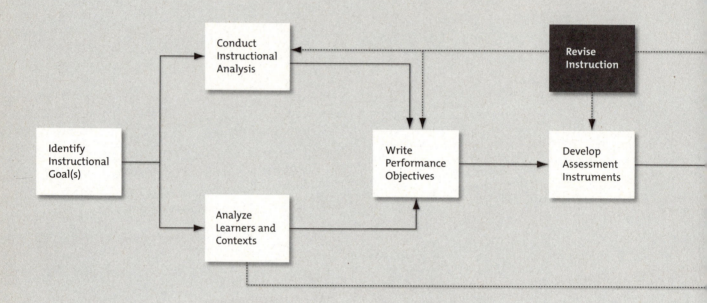

objectives

➤ Describe various methods for summarizing data obtained from formative evaluation studies.

➤ Summarize data obtained from formative evaluation studies.

➤ Given summarized formative evaluation data, identify weaknesses in instructional materials and instructor-led instruction.

➤ Given formative evaluation data for a set of instructional materials, identify problems in the materials, and suggest revisions for the materials.

Revising Instructional Materials

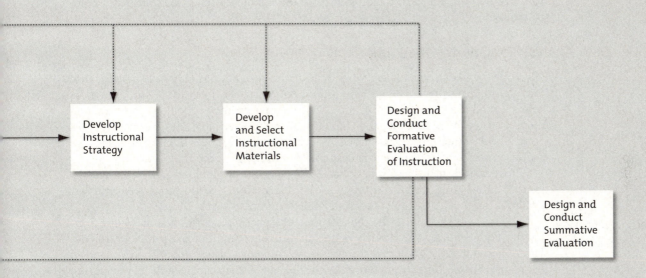

Develop Instructional Strategy → Develop and Select Instructional Materials → Design and Conduct Formative Evaluation of Instruction → Design and Conduct Summative Evaluation

Background

If you examine almost any instructional design model, you will find major emphasis on the concept of formative evaluation, that is, on collecting data to identify problems and to revise instructional materials. During the revision process, designers must keep a systems perspective on their work and remain open to possibilities that revisions may be warranted in any stage of the design process. Notice the broken feedback line in the model shown. From formative evaluation, the feedback line traces back through all stages of the design. Models often indicate that after data have been collected and summarized, you should revise the materials "appropriately." Although a number of studies have indicated the benefit of revising instructional materials, few have proposed any theories around which to gather the data. In our approach to formative evaluation, we interpret the data in light of our instructional strategy and then make changes that seem to be indicated by the data and our understanding of the learning process.

Two basic types of revisions you should consider with your materials are changes made to the content or substance of the materials to make them more accurate or more effective as a learning tool and changes related to the procedures employed in using your materials. In this chapter, we will point out how data from various formative evaluation sources can be summarized and used to identify portions of your materials that should be revised. Note that you need not be concerned about the use of complex statistics in this step of the instructional design process because simple descriptive summaries of the data are sufficient. Elaborate statistical tests are almost never employed in the formative evaluation and revision process.

Concepts

There are many different ways in which the data collected in a formative evaluation may be summarized to point to areas of learner difficulties and possible revisions. The methods we describe here are merely suggestions. As you begin to work with your own data, you may find other techniques that will help you derive more insight from them. We first look at what you can do with the data and information from a one-to-one formative evaluation and then consider the small-group and field-trial phases.

Data Analysis for One-to-One Trials

Following the one-to-one formative evaluation the designer has very little data because information typically is available for only three to five learners. Since these learners were selected based on their diversity, the information they provide will, in all likelihood, be very distinct, rather than blending into some type of group average. In other words, the designer must look at the similarities and differences among the responses of the learners and determine the best changes to make in the instruction.

The designer has five kinds of basic information available: learner characteristics and entry skills, direct responses to the instruction, learning time, posttest performance, and responses to an attitude questionnaire, if used.

The first step is to describe the learners who participated in the one-to-one evaluation and to indicate their performance on any entry-skill measures. Next, the designer should bring together all the comments and suggestions about the instruction that resulted from going through it with each learner, which can be done by integrating everything on a master copy of the instruction using a color code to link each learner to his or her particular problems. It is also possible to include comments from a subject-matter expert and any alternative instructional approaches that were used with learners during the one-to-one sessions.

Next posttest data are summarized by obtaining individual item performance and then combining item scores for each objective and for a total score. It is often of interest to develop a table that indicates each student's pretest score, posttest score, and total learning time. In addition, student performance on the posttest should be summarized, along with any comments, for each objective. The same type of summary can be used for examining the data on the attitude questionnaire, if one is used at this point in the instruction.

With all this information in hand, the designer is ready to revise the instruction. Of course, certain obvious revisions may have been made before completing the one-to-one sessions. Now the more difficult revisions must be made. Certainly the place to begin is within those sections that resulted in the poorest performance by learners and those that resulted in the most comments.

First, try to determine, based on learner performance, whether your rubric or test items are faulty. If flawed, then changes should be made to make them clearer or consistent with the objectives and the intent of the instruction. If the items are satisfactory, and the learners performed poorly, then the instruction must be changed. You have three sources of suggestions for change: learner suggestions, learner performance, and your own reactions to the instruction. Learners often can suggest sensible changes. In addition, the designer should carefully examine the *mistakes* made by learners in order to identify the kinds of misinterpretations they are making and, therefore, the kinds of changes that might be made. You should not ignore your own insights about what changes will make the instruction more effective. You have used systematic design procedures, so you have made careful descriptions of what is to be learned and have provided examples; you have offered students the opportunity to practice each skill and they have received feedback. The basic components are there! The usual revisions at this stage are ones of clarification of ideas and the addition or deletion of practice activities. Hopefully, the three sources of data will suggest the most appropriate steps to take.

There will be times when it is not obvious what to do to improve your instruction. It is sometimes wise simply to leave that part of the instruction as is and see how it works in the small-group formative evaluation. Alternatively, the designer can develop several approaches to solving the problem and try these out during the small-group evaluation.

Data Analysis for Small-Group and Field Trials

The small-group formative evaluation provides the designer with a somewhat different data summary situation. The data from eight to twenty learners are of greater collective interest than individual interest; that is, these data can show what problems and reactions this representative group of learners had. The available data typically include the following: item performance on the pretest, posttest, and responses to an attitude questionnaire; learning and testing time; and comments made directly in the materials.

The fundamental unit of analysis for all the assessments is the individual assessment item. Performance on each item must be scored as correct or incorrect. If an item has multiple parts, then each part should be scored and reported separately so that the information is not lost. This individual item information is required for three reasons:

1. Item information can be useful in deciding whether there are particular problems with the item or whether it is effectively measuring the performance described in its corresponding objective. The method for doing this will be described in a later section.
2. Individual item information can be used to identify the nature of the difficulties learners are having with the instruction. Not only is it important to know that, for example, half the learners missed a particular item, but it is also as important to know that most of those who missed it picked the same distractor in a multiple-choice item or made the same type of reasoning error on a problem-solving item.
3. Individual item data can be combined to indicate learner performance on an objective, and eventually, on the entire test. Sometimes, the criterion level for an objective is expressed in terms of getting a certain percentage of items correct on a set of items. The individual item data can be combined not only to show the percentage of items correct for an objective but also the number and percent of learners who achieved mastery.

After the item data have been collected and organized into a basic item-by-objective table, it is then possible to construct more comprehensive data tables.

Group's Item-by-Objective Performance   The first data summary table that should be constructed is an item-by-objective table, as illustrated in Table 11.1. Assume that we have a ten-item test that measures four objectives. Twenty learners were in the small-group formative evaluation.

Although any number of computer-based programs for data analysis can be used to create students' performance summaries, we recommend spreadsheet programs such as EXCEL because they are readily available and easy to use. Simply set up the analysis table in the program to reflect the structure of your test. Notice in Table 11.1

t a b l e | Item-by-Objective Analysis Table

11.1

Objectives		1		2		3		4			Items		Objectives	
ITEMS		1	2	3	4	5	6	7	8	9	10	#	%	#	%
Students	1	1	1	1	1	1	1	1	1	1	1	8	100	4	100
	2	1	1	1	1	1	1	1	1	1	1	8	100	4	100
	3		1	1	1	1	1	1	1	1	1	7	88	3	75
	4	1			1	1	1		1		1	4	50	0	0
	//														
	20	1	1			1	1	1	1			4	50	2	50
# students correct		18	19	15	17	17	6	18	18	10	9				
% students correct		90	95	75	85	85	30	90	90	50	45				
% mastering objectives			90		75			85			45				

(Summaries represent totals after items 6 and 8 were removed from the analysis.)

Note: Although there were twenty students in the analysis group, data for only five students are illustrated.

that the objectives are listed across the top of the table, and items are inserted in the second row within the objectives they measure. Learners are listed down the left side of the table, and their data are recorded in the rows beneath the items and objectives. A number 1 in the column beneath an item indicates a correct response, and a blank indicates an incorrect response for each learner. Using the number 1 to indicate correct answers makes it very easy to sum correct answers and calculate all the other summary data that you will need.

With the raw data displayed in this manner, we can use the table to create two summaries for analysis: item quality and learner performance. You should analyze item quality first, because faulty items should not be considered when analyzing learner performance. The bottom rows contain the data summaries needed for the item analysis. The first row contains the number of the twenty students who answered each item correctly. The next row contains the percentage of learners who answered each item correctly. These figures are obtained by dividing the total number of students in the evaluation into the number of students who answered correctly—that is, for item 1, 18/20 = .90 or 90 percent. The last row contains the percentage of the group that mastered each objective. This value is calculated by dividing the number of students who mastered each objective by the total number of students in the analysis. In this example, learners must correctly answer all the questions for an objective in order to master the objective.

The purpose for the item-by-objective analysis is threefold: to determine the difficulty of each item for the group, to determine the difficulty of each objective for the group, and to determine the consistency with which the set of items within an objective measures learners' performance on the objective. An item difficulty value is the percentages of learners who answer an item correctly. Item difficulty values above 80 percent reflect relatively easy items for the group, whereas lower values reflect more difficult ones. Similarly, consistently high or low values for items within an objective reflect the difficulty of the objective for the group. For example, the difficulty values for items 1 and 2 in Table 11.1 (90 and 95) indicate that nearly all the learners mastered the items associated with objective 1. If these data were from a posttest, we could infer that the instruction related to objective 1 is effective. Conversely, if they are low, they point to instruction that should be considered for revision.

The consistency of item difficulty indices within an objective typically reflects the quality of the items. If items are measuring the same skill, and if there is no inadvertent complexity or clues in the items, then learners' performance on the set of items should be relatively consistent. With small groups, differences of 10 or 20 percent are not considered large, but differences of 40 percent or more should cause concern. Notice in Table 11.1 that item data are consistent within objectives 1 and 2. In contrast, the data are inconsistent within objectives 3 and 4. For objective 3, two items are quite consistent (85 and 90), whereas one item, 6, yielded a much lower difficulty index (30). Such a pattern reflects either inadvertent complexity in the item or a different skill being measured. The pattern in objective 4 illustrates two consistent items (50 and 45) and one outlier (90). This type of pattern reflects either a clue in item 8 or a different skill being measured. When inconsistent difficulty indices are observed within an objective, it indicates that the items within the set should be reviewed and revised prior to reusing them to measure learner performance. If the item is judged sound, then it reflects an aspect of instruction that should be reconsidered.

Learners' Item-by-Objective Performance   The second type of analysis that can be conducted using the item-by-objective table is individual learner performance. Before conducting this analysis, you should eliminate any items judged faulty during the item analysis. The last four columns in the table contain the individual performance data. The first two of these columns contain the number and percent of items answered correctly by each learner. The last two columns contain the number and percent of objectives mastered by each learner. Answering all items within an objective was set as the criterion for mastery.

The hypothetical data for learners in Table 11.1 illustrate that individuals in the group performed quite differently on the test. Two individuals mastered all four objectives, and the scores for the other three learners range from no objectives mastered to 75 percent. If these data represented performance on entry behaviors or skills to be included in the instruction, then they would suggest who was ready for instruction and whether instruction was actually needed by some members of the sample. In contrast, if they reflected posttest performance, then the designer could make inferences about the necessity of revising the instruction. Data about learners' performance on items and objectives provide different information, and for the formative evaluator, data on objectives mastered are more informative than raw scores.

Learners' Performance across Tests   The item-by-objective table provides the data for creating tables to summarize learners' performances across tests. Table 11.2 illustrates how learner-by-objective mastery can be illustrated across tests administered. The data are presented for only five of the twenty students in the analysis, and a summary for the twenty students is presented at the bottom of the table. The first

table 11.2   Student Performance on the Pretest and Posttest by Objective

Objectives		1		2		3		4	
TEST		PR	PS	PR	PS	PR	PS	PR	PS
Students	1		1		1	1	1	1	1
	2		1		1		1		1
	3	1	1		1	1	1		
	4		1		1		1		1
	//								
	20		1		1	1	1		1
% mastering		20	100	10	100	50	100	40	60
diff.			80		90		50		20

PR = pretest; PS = posttest; 1 = mastered.

Note: Table includes data for only five of twenty students in the evaluation but summary percentages reflect data for entire group.

row identifies the objectives, the second row identifies the tests, and subsequent rows are used to record students' mastery of objectives on each test. The two summary rows at the bottom of the table contain the percentage of the twenty learners who mastered each objective on each test and the increase or decrease in percentages from pretest to posttest for each objective. Ideally, the percentages of learners who mastered each objective should increase from pretests to posttests. Such a pattern is illustrated for all four objectives in Table 11.2.

You may also want to summarize learners' performances across tests using the percentage of objectives mastered on each test, as illustrated in Table 11.3. The top row identifies the test and the number of objectives measured by each one. Subsequent rows contain the percentage of objectives mastered by each student on each test. The bottom row contains the average percentage of objectives mastered by the group on each test. From these data the designer could infer that: (1) the group selected was appropriate for the evaluation, (2) the instruction covered skills not previously mastered by the group, and (3) the instruction was effective in improving learners' skills.

Graphing Learners' Performances   Another way to display data is through various graphing techniques. A graph may show the pretest and posttest performance for each objective in the formative evaluation study. You may also want to graph the amount of time required to complete the instructional materials as well as the amount of time required for the pretest and posttest. An example of a pretest/posttest performance graph appears in Figure 11.1.

Another graphic technique for summarizing formative evaluation data involves the instructional analysis chart. This procedure requires the determination of the average pretest and posttest performance of learners participating in the formative evaluation on each of the skills indicated on the instructional analysis chart. The designer uses a copy of the instructional analysis chart without the statement of skills. See Figure 11.2 for an example of this technique. The pretest and posttest scores for each objective are entered in the appropriate boxes. This provides an interesting display of the interrelationships of the scores on the various skills in the instructional materials. It will become apparent if learners' performances decline as they approach the top of the hierarchy. You may also find a skill mastered by only a few learners that seems to have little effect on the subsequent mastery of superordinate skills.

Other Types of Data   There are other kinds of data to summarize and analyze in addition to learners' performance on objectives. It has been found that a good way to summarize data from an attitude questionnaire is to indicate on a blank copy of the questionnaire the percent of learners who chose each alternative to the various questions.

t a b l e

1 1 . 3

Entry Skill, Pretest, and Posttest Data Summarized by the Percent of Total Possible Objectives

Student Number	3 Entry Skill Objectives	9 Pretest Instructional Objectives	9 Posttest Objectives
1	100	11	89
2	100	22	89
3	100	22	89
4	100	11	100
//			
20	67	0	67
Mean	92	14	88

Note: The mean scores are based on the performance of all twenty students even though the data for only five are illustrated.

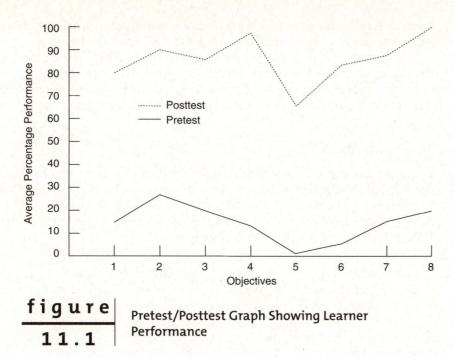

figure 11.1 | Pretest/Posttest Graph Showing Learner Performance

If you also request open-ended, general responses from the learners, then you can summarize them for each question.

Other important types of data are the comments obtained from learners, from other instructors involved in the formative evaluation, and from subject-matter experts who react to the materials. Data and information that are collected in performance context formative evaluations may have to be summarized in descriptive fashion. Since it is almost impossible to summarize these comments in tabular or graphic form, it is better to try to relate each of these comments to the instructional

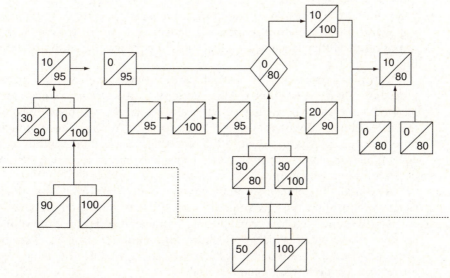

figure 11.2 | Summary of Pretest and Posttest Scores for a Hypothetical Instructional Analysis

materials themselves or to the objective in the materials to which they refer. These comments can be written directly on a copy of the materials.

The final type of data summary you may wish to prepare is related to any alternative approaches you may have used during either the small-group evaluations or field trials. These data may be performance on specific test items, responses on an attitude questionnaire, or even an indication of total learning time.

Sequence for Examining Data

As you prepare summaries of your data, you will quickly begin to get an overall picture of the general effectiveness of your instructional materials and the extent of revisions that may be required. Remember to be open to revisions of your design and materials in all steps of the model. After generally examining the data, we suggest that you use the data in the following sequence.

Instructional Analysis and Entry Skills   First, after removing data for any defective items, you should examine the remaining data with regard to the entry skills of learners. Did the learners in the formative evaluation have the entry skills you anticipated? If so, did they succeed with the instructional materials? If they did succeed, but did not have the required skills, then you must question whether you have identified critical entry skills.

Objectives, Pretests, and Posttests   The second step is to review the pretest and posttest data as displayed on the instructional analysis chart. If you sequenced the materials appropriately and if you identified skills that are hierarchically dependent on each other, then learners' pretest performances should decrease as you move upward through the hierarchy—that is, there should be poorer learner performance on the terminal objective than on the earlier skills. When the instruction is working well, there will, of course, be no decline in learner performance as learners complete the skills at the top of the analysis. These data will help you identify exactly where problems exist and perhaps even suggest a change in the instructional sequence for certain skills.

Third, you might examine the pretest scores to determine the extent to which individual learners, and the group as a whole, had already acquired the skills that you were teaching. If they already possess most of the skills, then you will receive relatively little information about the effectiveness of the instruction or how it might be improved. If they lack these skills, you will have more confidence in the analyses that follow.

By comparing pretest with posttest scores objective by objective, which is the usual procedure when you examine the instructional analysis chart, you can assess learner performance on each particular objective and begin to focus on specific objectives and the related instruction that appear to need revision. You may need to revise the conditions or the criteria specified in the objectives. Recall that conditions are used to control the complexity of performance tasks, and your criteria may be too lenient or harsh for the target group.

As you identify objectives on which the learners performed poorly, examine the exact wording of the objective and the associated test items and the exact student answers to the items. Before revising the instructional materials, refer to your item analysis table to see whether poor test items, rather than the materials, indicated poor learner performance. All that may be needed are revised test items rather than a major revision of the instructional materials.

Learning Components of Instructional Strategy and Materials   The next step is to examine the instructional strategy associated with the various objectives with which learners had difficulty. Was the planned strategy actually used in the instructional materials? Are there alternative strategies that might be employed? The final step is to examine the materials themselves to evaluate the comments about problem areas made by learners, instructors, and subject-matter experts.

Learning Time   An important concern in any formative evaluation is the amount of time required by students to complete the instructional materials. It may be necessary for you to revise the materials to make them fit within a particular time period. This is an extremely difficult task, and it must be done with great care. With individualized materials it is not unusual for the slowest learner to take two or three times longer than the fastest learner. Knowing what to remove from the materials or change without interfering with learning is very difficult to determine. Often the decision can be made only after a trial/revise/trial/revise process with target learners.

Media, Materials, and Instructional Procedures   Data that relate to the implementation of the instructional materials must also be examined. We suggested earlier that you might gather misleading data because of the faulty operations of media equipment. There may also have been disruptions in the classroom, an extended lunch break, or any one of a variety of other kinds of activities that are common to various instructional settings. Since these disruptions cannot be controlled, they simply must be noted and explained.

On the other hand, there are procedural concerns that can be controlled. Were learners hindered by the logistics required to use the materials? Were there questions about how to proceed from one step to the next? Were there long delays in getting test scores? These are the kinds of implementation procedural problems that often are identified in questionnaires and debriefing discussions. Solutions to such problems must be found and incorporated into either the instruction or the instructors' manual to make the instructional activity run more smoothly.

Revision Process

We suggest that as you begin the revision process, you summarize your data as suggested in this chapter. Table 11.4 contains a template designers can use for organizing the information gathered from all sources, and it uses the elements of the instructional strategy as the framework. In the table, the components of the instructional strategy are listed in the left column, and additional columns are provided for

table 11.4   **Template for Summarizing Information from a Formative Evaluation**

Instructional Strategy	Proposed Changes to		
COMPONENT	PROBLEM IDENTIFIED	INSTRUCTION	EVIDENCE AND SOURCE
Entry skills test			
Motivational material			
Pretest			
Information presentation			
Learner participation			
Posttest			
Attitude questionnaire			
Transfer to performance context			

summarizing (1) any problems identified with a component, (2) the changes that are being proposed based on the problems, and (3) the evidence gathered illustrating the problem. The evidence might name sources such as the materials, assessments, data summaries, observations, or interviews. Such a summary will help focus the designer on work to be done and when a design team is involved, it will enable conversations and negotiations about next steps in the project.

We recognize that the needs of instructional designers will differ according to the type of materials with which they are working; however, the strategy suggested here should apply to almost any instructional design effort. For example, if you have taught a psychomotor skill, then your posttest performance would be recorded on a rubric of some sort, and summarized on your instructional analysis chart. There might also be a paper and pencil test of subordinate skills and knowledge. These scores should be examined in connection with their associated motor skills. The use of attitude responses and learning time would be the same for any type of instruction.

Given all the data from a small-group evaluation or field trial, the designer must make decisions about how to make the revisions. It is almost always apparent where the problems are, but it is not always apparent what changes should be made. If a comparison of several approaches has been embedded in the formative evaluation, then the results should indicate the type of changes to be made. Otherwise, the strategies suggested for revising instruction following the one-to-one evaluations also apply at this point—namely, use the data, your experience, and sound learning principles as the bases for your revisions.

One caution: Avoid responding too quickly to any single piece of data, whether it is the learners' performance on a particular objective, a comment from an individual learner, or an observation by a subject-matter expert. They are all valuable pieces of information, but you should attempt to corroborate these data with other data. Look for performance as well as observational data that will help you focus on particular deficiencies in the instructional materials.

An additional suggestion: When summarizing data from the field evaluation, you should be careful to summarize it in an accurate and clear fashion. You will find that these data will be of interest not only to you as the instructional designer but will also serve as an effective vehicle to show others how learners performed with your instruction. The table and graphs can provide both a general and a detailed description of the overall performance of the learners.

Revision of Selected Materials and Instructor-Led Instruction

The data summary and revision procedures described previously are equally appropriate whether the instructor develops original instructional materials, uses a variety of selected materials, or works from an instructor's guide. The types of data that are collected, the ways in which they are summarized, and the ways in which they are used to direct the revision process are all similar. When working with selected materials, however, there is little opportunity to revise the materials directly, especially if they are commercially produced and copyrighted. With copyrighted materials, the instructor can consider the following adaptations for future trials: (1) omit portions of the instruction, (2) include other available materials, or (3) simply develop supplementary instruction. Procedures for the use of materials should also be reconsidered in light of formative evaluation data.

Instructors working from an instructor's guide have the same flexibility as the developer for changing instruction. A pretest and a posttest, together with an attitude questionnaire, should provide data for a thorough analysis of the instruction. Summary tables that indicate performance on each objective should be prepared. Examine learner performance on test items and objectives and then relate learner performance by objective to the instructional analysis diagram.

The instructor's notes from the guide should reflect questions raised by learners and responses to those questions. Learners' questions should be examined to determine whether basic misunderstandings have developed. Were the responses to the questions sufficient to provide adequate performance by learners on the related test items?

An instructor who used an instructor's guide is also likely to obtain a greater "spread" in the scores on tests and reactions on attitude questionnaires. Research data indicate that, by the very nature of group-paced, interactive instruction, some students are unlikely to understand the concepts as rapidly as others do during a given class period. Since there are typically no embedded remedial strategies in group instruction, such learners learn progressively less during a series of lessons, and receive progressively poorer scores; their attitudes will likely reflect this situation. In this interactive, group-paced mode, learners' performance is likely to resemble a bell curve distribution (i.e., a few high scores, a few low scores, and mostly average scores).

Identifying learners who are performing poorly and inserting appropriate activities are important components of the revision process for the instructor who is using an interactive instructional approach. Unlike using written instructional materials, the instructor can revise the presentation during its implementation and note the reasons for the change.

One final observation needs to be made. We have stressed that you are working with a systems approach to build an instructional system, and when you change one component of the system, you are changing the whole system. You need to be aware, therefore, that when you make changes through the revision process, you cannot assume that the remaining unchanged instruction will necessarily maintain its initial effectiveness. You may hope your changes are for the better, but you cannot assume that they always are.

Examples

Based on the degree of elaboration necessary to illustrate the process and products required for revising instructional materials, the examples within this chapter are all focused on the following case study related to leadership training.

Case Study: Group Leadership Training

Data from the instructional goal on leading group discussions is used to illustrate techniques for summarizing and analyzing data collected during formative evaluation activities. Examples provided in this case study are designed to illustrate procedures you might use for either a small-group evaluation or field trial of materials and procedures. Of course the types of tables, graphs, and summary procedures you actually use should be tailored to your instructional materials, tests, instructional context, and learners. These examples simply show some ways the information gathered could be summarized for the group leadership unit.

Recall that, based on interviews with learners in the performance context (current NCW leaders and police support personnel), some decisions were made about how these adult learners would be tested. Due to learner sensitivity, they would not be pretested on verbal information or leadership performance objectives; pretests would simply assess their ability to recognize leadership skills demonstrated by others during staged NCW meetings. The decision was also made not to have individual learners identify themselves on their pretest or practice exercise papers. Learners were identifiable on the posttests because these consisted of actual group leadership. Not having identified the learners, individual member performance cannot be traced across tests; however, total group performance can be monitored, which would provide evidence of instructional effectiveness.

Formative evaluation data for twenty learners were collected during a field trial of the instruction. Assessment data were collected for the twelve leader actions that encourage and stifle group cooperation contained within objectives 6.4.2 and 6.5.1. Recall that the same twelve actions are embedded within these two objectives. During the pretest, learners viewed a simulated NCW meeting on video and marked their observation form each time the leader exhibited one of the twelve enhancing or stifling actions (objective 6.4.2). Assessment data for objective 6.4.2 were also collected during learner participation activities within the instruction. Posttest data were collected only for the learners' group leadership actions exhibited during simulated NCW meetings (objective 6.5.1). Attitudinal data were collected using a questionnaire and debriefing at the end of session 10.

Analysis of Item-by-Objective Data across Tests

Table 11.5 contains a summary of learners' responses on the pretest for objective 6.4.2. There are twelve behaviors within the objective, and they were summarized similar to test items within an objective on an objective-style test. Each of the twelve encouraging and stifling actions is listed across the top of the table, and the twenty learners are listed in the far-left column. The first step in summarizing performance data from any test is to determine how to score learners' responses. When an objective-style test is administered, obtaining a score is relatively easy for each learner by counting the number of test items answered correctly. Scoring live performance assessments, however, requires some planning. (See the pretest in Figure 9.2, p. 240.)

In scoring the pretest, the designer made the following decisions. Each of the enhancing and stifling actions was exhibited by the leader three times during the simulated meeting. Learners were given credit if their tally was within one point of the exhibited actions; thus, a tally of 2, 3, or 4 occurrences earned credit, and a 1 was placed in the student-by-behavior cell in the summary chart in Table 11.5. Further, enhancing and stifling behaviors for each of the twelve actions were combined to create a total test score from 0 to 12. To receive credit for any one of the twelve actions, learners had to classify correctly both the enhancing and stifling behaviors within a skill. For example, if they correctly classified the enhancing behaviors for action 3 but not the stifling behaviors for action 3, they did not receive credit for action 3. Notice the shaded pairs of cells for each learner in the table. These pairs of cells reflect the skills for which learners received credit.

The row totals (each learner's score in the far-right column) were obtained by summing the shaded action pairs within each learner's row. The first row of column totals at the bottom of the table reflects the percentage of learners classifying each enhancing and each stifling action correctly. The last row on the bottom of the chart contains the percentage of the group that classified each of the twelve pairs of actions correctly.

With the pretest data summarized in this manner, the analysis and interpretation began. First, individual learner performance (far-right column) was examined. Was the group heterogeneous in their group leadership skills as anticipated? The designer concluded that their performance on the pretest was heterogeneous or very different. The highest possible score on the test was 12 points, and their scores ranged from 11 to 0. Three of the learners earned scores of 9 (75 percent) or above, four earned scores between 6 and 8, four earned scores of 4 and 5, and nine, or almost half the group, earned scores of 3 (25 percent) or less.

The next step was to examine the total group's performance on each of the behaviors (bottom row). A reasonable question to answer from pretest data was, "Do the learners need this instruction, or do they already possess the skills?" Between 10

table 11.5 — Pretest Data Summarized by Learners across Behaviors (Horizontal) and Behaviors across Learners (Vertical)

Encouraging (+) and Stifling (−) Behaviors Exhibited by Leaders

LRNS	1+	1−	2+	2−	3+	3−	4+	4−	5+	5−	6+	6−	7+	7−	8+	8−	9+	9−	10+	10−	11+	11−	12+	12−	TOTAL
1	1	1	1	1	1	1	1	1	1	1	1	1	1	1	1	1	1	1	1	1	1	1	1		11
2	1	1	1	1	1			1	1	1	1	1		1	1	1				1	1	1	1	1	7
3	1	1	1	1	1	1	1		1	1	1	1	1	1		1	1	1	1	1	1		1		8
4	1	1	1	1	1	1	1	1			1	1	1	1		1		1	1		1			1	6
5	1	1	1		1				1	1	1	1	1				1	1	1	1	1				5
6	1	1	1	1	1	1	1		1	1		1			1	1							1		5
7	1	1			1				1	1	1	1	1	1			1	1	1	1	1				6
8	1		1	1	1	1	1	1	1	1			1						1	1					4
9	1				1								1	1					1	1	1				2
10		1	1	1	1	1	1	1	1	1		1	1	1		1	1	1	1	1	1	1	1	1	9
11										1			1						1	1					0
12	1	1	1	1	1							1							1						2
13			1	1	1	1		1	1	1	1	1	1	1	1	1	1	1	1		1	1	1	1	9
14	1	1	1					1	1							1		1	1						2
15									1	1	1	1	1			1		1							2
16	1		1	1	1				1	1	1							1		1					3
17	1		1	1	1	1	1					1					1	1	1	1					3
18				1			1		1	1		1					1								0
19	1			1	1	1			1						1		1								1
20		1		1	1				1	1	1	1	1			1	1	1	1	1	1	1			5
*	70	50	70	60	85	55	40	30	30	50	55	55	80	60	50	35	45	25	70	50	80	60	55	15	
**	45		55		55		25		25		40		50		25		25		40		55		10		

*Percentage of learners receiving credit for correctly classifying each enhancing (+) and stifling (−) behavior

**Percentage of learners receiving credit for correctly classifying both the enhancing and the stifling actions within a skill.

and 55 percent of the group correctly classified each pair of skills. From these data the designer can conclude that, with the possible exception of learner 1, instruction in enhancing cooperative group interaction was warranted. In addition, their performance in classifying the enhancing and stifling actions (next to last row) was contrasted. The learners were better at recognizing the enhancing behaviors demonstrated than the stifling ones. In fact, they were better at classifying stifling behaviors for only one skill, 5, willingly turns over the floor to group members who interrupt rather than talking over interrupting members.

In this instruction, objective 6.4.2 was not included on the posttest since the posttest consisted of demonstrating the twelve encouraging actions and avoiding the stifling ones while leading a discussion group. The designer contrasted the learners' pretest performance for objective 6.4.2 with their performance on the participation exercise embedded within instruction. Although this is not typical, there were no other data following instruction that could be used to compare with their pretest performance. This contrast allowed loosely examining the effects of instruction for objectives 6.1.1 through 6.4.2. Learner participation data should always be considered tentative; however, it might provide some evidence of growth or change from the pretest. The observation sheet learners used in the learner participation exercise was scored in the same manner as the pretest, which made comparisons possible.

Analysis of Data across Tests

Figure 11.3 contains a graph of learners' achievement for objectives 6.4.2 and 6.5.1. The left side of the graph contains percentage levels used to identify the percentage of the twenty students who mastered each of the twelve behaviors. The twelve actions are listed along the bottom of the graph. With the data arranged as in Figure 11.3, the designer was able to make observations about instruction related to the encouraging actions and the learners' achievement.

The lower line in the figure represents learners' pretest performance on objective 6.4.2, and these data were transferred directly from the bottom row of Table 11.5. The top row of data illustrates their classification skills on the learner participation activity that was included within the instruction. This activity followed instruction on objectives 6.1.1 through 6.4.2. Notice that at this point in the instruction, 80 percent or more of the group correctly classified all twelve of the leader behaviors. This high level of performance across the twelve skills and the learners' growth between the pretest and the practice activity indicate that instruction was effective in helping learners recognize these encouraging and stifling actions when they are exhibited by others.

The center row of data illustrates learners' demonstration of the twelve behaviors during the posttest administered at the end of session 10. Setting the criterion for effective instruction at 80 percent of the group successfully demonstrating each skill, the designer concluded that instruction was adequate for eight of the twelve

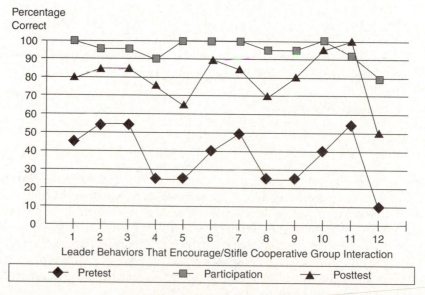

figure 11.3

Percentage of Group Recognizing Twelve Leader Actions That Encourage and Discourage Cooperative Group Interaction on the Pretest and Posttest (Objective 6.4.2) and Demonstrating Encouraging Behaviors as They Lead Group Discussions (Objective 6.5.1 Posttest Only)

behaviors. It was ineffective, however, for helping learners consistently demonstrate the following encouraging actions:

4. Hesitates and pauses between speakers rather than filling quiet gaps with personal points of view (75 percent)
5. Willingly turns over floor when interrupted rather than continuing to talk or interrupting group members (65 percent)
8. Uses comments to keep the discussion centered on the group rather than encouraging the discussion to flow through the leader (e.g., evaluating speaker's comments) (70 percent)
12. Praises group effort and accomplishment rather than singling out particular people for praise (50 percent)

Notice in this data that learners were better at recognizing the twelve encouraging or stifling behaviors in other leaders than they were at consistently exhibiting the actions themselves during a meeting. This differentiation is consistent with the hierarchical order of these two skills in the instructional goal analysis.

Analysis of Attitudinal Data

At the end of session 10, learners were asked to complete the attitudinal questionnaire contained in Figures 10.1 and 10.2 (pp. 272 and 238). The questionnaire was scored by summing the ratings of all learners (twenty) for each question and then dividing the sum by twenty to obtain the group's mean rating for each question. These values were then rounded to the nearest whole number. The range of responses (highest and lowest rating given for each question) was also identified.

These data are recorded on a blank copy of the questionnaire that is included in Figure 11.4. The mean rating for each item is circled on the questionnaire, and the range is indicated using a vertical line over the lowest and highest rating for each item. The mean rating is calculated by summing all learners' responses to an item and then dividing this sum by the number of learners who answered the item. At this point, items indicating potential problems can be flagged. In this instance, a potentially problematic question was defined as one having a mean or average score of 3 or lower and an asterisk was placed to the left of items with means in this area.

Related to learners' perceptions of their attention levels during instruction, they were attentive during all activities, and they believed all objectives covered were relevant to their new positions as NCW leaders (mean 4 or higher). Moving to the confidence questions, the range of responses, or distance between the lowest and highest rating, increased, and the mean score for their confidence in actually using these actions dropped to 3. Within the clarity category, all instruction was rated satisfactorily except for the videos of NCW meetings. For overall satisfaction, problems were identified for pace of instruction and self-satisfaction.

figure
────────
11.4

Summary of Field Test Group's Responses on the Attitude Questionnaire for Main Step 6: Manage Cooperative Group Interaction, Session 10, Objectives 6.1.1 through 6.5.1

Session 10: Engendering Cooperative Member Behaviors   Date: _____

Instructions: Use the following questionnaire to judge the effectiveness of today's session on engendering cooperative member behaviors. Please rate the quality of the instruction for you in each of the five main categories included on the form. For each of the instructional areas listed on the left, circle the response on the right that best reflects your perception of the quality level. At the bottom of the form, please comment on aspects of tonight's session that you consider to be particular strengths and/or problems.   Thank you.

(continued)

figure

11.4

Continued

I. **Attention:** To what degree did the following instructional activities hold your interest or attention?

Instructional Areas	**Attention Levels** (Circle one level for each area)
A. Reading and analyzing annotated diaglogues of NCW meetings illustrating the following:	
1. Member actions that aid cooperative interaction	Little 1 2 3 ④ 5 Very Attentive
2. Strategies leaders use to encourage group cooperation	Little 1 2 3 ④ 5 Very Attentive
B. Watching and analyzing videotapes of NCW meetings depicting the following:	
3. Positive member actions that aid cooperative interaction	Little 1 2 3 4 ⑤ Very Attentive
4. NCW leaders engendering cooperative member behaviors	Little 1 2 3 4 ⑤ Very Attentive
C. Acting as group leader to:	
5. Engender cooperative member behaviors in my group	Little 1 2 3 4 ⑤ Very Attentive

II. **Relevance:** To what degree do you believe the following skills are *relevant* for helping you provide effective leadership in NCW problem-solving meetings?

	Relevance Levels
6. Recognizing cooperative member behaviors during meetings	Little 1 2 3 4 ⑤ Very Relevant
7. Engendering cooperative member behaviors during meetings	Little 1 2 3 4 ⑤ Very Relevant

III. **Confidence:** What level of *confidence* do you have that you can effectively use these group interaction management skills in NCW problem-solving discussions?

	Confidence Levels
8. Recognizing cooperative member behaviors during meetings	Little 1 2 3 ④ 5 Very Confident
✱9. Engendering cooperative member behaviors during meetings	Little 1 2 ③ 4 5 Very Confident

IV. **Clarity:** What level of *clarity* do you believe the following instructional materials and activities have?

	Clarity Level
10. Session introduction	Little 1 2 3 ④ 5 Very Clear
11. Objectives for session	Little 1 2 3 4 ⑤ Very Clear
12. Annotated written dialogues of NCW meetings	Little 1 2 3 ④ 5 Very Clear
✱13. Videos of NCW meetings	Little 1 ② 3 4 5 Very Clear
14. Performing ourselves as group leaders	Little 1 2 3 4 ⑤ Very Clear
15. Instructions for our group leadership activity	Little 1 2 3 ④ 5 Very Clear

figure

11.4

Continued

16. Checklists we used to find positive leader actions	Little 1 2 3 ④ 5 Very Clear
17. Feedback on exercises for positive member and leader actions	Little 1 2 3 ④ 5 Very Clear
V. Satisfaction: Overall, how satisfied were you with the following:	**Satisfaction Level**
18. The facilities	Little 1 2 3 4 ⑤ Very Satisfied
19. The instructor(s)	Little 1 2 3 ④ 5 Very Satisfied
✳ 20. The pace	Little 1 2 ③ 4 5 Very Satisfied
21. The instruction	Little 1 2 3 ④ 5 Very Satisfied
✳ 22. Yourself, relative to the new skills you have developed/refined	Little 1 2 ③ 4 5 Very Satisfied

VI. Please comment on aspects of this session that were strengths and problems for you personally.

	Strengths	Problems
Introduction:	Good, interesting	Need food
Objectives:	Good; Clear; Liked outline format; Easy to follow	
Annotated dialogues:	Easy to follow; Easy to find actions; Relevant topics	
Video:	Relevant topics; Interesting new groups	Moved too fast; Would like to stop video while marking observation form; Help!
Interactive leadership session:	Liked problem areas; Relevant topics for our own meetings	Too hurried—not enough time to get into leadership role; Some people not serious
Assessments:	Like checklists; Like testing format— Seemed like part of instruction	Videos were too fast, missed stuff; Frustrating
Other:	Will be able to use skills on job for quality team	Some stifling actions conflict with good manners (e.g. should comment on speaker's ideas to demonstrate attentiveness and understanding)

At this point the four questions with means at or below the criterion for unsatisfactory ratings were examined. Instructional parts with potential problems are the following:

9. Confidence in engendering cooperative group behavior
13. Videos of meetings
20. Pace of instruction
22. Self-satisfaction with new skill levels

It is possible that these four questions were related. For example, questions 9 and 22, confidence and self-satisfaction, could have been linked; they could also have been related to the reported pacing and video problems.

Learners' open comments provided more information on these topics. Each learner's comments were content analyzed, similar comments were clustered across learners, and a summary of the issues they discussed were included on the questionnaire form. Related to the video problem, they thought the televised meetings went too fast for careful observation, and they were unable to watch the meeting progress and mark their observation forms at the same time. They also reported not having enough time to practice their leadership skills in the interactive meetings. Finally, several noted that they had trouble with some of the cooperation-stifling actions and believed the actions were in direct conflict with conventions of polite conversation. In follow-up interviews, the designer discovered that learners believed it was polite to comment when someone suggests a new idea because the comment illustrates to the speaker that others were listening and understood the comment. The difference between conventions of polite conversation and leader behaviors that stifle cooperative interaction could have accounted for learners' poor posttest performance in actions 4, 5, 8, and 12. It is typically not considered polite to leave a large, obvious gap in a conversation (4), allow others to interrupt (5), not comment on others' ideas (8), and not praise individuals for particularly good ideas and contributions (12). The designer concluded that the difference between cooperation-engendering behaviors in a group and conventions of polite conversation should be directly addressed in the instruction.

Plans for Revising Instruction

At this point in formative evaluation of the leadership training instruction, it was premature to make final decisions about changes in the materials for one segment of a total unit of instruction. Before actually making some changes, other lessons would be field-tested and analyzed. The changes would be made based on the overall effectiveness of the unit; however, data gathered in session 10 were used to create an instructional revision analysis table such as the one in Table 11.6. The table has four parts. The component being evaluated is listed in the left column. Problems identified and potential changes were described in the next two columns. The last column contains the evidence used to justify the change and its source. The resources used to complete the table were (1) test data and observations of students using the materials, (2) notes and remarks students made in the materials, and (3) information taken from the attitude questionnaire. The materials revision prescriptions were drawn directly from the verbal descriptions of each item analysis table made previously.

As the designers moved through the formative evaluation process, they noted that changes made in the materials could have consequences other than the ones anticipated. If extensive changes were made, such as inserting instruction for skills considered previously to be prerequisites for the leaders and excusing those with formal coursework and leadership experience from selected lessons, then another field trial should be conducted with these changes in place to see whether the desired impact was realized.

Appendix L, 1 through 7, contains the formative evaluation data summaries, and the revision prescriptions matrix is included in Appendix M for the case study on writing composition.

t a b l e | Instructional Revision Analysis Form

11.6

Instructional Strategy Source	Problem	Proposed Change in Instruction	Evidence and Source
Motivational, introductory material	None	None	Learners reported good attention levels, clarity of purpose, and relevance of instruction (attitude questionnaire and debriefing session).
Pretest	Video meeting was too quick; learners had difficulty watching meeting and marking their observation form at the same time.	Add instructions to pause video while marking the observation form.	Comments came from attitude questionnaires, instructor comments, and debriefing session.
Information presentation	Performance levels on skills 4, 5, 8, and 12 were inadequate.	Add more information and examples of these behaviors in the presentations.	Information came from the following sources: • Posttest scores for these skills • Attitude questionnaire • Debriefing session • Observation during interactive meetings
	Conflict was reported between stifling behaviors and conventions of polite conversation.	Directly address the differences between leadership actions that engender cooperative group behavior and conventions of polite conversation. State differences and explain the purpose for the differences.	
Learner participation	(6.4.2) Video meeting was too quick; learners had difficulty watching meeting and marking their observation form at the same time.	Add instructions to pause video while marking the observation form.	Attitude questionnaire
Posttest	There was inadequate time available for each learner to perform.	Move learners into groups as they finish individualized activities. Watch, however; this may tend to place all the strong performers together and the novices together.	Attitude questionnaire
Attitude questionnaire	None	None	Questionnaire did detect areas of weakness and obtain explanations for them. Information obtained was corroborated with posttest data, debriefing, and instructor's comments.

SUMMARY

The data you collect during the formative evaluation should be synthesized and analyzed in order to locate potential problems in the instructional materials. Your data summaries should include learners' remarks in the materials, their performance on the pretest and posttest, their responses on the attitude questionnaire, their comments during debriefing sessions, and information gained from the performance context. Once you get the data summarized you should perform the following analyses:

1. Examine the summarized data relative to entry skills and draw implications about the entry behaviors of students in your target group.
2. Review summarized pretest and posttest data both for total performance and objective-by-objective performance. Superimpose the averages on your instructional analysis chart. Draw inferences about your group's performance on each test item and each objective. You may want to compare data obtained from the entry skill items with pretest and posttest data as well.
3. Examine the objectives, test items, and instructional strategy for those objectives for which

student performance failed to meet your established criteria. Check the objectives, test items, vocabulary, sequence, and instructional strategy for those objectives prior to making direct changes in the instructional materials.

4. Check procedures and implementation directions as well as equipment required for instruction for possible guides to revision.
5. Develop a materials revision analysis table that describes problems, changes, evidence that changes are needed, and sources of evidence cited for each component in the materials.
6. Revise instruction based on your prescriptions in the materials revision analysis table. Delay any revisions that may depend on information from the field testing of other lessons.

These data synthesis and analysis activities are undertaken following each of the one-to-one, small-group, and field trial formative evaluations. If you make major revisions in your materials following the field trial, then another trial is advisable to check the effectiveness of your revisions.

RUBRIC FOR EVALUATING DATA SUMMARY AND INTERPRETATION

The following rubric contains criteria for evaluating data summary and interpretation. You can use it to plan data analysis for your own project, evaluate your analysis materials, or share with others for evaluating your materials.

Designer note: If an element is not relevant for your project, mark NA in the No column.

No	Some	Yes	
			A. Experts Do the information summaries include data from:
___	___	___	1. Content experts?
___	___	___	2. Managers and supervisors (performance context)?
___	___	___	3. Trainers/teachers (learning context)?
			B. Learners Do the information summaries include data from:
___	___	___	1. Readiness for instruction (entry skills)?
___	___	___	2. Pretest–posttest growth by skill?
___	___	___	3. Attitudes?
___	___	___	4. Comments within materials (clarity, sequence, chunk, etc.)?
___	___	___	5. Total learning times for each session?
			C. Procedures Do the information summaries include data about:
___	___	___	1. Media and equipment?
___	___	___	2. Personnel?
___	___	___	3. Facilities?
___	___	___	4. Budget?
___	___	___	5. Schedules?
___	___	___	6. Management of learners through materials?
			D. Analysis Were issues and problems summarized by and linked to:
___	___	___	1. Participants (e.g., experts, learners)?
___	___	___	2. Preinstructional activities?
___	___	___	3. Readiness/pretest?

No	Some	Yes	
—	—	—	4. Information presentation?
—	—	—	5. Learner participation?
—	—	—	6. Assessments?
—	—	—	7. Follow-through for transfer?

E. Revision Strategy Do suggested revisions reflect systematic thinking in that they are *logical* and *linked* to problems identified in the:

No	Some	Yes	
—	—	—	1. Design decisions (e.g., analysis of needs, solutions, goals, learners, contexts, instructional strategy)?
—	—	—	2. Instructional materials?
—	—	—	3. Instructional procedures?
—	—	—	4. Media and delivery system?
—	—	—	5. Resources (funding, personnel, time, facilities, equipment, etc.)?

The final revision of your materials should be effective in bringing about the intended learning with members of your target audience. Then you are ready to reproduce or publish an effective set of instructional materials.

PRACTICE

1. What data would you use to determine whether learners in your target group actually possessed the entry skills identified in your instructional analysis and whether those you identified were relevant to your instruction?

2. When should you develop instruction for prerequisite skills?

3. What type of data table should you create to provide the information necessary to determine the exact nature of problems that learners have with the instruction?

4. Why should you construct a narrative explanation from data tables of problems that are identified with each test?

5. Why should you summarize performance by objective across pretest and posttest?

6. What materials should you evaluate using an attitude questionnaire?

7. What information should you include in an instructional revision analysis table?

8. Table 11.7 contains an incomplete item-by-objective table for five learners. Use the raw data to calculate the following:
   - Raw score for each learner
   - Percent of items correct for each learner
   - Number of objectives passed by each learner

table 11.7 Item-by-Objective Analysis Table

Objective	_1_			_2_			_3_			_4_			RAW SCORE	PERCENT CORRECT	OBJECTIVES PASSED	PERCENTAGE OF OBJECTIVES PASSED
ITEM	1	2	3	4	5	6	7	8	9	10	11	12				
Student 1	1	1	1		1	1					1	1				
2	1	1	1	1	1	1	1	1	1	1	1	1				
3				1	1	1					1	1				
4	1			1	1	1	1	1	1	1	1	1				
5	1	1	1	1	1	1	1	1	1	1	1	1				
Total correct																
Percent correct																
Percent passing objective																

1 = Correct answer.

Incorrect answer is left blank.

To pass an objective, all items within the objective must be correct since each item was constructed to test a different facet of the objective.

- Number of learners answering each item correctly.
- Percent of learners answering each item correctly
- Percent of learners passing each objective

You may want to transfer the data to a spreadsheet such as EXCEL to complete your calculations.

Four students who participated in the field trial of the writing composition materials demonstrated on the entry skills test that they had not mastered the entry skills. They were included in the field trial to determine whether the subordinate skills identified as entry skills were correctly classified for the instructional goal. Figure 11.5 contains the percentage of these four students who mastered the declarative sentences sub-

ordinate skills on the pretest, embedded test, and declarative sentences portion of the posttest. Answer the following questions based on their performance data in the chart.

9. Did students appear to need instruction on all of the skills?

10. Based on pretest and posttest data, for which skills did students appear to benefit from the instruction?

11. Apart from those skills students had mastered prior to instruction, for which skills was instruction not effective?

12. Based on their achievement in the unit, what would you recommend as next steps for these students?

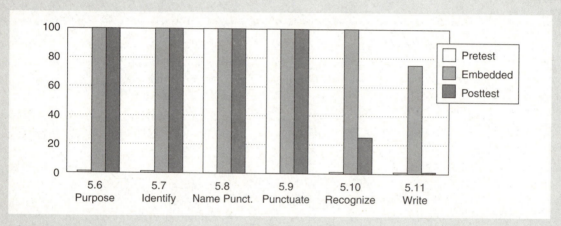

figure 11.5   Mastery of Each Objective on the Pretest, Embedded Items, and Posttest for Four Students Who Did Not Possess the Required Entry Skills

FEEDBACK

1. You would use item and objective analysis data from the items on the pretest and posttest. Data from the entry skills pretest would tell you whether students possessed the entry skills. Data from tests used with the instructional materials would tell you whether you had actually identified relevant entry skills. If students perform poorly on the entry skills items, yet are successful on subsequent tests, then you need to reexamine the entry skills you have identified.

2. You should *not* develop instruction for prerequisite skills prior to at least the one-to-one evaluation of your materials. As you could see in the Case Study section, data from the field test will tell you whether and for what specific objectives such materials are needed.

3. You should construct an item/objective analysis table. It should be constructed in a manner to enable you to analyze correct answers as well as incorrect answers. Correct answer analysis tells you whether your instruction was effective; incorrect answer analysis tells you what went wrong and helps you focus on revisions that might help.

4. You should construct a narrative analysis from the data for each test while the information is fresh in your mind, because this information becomes one basis for the instructional revisions analysis table. If you do not do it and have many raw data tables from several tests before you, it is very difficult to focus and pinpoint problems that have occurred.

5. The summary tables highlight trends in performance. If learners failed to master an objective on the pretest, was it mastered on the posttest?

6. All components of the materials should be evaluated on the attitude questionnaire. It is recommended that an attitude questionnaire be administered at the same time that materials are used by learners. We recommend embedding attitude questions within the lessons so students comment while the material is fresh in their minds. If this approach is used, then care must be taken not to disrupt the flow of learning.

7. An instructional revision analysis table should contain five types of information: (a) the name of the component, (b) problems identified with the component, (c) changes to be made in the instruction, (d) evidence from either test or questionnaire data, remarks in materials, and observations of how pro-

cedures worked, and (e) the source of evidence cited as the reason(s) for changes.

8. See Table 11.8.

9. Based on the pretest/posttest data in the chart, students do not appear to need instruction for subordinate skills 5.8 and 5.9.

10. Based on pretest and posttest data, students appeared to benefit from instruction for subordinate skills 5.6 and 5.7.

11. Instruction was not effective for subordinate skills 5.10 and 5.11.

12. These four students should be branched to individualized instruction covering recognizing the elements of complete sentences as well as additional instruction on recognizing and writing declarative sentences.

table 11.8 — Item-by-Objective Analysis Table

Objective	1			2			3			4			RAW SCORE	PERCENT CORRECT	OBJECTIVES PASSED	PERCENT OF OBJECTIVES PASSED
ITEM	1	2	3	4	5	6	7	8	9	10	11	12				
Student 1	1	1	1		1	1				1	1		7	58	1	25
2	1	1	1	1	1	1	1	1	1	1	1		11	92	3	75
3				1	1	1				1	1		5	42	1	25
4	1			1	1	1	1	1	1	1	1		9	75	1	50
5	1	1	1	1	1	1	1	1	1	1	1		11	92	3	75
Total correct	4	3	3	4	5	5	3	3	3	5	5	0				
Percent correct	80	60	60	80	100	100	60	60	60	100	100	0				
Percent passing objective		60			80			60			0					

1 = Correct answer.

Incorrect answer is left blank.

To pass an objective, all items within the objective must be correct since each item was constructed to test a different facet of the objective.

REFERENCES AND RECOMMENDED READINGS

All references at the end of Chapter 10, Designing and Conducting Formative Evaluations, are appropriate for this chapter on instructional materials revision. For additional resources on data synthesis, analysis, and interpretation, consult the references at the end of Chapter 7, Developing Assessment Instruments. These texts all address data synthesis, analysis, and interpretation in addition to instrument construction procedures and criteria.

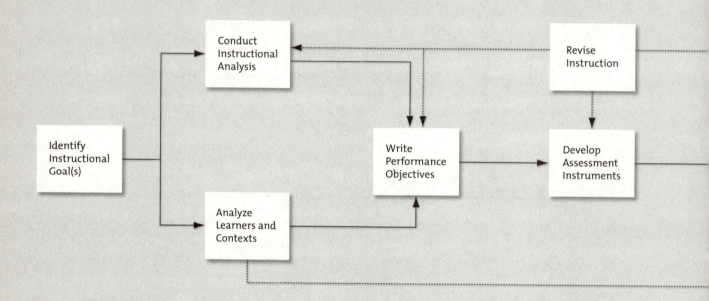

objectives

➤ Describe the purpose of summative evaluation.

➤ Describe the two phases of summative evaluation and the decisions resulting from each phase.

➤ Design a summative evaluation for comparing alternative sets of candidate instructional materials.

➤ Contrast formative and summative evaluation by purpose and design.

Designing and Conducting Summative Evaluations

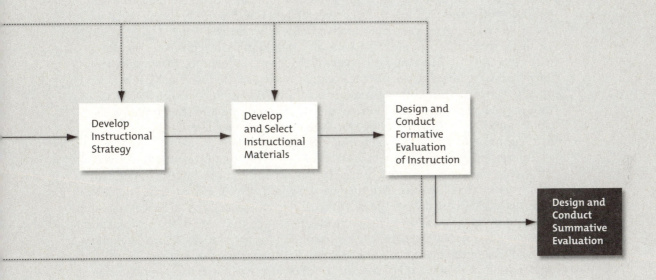

Background

You have learned that formative evaluation is the process of collecting data and information in order to improve the effectiveness of instruction. In sharp contrast, summative evaluation is the process of collecting data and information in order to make decisions about the acquisition or continued use of some instruction.

The distinction between formative and summative evaluation became important several decades ago when advocates for each new public school curriculum and each new media delivery system claimed that it was better than its competitors. Studies were conducted as soon as possible to determine the "winner." Often the innovation did not do as well as traditional instruction. This came as no surprise to experienced evaluators, who knew that the innovation was really in draft form whereas the traditional instruction had been used, and revised, for many years.

Persuasive arguments were made to postpone such comparisons until an innovation had been formatively evaluated and revised to the point that all the major problems were removed, and it was suitable for routine use. *Then* it would be appropriate to compare the innovation to other forms of instruction or to document exactly what the new innovation could do in terms of learner performance, attitudes, instructor reactions, costs, durability, and compatibility with other instruction in a curriculum or organization. It is not necessary to have a comparison between or among instructional products to have a summative evaluation. A summative study can be done to document the effects of a single innovation.

For the designer, the fundamental importance of formative evaluation for the effective use of the systematic design process cannot be overstated. Every designer should be able to conduct formative evaluations with confidence. Such is not as much the case with summative evaluation as it was originally conceived. When it came to an impartial study of the effects of an innovative delivery system or an innovative curriculum, or both, most decision makers did not want the study to be conducted by a developer or advocate for one of the competing formats of instruction; thus, external or third-party evaluators were often hired to conduct summative evaluations.

In recent years the tenor of summative evaluations has changed. The question is no longer "Which is better?" Instead it is "Did the intervention, including the instruction, solve the problem that led to the need for the instruction in the first place?" In other words, instruction is being considered as a solution to a problem, and the ultimate summative evaluation question is "Did it solve the problem?"

But is this not the question we were also asking in performance-context formative evaluation? Yes, it is, but with a very different purpose. In the formative evaluation phase we wanted to use the information to revise the instruction so it would promote use of skills and the effectiveness of the skills in the performance context. Now, in the summative evaluation, we are asking whether, after the formative evaluation (or whatever design strategy has been used by the developer) is complete, the instruction is effective in solving our performance problem.

Interest has shifted from comparisons of innovations and statements of posttest performance to demonstrations of learner performance in the context in which the skills were intended for use. Are they used, and do they work? In order to answer these questions, there are two phases of summative evaluation. The first focuses on the relationship between the instruction of interest and the needs of the organization. This analysis is done through the use of available documentation. The second phase is a field trial of the instruction that is similar to the third phase of formative evaluation, except it is now conducted for a different purpose—namely, to determine whether it produces the desired results for the decision maker.

In the sections that follow, we will refer at different times to *instruction* and *instructional materials*. We use these terms synonymously. Our intent is to refer to the summative evaluation of any form that instruction might take, whether that is video, instructor-guided, self-instructional materials, or computer-based instruction. So, when we use the terms *instruction* or *instructional materials,* you should consider them to mean any form of instruction.

Concepts

Summative evaluation is defined as the design of evaluation studies and the collection of data to verify the effectiveness of instructional materials with target learners. Its main purpose is to make go–no-go decisions about maintaining currently used instructional materials or about adopting materials that have the potential for meeting an organization's defined instructional needs. The materials evaluated may or may not have undergone formative evaluation and revision. Materials evaluated may come from commercial publishers, a consulting firm, or an individual. The scope of the materials varies as well. They may be intended for a one-day workshop, a short course of some type, or for a semester or year of instruction. The scope of the materials does not change the basic design of the study. Rather, it influences the amount of time required to complete it.

A summative evaluation has two main phases: expert judgment and field trial. The purpose of the expert judgment phase is to determine whether currently used instruction or other candidate instruction has the potential for meeting an organization's defined instructional needs. The purpose of the field trial phase is to document the effectiveness of promising instruction with target group members in the intended setting. The analyses and decisions to be made during each phase and the evaluation activities supporting each one are listed in Table 12.1.

The activities undertaken in the expert judgment phase to decide whether candidate instruction is promising include (1) evaluating the congruence between the organization's instructional needs and candidate instruction, (2) evaluating the completeness and accuracy of candidate instruction, (3) evaluating the instructional strategy contained in the candidate instruction, (4) evaluating the utility of the instruction, and (5) determining current users' satisfaction with the instruction. When instruction has been tailored to the defined needs of the organization, systematically designed and developed, and formatively evaluated prior to the summative evaluation, then the expert judgment phase has been accomplished. The expert judgment phase is imperative when the organization is unfamiliar with the instruction and its developmental history.

The field trial phase has two components. The first is *outcomes analysis,* which involves determining the effect of instruction on learners' skills, on the job (transfer), and on the organization (need resolution). The second component, called *management analysis,* includes assessing instructor and supervisor attitudes related to learner performance, implementation feasibility, and costs.

The field trial for the summative evaluation includes documenting learner performance and attitudes, documenting instructor/implementer attitudes, and documenting procedures and resources required to implement the instruction. The main

table 12.1	The Expert Judgment and Field Trial Phases of Summative Evaluation

Summative Evaluation	
EXPERT JUDGMENT PHASE	FIELD TRIAL PHASE
Overall Decisions	
Do the materials have the potential for meeting this organization's needs?	Are the materials effective with target learners in the prescribed setting?
Specific Decisions	
Congruence Analysis: Are the needs and goals of the organization congruent with those in the instruction?	**Outcomes Analysis:**
Content Analysis: Are the materials complete, accurate, and current?	**Impact on Learners:** Are the achievement and motivation levels of learners satisfactory following instruction?
Design Analysis: Are the principles of learning, instruction, and motivation clearly evident in the materials?	**Impact on Job:** Are learners able to transfer the information, skills, and attitudes from instructional setting to the job setting or to subsequent units of related instruction?
Feasibility Analysis: Are the materials convenient, durable, cost-effective, and satisfactory for current users?	**Impact on Organization:** Are learners' changed behaviors (performance, attitudes) making positive differences in the achievement of the organization's mission and goals (e.g., reduced dropouts, resignations; improved attendance, achievement; increased productivity, grades)?
	Management Analysis: 1. Are instructor and manager attitudes satisfactory? 2. Are recommended implementation procedures feasible? 3. Are costs related to time, personnel, equipment, and resources reasonable?

purpose of the field trial is to locate both the strengths and weaknesses of the instruction, to determine their causes, and to document the strengths and problems.

Both the expert judgment and the field trial can be focused on one set of instructional materials or on competing sets of materials. Typically the expert judgment phase is used to choose among available instruction in order to select one or two sets of materials that appear most promising for a field trial. Both phases are described in more detail in the following sections. In reading the material on the expert judgment phase, assume that the instruction to be evaluated is unfamiliar to you and that you are faced with the decision of whether to recommend expending additional effort and cost for a field trial.

Expert Judgment Phase of Summative Evaluation

Congruence Analysis

Organization's Needs. Regardless of whether the summative evaluation involves materials comparisons or is focused on one set of instructional materials, the evaluator must determine the congruence between the organization's needs, the characteristics of their target learners, and the needs and characteristics the candidate materials were designed to address. To perform the congruence analysis, you should first obtain a clear description of the organization's needs, which includes an accurate description of the entry skills and characteristics of the target learners. After obtaining this information, you should locate instructional materials that have potential for meeting the organization's needs. For each set of candidate materials identified, you should obtain a clear description of the goals and objectives of the instruction and the target audience for which it is intended. This information can sometimes be found in a foreword or preface in the materials themselves or in the instructor's manual. If these descriptions are too general, then you may wish to contact the publisher of the materials for more detailed information.

Resources. You should also analyze the congruence between the resources the organization has available for purchasing and implementing instructional materials and the costs of obtaining and installing candidate materials. Materials that are too costly, however effective, often cannot be considered by an organization. The facilities and equipment available in the organization and those required to implement the instruction should also be contrasted.

Once adequate descriptions are obtained, you should compare (1) the organization's needs versus needs addressed in the materials, (2) the organization's target groups versus target groups for the materials, and (3) the organization's resources versus requirements for obtaining and implementing the instruction. The information from your congruence analysis should be shared with appropriate decision makers. Although you may be asked to make recommendations, the persons who make the final decisions about which of the candidate materials to include in a summative evaluation, or whether to even continue the evaluation, will vary greatly from one organization to another.

Several groups of questions related to the design of quality materials should be addressed for any instruction selected for a summative evaluation. These questions should be answered prior to engaging in any field trials of the materials with learners.

1. Are the materials and any accompanying assessments accurate and complete?
2. Is the instructional strategy adequate for the anticipated types of learning outcomes?
3. Can the materials be used effectively?
4. Are current users of the materials satisfied?

If some or all of the candidate materials are judged to be unsound in these important aspects, then continuing the summative evaluation would be fruitless. Supervisors should be informed of your judgments following this phase of the summative evaluation, and again they should be asked whether they wish to continue the summative evaluation.

The manner in which we design and conduct this phase of the summative evaluation is similar to some of the strategies used in the one-to-one formative evaluation, but it has some distinctive features as well. Let's consider each cluster of questions in turn.

Content Analysis   Because you may not be a content expert in the materials you evaluate, it may be necessary to engage a content expert as a consultant. What you must consider is how best to use this expert. One strategy would be to provide the experts with copies of all candidate materials and ask them to judge the accuracy and completeness of the materials for the organization's stated goals. A better, more cost-effective strategy would be to work with the expert(s) to produce an instructional analysis of the stated goal. The document the expert(s) produces should include both the goal analysis and the subordinate skills analysis. A framework that identifies and sequences the main steps and subordinate skills in the goal would be a valuable standard against which you can evaluate the accuracy and completeness of any candidate materials.

How can the framework be used? The skills included in the framework can be converted to a checklist or rating scale the evaluator uses to review and judge the quality of the candidate materials and any accompanying tests.

Design Analysis   Similar to the one-to-one formative evaluation, you need to evaluate the adequacy of the components of the instructional strategy included in the candidate materials. As an external evaluator, you may not know whether particular components of the strategy are present, and if present, whether they have the potential for gaining and maintaining learners' attention. Again, checklists that can be used for reviewing and comparing candidate materials would be the most thorough and time-saving approach.

In developing the checklists, you should list the components of the instructional strategy in the far-left column and use the remaining columns for recording related information about candidate materials. Although the basic components of the strategy do not change, you may want to adopt criteria related to each component based on the type of learning outcome(s) addressed in the materials. The evaluator's response format can also be expected to vary based on the nature of the instruction.

Utility and Feasibility Analysis   The third area of questions about the instructional materials relates to the utility of the candidate materials. For each set, you should consider such factors as the availability of a learner guide or syllabus and an instructor's manual. Factors related to the durability of the materials are another consideration. Another is any special resources, such as instructor capabilities, equipment, or environments (e.g., learning centers) that are required. A utility concern is whether the materials require group or individual pacing. You may also wish to revisit the issue of the relative costs of obtaining and implementing the materials. In fact, any factors that might enhance or restrict the utility of the materials for the organization should be considered.

To design this part of the summative evaluation, you may need to interview the persons in the organization who requested the evaluation. Through discussions with them you can ensure that you have determined their needs, resources, and constraints. They may help to identify utility questions that you may not have considered.

Using the utility questions you select, you can design a summary form to focus your attention on each question as you reevaluate all the candidate materials. As in the previous examples, the important questions can be listed in the left column of your checklist and a separate response column provided for each set of materials. One possible difference between this checklist and the preceding ones is that you may need to include descriptive information related to each set of materials rather than simply judging the presence or absence of selected criteria. Briefly summarizing the descriptive information in tabular form will assist you in making the appropriate comparisons across materials and in formulating your recommendations.

Current User Analysis　One other analysis that you may wish to include in your design is to seek additional information about the candidate materials from organizations that are experienced in using them. The names of current users can often be obtained from the publishers of the materials.

What types of information should you seek from the users? One type of information involves data about the target learners in the other settings. For example, what are their entry skills and motivations for studying the materials? What are their pretest and posttest performance levels using the instruction? Finally, what are their attitudes about the materials?

Another type of information relates to the instructor's perceptions of the materials. For example, are the materials easy to use? What problems have they experienced in implementing the materials? What resources are required to use them? Do they plan to continue using the materials, and if not, why?

Depending on the logistics involved, you may wish to travel to the other organization, or you may decide to gather the information through questionnaires and telephone interviews. Either way you should plan carefully before obtaining the information.

At this point you have concluded the expert judgment phase of the summative evaluation. Based on the data you have gathered, you should be able to determine whether a field trial phase of the summative evaluation is warranted and to recommend the most promising set or sets of materials for the field trial phase. The evaluation design and procedures used to conduct this part of the evaluation should be documented in your evaluation report, together with your recommendations and rationale. Figure 12.1 illustrates the sequence of tasks involved in the expert judgment phase and the decisions summative evaluators make as they progress toward a field trial of given instruction.

Field Trial Phase of Summative Evaluation

Outcomes Analysis　The second phase of the summative evaluation is the field trial. During the trial the instruction is implemented as intended, within the organization, and with selected target learners. The field trial typically includes the following parts: planning for the evaluation, preparing for the implementation, implementing instruction and collecting data, summarizing and analyzing data, and reporting results.

Table 12.2 contains a matrix that summarizes the activities related to each part of the evaluation. Each column is headed by one of the main parts, and activities related to each are listed beneath. All activities in the first column, Planning, should be completed from top to bottom before beginning the activities in the second column, Preparing. Similarly, activities in the second column should be sequenced from top to bottom, and they should be completed prior to moving to the third column, Implementing/Collecting Data. At the point of instruction implementation and data collection, however, this top-to-bottom sequencing pattern within each part ceases. Data related to each area (across rows) should be collected using the most time- and cost-efficient schedule. This is true for the sequence of data summary and report sections, as well. The activities in the last three columns are presented in this sequence simply to illustrate their relationship to the activities named in the first two columns. The following paragraphs describe each of these summative field trial activities in more detail.

Planning.　The first planning activity is the design of your field trial. The exact nature of the design depends on several factors, including the needs assessment, the

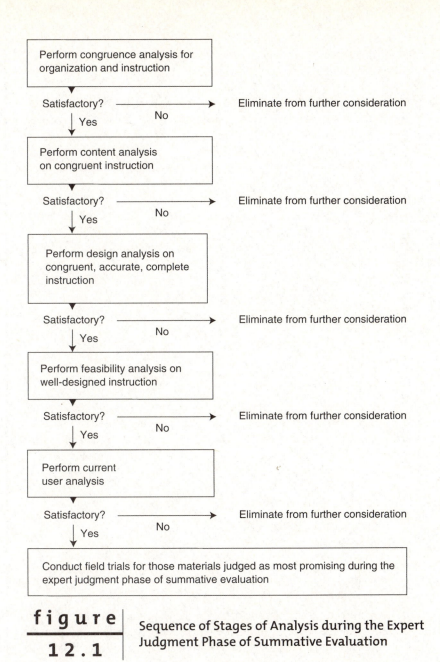

Perform congruence analysis for organization and instruction		

Satisfactory? ——————→ Eliminate from further consideration
   ↓ Yes   No

Perform content analysis on congruent instruction

Satisfactory? ——————→ Eliminate from further consideration
   ↓ Yes   No

Perform design analysis on congruent, accurate, complete instruction

Satisfactory? ——————→ Eliminate from further consideration
   ↓ Yes   No

Perform feasibility analysis on well-designed instruction

Satisfactory? ——————→ Eliminate from further consideration
   ↓ Yes   No

Perform current user analysis

Satisfactory? ——————→ Eliminate from further consideration
   ↓ Yes   No

Conduct field trials for those materials judged as most promising during the expert judgment phase of summative evaluation

figure
12.1

Sequence of Stages of Analysis during the Expert Judgment Phase of Summative Evaluation

nature of materials, and whether competing materials are included. You may need to evaluate only one set of materials using one group, one set of materials using several groups with different characteristics or in different settings, or competing sets of materials using comparable groups and settings.

Another design activity is to describe clearly the questions to be answered during the study. Basically, your questions should yield information for both outcomes analysis (impact on learner, job, and organization) and management analysis. Questions will undoubtedly relate to learners' entry-skill levels, their pretest and posttest performance on the objectives, and their attitudes. They may also relate to any resources, equipment, or facilities needed. They could relate to the skills and attitudes of those responsible for implementing the instruction. Others might relate to the implementation procedures and schedules. The precise areas of questions you include will depend on the nature of and resources for the study.

table 12.2

Overview of Activities for a Summative Evaluation Trial

Planning	Preparing	Implementing/Collecting Data	Summarizing and Analyzing Data	Reporting Results
Design evaluation	Obtain instruments Set schedule for instruction and testing Create/modify syllabus			Describe limitations of design
Outcomes analysis Describe resources, facilities, equipment needed	Obtain resources, facilities, equipment	Adequate? (Observation, Interview, Questionnaire)	Describe problems by resources, facilities, and equipment	Recommendations and rationale
Describe ideal entry skills/characteristics of target group	Select sample Verify entry skills (data)	Learner performance? (Pre-/Posttests) Learner attitudes? (Observation, Interview, Questionnaire) Learner performance in job context (Use, Effect?)	Item-by-objective analysis for group and individual Cross-test summary by group and individual by objective Attitude summary	Explanation, recommendations, rationale for learner, job, and organization impact
Describe number of groups and individuals needed	Schedule learners			
Management analysis Describe skills/ capabilities of instructors or managers	Select instructors Verify skills Schedule instructors	Validity of implementation? Modifications? (Observation, Interview)	Describe problems by instructor by objective	Recommendations and rationale
Describe number of instructors needed				
Plan and develop any training needed for instructors/managers	Provide training for instructors	Training effective? (Observation, Interview)	Describe implementation problems by objective and activity	Recommendations and rationale

In addition to the questions related to performance in the learning context, there is the whole set of questions about performance in the transfer context. Plans must be made to do follow-through activities with some or all of the participants in the instruction. Interviews, questionnaires, and observations can be used with learners and their managers, peers, and subordinates in order to determine the impact in the performance context. The same kinds of questions that were included in the field trial in the formative evaluation would also be asked here and should be planned for well in advance of the study.

With the instructional materials and a skeleton of the evaluation design in hand, you can describe the resources, facilities, and equipment appropriate for the study. This activity is included prior to planning for the sample, because any limitations you encounter in this area will undoubtedly influence the nature of the group you can use. Plan initially for the ideal requirements and then negotiate to determine the feasibility of these requests.

With the available resources issue settled, you can turn your attention to describing the ideal target learners. Your prescription should include their entry skills and any other characteristics that are relevant for the materials (e.g., prior experiences, present position, and personal goals). You also need to determine the number of learners you will need (or can afford) and how many groups you will need. In making this determination you should estimate conservatively, because quality and not quantity of data is the criterion. Often twenty to thirty carefully selected individuals who are truly representative of the target group will suffice. The term *group* is not intended to infer group-paced instruction; it refers to the number of individuals from whom data will be collected.

Once you know how many learners will be included in the study, you can decide how many instructors or managers you will need. Besides the ideal number to include, you should describe any skills they will need to implement the instruction. The availability of appropriate instructors may cause you to modify the number of learners in the design. If limiting learners is not feasible, then you may need to plan to train several instructors.

The final planning activity is to develop orientation and perhaps training for the instructors. A good summative evaluation will require the cooperation of those who are implementing the instruction. They must feel that they are an important part of the study, that they are informed, and that their opinions count. Developing initial rapport with this group and maintaining a cooperative relationship throughout the study will enhance the quality of the field trial and the data you are able to obtain. One final caution: the instructors must believe that you are not evaluating either them or the learners. From the outset the focus must be on evaluating the instruction. Building trust and being sensitive to learners' needs will help ensure your access to the setting and to the data. In fact, it may be a good idea to refer to them as implementer/evaluators throughout the study.

Preparing. The activities in the preparation stage flow from the decisions made during the planning stage. They involve obtaining all the materials, instruments, resources, and people prescribed. When a trade-off must be made between what is prescribed and what is available, you may need to note these changes in the limitations section of your report.

Implementing/Collecting Data. During the implementation of instruction you will need to collect all the types of data prescribed. You might include performance measures, observations, interviews, and questionnaires. The density of your data collection will depend both on your questions and on your resources. At a minimum you will want pretest–posttest data and information about learners' perceptions of the materials and procedures. This information usually can be obtained inexpensively and unobtrusively by the instructors. After an appropriate amount of time has passed, conduct the follow-up evaluation in the performance context.

Summarizing and Analyzing Data. The data summary techniques described for the formative evaluation field trial are appropriate for the summative field trial. At a minimum you will want to produce objective-by-item tables and to summarize learners' performance by group and individual. You will also want to create tables to compare individual and group progress from pretests to posttests and to describe their use in the performance context.

In analyzing the data, you will want to document areas of the instruction that were ineffective and the potential reasons for the weaknesses. You will also want to document areas of the instruction that were effective. During a summative evaluation field trial, it is important to provide a balanced analysis of both the strengths and weaknesses of the materials. Focusing only on weaknesses will result in a biased report of the worth of the materials.

Reporting Results. The nature of your summative evaluation report depends on your design. If you included both the expert judgment and the field trial phases, then both should be documented in the report. For each one you should describe the general purpose, the specific questions, the design and procedures, the results, and your recommendations and rationale. The rationale for your recommendations should be anchored in the data you present in the results section.

You should always consider the reader as you design and produce your report. After analyzing several program evaluation reports, Fitzpatrick, Sanders, and Worthen (2004) concluded that, although the reports were informative, they were also arsenic in print! You may want to follow their formatting suggestion for remedying this problem. They suggest beginning the report with an executive summary or abstract that highlights your final recommendations and rationale. Readers can then selectively read the remainder of the technical documentation to verify the quality of your procedures or the validity of your conclusions. (You can formatively evaluate technical reports just as you would formatively evaluate instruction.)

Comparison of Formative and Summative Evaluations

Formative and summative evaluations differ in several aspects. These differences are summarized in Table 12.3. The first difference is related to the purpose for conducting each type of evaluation. Formative evaluations are undertaken to locate weaknesses and

table 12.3 A Comparison of Formative and Summative Evaluation

	Formative Evaluation	Summative Evaluation
Purpose	Locate weaknesses in instruction in order to revise it	Document strengths and weaknesses in instruction in order to decide whether to maintain or adopt it
Phases or Stages	One-to-one Small group Field trial	Expert judgment Field trial
Instructional Development History	Systematically designed in-house and tailored to the needs of the organization	Produced in-house or elsewhere not necessarily following a systems approach
Materials	One set of materials	One set of materials or several competing sets
Position of Evaluator	Member of design and development team	Typically an external evaluator
Outcomes	A prescription for revising instruction	A report documenting the design, procedures, results, recommendations, and rationale

problems in the instruction in order to revise it. Summative evaluations are undertaken to locate both strengths and weaknesses in instruction and to document the findings for decision makers who must decide whether to maintain or adopt the materials.

The second difference involves the stages of the evaluations. The formative evaluation includes three stages—the one-to-one, small-group, and field trial—all conducted directly with target learners. During each stage, a great deal of time is spent observing and interviewing learners in order to understand the nature of problems they encounter with the instruction. The summative evaluation, conversely, contains only two stages: expert judgment and field trial. The expert judgment stage resembles evaluative decisions made by the designer and context expert during the design and development of materials. Target learners are not involved in this stage of summative evaluation. The field trial stage is conducted with target learners, but little if any time is spent interviewing learners to determine why they did or did not succeed with particular objectives in the instruction. Data are typically obtained through unobtrusive observations, questionnaires, and criterion-referenced tests, both at the end of instruction and in the performance context.

The materials subjected to formative and summative evaluations typically have different developmental histories. Instruction subjected to formative evaluations usually has been systematically designed and developed, and thus holds promise for being effective with target learners. Conversely, materials included in a summative evaluation may or may not have been developed following systematic design procedures. Those for which field trials are conducted, however, should have many of the characteristics of systematically designed instruction and thus should also hold promise for being effective with target learners.

Yet another difference between formative and summative evaluations is the number of sets of instruction that are evaluated. Formative evaluations are conducted on only one set of materials. Summative evaluations may focus on either one set of materials or on competing sets of promising materials. Summative evaluations may involve one set of materials and groups with different characteristics or several sets of materials and groups with similar characteristics.

Another contrast between formative and summative evaluations is the relationship of the evaluator to the materials. Typically, formative evaluators have a personal investment in the materials and thus seek valid judgments about the materials in order to produce the best materials possible. Evaluators with personal investments in the outcome of the evaluation are called internal evaluators. It is wise for summative evaluators not to have a personal investment in the materials being evaluated because such detachment helps them maintain objectivity in designing the evaluation and in describing both the strengths and weaknesses in the materials. Detached evaluators are commonly referred to as external evaluators.

A final difference between formative and summative evaluations is the outcome. The results of a formative evaluation include prescriptions for revising the instruction and the actual materials revisions between the three stages of the evaluation. The outcome of the summative evaluation is not a prescription for revisions. Instead it is a report for decision makers, which documents the strengths and weaknesses of the instruction that has been evaluated.

Examples

This section contains examples of the evaluation instruments for the expert judgment phase of the summative evaluation. Instrumentation and data analysis procedures required for the field trial phase were described in detail in the chapter on formative evaluation and will not be repeated here. Basically, the instruments required for the expert judgment stage consist of information summary charts and product evaluation checklists or rating scales to be completed by the evaluator.

Data Summary Form for the Congruence Analysis

Table 12.4 contains an example information summary form for completing the congruence analysis. The left-hand column is used to describe the instructional needs of the organization, the entry skills and characteristics of the target group in the organization, and the organization's resources for obtaining and implementing the instruction. Additional columns can be included to record related information about sets of potentially promising materials. Summarizing the information in this manner will enable both you and the decision makers to make judgments about the appropriateness of candidate materials.

Checklist for Content Analysis: Evaluating the Completeness and Accuracy of Materials

A hypothetical goal framework and materials checklist are illustrated in Figure 12.2. The goal analysis appears in the top portion of the table, and the checklist appears in the lower portion. Using such a checklist, the completeness of the materials and tests as well as the sequence of information in the materials can be evaluated. You could develop any number of response formats to record your judgments. In the example, three response columns are used for each set of materials. The first is for indicating the presence and sequence of subordinate skills in the instruction. The second and third columns are for indicating whether related test items are included in the pretest and posttest.

After evaluating each set of materials for accuracy and completeness, you can tally the number of positive marks for each one in the bottom row of the table and then compare the relative value of the candidate materials. In the hypothetical example, candidate instruction 2 appears to be the most promising because it includes

table 12.4 Congruence Analysis Information Summary Form

Statements of Organization's Characteristics	Candidate Materials (Set 1)	Candidate Materials (Set 2)	Candidate Materials (Set 3)
Organization's instructional needs (goals and main objectives)	Stated goals and objectives in materials	Etc.	Etc.
Entry skills of organization's target group	Stated entry skills for learners	Etc.	Etc.
Characteristics of organization's target group	Stated characteristics of learners and contexts	Etc.	Etc.
Characteristics of performance contexts			
Organization's resources available for obtaining and implementing instruction	Costs of purchasing and implementing materials	Etc.	Etc.
Organization's facilities and equipment available for implementing instruction	Facilities required to implement materials (learning centers, equipment)	Etc.	Etc.

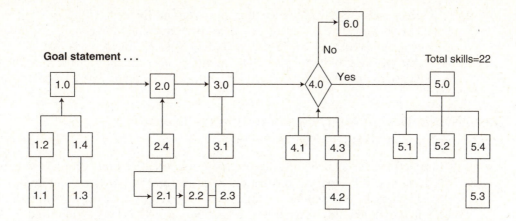

Subordinate Skill Statements	Candidate 1			Candidate 2			Candidate 3		
	MAT	PRE	POST	MAT	PRE	POST	MAT	PRE	POST
1.0	X	X	X	X	X	X			
1.1	X			X		X			
1.2	X		X	X	X	X			
1.3	X			X		X			
1.4	X		X	X	X	X			
2.0	X	X	X	X	X	X	X	X	X
2.1	X			X		X			
2.2	X			X		X			
2.3	X			X		X			
2.4	X		X	X	X	X	X	X	X
3.0	X	X	X	X	X	X	X	X	X
3.1				X	X	X			
4.0				X	X	X			
4.1				X		X			
4.2				X		X			
4.3				X		X			
5.0	X	X	X	X	X	X	X	X	X
Etc.									
Totals	16	5	11	22	16	22	4	4	4

Note: MAT = Instructional materials content; PRE & POST = test item contents; X = skill addressed in materials or tests

figure 12.2 | A Framework for Evaluating the Accuracy and Completeness of Candidate Instructional Materials and the Content Validity of Accompanying Tests

instruction on all twenty-two steps and subordinate skills identified by content experts. The accompanying tests also appear to be the most thorough in measuring the prescribed skills. Comprehensiveness, however, is only the second criterion for summatively evaluating instructional materials.

Following your data analysis, you may wish to use the data to answer questions about the instruction from a systematic instructional design perspective. Sample questions might include the following:

1. How clear are the goal(s) and the main objectives of this instruction?
2. How accurate and current is the information included in the instruction?

3. How logical is the sequence of information in the instruction?
4. How appropriate is the instruction for the entry skills and characteristics of target learners (skills; contexts; understandings; gender, racial, cultural bias)?
5. Are measures of performance (paper and pencil tests and rubrics) congruent with the goals and objectives in the instruction and the target learners' characteristics?

Checklists for Design Analysis: Evaluating the Learning and Instructional Strategies in Materials

Instructional designers who are conducting a summative evaluation of their own materials are keenly aware of the principles of learning and instruction foundations for their materials. Independent evaluators who were not involved in the production of the materials should determine whether these principles were employed in the creation of the instruction.

Effective instruction, regardless of whether it is for learning verbal information, intellectual skills, attitudes, or motor skills, has certain characteristics that are based on the research of cognitive and constructive psychologists and learning specialists. Quality instruction should gain the attention of the learner. It should also help the learner focus on the relevant aspects of what is learned, store the information logically in memory, and efficiently recall the information and skill at a later time. The summative evaluator should be aware of the current principles for designing effective instruction and transfer these design principles to criteria and standards for the evaluation of the materials. Areas of instructional principles that should be used in designing summative evaluations should at least include those from motivation, types of learning (i.e., intellectual skills, verbal information, attitudes, and motor skills), and the instructional strategy.

Motivation   You should particularly focus on the potential of the instruction for motivating learners and learners' perceptions of how interested they were in learning the information and skills presented. The ARCS model (Keller, 1987) provides a helpful summary of the motivational principles that can be used by designers in producing instructional materials and by evaluators in determining the quality of existing instruction. ARCS represents the principles for (1) gaining and then maintaining learner *attention* through instruction that is (2) perceived by the learners to be *relevant* for their personal needs and goals (3) at the appropriate level of difficulty so that learners are *confident* they can succeed if they try, and (4) perceived by learners as *satisfying* in terms of rewards for their investments. The concepts in this principle of motivation can be converted to complementary summative evaluation questions such as the ones presented in Table 12.5.

Types of Learning   The principles of instruction for different types of learning can be used as anchors for focusing the expert judgment phase of a summative evaluation. Table 12.6 contains a checklist based on principles of instruction for intellectual skills, verbal information, attitudes, and motor skills. The questions contained in the checklist are not intended to exhaust the list of learning principle–based questions that could be posed. Instead, they are intended to illustrate the role of these principles in the design of a summative evaluation. Readers who want more information on these principles or their derivation and use in instruction should consult texts on the principles of instruction.

Instructional Strategies   Table 12.7 on page 336 contains a checklist for evaluating the instructional strategies contained in the candidate materials. The left-hand column contains the parts of the instructional strategy, excluding pretests and posttests. Space is provided for two response columns for each set of materials. The first can

table **12.5**	Summative Evaluation Questions from Principles of Motivation (Attention, Relevance, Confidence, Satisfaction)						
ARCS Motivation Model	**Question Areas for Summative Evaluation**	**Instruction 1**		**Instruction 2**		**Etc.**	
		YES	NO	YES	NO	YES	NO
Attention:	1. Are strategies used to gain and maintain the learners' attention (e.g., emotional or personal appeals, questions, thinking challenges, human interest examples, etc.)?						
Relevance:	2. Is the instruction relevant for given target groups and how are learners informed and convinced of the relevance (e.g., information about new requirements for graduation, certification, employment, advancement, self-actualization, etc.)?	___	___	___	___	___	___
Confidence:	3. Are learners likely to be confident at the outset and throughout instruction so that they can succeed (e.g., learners informed of purposes and likely to possess prerequisites; instruction progresses from familiar to unfamiliar, concrete to abstract; vocabulary, contexts, and scope appropriate; challenges present but realistic; etc.)?	___	___	___	___	___	___
Satisfaction:	4. Are learners likely to be satisfied from the learning experience (e.g., relevant external rewards such as free time, employment, promotion, recognition; actual intrinsic rewards such as feelings of success, accomplishment, satisfaction of curiosity, intellectual entertainment, etc.)?						

be used to judge the presence or absence of each strategy component, and the second, marked Attention, can be used to judge the perceived motivational value of each component for the intended learners. Remember that the motivational value depends on the relevance of the material for the learners' interests and needs, their confidence that they can succeed, and the satisfaction they will gain from learning the skills and knowledge. You may choose to check each criterion separately instead of holistically, as formatted in the example. You might also prefer to use a rating scale instead of a Yes–No checklist.

t a b l e

1 2 . 6

Checklist for Examining Characteristics of Instruction Based on Principles of Instruction for Intellectual Skills, Verbal Information, Attitudes, and Motor Skills

I. Intellectual Skills	Instruction 1		Instruction 2		Etc.	
	YES	NO	YES	NO	YES	NO
1. Are learners reminded of prerequisite knowledge they have stored in memory?	___	___	___	___	___	___
2. Are links provided in the instruction between prerequisite skills stored in memory and new skills?	___	___	___	___	___	___
3. Are ways of organizing new skills presented so they can be recalled more readily?	___	___	___	___	___	___
4. Are the physical, role, and relationship characteristics of concepts clearly described and illustrated?	___	___	___	___	___	___
5. Are application procedures clearly described and illustrated for rules and principles?	___	___	___	___	___	___
6. Are quality criteria (characteristics) directly addressed and illustrated for judging adequate versus inadequate results such as answers, products, or performances?	___	___	___	___	___	___
7. Are obvious but irrelevant physical, relational, and quality characteristics and common errors made by beginners directly addressed and illustrated?	___	___	___	___	___	___
8. Do the examples and nonexamples represent clear specimens of the concept or procedure described?	___	___	___	___	___	___
9. Are examples and contexts used to introduce and illustrate a concept or procedure familiar to the learners?	___	___	___	___	___	___
10. Do examples, contexts, and applications progress from simple to complex, familiar to unfamiliar, and/or concrete to abstract?	___	___	___	___	___	___
11. Do practice and rehearsal activities reflect application of the intellectual skills or merely recall of information about the performance of the skill?	___	___	___	___	___	___
12. Does feedback to learners provide corrective information and examples, or does it merely present a correct answer?	___	___	___	___	___	___
13. When appropriate, are follow-through activities such as advancement, remediation, and enrichment present and logical (e.g., address prerequisites, focus on improved motivation, provide additional examples and contexts)?	___	___	___	___	___	___

II. Verbal Information	Instruction 1		Instruction 2		Etc.	
	YES	NO	YES	NO	YES	NO
1. Is new information presented in a relevant context?	___	___	___	___	___	___
2. Are strategies provided for linking new information to related information currently stored in memory (e.g., presentation of familiar analogies, requests for learners to imagine something, or to provide examples from their own experiences)?	___	___	___	___	___	___
3. Is information organized into subsets, and are the relationships of elements within and among subsets explained?	___	___	___	___	___	___
4. Are lists, outlines, tables, or other structures provided for organizing and summarizing information?	___	___	___	___	___	___
5. Are logical mnemonics provided when new information cannot be linked to anything stored in memory?	___	___	___	___	___	___
6. Does rehearsal (practice) include activities that strengthen elaborations and cues (e.g., generating new examples, forming images that will cue recall, refining organizational structure)?	___	___	___	___	___	___

table

12.6   Continued

		Instruction 1		Instruction 2		Etc.	
		YES	NO	YES	NO	YES	NO
7. Does feedback contain information about the correctness of a response as well as information about why a given response is considered incorrect?							
8. Does remediation include additional motivational strategies as well as more rehearsal for recall cues?							

	Instruction 1		Instruction 2		Etc.	
III. Attitudes	YES	NO	YES	NO	YES	NO
1. Are the desired feelings clearly described or inferred?						
2. Are the desired behaviors clearly described or inferred?						
3. Is the link (causality) between the desired feelings and behaviors and the link between them and the subsequent positive consequences clearly established?						
4. Is the link between the undesirable feelings and behaviors and the link between them and the subsequent negative consequences clearly established?						
5. Are the positive and negative consequences that are presented true and believable from the learners' perspective?						
6. Are the positive and negative consequences that are presented ones that are likely to be considered important by target learners?						
7. If vicarious learning is involved, are the target learners likely to generate emotions such as admiration, scorn, empathy, or pity for characters and situations presented to tap these emotions?						
8. If vicarious learning is involved, are the contexts and situations presented familiar and relevant to target learners?						
9. In the feedback, are the positive and negative consequences promised for specific actions experienced either directly or vicariously by learners?						

	Instruction 1		Instruction 2		Etc.	
IV. Motor Skills	YES	NO	YES	NO	YES	NO
1. Does the instruction address similar skills the learner can already perform?						
2. Does the instruction include a visual presentation of the motor skill that illustrates its sequence and timing?						
3. Are complex skills broken down into logical parts for learners' analysis, experimentation, and rehearsal?						
4. Is there provision for integrating the logical parts into performance of the complete skill?						
5. Are common errors and strategies for avoiding them directly addressed?						
6. Is repetitive practice provided to enable learners to smooth out the routine and automate the skill?						
7. Is immediate feedback provided to help learners avoid rehearsing inaccurate executions?						

t a b l e

12.7

Checklist for Evaluating the Learning Components of the Instructional Strategies in Candidate Materials

Learning Component	Candidate 1 PRESENT	Candidate 1 ATTENTION	Candidate 2 PRESENT	Candidate 2 ATTENTION	Candidate 3 PRESENT	Candidate 3 ATTENTION
I. Preinstructional						
A. Initial motivation	X	X	X	X		
B. Objectives	X	X	X	X		
C. Entry skills						
1. Described	X	X	X	X		
2. Sample items	X	X	X	X		
II. Information Presentation						
A. Organizational structures						
1. Headings	X	X	X	X	X	X
2. Tables and illustrations	X	X	X	X	X	X
B. Elaborations						
1. Analogies/synonyms	X	X	X	X		
2. Prompts to imagine/consider	X	X	X	X		
3. Examples and nonexamples	X	X	X	X	X	
4. Relevant characteristics of examples	X	X	X	X		
5. Summaries/reviews	X	X	X	X	X	
III. Learner Participation						
A. Relevant practice	X	X	X	X	X	X
B. Feedback						
1. Answers	X	X	X	X	X	X
2. Example solutions	X	X	X	X		
3. Common errors and mistakes	X	X	X	X		
IV. Follow-Through Activities						
A. Memory aids	X	X	X	X		
B. Transfer strategy	X	X	X	X		
TOTALS	17	17	17	17	6	4

A summary row is included at the bottom of the checklist to tally the number of positive responses given for each set of materials. Comparing the candidate materials in this way (Tables 12.4 through 12.7), you can begin to make recommendations about which set of materials appears to be most promising for the organization.

Form for Utility and Feasibility Analysis: Expert Judgment

Table 12.8 contains a form for summarizing and comparing expert judges' perceptions of the utility of the candidate materials. The elements to be judged for each set of materials are listed in the left-hand column, and space for noting the characteristics of each set of materials is included in subsequent columns. The particular elements you choose to compare across sets of materials will depend on the organization's stated needs and resources. The information you record about each set of materials will tend to be descriptive rather than a check indicating the presence or absence of an element or a rating of the quality of the element.

Form for Current Users' Analysis

Information collected about competing materials from current users is similar to that collected during a field trial. The difference is that most of these data are attitudinal rather than performance-based. Table 12.9 contains a summary of the types of information you may wish to gather from users.

The factors to consider are again listed in the left-hand column. The evaluator response format you use will differ from the previous ones for this data-gathering

| table 12.8 | Form for Documenting and Comparing the Utility of Competing Materials |

	Candidate 1				Candidate 2				
	MATERIALS		USERS' SATISF.		MATERIALS		USERS' SATISF.		ETC.
Feasibility Questions	Yes	No	Yes	No	Yes	No	Yes	No	
I. Characteristics of materials									
A. Do materials contain:									
1. Learner guides/syllabi?	___	___	___	___	___	___	___	___	
2. Instructor's manual?	___	___	___	___	___	___	___	___	
3. Test items or item bank?	___	___	___	___	___	___	___	___	
B. Can the materials be:									
4. Individually paced?	___	___	___	___	___	___	___	___	
5. Group paced?	___	___	___	___	___	___	___	___	
6. Used in a traditional classroom?	___	___	___	___	___	___	___	___	
7. Used in a learning center?	___	___	___	___	___	___	___	___	
8. Used at home or in library?	___	___	___	___	___	___	___	___	
C. Do the materials require:									
9. Special instructor capabilities?	___	___	___	___	___	___	___	___	
10. Special equipment?	___	___	___	___	___	___	___	___	
11. Special environments?	___	___	___	___	___	___	___	___	
D. How long does it typically take to:									
12. Complete one study session?	___	___	___	___	___	___	___	___	
13. Complete one unit?	___	___	___	___	___	___	___	___	
14. Complete the instruction?	___	___	___	___	___	___	___	___	
15. Complete the test?	___	___	___	___	___	___	___	___	
E. (Current users' opinions) Do the materials lead to:									
16. Expected achievement level?	___	___	___	___	___	___	___	___	
17. Expected attitude and motivation?	___	___	___	___	___	___	___	___	
18. Adequate transfer to job or next unit?	___	___	___	___	___	___	___	___	
19. Accomplished goals and mission?	___	___	___	___	___	___	___	___	
F. Costs	$ ___	___			$ ___	___			

| table 12.9 | Information Gathered from Current Users of the Materials |

	Candidate 1		Candidate 2		Candidate 3	
	USER 1	USER 2	USER 1	USER 2	USER 1	USER 2
1. Instructional needs for which materials are used?						
2. Entry skills of target learners?						
3. Characteristics of target learners?						
4. Achievement level of learners on pretests?						
5. Achievement level of learners on posttests?						
6. Achievement of learners in the performance context?						
7. Attitudes of learners about materials?						
8. Setting in which materials are used?						
9. Current satisfaction with materials?						
10. Plans for continuing use of materials?						

activity. You will need space to record the opinions of multiple users for each set of materials. Space for the responses for two users of each set of materials is included on the form in Table 12.9.

The reader will note that there is no Case Study: Group Leadership Training section in this chapter. The training program completed as part of the group leadership project would be a one-of-a-kind product for the Neighborhood Watch context, and thus would not be a candidate for any logical comparative analysis. The case study did, however, assume grant funding from the state to develop training for Neighborhood Crime Watch leaders, and most grants of this type would include requirements for project evaluation and reporting. One of the purposes for such an evaluation requirement would undoubtedly be documentation of the effectiveness of the training program. Summative evaluation methodology would be required, but lacking comparative analyses, would largely take the form of extended field trials within geographical locations and among trainee populations that were representative of training that occurred throughout the state. Evaluation procedures, therefore, would be similar to the field trial methodology described in Chapter 11.

SUMMARY

Summative evaluations are conducted to make decisions about whether to maintain or adopt instruction. The primary evaluator in a summative evaluation is rarely the designer or developer of the instruction; the evaluator is frequently unfamiliar with the materials, the organization requesting the evaluation, or the setting in which the materials are evaluated. Such evaluators are referred to as external evaluators; these evaluators are preferred for summative evaluations because they have no personal investment in the instruction and are likely to be more objective about the strengths and weaknesses of the instruction.

Instructional designers make excellent summative evaluators because of their understanding of the instructional design process, the characteristics of well-designed instruction, and the criteria for evaluating instruction. These skills provide them with the expertise for designing and conducting the expert judgment as well as the field trial phases of the summative evaluation.

The design of the expert judgment phase of summative evaluation is anchored in the model for systematically designing instruction. Similar to initially designing instruction, the materials evaluator begins by judging the congruence between the instructional needs of an organization and the goals for candidate instructional materials. Inappropriate materials are rejected, and promising materials are further evaluated. Next, the completeness and accuracy of the content presented in the materials are evaluated. The standard for this evaluation is an instructional goal analysis with required subordinate skills. Content experts are involved in either producing or verifying the quality of the skills diagram. Again, inappropriate materials are rejected, and promising materials are further evaluated. These materials are then evaluated for the quality of their instructional strategies, their utility, and their influence on current users. Materials that appear sound following these evaluation activities are then subjected to a field trial.

During the field trial phase, the instruction is evaluated for its effectiveness with the target group in the intended setting. Following the evaluation, both the strengths and the weaknesses of the instruction are documented in the areas of learner performance and attitudes, instructor attitudes, and implementation requirements. The report should be designed and written with the readers' needs in mind.

RUBRIC FOR EVALUATING SUMMATIVE EVALUATIONS

The following is a rubric designers can use to review summative evaluation procedures. The evaluation should include the expert judgment analysis (if one was conducted), the field trial phase of the evaluation, and an examination of the final evaluation report submitted to the organization.

Designer note: If an element is not relevant for your project, mark NA in the No column.

No	Some	Yes	**A. Expert Judgment Phase** Are the following analyses included:
___	___	___	1. Congruency (instructional goals, organizational needs, and resources)?
___	___	___	2. Content analysis (complete, accurate, and current)?
___	___	___	3. Design analysis (instructional strategy and motivation)?

No	Some	Yes	
—	—	—	4. Feasibility analysis (materials convenient, durable, cost-effective, appropriately paced, and acceptable to learners)?
—	—	—	5. Current user (target learners achievement/attitudes, instructors' skills/attitudes, resources, materials feasibility, problems, and plans)?
—	—	—	6. Clear data summaries and analyses in report to organization?

B. Field Trial Phase (Outcomes Analysis)   Are the following areas examined for their instructional impact:

No	Some	Yes	
—	—	—	1. Learners' achievement and attitudes?
—	—	—	2. Transfer of skills to performance context?
—	—	—	3. Organization better meeting mission and goals?
—	—	—	4. Management attitudes concerning utility, feasibility, and resources?
—	—	—	5. Instructors needed and training required?
—	—	—	6. Procedures needed (equipment, personnel, facilities, schedules)?
—	—	—	7. Data summaries and descriptions in a summary report?

C. Reports to Organization   Do reports contain clear:

No	Some	Yes	
—	—	—	1. Descriptions of evaluation procedures used?
—	—	—	2. Data summaries?
—	—	—	3. Impact analysis and conclusions?

D. Other

No	Some	Yes	
—	—	—	1.
—	—	—	2.

PRACTICE

1. What is the main purpose of a summative evaluation?

2. What are the two main phases of a summative evaluation?

3. Why is the first phase of a summative evaluation often necessary?

4. Name five different types of analyses conducted during the first phase of a summative evaluation and the types of instruments used to collect the information.

5. What is the main decision made following the second phase of a summative evaluation?

6. Name two different types of analyses conducted during the second phase of a summative evaluation and the procedures used to collect information for each type.

7. Contrast the purposes for formative and summative evaluations.

8. Contrast the position of the evaluator in formative and summative evaluations.

9. Contrast the final products of formative and summative evaluations.

FEEDBACK

1. Purpose: to document the strengths and weaknesses of instruction

2. Phases: expert judgment and field trial

3. Expert judgment: to determine the potential of candidate instruction for meeting the needs of the organization

4. Types of analyses conducted during expert judgment phase:
   - Congruence analysis—information summary form
   - Content analysis—product checklist or rating scale
   - Design analysis—product checklist or rating scale
   - Utility and feasibility analysis—information summary form, product checklist, or rating scale
   - Current users' analysis—information summary form, product checklist, or rating scale

5. Field trial: to document the effectiveness of instruction with target learners in the intended setting

6. Types of analyses conducted during the field trial:
   - Outcomes analysis (instructional impact on learner, job, organization)—criterion-referenced tests, attitude questionnaires, interviews, observations, company records
   - Management analysis (attitudes satisfactory, implementation feasible, costs reasonable?)—questionnaire, interview, observation, company records

7. Purpose:
   - *Formative evaluation:* To collect data in order to revise instruction
   - *Summative evaluation:* To collect data in order to document the strengths and weaknesses of the instruction

8. Evaluator Position:
   - *Formative evaluation:* Evaluators are typically designers with a personal investment in the improvement of the instruction
   - *Summative evaluation:* Evaluators are external personnel who can objectively evaluate the quality of instruction produced by others

9. Final Products:
   - *Formative evaluation:* Prescriptions for the revision of materials and revised materials
   - *Summative evaluation:* An evaluation report for decision makers that documents the purpose, procedures, results, and recommendations from the study

REFERENCES AND RECOMMENDED READINGS

Alexander, M. E., & Christoffersen, J. (2006). The total evaluation process: Shifting the mental model. *Performance Improvement, 45*(7), 23–28. The authors argue for establishing return on investment considerations during initial performance analysis work and then addressing considerations throughout design, development, and implementation.

Campbell, P. B., Perlman, L. K., & Hadley, E. N. (2003). Recommendations and voices from the field: Thoughts from the CLASS summative evaluation. In R. Bruning, C. A. Horn, & L. M. PytlikZillig (Eds.), *Web-based learning: What do we know? Where do we go?* Greenwich, CT: Information Age Publishing. Focus on learner perspectives in web-based instruction.

Carey, L. M., & Dick, W. (1991). Summative evaluation. In L. J. Briggs, K. L. Gustafson, & M. H. Tillman (Eds.), *Instructional design: Principles and applications.* Englewood Cliffs, NJ: Educational Technology Publications. Summary of summative evaluation procedures.

Cronbach, L., & Associates. (1980). *Toward reform of program evaluation.* San Francisco: Jossey-Bass. This book takes the position that the evaluator serves in a supportive role in the instructional design process.

Draper, S. W. (1997). The prospects for summative evaluation of CAI in HE. *Association of Learning Technology Journal, 5*(1), 33–39. Draper describes the utility of summative evaluation and some strategies for evaluating instructional software for computer assisted learning. His article can be accessed at the following web address: www.psy.gla.ac.uk/~steve/summ.html.

Fitzpatrick, J. L., Sanders, J. R., & Worthen, B. R. (2004). *Program evaluation: Alternative approaches & practical guidelines* (3rd ed.). Boston: Allyn & Bacon. Standards- and procedures-oriented, the focus of the text is program rather than instructional materials evaluation, although transfers can be made.

Gagné, R. M., Wager, W. W., Golas, K. C., & Keller, J. M. (2004). *Principles of instructional design* (5th ed.). Belmont, CA: Wadsworth/Thomson Learning. This test includes a brief description of the summative evaluation process from the instructional designer's point of view.

Keller, J. M. (1987). The systematic process of motivational design. *Performance and Instruction, 26*(9), 1–8. Focus on attention, relevance, confidence, and satisfaction from learners' perspective.

Kirkpatrick, D. L. (2006). *Evaluating training programs: The four levels* (3rd ed.). San Francisco: Berrett-Koehler. In Kirkpatrick's model, evaluation is the 10th of 10 steps that resemble the Dick & Carey ID process. The four levels of evaluation are reaction, learning, behavior, and results. The third edition describes the levels, includes considerations for e-learning and transfer of learning, discusses a fictitious model case, and provides case studies of a wide range of successful applications.

Morrison, G. R., Ross, S. M., & Kemp, J. E. (2007). *Designing effective instruction* (5th ed.). Hoboken, NJ: Wiley. This edition covers designs, data display's, and interpretations for summative evaluation.

Phillips, J. J. (1997). *Handbook of training evaluation and measurement methods* (3rd ed.). Houston, TX: Gulf

Publishing. Includes procedures for data management and has several chapters on analysis of return on training investment.

Phillips, J. J., & Stone, R. D. (2002). *How to measure training results: A practical guide to tracking the six key indicators.* New York: McGraw-Hill. Data analysis for relating six types of measures to an organization's bottom line and strategic goals.

Smith, M. E., & Brandenburg, D. (1991). Summative evaluation. *Performance Improvement Quarterly,* 4(2), 35–58. Summary of summative evaluation issues.

Stake, R. E. (2004). *Standards-based and responsive evaluation.* Thousand Oaks, CA: Sage Publications. Design, conduct, synthesis, and interpretation in evaluation studies. Also addresses ethics in evaluation.

Stufflebeam, D. L. (2001). *Evaluation models: New directions for evaluation.* San Francisco: Jossey-Bass. Reviews twenty-two evaluation models. Stufflebeam's CIPP model is the one now predominantly used in educational evaluation.

Stufflebeam, D. L., & Shinkfield, A. J. (2007). *Evaluation theories, models, and applications.* San Francisco: Jossey-Bass. A comprehensive evaluation resource that includes application of the Joint Committee *Program Evaluation Standards* to implementations.

APPENDIXES

Many readers of this textbook are educators using this book as a resource for developing their own instruction. The examples in this section relate to school curriculum to aid in applying the Dick and Carey Model to school learning. We thought it would be helpful for all readers to see abbreviated example products from each step in the design model collected together in one place. It should benefit those of you who are required to document your design process and develop materials as a course project. The following list will help you locate materials in the Appendixes.

Appendix A Design Decisions from Front-End Analysis and Instructional Goal for Writing Composition

Front-End Analysis	Design Decisions
I. Needs Assessment	During a middle school faculty meeting called to discuss problems of students' written composition, teachers decided to conduct a needs assessment study. Each teacher assigned a short essay for his or her students to be written on a common topic. A newly formed evaluation team of teachers from across the school district reviewed the themes to identify possible common problems. They reported that students typically use one type of sentence—namely, simple declarative sentences—to communicate their thoughts rather than varying their sentence structure by purpose or complexity. Additionally, punctuation other than periods and commas was absent from students' work, and commas were rare.
II. Instructional goal and relationship to needs	Teachers decided to design special instruction that focused students on • Writing a variety of sentence types based on sentence purpose • Writing using a variety of sentence structures that vary in complexity • Using a variety of punctuation to match sentence type and complexity Through instruction focused directly on the problems identified in the needs assessment, they hoped to change the current pattern of simplistic similarity found in students' compositions.
III. Clarifying the instructional goal	They decided to create two units of instruction with the following goals. In written composition, students will 1. Use a variety of sentence types and accompanying punctuation based on the *purpose* and *mood* of the sentence 2. Use a variety of sentence types and accompanying punctuation based on the *complexity* or *structure* of the sentence
IV. General description of the intended learners	The composition units with their special emphasis on sentence variety were judged most appropriate for sixth-grade classes that contain students presently achieving at average and above-average levels of language expression. These groups will be very heterogeneous in their current writing skill; therefore, instruction on writing sentence types as well as on using sentence types in compositions should be included in the materials.
V. General description of the performance context	The performance context is the school regardless of the subject area, any community group or organization where students may need to produce written work, and jobs they may have that require it.
VI. General description of the learning context, if different	The learning context is the school classroom and web-based instruction that can be accessed by students in the classroom, in the school media center/library, and at home.
VII. Description of any tools the learners will need to accomplish the goals	Students will need a personal computer with word processing to practice their writing skills, and they will need an instructional system (such as Blackboard) that delivers and manages instruction and assessments. Personal computers were loaned to all sixth-grade students in the district at the beginning of the year. Most schools in the district have wireless Internet connections within the upper grades classrooms, the learning center/libraries, and the teachers' workrooms. The district also has acquired Blackboard to enhance instruction within the schools and support student access to instruction from home.

Appendix B   Goal Analysis of the Instructional Goal on Writing Composition

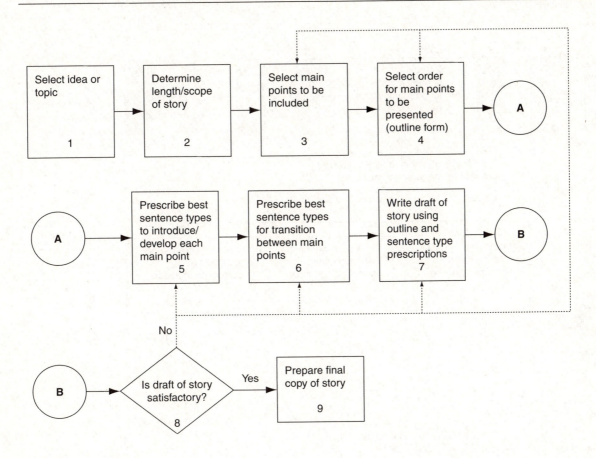

Appendix C Hierarchical Analysis of Declarative Sentence Portion of Writing Composition Goal with Entry Skill Lines

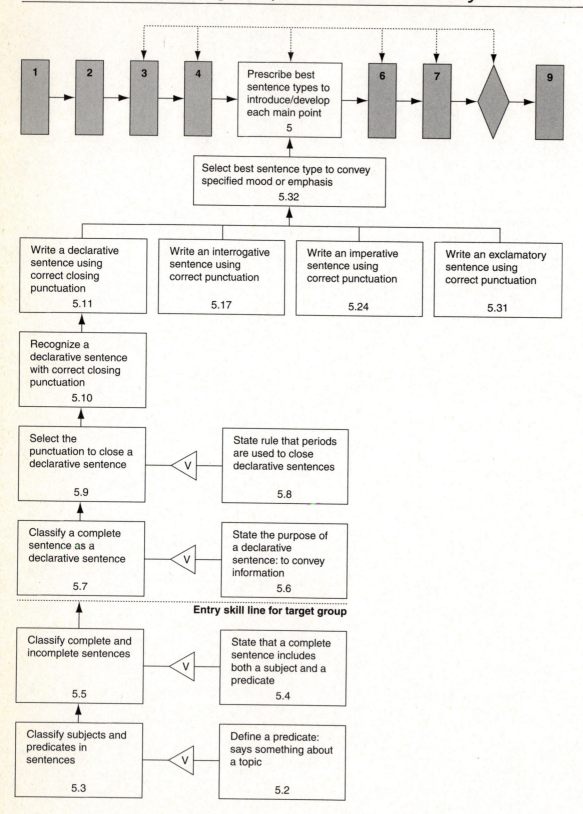

Appendix D   Analysis of Learner Characteristics, Performance Context, and Learning Context

Learner Characteristics for Sixth-Grade Students in Writing Instruction

Information Categories	Data Sources	Learner Characteristics
I. Abilities		
A. Entry skills	Needs assessment data from students' writing tests Interviews with teachers	Students tend • To write using simple, declarative sentences • To use only periods and commas to punctuate their work
B. Prior knowledge of topic area	Needs assessment data from students' writing tests Interviews with teachers	Students have completed five grades in school in which sentence types, structure, and punctuation have been covered in regular instruction.
C. Educational and ability levels	Permanent records Interviews with teachers	Students in the group are average and above average in their abilities (e.g., stanines 4–9 and percentile scores 27–99). Teachers indicate that all students in the group are very capable of learning and rehearsing the writing skills.
D. General learning preferences	Interviews with teachers and students	Students enjoy working with the computer and enjoy learner participation activities. They like working in class rather than being asked to complete large writing assignments as homework.
II. Attitudes		
A. Attitudes toward content	Interviews with teachers and tryout students	Teachers report that students vary widely in their receptivity to writing instruction and their willingness to practice their writing in journals and other writing assignments. Students interviewed verified this diverse opinion. For some it was their favorite subject, whereas for others it was their least favorite and a chore.
B. Attitudes toward potential delivery system	Interviews with teachers and tryout students	Teachers believe that the web-based instruction as well as the laptops students have for their writing assignments will be good motivators for students. They also think that an additional motivator or "hook" will be needed to motivate all of the students. Students want to be selected for the new writing program to gain access to computers in the classroom.
C. Motivation for instruction (ARCS)	Interviews with teachers and students	Students expect to pay attention to the computer. Most would like to write better (some said faster). They think they can learn to use sentence variety. Some think that learning to write better would make others respect them more. Teachers again indicate a diverse group with some students well motivated and others not motivated at all.
D. Attitudes toward training organization	Interviews with teachers and students	Varied perceptions of the effectiveness of the teachers and school. Most students are very positive while some appear negative and disgruntled with both school and teachers.
III. General group characteristics	Overall impressions	Group very heterogeneous in achievement and motivation. All in group can learn and improve their writing skills. Students need a writing vehicle (story, etc.), that is motivational and that will enable students to learn skills and practice in short rather than long writing assignments.

Performance and Learning Contexts for Writing Composition

Reader note: In this school, the learning and performance contexts are the same so no separate analysis of the performance context is required.

Information Categories	Data Sources	Performance Site Characteristics
1. Managerial/ supervisory support	Interviews with: Principals Teachers Parents	All are pleased with the use of computer-based, individualized instruction and the word processors as part of an overall program to improve students' writing skills. The principal has suggested creating a sixth-grade newsletter as a motivational tool and an outlet for students' writings, as long as all sixth graders are allowed to participate. She also suggested that the "newsletter" be distributed via the Blackboard system, perhaps as an "organization" space, thereby eliminating the costs of printing and distribution and initiating a "green" activity for the school. Parents are pleased with the new emphasis on writing, and they are willing to support their children's and the school's efforts. The PTA has agreed to fund a sixth-grade newspaper if articles are written by sixth graders but available to all grades in the school (supporting reading and writing). The leadership can be described as very positive and supportive of the planned writing initiative.
2. Physical aspects of the site	Interviews with: Students Teachers Media/library center directors Parents District director, Learning Support Center	All sixth-grade students were loaned personal computers at the beginning of the year. About 90 percent of the computers are working at any one time. Schools within the district, including the classrooms and learning centers, are wireless. The district Learning Support Center provides the Blackboard teaching/learning system to teachers and students throughout the district and provides regularly scheduled training for teachers in *using* the system and *managing* students receiving instruction through the system. Teachers are expected to teach their students how to use their computers, how to access the instructional system, and how to use the system. They are also expected to support students and provide elaboration when necessary.
3. Social and learning aspects of site	Interviews with: Students Teachers Media/library center directors	Students can work individually in Blackboard to access the direct instruction using their laptops. They can access the instruction from their classrooms, the media/library centers, and from home if they have a computer and Internet access. The direct instruction will provide • Preinstructional information including motivational material, performance objectives, and information about prerequisites • Presentation with examples and nonexamples • Rehearsal with feedback • Assessment to check whether students have acquired the skills at least at a basic level
4. A description of any tools the learners will have to accomplish the goals		Laptops (personal or school loaned)

Appendix E   Design Evaluation Chart for Subordinate Skills, Performance Objectives, and Parallel Test Items

Instructional Goal: In written composition, students will (1) use a variety of sentence types and accompanying punctuation based on the *purpose* and *mood* of the sentence and (2) use a variety of sentence types and accompanying punctuation based on the *complexity* or *structure* of the sentence.

Terminal Objective: In written composition, use a variety of sentence types and accompanying punctuation based on the *purpose, mood,* and *complexity* of the sentence. Sentences will be judged on format for sentence type, punctuation, sentence type by sentence purpose, and sentence variety within paragraphs.

Parallel Test Item: Write a one-page description or story that includes different kinds of sentences to hold your readers' interest. In your story, remember to use

1. At least *two* of each of the following types of sentences: declarative, interrogative, imperative, and exclamatory
2. Only complete sentences
3. Correct punctuation based on the type of sentence and mood
4. The best type of sentences to convey the idea you wish

Subordinate Skills	Performance Objectives	Parallel Test Items
5.1 Define *subject*.	5.1 Given the term *subject*, define the term by purpose.	1. Define the subject part of a sentence. 2. What does the *subject* part of a sentence do? The subject ○ Shows the sentence is beginning ○ Is capitalized ○ Shows action ○ Names the topic
5.2 Define *predicate*.	5.2 Given the term *predicate*, define the term. The definition must include that the predicate says something about the subject or topic.	1. Define the predicate part of a sentence. 2. What does the *predicate* part of a sentence do? The predicate tells something about the_____ ○ Subject ○ Verb ○ Adjectives ○ Prepositions

5.3 Classify subjects and predicates in complete sentences.	5.3 Given several complete simple declarative sentences, locate all the subjects and predicates.	1. Is the subject or the predicate underlined in these sentences? If neither is underlined, choose Neither.
		  a. <u>The carnival</u> was a roaring success.
		    ○ Subject ○ Predicate ○ Neither
		  b. <u>The</u> soccer team was victorious this season.
		    ○ Subject ○ Predicate ○ Neither
		  c. Susan got an <u>after-school job</u> weeding flower beds.
		    ○ Subject ○ Predicate ○ Neither

5.4 State that a complete statement includes both a subject and a predicate.	5.4 Given the term *complete sentence*, define the concept. The definition must name both the subject and the predicate.	1. A complete sentence contains both a(n) _____ and a(n) _____. 2. What is a complete sentence? A complete sentence contains a _____. ○ A subject ○ A predicate ○ Neither a subject nor a predicate ○ Both a subject and a predicate

continued

Subordinate Skills	Performance Objectives	Parallel Test Items

5.5 Classify complete and incomplete sentences.	5.5.1 Given several complete and incomplete declarative sentences, locate all those that are complete.	1. Are these sentences complete or incomplete?
		  a. John closely followed the directions.
		    ○ Complete ○ Incomplete
		  b. The team that was most excited.
		    ○ Complete ○ Incomplete
		  c. The dog sled bumped over the frozen land.
		    ○ Complete ○ Incomplete
		  d. Found the lost friends happy to see her.
		    ○ Complete ○ Incomplete

	5.5.2 Given several complete and incomplete declarative sentences, locate all missing subjects and missing predicates.	2. Are these sentences missing a subject *or* a predicate? If they have both a subject and predicate, mark Have both.
		  a. John closely followed the directions.
		    ○ Subject ○ Predicate ○ Have both
		  b. The team that was most excited.
		    ○ Subject ○ Predicate ○ Have both
		  c. The dog sled bumped over the frozen land.
		    ○ Subject ○ Predicate ○ Have both
		  d. Found the lost friends happy to see her.
		    ○ Subject ○ Predicate ○ Have both

5.6 State the purpose of a declarative sentence.	5.6 Given the terms *declarative sentence* and *purpose,* state the purpose of a declarative sentence. The purpose should include to convey/tell information.	1. The purpose of a declarative sentence is to
		  _____.
		2. What *purpose* does a declarative sentence serve? A declarative sentence _____ something.
		  ○ Tells
		  ○ Asks
		  ○ Commands
		  ○ Exclaims

5.7 Classify a complete sentence as a declarative sentence.	5.7 Given several complete simple sentences that include declarative, interrogative, and exclamatory sentences that are correctly or incorrectly closed using a period, locate all those that are declarative.	1. Tell whether these sentences are declarative.
		  a. Are you hungry
		    ○ Declarative ○ Not Declarative
		  b. Put down your pencils please
		    ○ Declarative ○ Not Declarative
		  c. The woods looked quiet and peaceful
		    ○ Declarative ○ Not Declarative
		  d. Wow, look at that huge fire
		    ○ Declarative ○ Not Declarative

5.8 State that periods are used to close declarative sentences.	5.8 Given the terms *declarative sentence* and *closing punctuation*, name the period as the closing punctuation.	1. The closing punctuation used with a declarative sentence is called a _____.
		2. Declarative sentences are closed using what punctuation mark?
		  ○ Quotation mark
		  ○ Exclamation point
		  ○ Question mark
		  ○ Period

5.9 Select the punctuation used to close a declarative sentence.	5.9 Given illustrations of a period, comma, exclamation point, and question mark and the terms *declarative sentence* and *closing punctuation*, select the period.	1. Circle the closing punctuation used to end a declarative sentence.
		  , ! . ? "
		2. Which one of the following punctuation marks is used to end a declarative sentence?
		  ○ , ○ ! ○ . ○ ? ○ "

Subordinate Skills	Performance Objectives	Parallel Test Items

5.10 Recognize a declarative sentence with correct closing punctuation.	5.10 Given several simple declarative sentences with correct and incorrect punctuation, select all the declarative sentences with correct closing punctuation.	1. Which of these sentences have the *correct* ending punctuation mark?
		 a. John likes to read space stories?
		  ○ Correct ○ Incorrect
		 b. I ride two miles to school on the bus.
		  ○ Correct ○ Incorrect
		 c. Sometimes I go skate boarding!
		  ○ Correct ○ Incorrect

5.11 Write declarative sentences with correct closing punctuation.	5.11 Write declarative sentences on: (1) selected topics and (2) topics of student choice. Sentences must be complete and closed with a period.	1. Write five declarative sentences that describe today's school assembly. 2. Choose an event that happened in our class during the last two weeks. Write five declarative sentences about the event that could be used in a "news" story.

Appendix F Instructional Strategy for Cognitive Instruction: The Objective Sequence and Clusters, Preinstructional Activities, and Assessment Activities

Objective Sequence and Clusters

Six lessons (each column below) with objectives clustered by lesson and sequenced within and across lessons. Allow one hour for each lesson

1	2	3	4	5	6
5.6	5.12	5.18	5.25	5.11	5.32
5.7	5.13	5.19	5.26	5.17	
5.8	5.14	5.20	5.27	5.24	
5.9	5.15	5.21	5.28	5.31	
5.10	5.16	5.22	5.29		
5.11	5.17	5.23	5.30		
		5.24	5.31		

Preinstructional Activities

Motivation

1. Learning Environment: The class will begin a school newsletter to be distributed throughout the school and perhaps the district using the district's Blackboard organization site. Sixth-grade students will plan for and manage the newsletter, and they will write the articles for it.
2. Writing Different Types of Sentences: A newsletter article will be used as an introduction. It will be on a topic of high interest to sixth graders, and it will contain all four sentence types to illustrate the point of variety and increased interest of the article through varying sentence type.

Objectives

Each of the four types of sentences in the sample story will be highlighted and described in the introduction. The purpose of the unit, learning to write stories that contain a variety of sentence types, will be included.

Entry Skills

1. Newsletter: Students will be reminded of the classes' problem-solving steps applied on previous assignments and use them for planning and developing the newsletter (clarify problem, look for solutions, try out and refine solutions, and monitor effectiveness).
2. Writing: Since there are several entry skills noted in the instructional analysis, a test including entry skills will be developed and administered to determine whether students have the required prerequisite skills.

Assessment

Entry Skills

The test will be short and consist of items covering skills 5.1, 5.2, 5.3, 5.4, and 5.5. If some learners do not have the prerequisites, then they will be directed to instruction for them as the first lesson (individualized through Blackboard). The assessment will be developed and administered through Blackboard.

Pretest

The pretest will have two parts. Students will be asked to write a short newsletter article using the four types of sentences, and their articles will be assessed using a scoring rubric. Each lesson (e.g., declarative sentences) will also have an objective test within Blackboard that is administered just prior to the lesson, and it will include only the subskills for that lesson. This assessment can eventually function as a branching mechanism for students who have previously mastered the skills. This test will be referred to using terms such as *recap* or *review* in directions to students.

Embedded Tests

An embedded test will be administered immediately following each lesson, and it will cover the subordinate skills from the lesson. These tests will be used to diagnose problems students may be having with these subordinate skills, and they will eventually become practice or rehearsal with feedback. In discussions with students, these assessments will also be referred to using terms such as *recap* or *review* in directions to students.

Posttests

Students will be administered two forms of posttests. One will be administered after instruction is completed for the unit, it will be objective in format, and it will enable checking whether students have the basic skills mastered. The second will be an alternative assessment format in the form of a newsletter article (monitor effectiveness step from problem-solving strategy). The instructor, young author, and young colleagues will review the article(s) and provide (1) praise for validation and (2) suggestions for improvement for each student. This particular review will focus on the use of the four sentence types. The article assessment will occur many times over the year and focus on a variety of writing skills (e.g., paragraphs, complex sentences, transition, sequence, elaboration, narratives, various sentence structures). The articles along with the reviews will become part of the students' writing portfolios. These portfolios will enable the teacher, student, and parents to monitor writing progress over the year.

Follow-Through Activities

Memory Aid

Students will develop a checklist of criteria for judging sentence types and articles they can use to evaluate their stories and articles. The teachers will provide the first simple rubric based on the lesson and students will modify it for their work. Students will be reminded to use the checklist in reviewing and editing their stories and in assisting their colleagues.

Transfer Strategy

There are two transfer strategies used: (1) applying their problem-solving strategy from a previous unit in this new newsletter environment and (2) reinforcing writing for reasons other than "the teacher assigned it."

Appendix G   Instructional Strategy for Content Presentation, Student Participation, and Lesson Time Allocation Based on the Strategy

Content Presentation		Student Participation	
CONTENT	EXAMPLES AND NONEXAMPLES	PRACTICE ITEMS	FEEDBACK

Objective 5.6
State Purpose of Declarative Sentence

Declarative sentences are used to convey information, to tell the reader something.	Use declarative simple sentences on the topics of interest students named in their newsletter interest inventory. Make all the example sentences on the same topic with a beginning, middle, and end sequence. For example: (1) Tom really enjoys space stories. (2) He has a subscription to a space fiction magazine. (3) He can't wait for each edition to come in the mail each month. (4) He reads it cover to cover before he will do anything else.	Direct students to tell what a declarative sentence does and what each of the sentences presented tells them. For example, What does a declarative sentence do? What does Tom like to read? Where does he get his information?	Tell again that a declarative sentence is used to convey information and point out *what* each of the sentences tells the reader.

Objective 5.7
Classify a Complete Sentence As Declarative

Declarative sentences are used to convey information to tell the reader something.	Use declarative simple sentences on the topics of interest students named in their newsletter interest inventory. Make all the example sentences on the same topic with a beginning middle, and end sequence. (See previous example in 5.6.) Use interrogative, imperative, and exclamatory sentences as nonexamples and point out why each is not an example without teaching about them. Stay focused on declarative sentences. For example: (1) What does Tom like to read? (2) Where does he get his stories? (3) What does he get in the mail? (4) Tom, stop reading right now.	Give students a list of sentences *on the same topic* and have them classify the declarative ones. Use interrogative, imperative, and declarative sentences in the set. *Remove the punctuation* from the sentences so they must classify using only the message as a clue.	Restate rule for declarative sentences and show *why* sentences presented are or are not declarative sentences.

Objective 5.8
State Periods Used to Close Declarative Sentences.

Periods are used to close declarative sentences.	Use three to five declarative simple sentences with their periods highlighted (e.g., bold print, color) on the topics of interest students named in their newsletter interest inventory. Make all the example sentences on the same topic with a beginning, middle, and end sequence. (See previous example in 5.6.)	Have students name *period* or select the name from among a list of punctuation mark names. For example: (1) What punctuation mark is used to close declarative sentences? (2) Does a period, comma, or exclamation point close a declarative sentence?	Restate that the period is used to close declarative sentences.

Content Presentation		Student Participation	
CONTENT	EXAMPLES AND NONEXAMPLES	PRACTICE ITEMS	FEEDBACK

Objective 5.9
Select Punctuation to Close Sentence

Periods are used to close declarative sentences.	Same format as subordinate skill 5.8 but different examples. Repeat the example sentences but replace the punctuation marks with punctuation from other sentence types and point out the mismatch between sentence content and incorrect punctuation mark.	Present three to five declarative simple sentences on the topics of interest with their periods omitted. Make all the example sentences on the same topic with a beginning, middle, and end sequence. (See previous example in 5.6.) Have students select the punctuation mark—period (.), question mark (?), or exclamation mark (!)—to close the sentences.	State that periods should be used to close all the declarative sentences. Show correct punctuation for illustration sentences.

Objective 5.10
Recognize Declarative Sentences with Correct Punctuation

Only periods are used to close declarative sentences.	Use three to five declarative simple sentences with their periods highlighted (e.g., bold print, color) on the topics of interest students named in their newsletter interest inventory. Make all the example sentences on the same topic with a beginning, middle, and end sequence. (See previous example in 5.6.) Present another set of simple declarative sentences on the same topic with correct and incorrect ending punctuation. Explain why each of the sentences is or is not correct.	Provide an additional set of simple declarative sentences on one topic of interest with correct and incorrect ending punctuation. Have students select the correctly punctuated declarative sentences.	Indicate *why* declarative sentences with incorrect punctuation are incorrect.

Content Presentation	Student Participation	
CONTENT	PRACTICE ITEMS	FEEDBACK

Objective 5.11
Write a Declarative Sentence with Correct Punctuation

The content for this skill was covered in its subordinate skills. At this point, students should be encouraged to write on a topic they know about. Figuring out what to write is a very different skill than recognizing correctly written declarative sentences. The content will be the directions of what to do.	**Practice 1:** Have students convert other types of sentences to declarative sentences. In their conversions, students should stay with the same topic but expand the meaning and add content as needed to change the format. Examples might be: Directions to students: Change the following sentences to declarative ones. Keep with the same topic, but expand or change the information in the sentence as you need to in order to convert the sentence to a declarative one. a. How did (somebody they know from film, or literature) look? b. Where did (somebody they know from town, class, story or literature) go? c. Watch out for lightening! d. Finish your chores before you go outside.	Show examples of how sample sentences can be rewritten as declarative sentences. Remember to tell them that there are many ways to convert the sentences correctly.

Content Presentation		Student Participation	
CONTENT	PRACTICE ITEMS		FEEDBACK

Objective 5.11 (continued)

Practice 2: Have students write a series of three to five declarative sentences on one topic of their choice. Topics they have chosen for their newsletter columns would be a good list of topics from which to choose. Another writing idea may be to describe events or places around the classroom or school.

Provide students with a brief list of criteria they can use to evaluate their sentences as they write them. For example, Do your sentences
- have a subject?
- have a predicate?
- tell something to the reader?
- have a period at the end?
- all describe the same topic?

Lesson Allocation Based on Instructional Strategy	Activity	Minutes Planned
Session 1	Introductory, motivational materials	
	Entry skills assessment	55
Session 2	Newsletter article writing pretest	
Session 3	Pretest and instruction on objectives 5.6–5.11, declarative sentences	55
Session 4	Pretest and instruction on objectives 5.12–5.17, interrogative sentences	55
Session 5	Pretest and instruction on objectives 5.18–5.24, imperative sentences	55
Session 6	Pretest and instruction on objectives 5.25–5.31, exclamatory sentences	55
Session 7	Review of objectives 5.11, 5.17, 5.24, and 5.31, all four sentence types	55
Session 8	Instruction on objective 5.32, selecting best sentence type for a particular purpose or mood	55
Session 9	Objective posttest on objectives 5.6–5.32	60

Student Groupings

Students will work individually using their laptops, and they may work with teacher or small group for question/answer, extra practice, and customized feedback.

Consolidation of Media Selection and Choice of Delivery System for Main Steps

The primary medium will be individualized web-based instruction, but the teacher will be prepared with extra examples, nonexamples, and practice to support small-group work when needed.

Appendix H   Plans for a Constructivist Learning Environment

Planning the Learning Environment

Designs and Materials Needed to Launch the CLE

Goal: Improved writing composition using a variety of sentence types

Learning Objectives: Main step 5: Prescribe best sentence types to introduce/develop each main point (in article)

Rationale: During a middle school faculty meeting called to discuss problems of students' written composition, teachers decided to conduct a needs assessment study. Each teacher assigned students a short essay to be written on a common topic. A newly formed evaluation team of teachers from across the school district reviewed the themes to identify possible common problems. They reported that students typically use one type of sentence—simple declarative sentences—to communicate their thoughts rather than varying their sentence structure by purpose or complexity. Additionally, punctuation other than periods and commas was absent from students' work, and commas were rare. Teachers decided to design special instruction that focused students on (1) writing a variety of sentence types based on sentence purpose, (2) writing using a variety of sentence structures that vary in complexity, and (3) using a variety of punctuation to match sentence type and complexity. Through instruction focused directly on the problems identified in the needs assessment, they hoped to change the current pattern of simplistic similarity found in students' compositions.

Constructivist Focus: Reasoning, critical thinking, problem solving, retention, understanding, and use

Pedagogical Model: Project-based learning

Scenario: The newsletter (suggested earlier by the needs assessment team and principal) will be used to create the desired learning environment. Students will work in cooperative teams to plan and produce their newsletters for student colleagues throughout the school and perhaps the district. The newsletter will provide opportunities for

- Natural motivation or a reason for practicing their writing skills
- Student-centered learning as students plan and manage their newsletter as well as plan what to write and how to write their articles (e.g., sports, nature, school events, community events, student heroes, health)
- Practicing, applying, and assessing sentence and paragraph construction skills in an authentic performance context
- Applying the classes' problem-solving strategies from earlier instructional units (i.e., prerequisite skills: clarify problem, seek solutions, try out ideas, refine, monitor effectiveness)
- Working cooperatively with their student colleagues and teacher advisors
- Applying criteria from multiple perspectives to judge their writing (e.g., format, content, interest, aesthetics, values or appropriateness, legal considerations)

Learning Resource Materials
- Structure for student activity for managing the newsletter (see section 2 following matrix)
- List of newsletter columns (topics) selected by students
- Individualized web-based instruction on writing various types of sentences (simple, complex, and compound), paragraphs, and articles
- Policies for use of the site to disseminate information established by district's legal personnel, administrators, and parents' advisory team including
  - Legal considerations the district has in providing the site
  - Individuals/groups given access to the site (e.g., students in class, across school, across district; teachers, parents, administrators)

- Types of access groups/individuals have (e.g., authorship; site leader for loading, editing, and deleting submitted materials; reader only)
- Content permitted in district disseminated materials (e.g., age appropriate, lacks bias, meets community and school values)
  - Job aids for
    - Sample middle school–level newsletters and newsletter articles on topics selected by students
    - Other products as identified during the production of the newsletter

Learner Groupings: There will be two different categories of work teams: the newsletter management teams (e.g., content, graphic design, editorial, production) and the column content (creative) teams (e.g., sports, science, school events). All students may choose to serve on one or more of the management teams based on their interest, and they may switch management teams for new experiences or colleagues. All members of the class will serve as writers on one or more of the column content (creative) teams. Students will monitor the monthly newsletter's progress to see whether they have the teams necessary for the tasks that evolve.

Delivery System, Media, and Personnel:
- Blackboard organization site for disseminating the newsletter created by district's Learning Support Center
- E-learning portal to deliver individualized web-based instruction on various types of sentences and composition
- Students' laptops for content research for articles
- Library/media specialists for assisting with topic research
- Sixth-grade language arts teachers
- District instructional designers and instructional technologists
- The teachers and students will identify other school personnel who want to become involved (e.g., art teachers for graphic design, physical education teachers for the sports column, social studies teachers for the history group, science teachers for the space group, music/drama/language arts teachers for the arts column, library/media specialists for content research and technology, and so forth).

Planning for Learner Engagement

Procedures and Activities Anticipated during Engagement

Engage: Engagement will be initiated by discussion within the classes about a middle school group who last year created and published their own newsletter. Positive benefits of the existing newsletter will be discussed, and the teacher will raise questions about whether the class would like to start their own newsletter this year. When, through their discussion with the teachers, the group decides to seek more information about publishing a newsletter, each class will choose one sixth-grade representative from each school to take a field trip to the county office to seek more information. At the school district office, the representatives will meet with the director of Learning and Technology and request permission for sixth graders to produce and publish their own newsletter. The representatives will report the content of the meeting to their classmates, and the classes will then wait one week to learn the verdict (prearranged) of the director's agreement to support the newsletter. Official letters will be sent from the director to the student representative, who will read the letters to their classmates.

Explore: Students seek information about the types of management teams that will be necessary to produce and publish the newsletter and the reading interests of sixth-grade students (columns and articles). They also seek information about the appearance of other student newsletters (graphics, distribution format) and the types of articles produced in them (e.g., topics, length, tone). They will also explore the types of articles they would like to write (e.g., sports, science, arts, school events, town history).

Explain: Students within work teams plan and explain the tasks to be accomplished and their ideas for articles to one another, to their parents, and to the teachers and advisors. They explore with the teacher whether they must write articles individually or can write in pairs or triads.

Elaborate: Their problem-solving, team work, and writing skills will be used in other classes in the school, at home, and for a few, on their jobs.

Evaluate: See authentic assessment in subsequent section

Planning Learning Guidance

Materials and Activities Anticipated for Adaptive Learning Guidance

Scaffolding
- Models
  - Newsletters
  - Articles
- Coaching, questioning by teachers and content advisors
- Peer tutoring from team members and editorial committee
- Individualized instruction in Blackboard on sentence, paragraph, and article types

Planning Authentic Assessment

Materials and Procedures Anticipated for Authentic Assessment

Individual Articles during Development: Students will reflect on the rubrics suggested by the teacher and add criteria they believe should be included. They will use writing format, content interest value, legal, and policy criteria to form and critique their articles individually. They will also work with their teacher advisors (e.g., art, physical education, media specialist) to reflect on and improve their articles.

Single Newsletter Issue Prepublication: Learners who serve on the editorial teams will work with writers to critique single issues of the newsletter prior to production and suggest ideas for revision and refinement.

Postpublication: Students will get "natural" feedback on their articles from siblings, parents, other students in the school, and other teachers.

Portfolio: Individual student's articles will be gathered over the year into a writing portfolio. Student and teacher will review the portfolio each grading period to examine writing progress overall and progress related to the particular lessons covered during the term (e.g., declarative sentences, transition).

Procedural Analysis for Management of Newsletter (Constructivist Learning Environment)

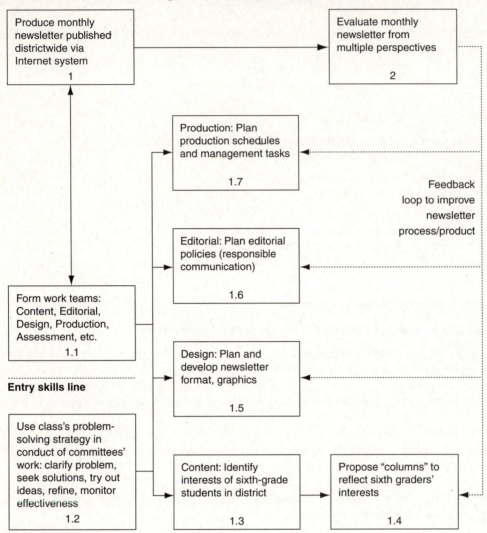

Appendix I   Session 1: Motivational Materials, Unit Objectives, and Assessment for Entry Skills

Designer note: These materials are intended to be delivered via Blackboard where space and color are not issues.

Component	Subskill	Text
Motivation		

Now that the work teams are busy planning for our newsletter, we can begin thinking about writing interesting articles for it. To make our articles interesting, we are going to use many different styles of writing and types of sentences. Are you wondering how you can make your articles most interesting for other sixth graders?

One way we can make our articles more interesting is to use *different types* of sentences when we write them. Using different types of sentences does not change the message, it only changes the way we tell it.

Different kinds of sentences help our readers know what we want to say and how we feel about what we have said. It involves them in what they are reading because it helps the article come alive.

To show you how using several different kinds of sentences makes a newsletter article more interesting, I have written the same article for the next science column two ways.

My story on the left side has only declarative sentences in it, while my story on the right side uses four different kinds of sentences.

Read both stories and compare them.

**There Is No Dark Side
of the Moon**

*by
Lauren Hauser*

**There Is No Dark Side
of the Moon!**

*by
Lauren Hauser*

They say there is no dark side of the moon. Next they will be telling us there is no boogey man or no tooth fairy. The source of ideas about the dark side of the moon needs some explanation. There must be something behind the idea. Rock bands sing about it, and it appears in space stories all the time.

The explanation is simple. Our Earth rotates on an axis. As it turns, it exposes all of its sides every day to anyone watching Earth from the moon. Unlike Earth, our moon does not rotate, so people looking at our moon from Earth always see the same side. When we go to the moon, we will see both daylight and darkness there, because both our Earth and our moon orbit the sun.

What songs and stories refer to as the moon's dark side is actually its far side. The side of the moon facing away from us is called the far side. The side facing us from space is called the near side. Go outside some night this week and look at the *near side* of the full moon.

What? There is no dark side of the moon? Next they will be telling us there is no boogey man or no tooth fairy! If there is no dark side of the moon, where did the idea come from? There must be something behind the idea! Rock bands sing about it, and it appears in space stories all the time.

The explanation is simple. Our Earth rotates on an axis. As it turns, it exposes all of its sides every day to anyone watching Earth from the moon! Unlike Earth, our moon does not rotate, so people looking at the moon from Earth always see the same side. When we go to the moon, will we see both daylight and darkness there? Yes, because both our Earth and our moon orbit the sun.

What songs and stories refer to as the moon's dark side is actually its far side. The side of the moon facing away from us is called the far side. What do you think the side we always see is named? The side facing us from space is called the near side. Go outside some night this week and look at the *near side* of the full moon.

Don't you think the second article tells exactly the same information, only it's more interesting to read? It makes me wonder whether I will ever see Earth from the moon. It also makes me wonder what is on the far side that I can't see. I hope Lauren writes about that in her next column.

When we write our own newsletter articles, we should remember that using several different kinds of sentences will make them more interesting for students all across town.

Component	Subskill	Text
Unit Objectives		

It will be fun to learn to write newsletter articles that have different kinds of sentences in them. Right now let's focus on the following kinds of sentences and choose the type that best fits what we want to say.

Four Types of Sentences

- Declarative sentences *tell* the reader something
- Interrogative sentences *ask* questions
- Imperative sentences *command,* direct, or request something
- Exclamatory sentences *show emotion* or excitement.

Of course, writing articles that have all four kinds of sentences will require some practice. I want to show each of the sentence types to you and help you practice writing each one.

After writing all four sentence types, we are going to use them to create interesting newsletter articles for our first edition.

Let's start with declarative sentences.

Component	Subskill	Text
Entry skills	5.1–5.5	

First, refresh your ideas about *complete* sentences because we will need to use them regardless of the type of sentence we write.

Please click on the **Review** button below to check your memory about complete sentences. To check your answers when you finish, click **Submit** and then click **OK.**

Review

Designer note: The skill codes in the left column would not be present on the entry skills test for students; they are included here to enable you to link the entry skills with the items.

Skills	Item
Entry Skills Test	

5.1.   1. What does the *subject* part of a sentence do? The subject
   ○ Shows the sentence is beginning
   ○ Is capitalized
   ○ Shows action
   ○ Names the topic

5.2.   2. What does the *predicate* part of a sentence do? The predicate tells something about the
   ○ Subject
   ○ Verb
   ○ Adjectives
   ○ Prepositions

5.3.   3. Is the subject or the predicate underlined in these sentences? If neither is underlined, choose Neither.
   a. American students <u>ride</u> Amtrak trains.   ○ Subject   ○ Predicate   ○ Neither
   b. <u>European students</u> ride Eurail trains.   ○ Subject   ○ Predicate   ○ Neither
   c. Students in Japan <u>ride white bullet trains</u>.   ○ Subject   ○ Predicate   ○ Neither

5.4.   4. What is a complete sentence? A complete sentence contains
   ○ A subject
   ○ A predicate
   ○ Neither a subject nor a predicate
   ○ Both a subject and a predicate

5.5.   5. Are these sentences complete or incomplete?
   a. The Iditarod Trail Sled Dog Race.   ○ Complete   ○ Incomplete
   b. Dry, bumpy, cold, dark, and wind-blown.   ○ Complete   ○ Incomplete
   c. The winner took about nine long, dark days to finish.   ○ Complete   ○ Incomplete

   6. Are these sentences missing a subject or a predicate? If they have both a subject and a predicate present, choose Have both.
   a. The Iditarod Trail Sled Dog Race.   ○ Subject   ○ Predicate   ○ Have both
   b. Dry, bumpy, cold, dark, and wind-blown.   ○ Subject   ○ Predicate   ○ Have both

Appendix J   Session 2: Pretest: Writing Newsletter Article and Using Rubric to Evaluate Article

Designer note: For space reasons in this book, we cannot continue the motivational aspect of direct instruction from peer tutors using photographs and dialog. We will continue here with straight text and use the symbol 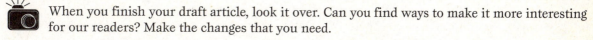 to indicate where a peer-tutor photograph is to be inserted and used with conversation callouts.

Pretest Directions to Students

Component	Subskill	Text
Alternative Assessment Pretest and Rubric	Instructional Goal	

It is time to write your first article for the newsletter because the Content Team has tallied the results of their survey on our interests and picked topics for columns. Choose any one of these column topics for your first article. If you have a better idea for a column, please name it and write your article for that column.

Newsletter Columns

- East Side West Side (All about the Town)
- Entertainment
- Environment
- Our Town in History
- Space
- Sports
- Technology in the News
- Upcoming School Events

Use your laptops and word-processing program to write a two or three paragraph article for the newsletter. Your article should include different kinds of sentences to hold your readers' interest. In your story, remember to use

1. At least *two* of each of the following types of sentences: declarative, interrogative, imperative, and exclamatory
2. Only complete sentences
3. Correct punctuation based on the type of sentence and mood
4. The best type of sentences to convey the idea you wish
5. Correct spelling. Remember to spell-check your work. Put any words you misspell (not typos) on your spelling list.

When you finish your draft article, look it over. Can you find ways to make it more interesting for our readers? Make the changes that you need.

Post your article to Mr. Brown electronically by the end of the period this morning.

You might want to use this rubric to help review your article.

Sample Rubric for Scoring Students' Pretest Articles

Criteria	Sentence Types			
	DECLARATIVE	INTERROGATIVE	IMPERATIVE	EXCLAMATORY
1. Total number of sentences				
2. Number of sentences complete				
a. Number of subjects missing				
b. Number of predicates missing				
3. Number of correct ending punctuation				
4. Number of sentences appropriate for idea				
5. Number of sentences appropriate for mood				

Designer note: Criteria not covered in this unit are omitted from the rubric purposefully.

Appendix K   Session 3: Pretest and Instruction in Subordinate Skills 5.6 through 5.11

Designer note: Recall that is used to indicate where a peer-tutor photograph will be inserted and used with conversation "callouts" to enter the text.

Component	Subskills	Text
Objective Pretest and Instruction	5.6–5.11	

Let's turn our attention to *declarative* sentences. First, refresh your ideas about them because they form the skeleton of all writing.

Please click on the **Review** button below to check your memory about declarative sentences. To check your answers when you finish, click **Submit** and then click **OK.**

Subordinate Skills Pretest

5.6   1. What *purpose* does a declarative sentence serve? A declarative sentence _____ something.
　　　○ Tells
　　　○ Asks
　　　○ Commands
　　　○ Exclaims

5.7   2. Ignore the missing punctuation marks and tell which of these sentences are declarative.
　　　a. Camping with the girl scouts was fun last Saturday   ○ Declarative   ○ Not Declarative
　　　b. Should we have pitched our tents in a circle   ○ Declarative   ○ Not Declarative
　　　c. Always clean up the dishes before campfire begins   ○ Declarative   ○ Not Declarative
　　　d. We heard scary stories about bears around the campfire   ○ Declarative   ○ Not Declarative
　　　e. Oh no, there's a bear outside the tent   ○ Declarative   ○ Not Declarative

5.8   3. Declarative sentences are closed using a
　　　○ Quotation mark
　　　○ Exclamation point
　　　○ Question mark
　　　○ Period

5.9   4. Which of these punctuation marks is used to end a declarative sentence?
　　　○ ,   ○ !   ○ .   ○ ?   ○ "
　　　5. Which of these punctuation marks is used to close a declarative sentence?
　　　○ .   ○ !   ○ ;   ○ ?   ○ :

5.10 6. Which of these declarative sentences ends with the correct punctuation mark?
　　　a. An Iditarod sled dog racer is called a *musher*? ○ Correct ○ Incorrect
　　　b. Last year's last-place musher had a team of 16 dogs. ○ Correct ○ Incorrect
　　　c. The losing musher took 16 days to finish the race. ○ Correct ○ Incorrect
　　　d. The race is so hard that even the last person gets a trophy? ○ Correct ○ Incorrect
　　　e. The trophy for the last musher is called the Red Lantern Award! ○ Correct ○ Incorrect

5.11 7. Choose any event that happened in our class during the last two weeks. In the space below, write four *declarative sentences* about the event that might be used in a "news" story.

SUBMIT

Student Management　　　Please go to Instruction and click on the title: Session 1 Declarative Sentences. *Designer note: Teacher should determine whether to split students for subsequent instruction based on mastery scores from the pretest.*

Component	Subskill	Text
Content Presentation	5.6	Declarative Sentences

 A declarative sentence is used *to tell the reader something or describe something*. When you want to state a fact or describe something in a direct manner, you write a declarative sentence.

Here are some declarative sentences used to state facts.

1. Chiniqua is growing a spice garden beside her back porch.
2. She has five different spices in her garden including mint and basil.
3. She has to finish her homework before she can go to the garden.
4. The whole family loves meals made with her spices.

 A declarative sentence tells us something. Notice that sentence 1 tells us *what* Chiniqua has. She has a garden. Sentence 2 tells us *what* she has in her garden. Sentence 3 tells us *when* she works in the garden, and sentence 4 tells us *how* her family feels about her garden. All these sentences *tell us something*.

 Declarative sentences can also be used *to describe something*. The following sentences are descriptions.

1. It rained really hard the day of the school picnic.
2. The sky was so dark the street lights in the park came on.
3. We were all soaking wet and so were the hot dogs.

 Sentence 1 *describes* the day as rainy, sentence 2 *describes* the picnic day as very dark, and sentence 3 *describes* the students and food.

Component	Subskill	Text
Content Presentation	5.7	

Look at the next two sentences. One is a declarative sentence and one is not. Can you tell the difference? Which one is the declarative sentence?

1. Georgia really enjoyed the soggy picnic.
2. What did Georgia enjoy?

Sentence 1 is the declarative sentence since it tells us *what* Georgia enjoyed. Sentence 2 is *not* declarative. After reading this sentence, we do not know what Georgia liked. Because sentence 2 does not give the reader information, it is *not* a declarative sentence.

Component	Subskill	Text
Practice and Feedback	5.6–5.7	

Let's practice. Read the following pairs of sentences. Which of the sentences are declarative and why?

1. a. What are Segway PTs?
   b. Segway PTs are battery-powered personal transporters.
2. a. Segway PTs can stand still, turn in place, and travel at the speed of walkers.
   b. What can you do with a Segway PT?

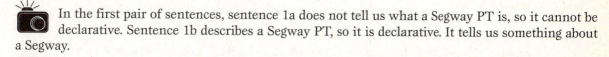 In the first pair of sentences, sentence 1a does not tell us what a Segway PT is, so it cannot be declarative. Sentence 1b describes a Segway PT, so it is declarative. It tells us something about a Segway.

In the second pair of sentences, the declarative sentence (2a) tells us what a Segway PT can do, but sentence 2b does not provide any clues about what we can do with one. Sentence 2b is *not* a declarative sentence.

Component	Subskill	Text
Content Presentation	5.8–5.9	Punctuation for Declarative Sentences

 Punctuation marks are used to close complete sentences. The *period* (.) is the punctuation mark that is *always* used to close a declarative sentence. When you see a period at the end of a sentence, it is a clue that the sentence may be a declarative one.

Other types of sentences may use a period, but a sentence that *provides information* and is *closed with a period* is always a declarative sentence.

 Here are some declarative sentences that are correctly punctuated with periods at the end.

1. Our solar system has the sun and eight planets that are bound to it by gravity.
2. The eight planets share well over 166 moons among them.
3. There are also three dwarf planets including Ceres, Pluto, and Eris.
4. The solar system has billions of small bodies that include asteroids, meteoroids, comets, and interplanetary dust.

 We know these four sentences are declarative because they *describe* our solar system and what it contains, and they are *closed using periods.*

If a sentence appears to be declarative because it tells something or describes something, yet the punctuation mark at the end of the sentence is *not* a period, then the sentence is *not* a declarative one.

Some sentences tell the reader something, and this is a clue that they *might* be declarative. *However,* when a period is *not* used to close the sentence, it is *not* declarative. Look at these sentences taken from a science fiction story.

1. The meteoroid may hit earth!
2. Earth will be destroyed for humans if it hits!

Neither one of these sentences is declarative because periods are *not* used to close them.

Remember, to be a declarative sentence, it must tell the reader something, and close with a period.

Component	Subskill	Text
Practice and Feedback	5.8–5.9	

 Let's practice! Look at these sentences. Which ones are declarative?

1. Welcome to Explore America Camp!
2. Welcome to Explore America Camp.
3. Where are you going to camp this summer?

 The first sentence is *not* declarative. Although it welcomes us to a new camp, it does *not* end with a period. The second sentence is declarative. It welcomes us to the new camp, and it ends with a period. The third sentence is not declarative because it does *not* convey information, and it does *not* end with a period.

Component	Subskill	Text
Embedded Test Items	5.6–5.11	

 Let's review declarative sentences. Please click on the **Review** button below to get the review questions. After you answer all of the questions, remember to **submit** your answers and carefully review the feedback for each question. Pay attention to any mistakes you see and try to figure out why. You may review the information you have just read about declarative sentences after your assessment if you wish.

Subordinate Skills

5.6   1. Why do we use declarative sentences in our writing? We use them to:
      ○ Ask something
      ○ Command something
      ○ Exclaim something
      ○ Tell something

5.7   2. Ignore the missing punctuation marks and tell which of these sentences are declarative.
      a. In the fifteenth century, Indians lived right here in our town
           ○ Declarative   ○ Not Declarative
      b. What kind of Indians were they   ○ Declarative   ○ Not Declarative
      c. Did they live near the school grounds   ○ Declarative   ○ Not Declarative
      d. Wow, I really wish I had known some of them   ○ Declarative   ○ Not Declarative
      e. Read the book about Indians first   ○ Declarative   ○ Not Declarative

5.8   3. Declarative sentences are closed using a
      ○ Question mark
      ○ Period
      ○ Exclamation point
      ○ Quotation mark

5.9   4. Which one of the following punctuation marks is used to end a declarative sentence?
      ○ ;   ○ !   ○ .   ○ ?   ○ :

5.10 5. Which of these declarative sentences end with the correct punctuation mark?
a. Each planet's distance from the sun determines how long its year lasts?
○ Correct   ○ Incorrect
b. An Earth year lasts about 365 Earth days!   ○ Correct   ○ Incorrect
c. Mercury's year lasts only about 88 Earth days.   ○ Correct   ○ Incorrect
d. Neptune's year lasts almost 165 Earth years?   ○ Correct   ○ Incorrect

5.11 6. Choose any one of the topic columns for our newsletter, and write four related *declarative sentences* in the space below that could be used in the column. The columns are: East Side West Side (All about the Town), Entertainment, Environment, Our Town in History, Space, Sports, Technology in the News, and School Events.

SUBMIT

Designer note: Assume that the portion of the objective posttest covering declarative sentences would be constructed using the prescriptions in the instructional strategy and formatted in the same manner as the pretest and embedded test. All test items on the posttest would contain different example sentences.

Appendix L   Group's and Individual's Achievement of Objectives and Attitudes about Instruction

Student-by-Item-by-Objective Data Array for Entry Skills

Obj	5.1	5.2		5.3		5.4		5.5						
Items	1	2	3	4	5	6	7	8	9	10	X	%	Obj	%
STUDENTS														
1							1		1		2	20	0	0
2			1	1	1		1		1		5	50	1	20
3			1	1	1		1		1		5	50	1	20
4	1		1	1	1		1		1		6	60	2	40
5	1	1	1	1	1		1	1	1	1	9	90	4	80
6	1	1	1	1	1	1	1	1	1	1	10	100	5	100
7	1	1	1	1	1	1	1	1	1	1	10	100	5	100
8	1	1	1	1	1	1	1	1	1	1	10	100	5	100
9	1	1	1	1	1	1	1	1	1	1	10	100	5	100
10	1	1	1	1	1	1	1	1	1	1	10	100	5	100
11	1	1	1	1	1	1	1	1	1	1	10	100	5	100
12	1	1	1	1	1	1	1	1	1	1	10	100	5	100
13	1	1	1	1	1	1	1	1	1	1	10	100	5	100
14	1	1	1	1	1	1	1	1	1	1	10	100	5	100
15	1	1	1	1	1	1	1	1	1	1	10	100	5	100
# students correct	12	11	14	14	14	10	15	11	15	11				
% students correct	80	73	93	93	93	66	100	73	100	73				
% obj	80	73		93		66			73					

Note: 1 = correct response; blank = incorrect response; obj = objective

Student-by-Item-by-Objective Data Array for Declarative Sentence Portion of Posttest

Obj	5.6	5.7				5.8	5.9	5.10				5.11						
Items	1	2	3	4	5	6	7	8	9	10	11	12	13	14	15	X	%	Obj
STUDENTS																		
1	1	1	1	1	1	1	1	1		1	1		1		1	12	80	5
2	1	1	1	1	1	1	1	1	1	1	1	1	1	1	1	15	100	6
3	1	1	1	1	1	1	1	1	1	1	1	1	1	1	1	15	100	6
4	1	1	1	1	1	1	1	1	1	1	1	1	1	1	1	15	100	6
5	1	1	1	1	1	1	1	1	1	1	1	1	1	1	1	15	100	6
6	1	1	1	1	1	1	1	1	1	1	1	1	1	1	1	15	100	6
7	1	1	1	1	1	1	1	1	1	1	1	1	1	1	1	15	100	6
8	1	1	1	1	1	1	1	1	1	1	1	1	1	1	1	15	100	6
9	1	1	1	1	1	1	1	1	1	1	1	1	1	1	1	15	100	6
10	1	1	1	1	1	1	1	1	1	1	1	1	1	1	1	15	100	6
11	1	1	1	1	1	1	1	1	1	1	1	1	1	1	1	15	100	6
12	1	1	1	1	1	1	1	1	1	1	1	1	1	1	1	15	100	6
13	1	1	1	1	1	1	1	1	1	1	1	1	1	1	1	15	100	6
14	1	1	1	1	1	1	1	1	1	1	1	1	1	1	1	15	100	6
15	1	1	1	1	1	1	1	1	1	1	1	1	1	1	1	15	100	6
# students correct	15	15	15	15	15	15	15	15	14	15	15	14	15	14	15			
% students correct	100	100	100	100	100	100	100	100	93	100	100	93	100	93	100			
% obj	100		100			100	100			100			93					

Note: 1 = correct response; blank = incorrect response; Obj = objective

Student Performance by Objectives on the Pretest, Embedded Items, and Posttest

Obj	5.6 Purpose			5.7 Identify			5.8 Select Punctuation			5.9 Punctuate			5.10 Recognize			5.11 Write		
STUDENTS	PR	EM	PO	PR	EM	PO	PR	EM	PO	PR	EM	PO	PR	EM	PO	PR	EM	PO
1		1	1		1	1	1	1	1	1	1	1		1				
2		1	1		1	1	1	1	1	1	1	1		1			1	
3		1	1		1	1	1	1	1	1	1	1		1			1	
4		1	1		1	1	1	1	1	1	1	1		1	1		1	
5		1	1		1	1	1	1	1	1	1	1		1	1		1	
6		1	1		1	1	1	1	1	1	1	1		1	1		1	1
7		1	1		1	1	1	1	1	1	1	1		1	1		1	1
8		1	1		1	1	1	1	1	1	1	1		1	1		1	1
9		1	1		1	1	1	1	1	1	1	1		1	1		1	1
10	1	1	1		1	1	1	1	1	1	1	1		1	1		1	1
11	1	1	1	1	1	1	1	1	1	1	1	1	1	1	1	1	1	1
12	1	1	1		1	1	1	1	1	1	1	1	1	1	1	1	1	1
13	1	1	1	1	1	1	1	1	1	1	1	1	1	1	1	1	1	1
14	1	1	1	1	1	1	1	1	1	1	1	1	1	1	1	1	1	1
15	1	1	1	1	1	1	1	1	1	1	1	1	1	1	1	1	1	1
# passing	6	15	15	4	15	15	15	15	15	15	15	15	5	15	12	5	14	10
% passing	40	100	100	27	100	100	100	100	100	100	100	100	33	100	80	33	93	66
diff		+60	0		+73	0		0	0		0	0		+67	−20		+60	−27

Note: 1 = objective mastered, blank = objective not mastered; Pr = pretest, Em = embedded test or rehearsal, Po = posttest; Diff = difference between students passing pretest and posttest on declarative sentences portion of goal; Students 1–5 had not mastered entry skills before beginning instruction

Percentage of All Fifteen Students Who Mastered Each Objective on the Pretest, Embedded Items, and Posttest

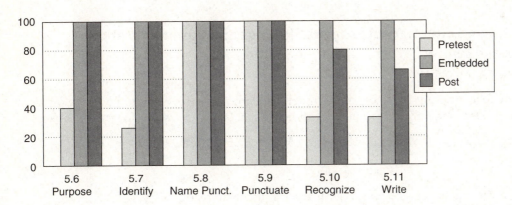

Percentage of Four Students (# 1–4) *Not* Possessing the Required Entry Skills Who Mastered Each Objective on the Pretest, Embedded Items, and Posttest

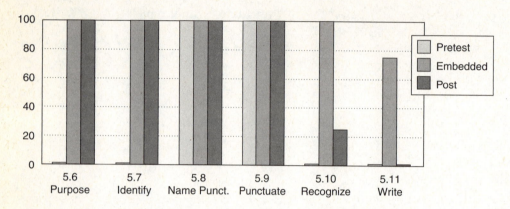

Percentage of Ten Students (#6–15) Possessing the Required Entry Skills Who Mastered Each Objective on the Pretest, Embedded Items, and Posttest

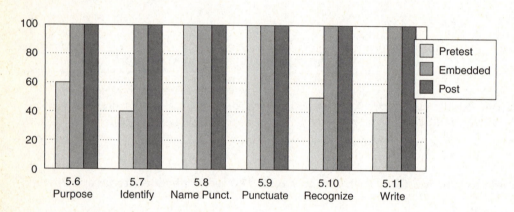

Attitude Survey and Summary of Students' Ratings and Comments about the Materials and Lesson

Help Us Make the Lesson Better

Please answer the following questions to help us understand what you think about the lesson on writing different kinds of sentences. Your comments will help us make better lessons for you. Thanks.

Name ___Summary___ Date ___1/6___ Class ___Small Group___

A. Motivation

1. Would you like to make a newsletter for sixth-grade students to read?   ◯ Yes   ◯ No
   Yes = ℍℍ ℍℍ ||| = 13; No = || = 2

2. Did you like the sixth graders in the lesson?   ◯ Yes   ◯ No
   Yes = ℍℍ ℍℍ ℍℍ = 15; No = 0

3. Do you enjoy working at your speed in Blackboard?   ◯ Yes   ◯ No
   Yes = ℍℍ ℍℍ ℍℍ = 15; No = 0

4. Did you enjoy the article about the dark side of the moon?   ◯ Yes   ◯ No
   Yes = ℍℍ ℍℍ ℍℍ = 15; No = 0

5. Did you think the story with all types of sentences was more interesting?   ◯ Yes   ◯ No

   Yes = ⊞⊞ ⊞⊞ ⊞⊞ = 15; No = 0

6. Would you like to write more interesting stories? ◯ Yes   ◯ No

   Yes = ⊞⊞ ⊞⊞ III = 13; No = II = 2

7. What types of stories do you most like to read?

   horses, pets, space, sports, nature, cars, mysteries

B. Objectives

1. Did you understand that you were going to learn to write interesting newsletter articles? ◯ Yes   ◯ No

   Yes = ⊞⊞ ⊞⊞ ⊞⊞ = 15; No = 0

2. Did you understand that you were going to learn to use the four different types of sentences in your stories?   ◯ Yes   ◯ No

   Yes = ⊞⊞ ⊞⊞ ⊞⊞ = 15; No = 0

3. Did you want to write different types of sentences?   ◯ Yes   ◯ No

   Yes = ⊞⊞ ⊞⊞ ⊞⊞ = 15; No = 0

C. Entry Behaviors

1. Were the questions about subjects, predicates, and complete sentences clear to you?   ◯ Yes   ◯ No

   Yes = ⊞⊞ ⊞⊞ ⊞⊞ = 15; No = 0

2. Did you already know about subjects, predicates, and complete sentences before you started? ◯ Yes   ◯ No

   Yes = ⊞⊞ ⊞⊞ IIII = 14; No = 1

3. Do you wish information about subjects, predicates, and complete sentences had been included in the lesson?   ◯ Yes   ◯ No

   Yes = 0 No = ⊞⊞ ⊞⊞ ⊞⊞ = 15

D. Tests

1. Were the questions on the pretest clear?   ◯ Yes   ◯ No

   Yes = ⊞⊞ III = 8; No = ⊞⊞ II = 7 Didn't know the answers, vocabulary clear

2. Did you know most of the answers on the pretest?   ◯ Yes   ◯ No

   Yes = ⊞⊞ IIII = 9; No = ⊞⊞ I = 6

3. Were the questions within in the lesson clear?   ◯ Yes   ◯ No

   Yes = ⊞⊞ ⊞⊞ ⊞⊞ = 15; No = 0

4. Were the questions on the posttest clear?   ◯ Yes   ◯ No

   Yes = ⊞⊞ ⊞⊞ ⊞⊞ = 15; No = 0

E. Instruction

1. Was the lesson on declarative sentences interesting?   ◯ Yes   ◯ No

   Yes = ⊞⊞ ⊞⊞ ⊞⊞ = 15; No = 0

2. Was the lesson clear to you?   ◯ Yes   ◯ No

   Yes = ⊞⊞ ⊞⊞ ⊞⊞ = 15; No = 0

   If not, what wasn't clear?

Where were the newsletter articles?

3. Were the example questions helpful?   ○ Yes   ○ No
   Yes = ₩₩ ₩₩ = 10; No = ₩₩ = 5

4. Were there too many examples?   ○ Yes   ○ No
   Yes = ₩₩ = 5; No = ₩₩ ₩₩ = 10

5. Were there too few examples?   ○ Yes   ○ No
   Yes = ||| = 3; No = |||| = 4

6. Did the practice questions in the lesson help you?   ○ Yes   ○ No
   Yes = ₩₩ ₩₩ = 10; No = ₩₩ = 5
   If not, why not?

7. Did the feedback for the questions in the lesson help you?   ○ Yes   ○ No
   Yes = ₩₩ ₩₩ = 10; No = ₩₩ = 5
   If not, why not?

F. Overall

1. Generally, did you like the lesson?   ○ Yes   ○ No
   Yes = ₩₩ ₩₩ ₩₩ = 15; No = 0

2. Did you learn to do things you couldn't do before?   ○ Yes   ○ No
   Yes = ₩₩ ₩₩ 10; No = ₩₩ = 5

3. What do you think would improve the lesson most?
   More example articles to see; The lesson wasn't about writing articles. We learned this before.

Appendix M   Materials Revision Matrix Analysis

Instructional Strategy	Problem Identified	Proposed Changes to Instruction	Evidence and Source
Preinstruction Motivation	OK	None	Questionnaire Interview
Entry skills	Four students did not have required entry skills (1, 2, 3, & 4); Student 5 missed skill 5.4, was able to classify sentences (skill 5.5), but had problems writing (5.11). Students without entry skills performed well on embedded tests, but did not retain skills for posttest. Students who did not have entry skills did not want to make a newsletter.	Ensure all students entering the instruction possess entry skills. Develop lesson on entry skills for students who need it.	Entry skills test Embedded test Posttest Observation
Presentation	Group appears not to need instruction in skills 5.8 and 5.9. Five students (11–15) in group did not need instruction, and another five (6–10) only needed to review. Several students said they already knew how to write declarative sentences. High-ability students dissatisfied with lesson.	Move 5.8 and 5.9 to entry skills for unit and remove from instruction and assessments. Branch students based on pretest data; instruction is individualized.	Pretest Embedded test Posttest Questionnaire
Student Participation (Practice with Feedback)		Students wanted more information about newsletter. Refocus objective items and/or examples/nonexamples toward newsletter content. Remove imperative items as distractors in assessments because they are too difficult to distinguish at this point. Reintroduce them following instruction on content differences between declarative and imperative sentences.	Embedded Test Posttest Questionnaire Interview
Assessment	None	None	Pretest separated skilled and unskilled in objective and alternative assessment. Vocabulary OK Time OK Scoring within Blackboard OK. Students liked the name *review* rather than *quiz,* and they liked the immediate feedback they could check themselves.

continued

Instructional Strategy	Problem Identified	Proposed Changes to Instruction	Evidence and Source
Transfer	Students without entry skills did not think the newsletter would be a good idea; those with entry skills liked it very much.		Questionnaire Interview
General	Most students could master the items on the objective posttest but many still struggle with coming up with their own ideas and writing their own content. Practice using the newsletter and working in writing teams should help. Work with library/media specialist to work with article research in the library/media center. Monitor writing to ensure that all students are participating rather than allowing others to accomplish their writing for them.		

GLOSSARY

Alternative assessment   Describes evaluation instruments and procedures other than objective-style tests; includes the evaluation of live performances, products, and attitudes; format includes directions for the learner and a scoring rubric.

ARCS   Acronym for Keller's theory of motivation (attention, relevance, confidence, and satisfaction).

Assessment-centered criteria   Test or item criteria used to judge item writing qualities such as grammar, spelling, punctuation, clarity, parsimony, and the use of recommended item formatting rules.

Assessment instruments   Materials developed and used to assess learners' status and progress in both achievement and attitudes. For achievement, objective tests, product development activities, and live performances are included. For attitudes, both observation and self-report techniques are included.

Attitude   An internal state that influences an individual's choices or decisions to act under certain circumstances. Attitudes represent a tendency to respond in a particular way.

Authentic assessment   Assessment in meaningful real-life contexts (or simulations thereof) in which newly acquired skills will ultimately be applied.

Behavior   An action that is an overt, observable, measurable performance.

Behavioral objective   See Objective.

Candidate media   Those media that can present the desired information, without regard to which may be the most effective. The distinction is from *noncandidate media*. A book, for example, cannot present sound and thus would be an inappropriate choice for delivering instruction for certain objectives.

Chunk of instruction   All the instruction required to teach one objective or a combination of two or more objectives.

Cluster analysis   A technique used with goals in the verbal information domain to identify the specific information needed to achieve the goal and the ways that information can best be organized or grouped.

Cognitive flexibility   The ability to adapt and change one's mental organization of knowledge and mental management of solution strategies for solving new, unexpected problems.

Cognitive strategy   Metaprocesses used by an individual to manage how he or she thinks about things in order to ensure personal learning.

Cognitivism   A learning theory in which learning is viewed as active mental processing to store new knowledge in memory and retrieve knowledge from memory. Cognitivism emphasizes the structure of knowledge and external conditions that support internal mental processes.

Complex goal   A goal that involves more than one domain of learning.

Concept   A set of objects, events, symbols, situations, and so on, that can be grouped together on the basis of one or more shared characteristics and given a common identifying label or symbol. Concept learning refers to the capacity to identify members of the concept category.

Conditions   A main component of a performance objective that specifies the circumstances and materials required in the assessment of the learners' mastery of the objective.

Congruence analysis   Analyzing the congruence among (1) an organization's stated needs and goals and those addressed in candidate instruction; (2) an organization's target learners' entry skills and characteristics and those for which candidate materials are intended; and (3) an organization's resources and those required for obtaining and implementing candidate instruction. Conducted during the expert judgment phase of summative evaluation.

Constructivism   A learning theory in which learning is viewed as an internal process of constructing meaning by combining existing knowledge with new knowledge gained through experiences in the social, cultural, and physical world. Constructivism emphasizes the processes and social interactions in which a student engages for learning.

Constructivist learning environment   Learners in collaborative groups with peers and teachers consulting resources to solve problems. Collaboration can be face to face or managed at a distance by media. Collaboration can be real or simulated in virtual learning spaces.

Content stability   The degree to which information to be learned is likely to remain current.

Context-centered criteria   Test or item criteria used to judge the congruence between the situations used in the assessments and the learning and performance contexts. Authenticity of examples and simulations is the main focus.

Criterion   A standard against which a performance or product is measured.

Criterion-referenced test items   Items designed to measure performance on an explicit set of objectives; also known as objective-referenced test items.

Delivery system   Term used to describe the means by which instruction will be provided to learners. Includes instructor-led instruction, distance education, computer-based instruction, and self-instructional materials.

Design evaluation chart   A method for organizing design information to facilitate its evaluation. The chart relates skills, objectives, and associated test items, allowing easy comparison among the components of the instructional design.

Discrimination   Distinguishing one stimulus from another and responding differently to the various stimuli.

Domain of learning   A major type of learning outcome that can be distinguished from other domains by the type of learned performance required, the type of mental processing required, and the relevant conditions of learning.

Embedded attitude question   Question asked of learners about the instruction at the time they first encounter it.

Entry skills   Specific competencies or skills a learner must have mastered before entering a given instructional activity.

Entry-skill test item   Criterion-referenced test items designed to measure skills identified as necessary prerequisites to beginning a specific course of instruction. Items are typically included in a pretest.

EPSS   Acronym for electronic performance support system. An application embedded in a software system that can be accessed as needed to support job performance. The application could supply algorithms, expert systems, tutorials, hyperlinked information, and so forth.

Evaluation   An investigation conducted to obtain specific answers to specific questions at specific times and in specific places; involves judgments of quality levels.

Expert judgment evaluation   Judgments of the quality of instructional materials made by content experts, learner specialists, or design specialists. The first phase of summative evaluation.

Feedback   Information provided to learners about the correctness of their responses to practice questions in the instruction.

Field trial   The third stage in formative evaluation, referring to the evaluation of the program or product in the setting in which it is intended to be used. Also, the second phase of summative evaluation.

Formative evaluation   Evaluation designed to collect data and information that is used to improve a program or product; conducted while the program is still being developed.

Front-end analysis   A process used for evaluating instructional needs and identifying alternative approaches to meeting those needs. It includes a variety of activities including, but not limited to, performance analysis, needs assessment, job analysis, training delivery options, and feasibility analysis.

General learner characteristics   The general relatively stable (not influenced by instruction) traits describing the learners in a given target population.

Goal   A broad, general statement of an instructional intent, expressed in terms of what learners will be able to do.

Goal analysis   The technique used to analyze a goal to identify the sequence of operations and decisions required to achieve it.

Goal-centered criteria   Test or item criteria used to judge the congruence between the instructional goal, performance objectives, and test items of any format that is used to monitor learning.

Group-based instruction   The use of learning activities and materials designed to be used in a collective fashion with a group of learners; interactive group-paced instruction.

Hierarchical analysis   A technique used with goals in the intellectual skills domain to identify the critical subordinate skills needed to achieve the goal and their interrelationships. For each subordinate skill in the analysis, this involves asking "What must the student know how to do in order to learn the specific subskills being considered?"

Individualized instruction   The use by students of systematically designed learning activities and materials specifically chosen to suit their individual interests, abilities, and experience. Such instruction is usually self-paced.

Instruction   A set of events or activities presented in a structured or planned way, through one or more media, with the goal of having learners achieve prespecified behaviors.

Instructional analysis   The procedures applied to an instructional goal in order to identify the relevant skills and their subordinate skills and information required for a student to achieve the goal.

Instructional materials   Print or other mediated instruction used by a student to achieve an instructional goal.

Instructional strategy   An overall plan of activities to achieve an instructional goal. The strategy includes the sequence of intermediate objectives and the learning activities leading to the instructional goal as well as specification of student groupings, media, and the delivery system. The instructional activities typically include preinstructional activities, content presentation, learner participation, assessment, and follow-through activities.

Instructor's manual   The collection of written materials given to instructors to facilitate their use of the instructional materials. The manual should include an overview of the materials, tests with answers, and any supplementary information thought to be useful to the instructors.

Intellectual skill   A skill that requires some unique cognitive activity; involves manipulating cognitive symbols, as opposed to simply retrieving previously learned information.

Item analysis table   A means of presenting evaluation data that show the percentage of learners who correctly answered each item on a test.

Item difficulty index   The percentage of learners who answer a test item or perform a task correctly.

Job aid   A device, often in paper or computer form, that is used to relieve the learner's reliance on memory during the performance of a complex task.

Job analysis   The process of gathering, analyzing, and synthesizing descriptions of what people do, or should do, on their jobs.

Learner analysis   The determination of pertinent characteristics of members of the target population. Often includes prior knowledge and attitudes toward the content to be taught, as well as attitudes toward the organization and work environment.

Learner-centered criteria   Criteria used to judge the congruence between the appropriateness of achievement level, language, contexts, and experiences of target learners and that presented in instructional materials.

Learner performance data   Information about the degree to which learners achieved the objectives following a unit of instruction.

Learner specialist   A person knowledgeable about a particular population of learners.

Learning context   The actual physical location (or locations) in which the instruction that is under development will be used.

Mastery level   A prespecified level of task performance, with no gradations below it, that defines satisfactory achievement of an objective.

Media   The physical means of conveying instructional content. Examples include drawings, slides, audio, computer, person, model, and so on.

Mindful reflection   In constructivist learning it is the internal mental process in which learners consider their own past and present process of learning for the purpose of confirming or adjusting the process for future learning encounters.

Model   A simplified representation of a system, often in picture or flowchart form, showing selected features of the system.

Module   An instructional package with a single integrated theme that provides the information needed to develop mastery of specified knowledge and skills and serves as one component of a total course or curriculum.

Need   A discrepancy between what should be and the current status of a situation.

Needs assessment   The formal process of identifying discrepancies between current outcomes and desired outcomes for an organization.

Noninstructional solution   Means of reducing performance discrepancies other than the imparting of knowledge; includes motivational, environmental, and equipment factors.

Objective   A statement of what the learners will be expected to do when they have completed a specified course of instruction, stated in terms of observable performances. Also known as performance objective; behavioral objective; instructional objective.

One-to-one evaluation   The first stage in formative evaluation, referring to direct interaction between the designer and individual tryout student.

Performance analysis   An analytical process used to locate, analyze, and correct job or product performance problems.

Performance-based instruction   The use of job performance measures or estimates as inputs for designing training and assessing learning.

Performance context   The setting in which it is hoped that learners will successfully use the skills they are learning; includes both the physical and social aspects of the setting.

Performance objective   See Objective.

Performance technology   Application of relevant theories of human learning and behavior to improve human performance in the workplace. Synonymous with *human performance technology*. A *performance technologist* practices performance technology.

Portfolio assessment   The process of meta-evaluating a collection of work samples or assessments to determine observable changes over time in skill level and/or attitudes. All test formats can be used including objective tests, products, and live performances.

Posttest   A criterion-referenced test designed to measure performance on objectives taught during a unit of instruction; given after the instruction. Typically does not include items on entry behaviors.

Practice test   A criterion-referenced assessment, typically at the skill or lesson level, used to provide the learner with active participation and rehearsal opportunities and the designer with opportunities to monitor learner progress.

Preinstructional activities   Techniques used to provide the following three events prior to delivering instructional content: (1) get the learners' attention; (2) advise them of the prerequisite skills for the unit; and (3) tell them what they will be able to do after the instruction.

Prerequisite skills   Another term used to describe entry skills.

Pretest   A criterion-referenced test designed to measure performance on objectives to be taught during a unit of instruction and/or performance on entry skills; given before instruction begins.

Problem, ill-structured   Situation in which neither the exact rules to be applied nor the exact nature of the solution is identified in the problem statement. Multiple solutions may be acceptable.

Problem, well-structured   Situation in which the nature of the solution is well understood, and there is a generally preferred set of rules to follow to determine the solution.

Procedural approach (for goal analysis)   The process of listing chronologically, in a step-by-step manner, all the substeps required to perform an instructional goal.

PST   Acronym for performance support tool. A small-scale, usually stand-alone electronic performance support system designed to support a limited range of job tasks.

Psychomotor skill   Execution of a sequence of major or subtle physical actions to achieve a specified result. All skills employ some type of physical action; the physical action in a psychomotor skill is the focus of the *new* learning, and is not merely the vehicle for expressing an intellectual skill.

Rapid prototyping   In software development it is also called rapid application design (RAD) and is the process of using prototype approximations of a software design in order to test whether the application meets the design specifications.

Reliability   The consistency or dependability of a measure.

Research   An investigation conducted to identify knowledge that is generalized.

Revision   The process of producing an amended, improved, or up-to-date version of a set of instructional materials.

ROI   Acronym for return on investment. In training and development it is a comparison between the costs incurred for training and the benefits realized from training.

Rough draft materials   The development of instructional materials in quick, inexpensive media formats for formative tryout.

Scaffolding   Teacher, peer, or mediated guidance for students' learning that is provided when support is needed for progress and withdrawn as students develop proficiency.

SCORM   Acronym for Sharable Content Object Reference Model. SCORM is a series of e-learning standards for ensuring interchangeability of course objects within SCORM-compliant course management systems.

Situated learning The concept that learning occurs best through engagement in a process or activity that should be placed in (situated in) a context that is relevant to the learner and the knowledge to be gained.

Skill An ability to perform an action or group of actions; involves overt performance.

Small-group evaluation The second stage of formative evaluation, referring to the use of a small number of tryout students who study an instructional program without intervention from the designer and are tested to assess the effectiveness of the instruction.

Step One skill identified in the analysis of an instructional goal. Describes a complete task, behavior, or decision that must be completed when someone performs the instructional goal. Most goals include five or more steps (see Substep).

Strategic planning A planning process used to determine and describe future organizational directions, how to achieve the prescribed directions, and how to measure whether the directions are achieved. Strategic planning encompasses a variety of models and processes.

Subject-matter expert (SME) See Subject-matter specialist.

Subject-matter specialist A person knowledgeable about a particular content area. Also known as content specialist; subject-matter expert (SME).

Subordinate objective An objective that must be attained in order to accomplish a terminal objective. Also known as enabling objective; intermediate objective.

Subordinate skill A skill that must be achieved in order to learn a higher-level skill. Also known as subskill or enabling skill.

Substep One component of a major step in a goal. There must be two or more substeps to justify a substep analysis. Performing each of the substeps in sequence is equivalent to performing the step from which they were derived.

Summative evaluation Evaluation designed and used after an instructional program has been implemented. The purpose is to present conclusions about the worth of the program or product and make recommendations about its adoption or retention. It includes two phases: expert judgment and field trial. The expert judgment phase includes congruence, content, design, and feasibility analyses. The field trial phase includes analyses of management and impact on learners, job, and organization.

Superordinate skill Higher-level competency that is composed of and achieved by learning subordinate skills.

System A set of interrelated parts working together toward a defined goal.

Systems approach Procedure used by instructional designers to create instruction. Each step requires input from prior steps and provides input to the next step. Evaluation provides feedback that is used to revise instruction until it meets the original need or specification.

Systems approach and models for instruction A logical, iterative process of identifying all the variables that can impact the quality of instruction, including delivery, and then integrating information about each variable in the design, development, evaluation, and revision of the instruction.

Table of test specifications Prescriptions for a test that include information such as level of learning, the task, performance objective, test item format, and the number of items to present for each task.

Target population The total collection of possible users of a given instructional program.

Terminal objective An objective the learners will be expected to accomplish when they have completed a course of instruction, made up of subordinate objectives. Often, a more specific statement of the instructional goal.

Training   A prespecified and planned experience that enables a person to do something that he or she could not do before.

Transfer of learning   The process whereby the learner applies skills learned in one context to another, similar context. Also referred to as transfer of training.

Tryout students   A representative sample of the target population; may be used to test an instructional program prior to final implementation.

Validity   The degree to which a measuring instrument actually measures what it is intended to measure.

Verbal information   Requirement to provide a specific response to relatively specific stimuli; involves recall of information.

INDEX